THE ROUTLEDGE COMPANION TO CULTURAL PROPERTY

The Routledge Companion to Cultural Property contains new contributions from scholars working at the cutting edge of cultural property studies, bringing together diverse academic and professional perspectives to develop a coherent overview of this field of enquiry. The global range of authors use international case studies to encourage a comparative understanding of how cultural property has emerged in different parts of the world and continues to frame vital issues of national sovereignty, the free market, international law, and cultural heritage. Sections explore how cultural property is scaled to the state and the market; cultural property as law; cultural property and cultural rights; and emerging forms of cultural property, from yoga to the national archive. By bringing together disciplinary perspectives from anthropology, archaeology, law, Indigenous studies, history, folklore studies, and policy, this volume facilitates fresh debate and broadens our understanding of this issue of growing importance. This comprehensive and coherent statement of cultural property issues will be of great interest to cultural sector professionals and policy makers, as well as students and academic researchers engaged with cultural property in a variety of disciplines.

Jane Anderson is Assistant Professor of Anthropology and Museum Studies at New York University. Her research is focused on property law, Indigenous rights and sovereignty, colonial archives, repatriation, digital return, collaborative research, and transformative practice for social change.

Haidy Geismar is Reader in Anthropology and Vice Dean for Strategic Projects at University College London where she co-directs the Digital Anthropology Program. Her research interests focus on digital collections, Indigenous intellectual and cultural property, critical museum studies, the anthropology of economy and exchange, material culture and materiality, and digital anthropology.

THE ROUTLEDGE COMPANION TO CULTURAL PROPERTY

Edited by
Jane Anderson and Haidy Geismar

Routledge
Taylor & Francis Group
LONDON AND NEW YORK

First published 2017 by Routledge

2 Park Square, Milton Park, Abingdon, Oxon, OX14 4RN
605 Third Avenue, New York, NY 10017

Routledge is an imprint of the Taylor & Francis Group, an informa business

First issued in paperback 2020

British Library Cataloguing in Publication Data
A catalogue record for this book is available from the British Library

Library of Congress Cataloging in Publication Data
Names: Anderson, Jane L., editor. | Geismar, Haidy, editor.
Title: The Routledge companion to cultural property / edited by Jane Anderson and Haidy Geismar.
Other titles: Cultural property
Description: Abingdon, Oxon ; New York, NY : Routledge, an imprint of the Taylor & Francis Group, an informa business, 2017. | Includes bibliographical references and index.
Identifiers: LCCN 2016039420 | ISBN 9781138812642 (hardback : alk. paper)
Subjects: LCSH: Cultural property.
Classification: LCC CC135 .R68 2017 | DDC 363.6/9--dc23
LC record available at https://lccn.loc.gov/2016039420

ISBN: 978-1-138-81264-2 (hbk)
ISBN: 978-0-367-78398-3 (pbk)

Typeset in Bembo
by Taylor & Francis Books

CONTENTS

FIGURES

ACKNOWLEDGEMENTS

Thanks to Ryan O'Byrne, Anna Weinrich and Matt Canfield for editorial assistance in the last phases of production, to Matthew Gibbons for the invitation to put the volume together and Lola Harre for support and editorial assistance during the book's production. Special thanks to Andrea Geyer. Thanks to the Departments of Anthropology at University College London and New York University for supporting both editors during the time it took to put the book together.

The editors will donate all royalties from the sale of this book to the International Repatriation Project, Association of American Indian Affairs, www.indian-affairs.org.

CONTRIBUTORS

Jane Anderson is Assistant Professor of Anthropology and Museum Studies at New York University. Her work is focused on the philosophical and practical problems of intellectual property law, repatriation and Indigenous rights. She works with a variety of Native American communities negotiating control and ownership over tribal knowledge resources and cultural heritage held within archives and museums. Her most recent project, with Kim Christen, is Local Contexts (www.localcontexts.org). This project includes the new Traditional Knowledge (TK) Labels as an educational intervention to address the needs of Indigenous communities to manage their intellectual property rights and cultural heritage specifically within the digital environment.

Regina F. Bendix has taught at the Department of Cultural Anthropology/European Ethnology at the University of Göttingen, Germany since 2001. The conceptual and historical work she carried out for her monograph *In Search of Authenticity* (Madison 1997) fostered her interest in questions at the intersection of culture, the economy and politics. She worked on tourism and heritage and led the multi-year, interdisciplinary research group on 'The Constitution of Cultural Property', in whose framework a number of co-edited volumes such as *Heritage Regimes and the State* (Göttingen 2013) and *Between Imagined Communities and Communities of Practice* (Göttingen 2015) have appeared.

Susan Benton holds a Juris Doctor degree in law and a PhD in anthropology. Susan has been active in private law practice in the United States since 1987 with a focus on issues affecting the cultural and creative sectors. For more than a decade, she has focused her research on issues involving indigenous cultural heritage, arts, and the law, including the processes of repatriation and their effects on groups and individuals. For more than 20 years, Susan has also taught courses at the doctoral and master's levels on issues involving cultural heritage law, museum law, and the international arts and antiquities trade. Currently residing in Melbourne, Australia, Susan is active internationally with research, law practice, teaching, and speaking engagements.

Boatema Boateng is Associate Professor in the Department of Communication, University of California San Diego. Her research interests include critical legal studies, cultural studies, transnational gender studies, and African diaspora studies. She has published several articles and book chapters on the political and cultural dimensions of intellectual property law and her book *The Copyright Thing Doesn't Work Here: Adinkra, Kente Cloth and Intellectual Property in Ghana* was published by the University of Minnesota Press in 2011.

John Bradley is the Deputy Director of the Monash Indigenous Centre and has worked for 35 years in the Northern Territory of Australia. His research has centred on working with Indigenous peoples to record their own Indigenous knowledges in ways that are useful to them. He has also worked on a number of land and sea claims assisting Indigenous peoples in regaining their traditional lands. More recently he has been developing ways in which his own fieldwork can be returned to Indigenous communities, the animations project of which he is the director having been a part of this.

Neil Brodie is Senior Research Fellow in the School of Archaeology at the University of Oxford. He graduated from the University of Liverpool with a PhD Archaeology in 1991 and has held positions at the British School at Athens, the McDonald Institute for Archaeological Research at the University of Cambridge, where he was Research Director of the Illicit Antiquities Research Centre, Stanford University's Archaeology Center, and the Scottish Centre for Crime and Justice Research, at the University of Glasgow. He has published widely on issues concerning the illegal trade of cultural property, and has worked on archaeological projects in the United Kingdom, Greece and Jordan.

Rosemary J. Coombe is the Tier One Canada Research Chair in Law, Communication and Culture at York University in Toronto, where she teaches in the Department of Anthropology, the York and Ryerson Joint Graduate Program in Communication and Culture, and the Graduate Program in Socio-legal Studies. She holds a joint doctorate in Law and Anthropology from Stanford University. She has been awarded visitorships at Harvard, MIT, Iowa, American, De Paul, the University of Chicago and the University of California and has held research fellowships at the University of Utrecht, the Stellenbosch Institute for Advanced Study, and the University of Göttingen. Her award-winning book *The Cultural Life of Intellectual Properties* (1998) was reprinted in 2008 by Duke University Press. Other publications and works in progress may be found at http://rcoombe.blog.yorku.ca/.

Lee Douglas is a doctoral candidate in Sociocultural Anthropology and a graduate of the Culture and Media Program at New York University. She holds an MSc in Visual Anthropology from the University of Oxford. Her research focuses on the intersection of forensic science, archival practice, and photographic documentation during the excavation of mass graves and the identification of remains in post-Franco Spain. Paying close attention to engagements with forensic evidence, her research considers what the entanglement between science, documentary practice, and visual representation reveals about the production and mobilization of knowledge in times of economic austerity and political change.

Shannon Faulkhead's research concentrates on the location of Koorie peoples and their knowledge within the broader Australian society and its collective knowledge as reflected through narratives and records. To date Shannon's multi-disciplinary research has centred on community and archival collections of records. Being the Finkel Fellow, attached to Monash Country Lines Archive, Monash University, will allow for greater exploration and development in the area of Indigenous archiving.

Aaron A. Fox is Associate Professor of Music and Director of the Center for Ethnomusicology, Columbia University. He is the author of *Real Country: Music and Language in Working-Class Culture* (Duke University Press, 2004). He holds a PhD in Social Anthropology from the University of Texas at Austin.

Haidy Geismar is Reader in Anthropology and Vice Dean for Strategic Projects at University College London where she co-directs the Digital Anthropology Program. With extensive fieldwork experience in Vanuatu, New Zealand and in numerous museums in Europe and North America her research interests focus on digital collections, indigenous intellectual and cultural property, critical museum studies, the anthropology of economy and exchange, material culture and materiality, and digital anthropology. Her most recent book is *Treasured Possessions: Indigenous Interventions into Intellectual and Cultural Property* (Duke University Press, 2013). Geismar is Associate Editor of the *International Journal of Cultural Property* and edits the popular weblog www.materialworldblog.com.

Patty Gerstenblith is distinguished research professor of law at DePaul University College of Law. She is secretary of the US Committee of the Blue Shield and was formerly president of the Lawyers Committee for Cultural Heritage Preservation and editor-in-chief of the *International Journal of Cultural Property*. In 2011, President Obama appointed her chair of the President's Cultural Property Advisory Committee in the US Department of State. Her publications include the casebook *Art, Cultural Heritage and the Law*. Gerstenblith received her AB from Bryn Mawr College, PhD in art history and anthropology from Harvard University, and JD from Northwestern University.

D. Rae Gould is a member of the Nipmuc Nation of Massachusetts and holds a PhD in Anthropology from the University of Connecticut, with a research focus on southern New England Native American culture and history. She has worked in New England and Washington, DC over the past 20 years on issues related to federal acknowledgement, NAGPRA and historic preservation.

Stefan Groth is a European Ethnologist/Cultural Anthropologist working on cultural heritage, normative dimensions of everyday culture, sports, and multilateral negotiations. He is a senior researcher and head of the Laboratory of Popular Culture Studies at the Institute of Social Anthropology and Cultural Studies, University of Zurich. Author of *Negotiating Tradition: The Pragmatics of International Deliberations on Cultural Property* (Göttingen 2012), he has published on normative dimensions of cultural property, traditional knowledge and intellectual property, and collaborative aspects of cultural heritage.

Valdimar Tr. Hafstein is Professor in the Department of Ethnology, Folklore, and Museum Studies at the University of Iceland, and current president of SIEF (International Society for Ethnology and Folklore). He holds an MA and a PhD from the University of California, Berkeley. Valdimar chaired the Icelandic National Commission for UNESCO from 2011 to 2012. He has published on topics ranging from heritage theory to copyright, from UNESCO to medieval legends, and from traditional wrestling to CCTV surveillance. His work has been translated into French, Italian, Portuguese, Croatian, and Danish.

Morag M. Kersel is Associate Professor of Anthropology at DePaul University and a visiting fellow with the Neubauer Collegium at the University of Chicago. She co-directs the

Follow the Pots Project (followthepotsproject.org), which traces the movement of Early Bronze Age pots from the Dead Sea Plain in Jordan. She recently co-authored (with Christina Luke) *US Cultural Diplomacy and Archaeology: Soft Power, Hard Heritage* (Routledge 2013) and co-edited (with Matthew T. Rutz) *Archaeologies of Text: Archaeology, Technology and Ethics* (Oxbow 2014).

Jennifer Kramer holds a joint position at the University of British Columbia as Associate Professor in the Department of Anthropology and Curator, Pacific Northwest at the Museum of Anthropology. She works with First Nations on the Central Northwest Coast of British Columbia. Her research focuses upon art market economies, identity production, representation, repatriation, Aboriginal cultural tourism, Indigenous modernity, and collaborative and critical museology. Kramer is co-editor with Charlotte Townsend-Gault and Ki-ke-in of the multiple award-winning anthology *Native Art of the Northwest Coast: A History of Changing Ideas* (UBC Press 2013). She curated the exhibition 'Kesu': The Art and Life of Doug Cranmer' (with a complementing book of the same title with Douglas & McIntyre Press 2012) and authored *Switchbacks: Art, Ownership, and Nuxalk National Identity* (UBC Press 2006).

Brent McKee is a graduate and researcher in the Faculty of Information Technology, Monash University. Brent is the lead animator on the Monash Country Lines Archive and the 3D animator and postproduction editor on the Visualising Angkor project.

Maria Montenegro has a Master's in Museum Studies from New York University and is a PhD candidate in Information Studies at University of California, Los Angeles. Her work is focused on the digital collaborations between museums and Native communities at the intersections of Indigenous knowledge systems with intellectual property law. She also works with Jane Anderson at Local Contexts and with Kim Christen at the Sustainable Heritage Network.

Marama Muru-Lanning is Acting Director and a Senior Research Fellow at the James Henare Māori Research Centre for the University of Auckland. She is also an advisor of elderly health projects in the Faculty of Medical and Health Sciences. Her research is concerned with debates and critical challenges in social anthropology where she focuses on the cultural specificity of Maori and their unique sense of place and belonging in New Zealand. What distinguishes Marama as a social scientist is her specialisation in water rights, environment and Indigenous issues. She holds a Royal Society Marsden Research Grant, is Chair of the Association for Social Anthropology in Oceania and is a Council member of the *Journal of the Polynesian Society*, New Zealand's oldest scholarly journal.

Fred Myers, Silver Professor of Anthropology at New York University, has written on Indigenous Australian culture, objects, and identity as they are understood both within local communities and circulated through different regimes of value. His books include *Pintupi Country, Pintupi Self: Sentiment, Place and Politics among Western Desert Aborigines* (1986), *Painting Culture: The Making of an Aboriginal High Art* (2002), and edited volumes *The Traffic in Culture: Refiguring Anthropology and Art* (co-edited with George Marcus, 1995), and *The Empire of Things* (2001). His current project involves the repatriation and 're-documentation' of film footage from 1974 with the current Pintupi communities.

George Nicholas is a Professor of Archaeology at Simon Fraser University (SFU) and an adjunct professor of Archaeology at Flinders University. He was the founding director of

SFU's Indigenous Archaeology Program in Kamloops (1991–2005), and has worked closely with Indigenous peoples for 30 years. Nicholas' research focuses on Indigenous peoples and archaeology, intellectual property, the archaeology and human ecology of wetlands, and archaeological theory. He directed the Intellectual Property Issues in Cultural Heritage (IPinCH) project (2008–2016), an eight-year, international collaboration concerned with the theoretical, ethical, and practical implications of commodification and appropriation of heritage, and other flows of knowledge about the past, and with how these may affect communities, researchers, and other stakeholders. In 2013, he received the first 'Partnership Impact Award' from Canada's Social Sciences and Humanities Research Council.

Sita Reddy is a cultural sociologist, museum curator, and heritage policy worker, in no particular order but sometimes all at once. She writes on topics ranging from the history of Ayurveda, Yoga, and botanical art, to museum practices such as the decolonization of heritage archives and music repatriation. She has been Fellow at the Smithsonian Institution and the Library of Congress, and most recently was Visiting Professor at the University of Hyderabad. Her curatorial experience includes a variety of exhibitions at the Sackler Gallery (Yoga: The Art of Transformation), NLM (Visible Proofs), Provisions Library (The Innocents), and the Salar Jung Museum, Hyderabad. She blogs occasionally at ajeebghar.com

Michael Rowlands is Emeritus Professor of Anthropology and Material Culture Studies at UCL. Recent field research has been on the histories and development of postcolonial museums and heritage conflicts in West Africa (Cameroon, Liberia, Mali). He is currently a co-investigator of a Leverhulme-funded research project on 'Conflicts in Cultural Value: Localities and Heritage in South West China.' He is also a co-director of UCL/CREDOC (Centre for Research in the Dynamics of Civilisation) seeking to reintroduce the concept of 'civilization' in the study of ancient and modern worlds.

Sandra Rozental received her PhD in Anthropology from New York University in 2012 and is an Assistant Professor at the Universidad Autónoma Metropolitana in Mexico City. Her work explores the tangible residues of pre-Hispanic civilizations in Mexico by way of national patrimony claims on artifacts, territories and landscapes. She co-directed the feature-length documentary 'The Absent Stone' (2013) with Jesse Lerner; has published 'In the Wake of Mexican Patrimonio: Material Ecologies in San Miguel Coatlinchan', *Anthropological Quarterly* 89.1 (2016) and 'Stone Replicas: The Iteration and Itinerancy of Mexican Patrimonio', *Journal of Latin American and Caribbean Anthropology* 19.2 (2014); and co-edited the special dossier 'Matters of Patrimony: Anthropological Theory and the Materiality of Replication in Contemporary Latin America', *Journal of Latin American and Caribbean Anthropology* 21.1 (2016).

Neil Asher Silberman is a historian and heritage scholar who is the author of more than a dozen books, from *Digging for God and Country* (1982) to *The Bible Unearthed* (2001). He is an adjunct faculty member of the Department of Anthropology of the University of Massachusetts Amherst. From 2004 to 2007 he served as director of the Ename Center in Belgium, and also served as president of the ICOMOS International Scientific Committee on Interpretation and Presentation and as a member of the ICOMOS International Advisory Committee from 2005 to 2015. He is a managing partner of Coherit Associates, an international heritage consultancy.

Martin Skrydstrup, formerly a postdoc at the Department of Food and Resource Economics, Section for Global Development, University of Copenhagen, is affiliated with the Saxo Institute, University of Copenhagen. He holds an MA in cultural anthropology from the University of Copenhagen and a PhD also in cultural anthropology from Columbia University based on his dissertation entitled 'Once Ours: The Making and Unmaking of Claims to Cultural Property' (2010). He has served on the Board of Directors for ICME and as Adviser to ICOM's Ethics Committee. His research straddles the disciplines of anthropology, science studies and history and is concerned most generally with relationships between expertise, governance and the constitution of natural and cultural resources.

Paul Tapsell is Chair of Māori Studies and a former Dean of Te Tumu, the School of Māori, Pacific and Indigenous Studies, at the University of Otago. Paul's Māori ancestry originates out of the Bay of Plenty and Waikato regions. His research interests include Māori youth identity in twenty-first-century New Zealand, the role of cultural heritage and museums in nation states, and taonga trajectories in and beyond tribal contexts. Paul continues to build on his past museum experiences at Rotorua Museum (curator), Pitt Rivers Museum (doctoral research), post-doctoral studies (CCR/ANU) and Auckland War Memorial Museum (Director Māori). He is a former co-Chair of Museums Aotearoa and sat on Te Māori Manaaki Taonga Trust. Today he serves on the Otago Museum Trust Board, Pukaki Trust, Sir Hugh Kawharu Foundation, Te Potiki National Trust and as an Eisenhower Fellow (NZ). Paul's most notable exhibitions are The New Dawn (1991), The Legacy of Houmaitawhiti (1993–1997), Ko Tawa – Maori Ancestors of New Zealand (2005–2008) and Te Ara – Māori Pathways of Leadership (2010–2014). His publications are not only academic in nature, but also include very accessible books on taonga and leadership (*Pukaki*, 2000, *Ko Tawa*, 2006, *The Art of Taonga*, 2011, and *Te Ara*, 2013) and most recently a digital web service, designed to assist urban-raised Māori youth reconnect to their ancestral communities (www.maorimaps.com).

Ana Filipa Vrdoljak is Professor of Law, Faculty of Law, University of Technology Sydney. She is the author of *International Law, Museums and the Return of Cultural Objects* (CUP, 2006) and editor of *Culture and Human Rights* (OUP, 2013) and *International Law for Common Goods: Normative Perspectives in Human Rights, Culture and Nature* (Hart, 2014). She is co-General Editor of the Oxford University Press book series Cultural Heritage Law and Policy and member of the Advisory Board of the *International Journal of Cultural Property*. She is a member of the Cultural Heritage Law Committee, International Law Association and secretary of the International Cultural Property Society.

Shu-Li Wang is assistant research fellow of the Institute of Ethnology, Academia Sinica, Taiwan. Wang obtained her PhD in anthropology from University College London. Her research interests lie in critical heritage studies, comparative museology, cultural memory and anthropology of nationalism, and her goal is to present an ethnography on archaeological and heritage works as the place to explore knowledge production and nation building in contemporary China. Currently, she is working towards the transformation of her PhD thesis into book form as *The Heritage Complex in China – Yinxu Archaeological Park in the Making* (to be published in the Routledge Critical Heritage series); she is also co-editing a volume entitled *Heritage as Aid and Diplomacy in Asia*.

1
INTRODUCTION

Jane Anderson and Haidy Geismar

The many faces of cultural property

This book is both a reader and an extended argument for how to think about cultural property today. Cultural property is a term that has different meanings across scholarly disciplines, governmental and policy environments, within museums and collections, and within communities of practice. A curious hybrid of culture (the evanescent and immaterial systems and structures of knowledge that bind human beings together) and property (the ideologies, political regulations, customs and popular consensus that establish entitlement and sovereignty, and determine claims and power over a range of tangible and intangible resources), cultural property is an evolving category used to describe ways of talking about collective entitlement, shared inheritance, the material nature of identity, and in more recent years, to debate the ethics of the commoditization of culture.

This collection of commissioned essays demonstrates how cultural property is more than valuable artefacts embedded within varied forms of control and allocations of rights. Collectively, the chapters in this volume argue that cultural property is also popular discourse, a way of describing culture, a form of sovereignty, a unit of power, a measure of value, a political instrument, and that it refers to a wide range of different things, both material and immaterial. This book is therefore primarily an argument for *multiple* perspectives on cultural property. Our ambition has been to curate a selection of chapters that reflect the ways in which cultural property is described and discussed from different vantage places, academic disciplines, forms of governance, and practice. Taken together, these essays demonstrate how cultural property's collective nature, as well as the ways in which relationships of rights and authority are activated, emerges around the world in many different ways. We recognize that the volume reflects the ways we are situated in this landscape, as scholars who work and teach in the United Kingdom and North America, with research backgrounds in Australia and the Pacific, and with disciplinary backgrounds in anthropology, critical legal studies, and Indigenous studies.

For the purposes of this Introduction we define cultural property very broadly as the recognition of collective rights in both material and intangible culture within international policy, national law, cultural institutions, local contexts, and everyday practices. As the history of cultural property we present in this Introduction demonstrates, cultural property as an idea, as a legal category, and as something tangible in need of protection has emerged historically out of armed conflict and has been conceptually embedded within the modern nation-state. The threat, through the violence of warfare to churches, libraries, works of art, and monuments, both demanded and constituted a new category of national property, which needed international recognition in order to be preserved. The language of cultural property therefore emerged predominantly in the nineteenth century as a means to position the nation-state as the *owner* of particular kinds of artefacts and institutions. Breaking open a space between traditional ideas of private property and of public property, this category of national property produced a new understanding of the inalienable relationship between the state and its possessions. However, by the end of the twentieth century, challenges to this jurisdiction had emerged from many directions. The language of cultural property has been adopted and adapted by collectivities that actively resist the authority of the state over diverse cultural resources.

The essays in this volume demonstrate that the rights and relations of cultural property are multiple and need to be understood as engaging a range of actors with varied power and agency. Despite its history, nation-states and national institutions are not the only arbiters of the definition and value of cultural property. As such we must also be attentive to the ways in which cultural property has been able to offer itself as a vehicle to articulate complex identity politics and painful histories of exploitation and appropriation both within and between states. We are committed here to exploring the diverse languages, interpretations, materialities, and politics of cultural property and to understanding the power of global concepts and values as well as local differences in both the implementation and interpretation of cultural property. It is crucial to recognize that whilst cultural property policy and legislation, particularly from within Anglophone traditions, may be seen to be relatively similar across the globe, the interpretation and implementation of cultural property vary from place to place, and are in turn continually altering mainstream understandings and definitions (see Coombe 2009; Geismar 2013b; Myers 2005). Canonical contests over cultural property such as the destruction of the Bamiyan Buddhas by the Taliban in 2001; the restitution of art stolen from Jewish families during the Holocaust; the loss of cultural heritage in the building of the Aswan High Dam in the 1960s; the 2012 settlement by Yale University over artefacts collected from Machu Picchu in Peru in 1912–1915; the appropriation of Navajo designs by Urban Outfitters in the United States; the fight by the British Museum to justify keeping the Greek Elgin/Pantheon Marbles; and Indigenous anxieties over the distortion of Quileute tribal narratives by Stephanie Myers in the *Twilight* trilogy demonstrate how it is vital to pay attention to local differences as well as global histories, to appreciate the discontent with the assumption of national sovereignty from both within and across nation-states, and to understand that the phrase 'cultural property' does not simply reference an international category and bureaucratic order, but is itself an active site of claim making that is about political recognition, cultural memory, and identity formation.

Genealogies of cultural property

To understand the diverse strands of engagement and the questions provoked by cultural property, it is important to understand the key historical moments that constitute a genealogy of mainstream understandings of cultural property. Despite the complex global history of cultural property, inflected by multiple locations and histories, the category and concept has historically been bound to elite institutions and the emergence of (largely European) nation-states. This history has established an authoritative and disciplinary framework, grounded in cultural institutions such as museums, in material culture that is monumental, sacred, and antique, and in languages of law, policy, and governance.

As the very term itself suggests, cultural property develops out of longstanding traditions of property theory, but it also departs from mainstream trajectories of property thinking, pushing against familiar ideas of private property and possessive individualism whilst marking interests in collective identities, social relationships with tangible and intangible objects, and discourses of cultural rights. Property is traditionally understood as a right or 'an enforceable claim to some use or benefit of something' (Macpherson 1978: 3). Just what this right is, how it is developed, justified, and elaborated has been the primary focus of property and social theorists at least since the seventeenth century.

It is possible to trace a pre-history of cultural property as Marcel Mauss does in his classic essay *The Gift* (1990 [1925]) into Roman codes of patronage; as Merryman (2005) does to the writings of Polybius of Athens about plunder in ancient Greece; and to medieval discourses of the commons (Boyle 2008). However, for the purposes of this volume, we focus on the emergence of modern cultural property thinking as it emerged from the seventeenth century onwards in response to a variety of social, economic, and cultural factors, including the interests and effects of colonization, concerns for articulations of nascent national and ethnic collectivities and the increasing technological capacity for the destruction of valuable sites of memory and identity. The modern definition of property is usually recognized to have emerged during the European Enlightenment (Macpherson 1978; Macpherson, Parel and Flanagan 1979). Enlightenment philosophies posited that property was an exclusive right of individuals over the things that were produced through their own efforts or labour. Property and personhood were thus intimately entangled from the very beginning (Radin 1993). This position was argued most famously by the philosopher and political theorist John Locke in his *Two Treatises of Government* (2011, first published in 1689). Locke's description of property posited it as a natural right – that is, an inherent and original right existing by virtue of human existence. The key point of the natural right thesis expanded by political theorists in this period is that certain rights exist automatically in distinction from those established through government. As a natural right, property pre-exists government and therefore the state. Locke argued that government should not, and could not wind back, reduce, or take away already existing rights to property for individuals.

Lockean ideas about 'first possession' and that property is produced through the active action of individual labour still have influence within the debates and claims of a range of modern property theorists, including in the domain of cultural property (e.g. Rose 1994). These European, and later North American, understandings of property were exported around the world during the nineteenth century through colonial expansion, and via international law and policy within the twentieth century. In fact, these theories of property were crucial for the colonial appropriation of territory and resources, especially from peoples whose lands were not perceived to be noticeably transformed through culturally specific ideas of what exerting labour on lands (for instance cultivation) looked like. As a result, these peoples were deemed to be without property, and therefore without history or culture (Wolf 1982). These legal definitions were bolstered by a nascent evolutionary anthropology (not without its critics) and by contemporary theories of race (Pels 1997; Asad 1973). For instance, when the British first arrived in Australia in 1788, they claimed the territory on behalf of the British Crown as *terra nullius* – the political concept that 'previously empty "waste" lands could be settled without conquest' (Benton 2001: 168). Whilst this legal doctrine was a strategy built out of prior histories of colonialism, it was maintained effectively because it was based upon a narrow cultural understanding of how property in land was acquired and justified. The doctrine of *terra nullius* in Australia was only overturned, through the famous Mabo case brought by Torres Strait Islander Eddie Mabo, in 1992. The consequences of this form of settler colonialism reached much further than just the taking of lands. In Australia, it included the taking and disciplining of Aboriginal and Torres Strait Islander bodies and targeted attempts to destroy complex social relationships and cultural practices through directed governmental policy (Nakata 2007). Aboriginal and Torres Strait Islanders only became legal citizens of the nation in 1967; prior to that they were considered 'wards of the state' with almost no rights. Eileen Moreton-Robinson has thoughtfully observed that the Australian nation, once it became a white possession, was renamed and mapped according to prevailing European logic of ownership. It is this logic of ownership that has produced invisible borders that continue to deny Indigenous sovereignty (Moreton-Robinson 2015).

Cultural property as political theory

Locke's natural rights thesis for the foundation and justification of property emerged within complex political debates about the nature of existence and the authority of the Crown. Yet Locke's idea of the individual and his property, which was implicitly gendered and racialized (Harris 1993), generated a parallel conversation around the form of the collective rights that were necessary to support the rights of individuals. Colonial expansion enabled European social theorists to contemplate the telos of their own social forms by placing them in both comparative and historical context. The English philosopher Thomas Hobbes argued in *Leviathan* (1996 [1651]) that rights were not natural but rather produced by the sovereign state. Later, French philosopher Jean-Jacques Rousseau who also started from a natural rights position, modified and refined his ideas of property as an unlimited right through his own emergent ideas of evolutionary change and equity. He developed Hobbes' notion of a 'social contract', in order to explore the ways in which the natural rights of man could be consensually organized into enlightened government in order to combat the inequalities enshrined within the more individualistic orientation of commerce and property theory (1998 [1762]). Rousseau's concern was that the idea of an unlimited property right (like the one that Locke had advanced) actually deprived most people of property: unequal private property enslaved some men to others. Importantly for our purposes, the archetypal property form, the 'thing' in these theories, was still largely land, which became property through the application of a culturally specific idea of human labour and organization, and through an increasingly naturalized relation between territory and political authority (Hann 1998b).

Lockean ideas of property were also picked up, adapted and moved into other areas of developing property law which was influential on emerging understandings of cultural property. For instance, in the literary property and copyright debates of the eighteenth century, Locke's ideas of first occupancy (of property) and natural rights were strategically deployed by the English jurist William Blackstone who was a central figure in arguing these cases and in producing one of the most significant corpus of legal writing that influenced both English and colonial jurists and lawyers – the 1797 *Commentaries of the Laws of England*. In the cases that are foundational to our modern idea of copyright, Blackstone strategically redeployed Lockean concepts, arguing how the original work of an author was akin to the first occupancy of an idea, and that therefore very specific legal protections were necessary (Drahos 1996).

These emerging European ideas of property inevitably engaged questions around who could constitute a property owner, the governance of one's body and labour, and of territory, establishing a link through property to many different kinds of rights: human, cultural, and political. This specific genealogy of property directly connects to the emergence of discourses of human and cultural rights (Cowan et al. 2001; Goodale and Merry 2007). As Margaret Radin makes clear in her seminal work on property and personhood, it is because a person can be bound up with an external 'thing' in intricate and intimate ways that questions of personal liberty and the capacity to exert control over that 'thing' arise (Radin 1982).

Theories of property are deeply entangled with ideas about political sovereignty (Agamben 1998). Property rights are therefore by definition human rights, framed increasingly as the rights of citizens. During the Enlightenment discussions of natural rights displaced discourses about spiritual authorization of inheritance by God. By the nineteenth century, as property became institutionalized at the level of the state and with regard to law and legislation, it also opened up new conceptions of public and private property and notions of collective inheritance became linked to burgeoning theories of cultural identity and cultural progress.

Social theorists have continued to be concerned around the inequities embedded within the institution of property. For instance Karl Marx's 'law of value' (1992 [1847]), which owes a significant debt to Locke's original conceptualization of the relationship between labour and property, focused on the ways in which value was produced through both human labour and the political systems that emerged to regulate it. His writing, influenced by legal theorists such as Louis Henry Morgan (1877), explored how different political and economic systems constitute the relationships between people, labour, and things. Marx detailed how capitalism had emerged in the nineteenth century to dominate political and economic theories of ownership, entitlement, and rights, and his influential writing (e.g. 1976 [1867]) exposes the salience of the commodity form in modern understandings about value, property, and ownership. Marx's notion of 'commodity fetishism' exposed how capitalism displaced value from the physical labour and social relations of production to the site of the commodity itself. People become subordinate in their relations to these commodities and in this sense, 'under capitalism, property itself is anti-personhood' (Radin 1982: x). Marx, and Marxist perspectives on property also highlight the ways in which very particular capitalist interests in protecting private property inform and are upheld within modern legal systems, with their emphasis on the exclusive rights of individual owners (whether they be people or corporations). The genealogy of thinking about property as the exercise of exclusive ownership has been famously termed by Macpherson (2010 [1962]) as 'possessive individualism', a political theory that in turn increasingly underpins a liberal political system which focuses on protecting the rights of individuals, potentially at the expense of broader definitions of collective rights and obligations. This privileging of the individual as both the human and singular owner of property is not a universally held position. The 2007 *United Nations* Declaration on the Rights of Indigenous Peoples makes this very clear in its articulation of the multiple cultural and political subjectivities that influence and condition ideas of property:

> Article 31
>
> 1. Indigenous peoples have the right to maintain, control, protect and develop their cultural heritage, traditional knowledge and traditional cultural expressions, as well as the manifestations of their sciences, technologies and cultures, including human and genetic resources, seeds, medicines, knowledge of the properties of fauna and flora, oral traditions, literatures, designs, sports and traditional games and visual and performing arts. They also have the right to maintain, control, protect and develop their intellectual property over such cultural heritage, traditional knowledge, and traditional cultural expressions.
>
> *(http://www.un.org/esa/socdev/unpfii/documents/DRIPS_en.pdf)*

The nation and other collectives

In the nineteenth century, the concept of cultural property emerged as a way to think about social orders of entitlement and ownership that could not be encapsulated through either the model of pre-modern collectives, exclusive rights, or individual ownership. Cultural property became one way to articulate a political theory of society that was constituted not simply by the recognition of individual rights, but by the recognition of collective entitlements triangulated through ethnicity, territory, and citizenship in the context of the modern nation-state. In turn, cultural property, in the form of museum collections, libraries, monuments, and the archaeological record, became a crucial form with which to imagine, and communicate, the idea of the nation (Anderson 1991). Cultural property as a distinct category of objects with accompanying sets of obligations, emerged as a way to theorize the ethics of relationship between polities, and an important discourse of diplomacy and respect between nations. The triangulation of sovereignty, national identity, and anthropological notions of culture (see the section on culture below), underpinned by entangled articulations of race, ethnicity and territory, framed the emergence of the nation-state in the nineteenth century and started to forge the very notion of the modern international community (Gellner 1983; Hobsbawn 2012; Kuper 2000; Stocking 1982).

The common coupling and indeed production of cultural property for the European-modelled nation-state can, however, obscure alternative histories and ways of framing cultural property both between and within nations, and the critique of cultural property from *within* the nation-state is an important theme in this volume. For instance, the Treaty of Waitangi, signed in 1840 between some Māori chiefs and representatives of the British Crown, brought the state of New Zealand as a British colony into being, and at the same time, established in two versions, English and Māori, that Māori would retain 'tino rangatiratanga' – full sovereign authority – over their lands, forests, fisheries, and 'me o rātau taonga katoa', everything that they valued (Henare 2007). The term 'taonga' which is now used colloquially to refer to Māori cultural property or treasured cultural possessions (exemplified by the incorporation of the category Nga taonga tūturu as one of nine kinds of object in need of protection in the New Zealand Protected Objects Act of 2012 [1975]), referred, in the nineteenth century, in a much broader sense to the Māori estate (Henare 2003; Tapsell 1997). This historical framing in both European and Māori registers informs contemporary debates, about sovereignty and the property rights that it enables, for instance, recent claims to the Waitangi Tribunal (the agency set up in 1975 to evaluate treaty violations) about whether the radio spectrum is a taonga (and therefore part of the Māori estate) and if indigenous flora and fauna and the intellectual property related to them are also Māori cultural property (Van Meijl 2009). These contestations over the definition and scope of sovereignty have very real ramifications for the evaluation of how to redress violations of the Treaty as well as how to recognize the responsibilities of the state to uphold specifically Māori rights (Belgrave et al. 2005; Rata 2003). The example of New Zealand shows that from the beginning the concept of cultural property has contained the stakes of sovereignty in both intra- and inter-national frameworks, and emphasizes the power of the category to colonize alternative frameworks of collective ownership, authority and entitlement.

Cultural property, allied with discourses of the 'commons' or 'public domain' has also emerged as a zone of idealized collective entitlement that transcend the interests of individuals (Ostrom 1990; Hardt and Negri 2009; Hyde 2012a and 2012b). Like the notion of the public domain, which emerges in the spaces opened by the expiration, or rejection, of intellectual property rights (Boyle 2010), cultural property theory builds on the traditions of both property law and state sovereignty in order to constitute a genre of property owned by collectives, defined through identities and values described using the notion of culture, ethnicity, race, and heritage, that transcends the interests of private property for the benefit of the public sphere. One of our arguments here is that cultural property operates as a 'third space' between private and public property, by bringing national property and international community together, forging an international and global ethical environment emphasizing an idea of shared cultural resources and values (Merryman 1998). This builds explicitly on more anthropological understandings of the ways in which property constitutes identity through culture.

Whilst the reference point for this collective inheritance and entitlement has been the nation-state, cultural property is increasingly used as a way to discuss the sovereignty and rights of non-state groups. In present-day theorizing, a stringent body of work has emerged which critiques and unpacks property theory from the vantage point of culture. Legal scholars such as Carpenter, Katyal, and Riley (2009) and Sunder (2012), and anthropologists such as Handler (1988, 2003) and Myers (1989, 2005, 2012) have argued for recognition of the collective and cultural rights that underscore all property regimes. At the same time, theorists such as John and Jean Comaroff highlight the growing move towards what they term 'Ethnicity, Inc.', the 'process of cultural commodification, and the incorporation of identity in which it is imbricated … the rendering of ethnicized population into corporations or one kind or another … the creeping commodification of their cultural products and practices' (2009: 20–21) that characterizes the global expansion of neo-liberal property theory (see also Coombe and Weiss 2015; Coombe 2011). Carpenter, Katyal, and Riley (2009, 2010) argue that cultural property extends property logics away from personhood towards the construction of 'peoplehood'. Within this third space of property, the singular relationship between a person and a thing is displaced in favour of collective interests and rights. For the nation, cultural property protections and claim-making serve an agenda that shores up very precise boundaries and legitimacies of the state. Many Indigenous claims to cultural property function as a necessary mechanism for political recognition within and beyond the state whilst at the same time offer a refusal of state control and its varied attempts at legitimization.

Codifying cultural property

The language of cultural property was from the outset an expression of collective entitlement and identity referencing the borders of state sovereignty and focused on high culture: art, architecture, classically valued artefacts. One of the first formal codifications of the idea of cultural property can be found in the Leiber Code (1863), or the *Instructions for the Government of Armies of the United States in the Field*, which was established by Abraham Lincoln to govern the ethical behaviour of soldiers in the United States Civil War. The Leiber Code was the first modern instance in which 'public moveable property' referring specifically to religious and art objects, was reified as a category of protection and an ethical frame of reference in situations of conflict between polities showing a concern for managing the expectations over 'spoils of war'. This way of thinking about cultural property was continued into key legislation that aimed to ameliorate the potential for total destruction within the wars that originated in twentieth-century Europe. The Leiber Code was used as the template for the Hague Conventions of 1899, 1907, and 1954, which were the first multilateral and international efforts to develop codes of conduct and law during international conflict.

While we have been using the term cultural property to signify a discourse of rights and ownership through collectively owned practices and artefacts throughout this genealogy, it is important to realize that the term is relatively recent. Neither the Leiber Code nor the 1899 or 1907 Hague Conventions explicitly utilize the phrase 'cultural property'. Instead the concept is expressed in the following way in Article 56 of the 1899 Hague Convention (with very little change in language):

> The property of municipalities, that of institutions dedicated to religion, charity and education, the arts and sciences, even when State property, shall be treated as private property.
>
> All seizure of, destruction or wilful damage done to institutions of this character, historic monuments, works of art and science, is forbidden, and should be made the subject of legal proceedings.

Naming this kind of property as a correlated, but distinct from, private property marks the turn towards a new language of 'cultural property'. It is only in the 1954 Hague Convention that the first international definition of cultural property is found. The *Convention for the Protection of Cultural Property in the Event of Armed Conflict* reflects the emergence of cultural property as a political concept and new quasi-legal category in the aftermath of World War Two. For nation-states there had not previously been such a scale of destruction, looting, and loss of life with a deliberate 'cultural' focus over such a short period of time in the modern era. Crafted as a response to these recent events, cultural property emerged as a category that constituted a new sense of international community forged through the recognition of shared material values. The first international definition of cultural property, enshrined in the Hague Convention thus reads:

> Article 1. Definition of cultural property
>
> For the purposes of the present Convention, the term 'cultural property' shall cover, irrespective of origin or ownership:
>
> (a) movable or immovable property of great importance to the cultural heritage of every people, such as monuments of architecture, art or history, whether religious or secular; archaeological sites; groups of buildings which, as a whole, are of historical or artistic interest; works of art; manuscripts, books and other objects of artistic, historical or archaeological interest; as well as scientific collections and important collections of books or archives or of reproductions of the property defined above;
>
> (b) buildings whose main and effective purpose is to preserve or exhibit the movable cultural property defined in sub-paragraph (a) such as museums, large libraries and depositories of archives, and refuges intended to shelter, in the event of armed conflict, the movable cultural property defined in sub-paragraph (a);
>
> (c) centers containing a large amount of cultural property as defined in sub-paragraphs (a) and (b), to be known as 'centers containing monuments'.

As an international convention emanating from the United Nations, this document establishes relationships of obligation and care for material culture between nations. Each state retains authority to designate which material is of concern to the state and consequently where it is willing to take action.

Since the drafting of the Leiber Code, this particular codification of cultural property has been at the heart of imaginaries of international community and consensus, and has been used as a shorthand to signal both the rights of nations and their global obligations to one another, not just in terms of economic and political entitlement but in terms of cultural recognition and respect. This sense of ethical obligation to the international community began its circulation in 1954. Since then however it has been redirected and stewarded most prominently by another UN agency, the United Nations Educational, Scientific and Cultural Organization. The UNESCO 1970 *Convention on the Means of Prohibiting and Preventing the Illicit Import, Export and Transfer of Ownership of Cultural Property* has perhaps more than any other single law or convention moulded official cultural property discourse and practice into the present day. In this Convention, again developed for quite specific concerns about the non-state-sanctioned movement of items of collective cultural value, the scope of what constitutes cultural property is substantially expanded and the role of the state in making particular designations is affirmed. So expansive is the new list of what cultural property could entail – including rare collections and specimens of flora and fauna; antiquities; historical monuments, postage and archives – that it is no surprise that the Convention has been influential in defining and broadening the scope of tangible and moveable cultural property.

From the Hague to UNESCO

The shift within cultural property thinking away from definitions that focus only on fine art and antiquities can be tracked most visibly in the reworking of UNESCO definitions of cultural property as it is increasingly entangled with notions of heritage. Following the Hague Conventions which set a focus on art and antiquities and largely moveable cultural property, they have grown to include site-specific heritage, the natural as well as cultural, in the form of the 1972 UNESCO *Convention Concerning the Protection of the World Cultural and Natural Heritage*, and finally shifted to a focus on the immaterial in the 1994 *Nara Document on Authenticity* and the 2003 UNESCO *Convention for the Safeguarding of Intangible Cultural Heritage*. In particular these later Conventions shift the emphasis of cultural property discourse and policy 'from historical monuments, archaeological sites and natural parks to living traditions, embodied skills and oral expressions … widely heralded as more inclusive and people oriented' (Alivizatou 2012: 15; Hafstein 2009; Alivizatou 2011; Smith and Akagawa 2009). UNESCO increasingly galvanizes relations of authority and ownership over embodied skills, expressions, and practices, and these conventions mark an important shift from the singular (building or property owner for instance) to the collective, stretching definitions of cultural property into rights and relationships around a notion of 'peoplehood' as developed by Riley, Carpenter and Katyal (noted above).

In the latter part of the twentieth century, UNESCO continued as one of the principal agents producing international consensus around cultural property ensuring that ideas of cultural property and cultural heritage have blurred together becoming almost synonymous with the idea of international community (Di Giovine 2009; Meskell et al. 2015). During this same period the calibration of UNESCO to the scale of the nation also started to unravel. The claims of Indigenous groups and to some extent unrecognized states, such as Palestine, have found increasing voice within this international bureaucratic domain, with the Permanent Forum on Indigenous Issues, the World Intellectual Property Organization, and the 1993 Convention of Biological Diversity operating as the primary sites of direct dialogue and engagement on issues of cultural property and heritage protection. There is a new kind of political power offered via these sites, which is evident in the way that Indigenous peoples, for instance, have been using them (Simpson 2014).

Perhaps because of these shifts in who is able to participate within international political spaces as well as an opening up, post-World War Two, of who constitutes the 'international community', United Nations agencies are increasingly incorporating cultural rights within their remit. For instance, the United Nations now has a special Cultural Rights Rapporteur charged with reporting on cultural rights and their various vulnerabilities. The reports that have been generated since the inception of this position set through the Human Rights Council resolution 10/23 have included themes that easily map onto the terrain of cultural property. They include issues around access to cultural heritage, the right to artistic freedom, history and memory, intellectual property regimes, and since 2016 the intentional destruction of cultural heritage. Here we have an almost full circle return to the concerns of the 1954 Hague Convention that mobilize cultural property as a recognized vulnerability and consequence of armed conflict, except the focus here is less on the ways in which nation-states should be accountable to one another, than on how to manage the claims to sovereignty by non-state entities such as Daesh (or Islamic State). This has been exemplified by the concern expressed by UNESCO Director Irina Bokova about the destruction and illegal trading of antiquities by Daesh which rejects the international norms around cultural property that have been developed by UNESCO (Abu-Fadil 2013). The return to tangible property as a priority of state concern shows how important these forms are to the very idea of cultural property and highlights the anxieties about cultural property that emerge at the edge of state sovereignties.

Cultural property and intellectual property

If there are questions about the relationship between cultural rights, human rights, and cultural property, so too are there further questions about the intersections of cultural property and intellectual property. Like cultural property and heritage, intellectual property and cultural property are increasingly allied as concepts. In legal and policy domains, intellectual property is a space where the rights and sovereignties of cultural collectives are also being claimed and recognized.

For instance, in Australia, Aboriginal artists in the 1990s successfully used copyright law to secure protection for their cultural expressions as recognized works of 'art'. Initiated in the early 1960s by specialized in-country meetings by UNESCO about heritage and taken up and strategically re-positioned by Aboriginal advocates like Wandjuk Marika and Lin Onus in the 1970s and early 1980s, the artists, their communities, their lawyers, and their expert witnesses consistently expressed their complaint against the copying of styles, designs, and stories as a distinct form of cultural property, as a breach of legal rights that derived from their collective interests and community relationships and obligations. The key in understanding this move was that copyright actually provided legal redress and a very specific kind of public recognition of Aboriginal rights. The argument presented in court and in the popular writing available at the time explained that alternative structures of ownership and entitlement, based on ritual, spiritual authorization and kinship, already regulated the transmission of Aboriginal images (Myers 2005). The success of artists such as Banduk Marika, Johnny Bulun Bulun, and George Milpurrurru in getting the Australian courts to recognize Aboriginal law managing the circulation of culture, led to substantial governmental policy discussion within Australia about how and to what extent intellectual property law could be used as a tool to protect Aboriginal cultural works that were collectively and inter-generationally produced (Anderson 2009). This question was later picked up by the World Intellectual Property Organization, where the experience in Australia provided an important national 'case study'. Within Australia, these cases led to the new terminology, 'Indigenous intellectual and cultural property', which merged both ideas and expectations of intellectual property and cultural property together for a new political agenda that continues to hold significant traction. The strategic shifts between cultural property – which offered no specific legislation to leverage for direct action, and intellectual property – which offered the legal paradigm of copyright, speaks to the complex manoeuvring required at a local level to make concerns about cultural property legible and recognizable at a national and later international level.

Broad national attention to Indigenous intellectual and cultural property in Australia has had significant consequences. One example has been the development of the domain of cultural protocols as a non-legal way of articulating cultural property rights. Cultural protocols offer a paradigm for recognizing pre-existing, non-state-held rights and responsibilities towards Aboriginal cultural production and transmission. Illustrating the capacity of movement from the local to the international, there has been an increased pick-up of cultural protocols outside Australia as a deliberate mechanism for establishing and managing rights and relationships around cultural property, especially for making visible different cultural expectations for access and sharing particular kinds of cultural material (Myers 2011, 2014, 2015; Raven 2006, 2010; Anderson and Younging 2015). The adoption of cultural protocols within contexts like museums and archives that hold collections of Indigenous tangible and intangible cultural property highlights the multiple trajectories that localized concerns for appropriate recognition of, ongoing sovereignty over and acknowledgement of the conditions that led to the taking of this kind of cultural property to start with have produced.

The concern for Indigenous interests in the protection of culture has also been carried into the international arena and has led to the emergence of new categories such as 'Traditional Knowledge', 'Traditional Cultural Expressions', and 'Intangible Cultural Heritage'. In addition to UNESCO, the World Intellectual Property Organization's 15-year Intergovernmental Committee on Traditional Knowledge, Genetic Resources and Traditional Cultural Expressions has worked to develop the triangle of culture as a resource, a vehicle for articulations of sovereignty, and as a form of property. In these articulations there is a fusing of models as well as the development of what might be termed a legal creole – the various strategic manoeuvring around national legislation on one hand and international conventions on another – that understands cultural property as integral to the collective sovereignty of a people (modelled on the nation but extended to other polities) *and* those who draw on the constitution of culture as a commercial as well as spiritual resource to be managed and protected (Anderson 2010; Geismar 2013b).

Despite the expansion of definitions of cultural property, especially in UN policy contexts, there are many slippages between discourses of cultural property, cultural heritage, and intellectual property. By considering the motivations behind using one term or another, as well as what each enables (a certain kind of claim-making for example), it is possible to see various social and political strategies at play. For instance, when the nature of the claim being made is one of return, the return of an item of cultural significance to a community, cultural *property* offers a strategically powerful language for that claim as well as access into legal spaces where it reverberates. Claims for preservation of an item, a monument or a natural site, for instance, tend to harness the language of cultural *heritage*, which offers a different register of safeguarding and/or preserving a 'common' and universal good (see Hafstein and Skrydstrup this volume).

Cultural property and the market

Alongside the destruction of cultural property during armed conflict, the other major arena for cultural property policy and law has been controlling the market for cultural property.

John Merryman's influential piece, *Two Ways of Thinking About Cultural Property* (1986, 2005), summarizes the tensions that emerge between international conventions and their translation into national legislation by contrasting theories of 'cultural nationalism' (in which cultural property belongs first and foremost of the territories in which it was found) with theories of 'cultural internationalism' (the assertion that cultural property transcends such nationalistic claims to ownership and belongs to global communities as a shared inheritance of humanity). In addition to provoking tensions regarding collective entitlement – both within the nation and between national and international interests – cultural property may be seen as a commentary on the relationship between the market and the state. These legacies are challenged not just through the international community, but by models of private property that work to unravel nationalistic models of governance and regulation of the marketplace, and promote a 'free market' perspective on the regulation of both culture and identity. Museums, sitting between the two constituencies of private collector and public institution have had to carefully re-calibrate their collecting practices, especially in the wake of a number of high profile scandals at key institutions such as the Getty, whose curator Marion True was tried by the Italian courts after it came to light that she knowingly purchased illegally trafficked antiquities (Watson and Todeschini 2006). In the context of economic markets, cultural property thinking still tends to fall into binaries (national/international; free-market/state-regulated market) even as national borders are increasingly disrupted by supranational entities, and as communities within the nation contest whether this entity has ever really had their interests in mind.

A significant body of cultural property law beyond UNESCO 1970 focuses on the constitution and management of markets for cultural property. The UNIDROIT 1995 *Convention on Stolen or Illegally Exported Cultural Objects* recognizes a need to develop more private law controls over the circulation of cultural property not just within and between nation-states, but especially also within the private marketplace. In the 25 years after the passing of UNESCO 1970, the theft of cultural objects from museums, private collections, churches, and archaeological sites radically increased, especially in light of the growing standards around preservation, protection, and export. As Lyndel Prott has clearly explained, the UNIDROIT Convention focuses on private law-making which allows for a claim of 'theft' of a cultural object to be 'brought before a court or other competent tribunal … [t]his means that a private owner may make use of the normal legal channels available in the country where the object is located' (Prott 1996: 65). In shifting the legislative framework beyond UNESCO to UNIDROIT, ratifying states increasingly understood the necessity of developing more refined processes of addressing the complex networks that cultural property circulates within. The UNIDROIT Convention is also the first international cultural property convention that explicitly identifies Indigenous peoples as having unique types of claims that could require a private law response from states. With the expansion of markets for Native, First Nation, Aboriginal, and Indigenous artefacts, and for artefacts from the generally under-resourced global south, UNIDROIT begins to acknowledge some of the unequal and largely unethical circumstances of collection and exchange. It is, however, noticeable that there is not yet one instance where UNIDROIT has been used by a state to circumvent the sale of Native, First Nation, or Indigenous artefacts despite an increase in public auctions and private sales.

In another instance of increasing regulation of cultural property markets, the 1994 *Agreement on Trade Related Aspects of Intellectual Property Rights* (TRIPS), brought into being through the World Trade Organization (WTO) strategically tied trade to the international regulation of intellectual property. In mandating an international consensus around intellectual property rights which have expanded globally to include geographical indicators, new plant varieties, trade dress and so on – all of which in many contexts are also understood as cultural property – new markets as well as new property have been created. The growing acceptance of culture as a profit-generating resource crosscuts the rights and entitlements claimed by the state on behalf of its citizens. As Marama Muru Lanning discusses in this volume, the privatization of water rights in New Zealand has joined discussion about whether water, fisheries, the radio spectrum, and the foreshore and seabed are Māori taonga (Māori cultural property), state cultural property, Māori private property, or simply private property (see Goldsmith 2009).

The genealogy and current trajectories of cultural property thus lie within the broader history of thinking about the entanglement of property rights and national social orders, the tension between collective and individual rights, and the place for ethics and accountability within a global conversation about international community, value and international markets for culture. As well as becoming a shorthand for talking about systems of governance, especially within the frame of the nation-state, cultural property has also become a way of describing culture and cultural identities. Tensions around culture as a commodity versus culture as a common good continue to inflect understandings of culture as property, as does the acknowledgement that all property is cultural (Bodenhorn 2004).

Disciplinary engagements as sites of meaning

We have so far established the genealogy of cultural property as both a series of ideas and ideologies about how different kinds of collective identity authorize ownership over cultural resources, as well as a set of practical engagements in law and policy. We have focused on some of the key discourses, philosophical questions, conventions, and laws that have brought cultural property into being in both national and international contexts, and have highlighted some of the conceptual underpinnings around culture, nationalism, and property that are built into them. A primary objective of this volume is to allow the reader to appreciate how cultural property is brought into being in a wide number of different contexts, most especially through varied disciplinary and academic engagements, through policy and governance, and within particular sites of meaning (predominantly law courts, museums, archaeological sites, communities, and international organizations).

One of our aims in this Introduction and in the reader as a whole, including the accompanying website, is to provide a resource that transcends the assumptions and perspectives of any single academic discipline, and to draw different disciplines into conversation with one another. There are long traditions of thinking about cultural property that emerge from the key disciplines of law, anthropology, archaeology, economics, art history, and philosophy, amongst others, that are supplemented by work within the newer fields of museum studies, heritage studies, and cultural policy and management. It is often the case that these disciplines bound conversations and may talk about very similar issues in completely different languages, diminishing the opportunity to learn from, and communicate with, one another. For example, a specific legal case around cultural property might lead anthropologists to discuss the dynamics of the courtroom, the way in which particular claims are phrased, the performative nature of the actors and their various representatives, the regimes of value circulating and produced around the 'object' that is the centre of the case and the hierarchies of power in any legal decision making. A legal analyst might instead focus on the way the case is itself presented, the different jurisdictional questions that arise and the specific technicalities in the law that is being presented before the court. Both these approaches are rich with insight, but they do different work for their different audiences. As such they are bound by certain kinds of disciplinary logics and conventions. Journals such as the *International Journal of Cultural*

Property and the *International Journal of Heritage Studies* have been crucial in creating spaces to facilitate a conversation across disciplines, and in linking academic scholarship to law, policy, and practice. In this section, we focus particularly on the fields of anthropology, law, and archaeology, as they have been particularly dominant in creating a vibrant academic field for cultural property. We hope that students and scholars reading this volume will be able to develop a fluency in reading from the vantage point of different disciplinary perspectives and develop their own hybrid voice with regards to cultural property.

Anthropology

Anthropological engagements with cultural property have unravelled many of the often ethnocentric assumptions that are built into the term. These works question the very idea that culture can be owned in any tangible and fungible sense, as well as the models of ownership that underpin this claim. Marcel Mauss' influential writing on *The Gift* exemplifies an analytic trajectory in which cross-cultural and comparative cultural histories of exchange have been used to critique and denaturalize modern-day logics of private property, commodity exchange, and the relation between politics and economics that they suggest. Drawing on examples of global exchange from the potlatch of North-West Coast British Columbia, Māori understandings of the spirit of exchange (*hau*) in New Zealand, and traditions from the Ancient and Eastern world, Mauss demonstrated the cultural nature of all property relations and emphasized that capitalist commodity exchange was not simply the most evolved form of property relation but existed in tandem with a parallel tradition that emphasized social obligation and ethics of connection (Hart 2007). Recent influential works of economic and social theory have continued this tradition, with David Graeber demonstrating in his book *Debt: The First Five Thousand Years* (2013) that millennia of social relations organized around debt and obligation underpin the foundations of the modern credit economy (see also Graeber 2001).

A large body of literature focused specifically on cultural property develops this relative and comparative perspective, expanding our lexicon of exchange and value (e.g. Appadurai 1988; Myers 2001). Volumes such as Verdery and Humphrey (2004) and Strang and Busse (2011) present cultural property as an analytic frame that has come to have a wide variety of different meanings in different parts of the world, in many cases instantiating a form of what Lisa Breglia has termed 'monumental ambivalence' (2006) to the systems of governance, law, and policy that constitute official, often colonial, cultural property. The anthropological commitment to challenging analytic frameworks for property that normalize the values and modes of exchange within capitalism has led to a reframing of some of the conventional vocabularies of cultural property, often from the perspective of different contexts. For instance, engagements with Indigenous communities and museums has led to the development of new languages of 'stewardship' and 'guardianship' as substitutes for the commodity logic of ownership with regards to cultural material. In turn this has altered the normative practices of collections management in institutions with these collections (Brown 2006; Marstine 2011).

Anthropologists, drawing on the primary methodology of the discipline, participant-observation, also use ethnography to present the everyday experiences of people living within cultural property regimes. Many ethnographies present how people work to interpret and implement cultural property laws and policies on the ground (Breglia 2006; Butler 2007; Hviding and Rio 2011). Other accounts focus on how cultural property frameworks become avenues for those seeking to appropriate the economic and political capital that comes from having one's cultural artefacts and practices recognized in this framework and on the international stage (see Byrne 2014; Comaroff and Comaroff 2009; Hayden 2003; Geismar 2008; Geismar 2015a). The contribution that anthropological accounts of property have made really point to a shift in meaning and focus, where cultural property is not something that is owned, but rather functions to mark difference and identity. This moves beyond an assumed use-value of an object, and helps explain the multiple politics folded into the cultural property category and how this is rendered meaningful in diverse contexts (see Myers this volume).

The contributions of Melanesian/Polynesian ethnography to the rethinking of property relations from Mauss onwards cannot be underestimated. In particular, the work of Marilyn Strathern (e.g. 1999) and her students (e.g. Kalinoe and Leach 2001; Strathern and Hirsch 2004) have interrogated notions of rights, entitlement, and property from the vantage point of Melanesian exchange, ritual, and kinship. For instance, James Leach's ethnography of Nekgini articulations of cultural property (2003) argues that ideas about owning creativity in Papua New Guinea are incompatible with the objectifying language of cultural property and the ways cultural traditions are promoted by UNESCO. For Nekgini speakers, the term 'kastom' (a *tok pisin* transliteration of custom) signifies a far greater flexibility and fluidity of cultural practice that is located within local systems of entitlement and accountability and which cannot be codified or objectified. Leach's work signifies an important trend in anthropology that asserts that local terms do not map onto global terms such as cultural property, and which also accentuates the risks of local values and concepts being overwritten or ignored (see also Errington and Gewertz 2001).

An anthropological focus insists that we pay attention to the politics and the differences between local and global definitions of cultural property as well as local understandings of ownership and entitlements to culture in the creation and the production of new laws (see Aragon and Leach 2008). Many anthropologists are also critical of the bureaucracies that emerge to bolster state control of cultural property as well as promoting an official discourse and language. Michael Brown, for instance has developed a corpus of work that is critical of the application of legal frameworks to the sphere of cultural production and exchange, asking 'Can Culture be Copyrighted?' (1998) and exploring the 'heritage trouble' inherent in global policy and bureaucracies (2005). In particular, Brown took on the question of ownership over Native American culture and analysed various kinds of claim-making, arguing that culture should be managed through the civility of the cultural commons, rather than being subjected to an intensification of legal and bureaucratic protections. In a trenchant review, Mohawk anthropologist Audra Simpson accuses Brown of perpetuating a kind of cultural *terra nullius* by normalizing what are in fact colonial notions of the cultural commons (Simpson 2007). Here she points to the already erased complexities of Indigenous sovereignty over cultural sharing that make the idea of the cultural commons open and free (and without history) to start with. The opening up of anthropology to new generations of Indigenous anthropologists has also added a new layer of deconstruction and critique of the category of cultural property. This has helped re-position questions of sovereignty, control, and the difficult negotiations that Indigenous peoples must engage in within this discourse (Tsosie 1997; Mihesuah 2000; Deloria 2004).

Law

If anthropology can be glossed as a relativizing discipline, it might be easy to gloss law as a universalizing discipline and practice, committed to developing standardized languages for cultural property that can transcend local differences. However, the field of law has, often in close dialogue with anthropology, been committed to not only creating a series of normative definitions for cultural property, but to exploring cultural property in the context of both legal pluralism and alternative cultural systems (Merry 2000; Brenneis and Merry 2004; Carpenter, Katyal and Riley 2009; Riley 2004; Coombe 1998; Anderson 2009; Boateng 2011). At the same time, there are still tensions between critical legal studies, the field that emerged in the 1970s to analyse the cultural frameworks of law, and the branches of law that bring cultural property into being as an index of national and international interest in protecting and valorizing rights to culture.

Depending on where they study, law students may or may not be trained to think critically about law as a social phenomenon that may be implemented imperfectly and in continual dialogue with other social and cultural mores, including the agenda of elected politicians, minority interest groups, and the media. By criminalizing certain activities (such as the illicit trafficking of cultural heritage), defining the objects of cultural property, and laying out the rules of ownership, law implements core definitions of cultural property and supports certain cultural, social, and political values. Law is a distributed system made up of many different sites of articulation and dispensation, and with multiple actors who participate, produce, refine, and recirculate legal meaning. Each site, whether it be national or international for instance, carries its own internal logics of operation and of authority. How legal reasoning and decision making is made is largely dependent upon different principles and traditions within each locale – for instance in common law jurisdictions (like England, Australia, Canada (except Quebec), and India) the primary source and authority for law is found in case law and the establishment of precedent which treats legislation as something that is open to interpretation. This is different to how civil law jurisdictions (like France, Germany, Russia, and Turkey) approach legislation and the interpretative capacities of judges and of courts. Countries that have a blend of both common law and civil law do not necessarily find contradiction here, but instead have refined their ideas about the source and authority of law and how this impacts the various modalities of legal decision making.

At an international level, law functions to set global standards at the level of the nation, rather than regulating individual behaviour – the purview of private law making in each country. Treaties, conventions, and declarations all seek to affect forms of legal ordering in different ways. Treaties for instance set particular standards to be incorporated at the national level and are binding upon nations that are signatories. Conventions are agreements to act in certain ways and are also binding upon signatories but are less prescriptive, open to each state's own interpretation of action. Declarations are documents where nation-states agree to appropriate standards, but they are not legally binding. Conventions such as UNESCO 1970 attempt to create international consensus by developing requirements to adopt certain standards within national law. The implementation of international conventions reveals some of the social and political tensions that surround processes of claim-making as they are activated within legal fields. This is especially the case for cultural property disputes that are often international in their make-up. What is interesting in these instances is where the initial claims are made, how previous jurisdiction and control over the property is accommodated, and how competing state and non-state positions are recognized.

One rich site for thinking about this interplay is in the context of increasing cultural property suits around art looted during World War Two. The case of the restitution of Gustav Klimt's portrait of Adele Bloch-Bauer to Maria Altmann from the Austrian National

Collection is complicated not only because of the original facts surrounding the case, namely that the systematic looting and stealing of Jewish private property was legal and sanctioned at the German and Austrian state level when the painting was taken from the Bloch-Bauer family during the Nazi era. But also because this case proceeded through the US courts rather than courts in Austria because the filing fee for this kind of lawsuit in Austria, a portion of what would be understood as the recoverable amount of how much the paintings were worth, was impossible for Altmann to raise. As a US citizen Altmann instead made a claim against the Austrian government within the US court and so first had to make an argument under the Federal Sovereign Immunities Act – wherein a claim against one state can be made by another on behalf of an individual. Altmann won this case and it allowed her to file against the Austrian government. Following this decision, Altmann and Austria decided against further litigation and instead entered into a binding arbitration with three Austrian judges. The ruling in 2006 was that Austria was legally required to return the art to Altmann. What makes this case, and others like it, so interesting is the intersection of state claims; the different kinds of strategy and manoeuvring around national legislation; the changing social and political environments as Austria re-evaluated its relationship to its Nazi past; and the upholding of Altmann's private property rights that enabled her to sell the paintings upon their return to her in the US (Republic of Austria v. Altmann, 541 U.S. 677 (2004)).

Other high profile cases dealing with artwork stolen during the Holocaust from Jewish families have been heard in US courts partly because many of these artworks have ended up, through various legal and illegal channels, in the US (see also for instance United States v. Portrait of Wally, 105 F. Supp. 2d 288 (Southern District of New York 2000)). This has led to the US, especially New York City, becoming an amenable environment for debating and interpreting international law, as well as a global site of economic power particularly within the art market and museum world (Gerstenblith 2012). By way of contrast, it has taken nearly the same amount of time, forty years, for New Zealand claims for the restitution of the Māori carvings illegally exported to Switzerland by George Ortiz in 1973 to be upheld. This was, in part, a result of a lack of familiarity in the courtroom with Māori framings of cultural property as well as confusions around the status of New Zealand law in the UK during this period (Prott 2005). These cases demonstrate that cultural property claims need to develop the right combination of international community, agreed-upon logics and languages and recognizable national law in order to be successful. The situatedness, or place, of law, like the historical moments of its emergence and subsequent enforcement, therefore adds much nuance to its effectiveness, even though this may not be made explicit in discussions of legal suits and decisions about cultural property.

Law continues to shape cultural property debates in very particular ways. It structures fields of action, and affects how claims are imagined and then made, where they are legitimated and also where they are heard. Law is also involved in circulating phrases and generating meaning, and this includes the consistent reworking of the concept of cultural property itself.

Archaeological sites of meaning

Archaeologists, through their work on the ground in excavation and site management, and in the publication of site reports and archaeological analyses, have been at the forefront of many core issues and debates around cultural property. This has also been because of increased questions about where the 'objects' that come out of the ground reside, how they are documented and classified within museums/archives, how they enter into public, private, and other markets of exchange, and whose histories, identities, and memories they represent.

The archaeological record has historically been used as the very definition of what cultural property is, the paradigmatic 'object lesson' within legislation, and archaeological sites are often the primary domains of conflict and contestation over cultural property (see Brodie this volume; Renfrew 2000). Archaeologists, by defining and evaluating the archaeological record, play a vital role in establishing the scientific validation of space, time, and location and thus the very possibility of both provenance and provenience. They are in a privileged position to document the illicit trafficking of artefacts and the multiple claims that different stakeholders bring to questions of ownership of archaeological material (LaRoche and Blakey 1997; Harrison 1991; Agbe-Davies 2003; Battle-Baptiste 2011). The challenges of looting, illicit export, wilful destruction, fossicking, and balancing the interests of different communities (from collectors and curators through to people living on and around archaeological sites) have informed much recent archaeological commentary (Atalay 2012; Bruchac, Hart and Wobst 2010; Brodie, Kersel, Luke and Tubb 2006; Zimmerman 1997; Watkins 2001). Archaeologists have been active within debates (in policy environments, law courts, museums, universities, and in the media) around the efficacy of national and international law, often passionately advocating for regulation and education to prevent the destruction of artefacts and their promiscuous circulation within a free market (Brodie et al. 2000, 2008). Archaeological writing on illicit trafficking and collecting, and on the relationships between the state and the valuation of the archaeological record frames cultural property as a series of contests around the boundaries of both law and the valuing of objects from the past. This literature also engages with the tensions around the free market that underscore the terms of thinking that inhabit categories such as 'cultural nationalism' and 'cultural internationalism' (Bauer 2008).

There is a striking connection between advocates of cultural internationalism in cultural property legislation, theories of universal cultural heritage, and proponents of market deregulation (e.g. Appiah 2006; Cuno 2008). In his influential book *Against Cultural Property* (2005) John Carman argues that the very category of cultural property perpetuates the exploitation of heritage and the looting and expropriation of archaeological material and antiquities because of the dominant assumptions about private property, value, and commoditization he reads as being built into the language of property. In the UK context, prominent archaeologists such as Neil Brodie, Colin Renfrew, David Gill, and Christopher Chippindale have argued strongly in favour of regulation of the marketplace for antiquities, arguing that managing the collector's market fundamentally influences the production of archaeological knowledge and the preservation of archaeological sites (Renfrew 2000; Chippindale and Gill 2000). Chippindale's discussion of Stonehenge (1990), for instance, explores the interpretive frameworks that lead to understandings of ownership as they change over time, shifting a sense of entitlement through the state, and working in part to constitute organs of governmentality including the National Trust, English Heritage (now Heritage England) and even the public (see also Bender 1999). Part of his argument is to articulate strong collective interests in heritage and for a turn away from the market to support the maintenance of key heritage sites and cultural property. In more mainstream heritage environments, this approach has not been borne out in the ways in which heritage increasingly relies on consumer markets for direct financial support.

The significance of an archaeological mediation of cultural property comes through most clearly in the emergence of a new role for the archaeologist as an expert witness within land claim cases. Within the confines of the court, archaeologists (and anthropologists) have come to hold a specialized knowledge about Indigenous pasts and presents in places like the US and Australia, mediating these knowledges in ways that the (non-Native) court could hear and accommodate. Much more than the testimony from claimants themselves, archaeologists and anthropologists came to occupy a privileged if not also uncomfortable position for the possibility of the recognition of different land titles (Edmond 2004). This position speaks to inherent exclusions embedded within the law, and especially property law. Both anthropologists and archaeologists have played pivotal roles in Aboriginal land claims in Australia (see Layton 1994; Watkins 2001), for example being used to both legitimate and de-legitimate the notion of traditional Aboriginal culture in a suit to recognize Aboriginal cultural and political rights in claims to areas such as Alligator River (Tatz and Lambert 2006) and Hindmarsh Island (Kenny 1996; Bell 2008). Archaeologists have also been at the forefront of a critical turn towards the notion of heritage in which they unpack the core values, structures of government, and modes of practice that constitute both cultural heritage and cultural property (Smith 2006; Meskell 2015a; Harrison 2013).

Both cultural property and heritage are understood to be the collective belongings and patrimony of a described polity, the base unit of which is still that of the nation-state even as the ethnic tensions underpinning the formation of the nineteenth-century state remain as volatile today as they were two hundred years ago. Much of these debates focus on the ancient past, but a growing archaeology of the contemporary inscribes these issues into present-day contests over authority and ownership (Dawdy 2016; Harrison 2011; Byrne 2014; Atalay 2012). For instance, Rathje (2002) draws on his long-standing garbology project to argue that using the theories and methods of archaeology to analyse the things we throw away can open us up to new understandings of value, and new modes of analysis for understanding the relation of cultural practices to the artefactual world. Archaeology continues to inflect our understanding of cultural property, highlighting tensions between the material and the immaterial, the past and the present, and the social and political construction of value. Nadia Abu El Haj's work on the history and practice of archaeology in Israel demonstrates how archaeological practice 'inscribes the landscape with the concrete signs of particular histories and historicities ... producing an archaeological record for those eras considered central to a Jewish national heritage' (1998: 168–169). In Israel, the convergence of heritage regimes and material culture therefore becomes 'facts on the ground.'

The museum life of cultural property

Museums are critical sites in which cultural property is brought into being and given multiple meanings. Museum collections have been a primary reference point for the establishment of international definitions of cultural property, with a particular focus on archaeology and antiquities (Barkan and Bush 2003). In addition to providing an object lesson in the construction of national cultural property, museums have in the present day become sites of critique of nineteenth-century legacies of colonial collecting, of the national appropriation of cultures (Deloria 1969; Krech and Hail 1999; Jacknis 1985; Peers and Brown 2003; Clifford 1997, 2013; Turnbull and Pickering 2010; Silverman 2015; Krmpotich and Peers 2013).

Museums and their collections provide key venues for thinking through different models of cultural property. Some of the earliest cultural property laws (from the National Antiquities Act that was passed in the United States in 1906 (16 USC 431–433) through to the 1954 Hague Convention) were drafted with explicit reference to museum collections, as well as monuments and other moveable items. Yet there is an ongoing debate about the legitimacy of museums as the 'owners' of cultural property (e.g. Ames 1992; Cooper 2008; Tapsell 2006). The extensive critical writing about museums and communities and the various re-assemblage of collections *viz* community rights and expectations of inclusion, participation, and co-management mark a new and distinct turn in questions about exhibiting and display, and who gets to speak and has the right to do so. It has also opened up extensive dialogue about collaboration and who the 'publics' of museums are and have been presumed to be (Karp, Kreamer and Lavine 1992; Edwards et al. 2006; Golding and Modest 2013; Harrison et al. 2013; see also Anderson and Montenegro in this volume).

In response to this interrogation of the function and status of museums and the nature of their relationship to their collections, in 2003 the directors of several major art museums including the Chicago Art Institute, the Metropolitan Museum, and the British Museum published the *Declaration on the Importance and Value of Universal Museums*. They asserted that:

> Over time, objects so acquired – whether by purchase, gift, or partage – have become part of the museums that have cared for them, and by extension part of the heritage of the nations which house them. Today we are especially sensitive to the subject of a work's original context, but we should not lose sight of the fact that museums too provide a valid and valuable context for objects that were long ago displaced from their original source. The universal admiration for ancient civilizations would not be so deeply established today were it not for the influence exercised by the artifacts of these cultures, widely available to an international public in major museums.
>
> *(ICOM 2004)*

This argument was a direct response to paradigmatic shifts in the formulation of museum collections as cultural property. UNESCO 1970 demanded an unprecedented level of accountability and transparency in the collection of cultural property, requiring proof of export after 1970 and proof of provenance before 1970 in order to legitimate the transfer of ownership of cultural property. The passing of the 1990 *Native American Grave Protection and Repatriation Act* (NAGPRA) in the United States required all federal institutions to inventory their holdings of Native American human remains, materials collected from graves, and other associated items of cultural patrimony, and to make these inventories publicly available to federally recognized tribes for repatriation requests (Mihesuah 2000; Fine-Dare 2002; Chari and Lavallee 2013). This piece of national legislation has inculcated more accountability for the recognition of histories of colonial exploitation and dispossession, looting, theft, and straight-up dodgy dealing, and has situated the process and practice of repatriation of museum collections as one of the biggest issues for both cultural property law and policy as well as museums confronting the colonial legacies of many cultural property claims (e.g. Coombes 2003). Even the most conservative of museums are entering into negotiations around the ownership of collections focusing on relations of reciprocity and exchange rather than finite ownership, with long-term loans becoming a new norm in the return of cultural property. The language and practice of the 'loan' is important here and should also alert us to how rights are being negotiated and the way in which the very idea of property itself is also being both troubled and perpetuated. Paradigmatic tangible returns such as the returned potlatch treasures that founded the U'mista Cultural Centre (Clifford 1991, 2013), the return of the G'psgolox pole from Stockholm to British Columbia (Jessiman 2011), the return of Icelandic manuscripts from Denmark (Hafstein and Skysdrup this volume), and the return of the Euphronios Krater to Italy from the Metropolitan Museum of Art (Geismar 2008), signify new paradigms for the circulation of cultural property. All of these objects were collected in times of conflict or duress, or were exported illegally, and their return highlights the development of an international moral consensus embodied in national repatriation legislation and in conventions such as UNESCO 1970.

In turn, NAGPRA has also signalled a shift in the classification of human remains as collections. Cultural property, which challenges the alienability of material, and the domination of private property rights, has been a crucial part of claim-making to resist the cooption of human remains as collections, precipitating all kinds of contestations about the interpretation of human remains as ancestors in contradistinction to objects of scientific enquiry (Jenkins 2014; Fforde et al. 2004; Gould this volume). It is striking how cultural property law has developed alongside ethical guidelines and protocols facilitating a changing culture of respect and practice within museum collecting as well as in display and curation. This speaks to the complex matrix of formal and informal law that is required for shifting expectations and behaviour towards collections as well as to the communities from which they derived and continue to maintain meaning and memory.

This ethical framework is by no means universal and is contested from a number of different perspectives. Recent efforts by the Hopi Nation to block the sale of sacred Kachina or Katsinam were stymied by the French courts, who continued to frame Kachina as commodities rather than sacred material, upholding the rights of private property, and excusing private collectors from the responsibilities now increasingly demanded of state-run collections (*New York Times* 29 June 2014, and Association on American Indian Affairs Press Release 2016). Moreover, and to further highlight the very different registers of legitimacy that are a product of settler colonialism, French judges continue to reject the Hopi Nation as having any legal standing in France. This leaves the Hopi and the other tribes like the Zuni, Navajo, and Acoma Pueblo that are recognized in the US as sovereign nations requesting intervention by the US State Department in matters of international repatriation. From the very beginning of NAGPRA, private collections were recognized as a problem that this legislation could not address or regulate. In the wake of this reality and the contest of value around private collections, noted art collector and philanthropist Elizabeth Sackler founded the American Indian Ritual Object Repatriation Foundation, which aimed to reunite objects with their descendent communities through, rather than despite, the art market (American Indian Ritual Object Repatriation Foundation 1996). Restitution, the return of stolen property to its rightful owner, intersects with repatriation (the return of property to its rightful owner *in place*) around claims to stolen art, most famously the return of artwork looted or appropriated during World War Two (Nicholas 2009; Woodhead 2014).

Glass (2004) argues that there are many similarities between Native American and Jewish claims to museum collections as their cultural property in that both repatriation and restitution redress historical injustice in the present, allowing for closure for both individuals and communities. However, most cases of restitution are heavily mediated by the art market, and many works end up being re-sold, highlighting the alienability of their definition of property rather than the enduring relations drawn through the discourse of culture. Stolen art is recognized as the property of individuals first and cultural groups who were discriminated against second, and it is rarely produced by those groups. Glass asks why some collections might be recognized as cultural property and others as stolen works of art? There is a politics of recognition that generally still tends to gloss over cultural communities as individual owners, and privileges social and economic capital in the recognition of ownership rights.

This is the context within which the declaration of universal museums must be read: a context in which individual rights are presented as alternative to collective rights, and the entitlements of private property are still in tension with the requirements of a 'public good'. In response to a shifting legislative climate and a shift in the ethics of collection and display (Marstine 2011), and also the thrust of decolonization, the self-defined encyclopaedic or universal survey art museums assert that collecting practices of the past should not be judged by the morals of the present and highlight, as then-director Neil Macgregor commented on behalf of the British Museum, that they themselves were centres of world culture, rather than partisans of nationalist sentiment (Macgregor 2004). The idea that these institutions are uniquely situated as holders of world culture, however, is tempered by the emergence of new museums and cultural centres that establish sites of ownership and responsibility outside national capital cities. New museums such as the U'mista Cultural Centre in British Columbia, founded using a repatriated potlatch collection as mentioned above (Webster 1990), numerous tribal museums in North and South America like the Ziibiwing Center for Anishinabe Culture and Lifeways (Lonetree 2012), and local memory initiatives such as the District Six Museum in Cape Town in South Africa (Rassool 2006a) highlight a decentralizing and decolonizing move which has, in many instances, been supported by repatriation. These institutions have become vibrant community centres demonstrating the significance of historical collections to source communities (see Karp et al. 2006; Karp, Kreamer, and Lavine 1992).

There remain ongoing tensions that the framework of cultural property inculcates in museums. In addition to playing a crucial role in a new politics of restitution, reparation, and repatriation, museum practices of exhibition and display have become primary interlocutors themselves in debates about cultural property. Exhibitions – weaving objects, narratives, and representational technologies together – are increasingly recognized as a kind of cultural property, reflected in the growing recognition that sharing representational and curatorial authority is a form of self-determination, or even sovereignty in museum contexts, that may be as important as the repatriation of objects (Shannon 2014). For instance, the landmark controversy around the exhibition *The Spirit Sings* held at the Glenbow Museum in Calgary during the 1988 Winter Olympics continues to reverberate (Cooper 2008). The protests of the Lubicon Lake Band of Cree of Peace River were against the sponsorship of the exhibition by Shell Oil, a company they perceived to be directly damaging to the communities that the exhibition was celebrating through their art and material culture. The protests caused several sponsors and lenders to withdraw from the exhibition and damaged the relations between the museum and the community for many years. They also highlighted how self-determination over land and resources was tied to the politics of representing First Nation cultural collections or cultural property (Kisin 2013). The idea that representational frameworks within museums are themselves constitutive of cultural property continues to resonate, for example in recent protests surrounding the installation piece *Exhibit B*, by South African artist Brett Bailey, which continues a long trajectory of using the tactics of exhibitions to critique past politics of exhibitions, presenting a self-styled 'human zoo' referencing the colonial history of collecting and displaying African people. *Exhibit B* was eventually cancelled by the Barbican Gallery in London in the wake of an intense boycott movement by protestors who argued that the exhibition continued the racist oppression of past museum displays (Odunlami and Andrews 2014).

Digital technology in museums has become a space that unites these two domains – repatriation and the ownership of representational narratives – bringing together important conversations about ethics, ownership, and the materiality of cultural property. It also extends the reach of ideas around cultural property into other kinds of material, for instance ethnographic collections of sound and audio-visual materials. Field-notes that contain the documentation of language material, for instance, are increasingly a site for claim-making and for negotiations around ownership and control (Henderson et al. 2006; Anderson 2005; Anderson and Francis forthcoming). The emergence of new practices of digital 'repatriation' (Bell 2003; Christen 2011), 'return' (Bell et al. 2013), and 'e-patriation' (Glass 2015) demonstrates how definitions of cultural property continue to oscillate between a focus on material culture and a focus on immaterial knowledge and practice. Boast and Enote (2012) are stringently critical of the term 'digital repatriation' to refer to the return of digital versions of collections to communities. They argue 'the appropriation of *virtual repatriation* for projects of data sharing confuses the context of sharing with programs of restitution, thus potentially playing into the hands of those voices which seek to maintain the centralized, universal enlightenment collection' (2012: 111). The circulation of cultural property in digital form has raised a number of provocative questions: does the return of digital material count as repatriation? What issues of power, skills, and knowledge are exposed within these projects? What does it mean to 'own' digital files of cultural forms and practices? What exactly is the property and how is it regulated? And how can digital connectivity facilitate a more expansive definition of ownership, facilitating practices of guardianship, and extending custodial care beyond the borders of the museum (Geismar 2015b; Were 2014; Hogsden and Poulter 2012; Ngata et al. 2012; Anderson and Christen 2013; Isaac 2015)?

Cultural property into the future

If the years prior to the end of World War Two in 1945 signified an investment in the nation as owner of cultural property, the end of World War, the beginning and end of the Cold War era, the era of decolonization, and the emergence of diverse rights movements around the world challenged the supremacy of national interests from both the standpoint of a nascent international community but also from within nation-states. The nation has re-fractured into interest groups defined by categories of race and ethnicity. This complex cultural framework can only be summarized here: important trajectories of critique within the spectrum of cultural property discourse have been mounted by Indigenous peoples in settler-colonies such as Brazil, New Zealand, Canada, United States, Australia, and South Africa (e.g. Barker 2011; Cadena and Starn 2007); the descendants of African slaves in the Americas (Teye and Timothy 2004); and Queer activists who have all challenged the representational authority of the state and its right to mobilize and speak for them through the material record and archive (Vincent 2014; Marshall et al. 2014; Drabinski 2013). The legitimacy of national ownership of museum collections, national parks, and public spaces has been challenged from a number of different directions: through student protests and popular revolutions, the globally reaching Women's Rights Movements, the Civil Rights Movements, including the Black and Red Power Movement and the American Indian Movement in the USA (Message 2014). Projects to assert or reclaim memory politics in spaces of historical trauma (Williams 2007) have all challenged state ownership of cultural property, and by extension of the power to make and represent history. Core concerns of cultural property – to establish state recognition and governance through the channelling of rights to cultural forms and practices; to create collective modes of engagement through entitlement; and, for many, to instantiate a critique of private property – are now extended to a perhaps surprising array of new forms. For instance, Lee Douglas' contribution to this volume explores the ways in which ordinary Spaniards seek to construct a new genre of cultural property – evidence in documentation, oral testimony, and forensic material – to reassert historical memory in Post-Franco Spain. There, cultural property increasingly becomes a way to resist and reclaim the representational authority of the State's monopoly over the past.

From the start, cultural property as a category emerged at moments of conflict, and out of tensions of global engagement across often contested national and local borders. As we move towards the third decade of the twenty-first century, familiar models of national authority and sovereignty over cultural properties are starting to break down under pressure from groups within states who call into question this authority and its operating logics, challenging the remit and boundaries of the nation-state itself. The challenge to the authority of the nation emerges not only from within states but also within the global arena as the recent destruction of specific world heritage sites in Afghanistan and Syria demonstrates. Debates around the preservation of cultural property sit squarely at the centre of theorizations of the powers of 'international community', global consensus, and the limits of international policy (see Flood 2002). The emergence of new political entities such as Daesh, that reject existing parameters of nation-states and international conventions, and the uncertainties about supranational alliances (from NATO to the European Union) are slowly unravelling the traditional forums for the definition and recognition of cultural property – the nation, or the international community (Byrne 2014). If World War Two strongly influenced our current international and national regimes, we may well ask what the effect of this new kind of non-state conflict and politics will produce, what kinds of new models and formulations for cultural property governance will be developed, and what the changing nature of cultural property will be? Within the current flux and decomposition of the nation-state as the ultimate unit of economic and political authority, the different policies and orders informing the international governance of cultural property may need to be remade. As such, future lives for cultural property claims and constituents are in motion. This volume sits at a moment in which cultural property is being redefined, its borders (economic, political, and material) reconfigured. We hope that the collection of essays here will provide a blueprint for understanding cultural property in relation to its past and taking account for its present as we steadily move into unanticipated and unpredictable futures.

Acknowledgements

Sincere thanks to Alex Bauer, Joshua Bell, Rosemary Coombe, Fred Myers, and David Wengrow for critical readings and advice on framing what is a broad and unruly field. Thanks to Faye Ginsburg, Sonia Das, Emily Martin, Mathilde Cohen, John Hadfield, Maria Montenego and Andrea Geyer. Thanks to Ryan O'Byrne and Anna Weinreich for their research assistance.

Bibliography

Abu El-Haj, Nadia. 1998. "Translating Truths: Nationalism, the Practice of Archaeology, and the Remaking of Past and Present in Contemporary Jerusalem." *American Ethnologist* 25(2): 166–188.

Abu-Fadil, Magda. 1 November 2013. "War Threatens Palmyra, UNESCO Pleads for Syrian Heritage Protection." *Huffington Post.*

Agamben, Giorgio. 1998. *Homo Sacer: Sovereign Power and Bare Life.* Stanford, CA: Stanford University Press.

Agbie-Davis, Anna. 2003. "Archaeology of the Old Elliott School." *Bermuda Journal of Archaeology and Maritime History* 13: 129–154.

Alvizatou, Marilena. 2011. "Intangible Cultural Heritage and Erasure: Rethinking Cultural Preservation and Contemporary Museum Practice." *International Journal of Cultural Property* 18: 37–60.

Alivizatou, Marilena. 2012. *Intangible Heritage and the Museum: New Perspectives on Cultural Preservation.* Walnut Creek, CA: Routledge.

American Indian Ritual Object Repatriation Foundation, and United States, eds. 1996. *Mending the Circle: A Native American Repatriation Guide: Understanding and Implementing NAGPRA and the Official Smithsonian and Other Repatriation Policies.* New York: American Indian Ritual Object Repatriation Foundation.

Ames, Michael M. 1992. *Cannibal Tours and Glass Boxes: The Anthropology of Museums*. Vancouver, BC: University of British Columbia Press.
Anderson, Benedict. 1991. *Imagined Communities: Reflections on the Origin and Spread of Nationalism*. London and New York: Verso.
Anderson, Jane. 2005. "Access and Control of Indigenous Knowledge in Libraries and Archives: Ownership and Future Use." American Library Association and The MacArthur Foundation. Correcting Course: Copyright for Libraries in the National and International arena. www.ccnmtl.columbia.edu/projects/alaconf2005/paper_anderson.pdf.
Anderson, Jane. 2009. *Law, Knowledge, Culture: The Production of Indigenous Knowledge in Intellectual Property Law*. Cheltenham: Edward Elgar.
Anderson, Jane. 2010. "Indigenous/Traditional Knowledge and Intellectual Property." Durham, NC: Duke University School of Law.
Anderson, Jane, and Kimberly Christen. 2013. "'Chuck a Copyright on It': Dilemmas of Digital Return and the Possibilities for Traditional Knowledge Licenses and Labels." *Museum Anthropology Review* 7(1–2): 105–126.
Anderson, Jane, and James Eric Francis, Sr. forthcoming. "Decolonial Futures of Sharing: Protecting Our Voice, Intellectual Property and Penobscot Language Materials." *Proceedings from the American Philosophical Society*.
Anderson, Jane, and Greg Younging. 2015. "Renegotiated Relationships and New Understandings: Indigenous Protocols." In *Free Knowledge: Confronting the Commodification of Human Discovery*, edited by Patricia Elliott and Daryl Hepting, 180–198. Regina, SK: University of Regina Press.
Appadurai, Arjun, ed. 1988. *The Social Life of Things: Commodities in Cultural Perspective*. New edition. Cambridge and New York: Cambridge University Press.
Appiah, Kwame Anthony. 2006. *Cosmopolitanism: Ethics in a World of Strangers*. New York: W.W. Norton.
Aragon, Lorraine V., and James Leach. 2008. "Arts and Owners: Intellectual Property Law and the Politics of Scale in Indonesian Arts." *American Ethnologist* 35(4): 607–631.
Asad, Talal. 1973. *Anthropology and the Colonial Encounter*. Ithaca, NY: Ithaca Press.
Atalay, Sonya. 2012. *Community-Based Archæology: Research with, by, and for Indigenous and Local Communities*. Berkeley: University of California Press.
Barkan, Elazar, and Ronald Bush. 2003. *Claiming the Stones, Naming the Bones: Cultural Property and the Negotiation of National and Ethnic Identity*. Los Angeles, CA: Getty Publications.
Barker, Joanne. 2011. *Native Acts: Law, Recognition, and Cultural Authenticity*. Durham, NC: Duke University Press.
Battle-Baptiste, Whitney. 2011. *Black Feminist Archaeology*. Walnut Creek, CA: Routledge.
Bauer, Alex. 2008. "New Ways of Thinking about Cultural Property: A Critical Appraisal of the Antiquities Trade Debate." *Fordham International Law Journal* 31: 690–724.
Belgrave, Michael, Merata Kawharu, and David Williams. 2005. *Waitangi Revisited: Perspectives on the Treaty of Waitangi*. Oxford: Oxford University Press.
Bell, Diane, ed. 2009. *Listen to Ngarrindjeri Women Speaking: Kungun Ngarrindjeri Miminar Yunnan*. North Melbourne: Spinifex Press.
Bell, Joshua A. 2003. "Looking to See: Reflections on Visual Repatriation in the Purari Delta, Gulf Province, Papua New Guinea." In *Museums and Source Communities: A Routledge Reader*, edited by Laura L. Peers and Alison K. Brown, 111–122. London: Routledge.
Bell, Joshua A., Kimberly A. Christen, and Mark Turin. 2013. "Introduction: After the Return." *Museum Anthropology Review* 7(1–2): 1–21.
Bender, Barbara. 1999. *Stonehenge: Making Space*. Oxford and New York: Berg 3PL.
Benton, Lauren. 2001. *Law and Colonial Cultures: Legal Regimes in World History, 1400–1900*. Cambridge and New York: Cambridge University Press.
Boast, Robin, and Jim Enote. 2012. "Virtual Repatriation: It is Neither Virtual nor Repatriation." In *Heritage in the Context of Globalization, Vol. 8*. Springer, NY: Springer Briefs in Archaeology.
Boateng, Boatema. 2011. *Copyright Thing Doesn't Work Here: Adinkra and Kente Cloth and Intellectual Property in Ghana*. Minneapolis: University of Minnesota Press.
Bodenhorn, Barbara. 2004. "Is Being 'Really Inupiaq' a Form of Cultural Property?" In *Properties of Culture – Culture as Property. Pathways to Reform in Post-Soviet Siberia*, 35–50. Berlin: Dietrich Reimer Verlag. http://www.siberian-studies.org/publications/PDF/cpbodenhorn.pdf.
Boyle, James. 2010. *The Public Domain: Enclosing the Commons of the Mind*. New Haven, CT; London: Yale University Press.

Breglia, Lisa. 2006. *Monumental Ambivalence: The Politics of Heritage*. Austin: University of Texas Press.
Brenneis, Donald Lawrence, and Sally Engle Merry. 2004. *Law and Empire in the Pacific: Fiji and Hawai'i, Vol. 1*. Oxford: James Currey.
Brodie, Neil, Jennifer Doole, Peter Watson, and Museums Association. 2000. *Stealing History: The Illicit Trade in Cultural Material*. Cambridge: McDonald Institute for Archaeological Research.
Brodie, N., M. Kersel, C. Luke and K. W. Tubb. 2006. *Archaeology, Cultural Heritage and the Antiquities Trade*. Gainesville: University of Florida Press.
Brown, Alison K., and Laura Peers. 2006. *Pictures Bring Us Messages/Sinaakssiiksi Aohtsimaahpihkookiyaawa: Photographs and Histories from the Kainai Nation*. Toronto: University of Toronto Press.
Brown, Deidre. 2006. "Museums as Cultural Guardians." In *South Pacific Museums: Experiments in Culture*, edited by Chris Healy and Andrea Witcomb, 238–260. Clayton: Monash University ePress.
Brown, Michael F. 2005. "Heritage Trouble: Recent Work on the Protection of Intangible Cultural Property." *International Journal of Cultural Property* 12(01): 40–61.
Brown, Michael F., J. A. Barnes, David A. Cleveland, Rosemary J. Coombe, Phiilippe Descola, L. R. Hiatt, Jean Jackson, Bengt Karlsson, Darryl A. Posey, Lawrence Rosen, Fernando S. Granero, Carlo Severi, David Stephenson, Marilyn Strathern, and Donald Tuzin. 1998. "Can Culture Be Copyrighted? [and Comments and Reply]." *Current Anthropology* 39(2): 193–222.
Bruchac, Margaret, Siobhan Hart, and H. Martin Wobst, eds. 2010. *Indigenous Archaeologies: A Reader on Decolonization*. Reprint edition. Walnut Creek, CA: Routledge.
Butler, Beverley. 2007. *Return to Alexandria: An Ethnography of Cultural Heritage, Revivalism, and Museum Memory*. Publications of the Institute of Archaeology, University College London. Walnut Creek, CA: Left Coast Press.
Byrne, Denis. 2014. *Counterheritage: Critical Perspectives on Heritage Conservation in Asia*. New York: Routledge.
Cadena, Marisol de la, and Orin Starn, eds. 2007. *Indigenous Experience Today*. Oxford: Berg.
Carman, John. 2005. *Against Cultural Property: Archaeology, Heritage and Ownership*. London and New York: Bloomsbury Academic.
Carpenter, Kristen A., Sonia K. Katyal, and Angela R. Riley. 2009. "In Defense of Property." *Yale Law Journal* 118(6): 1022–1125.
Carpenter, Kristen A. 2010. "Clarifying Cultural Property." *International Journal of Cultural Property* 17(3): 581–598.
Cattelino, Jessica. 2010. "The Double-Bind of American Needs-Based Sovereignty." *Cultural Anthropology* 25(2): 235–262
Chari, Sangita, and Jaime M. N. Lavallee. 2013. *Accomplishing NAGPRA: Perspectives on the Intent, Impact, and Future of the Native American Graves Protection and Repatriation Act*. Corvallis: Oregon State University Press.
Chippindale, Christopher. 1990. *Who Owns Stonehenge?* London: Batsford.
Chippindale, Christopher, and David W. J. Gill. 2000. "Material Consequences of Contemporary Classical Collecting." *American Journal of Archaeology* 104(3): 463.
Christen, Kimberly. 2011. "Opening Archives: Respectful Repatriation." *American Archivist* 74(1): 185–210.
Clifford, James. 1991. "Four Northwest Coast Museums: Travel Reflections." In *Exhibiting Cultures: The Poetics and Politics of Museum Display*, 212–254. Washington, DC: Smithsonian Institution Press.
Clifford, James. 1997. *Routes: Travel and Translation in the Late Twentieth Century*. Cambridge, MA: Harvard University Press.
Clifford, James. 2013. *Returns*. Cambridge, MA: Harvard University Press.
Collins, John. 2012. "'But What If I Should Need to Defecate in Your Neighborhood, Madame?': Empire, Redemption, and the 'Tradition of the Oppressed' in a Brazilian World Heritage Site." *Cultural Anthropology* 23(2): 279–238.
Comaroff, John L., and Jean Comaroff. 2009. *Ethnicity, Inc.* Chicago: University of Chicago Press.
Coombe, Rosemary J. 1998. *The Cultural Life of Intellectual Properties: Authorship, Appropriation and the Law*. Durham, NC: Duke University Press.
Coombe, Rosemary J. 2009. "The Expanding Purview of Cultural Properties and Their Politics." *Annual Review of Law and Social Science* 5(1): 393–412.
Coombe, Rosemary J. 2011. "Possessing Culture: Political Economies of Community Subjects and Their Properties." In *Ownership and Appropriation*, edited by Mark Busse and Veronica Strang, 105–127. London: Berg Publishers.

Coombe, Rosemary J., and Lindsay M. Weiss. 2015. "Neoliberalism, Heritage Regimes, and Cultural Rights." In *Global Heritage: A Reader*, edited by Lynn Meskell, 43–69. Chichester and Malden, MA: Wiley-Blackwell.

Coombes, Annie E. 2003. *History after Apartheid: Visual Culture and Public Memory in a Democratic South Africa*. Durham, NC: Duke University Press.

Cooper, Karen Coody. 2008. *Spirited Encounters: American Indians Protest Museum Policies and Practices*. Lanham, MD: AltaMira Press.

Cowan, Jane K., Marie-Bénédicte Dembour, and Richard Wilson, eds. 2001. *Culture and Rights: Anthropological Perspectives*. Cambridge and New York: Cambridge University Press.

Cuno, James B. 2008. *Who Owns Antiquity?: Museums and the Battle over Our Ancient Heritage*. Princeton, NJ: Princeton University Press.

Dawdy, Shannon Lee. 2016. *Patina: A Profane Archaeology*. Chicago: University of Chicago Press.

Deloria, Philip J. 2004. *Indians in Unexpected Places*. Lawrence: University Press of Kansas.

Deloria, Vine. 1969. *Custer Died For Your Sins*. New York: Macmillan.

Di Giovine, Michael A. 2009. *The Heritage-Scape: UNESCO, World Heritage, and Tourism*. Lanham, MD: Lexington Books.

Drabinski, Emily. 2013. "Queering the Catalog: Queer Theory and the Politics of Correction." *Library Quarterly*. 3(2): 94–111.

Drahos, Peter. 1996. *A Philosophy of Intellectual Property*. New edition. London and New York: Routledge.

Edmond, Gary. 2004. "Thick Decisions: Expertise, Advocacy and Reasonableness in the Federal Court of Australia." *Oceania* 74(3): 190–230.

Edwards, Elizabeth, Chris Gosden, and Ruth Phillips, eds. 2006. *Sensible Objects: Colonialism, Museums and Material Culture*. English edition. London and New York: Bloomsbury Academic.

Eriksen, Thomas Hylland. 2001. "Between Universalism and Relativism: A Critique of the UNESCO Concept of Culture." In *Culture and Rights: Anthropological Perspectives*, 127–148. Cambridge: Cambridge University Press.

Errington, Frederick, and Deborah Gewertz. 2001. "On the Generification of Culture: From Blow Fish to Melanesian." *Journal of Royal Anthropological Institute* 7(3): 509–525.

Fforde, Cressida, Jane Hubert, and Paul Turnbull, eds. 2004. *The Dead and Their Possessions: Repatriation in Principle, Policy and Practice*. New York: Routledge.

Fine-Dare, Kathleen S. 2002. *Grave Injustice: The American Indian Repatriation Movement and NAGPRA*. Lincoln: University of Nebraska Press.

Flood, Barry. 2002. "Between Cult and Culture: Bamiyan, Islamic Iconoclasm, and the Museum." *The Art Bulletin* 84(4): 641–659.

Geismar, Haidy. 2008. "Cultural Property, Museums, and the Pacific: Reframing the Debates." *International Journal of Cultural Property* 15(2): 109.

Geismar, Haidy. 2013a. "Defining the Digital." *Museum Anthropology Review* 7(1–2): 254–263.

Geismar, Haidy. 2013b. *Treasured Possessions: Indigenous Interventions into Cultural and Intellectual Property*. Durham, NC: Duke University Press.

Geismar, Haidy. 2015a. "Anthropology and Heritage Regimes." *Annual Review of Anthropology* 44(1): 71–85.

Geismar, Haidy. 2015b. "Post-Photographic Presences, or How to Wear a Digital Cloak." *Photographies* 8(3): 305–321.

Gellner, Ernest. 1983. *Nations and Nationalism*. Ithaca, NY: Cornell University Press.

Gerstenblith, Patty. 2004. "The Licit and Illicit Trade in Antiquities." In *It's Legal but It Ain't Right*, edited by Nikos Passas and Neva Goodwin, 138–167. Ann Arbor: University of Michigan Press.

Gerstenblith, Patty. 2012. *Art, Cultural Heritage, and the Law: Cases and Materials*. Durham, NC: Carolina Academic Press.

Gibbon, Kate Fitz. 2005. *Who Owns the Past?: Cultural Policy, Cultural Property, and the Law*. New Brunswick, NJ: Rutgers University Press.

Glass, Aaron. 2004. "Return to Sender: On the Politics of Cultural Property and the Proper Address of Art." *Journal of Material Culture* 9(2): 115–139.

Glass, Aaron. 2015. "Indigenous Ontologies, Digital Futures: Plural Provenances and the Kwakwaka'wakw Collection in Berlin and Beyond." In *Museum as Process: Translating Local and Global Knowledges*, edited by Raymond Silverman, 19–44. Oxford and New York: Routledge.

Golding, Viv, and Wayne Modest, eds. 2013. *Museums and Communities: Curators, Collections and Collaboration*. London and New York: Bloomsbury Academic.

Goldsmith, Michael. 2009. "Who Owns Native Nature? Discourses of Rights to Land, Culture, and Knowledge in New Zealand." *International Journal of Cultural Property* 16 (Special Issue 03): 325–339.
Goodale, Mark, and Sally Engle Merry, eds. 2007. *The Practice of Human Rights: Tracking Law Between the Global and the Local.* Cambridge and New York: Cambridge University Press.
Graeber, David. 2001. *Toward an Anthropological Theory of Value: The False Coin of Our Own Dreams.* New York: Palgrave.
Graeber, David. 2013. *Debt: The First 5,000 Years.* Reprint edition. Brooklyn, NY: Melville House Publishing.
Greene, Shane. 2004. "Indigenous People Incorporated?: Culture as Politics, Culture as Property in Pharmaceutical Bioprospecting." *Current Anthropology* 45(2): 211–237.
Hafstein, Valdimar Tr. 2009. "Intangible Heritage as a List: From Masterpieces to Representation." In *Intangible Heritage*, 93–111. Oxford: Routledge.
Hamilton, Jennifer A. 2008. *Indigeneity in the Courtroom: Law, Culture, and the Production of Difference in North American Courts.* New York: Routledge.
Handler, Richard. 1988. *Nationalism and the Politics of Culture in Quebec.* Madison: University of Wisconsin Press.
Handler, Richard. 2003. "Cultural Property and Culture Theory." *Journal of Social Archaeology* 3(3): 353–365.
Hann, Chris M. 1998a. "Introduction: The Embeddedness of Property." In *Property Relations: Renewing the Anthropological Tradition*, 1–47. Cambridge: Cambridge University Press.
Hann, Chris M. 1998b. *Property Relations: Renewing the Anthropological Tradition.* New York: Cambridge University Press.
Hardt, Michael, and Antonio Negri. 2009. *Commonwealth.* Cambridge, MA: Harvard University Press.
Harris, Cheryl I. 1993. "Whiteness as Property." *Harvard Law Review* 106(8): 1707–1791
Harrison, Faye. 1991. *Decolonizing Anthropology: Moving Further Toward an Anthropology of Liberation.* Arlington, VA: American Anthropological Association.
Harrison, Rodney. 2011. "Surface Assemblages. Towards an Archaeology in and of the Present." *Archaeological Dialogues* 18(2): 141–161.
Harrison, Rodney. 2013. *Heritage: Critical Approaches.* New York: Routledge.
Harrison, Rodney, Sarah Byrne, and Anne Clarke, eds. 2013. *Reassembling the Collection: Ethnographic Museums and Indigenous Agency.* Santa Fe, NM: School for Advanced Research Press.
Hart, Keith. 2007. "Marcel Mauss: In Pursuit of the Whole. A Review Essay." *Comparative Studies in Society and History* 49(2): 473.
Hayden, Cori. 2003. "From Market to Market: Bioprospecting's Idioms of Inclusion." *American Ethnologist* 30(3): 359–371.
Henare, Amiria. 2007. "Taonga Maori: Encompassing Rights and Property in New Zealand." In *Thinking Through Things: Theorising Artefacts in Ethnographic Perspective*, edited by Amiria Henare, Martin Holbraad, and Sari Wastell, 57–83. London: University College London.
Henare, Manuka. 2003. "The Changing Images of Nineteenth Century Māori Society: From Tribes to Nation: A Thesis Submitted to the Victoria University of Wellington in Fulfilment of the Requirements for the Degree of Doctor of Philosophy in Maōri Studies." Wellington: Victoria University.
Henderson, John, Hannah McGlade, Kim Scott, and Denise Smith-Ali. 2006. *A Protocol for Laves' 1931 Noongar Field Notes.* Nedlands: University of Western Australia.
Hobbes, Thomas. 1996. *Hobbes: Leviathan.* Edited by Richard Tuck. Cambridge: Cambridge University Press.
Hobsbawm, E. J. 2012. *Nations and Nationalism Since 1780: Programme, Myth, Reality.* Cambridge: Cambridge University Press.
Hogsden, Carl, and Emma K. Poulter. 2012. "The Real Other? Museum Objects in Digital Contact Networks." *Journal of Material Culture* 17(3): 265–286.
Hviding, Edvard, and Knut Rio. 2011. *Social Movements, Cultural Heritage and the State in Oceania.* Oxford: Sean Kingston Publishing.
Hyde, Lewis. 2012a. *Common as Air: Revolution, Art and Ownership.* New York: Farrar, Straus and Giroux.
Hyde, Lewis. 2012b. *The Gift: How the Creative Spirit Transforms the World.* Edinburgh: Canongate Canons.
ICOM. 2004. "Declaration on the importance and value of universal museums." ICOM News 1:4. http://icom.museum/fileadmin/user_upload/pdf/ICOM_News/2004-1/ENG/p4_2004-1.pdf (accessed 29 March 2017).
ICTMN Staff. 2015. "Selling the Sacred, Again: Another Auction of Hopi Katsinam Takes Place in Paris." *Indian Country Today Media Network.com.* 1 June. http://indiancountrytodaymedianetwork.com/2015/06/01/selling-sacred-again-another-auction-hopi-katsinam-takes-place-paris-160568 (accessed 29 March 2017).
Isaac, Gwyneira. 2015. "Perclusive Alliances." *Current Anthropology* 56(S12): S286–296.

Jacknis, Ira. 1985. "Franz Boas and Exhibits: On the Limitation of the Museum Method of Anthropology." In *Objects and Others: Essays on Museums and Material Culture*, edited by George Stocking, 75–111. Madison: University of Wisconsin Press.

Jenkins, Tiffany. 2014. *Contesting Human Remains in Museum Collections: The Crisis of Cultural Authority*. New York: Routledge.

Jessiman, Stacey R. 2011. "The Repatriation of the G'psgolox Totem Pole: A Study of Its Context, Process, and Outcome." *International Journal of Cultural Property* 18(3): 365–391.

Kalinoe, Lawrence Kuna, and James Leach. 2001. *Rationales of Ownership: Ethnographic Studies of Transactions and Claims to Ownership in Contemporary Papua New Guinea*. New Delhi: UBS Publishers' Distributors.

Karp, Ivan, Christine Mullen Kreamer, and Steven Levine, eds. 1992. *Museums and Communities: The Politics of Public Culture*. Washington, DC: Smithsonian Books.

Karp, Ivan, Corinne A. Kratz, Lynn Szwaja, and Tomas Ybarra-Frausto. 2006. *Museum Frictions: Public Cultures/Global Transformations*. Durham, NC: Duke University Press.

Kenny, Chris. 1996. *Women's Business*. Potts Point: Duffy & Snellgrove.

Kirsch, Stuart. 2001. "Lost Worlds: Environmental Disaster, 'Culture Loss,' and the Law." *Current Anthropology* 42(2): 167–198.

Kisin, Eugenia. 2013. "Unsettling the Contemporary: Critical Indigeneity and Resources in Art." *Settler Colonial Studies* 3(2): 141–156.

Krech, Shepard and Barbara A. Hail, eds. 1999. *Collecting Native America 1870-1960*. Washington, DC: Smithsonian Institution Press.

Krmpotich, Cara, and Laura Peers. 2013. *This Is Our Life: Haida Material Heritage and Changing Museum Practice*. Vancouver, BC: University of British Columbia Press.

Kuper, Adam. 2000. *Culture: The Anthropologists' Account*. New edition. Cambridge, MA: Harvard University Press.

La Roche, Cheryl J., and Michael L. Blakey. 1997. "Seizing Intellectual Power: The Dialogue at the New York African Burial Ground." *Historical Archaeology* 31(3): 84–106.

Layton, R. 1994. *Conflict in the Archaeology of Living Traditions*. London: Taylor & Francis.

Leach, James. 2003. "Owning Creativity: Cultural Property and the Efficacy of Custom on the Rai Coast of Papua New Guinea." *Journal of Material Culture* 8(2): 123–143.

Locke, John. 2011. *Second Treatise of Government*. Seaside, OR: Watchmaker Publishing.

Lonetree, Amy. 2012. *Decolonizing Museums: Representing Native America in National and Tribal Museums*. Chapel Hill, NC: UNC Press.

MacGregor, Neil. 2004. "The Whole World in Our Hands." *The Guardian*, 24 July. http://www.theguardian.com/artanddesign/2004/jul/24/heritage.art.

Macpherson, C. 2010. *The Political Theory of Possessive Individualism: Hobbes to Locke*. Don Mills: Oxford University Press Canada.

Macpherson, Crawford Brough 1978. *Property: Mainstream and Critical Positions*. Oxford: Blackwell.

Macpherson, Crawford Brough, Anthony Parel, and Thomas Flanagan. 1979. *Theories of Property: Aristotle to the Present: Essays*. Waterloo: published for the Calgary Institute for the Humanities by Wilfrid Laurier University Press.

Marshall, Daniel, Kevin Murphy, and Zeb Tortorici. 2014. *Queering Archives: Historical Unravelings*. Durham, NC: Duke University Press.

Marstine, Janet, ed. 2011. *The Routledge Companion to Museum Ethics: Redefining Ethics for the Twenty-First Century Museum*. Milton Park, Abingdon and New York: Routledge.

Marx, Karl. 1976. "The Fetishism of Commodities and the Secret Thereof." In *Capital: A Critique of Political Economy, Vol. 1*. New York: Vintage Press.

Marx, Karl. 1992. *The Poverty of Philosophy*. New York: International Publishers.

Mashberg, Tom. 2014. "Despite Legal Challenges, Sale of Hopi Religious Artifacts Continues in France." *New York Times*, 29 June. http://www.nytimes.com/2014/06/30/arts/design/sale-of-hopi-religious-items-continues-despite-us-embassys-efforts.html.

Mauss, Marcel. 1990 [1925]. *The Gift: The Form and Reason for Exchange in Archaic Societies*. London: Routledge.

Merry, Sally Engle. 1988. "Legal Pluralism." *Law and Society Review* 22(5): 869–896.

Merry, Sally Engle. 2000. *Colonizing Hawai'i: The Cultural Power of Law*. Princeton, NJ: Princeton University Press.

Merryman, John Henry. 1986. "Two Ways of Thinking about Cultural Property." *American Journal of International Law* 80(4): 831–853.

Merryman, John Henry. 1998. "Cultural Property Ethics." *International Journal of Cultural Property* 7(1): 21–31.
Merryman, John Henry. 2005. "Cultural Property Internationalism." *International Journal of Cultural Property* 12(1): 11–39.
Merryman, John Henry. 2006. *Imperialism, Art and Restitution*. Cambridge: Cambridge University Press.
Meskell, Lynn. 2015a. *Global Heritage: A Reader*. Hoboken, NJ: John Wiley & Sons.
Meskell, Lynn, ed. 2015b. *Global Heritage: A Reader*. Chichester: Wiley-Blackwell.
Meskell, Lynn, Claudia Liuzza, and Nicholas Brown. 2015. "World Heritage Regionalism: UNESCO from Europe to Asia." *International Journal of Cultural Property* 22(04): 437–470.
Message, Kylie. 2014. *Museums and Social Activism: Engaged Protest*. Museum Meanings. London and New York: Routledge/Taylor & Francis Group.
Mihesuah, Devon Abbott, ed. 2000. *Repatriation Reader: Who Owns American Indian Remains?* Lincoln, NE: University of Nebraska Press.
Moreton-Robinson, Aileen. 2015. *The White Possessive: Property, Power, and Indigenous Sovereignty*. Minneapolis: University of Minnesota Press.
Morgan, Lewis Henry. 1877. *Ancient Society; Or, Researches in the Lines of Human Progress from Savagery, Through Barbarism to Civilization*. New York: H. Holt.
Myers, Fred. 1989. "Burning the Truck and Holding the Country: Pintupi Forms of Property and Identity." In *We Are Here: Politics of Aboriginal Land Tenure*, edited by Edwin N. Wilmsen, 15–42. Berkeley: University of California Press.
Myers, Fred, ed. 2001. *The Empire of Things: Regimes of Value and Material Culture*. Santa Fe, NM: School of American Research Press.
Myers, Fred. 2005. "Some Properties of Art and Culture." In *Materiality*, edited by Daniel Miller, 88–117. Durham, NC: Duke University Press.
Myers, Fred. 2011. "Translating Indigenous Protocol." In *Tjukurrtjanu: Origins of Western Desert Art*, edited by Philip Batty and Judith Ryan, ix–xi. Melbourne: National Gallery of Victoria.
Myers, Fred. 2012. "Censorship from Below: Aboriginal Art in Australian Museums." In *No Deal! Indigenous Arts and the Politics of Possession*, edited by Tressa Berman, 174–187. Santa Fe, NM: School for Advanced Research Press.
Myers, Fred. 2014. "Showing Too Much or Too Little: Predicaments of Painting Indigenous Presence in Central Australia." In *Performing Indigeneity*, edited by Glenn Penny and Laura Graham, 351–389. Lincoln, NE: University of Nebraska Press.
Myers, Fred. 2015. "Paintings, Publics, and Protocols: The Early Paintings from Papunya." *Material Culture Review/Revue de la Culture Matérielle* 79 (March): 78–91.
Nakata, Martin. 2007. *Disciplining the Savages: Savaging the Disciplines*. Canberra: Aboriginal Studies Press.
Ngata, Wayne, Hera Ngata-Gibson, and Amiria Salmond. 2012. "Te Ataakura: Digital Taonga and Cultural Innovation." *Journal of Material Culture* 17(3): 229–244.
Nicholas, Lynn H. 2009. *The Rape of Europa: The Fate of Europe's Treasures in the Third Reich and the Second World War*. New York: Knopf Doubleday Publishing Group.
Odunlami, Stella, and Kehinde Andrews. 2014. "Is Art Installation Exhibit B Racist?" *The Guardian*, 27 September. https://www.theguardian.com/commentisfree/2014/sep/27/is-art-installation-exhibit-b-racist.
Ostrom, Elinor. 1990. *Governing the Commons: The Evolution of Institutions for Collective Action*. Cambridge and New York: Cambridge University Press.
Peers, Laura L., and Alison K. Brown. 2003. *Museums and Source Communities: A Routledge Reader*. London and New York: Routledge.
Pels, Peter. 1997. "The Anthropology of Colonialism: Culture, History, and the Emergence of Western Governmentality." *Annual Review of Anthropology* 26(1): 163–183.
Prott, Lyndel V. 1996. "UNESCO and UNIDROIT: A Partnership against Trafficking and Cultural Objects." *Uniform Law Review* 1: 59–71.
Prott, Lyndel V. 2005. "The International Movement of Cultural Objects." *International Journal of Cultural Property* 12(02): 225–248.
Radin, Margaret Jane. 1982. "Property and Personhood." *Stanford Law Review* 34: 957–1015.
Radin, Margaret Jane. 1993. *Reinterpreting Property*. Chicago: University of Chicago Press.
Rassool, Ciraj. 2006a. "Community Museums, Memory Politics, and Social Transformation in South Africa: Histories, Possibilities and Limits." In *Museum Frictions: Public Cultures/Global Transformations*, 286–321. Durham, NC: Duke University Press.
Rassool, Ciraj. 2006b. "Making the District Six Museum in Cape Town." *Museum International* 58(1–2): 9–18.

Rata, Elizabeth. 2003. "The Treaty and Neotribal Capitalism." *Public Sector* 26(3): 2–6.
Rathje, William. 2002. "Integrated Archaeology: A Garbage Paradigm." In *Archaeologies of the Contemporary Past*, edited by Victor Buchli and Gavin Lucas, 63–76. New York: Routledge.
Raven, Margaret. 2006. "Protocols & ABS: Recognising Indigenous Rights to Knowledge in Australian Bureaucratic Organisations." *Indigenous Law Bulletin* 6(20): 13–16.
Raven, Margaret. 2010. "Protocols: Devices for Translating Moralities, Controlling Knowledge, Defining Actors in Indigenous Research, and Critical Ethical Reflection." *Australian Aboriginal Studies* Fall(2): 33–47.
Renfrew, Colin. 2000. *Loot, Legitimacy and Ownership: The Ethical Crisis in Archaeology*. London and New York: Bloomsbury Academic.
Riley, Mary, ed. 2004. *Indigenous Intellectual Property Rights: Legal Obstacles and Innovative Solutions, Vol. 10.* Walnut Creek, CA: AltaMira Press.
Rose, Carol M. 1994. *Property and Persuasion : Essays on the History, Theory, and Rhetoric of Ownership.* Boulder, CO: Westview Press.
Rousseau, Jean-Jacques. 1998. *The Social Contract.* New edition. Ware: Wordsworth Editions.
Shannon, Jennifer A. 2014. *Our Lives: Collaboration, Native Voice, and the Making of the National Museum of the American Indian.* Santa Fe, NM: School for Advanced Research Press.
Silverman, Raymond Aaron, ed. 2015. *Museum as Process: Translating Local and Global Knowledges.* Museum Meanings. London and New York: Routledge.
Simpson, Audra. 2007. "On the Logic of Discernment." *American Quarterly* 60(2): 251–257.
Simpson, Audra. 2014. *Mohawk Interruptus: Political Life Across the Borders of Settler States.* Durham, NC: Duke University Press.
Smith, Laurajane. 2006. *Uses of Heritage.* New York: Routledge.
Smith, Laurajane, and Natsuko Akagawa. 2009. *Intangible Heritage.* London: Routledge.
Stocking, George W. 1982. *Race, Culture, and Evolution: Essays in the History of Anthropology: With a New Preface.* Chicago: University of Chicago Press.
Strang, Veronica, and Mark Busse, eds. 2011. *Ownership and Appropriation.* London and New York: Bloomsbury Academic.
Strathern, Marilyn. 1999. *Property, Substance, and Effect : Anthropological Essays on Persons and Things.* London and New Brunswick, NJ: Athlone Press.
Strathern, Marilyn, and Eric Hirsch. 2004. *Transactions and Creations: Property Debates and the Stimulus of Melanesia.* New York: Berghahn Books.
Sullivan, Lawrence Eugene, and Alison Edwards. 2004. *Stewards of the Sacred.* Washington, DC: American Association of Museums in cooperation with the Center for the Study of World Religions, Harvard University.
Sunder, Madhavi J. 2012. *From Goods to a Good Life: Intellectual Property and Global Justice.* New Haven, CT: Yale University Press.
Tapsell, Paul. 1997. "The Flight of Pareraututu: An Investigation of Taonga from a Tribal Perspective." *Journal of the Polynesian Society* 106(4): 323–374.
Tapsell, Paul. 2006. "Taonga, Marae, Whenua – Negotiating Custodianship: A Maori Tribal Response to Te Papa: The Museum of New Zealand." In *Rethinking Settler Colonialism: History and Memory in Australia, Canada, Aotearoa New Zealand and South Africa*, 86–99. Studies in Imperialism. Manchester and New York: Manchester University Press and Palgrave.
Tatz, Colin, and Jacquie Lambert. 2006. "Eaglehawk and Crow." In *A Future for Archaeology: The Past in the Present*, edited by Robert Layton and Stephen Shennon, 17–30. London: University College London Press.
Teye, Victor B., and Dallen J. Timothy. 2004. "The Varied Colors of Slave Heritage in West Africa White American Stakeholders." *Space and Culture* 7(2): 145–155.
Tsosie, Rebecca. 1997. "Indigenous Peoples' Claims to Cultural Property: A Legal Perspective." *Museum Anthropology* 21(3): 5–11.
Turnbull, Paul, and Michael Pickering. 2010. *The Long Way Home: The Meaning and Values of Repatriation.* New York: Berghahn Books.
Van Meijl, Toon. 2009. "Māori Intellectual Property Rights and the Formation of Ethnic Boundaries." *International Journal of Cultural Property* 16 (Special Issue 03): 341–355.
Verdery, Katherine, and Caroline Humphrey. 2004. *Property in Question: Value Transformation in the Global Economy.* Oxford and New York: Berg Publishers.
Vincent, John. 2014. *LGBT People and the UK Cultural Sector: The Response of Libraries, Museums, Archives and Heritage since 1950.* New York: Ashgate Publishing.

Watkins, Joe. 2001. *Indigenous Archaeology: American Indian Values and Scientific Practice*. Walnut Creek, CA: AltaMira Press.
Watson, Peter, and Cecilia Todeschini. 2006. *The Medici Conspiracy: The Illicit Journey of Looted Antiquities, from Italy's Tomb Raiders to the World's Greatest Museums*. New York: BBS Public Affairs.
Webster, Gloria Cranmer. 1990. "The U'mista Cultural Centre." *The Massachusetts Review* 31(1–2): 132–143.
Were, Graeme. 2014. "Digital Heritage, Knowledge Networks, and Source Communities: Understanding Digital Objects in a Melanesian Society." *Museum Anthropology* 37(2): 133–143.
Westfall, Sylvia. 2015. "ISIS' Destruction of Palmyra Temple Is a War Crime, UNESCO Says." *The Huffington Post*, 24 August. http://www.huffingtonpost.com/entry/isis-palmyra-baal-shamin_us_55db3a4be4b04ae49703b4ff.
Williams, Paul Harvey. 2007. *Memorial Museums: The Global Rush to Commemorate Atrocities*. Oxford and New York: Berg Publishers. http://www.loc.gov/catdir/enhancements/fy0801/2007039580-b.html.
Wolf, Eric R. 1982. *Europe and the People Without History*. Berkeley and Los Angeles: University of California Press.
Wolfe, Patrick. 2006. "Settler Colonialism and the Elimination of the Native." *Journal of Genocide Research* 8(4): 387–409
Woodhead, Charlotte. 2014. "Redressing Historic Wrongs, Returning Objects to Their Rightful Owners or Laundering Tainted Objects? 21st-Century UK Remedies for Nazi-Era Injustices." *International Journal of Cultural Property* 21(2): 113–142.
Zimmerman, Larry. 1997. "Remythologizing the Relationship Between Indians and Archaeologists." In *Native Americans and Archaeologists: Stepping Stones to Common Ground*, edited by Roger Anyon, Nina Swidler, Kurt E. Dongoske, and Alan S. Downer, 44–56. Walnut Creek, CA: AltaMira Press.

PART I

Legal ordering of cultural property

Jane Anderson and Haidy Geismar

In any discussions of cultural property, legislation and policy matter significantly because together they have produced a key authoritative discourse directing how specific meaning about cultural property is made and circulated within national and international contexts. As we discussed in our genealogy of cultural property in the Introduction, law plays a significant role in configuring and reworking European ideas of property as well as providing a dominant platform for the expression of nation-state interests. For instance, policy developed at an international level greatly impacts legislation developed at a national level to implement that policy. As such, particular kinds of values and priorities are privileged (such as 'preservation' for instance) and this facilitates the development of new bureaucratic apparatuses (cultural preservation departments for example), which in turn shape the identification of some sites for supported preservation at the expense of others. As Joseph Sax has aptly demonstrated in his series of articles tying the development of concepts of cultural property with nationalism, preservation policy 'goes beyond simply saving certain objects and becomes a symbolic shaping of the national agenda' (Sax 1990: 1544)

International conventions like the 1954 Hague Convention and the 1970 UNESCO Convention have worked to formalize the idea of cultural property that most readers will be familiar with. These Conventions developed most directly out of the devastation of the Second World War, especially in Europe with the targeted destruction of sites of cultural significance as well as the large-scale looting of art and objects of cultural significance (Nicholas 2009). As a result, these Conventions must be read with this history in mind – they were crafted in the post-war political climate that was also striving to rebuild international consensus around culture as a site of value which required specific forms of 'preservation' and 'protection'. These Conventions were also built out of prevailing concepts about the nature of warfare itself, including imagining what could be likely future targets of destruction and theft, and therefore how 'properties' of the nation could be identified, avoided and saved. Both Conventions are good examples of how law and legislation are not made external to political events, but instead are developed in response to them. In many ways current international cultural property policy and legislation might be considered to be reactive and quite specific. It is responding to these past events in preparation for the future, but that future is hard to predict, can be romanticized for political purposes and can fold ideologies of nationalism or nation building into it.

It is in this temporal struggle to develop universal forward-looking policy that certain gaps or limits are produced. One obvious example is in the recent efforts by the Association on American Indian Affairs in the United States to leverage these same Conventions in support of the return of Native American cultural patrimony on sale currently in auction houses in France. Here there is a problem of both translation and political recognition. Long-term colonial violence perpetuated against Indigenous peoples and cultures does not map easily onto the violence of the Second World War or even extreme state violence against a specific group within that country. Despite the alliance made between the Hopi Nation and the Holocaust Art Restitution Project over the 2015 auction in Paris, drawing an equivalence between the theft of Jewish art and the theft of Native cultural expressions has been very difficult (Native News 2015). But the real stumbling block remains one of political recognition because the Conventions clearly demarcate the obligations of signatories as being from states to other states. Thus the French courts will not grant Native nations any legal standing as sovereign nations. This is despite 566 Native tribes holding this status as independent nations within the United States (Kaplan 2016).

When thinking about legal orders and their distributive effects we are following critical legal and legal anthropology scholars in encouraging a reflexivity about the way in which laws are crafted, who the parties are that are doing the creating as well as whose interests are represented (Merry 2011; Barker 2011; Comaroff and Comaroff 2006; Riles 2000; Coombe 1998; Mezey 2001; Echo-Hawk 2010; Anderson 2009). We are interested in what law is understood to be and by whom, as well as the embedded networks of politics and power that underpin the identification of a 'problem' that needs some kind of legal or public policy 'solution'. What that 'solution' is and how it mobilizes very particular actions and agents at the expense of other initiatives is critical here. Tracking the flows and overlaps between the local, the national and the international also opens up productive spaces for seeing actors who might be otherwise obscured. It helps in understanding certain sites of tension (between heritage and property for instance) and why some political claims leveraged by or within states mobilize a language of property and why others find the international framing of heritage more strategically powerful.

Valdimar Hafstein and Martin Skrydstrup explore this dynamic by contrasting the parallel discourses of cultural property and cultural heritage. As Hafstein and Skydstrup argue, the choice to turn to either property or heritage in thinking about the governance of culture signals different, often competing, state regimes and technologies of governmentality. They argue that cultural *property* is associated with technologies of *sovereignty*, asserting claims and modes of ownership, and cultural *heritage* with technologies of *reformation*, asserting modes of relationality, participatory experience, practice and modulating senses of community. Whilst both cultural heritage and cultural property evoke discourses of rights, focusing on the way in which they prioritize their mobilization into very specific frameworks allows us to disentangle and better understand the ways in which they are strategically advanced on the ground. The sovereignty thinking of cultural property and the reforming tendencies embedded in cultural heritage policies and practices speak to the future where both are increasingly challenged by the resistance of market logics and processes of commoditization to the territorialization of the state. We therefore see emerging strategies to assert territory within cultural heritage regimes, increasingly importing the language of national sovereignty from cultural property in heritage. Understanding this initial separation therefore allows us to appreciate why *terroir* has emerged, for example, as a way to assert heritage in property claims as in the example of geographical indications, an enterprise shared across two international bureaucratic sites of the World Intellectual Property Organization and UNESCO for instance.

The 1970 UNESCO Convention requires that all state signatories implement protective legislation to prevent the illicit trafficking of cultural property and is committed to the three fields of prevention, restitution and international cooperation, responding in particular to a growing inequality between nations understood to be 'sources' (countries with rich archaeological and cultural heritage) and those understood to be 'market' or 'collector' nations, countries with wealthy private collectors and museums keen to consolidate their holdings. Ana Filipa Vrdoljak contextualizes UNESCO 1970 within a set of international efforts to respond to the effects of armed conflict on the safety of cultural property and heritage, working through World War Two towards the Hague Convention of 1954, and then to UNESCO 1970. She argues that Allied responses to the ways in which the Nazis incorporated cultural property into their ideological agenda became part of the creation of a new sense of international community in the wake of the Nuremberg trials. This led to a stronger connection between rights to cultural property and human rights, and formed a cornerstone in the expansive development in international humanitarian law from this period. In considering the criminalization of the illicit traffic of cultural objects in international law, and the obligation, following the 2014 UN Security Council Resolution condemning human and cultural rights violations in Syria and Iraq, to prosecute these acts in domestic courts, this chapter charts the relationship between cultural property policy after the Second World War and how these ideas have been carried into the present. Here we have a good illustration of the temporal struggles within international policy and the unimagined futures that create dissonance for action – in this instance how states are to respond to a non-state actor like Daesh.

As Vrodjolak's piece details, alongside the continued commitment to a discourse about international community, UNESCO 1970 highlights how cultural property continues to galvanize debates as well as organizing language and logics about the relations between cultural rights and national sovereignties. It also raises tensions between theories of property and exchange, most prominently between those who think that a free market of exclusive property rights should dominate the exchange of cultural property and those who think that there are some artefacts which should transcend the ownership of any individual in favour of values of either national or international heritage.

The US was one of the first signatories of UNESCO 1970, subsequently passing in 1982 the *Cultural Property Implementation Act* (CIPA). This national legislation substantially implements two sections of the 1970 Convention. Article 7(b) addresses the return of stolen cultural property that had been inventoried in the collection of a public secular or religious institution, and Article 9 provides a mechanism by which state parties may call upon each other for assistance in cases of jeopardy to cultural heritage through the looting of archaeological and ethnological materials. CIPA offers itself as a national example of a method of implementation. CIPA essentially pushed cultural property protection into a national and criminal framework around border control and customs. It also set up the capacity for the US to enter bilateral relations with other nations in order to address the issue of the movement of cultural heritage. Bilateral agreements effectively work to find consensus across national difference and in this sense also work to streamline process and policy. Patty Gerstenblith provides a detailed account of US implementation and also surveys other national responses to UNESCO 1970, such as those that cluster their efforts through "across-the-board import regulations" (e.g. Canada, Australia), the use of bilateral agreements (US, Switzerland), and "hybrid" approaches that merge UNESCO 1970 with the 1995 UNIDROIT Convention on Stolen or Illegally Exported Cultural Objects (e.g. Netherlands, United Kingdom). By surveying the nuanced ways in which different member nations interpret and implement the UNESCO Convention,

Gerstenblith demonstrates both the complexity of the international field of cultural property legislation and that there is always a tension between cultural nationalism and internationalism within any such legislation and developed systems of cultural property governance.

The limits on the marketplace and the international compliance in protecting the national borders of cultural heritage and property instantiated in UNESCO 1970 have been broadly supported by many archaeologists and countries with rich archaeological holdings, and have also been decried by many art dealers and collectors (Fitz Gibbon 2005). A very different perspective on the implications of this legal framework is provided by Neil Brodie. Brodie argues stringently that current international cultural property policy is largely ineffective in that it fails to address the source of much illicit trafficking, namely demand and the private market. As Brodie clearly states, the illegal trade is a commercial construct and as such seems the most open to control, as well as being completely predictable. Yet the focus of current policy on the preservation of cultural property *in situ* has largely left a blind spot in terms of how this kind of property is valued and the extent of the illegal markets that respond to significant demand. Drawing upon long-term research in the Middle East-North Africa (MENA) region between 1990 and 2015, Brodie offers some compelling arguments for why international cultural property policy has failed. He demonstrates that the marketplace for illicit antiquities is not bounded within national territories; it is often associated with other illegal activities, and thrives in local conditions of political and economic instability. He argues that international policy needs to be supported by what he describes as a 'market reduction approach (MRA), an interrelated set of pragmatic initiatives aiming to create a more inhospitable commercial environment by increasing levels of risk for all market participants'. His is one of the clearest and most forceful arguments for a shift away from the logic of nationalism or internationalism into a more concerted politics of regulation and deliberate and specific intervention at the level of demand and the market. He argues, contra Vrdoljak, that a greater emphasis on criminalization is necessary in cultural property law and that the focus needs to shift away from source nations into collectors' markets.

At an international level there are only a handful of conventions or declarations providing the overarching governing apparatus for conceptualizing and formalizing definitions of cultural property. In contrast, at the national level there can be multiple. In the United States for example, there are at least 12 separate pieces of legislation beginning with the *Antiquities Act* of 1906 (Pub.L. 59–209, 34 Stat. 225, 16 U.S.C. § 431–433) that could be classified as cultural property legislation. One of the most significant of these is the 1990 *Native American Graves and Repatriation Act* (NAGPRA) (Pub.L. 101–601). This unique piece of legislation does not refer to preservation or protection of cultural property under threat outside the country. Instead the focus is on the history of internal national violence perpetuated against Native American people and communities through the deliberate destruction and looting of graves and burial sites. The focus of this legislation is to facilitate the return to present-day communities of the enormous collections of this highly sensitive material, renamed by Native activists as ancestors and belongings, from all federal institutions as well as all institutions, including universities, that receive any federal funding. Susan Benton explores the development of this legislation and the tensions within it that affect its success. Benton draws attention to the historical injustices that underpin the development and ambitions of this legislation, as well as how these continue to shape the possibilities of action and return. Pointing to the very real cultural differences that can be hidden by the universalizing value systems embedded at the international levels, Benton highlights a significant ill fit with property logics and Native perspectives of this past and of this material. NAGPRA is not without its difficulties and is largely constricted by its own language and the realities of negotiating with bureaucracies.

Yet because it is federal legislation, it organizes and sets out deliberate steps and process. These actions still require negotiation and engagement, but this would be much more difficult for Native American communities to undertake without such legislative support. NAGPRA offers itself as a unique example of a national cultural property intervention. It works to organize communities and institutions in relationship to each other. What is also interesting here is that it has no reach outside of a US jurisdiction, either to communities situated outside the US, or to overseas institutions that hold US tribal material. In contrast to the direct implementation of UNESCO 1970 in the US and the bilateral agreements that have been established as discussed by Gerstenblith, there have been no bilateral arrangements or discussions following NAGPRA. This is despite significant collections of this material being held outside the country, especially in Europe.

In rendering visible internal mechanics crucial for the making of law it is possible to see very particular kinds of authority and value. This allows us to better distinguish sources of legal authority, as well as why certain legal concepts (like property for instance) continue to wield such force. Importantly, law is made and distributes its effects in a range of haphazard and unpredictable ways. This helps explain why it can be mobilized by different parties with diverse political registers and agendas. Keeping alert to the appropriation of law and policy by groups that have historically been excluded helps understand its malleability, its productive power and its source of authority within the larger field of cultural property.

Bibliography

Anderson, Jane. 2009. *Law, Knowledge, Culture: The Production of Indigenous Knowledge in Intellectual Property Law*. Cheltenham: Edward Elgar.

Barker, Joanne. 2011. *Native Acts: Law, Recognition and Cultural Authenticity*. Durham, NC: Duke University Press.

Coombe, Rosemary J. 1998. *The Cultural Life of Intellectual Properties: Authorship, Appropriation and the Law*. Durham, NC: Duke University Press.

Comaroff, John, and Jean Comaroff (eds.). 2006. *Law and Disorder in the Post-Colony*. Chicago: Chicago University Press.

Echo-Hawk, Walter. 2010. *The Courts of the Conqueror: The Ten Worst Indian Law Cases Ever Decided*. Golden, CO: Fulcrum Publishing.

Fitz Gibbon, Kate. 2005. *Who Owns the Past?: Cultural Policy, Cultural Property and the Law*. New Brunswick, NJ: Rutgers University Press.

Kaplan, Isaac. 2016. "Native Americans Want the French to Stop Selling Their Sacred Objects – Here's Why They Won't." *Artsy*, 27 May 2016. https://www.artsy.net/article/artsy-editorial-native-americans-want-the-french-to-stop-selling-their-sacred-objects-here-s-why-they-won-t.

Merry, Sally. 2011. "Measuring the World: Indicators, Human Rights, and Global Governance." *Current Anthropology* 52(Supplementary Issue 3): S83–S95.

Mezey, Naomi. 2001. "Law as Culture." *Yale Journal of Law and Human Rights* 13, 35–67.

Native News. 2015. "Hopi Chairman and the Holocaust Art Restitution Project Denounce French Government's Decision to Allow Auction of Sacred Hopi Objects." *Native News*, 2 June 2015. http://nativenewsonline.net/currents/hopi-chairman-the-holocaust-art-restitution-project-denounce-french-governments-decision-to-allow-auction-of-sacred-hopi-objects/.

Nicholas, Lynn H. 2009. *The Rape of Europa: The Fate of Europe's Treasures in the Third Reich and the Second World War*. New York: Knopf Doubleday Publishing Group.

Riles, Annalise. 2000. *The Network Inside Out*. Michigan: Michigan University Press.

Sax, Joseph 1990. "Is Anyone Minding Stonehenge? The Origins of Cultural Property Protection in England." *California Law Review* 78: 1543–1567.

2
HERITAGE VS. PROPERTY
Contrasting regimes and rationalities in the patrimonial field

Valdimar Tr. Hafstein and Martin Skrydstrup

A persisting problem for the critical study of cultural property is how to conceptualize differences in the ways in which national and indigenous claims are shaped and legitimated. The coupling of identity and indigeneity with ownership and rights mobilized in claims have been read analytically as identity politics (Handler 1988), nation building (Li 2001), resistance (Miller 1995), postcolonial mimesis (Bhabha 1994), alternative modernities (Coombe 2003), forms of ethno-commodification (Comaroff and Comaroff 2009), and as a "provincializing move that destabilizes our certainty about what is local and what is global" (Geismar 2013). It seems to us that such readings hinge on how we analytically configure "case studies" vis-à-vis larger processes of state formation; that is, how we relate biographies of contested artifacts and the lives of intellectual properties to the distinct regimes of governmentality, which perform the work of (non-)recognition of such claims.

In this chapter, we cut a different pathway through these conundrums. We present a sustained argument, which reframes the debate about how to read claims. Our argument is based on contrasts between property and heritage and between distinct technologies of governmentality, which we argue are associated with these terms. Thus, specific technologies of governmentality produce distinct set of claims. The stepping stones in our argument are the following: firstly we set out the nominal distinctions between property and heritage, then we show how *property* is associated with technologies of *sovereignty* and *heritage* with technologies of *reformation*, and finally we discuss how these technologies of governmentality can co-exist in single case trajectories.

Nominalism

In an article published in the first volume of the *International Journal of Cultural Property* in 1992, Lyndel V. Prott and Patrick J. O'Keefe contrast the terms cultural property and cultural heritage. Whereas cultural property denotes ownership and exclusivity, they contend, cultural heritage denotes a relationship of responsibility, custodianship, and sharing. The thrust of their argument is that the time had come for the latter concept to supersede the former (Prott and O'Keefe 1992).

Eight years later, Janet Blake, legal scholar and long-term UNESCO consultant, suggests that although the "relationship between 'cultural property' and 'cultural heritage' is unclear, appearing interchangeable in some cases, … 'cultural heritage' has now become the term of art in international law since it is capable of encompassing [a] much broader range of possible elements" (Blake 2000: 67). In a book on *International Cultural Heritage Law* from 2015, Blake reaffirms that "cultural property" is "far too limited a term" and therefore now "much less widely used and the alternative cultural heritage is generally favoured" (Blake 2015: 8).

On the other hand, Manlio Frigo, another legal scholar, observes that "the concepts of cultural heritage and cultural property practically never appear simultaneously as complementary notions in the same legal text" (Frigo 2004: 376), which may be taken to indicate that in fact they have distinct functions and relate to legal regimes that are at least partly separate. Frigo suggests that this relationship is further complicated by different national terminologies (2004: 370), a claim which legal anthropologist Rosemary Coombe dismisses, along with any attempts to draw a legal distinction between the two concepts:

> Such interpretive difficulties now seem provincial. In any case, these promise only to proliferate as these categories expand, their distinction implodes, and their subject matter and fields of reference proliferate.
>
> *(Coombe 2009: 394)*

As we understand them, these concepts operate within a global patrimonial field with a proliferating variety of actors: states, intergovernmental organizations, transnational NGOs, indigenous peoples, local communities, museums, archives, institutions, universities, scholars, and experts. The patrimonial field is governed by national and international regimes, some of which gravitate towards a rights-based approach to protection and dispute management under the sign of cultural property, while others gravitate towards an ethical approach to conservation and safeguarding under the sign of cultural heritage. Rights-based regimes of cultural property come with their own set of national laws and international conventions, committees, discourses, and forms of expertise, and while there are certainly overlaps, these can be distinguished from corresponding institutions of the ethical regimes of cultural heritage operating in the same global patrimonial field. We will argue in the following pages that the two correspond to distinct governmental rationalities and modes of subject formation: that cultural property is a technology of sovereignty and cultural heritage a technology of reformation.

Cultural property as a technology of sovereignty

When she and Patrick O'Keefe set out the contrast between cultural property and cultural heritage, Lyndel V. Prott had recently been appointed Chief of the International Standards Section in the Division of Cultural Heritage of the United Nations Educational, Scientific, and Cultural Organization (UNESCO), where she was in charge of conventions for cultural property and cultural heritage. Since its founding in 1946, UNESCO has developed a series of such legal instruments, beginning in 1954 with the Convention for the Protection of Cultural Property in the Event of Armed Conflict, often referred to as the Hague Convention for short. "Recognizing that cultural property has suffered grave damage during recent armed conflicts," the Hague Convention begins, and "Being convinced that damage to *cultural property belonging to any people whatsoever* means damage to the *cultural heritage of all mankind*" (our emphasis), the states parties to the convention agree to take on various obligations to protect cultural property from theft and destruction. As is evident from the preamble, cultural property and cultural heritage both emerged in international law through the Hague Convention, already recognizably distinct: in the sentences quoted above, cultural property belongs to a people, whereas cultural heritage is attributed to mankind. Cultural heritage and cultural property were thus coined as international legal concepts within a decade of the end of the Second World War and as part of a new world order represented by the United Nations.

Since its inception, UNESCO has been the engine driving the development of regimes of cultural property and cultural heritage. Up until the 1970s, its efforts focused on the legal protection of cultural property. Following up on the Hague Convention, UNESCO's member states adopted in 1970 the Convention on the Means of Prohibiting and Preventing the Illicit Import, Export and Transfer of Ownership of Cultural Property (based on UNESCO's Recommendation of the same name from 1964) and founded in 1978 an Intergovernmental Committee for Promoting the Return of Cultural Property to its Countries of Origin or its Restitution in Case of Illicit Appropriation. As the titles of the convention and the committee make clear, cultural property is at its inception a national concept, used in the context of claims for the return or restitution of historical artifacts from one state to another. UNESCO's instruments, binding for states that ratify them, lend to such claims the force of international law. At the national level, some regimes of cultural property also provide legal grounds for peoples, tribes, or communities within national borders to stake claims on state institutions for the repatriation of artifacts from their collections to their original holders. In the patrimonial field, the very term "repatriation" was first inscribed into law by the passage of the National Museum of the American Indian Act (NMAIA) in 1989, followed by the Native American Graves Protection and Repatriation Act (NAGPRA) one year later. The term repatriation – literally meaning back to the father's land – has since then diffused into a general designation for acts of return, albeit its legal use is restricted to the national domains of settler-colonies. Historically, NMAIA and NAGPRA may represent the apex of the idea of cultural property, as the exclusive property of lineal descendants or tribes (*patria*) through a technology, which produces and asserts the sovereignty of its claimants.

The claims that regimes of cultural property recognize and validate are claims to objects which colonialism, capitalism, and science have transported in their common luggage. These claims propose now to reverse their trajectories and return the objects to their countries of origin or to their rightful owners within settler-colonial societies. Claims to cultural property are usually staked in the aftermath of violence: of war or colonial rule, or both. The claims assert sovereign powers and they affirm cultural integrity in the face of foreign invasion and foreign rule, globalized markets and foreign science. Cultural property claims thus help form sovereign subjects, whether independent peoples or semi-autonomous social collectives such as communities and tribes. In other words, claims to cultural property are a technology of sovereignty.

Sovereignty is typically understood as a property of nation-states, often taken to mean that a state is sovereign when it governs its own *dominium* independently; what Hannah Arendt called "uncompromising self-sufficiency and mastership" (Arendt 1958: 234). The various congruencies between notions of liberal individualism and Arendt's modernist notion of sovereign state agency became – not surprisingly – the target for postmodern critiques of various bents. Perhaps most famously, Giorgio Agamben argued that sovereignty is in fact indistinguishable from a permanent state of exception (Agamben 1998), drawing on Carl Schmitt's idea of sovereignty as the exception to rules (Schmitt 2005 [1922]). Less well known is the intervention by Jacques Derrida, who argued that "sovereignty" designates "unconditional expenditure" (Derrida 1978), drawing on George Bataille; that is, sovereign action is a form of agency undertaken without any expectations of reciprocity/compensation. Michael Brown's critique of the "talismanic properties" of the principle of sovereignty (2003: 224), which he finds antithetical to "complex cultural flows" (ibid.: 225) and which according to him "has led proponents of Total Heritage Protection to focus on customary law as the solution for conflicts over intellectual property" (op.cit.), clearly leans on Arendt's modernist notion of sovereignty.

Our concept of "technologies of sovereignty" builds in part on Haidy Geismar's argument that "property is an implementation of sovereignty everywhere, whether or not it is acknowledged as such" (2013: 18). However, where Geismar aims to capture indigenous aspirations to sovereignty – where property is the necessary medium and recognition sets the terms for acknowledgement – our analytical prism anchors sovereignty in *technologies of governmentality*. By this we mean sovereignty *through* the technology of recognition, infused by expertise. Contrary to Brown's modernistic concept of sovereignty, technologies of sovereignty remain open to ethnographic surprises and historical transformations.

A small but telling example of how claims to cultural property are enlisted in the formation of sovereign subjects may be gleaned from a statement by Alex Salmond, Scotland's First Minister in 2007, in which he deplores the fact, unacceptable in his view, that the Lewis Chessmen (a medieval collection of 93 chess pieces) are still "scattered around." "And you can be assured," Salmond declares, "that I will continue campaigning for a united set of Lewis Chessmen in an independent Scotland" (qtd. in Fincham 2010: 679). Salmond's demand for the return of cultural property is inseparable from his claim to national sovereignty; the former is a technology to produce the latter.

The case of the Parthenon sculptures also lends itself as an instructive touchstone for our argument. The case has generated its own comprehensive scholarship, which has predominantly focused on the historical trajectories of the monument (Clair 1998), the justification or not for Lord Elgin's removal of the sculptures in the opening decade of the nineteenth century, and contemporary arguments pro and con return (Hitchens 1987; Greenfield 2013 [1989]; Webb 2002). Much less has been written about the shifting history of the claim, since Greece was recognized as a sovereign nation-state in 1830 and restoration work began on the Acropolis. The first formal claim to the sculptures was filed through official diplomatic protocols as late as 1983. It referred to a UNESCO recommendation in favor of return adopted in Mexico City in 1982 and was justified by recourse to three ideas: 1) the aesthetic argument that the sculptures are integral to the monument; 2) the political argument that the sculptures belong to the cultural context in which they were created; and 3) the legal property argument that the sculptures had been removed during occupation. A year later, the British government responded only to the last part of the claim, which they formally declined on the grounds that the sculptures were "secured" by Lord Elgin "as the result of a transaction conducted with the recognized legitimate authority at the time" (Greenfield 2013 [1989]: 87). Subsequently, Greece filed a formal claim to UNESCO's Intergovernmental Committee for Promoting the Return of Cultural Property to its Countries of Origins or its Restitution in Case of Illicit Appropriation.

Throughout the 1990s, UNESCO (which carries a picture of the Parthenon as its emblem) has adopted a series of recommendations to encourage bilateral negotiations and ultimately return or restitution of the sculptures, which have led nowhere. In 2002, the directorship of the British Museum changed and so did the response to the Greek claim. The museum along with eighteen sister institutions now reinvented itself as a "universal museum" housing encyclopedic collections embodying all the arts of all the civilizations, which could only be justly appreciated under one single roof. In the meantime, the Greek claim has caught up, so to speak, with the idea of universalism. Thus, in 1983 the British Museum made the case for retention on the basis of legalities recognized by the (Ottoman) authorities at the time of acquisition. The contemporary Greek claim, as well as the British Museum's current case for retention, is couched in very different terms. In March 2008, the Hellenic Ministry of Culture and UNESCO convened the Athens International Conference on the Return of Cultural Objects to their Countries of Origin, in conjunction with a pre-opening of the New Acropolis Museum, its partly empty galleries making clearly visible what marbles are considered to be "in exile." At this world event, Michalis Liapis, Greece's Minister of Culture, reiterated the aesthetic claim from 1983 for return as a "re-unification of the Parthenon sculptures." According to Liapis, however, that claim is not made merely as a property claim on behalf of the Greek nation, but "in the name of the world's cultural heritage; a universal demand and a global debt to Greece." The Minister closed his inauguration speech contending that the best supporters for the claim would be the thousands of visitors, who would see the New Acropolis Museum and "will be thinking that some pieces of these artefacts are 4,000 miles away from their destination point" (conference recording on file with the authors). Partly through extravagant expenditure on this event in the shadow and light of the Acropolis, a nation-state asserted its sovereign right. Interestingly, from our point of view, the rhetorical tactics of the claim have shifted from Minister Mercouri's claim for the restitution of cultural property in the course of the 1980s to Minister Liapis' claim for the return of the "world's cultural heritage" as a "global debt" to Greece. After all, the very premise of European Enlightenment thinking upon which the British Museum's appeal to universalism and encyclopedic collections rests is Hellenic. Nevertheless, although the Greek government of late deploys the term cultural heritage, we maintain that at its core the case still turns on the congruence between the artifacts and the territoriality from which they were removed and involves centrally the production of sovereignty of the claimant. In other words, claims made under the sign of cultural property produce and assert territoriality and sovereignty, even when they are cast in the language of world heritage.

The event in Athens closed with a moving case, which projected the same technology of sovereignty couched in the same evocative language of original wholes, scattered parts and contemporary need for re-unification as in the aforementioned Scottish and Greek cases. To build an international precedent for returns, Andrea Sanborn from the Kwakwaka'wakw First Nation was called to present a temporary loan of a transformation mask, which was formally held by the British Museum:

> Our story begins with the creation of our ancestors in our territories. . . . We have come to understand that the very soul of our culture remains fragmented until all the pieces can be reunited, repatriated and returned home. . . . Give us back our cultural ceremonial masks and regalia. . . . Only then can the spirits of our ancestors be at rest, as we will have *u'mista* [*historically, Kwakwaka'wakw people who were held captive by neighboring tribes and then returned to their homes were said to have u'mista*] and we can continue rebuilding our culture and our lives and become whole again.
>
> *(Sanborn 2008, Athens)*

What we have here is the same assertion of territoriality, sovereignty, and origins as in the Parthenon case; spiritual wholeness has merely replaced aesthetic integrity. Common cause makes the Greek nation and the Kwakwaka'wakw First Nation contemporary subaltern allies set against the same institution. This alliance between nation-states and First Nations illustrates the affinities between claim-making as a technology of sovereignty at different scales, which enables new types of alliances across the world. Extending the analogy to other settler-colonies, NAGPRA (Native American Graves Protection and Repatriation Act 1990) could be viewed as a machine that produces sovereignty at the sub-national level. That is apparent in Hawai'i where repatriation claims are often coupled with notions of "Native Soil," the "Hawaiian cultural renaissance" and the various movements for sovereignty, both royalist and otherwise. The same goes without saying for Native Americans on the mainland or "Lower 48 States"; claims staked through NAGPRA assert and help produce tribal sovereignty in the various configurations ("homelands," "shared sovereignty," and "shared tribal management of repatriation/burial sites"), which Thomas Biolsi (2004) has outlined vis-à-vis the federal government.

Cultural heritage as a technology of reformation

Starting in the 1970s, UNESCO began developing a separate regime, with its own legal instruments and bodies, for what it calls the safeguarding of cultural heritage (as opposed to the protection of cultural property). Cultural heritage is the preferred term in contexts that stress the general safeguarding (as opposed to legal protection) of artifacts, buildings, sites, and, most recently, cultural practices. UNESCO is today best known in many parts of the world for its Convention Concerning the Protection of the World Cultural and Natural Heritage (a.k.a the World Heritage Convention) from 1972, the associated World Heritage Committee, and especially the World Heritage List. Rather than acknowledging the rights of states, the World Heritage Convention recognizes their responsibilities to current and future generations and to humanity as a whole. In Article 5, states parties are urged "to adopt a general policy which aims to give the cultural and natural heritage a function in the life of the community," while the following article makes plain their responsibility:

> Whilst fully respecting the sovereignty of the States on whose territory the cultural and natural heritage . . . is situated . . . the States Parties to this Convention recognize that such heritage constitutes a world heritage for whose protection it is the duty of the international community as a whole to co-operate.

With respect to cultural heritage, UNESCO's regime is thus not so much rights-based as it is ethical: World Heritage is designed to mobilize international opinion and to create state practice through moral and rhetorical pressure, dangling the prospect of a place on the List before states as an incentive, while removal from the List, even the threat of removal, is an effective form of shaming.

If the primary concerns of UNESCO conventions for protecting cultural property are conflicting national claims and the settlement of international disputes over transfer, then conversely, conventions for safeguarding cultural heritage organize international cooperation around the common goal of keeping safe and bequeathing to posterity those monuments and expressions that are considered of value to humanity as a whole, regardless of where they are located or who may use them. One way to put this might be to say that under UNESCO's respective regimes, cultural property belongs to an exclusive "us" but cultural heritage belongs to an inclusive "us." In other words, while claims staked within both regimes help to constitute collective subjects, the subject of cultural property is exclusive, subject to misappropriation and entitled to restitution; the subject of cultural heritage tends rather to be inclusive, a collective "we" that conventions entreat to take responsibility and stand together to prevent degradation and loss, rather than theft by an other. Compared with cultural property, we might say that cultural heritage is subtler in both its perpetuation and its disruptions of state hegemony.

This distinction is clearly recognized by Prott and O'Keefe, who contrast the ownership and exclusivity of cultural property with the responsibilization, custodianship, and sharing characteristic of cultural heritage (1992). One is left wondering, therefore, after teasing out the different uses of the two concepts and their associated regimes, why the authors argue for dropping the one in favor of the other.

Of course, the terms are not unequivocal and we should be careful not to reify them. Indeed, their distinction is often blurred, as we saw above in the shifting language in which Greek claims to the Parthenon sculptures have been couched. As anthropologist Haidy Geismar has recently noted, cultural heritage, "like its older sister, cultural property, is a tangle of ideology and expectation; an analytic term and a tool of governance; . . . [and] a foundational category for a political economy, the 'heritage industry'" (Geismar 2015: 72). Social actors across the globe participate in new opportunities offered by both concepts, and help to shape new options in markets and politics that have come to be imaginable through instruments such as inscriptions and lists. But even so, in the international regimes the distinction is fairly clear-cut, and one should not underestimate the importance of these regimes in diffusing a conceptual matrix and shaping local practices. The term cultural property gained universal currency following the adoption of the Hague Convention in 1954, not the other way around, and likewise the proliferation of cultural heritage in recent decades only gained momentum as a result of the adoption of the World Heritage Convention in 1972.

In recent years, intangible cultural heritage exemplifies how international conventions, when successful, can act as catalysts; this term, concocted in the assembly halls of UNESCO in the 1990s, has rapidly gained acceptance following the adoption in 2003 of the convention dedicated to safeguarding it. Its widespread use is in some ways confounding, considering its negative semantics and bureaucratic etymology, not to mention that it is enough of a mouthful that it has in many contexts been replaced with the acronym ICH. And yet in tens of thousands of scattered places all over the world, people now refer to their traditional practices as intangible cultural heritage, or as ICH, and in so doing they make claims that are recognizable with reference to an international regime and validated by a proliferating production of expert knowledge on intangible heritage.

Based to a large extent on the World Heritage Convention, the Convention for the Safeguarding of the Intangible Cultural Heritage from 2003 extends the reach of the international heritage regime to a new domain of cultural practices and expressions, and comes complete with an Intangible Heritage Committee and a Representative List of the Intangible Cultural Heritage of Humanity, to match the World Heritage List. With thirty years of world heritage under their belt, UNESCO's member states proved ready to take a much larger step away from state sovereignty over heritage and toward the responsibilization of populations, conceived of in the Intangible Heritage Convention as "communities, groups, and in some cases individuals" and entrusted with identifying and managing their intangible heritage in cooperation with state institutions and experts.

Deferring even the definition of its subject matter to the populations that it addresses ("The 'intangible cultural heritage' means the practices, representations, expressions, knowledge, skills . . . that communities, groups and, in some cases, individuals recognize as part of their cultural heritage"; Art. 2), the Intangible Heritage Convention testifies to an important development in the regime of heritage. From the reference to the "function" of heritage in "the life of the community" (Art. 5) in the 1972 convention, "participation" has come to play an ever-larger role in the discourse and practice of heritage from the 1970s to the present time. The Intangible Heritage Convention of 2003 prevails on states to ensure "the widest possible participation of communities, groups and, where appropriate, individuals that create, maintain and transmit such heritage, and to involve them actively in its management"

(Art. 15). Two years later, with the Council of Europe's Faro Convention on the Value of Cultural Heritage for Society, states undertook to:

> a) encourage everyone to participate in: the process of identification, study, interpretation, protection, conservation and presentation of the cultural heritage; public reflection and debate on the opportunities and challenges which the cultural heritage represents; b) take into consideration the value attached by each heritage community to the cultural heritage with which it identifies; c) recognise the role of voluntary organisations both as partners in activities and as constructive critics of cultural heritage policies.
>
> *(Art. 12)*

And in 2011, UNESCO's General Conference adopted the Recommendation on the Historic Urban Landscape, calling on all parties to develop "civic engagement tools" to "involve a diverse cross-section of stakeholders, and empower them to identify key values in their urban areas, develop visions that reflect their diversity, set goals, and agree on actions to safeguard their heritage" (Art. 24).

Starting in the 1970s, a turn to "participation" may be observed in widely disparate fields of policy and practice, from urban planning to international development and from environmental protection to humanitarian aid, at international, national, as well as municipal levels. As anthropologist Ellen Hertz notes, the "participatory approach is at the center of a semantic field filled with familiar if vague notions: 'engagement,' 'ownership' and 'empowerment,' are the desired or imagined results of administrative and political processes that range from 'capacity building' and 'consultation' to the use of 'focus groups,' 'lay experts' and 'hybrid forums' in the formulation and application of policy" (Hertz 2015: 25). While deferring to an "unimpeachable political subject – 'the community'" (ibid.) – the turn to participation has effectively compelled states and intergovernmental organizations to identify, label, and organize these new subjects as political partners. In this way, heritage regimes reconfigure cultural agency and assist in a "proliferation of the social" (Callon, Barry, and Slater 2002), populating the patrimonial and the political field with heritage communities (and "groups and, in some cases, individuals") charged with identifying and safeguarding their own heritage. In objectifying their practices and expressions as "intangible heritage," for example, through the intervention of experts and administrators deployed from metropolitan centers, population groups are invited to subjectify themselves as communities that identify with their cultural heritage and take responsibility for keeping practices and expressions "safe" from change. Government can then act on the social field through communities and by means of, among other things, heritage policies.

This parallels recent developments in environmental conservation, where there is widespread preoccupation with community, and programs proliferate that devolve to communities the responsibility for putting environmental policy into practice. Political scientist Arun Agrawal coined the term "environmentality" to describe this governmental rationality in which communities are interpellated as "environmental subjects" (Agrawal 2005): populations learn to conceive of their habitat as "the environment" and to appreciate the need for its conservation, and – through an infusion of expertise and in cooperation with state, nongovernmental, and intergovernmental organizations – they are charged with administering themselves and their environmental practices (e.g. Agrawal and Gibson 2001; Li 2001; McDermott 2001).

In much the same way, cultural heritage may be described as a technology of reformation. Teaching people to have a heritage, to value it, and keep it safe is a project of *Bildung* or self-cultivation, fostering new forms of subjectivity and cultivating the capacity for action. It is a transformative process, calibrating people's relationship with their practices and their built environment and, as a consequence, their relationships with one another (mediated through those practices and that environment). Thus, for example, UNESCO convened an "Expert Meeting on Community Involvement in Safeguarding Intangible Cultural Heritage" in 2006, which urged that: "the community should be provided with the means to elaborate safeguarding measures aiming at maintaining or improving their capacity of transmitting their ICH, rather than having plans elaborated by external experts in the first place" (UNESCO 2006). Nevertheless, the Expert Meeting recognized the necessity of involving experts from outside the community in the task and the role played by state institutions. Cultural heritage, in this sense, requires both the intervention of outside experts and the training of local experts. Their task is always in part pedagogic, their goal to reform the practices of local populations and reframe their relationships to their (tangible) habitat and (intangible) habitus in terms of heritage. By means of such interventions, populations learn to conceive of buildings and practices as their heritage and to appreciate the need for safeguarding them from change or destruction. Through an infusion of expertise and in cooperation with state, non-governmental, and intergovernmental organizations, they are consequently charged with administering themselves and their cultural heritage.

In such ways, projects of safeguarding connect agendas in political centers to those dispersed sites where operations of power connect with the population. The experts, councils, committees, museums, workshops, awareness raising, and grassroots organizations that the heritage regime summons into being or summons on site all help to establish lines of communication between the calculations of authorities and the aspirations of free citizens, to mold the ambitions and shape the desires of the latter to safeguard their heritage of their own free accord and initiative. Appealing to their civic duty and moral responsibility for maintaining a particular alignment between the past and the present, in which strong emotions and identities are vested, projects for safeguarding cultural heritage thus are designed to modify behavior, sensitivities, and ideas about preservation and history. As a technology of reformation, then, safeguarding is part of the arts of governing by means of what Michel Foucault called the "conduct of conduct."

From Kutiyattam theater in Kerala, and Vimbuza healing in Malawi, to the Jemaa el-Fna marketplace in Marrakesh, the recognition of traditional practices as intangible heritage across the globe and their inscription on the Representative List of the Intangible Cultural Heritage has brought into being new collective subjects and institutions to represent them, involving (some) local actors in new capacities, making them responsible for safeguarding the practices and making sure they continue, and in many cases vesting them with power to make decisions that was previously distributed among other social actors or else was simply unthinkable before the practices came under the sign of heritage. In Malawi, for example, the Ministry of Culture has "convened an official body, the National Intangible Cultural Heritage Committee that comprises cultural workers, academics, and ethnic association members among others" (Gilman 2015: 214). Moreover, the inscription of Vimbuza on the Representative List occasioned the creation of a Vimbuza Healers and Dancers Association of Malawi, which immediately established a code of conduct for its members with the proclaimed purpose of countering "the negative image of Vimbuza caused by inappropriate practice" (ibid.: 206).

In 2008, when presenting the first Representative List of the Intangible Cultural Heritage of Humanity, Koichiro Matsuura, UNESCO's Director-General, declared his confidence that "with time, this List – designed to give more visibility to our living heritage – will contribute to raising awareness of its importance and instill a sense of pride and belonging to custodian communities" (UNESCO 2008). The prestige of international recognition that comes with listing is thus designed to elicit the self-recognition of communities as custodians of their own heritage. It is supposed to induce in people a desire to have a heritage and to take care of it; to curate their own practices, or those of other segments of the local population.

Kutiyattam Sanskrit theater was among the first cultural practices to be inscribed on UNESCO's Representative List in 2008, but had previously been recognized in UNESCO's Proclamation of Masterpieces of the Oral and Intangible Heritage of Humanity in 1999, a pilot program that helped pave the way for the Intangible Heritage Convention. Making good on India's commitment to safeguard Kutiyattam, a national center (Kutiyattam Kendra) was founded in Kerala's capital in 2007 to administer an action plan for safeguarding the theatrical tradition (Lowthorp 2015). Moreover, its recognition and listing has led to the founding of four new teaching institutions, the coordination of a Kutiyattam network that holds regular meetings, the organization of public awareness raising workshops and seminars, and public promotion activities including an annual performance festival, documentaries, and school outreach programs (ibid.: 164). According to folklorist Leah Lowthorp, the greatest impact of the recognition is felt in the way Kutiyattam artists relate to their art. In an interview with Lowthorp, one of these artists seems to confirm Matsuura's prediction: "The greatest effect was that working artists had an awakening, they found a belief in themselves. That was the greatest. Now we're really proud to be in Kutiyattam. It has gained value" (ibid.: 167). At the same time, the recognition of Kutiyattam as intangible heritage prompts increased administration, surveillance, and accountability, shaping the conduct of Kutiyattam performers as well as their social organization. In this it provides a textbook example of cultural heritage as a technology of reformation, reforming both the subjects and objects of intangible heritage, the practices themselves as well as the practitioners and their communities. Another artist whom Lowthorp spoke with reflects: "Now we have a condition of normal working people. It is good for an office but bad for art" (ibid.: 170).

The president of UNESCO's first jury for the Proclamation of Masterpieces of the Oral and Intangible Heritage of Humanity was Juan Goytisolo, the Spanish novelist and Nobel laureate. Goytisolo spearheaded an effort in the second half of the 1990s to protect Jemaa el-Fna, a busy marketplace in Marrakesh that is the site of myriad performances – storytelling, snake-charming, fortune-telling, preaching, acrobatics, and musical performances, to name a few (Kapchan 2014). At the time, the city and its contractors were planning to get rid of the marketplace and kick out the peddlers and performers to make way for a shopping mall and a parking lot. Goytisolo and likeminded intellectuals in Marrakesh enlisted the aid of UNESCO and its "critical gaze" (Foster 2015: 229) to save Jemaa el-Fna. In Goytisolo's analysis, the key to saving the square was to change the relationship of the local population (in particular its wealthier, more powerful elements) to Jemaa el-Fna:

> The bourgeois "society" of Marrakesh looks at the square with disdain and has on various occasions attempted to do away with it because they think it is a symbol of backwardness and decay. . . . Well, what we are attempting – and UNESCO's decision will help us in this – is to change the way that many of Marrakesh's own inhabitants look at the square. So that they feel a justified sense of pride.
>
> *(Espada; our translation)*

By means of new social institutions and using genres of display characteristic of intangible heritage (lists, festivals, brochures, competitions, exhibitions, school programs, etc.), Jemaa el-Fna has been reformed from a rogue element to a public theater of power and Marrakesh-ness.

Existing practices and expressions have become objects of safeguarding. As part of UNESCO's proclamation of Jemaa el-Fna, Moroccan and international experts drew up a ten-year safeguarding plan and local authorities created a special commission to implement this plan, which included an urban planning study, a research facility, the identification and inventorying of traditional knowledge holders and their skills, weekly storytelling sessions, prize competitions, and festivals. To ethnomusicologist Tom Beardslee, it "is no surprise that the first of the larger, more formalized multi-genre [associations] . . . the *Association des Maitres du ḥalqa*, was formed in 2002 following the first of these festivals, in part as a way of negotiating collectively over the pay for the festival and anticipated benefits coming from the UNESCO designation" (Beardslee 2014: 276). In addition, several smaller associations have formed on the square, "dedicated to a particular genre or ethnicity – one Berber association, two Aissawa, two with assorted musicians and other performers, four Gnawa, and one of storytellers. Most ḥlayqiya [i.e. performing artists] claimed to have membership in an association" (ibid.: 266–7; cf. Beardslee 2016). Thus, as Beardslee recognizes, intangible heritage has proved to be an effective technology of reformation in Jemaa el-Fna, "fostering the growing sense the ḥlayqiya have of themselves as being a community – a body that is more readily able to act upon and be acted upon by government than would be a population of ungrouped individuals" (Beardslee 2014: 224).

Different patrimonialities

This is our principal argument: that while their boundaries are often blurred and there are certainly overlaps and overflows between cultural property and cultural heritage, the two represent nonetheless fundamentally different approaches to subject formation, produce distinct bodies of expertise, and belong to different rationalities of government in the patrimonial field, or different "patrimonialities."

Protecting cultural property is a technology of sovereignty. As such, it forms part of the order of the modern liberal state. Regardless even of whether or not they are recognized within legal regimes of cultural property, claims to cultural property help to form sovereign subjects with their own exclusive cultures and autonomous histories: nations, peoples, tribes, etc. Conversely, safeguarding cultural heritage is a technology of reformation, cultivating responsible subjects and entangling them in networks of expertise and management. The historical ascendancy of the cultural heritage regime coincides with a shift in political economy, from the liberal capitalism of the modern state to neoliberalism with its projects of responsibilization, its delegation of tasks of governance from the state, and its cultivation of "self-governing capabilities" (Rose 1996). It is therefore a small step from describing heritage as a technology of reformation to linking the regime of cultural heritage to neoliberal politics and forms of subjectivity (Coombe and Weiss 2015).

Hence, when Prott and O'Keefe suggested in 1992 that it was time for cultural heritage to supersede cultural property as a term of art, this represents in our view a political position that reaches well beyond semantics. One might add that this position points in the direction that UNESCO has been heading since the 1970s, with a focus on developing regimes of cultural heritage with an ever more pronounced emphasis on participation, bottom-up approaches, and community involvement. Indeed, we would suggest that this is part of a larger turn to governmentality in the politics of the past decades.

This larger turn, as well as its inherent contrasts, could be exemplified at the case level with reference to the historical trajectories of cultural property/cultural heritage in the North Atlantic. The transfer of medieval manuscripts from Denmark to Iceland (1971–1997) featured prominently in Greenfields' magisterial work *The Return of Cultural Treasures* (2013 [1989]) as an "outstanding example of a major state-to-state return of cultural property," which Icelandic editorial opinion hailed as "a unique step in Nordic and world history – an example and incentive for the rest of the world on how to resolve sensitive disputes" (Greenfield 2013 [1989]: 46). This case spans several decades, from the first official requests in the 1930s to a political agreement in 1961 about a partition of the collection, followed by two court cases in the Danish Supreme Court about constitutional breach and compensation to the holding institution. Then, in 1971, the first two manuscripts were handed over to Iceland as "priceless gifts," while the holding institution in Denmark flagged at half-mast to signal its dismay with Danish politicians as the final arbitrators of the case. Like the Parthenon, the case has generated its own bibliography (Davíðsdóttir 1999; Nebelong 2002; Prott 2009: 343–346; Ólason 2002; Kjær 2002; Sigurðsson and Ólason 2004), but what is significant for our argument here is that the Icelandic claim for archival materials in the course of the first half of the twentieth century falls squarely within the technology of sovereignty, as a cultural property claim for everything Icelandic held by Danish institutions (documents, manuscripts, letters). More specifically, the case trajectory begins with a more or less informal request in 1837 for archival documents, which is formally asserted again in 1907 (Iceland having gained home-rule in 1904) and in 1925. In between, Denmark formally recognized Icelandic sovereignty in 1918 and the substantial claim for all medieval manuscripts in the holdings of the former colonizer was articulated in 1930 by a sovereign government. Denmark's occupation by Germany during WWII interrupted the negotiations (and the Republic of Iceland was founded in 1944), but in postwar Denmark the case took on certain urgency and became an object of domestic debate, which roughly pitted progressive liberals (*kulturradikale*) in favor of repatriation against conservatives and academics advocating retention. Roughly, the former argued for return on the basis of moral rights and Nordic solidarity and the latter were against return with recourse to the loss for science, the legitimacy of the acquisition and the lack of international precedence (Davíðsdóttir 1999).

These debates sparked an intricate process, which culminated in a Danish proposal to Iceland for the partition of the collection according to scholarly criteria of provenience and the idea of "common stewardship" of the collection. However, to Icelanders in the first half of the twentieth century, the only acceptable outcome was that all medieval manuscripts were returned to Iceland and the proposed "common stewardship" notion did not sit well in postcolonial Iceland. In the course of the 1960s, the parties eventually reached an agreement, which ultimately led to the adoption of a law that circumvented the question of ownership, but instead introduced the notion of "Icelandic cultural heritage." The parties agreed to form an expert committee, charged with partitioning the collection according to a set of criteria for what constituted "Icelandic cultural heritage." Those manuscripts that met the criteria would then be transferred to the Árni Magnússon Manuscript Institute in Reykjavik, newly created for this purpose and named for the same seventeenth–eighteenth-century collector as the Arnamagnean Institute in Copenhagen, a sister institute that houses most of the manuscripts still in Denmark. Scholars and technicians at the new Manuscript Institute, by and large trained at the Danish Arnamagnean Institute and the University of Copenhagen, were charged with curating and administering the manuscripts after their arrival in Iceland, and special travel grants and scholarships were set up to encourage exchange and cooperation between the sister institutes.

From 1972 to 1983, the expert committee convened 41 times to resolve the issues relating to the partition and their work came to an end in 1997, when the last manuscripts were transferred and Iceland signed a protocol in which it accepted that the case was closed. In the fall of 2002, a comprehensive exhibition entitled "The Manuscripts of Iceland" opened in the Culture House in Reykjavik. As Vésteinn Ólason states in the accompanying catalogue: "When Iceland had recovered a great part of the ancient manuscripts that had been kept in Danish libraries for centuries and it had established an institution dedicated to preserving and propagating this treasure, it was only natural for the nation to take an interest in seeing them" (Ólason 2004: IV).

What we have here is a case trajectory that shifts from a technology of sovereignty to a technology of reformation; that is, from a sovereign claim for "cultural property" to a partition of the collection, which is associated with the infusion of expertise and institution building around the notion and definition of "Icelandic cultural heritage." Although the Icelandic government officially accepted the manuscripts as gifts, the local interpretation of their transfer is still very much under the sign of cultural property – as the return to a newly sovereign people of its rightful property from a former colonial ruler (Hálfdanarson 2015).

This case trajectory exemplifies the complementarity of these two technologies of governance. The Icelandic case then delivered a blueprint for the so-called UTIMUT case (1984–2001), which comprised the transfer of more than 35,000 ethnographic and archaeological objects from the National Museum of Denmark to the National Museum of Greenland, according to curatorial criteria worked out between the two institutions (Pentz 2004). Unlike the Icelandic case, no political or legal claims were ever raised in the Greenlandic case. It unfolded within formal and informal networks in the museum sector. Greenland had to meet a number of conditions with regard to professional curatorial standards, before the National Museum of Denmark would consider any deposits or returns of artifacts. This museum then facilitated "capacity building" in Nuuk, which resulted in a National Museum and an associated archive, with all the necessary expertise. After these infrastructures had been put into place, the UTIMUT project of return could commence. Significantly, the physical return of objects was accompanied by a new research centre (SILA) established in the year 2000 at the sending institution in Copenhagen. In connection with the return of the last object in June 2001, a binding document was signed, which set out the regulations for continuous collaboration and mutual access to the divided collection (Pentz 2004). Moreover, the physical return of objects was accompanied by all available archival information, including excavation reports, letters, field reports and the like, which effectively means the transfer of Danish expertise about Greenland to Greenland. In a jointly penned article the two museum directors at the time state that: "This continued cooperation between Denmark and Greenland in the museum field expresses the recognition that the return of the quantities in question involves an obligation for both parties" (Rosing and Pentz 2004: 29). By now it should be clear that the "capacity building" was part of UTIMUT and shows how the technology of reformation responsibilized and formed a new Greenlandic subjectivity, and taught it to have a heritage, to value it, and to care for it in particular ways that instilled "obligations" to the Danish State. More generally, UTIMUT embodies the completion of the shift from a technology of sovereignty to a technology of reformation, which is also exemplified by the fact that the Greenlandic case – in contrast to the Icelandic one – never became the subject matter for legal action or parliamentary debates and motions. UTIMUT remains throughout confined to archaeological expertise within museum networks.

As such, this case seems to corroborate the suggestion by Prott and O'Keefe in 1992, that cultural heritage would supersede cultural property, later affirmed as fact by other legal scholars. We propose, however, to complicate such linear, teleological narratives by moving from a legal to an historical definition of cultural property and cultural heritage as distinct, if overlapping, formations within an overarching patrimonial field, developing under distinct historical conditions (the one in the aftermath of World War II, the other in the aftermath of decolonization) and producing separate regimes (the one proceeding from the Hague Convention, the other from the World Heritage Convention) and distinct forms of expertise (the one primarily legal, the other primarily curatorial), which belong to different rationalities of government (the one liberal, the other neoliberal) and take a very different approach to the formation of patrimonial and political subjects (the one producing sovereign subjects in the mold of the liberal modern state, with rights, territories, borders, and property, the other producing subjects entangled in dense networks of neoliberal/postcolonial forms of governance). The one employs return, restitution and repatriation as a technology of sovereignty, the other employs capacity building, education, collaboration and the infusion of expertise as a technology of reformation.

The transfer of the manuscripts from Denmark to Iceland and the non-transfer of the Parthenon sculptures from the British Museum to Greece illustrate how particular case trajectories may shift back and forth from rights-based claims and resolutions under the sign of cultural property to ethical claims and solutions under the sign of cultural heritage. Far from portraying such shifts in terms of either linear progress (as legal scholars like Prott and O'Keefe or Janet Blake propose) or as an implosion of any meaningful distinction (as anthropologists such as Coombe and Geismar seem to suggest), we argue that there is significant analytical purchase to be gained from an historically grounded and theoretically informed understanding of the distinction between the two terms.

Bibliography

Agamben, Giorgio. 1998. *Homo Sacer. Sovereign Power and Bare Life.* Stanford: Stanford University Press.

Agrawal, Arun. 2005. "Environmentality. Community, Intimate Government, and the Making of Environmental Subjects in Kumaon, India." *Current Anthropology* 46(2): 161–190.

Agrawal, Arun, and Clark C. Gibson. 2001. "The Role of Community in Natural Resource Conservation." In *Communities and the Environment. Ethnicity, Gender, and the State in Community-Based Conservation*, edited by Arun Agrawal and Clark C. Gibson, 1–31. New Brunswick: Rutgers University Press.

Arendt, Hannah. 1958. *The Human Condition.* Chicago: University of Chicago Press.

Beardslee, Thomas. 2014. "Questioning Safeguarding: Heritage and Capabilities at the Jemaa El Fnaa." Ph.D. dissertation. The Ohio State University.

Beardslee, Thomas. 2016. "Whom does heritage empower, and whom does it silence? Intangible cultural heritage at the Jemaa el Fnaa, Marrakech." *International Journal of Heritage Studies* 22(2): 89–101.

Bhabha, Homi K. 1994. "Of Mimicry and Man: The Ambivalence of Colonial Discourse." In *The Location of Culture.* London: Routledge.

Biolsi, Thomas. 2004. "Political and Legal Status 'Lower 48' States." In *A Companion to the Anthropology of American Indians*, edited by Thomas Biolsi, 231–247. New York: Blackwell.

Blake, Janet. 2000. "On Defining the Cultural Heritage." *International and Comparative Law Quarterly* 49(1): 61–85.

Blake, Janet. 2015. *International Cultural Heritage Law.* Oxford: Oxford University Press.

Brown, Michael. 2003. *Who Owns Native Culture?* Cambridge, Mass: Harvard University Press.

Callon, Michel, Andrew Barry, and Don Slater. 2002. "Technology, Politics and the Market: An Interview with Michel Callon." *Economy and Society* 31(2): 285–306.

Clair, William St. 1998. *Lord Elgin and the Marbles.* Oxford: Oxford University Press.

Comaroff, John L., and Jean Comaroff. 2009. *Ethnicity, Inc.* Chicago: University of Chicago Press.

Coombe, Rosemary J. 2003. "Works in Progress: Traditional Knowledge, Biological Diversity, and Intellectual Property in a Neoliberal Era." In *Globalization under Construction: Governmentality, Law and Identity*, edited by Richard Warren Perry and Bill Maurer, 273–314. Minneapolis: University of Minnesota Press.

Coombe, Rosemary J. 2009. "The Expanding Purview of Cultural Properties and their Politics." *Annual Review of Law and Social Science* 5: 393–412.

Coombe, Rosemary J., and Lindsay M. Weiss. 2015. "Neoliberalism, Heritage Regimes, and Cultural Rights." In *Global Heritage: A Reader*, edited by Lynn Meskell, 43–69. Hoboken, NJ: Wiley-Blackwell.

Davíðsdóttir, Sigrún. 1999. *Håndskriftsagens saga i politisk belysning*. Odense: Odense Universitetsforlag.

Derrida, Jacques. 1978. "From Restricted to General Economy: A Hegelianism without Reserve." In *Writing and Difference*. Chicago: University of Chicago Press.

Espada, Arcadi. 2004. "Entrevista de Arcadi Espada a Juan Goytisolo." La espía del sur. http://web.archive.org/web/20050516010332/http://www.geocities.com/laespia/goytisolo2.htm. Accessed 9 April 2017.

Fincham, Derek. 2010. "Distinctiveness of Property and Heritage." *The Penn State Law Review* 115(3): 641–684.

Foster, Michael Dylan. 2015. "Imagined UNESCOs: Interpreting Intangible Cultural Heritage on a Japanese Island." *Journal of Folklore Research* 52(2): 217–232.

Frigo, Manlio. 2004. "Cultural Property v. Cultural Heritage: A 'Battle of Concepts' in International Law?" *Revue Internationale de la Croix-Rouge/International Review of the Red Cross* 86(854): 367–378.

Geismar, Haidy. 2013. *Treasured Possessions: Indigenous Interventions into Cultural and Intellectual Property*. Durham, N.C.: Duke University Press.

Geismar, Haidy. 2015. "Anthropology and Heritage Regimes." *Annual Review of Anthropology* 44: 71–85.

Gilman, Lisa. 2015. "Demonic or Cultural Treasure?: Local Perspectives on Vimbuza, Intangible Cultural Heritage, and UNESCO in Malawi." *Journal of Folklore Research* 52(2): 199–216.

Greenfield, Jeanette. 2013 [1989]. *The Return of Cultural Treasures, 3rd Edition*. Cambridge: Cambridge University Press.

Hálfdanarson, Guðmundur. 2015. "Þjóðnýting menningararfsins. Norræn miðaldamenning og sköpun nútímaþjóðernis." In *Menningararfur á Íslandi. Gagnrýni og greining*, edited by Ólafur Rastrick and Valdimar Tr. Hafstein, 39–70. Reykjavik: University of Iceland Press.

Handler, Richard. 1988. *Nationalism and the Politics of Culture in Quebec*. Madison: University of Wisconsin Press.

Hertz, Ellen. 2015. "Bottoms, Genuine and Spurious." In *Between Imagined Communities and Communities of Practice. Participation, Territory and the Making of Heritage*, edited by Nicolas Adell, Regina F. Bendix, Chiara Bortolotto and Markus Tauschek, 25–58. Göttingen: Universitätsverlag Göttingen.

Hitchens, Christopher. 1987. *The Elgin Marbles: Should They be Returned to Greece?* London: Verso.

Kapchan, Deborah. 2014. "Intangible Heritage in Transit: Goytisolo's Rescue and Moroccan Cultural Rights." In *Cultural Heritage in Transit. Intangible Rights as Human Rights*, edited by Deborah Kapchan, 177–194. Philadelphia: University of Pennsylvania Press.

Kjær, Birgitte. 2002. "Håndskriftsagen' set fra Danmark." *Nordisk Museologi* 2: 8–16.

Li, Tania Murray. 2001. "Boundary Work. Community, Market, and State Reconsidered." In *Communities and the Environment. Ethnicity, Gender, and the State in Community-Based Conservation*, edited by Arun Agrawal and Clark C. Gibson, 157–179. New Brunswick: Rutgers University Press.

Lowthorp, Leah. 2015. "Voices on the Ground: Kutiyattam, UNESCO, and the Heritage of Humanity." *Journal of Folklore Research* 52(2): 157–180.

McDermott, Melanie Hughes. 2001. "Invoking Community. Indigenous People and Ancestral Domain in Palawan, the Phillippines." In *Communities and the Environment. Ethnicity, Gender, and the State in Community-Based Conservation*, edited by Arun Agrawal and Clark C. Gibson, 32–62. New Brunswick: Rutgers University Press.

Miller, Daniel, ed. 1995. *Worlds Apart: Modernity through the Prism of the Local*. London; New York: Routledge.

Nebelong, Henrik. 2002. "Haandskriftssagerne' i bagklogskabens lys." In *Mindevaerdige Retssager*, edited by Peter Garde, Mogens Koktvedgaard and Oluf Engell, 127–142. Copenhagen: Forlaget Thomson, Gad Jura.

Ólason, Vésteinn. 2002. "Håndskriftenes Hjemkomst – Vitenskapelig og Ideologisk Belysning." *Nordisk Museologi* 2: 3–7.

Ólason, Vésteinn. 2004. "The Manuscripts of Iceland." In *The Manuscripts of Iceland*, edited by Gísli Sigurðsson and Vésteinn Ólason, III–VI. Reykjavik: Árni Magnússon Institute in Iceland.

Pentz, Peter, ed. 2004. *Utimut – Return: The Return of More Than 35.000 Cultural Objects to Greenland*. Gylling: The National Museum of Denmark, Greenland National Museum and Archives and UNESCO.

Prott, Lyndel V., ed. 2009. *Witnesses to History: A Compendium of Documents and Writings on the Return of Cultural Objects*. Paris: UNESCO.

Prott, Lyndel V., and Patrick J. O'Keefe. 1992. "'Cultural Heritage' or 'Cultural Property'?" *International Journal of Cultural Property* 1(2): 307–320.

Rose, Nikolas. 1996. "Governing 'Advanced' Liberal Democracies." In *Foucault and Political Reason: Liberalism, Neo-Liberalism and Rationalities of Government*, edited by A. Barry, T. Osbourne and N. Rose, 37–64. Chicago: University of Chicago Press.

Rosing, Emil, and Peter Pentz. 2004. "The Museum Collaboration of Denmark and Greenland." In *UTIMUT-RETURN*, edited by Peter Pentz, 23–30. Gylling, Denmark: The National Museum of Denmark, Greenland National Museum & Archives, and UNESCO.

Sanborn, Andrea. 2008. Oral presentation in Athens, Greece, quoted in Martin Skrydstrup. "Once Ours: The Making and Unmaking of Claims to Cultural Property" (2010: 10). PhD dissertation, Columbia University.

Schmitt, Carl. 2005 [1922]. *Political Theology: Four Chapters on the Concept of Sovereignty*. Chicago: University of Chicago Press.

Sigurðsson, Gísli, and Vésteinn Ólason, eds. 2004. *The Manuscripts of Iceland*. Reykjavik: Árni Magnússon Institute in Iceland.

UNESCO. 2006. Expert Meeting on Community Involvement in Safeguarding Intangible Cultural Heritage: Towards the Implementation of the 2003 Convention. 13–15 March 2006, Tokyo, Japan. Report. Intangible Heritage Section, Division of Cultural Heritage, Sector for Culture, United Nations Educational, Scientific and Cultural Organisation (UNESCO) and the Asia/Pacific Cultural Centre for UNESCO (ACCU).

UNESCO. 2008. Press Release No. 112. UNESCOPRESS.

Webb, Timothy. 2002. "Appropriating the Stones: The 'Elgin Marbles' and the English National Taste." In *Claiming the Stones – Naming the Bones*, edited by Elazar Barkan and Ronald Bush, 51–96. Los Angeles: Getty Research Institute.

3
THE CRIMINALISATION OF THE ILLICIT TRADE IN CULTURAL PROPERTY

Ana Filipa Vrdoljak

Introduction

In August 2014, the UN Security Council condemned the gross, systematic and widespread violation of international humanitarian and human rights law by various armed groups in Syria and Iraq including:

> [I]ndiscriminate killing and deliberate targeting of civilians, numerous atrocities, mass executions and extrajudicial killings, including of soldiers, persecution of individuals and entire communities on the basis of their religion or belief, kidnapping of civilians, forced displacement of members of minority groups, killing and maiming of children, recruitment and use of children, rape and other forms of sexual violence, arbitrary detention, attacks on schools and hospitals, destruction of cultural and religious sites and obstructing the exercise of economic, social and cultural rights, including the right to education.
>
> *(UN 2014a: para. 2).*

Through its inclusion of acts directed against cultural heritage in this list, the Security Council reaffirmed the opprobrium with which the international community holds them. In later resolutions, and in line with existing customary international law, it condemned the incidental or deliberate destruction and pillage of cultural heritage. More significantly, it recognised that looting and the illicit traffic of cultural objects is used by these groups to raise funds, as they do with other economic resources (oil, precious metals) and illicit activities (kidnapping for ransom). Viewing them as facilitating acts which threaten international peace and security, it calls on Member States to repress these activities and ensure that those who engage in such acts be 'brought to justice' (UN 2015a).

This chapter considers the criminalisation of illicit traffic of cultural objects in international law and its impact for domestic law. The regulation of the trade in cultural objects has long been resisted in so-called market states, which host major auction houses and art and antiquities dealers. The lobbying was particularly directed against the enforcement of foreign public laws covering export controls in domestic courts (NADAOPA *et al.* 2002). However, the Security Council's adoption of resolutions that condemned the pillage of Iraqi and Syrian cultural sites has transformed this debate. These resolutions enunciate an obligation to prosecute in domestic courts which covers all UN Member States. It is no longer confined to States Parties of the relevant international conventions including the Convention on the Means of Prohibiting and Preventing the Illicit Import, Export and Transfer of Ownership of Cultural Property (UNESCO 1970) and Convention for the Protection of Cultural Property in the Event of Armed Conflict (1954 Hague Convention) and First Hague Protocol (UNESCO 1954a and 1954b). This is a significant shift in the criminalisation of the illicit trade in cultural objects. While this chapter does not address in detail the deliberate destruction of cultural heritage, the destruction of cultural diversity through the targeting of cultural patrimony of religious and ethnic groups, and the targeting and killing of heritage professionals, these acts are entwined with the illicit traffic in cultural objects and are increasingly condemned by the international community in the same instruments.

To examine this development in international law, I focus on two seemingly unrelated, recent events. The first part of this chapter examines the discovery of the hoard of artworks held by Cornelius Gurlitt in Germany in 2012. It serves as a reminder not only of the systematic confiscation of artworks by the Nazi regime during the 1930s and 1940s, and the complicity of art dealers and auction houses, but its lingering legacy. The lessons learned during the mid-twentieth century which transformed international law including human rights law and cultural heritage protection are revisited in the second part. It details the response of the international community in the twenty-first century to atrocities committed in Iraq and Syria and funded by illicit activities including the looting of and trade in cultural objects. In 1943 and 2015, the international community condemned such acts, and put those engaged in these activities on notice that they would be held to account and that these transfers of property would not be recognised as licit. The continued large-scale looting and limited success in returning cultural materials which have been illicitly removed emphasises the need for effective, systematic cooperation among states and other stakeholders in ways which are increasingly being articulated in international instruments.

Lessons from the 1930s and Second World War

The list enumerated by the Security Council in 2014 concerning violations of international law committed in Iraq and Syria, and its inclusion of the acts against cultural heritage, was reminiscent of the indictment of the major war criminals before the International Military Tribunal in Nuremberg at the close of the Second World War. The Nuremberg Tribunal's judgment, and the Allied governments' announcements that preceded it, serve as an important precursor for the international community's response to atrocities being committed today.

Confiscation and forced sales by the Nazi regime

The search by German authorities of Cornelius Gurlitt's Munich apartment in 2012 uncovered a cache of approximately 1,400 paintings and drawings by numerous, celebrated Impressionist and Modernist artists (Eddy et al. 2013). Gurlitt had inherited the artworks from his father, Hildebrand Gurlitt, a prominent German art dealer during the 1930s, who had died in 1956 (Bohr et al. 2013) and was one of four art dealers appointed by Joseph Goebbels to sell artworks confiscated from German public collections and Jewish collectors which were designated 'degenerate' because they did not conform to the regime's national cultural narrative (Nicholas 1995: 24–5; Chechi 2013: 203). Despite the resurgent awareness of restitution claims by Holocaust survivors and their heirs since the end of the Cold War, this discovery again laid bare the complex history and unresolved legacy of Nazi art confiscations during the 1930s and 1940s.

Much contemporary discourse concerning Nazi depredations of artworks focuses on the Shoah and the question of restitution for victims and their heirs; but the regime's confiscation and destruction of artworks went beyond the Jewish community. After coming to power in 1933 and until the end of the Second World War, the Nazi regime 'acquired' artworks through a number of means (IMT 1946; Simpson 1997). Despite the dislocation, loss and destruction of cultural heritage that these acts wrought, they were not necessarily all illegal (according to the legal framework within Germany at the time). In international law, it is important to distinguish the de-accession of artworks designated as 'degenerate' from German public collections prior to (and indeed, during) the Second World War by its national authorities which was a matter for domestic law. From their accession to power, the National Socialists commenced a campaign of systematically denuding German public collections of (mainly modern) artworks that were deemed 'degenerate' and did not conform with their vision of an appropriate national culture and the attendant propaganda (Peters 2014). Indeed, the removal of Hildebrand Gurlitt as a director of the Zwichau Museum in 1930 for 'pursuing an artistic policy affronting the healthy folk feeling of Germany' because of a show of 'New German Painting', highlighted that the die was cast prior to 1933 (Nicholas 1995: 9).[1] By contrast, as explained below, similar acts which led to the looting of public and private collections in territories occupied by Germany were contrary to international humanitarian law as codified in the late nineteenth and early twentieth centuries. Gurlitt re-emerged by the late 1930s as one of the few dealers sanctioned by the Nazi regime to handle artworks confiscated in Germany and occupied territories, in particular, France (Nicholas 1995: 24). Initially, and by contrast, the confiscation of private collections of targeted ethnic, religious, political or other groups in Germany and occupied territories was a thornier legal issue for the Allied governments and their legal advisers. The acts of the Nazi regime against German nationals were viewed as entirely a domestic concern, falling outside the purview of international law. However, as the scale of the Shoah emerged at the close of the hostilities, these acts were found to be illegal because they were intimately related to crimes against humanity and genocide (Lemkin 1944). The hoard discovered by authorities in Cornelius Gurlitt's apartment shed light on the multiplicity of sources from which his father had 'acquired' the artworks, the complexity in determining provenance and the legality or otherwise of his title in them.[2] It is also why he (and upon his death, his estate) legally retained parts of the collection.[3]

The Nazi regime's policies and practices towards these artworks invariably involved their forced sale to raise funds or deliberate, public destruction for propaganda purposes. Despite their distaste for the artworks and/or their owners, the Nazi regime recognised their revenue-raising potential through its Commission for the Exploitation of Degenerate Art, whose membership included Alfred Rosenberg, as chair, and Berlin art dealer Karl Haberstock among others (Nicholas 1995: 23). The Commission, in turn, officially sanctioned a select few leading art dealers (including Gurlitt, Karl Buchholz, Ferdinand Möller and Bernhard Boehmer) and auction houses to sell the confiscated artworks on behalf of the regime (Nicholas 1995: 24). So for example, by November 1941, the Reich Minister in pursuing *Abschiebung* (pushing out of the Jews) had ordered that Jewish property seized which was of value needed to be reported if it was of 'museum value', so that special instructions could be given, with the remainder to be sold (Treue 1952: 238).

Early sales of works seized from German public and private collections realised minimal returns not the least because of the refusal of some foreign buyers, including US and French public institutions, to be seen to be condoning the confiscations and forced sales. This phenomenon was reflected in the infamous auction held at the Grand Hotel Lucerne, organised by Haberstock, on the eve of the Second World War (Nicholas 1995: 4). It had been preceded by the burning of almost 4,000 artworks in the courtyard of the Berlin Fire Department's headquarters (Nicholas 1995: 25). This act of destruction spurred on efforts to sell artworks even for minimal sums to buyers outside Germany, often on the pretext of trying to save them from destruction. This cycle of confiscation from private and public collections, dislocation and destruction, and forced sales to raise revenue to fund the war effort only escalated and spread beyond Germany to occupied territories during the war. Indeed, with civilian populations under occupation in the Netherlands, Belgium and France desperate to realise their assets and flee or just survive, many prominent auction houses reported the war years as their most prosperous (Nicholas 1995: 153). The four sanctioned German art dealers were among the chief buyers as they sourced works for the new museum to be established under the Führer's watchful eye in Linz (Bohr et al. 2013). However, they did not only confine themselves to artworks approved by the regime. Instead, for example, Gurlitt continued to purchase modern works, which were later inherited by his son.

1943 London Declaration and Nuremberg Trials

As the tide of war began to turn and conscious of the ever-heightening risk to artworks by Axis authorities and forces as the war intensified, the Allied forces issued the Inter-Allied Declaration against Acts of Dispossession Committed in Territories under Enemy Occupation or Control (1943 London Declaration) on 5 January 1943. It put the governments and individuals in Axis and occupied territories and neutral states on notice that acts of looting and subsequent sale of these art objects would be held to account and these transfers of property would not be recognised at the end of hostilities. It stated that:

> This warning applies whether such transfers or dealings have taken the form of open looting or plunder, or of transactions apparently legal in form, even when they purport to be voluntarily effected.

The Regulations annexed to the Convention IV respecting the Laws and Customs of War on Land (1907 Hague IV Regulations)[4] had outlawed the confiscation of private property (Article 46) and forbidden pillaging (Article 47) and the 'seizure of, destruction or wilful damage' of public property including artworks held by the state or religious, charitable or educational institutions (Article 56) from territory under belligerent occupation. They provided that perpetrators would be 'subject to legal proceedings' and liable to pay compensation (Article 56 Annex; Article 3 Hague IV Convention). The International Military Tribunal at Nuremberg when handing down its judgment on the war crimes count of the indictment of the major Nazi war criminals found that the 1907 Hague IV Convention represented customary international law, binding not only those states that had ratified the treaty but all states (IMT 1947: 248–9). The more ground-breaking (and contentious) aspect of the indictment was the inclusion of the crimes against humanity count. This count covered acts perpetrated before the commencement of the war and encompassed the confiscation of property (including artworks) from targeted civilian populations in Germany and occupied territories before and during the armed conflict (IMT 1946: vol.1, 10–11).

Some months before the commencement of the Nuremberg Trial, the US Army in Bavaria had come upon Haberstock and Gurlitt living with their families. Not long afterwards they located a warehouse full of artworks (Nicholas 1995: 379). These dealers came within the purview of the US Army's Monuments, Fine Arts and Archives (MFAA) Section, which had been established to locate and facilitate the return of confiscated artworks. Already on the Office of Strategic Services (OSS) (a precursor to the CIA) wanted list, Haberstock was described by MFAA officers as 'Hitler's private art collector [who], for years, seized art treasures in France, Holland, Belgium and even Switzerland and Italy, using illegal, unscrupulous and even brutal means' (Bohr et al. 2013). They described Gurlitt as an 'art dealer to the Führer', who 'acted on behalf of other Nazi officials and made trips to France, from where he brought home art collections' (Bohr et al. 2013). Haberstock was taken into custody, relocated and interrogated. The resulting testimony was vital in the trial of the major war criminals at Nuremberg, particularly Alfred Rosenberg. Haberstock was turned over for trial before German courts, where he was exonerated. Gurlitt was placed under house arrest and later released. With the onset of the Cold War, both men and others like them were 'de-nazified' and successfully re-emerged after the war as respected art dealers (Nicholas 1995: 376, 435–6). Nonetheless, their testimonies facilitated the conviction of Alfred Rosenberg, and other war criminals, who had been actively involved in the confiscation and forced sale of public and private art collections.

The indictment of the major German war criminals at Nuremburg charged that as part of their 'plan of criminal exploitation', they had destroyed 'cultural monuments, scientific instruments, and property of all types in the occupied territories' (IMT 1946: vol.1, 11–30). The International Military Tribunal found that Alfred Rosenberg was in charge of the 'entire spiritual and ideological training' of the National Socialist Party. To this end, he had established the 'Hohe Schule' (Centre of National Socialistic Ideological and Educational Research), which instigated the 'Einsatzstab Rosenberg', 'which plundered museums and libraries, confiscated art treasures and collections, and pillaged private houses' (IMT 1947: 237). He extended these activities to the occupied territories in Central and Eastern Europe where he directed the Hague Regulations 'were not applicable' (IMT 1947: 287). The Court found that this plunder was also driven by a need to raise revenue for the war effort and that these acts constituted war crimes (IMT 1947: 274).

The activities of the 'Einsatzstab Rosenberg' also led to Rosenberg being indicted for crimes against humanity before the Nuremberg Tribunal. Article 6(c) of the Charter of the International Military Tribunal of 8 August 1945 (London Charter) provided that crimes against humanity included 'persecutions on political, racial or religious grounds in execution of or in connection with any crime within the jurisdiction of the Tribunal, whether or not in violation of the domestic law of the country where perpetrated.'[5] Count Four of the Nuremberg Indictment addressed the persecution of Jews 'since 1933 . . . from Germany and from the occupied Western Countries and where sent to the Eastern Countries for extermination' (IMT 1947: 243–7). It found that the deliberate, systematic and discriminatory confiscation of the property, including cultural objects, of Jewish populations in occupied territories was designed to remove them from the economic life of the nation and was part of policies which were designed to lead to their extermination (IMT 1947: 287–8). Rosenberg was found guilty of crimes against humanity, war crimes and other counts of the indictment and sentenced to death. This legal precedent proved vital to the future codification of protection of cultural heritage and criminalisation of these acts in international law.

Restitution and codification after the Second World War

In keeping with the 1907 Hague Regulations, the 1943 London Declaration flagged that perpetrators involved in the confiscation of cultural property would be held criminally responsible and that the resulting transfers of property would not be recognised after the war. The post-war Allied restitution programme covered acts encompassing not only war crimes, that is, the plunder of public and private property in occupied territories, but crimes against humanity, namely the confiscation of private property of persecuted groups in Germany from 1933 to 1945 and occupied territories during the war (Nicholas 1995:407–44).

Reflecting the scale of dislocation of cultural property and recognition that the legal obligation concerning restitution went beyond Germany, the legal instruments adopted or enacted to realise it covered multilateral agreements between the Allied governments covering Germany; domestic laws of the four occupying powers of Germany (and for Austria); dedicated provisions in peace treaties with Italy, Romania, Bulgaria and Finland; and domestic laws of neutral states (Switzerland and Sweden) (Vrdoljak 2012:165–87). They encapsulate the obligation of solidarity and cooperation contained in the London Declaration, which transformed long-held principles in domestic legal systems (like the *bona fide* purchaser, statute of limitations, etc.) that governed the transfer of property but would have impeded restitution.

A few years after the Nuremberg Judgment, UNESCO commenced work on the codification of the protection of cultural property during armed conflict and belligerent occupation which led to the adoption of the 1954 Hague Convention and First Protocol. A preliminary study prepared by jurist Georges Berlia, which proposed the inclusion of preventative and punitive measures, also referenced the findings of the Nuremberg Tribunal in respect of acts directed against cultural property (Berlia 1950:12). The Convention's preparatory documents noted that the armistice agreements and peace treaties following the Second World War which enabled restitution of cultural property and the Nuremberg Tribunal had 'introduced the principle of punishing attacks on the cultural heritage of a nation into positive international law' (UNESCO 1952:5).

The 1954 Hague Convention was the first binding, specialist multilateral agreement for the protection of cultural property during war. It covers publicly and privately owned movable and immovable cultural heritage including 'archaeological sites' and 'works of art, books, scientific collections, archives' (Article 1). High Contracting Parties are required to refrain from acts of reprisal against cultural property, and to prohibit, prevent and stop the theft, pillage and misappropriation of and acts of vandalism towards cultural heritage during armed conflict (Article 4). During belligerent occupation, the occupying power must cooperate with and support the competent national authorities for the protection of cultural heritage (Article 5). The First Hague Protocol, which covers the removal and return of cultural objects, draws on the principles contained in the 1943 London Declaration and the post-war restitution programmes. It requires High Contracting Parties to prevent the export of cultural property from territory under their control (para.1). Those not involved in a conflict must take cultural objects removed from occupied territory into their custody for safekeeping (para.2). Cultural objects removed in contravention of the Protocol must be returned to the competent authorities of the territory immediately after occupation has ceased (para.3). For international armed conflicts, if one of the combatants is not a High Contracting Party, the Convention is binding on any High Contracting Party and any other party that declares that it accepts the obligations (Article 18(3)). For civil war occurring on the territory of a High Contracting Party, each party to the conflict must apply the provisions of the Convention as a minimum standard (Article 19(1)).

The Convention contains a duty to prosecute violations (Article 28), which is elaborated by the 1999 Second Hague Protocol (UNESCO 1999a). This second protocol to the 1954 Hague Convention was adopted in response to the shortcomings of the Convention and First

Protocol exposed by the Yugoslav conflicts of the 1990s. High Contracting Parties under the Second Protocol are required to introduce domestic penal law (establishing jurisdiction and appropriate penalties) concerning serious violations occurring within their territory or perpetrated by nationals (Articles 15(2) and 16(1)). Serious violations cover acts committed intentionally and in contravention of the Convention or Second Protocol, including extensive destruction or appropriation of cultural property, and its theft, pillage or misappropriation (Article 15(1)). If a High Contracting Party does not prosecute, it must extradite the perpetrator to a country that can and which meets the minimum standards of international law (Articles 17 and 18). Further, it may introduce legislative, administrative or disciplinary measures which suppress the intentional use of cultural property in violation of the Convention or Second Protocol, and the illicit export, removal, or transfer of ownership of cultural property from occupied territory in violation of the Convention or Protocol (Article 21).

By the close of the twentieth century, international legal obligations prohibiting the deliberate destruction and pillage of cultural property were broadly reaffirmed in the governing statutes of several international criminal tribunals. The related case law has reiterated and elaborated upon the Nuremberg Tribunal's jurisprudence a half century earlier. The Statute of the International Criminal Tribunal for the former Yugoslavia (ICTY) (UN 1993) covers '*seizure* of, destruction, or wilful damage done to institutions dedicated to religion, charity, education, the arts and sciences, historic monuments, and works of art and science' (Article 3 (d)). The ICTY's case law in respect to relationship of acts directed towards the destruction of cultural property as constituting war crimes, crimes against humanity (namely persecution) and evidencing the crime of genocide, were reaffirmed by the International Court of Justice (ICJ 2007; ICJ 2015; Vrdoljak 2011: 37–9; O'Keefe 2010: 47–50; Novak 2014). The instruments for the Extraordinary Chambers in the Court of Cambodia for the Prosecution of Crimes perpetrated during the Khmer Rouge regime in the late 1970s specifically cover violations of obligations under the 1954 Hague Convention (Ehiert 2013: 193–228).[6] In *Case 002–02*, ECCC Trial Chamber is considering the indictment against high-ranking officials of Democratic Kampuchea for crimes against humanity and genocide against Buddhist and Cham people, including destruction of religious sites and sacred texts (ECCC 2010, 2014).

The International Criminal Court (ICC) in The Hague has also been called to consider the link between deliberate destruction of cultural property and looting as war crimes. The Rome Statute defines war crimes to include 'destroying or seizing the enemy's property' and 'pillage' covering international conflicts (Article 8(2)(b)(xiii) and (xvi)) and 'pillage' during non-international conflicts (Article 8(2)(e)) (UN 1998). In 2012, Mali requested that the ICC Prosecutor investigate and indict the perpetrators of attacks on religious and cultural sites in Timbuktu (Coulibaly 2012). The UN Secretary General called on the Security Council to impose sanctions on the perpetrators of attacks on sites that are designated as 'part of the indivisible heritage of humanity' (Ki-moon 2012: 1). The ICC Prosecutor found a prima facie case for war crimes in respect of acts including direct attacks against protected objects and pillaging of sites and objects whose 'value transcends geographical boundaries, and which are unique in character and are intimately associated with the history and culture of the people' (ICCP 2013: 31, 34). The defendant was found guilty and sentenced in 2016.

Iraq, Afghanistan and Syria: illicit traffic in the twenty-first century

The obligation to cooperate contained in the 1943 London Declaration was revisited in the twenty-first century with UN Security Council resolutions covering Iraq, Afghanistan and Syria, and the UNESCO Declaration covering the intentional destruction of cultural heritage.

These resolutions are significant because they take this obligation beyond the States Parties to the 1954 Hague Conventions and its Protocols, or the 1970 UNESCO Convention. They reinforced the application of a legally binding obligation on all UN Member States whether or not they are parties to these conventions.

UN Security Council Resolution 1483 of 2003 on Iraq: An obligation for all

The obligations contained in the 1954 Hague Protocol were largely replicated in Security Council resolutions on Iraq during the Gulf War in 1991 and the Iraq War of 2003, which provided for the safekeeping and restitution of cultural heritage removed from that country (UN 2003: para.7). They bound all UN Member States and not just States Parties to the Hague Protocol.

In the months preceding the Iraq War, archaeologists raised fears concerning cultural losses caused by looting following the ensuing civil unrest. A petition by international Near East scholars to the United Nations and UNESCO urged the international community to ensure that archaeological sites and museum collections be secured by armed personnel as soon as practicable to prevent theft (UNESCO 2003b). US Major Christopher Varhola, a cultural anthropologist, acknowledged: 'The US military [was] eager to coordinate the task of preservation, which transcend[ed] military and operational necessity' ('Army Takes Steps' 2003).

Archaeologists' fears regarding looting were heightened when news filtered out that representatives of the American Council for Cultural Policy (ACCP), a group representing antiquities dealers and art lawyers, met with the US Defense officials and the Department of State prior to the commencement of hostilities (D'Arcy 2002). The ACCP had been vocal in its campaign to persuade the US government to amend the Convention on Cultural Property Implementation Act (19 US 2603) to lessen the impact of efforts of other States to stem the flow of antiquities from their territories into overseas markets, particularly the United States (McDougall 2003). Andre Emmerich (2003), dealer of Classical, pre-Columbian and contemporary art, wrote: 'The major lesson to be learned from the Iraq disaster is the desirability of dispersing widely the art of past civilizations. . . . Contrary to what some believe, trade in ancient objects is not the enemy of preservation. . . . In fact, higher morality, as so often, is best served by the free market.' On 14 April 2003, several eminent archaeologists co-signed a letter published in the *Guardian* (UK) that flagged the imminent danger of large-scale looting of cultural sites and institutions and noted that lobbying by the ACCP was designed to persuade the US government to 'relax legislation that protects Iraq's heritage by prevention of sales abroad, arguing that antiquities will be safer in American museums and private collections than in Iraq' (Lambrick et al. 2003). When looting did occur, then-US Attorney-General John Ashcroft advised that: '[T]here is evidence that organized criminals were behind the looting of select, high value items, possibly stolen to order for international clients' ('Looted Iraqi Artefacts' 2003).

Like the London Declaration 60 years before it, Security Council Resolution 1483 of 2003 recalled the 1907 Hague IV Convention and encompassed a request for cooperation to repress certain acts and to hold perpetrators to account. Paragraph 7 provided:

> [A]ll Member States shall take appropriate steps to facilitate the safe return to Iraqi institutions of Iraqi cultural property and other items of archaeological, historical, cultural, rare scientific and religious importance illegally removed from Iraq … including by establishing a prohibition on trade in or transfer of such items and

> items with respect to which reasonable suspicion exists that they have been illegally removed.
>
> *(UN 2003)*

It also called on them to cooperate with relevant international organisations like UNESCO and INTERPOL. When transposing this obligation into their domestic laws states have often adopted approaches which are stricter than the obligations under the Hague Convention and Protocols or the 1970 UNESCO Convention. For example, *Iraq (United Nations Sanctions) Order 2003 (UK)* shifted the burden of proof from the prosecution to the defendant. He or she had to prove that they 'did not know and had no reason to suppose' that the object was removed illegally from Iraq after the relevant date (Section 8(2) and (3)). In the United States, the Emergency Protection for Iraqi Cultural Antiquities Act of 2004 extended the application of the existing law to cultural material covered by the Resolution regardless of whether Iraq is a State Party to the 1970 UNESCO Convention. Persistent civil strife and hostilities in Iraq resulted in the Security Council reaffirming these obligations in 2015, discussed below.

UNESCO Declaration on Intentional Destruction of 2003

The rationale contained in the preamble of the 1954 Hague Convention was reaffirmed by the Declaration Concerning the Intentional Destruction of Cultural Heritage adopted by the UNESCO General Conference in 2003 (UNESCO 2003a). Adopted in response to the destruction of the monumental Buddhas at Bamiyan, Afghanistan, it states that these acts 'affected the international community as a whole' (Francioni and Lenzerini 2003; O'Keefe 2004). It also draws on lessons learned from the mid-twentieth century when it states that: '[C]ultural heritage is an important component of the cultural identity of communities, groups and individuals, and of social cohesion, so that its intentional destruction may have adverse consequences on human dignity and human rights' (UNESCO 2003a). The Declaration covers acts occurring outside the theatre of war and within the territory of a state. In support it invokes, not only the 1954 Hague Convention, 1899 Hague II and 1907 Hague IV Conventions, but the relevant provisions of the Rome Statute and the ICTY Statute and related jurisprudence.

While the 2003 Declaration calls on UNESCO Member States to adhere to conventions and recommendations covering the protection of cultural heritage, the 1970 UNESCO Convention on illicit traffic was not one of them. Nevertheless, during the drafting process the UNESCO General Conference adopted a resolution which did refer to this treaty and 'note[d] the fundamental principles included in these instruments to prevent the destruction of cultural heritage including looting and illicit excavations' (UNESCO 2001).

Accordingly, the 2003 Declaration is an important reference point because it provides for state and individual responsibility for intentional destruction of cultural heritage (Articles VI and VII), and outlines the obligation to cooperate in respect of protecting cultural heritage against intentional destruction (Article VIII). It calls on States Parties to the 1954 Hague Convention to establish jurisdiction and effective criminal sanctions against individuals who commit or order others to commit such acts. It calls on states to cooperate with one another and UNESCO including through information sharing; consultation in cases of actual or impending destruction; assistance in respect of educational, awareness-raising and capacity-building programmes for prevention and repression; and assistance of judicial and administrative processes. These modalities of international cooperation are important in defining expectations in other contexts including those covering illicit traffic.

UN Security Council Resolution 2199 of 2015: Deliberate destruction and looting

The deliberate destruction of cultural heritage again became the focus of international attention in 2014 with atrocities committed by extremist groups, including Al Nusrah Front (ANF) and Islamic State of Iraq and the Levant (ISIL), in Iraq and Syria. The Security Council strongly condemned the 'destruction of cultural and religious sites and obstruct[ion] of the exercise of … cultural rights' (UN 2014a: para. 2). The Human Rights Council likewise expressed deep concern for the 'rampant destruction of monuments, shrines, churches, mosques, and other places of worship, archaeological sites and cultural heritage sites' (Human Rights Council 2014).

The Security Council tasked the UN Analytical Support and Sanctions Monitoring Team with reporting back on this and other threats. Its report recommended that that the Security Council build on SC Resolution 1483 of 2003 and mandate 'a world-wide moratorium on the trading of antiquities from the Syrian Arab Republic or Iraq since the passing of resolution 2170 (2014) that *lack clear, certified provenance*' (UN 2014b: 23–4). The report observed that ANF and ISIL could raise funds from the trade in antiquities and while the ban would not eliminate the illicit market, it could depress it. The UNESCO Executive Board noted that such acts 'damage[d] the cultural heritage of all humankind' and were a war crime under the Rome Statute (UNESCO 2014a: para. 6). It called on 'all countries and all professional groups involved in the areas of customs and trade, as well as individuals and tourists, to *verify the origin* of cultural property that may have been imported, exported or offered for sale illegally' (UNESCO 2014a: para. 18 (emphasis added)). UNESCO adopted an Emergency Response Action Plan which put Member States, museums and auction houses on notice of the pillaging of Iraqi cultural heritage and called on them to support the international effort to repress it (UNESCO 2014b: 3).

The Security Council adopted the Monitoring Team's recommendation in SC Res. 2199 of 12 February 2015. It is binding on UN Member States and takes precedence over any conflicting treaty obligations (Negri 2015: 5–6). The resolution dealing with UN Member States' obligations concerning atrocities being committed by ANF and ISIL brings together condemnation of the acts of destruction and looting of cultural heritage in the one instrument. It recognises that their impact is identical – systematic and irreversible loss of cultural heritage. The Security Council condemned incidental or deliberate destruction of religious and cultural sites and objects (para. 15). It then noted with concern that ISIL, ANF and other groups and individuals were either directly or indirectly engaged in the 'looting and smuggling of cultural heritage items from archaeological sites, museums, libraries, archives, and other sites in Iraq and Syria' (para. 16). Since ancient times both acts were designed to demoralise the enemy and civilian populations into submission. As noted earlier, it is a strategy condemned and prohibited by the international community since the late nineteenth century.

However, the Security Council acknowledged that cultural heritage has another significant potential for these groups. Like the National Socialists in the mid-twentieth century, the SC Res. 2199 of 2015 makes clear that ISIL and ANF have facilitated the looting and illicit trade in cultural objects in Iraq and Syria to generate revenue 'to support their recruitment efforts and strengthen their operational capability to organize and carry out terrorist attacks' (para. 16). The deliberate destruction of historic sites for propaganda value had successfully garnered worldwide attention through social and traditional media. However, as Syrian archaeologist Amr Al-Azm explained, the large-scale, systematic looting of archaeological sites by all parties in the Syrian conflict was driven not by 'ideology, but income' (Kohn 2014).

Indeed, the US State Department advised that a cache of archaeological objects had been found with ISIL's deceased finance chief in a raid in Syria in May 2015 (Duray 2015). The push into the trade in antiquities was seen as precipitated by the bombing of key economic sites like oil fields (Symmes 2015). The Director of Compliance and Facilitation, World Customs Organisation noted that 'plundering of cultural property is one of the oldest forms of organised cross-border crime' and that its financing of terrorist groups through the trade in cultural objects has become a focus for his organisation (Zhu 2014). SC Res. 2199 of 2015 (with SC Res. 2170 of 2014) is primarily designed to ensure the cooperation of UN Member States in curbing the sources of funding to terrorist organisations which are viewed as 'serious threats to international peace and security' (Preamble). For this reason, it is incorporated in a Security Council resolution adopted under Chapter VII of the UN Charter.

Moving beyond war crimes, these acts of looting to finance terrorist activities are recalibrated by the Security Council more broadly as 'criminal and unjustifiable regardless of their motivation, whenever, and by whomever they are committed' (United Nations 2015, Preamble). SC Res. 2199 of 2015 noted that any 'direct or indirect trade with ISIL and ANF' could be a violation of obligations imposed to combat terrorist activities, including to 'ensure that any person who participates in financing ... of terrorist acts or in supporting terrorist acts is brought to justice' (Preamble). The criminalisation of illicit trade in cultural property was reinforced by the UN General Assembly when it reaffirmed obligations under cultural heritage instruments (including the 1954 Hague Convention and Protocols, 1970 UNESCO Convention and 2003 Declaration on Intentional Destruction) and those in the field of organised crime prevention, including the International Guidelines for Crime Prevention and Criminal Justice Responses with Respect to Trafficking in Cultural Property and Other Related Offences, in respect of international and national efforts to protect Iraqi cultural heritage (UN 2015b; Bokova 2015: 3). These guidelines provide detailed strategies in respect of crime prevention, criminal justice policies and international cooperation.

Like prior Security Council resolutions, SC Res. 2199 of 2015 calls on UN Member States to 'prevent the trade in Iraqi and Syrian cultural property and other items of archaeological, historical, cultural, rare scientific, and religious importance illegally removed' from these countries by prohibiting the cross-border trade, facilitating their safe return, and cooperating with international organisations like UNESCO and Interpol (para. 17). Under the resolution, Member States are required to report back to the UN Sanctions Committee concerning their compliance with these measures (para. 29).[7] The State Department emphasised that the United States is working with 'transit and market countries' to take measures to curb trafficking and aid return 'to the country of origin when it is safe to do so', and to 'collaborate with international and national law enforcement, customs officials, and ministries of culture to alert art dealers and collectors' to plundered artefacts circulating illegally in the market (Ryan 2015). The Federal Bureau of Investigation alerted art collectors and dealers about antiquities from the region that may be in circulation (Duray 2015). Further, there are efforts to transpose these obligations into US domestic law with the tabling of legislation before Congress referencing the deliberate destruction and looting of cultural heritage in Syria, Iraq, Mali and by the Nazi regime in support of the establishment of a US Coordinator for International Cultural Property Protection.[8]

Despite these initiatives, cultural objects from Syria and Iraq continue to be traded illicitly in transit and market countries (Shabi 2015). For instance, the US Department of Homeland Security in early 2015 returned 60 cultural artefacts including the head from a statute of the Assyrian King Sargon II to the government of Iraq. US Assistant Secretary of State, Evan Ryan (2015), explaining the State Department's actions, observed: 'ISIL actions equate to nothing less than ethnic cleansing . . . The American people stand with the people of Iraq in their battle against ISIL and others whose goal is to destroy and deny our common humanity.'

Codes of conduct and criminalisation

Reminiscent of the 1943 London Declaration, the General Assembly in its 2015 Resolution on saving Iraqi cultural heritage urged:

> [A]ll States to take appropriate measures to ensure that all actors involved in the trade in cultural property, including but not limited to auction houses, art dealers, art collectors and museum professionals, are required to provide verifiable documentation of provenance as well as export certificates related to any cultural property imported, exported or offered for sale, including through the internet.

The standard of conduct expected of those dealing with cultural objects has been defined in codes of ethics or good practice adopted by intergovernmental organisations in the field. The UNESCO International Code of Ethics for Dealers in Cultural Property calls on 'traders' not to facilitate the trade in stolen, illegally alienated, clandestinely excavated or illegally exported cultural property and if in possession of such an object to take all legally permissible steps to cooperate in its return to the country of origin in a reasonable time (UNESCO 1999b). The UNESCO Code is closely aligned with the International Council of Museums (ICOM) Code of Ethics for Museums (ICOM 2004). The ICOM Code provides that museum professionals must not directly or indirectly support the illicit trade in cultural objects and cooperate with police and authorities in curbing it (paras 8.5 and 8.8). However, museums are not prevented from 'acting as an authorised repository for unprovenanced, illicitly collected or recovered specimens or objects from the territory over which it has lawful responsibility' (para. 2.11).

Further guidance as to the requisite standard of conduct expected of persons engaged in the trade in cultural objects is provided by the UNIDROIT Convention on Stolen or Illegally Exported Cultural Property in its definition of due diligence (UNIDROIT 1995). In determining whether the possessor has exercised due diligence in the circumstances consideration should be given to the 'character of the parties', the purchase price, whether the possessor sought information from established databases of stolen or missing cultural property, or consulted relevant agencies, or 'took any other step that a reasonable person would have taken in the circumstances' (Article 4(4)). A number of countries that host large auction houses have also adopted laws defining due diligence. For example, the Swiss Federal Act on the International Transfer of Cultural Property of 2003 provides that those engaged in the art trade and auction businesses can only transfer cultural property that is not stolen, removed against the will of the owner, or illegally excavated or illicitly exported (Article 16). They must act with due diligence by establishing the identity of the seller, obtaining their written consent that they have a right to transfer the property, advising the customers of current import and export regulations, maintaining written sales records for 30 years, and providing data to a central body (Article 16(2)).

The UNESCO Code requires violations to be investigated by a body nominated by participating dealers, with its decision to be made publicly available. By contrast, the 2015 International Guidelines call for states to introduce criminal, civil and administrative sanctions against individuals and corporations engaged in the illicit import and export, theft, looting, or laundering of such cultural property (Guidelines 20–31). Leading market states introduced criminal and civil sanctions for the trade in stolen cultural property in response to

SC Res. 1483 of 2003 and penal codes that cover handling of stolen property. Nonetheless, experience shows that in the period from the Nuremberg Trials to the present day, the successful criminal prosecution of those engaged in the illicit trade of cultural property is rare (Gerstenblith 2013).

Conclusion

The UN Sanctions Monitoring Team when preparing its report in 2014 on the fate of cultural heritage in Syria and Iraq observed that: '[T]here is a risk that local dealers will stockpile the artefacts until the world is no longer focused on this issue. On this basis, the Monitoring Team recommends a preventative approach' (UN 2014b: 24). The story of Cornelius Gurlitt and the hoard of artworks collected by his art dealer father during the Nazi period and kept by him in secret during his lifetime bears witness to the reality of this risk. Some art dealers, auction houses, collectors and museum officials then and now have argued that they are seeking to 'save' cultural objects which would otherwise be lost forever.

However, the international community in the mid-twentieth and early twenty-first century recognised that far from 'saving' cultural heritage, the fostering of the market in cultural objects from territories subject to war, occupation or civil strife fuelled its ever-increasing dislocation and loss. There has been recognition too that groups and regimes that have engaged in illicit trade in cultural objects have often been motivated by the same nihilist tendencies which drive their destruction of cultural, religious and historic sites and monuments *and* the need to raise funds. It is for this reason that the international community has grouped those who participate in the illicit trade of these cultural objects with those who facilitate and engage in other illicit means of funding gross, systematic and widespread abuses of human rights and international humanitarian law. It had led to the criminalisation of this illicit trade in cultural objects and called on all states to repress the export of cultural objects from these territories, refuse to recognise any transfers as legal, prosecute those engaged in this illicit trade and cooperate with other states and intergovernmental organisations to this end. These principles were affirmed in Security Council Resolution 2347 of 24 March 2017, the first resolution specifically dedicated to condemnation of the looting and smuggling of cultural property during armed conflict and recognizing it as a threat to international peace and security.

Notes

1 After 1933, laws were passed which covered the public service including museum directors and other public officials engaged in the arts, and those outside the public sector (including art dealers) were covered by the *Reichkulturkammer* (Reich Chamber of Culture). Those excluded by these acts (including Jews, Communists) could neither produce, exhibit or sell artworks nor hold any job in the field.

2 See database established by the German and Bavarian taskforce: < http://www.lostart.de/Webs/EN/Datenbank/KunstfundMuenchen.html> [22 August 2015]; and for the difficulties arising under German civil law: Chappell and Hufnagel (2015: 221).

3 A confidential agreement was reached with Cornelius Gurlitt and Federal German and Bavarian authorities to return artworks to him where it was found that he had legal title in exchange for his cooperation in establishing the provenance of art objects in his possession in Germany: Federal German Commissioner for Culture and the Media et al. (2014); and similar agreement with the museum bequeathed the collection upon his death: Agreement between the Federal Republic of Germany, the Free State of Bavaria and the

Stiftung Kunstmuseum Bern, 24 November 2014, at <http://www.bundesregierung.de/Content/DE/_Anlagen/BKM/2014-11-24-zusammenfassung-englisch.pdf?__blob=publicationFile> [22 August 2015].

4 18 October 1907, in force 26 January 1910, in *American Journal of International Law* (1908), vol. 2 (supp.), p.90.

5 Signed and entered into force 8 August 1945, 82 UNTS 279, reprinted in *American Journal of International Law* (1945) vol. 39 (supp.), p. 258.

6 Art. 9, Agreement Between the United Nations and the Royal Government of Cambodia Concerning the Prosecution under Cambodian Law of Crimes Committed During the Period of Democratic Kampuchea, GA Res 57/228B of 22 May 2003, UN Doc.A/RES/57/228B (2003) Annex; Arts 6 and 7, Law on the Establishment of Extraordinary Chambers in the Court of Cambodia for the Prosecution of Crimes committed during the period of Democratic Kampuchea, with the inclusion of amendments as promulgated on 27 October 2004 (NS/RKM/1004/006).

7 As of September 2015, the Committee and UNESCO were processing these reports of some Member States.

8 Act to protect and preserve international cultural heritage at risk due to political instability, armed conflict, or natural or other disasters, and for other purposes (H.R. 1493).

Bibliography

'Army Takes Steps to Protect Iraq's Cultural Heritage', 6 April 2003. Available at: <users.ox.ax.uk> [11 April 2003]

Berlia, G. (1950). 'Report on the International Protection of Cultural Property by Penal Measures in the Event of Armed Conflict', 8 March 1950, UNESCO Doc.5C/PRG/6, Annex I.

Bohr, F., Gorris, L., Knofel, U., Robel, S., and Sontheimer, M. (2013). 'Art Dealer to the Fuhrer: Hildebrand Gurlitt's Deep Nazi Ties', 23 December 2013, *Der Speigel Online International.* Available at: <http://www.spiegel.de/international/germany/hildebrand-gurlitt-and-his-dubious-dealings-with-nazi-looted-art-a-940625.html> [16 August 2015]

Bokova, I. (2015). Address by Director-General of UNESCO, on the Occasion of the Stakeholders' Roundtable 'Despoiled and Destroyed: Ancient Civilizations of Iraq and Syria', UNESCO Paris, 1 June 2015, UNESCO Doc.DG/2015/105

Chappell, D. and Hufnagel, S. (2015). 'The Gurlitt Case: German and International Responses to Ownership Rights in Looting Cases', in E. Moustaira (ed.) *Art Collections, Private and Public: A Comparative Legal Study*, Springer, Berlin, p. 221.

Chechi, A. (2013). 'The Gurlitt Hoard: An Appraisal of the Role of the International Law with Respect to Nazi-Looted Art', *Italian Yearbook of International Law*, vol. 23, p. 199.

Coulibaly, M. (2012). 'Referral under Article 14 ICC Statute from Malian Minister for Justice to ICC Prosecutor, 13 July 2012', Available at: <http://www.icc-cpi.int/NR/rdonlyres/A245A47F-BFD1-45B6-891C-3BCB5B173F57/0/ReferralLetterMali130712.pdf > [30 January 2014]

D'Arcy, D. (2002). 'Legal Group to Fight "Retentionist" Policies', *The Art Newspaper*, 24 October 2002. Available at: <www.theartnewspaper.com/news/article.asp?idart=10176> [26 April 2003].

Duray, D. (2015). 'Just What is ISIL looting in Syria?', *The Art Newspaper*, 26 August 2015.

ECCC. (2010). Trial Chamber Closing Order Relevant to Case 002/02, D427, 15 September 2010.

ECCC. (2014). Trial Chamber Decision on Additional Severance of Case 002 and Scope of Case 002/02, E301/9/1, 4 April 2014, p. 21.

Eddy, M., Smale, A., Cohen, P., and Kennedy, R. (2013). 'German Officials Provide Details on Looted Art', *New York Times*, 5 November 2013. Available at: <http://www.nytimes.com/2013/11/06/arts/design/german-officials-provide-details-on-looted-art-trove.html> [3 September 2015].

Ehiert, C. (2013). *Prosecuting the Destruction of Cultural Property in International Criminal Law: A Case Study on the Khmer Rouge's Destruction of Cambodia's Heritage*, Martinus Nijhoff, London.

Emmerich, A. (2003). 'Let the Market Preserve Art: What Were All Those Antiquities Doing in Iraq Anyway?' *Wall Street Journal*, 24 April 2003. Available at: <www.opinionjournal.com> [26 April 2003].

Federal German Commissioner for Culture and the Media, Bavarian State Ministry of Justice and C. Edel (Gurlitt's legal representative). (2014). Joint Press Release, 6 April 2014. Available at: <http://www.lostart.de/Content/02_Aktuelles/2014/14-04-07%20PM%20Agreement%20for%20the%20Schwabing%20Art%20Trove.html?nn=67126> [22 August 2015].

Francioni, F., and Lenzerini, F. (2003). 'The Destruction of the Buddhas of Bamiyan and International Law', *European Journal of International Law*, vol. 14, p. 619.

Gerstenblith, P. (2013). 'Enforcement by Domestic Courts: Criminal Law and Forfeiture in the Recovery of Cultural Objects', in *Enforcing International Cultural Heritage Law*, F. Francioni and J. Gordley (eds.), Cambridge University Press, Cambridge, pp. 150–167.

Human Rights Council. (2014). 'Res S-22/1 on the Human Rights Situation in Iraq in the Light of Abuses Committed by the So-Called Islamic State in Iraq and the Levant and Associated Groups', 3 September 2014, UN Doc.A/HRC/RES/S-22/1.

Inter-Allied Declaration against Acts of Dispossession Committed in Territories under Enemy Occupation or Control, 5 January 1943 (1943 London Declaration), London and Washington, DC, British Foreign Office, Misc. No. 1 (1943), Cmd 6418; and *Department of State Bulletin* (1943) vol. 8, p. 21.

International Council of Museums (ICOM). (2004). 'Code of Ethics for Museums'. Adopted by 1986 and revised 2004. Available at: <http://icom.museum/the-vision/code-of-ethics/> [19 September 2015].

International Court of Justice (IJC). (2007). 'Application of the Convention on the Prevention and Punishment of the Crime of Genocide, (Bosnia and Herzegovina v. Serbia and Montenegro)', *Judgment*, 26 February 2007.

International Court of Justice (IJC). (2015). 'Application of the Convention on the Prevention and Punishment of the Crime of Genocide, (Croatia v. Serbia)', *Judgment*, 3 February 2015.

International Criminal Court Prosecutor (ICCP). (2013). 'Situation in Mali, Article 53(1), Report', 16 January 2013.

International Military Tribunal (IMT), Nuremberg. (1947). 'Judgment', *American Journal of International Law*, vol. 41, pp. 172–333.

International Military Tribunal (IMT), Nuremberg, Germany, Office of the US Chief Counsel for the Prosecution of Axis Criminality. (1946). *Nazi Conspiracy and Aggression*, USGPO, Washington, DC, 8 volumes.

Ki-moon, B. (2012) Secretary-General's Remarks to the Security Council on Mali. Speech delivered at the UN Security Council, New York, 8 August 2012. Available at: http://www.un.org/sg/statements/index.asp?nid=6232 [30 January 2014]

Kohn, D. (2014). 'ISIS's Looting Campaign', *The New Yorker*, 14 October 2014.

Lambrick, G., Hinton, P., Pellew, R., Thackary, D., Wainwright, G., Lord Redesdale, Hassall, M., Catling, C., and Hassall, T. (2003). 'Letter to the Editor', *The Guardian*, 14 April 2003. Available at: <www.guardian.co.uk> [23 April 2003].

Lemkin, R. (1944). Axis Rule in Occupied Europe. Laws of Occupation, Analysis of Government, Proposals for Redress, Carnegie Endowment for International Peace, Washington, DC.

'Looted Iraqi Artefacts "Returned"', *BBC News*, 9 May 2003. Available at: <news.bbc.co.uk/go/pr/fr/-/2/hi/middle_east/3009587.stm> [9 May 2003].

McDougall, L. (2003). 'US Accused of Plans to Loot Iraqi Antiquities', *Sunday Herald*, 6 April 2003.

National Association of Dealers in Ancient, Oriental and Primitive Art, Inc (NADAOPA) et al. (2002). Brief of Amici Curiae in support of the Appeal of Defendant-Appellant Frederick Schultz, 20 September 2002, in United States v. Schultz, 333 D. 3d 393, C.A.2 (N.Y.) 2003 (25 June 2003).

Negri, V. (2015). *Legal Study on the Protection of Cultural Heritage Through the Resolutions of the Security Council of the United Nations*. UNESCO, Paris.

Nicholas, L. H. (1995). *The Rape of Europa: The Fate of Europe's Treasures in the Third Reich and the Second World War*, Papermac, London.

Novak, E. (2014). 'The Concept of Cultural Genocide: An International Law Perspective', PhD thesis, Law Department, European University Institute, Florence.

O'Keefe, R. (2004). 'World Cultural Heritage Obligations to the International Community as a Whole?', *International and Comparative Law Quarterly*, vol. 53, p. 189.

O'Keefe, R. (2010). 'Protection of Cultural Property under International Criminal Law', *Melbourne University Journal of International Law*, vol. 11, p. 1.

Peters, O. (2014). *Degenerate Art: The Attack on Modern Art in Nazi Germany 1937*, Prestel and Neue Galerie, New York.

Ryan, E. (2015). Assistant US Secretary of State, Bureau of Educational and Cultural Affairs, 'Repatriation of Iraqi Artifacts', 21 March 2015. Available at: <http://blogs.state.gov/stories/2015/03/21/repatriation-iraqi-artifacts> [5 September 2015].

Shabi, R. (2015). 'Looted in Syria – and Sold in London: The British Antiquities Shops Dealing in Artefacts Smuggled by Isis', *The Guardian*, 3 July 2015.

Simpson, E. (ed.). (1997). *The Spoils of War: World War II and Its Aftermath: The Loss, Reappearance and Recovery of Cultural Property*, Harry N. Abrams, New York.

Symmes, P. (2015). 'The Ancient Ruins Terror Can't Destroy', *New York Times*, 23 May 2015.

Treue, W. (1952). *Art Plunder: The Fate of Works of Art in War and Unrest*, The John Day Company, New York.

UNESCO. (1945). Constitution of UNESCO, signed on 16 November 1945, entered into force 4 November 1946, 4 UNTS 275.

UNESCO. (1952). Draft International Convention for the Protection in the Event of Armed Conflict of Monuments, Collections and other Cultural Property, 30 September 1952, UNESCO Doc.7C/PRG/7, Annex I: Report of the rapporteur, with comments on the drafts worked out by the Committee.

UNESCO. (1954a). Convention for the Protection of Cultural Property in the Event of Armed Conflict (1954 Hague Convention), 14 May 1954, entered into force 7 August 1956, 249 UNTS 240.

UNESCO. (1954b). Protocol for the Protection of Cultural Property in the Event of Armed Conflict (First Hague Protocol), 14 May 1954, entered into force 7 August 1956, 249 UNTS 358.

UNESCO. (1966). Declaration of Principles of International Cultural Cooperation (1966 UNESCO Principles), resolution adopted by at the UNESCO General Conference, 4 November 1966.

UNESCO. (1970). Convention on the Means of Prohibiting and Preventing the Illicit Import, Export and Transfer of Ownership of Cultural Property (1970 UNESCO Convention), 14 November 1970, entered into force 24 April 1972, 823 UNTS 231.

UNESCO (1999a) Second Protocol to The Hague Convention for the Protection of Cultural Property in the Event of Armed Conflict (1999 Hague Protocol) 26 March 1999, entered into force 9 March 2004, 2253 UNTS 212.

UNESCO. (1999b). International Code of Ethics for Dealers in Cultural Property. Adopted by the UNESCO Intergovernmental Committee for Promoting the Return of Cultural Property to its Countries of Origin or its Restitution in Case of Illicit Appropriation at its Tenth Session, January 1999 and endorsed by the 30th General Conference of UNESCO, November 1999.

UNESCO. (2001). General Conference Res. 26/20 of 2 November 2001 on Acts Constituting a Crime against the Common Heritage of Humanity.

UNESCO. (2003a). Declaration concerning the Intentional Destruction of Cultural Heritage (2003 Declaration). 17 October 2003, UNESCO Doc. 32C/Res. 39.

UNESCO. (2003b). Experts' Meeting, UNESCO Press Release, 17 April 2003.

UNESCO. (2014a). Executive Board, Protection of Iraqi Heritage, 1 October 2014, UNESCO Doc. 195 EX/31.

UNESCO. (2014b). Comments by the Director-General on Items Presented by Member States which may have Administrative and Financial Implications, 10 October 2014, UNESCO Doc. 195 EX/DG.INF.

UNIDROIT. (1995). Convention on Stolen or Illegally Exported Cultural Property, 24 June 1995, in force 1 July 1998, (1995) 34 ILM 1322

United Nations. (1993). Statute of the International Criminal Tribunal for the former Yugoslavia (ICTY). GA Res. 827, 25 May 1993, amended by GA Res. 1166(1998), 1329(2000), 1411(2002), 1431(2002) 1481(2003), 1597(2005), 1660(2006), 1837(2008), 1877(2009).

United Nations. (1998). Rome Statute for the International Criminal Court (Rome Statute). 17 July 1998, entered in force 1 July 2002, 2187 UNTS 90.

United Nations. (2003). SC Res. 1483 of 22 May 2003 on Iraq, UN Doc.S/RES/1483(2003).

United Nations. (2014a). SC Res. 2170 of 15 August 2014 on Threats to International Peace and Security Caused by Terrorist Acts, UN Doc. S/RES/2170 (2014).

United Nations. (2014b). UN Analytical Support and Sanctions Monitoring Team, Islamic State in Iraq and the Levant and the Al-Nusrah Front for the People of the Levant: Report and Recommendations submitted pursuant to resolution 2170(2014), 14 November 2014, UN Doc.S/2014/815, p. 32.

United Nations. (2015a). SC Res. 2199 of 12 February 2015 on Threats to International Peace and Security Caused by Terrorist Acts, UN Doc.S/RES/2199(2015).

United Nations. (2015b). International Guidelines for Crime Prevention and Criminal Justice Responses with Respect to Trafficking in Cultural Property and Other Related Offences. GA Res. 69/281 of 28 May 2015, UN Doc. A/RES/69/281.

United Nations. (2015c). GA Res. 69/281 of 28 May 2015 on Saving Iraqi Cultural Heritage.

Vrdoljak, A. F. (2012). 'Gross Violations of Human Rights and Restitution: Learning from Holocaust Claims', in L. V. Prott (ed.), *Realising Cultural Heritage Law: Festschrift for Patrick O'Keefe*, IAL, Builth Wells.

Vrdoljak, A. F. (2011). 'Genocide and Restitution: Ensuring Each Group's Contribution to Humanity', *European Journal of International Law*, vol. 22, p. 17.

Zhu, G. (2014). Comment, in UNESCO, 'Heritage and Cultural Diversity at Risk in Iraq and Syria: Report', 3 December 2014, p. 16.

4

IMPLEMENTATION OF THE 1970 UNESCO CONVENTION BY THE UNITED STATES AND OTHER MARKET NATIONS

Patty Gerstenblith[1]

Introduction

The major threats to cultural heritage come in the twin forms of destruction during military conflict and looting of sites and collections. Both in antiquity and in contemporary times, we see these destructive activities often going hand-in-hand (Miles 2008, 33–104). While the Roman authors Cicero and Polybius provide antecedents for the protection of cultural heritage, these ideas appeared first in modern history in the writings of the international legal theorist Emmerich de Vattel in the mid-eighteenth century (Miles 2008, 300–2). The Hague Conventions and Regulations of 1899 and 1907, which were influenced by the Lieber Code, drafted for the Union Army in 1863 during the American Civil War, engrained concepts of protection into international law.

It was only with the end of the Second World War and the ruin wreaked upon Europe from both a humanitarian and cultural perspective by the Nazi forces that the international community approached international humanitarian law from a comprehensive perspective. The late 1940s saw the large-scale development of international humanitarian law principles, embodied primarily in the Geneva Conventions. The subject of cultural property protection was separated into its own distinct convention, the 1954 Hague Convention on the Protection of Cultural Property during Armed Conflict. While the First Protocol to the 1954 Hague Convention addresses the subject of movable cultural property, it does so only under very narrow circumstances of illegal removal of cultural objects from occupied territory and the deposit of cultural objects by one State in another State for the purpose of safekeeping.

However, in the post-Second World War period, the appetite of the international art market for works of art, including archaeological objects, grew commensurately with the increase in wealth of the European and North American countries. Unlike contemporary works of art, the corpus of archaeological objects available on the market can increase only by the addition of fakes and forgeries or by the looting of archaeological sites. At the same time, the increasing application of scientific methodologies, including stratigraphic retrieval and scientific analyses, meant that greater quantities of information could be recovered from the proper excavation of sites. Therefore, the looting of sites caused an increasing loss to our knowledge and understanding of the past. Finally, with the end of colonialism in much of the world, particularly Africa and Asia, the new countries sought legal means to conserve at home what remained of their heritage, after so much had been lost to the colonial powers.

Sparked in particular by the work of Professor Clemency Coggins (1969), who brought world attention to the destruction of Maya architectural and monumental sculptural remains in Central America, and of Karl E. Meyer (1977), the world community under the leadership of UNESCO sought to draft a new international convention to confront the illegal trade in artworks, antiquities, and ethnographic objects. These efforts culminated in the 1970 UNESCO Convention on the Means of Prohibiting and Preventing the Illicit Import, Export and Transfer of Ownership of Cultural Property ("the 1970 UNESCO Convention" or "the Convention"). The Convention currently has 131 States Parties. Depending on how a country views a particular convention, it may need to enact implementing legislation to give the convention domestic legal effect. The extent to which a convention is legally binding within a nation then depends on the parameters of this domestic legislation. This chapter will consider the nature of the implementing legislation for the 1970 UNESCO Convention enacted by several of the most significant market nations for archaeological objects. The method by which the United States implements the 1970 UNESCO Convention is examined first and then several paradigms of implementation used by other states are considered in briefer detail.

Implementation by the United States

The United States was one of the first market countries to take steps toward ratification of the 1970 UNESCO Convention when the Senate gave its unanimous consent to ratification in 1972. However, it stated one reservation and six "understandings" to its ratification. One of these understandings provided that the United States viewed the convention as executory in nature. This meant that for the convention to have domestic legal effect, Congress would have to enact legislation by which it would be implemented into domestic law.[2] Such legislation was proposed and passed in the House of Representatives during the late 1970s, but it was largely held hostage in the Senate through the efforts of the late Senator Daniel Patrick Moynihan of New York, who represented the heart of the United States art and antiquities market and was himself involved in the antiquities collecting world.

The implementing legislation, known as the Convention on Cultural Property Implementation Act (CPIA), 19 U.S.C. §§2601–13, was finally enacted in December 1982 and signed into law by President Reagan in January 1983. Among the reasons given by Congress for enactment of the CPIA and ratification of the 1970 UNESCO Convention were that:

> The increasing demand in recent years for archaeological and ethnological materials and antiquities has spurred, in most experts' opinions, a great increase in the international exchange of such materials. But unlike other commodities, increased or new production of these articles cannot rise to meet the demand. Instead, the increased supply results from the sales of known artifacts and those newly recovered from

> archaeological sites. The unique origin and character of these articles raises serious trade issues distinct from the normal concerns of the reciprocal trade agreements program or US trade law. . . . [T]he demand for cultural artifacts has resulted in the irremediable destruction of archaeological sites and articles, depriving the situs countries of their cultural patrimony and the world of important knowledge of its past. Further, because the United States is a principal market for articles of archaeological or ethnological interest and of art objects, the discovery here of stolen or illegally exported artifacts in some cases severely strains our relations with the countries of origin, which often include close allies.

The Senate Report also recognized that archaeological and historical sites in the United States were equally subject to pillage and looting. "The destruction of such sites and the disappearance of the historic records evidenced by the articles found in them has given rise to a profound national interest in joining other countries to control the trafficking of such articles in international commerce" (US Senate Report 1982).

The CPIA substantively implements only two sections of the 1970 UNESCO Convention – Article 7(b), which addresses return of stolen cultural property that had been inventoried in the collection of a public secular or religious institution, and Article 9, which provides a mechanism by which States Parties may call upon each other for assistance in cases of jeopardy to cultural heritage through the looting of archaeological and ethnological materials. The CPIA incorporates other sections, including the definition of cultural property in Article 1 of the Convention and measures that a State Party should take to protect its cultural heritage outlined in Article 5. The United States explicitly failed to view Article 3, which other countries consider to be the Convention's core obligation, as substantive in nature and therefore refused to include it within the US implementing legislation (O'Keefe 2007, 41, 108). The view of the United States was likely the result of Article 3's across-the-board adherence to the Convention's provisions, in particular the recognition of all other States Parties' export controls on cultural objects.

"Stolen Cultural Property": Article 7(b)

Of the two substantive provisions of the CPIA, the more straightforward concerns cultural property stolen from public or religious institutions, reflecting Article 7(b) of the Convention. This section of the CPIA states:

> No article of cultural property documented as appertaining to the inventory of a museum or religious or secular public monument or similar institution in any State Party which is stolen from such institution after the effective date of this title, or after the date of entry into force of the Convention for the State Party, whichever is later, may be imported into the United States.
>
> *(19 U.S.C. §2607)*

The term "cultural property" is defined in reference to the Convention as "includ[ing] articles described in article 1 (a) through (k) of the Convention whether or not any such article is specifically designated as such by any State Party for the purposes of such article" (19 U.S.C. §2601(6)). The Convention definition is very broad and includes virtually every sort of cultural object that might be housed in a museum or other type of public secular or religious institution.

The primary change in United States domestic law that this section of the CPIA produced was essentially one of remedy. It had always been possible for private litigants, including foreign governments recognized by the United States, to enter United States courts to reclaim their stolen property in a civil replevin action. The United States interpreted the Convention's admonition to prohibit the import of cultural property stolen from an institution to mean that such import should be prohibited at the border. The CPIA thus gives to the Department of Homeland Security (formerly Customs) the authority to seize and forfeit such property at the border, although such property can also be seized and forfeited after it has entered the country.

The only elements that the government must prove in order to seize and forfeit such cultural property are that the cultural property came from a documented public collection and that it was stolen from the institution after the date on which both the United States and the country of origin became parties to the Convention (whichever date is later). There is no need for the government to establish that the importer had any knowledge of or intent to commit any wrongdoing. This provision can also prove useful in the case of recovery of documented cultural property that is stolen from a State Party which cannot maintain a suit in US courts. This provision of the CPIA thus grants significant "enhanced" protection.

Import restrictions for undocumented archaeological and ethnological materials: Article 9

The United States' implementation of Article 9 is complex and splits this provision into two sections of the CPIA. The first of these statutory provision, 19 U.S.C. §2602, provides a mechanism by which the United States can enter into bilateral agreements or memoranda of understanding (MOU) with other States Parties for the imposition of import restrictions on designated categories of archaeological or ethnological materials. The CPIA allows the United States to enter such an agreement with a requesting State Party without the necessity of Senate ratification of a new treaty. These agreements pertain only to archaeological and ethnological materials, rather than to the broader category of cultural property defined in Article 7(b) of the Convention.

Unlike the Convention, the CPIA offers a definition of the archaeological and ethnological materials to which the Article 9 provisions may apply.

> The term "archaeological or ethnological material of the State Party" means –
>
> (A) any object of archaeological interest;
> (B) any object of ethnological interest; or
> (C) any fragment or part of any object referred to in subparagraph (A) or (B), which was first discovered within, and is subject to export control by, the State Party. For purposes of this paragraph –
> (i) no object may be considered to be an object of archaeological interest unless such object –
> (I) is of cultural significance;
> (II) is at least two hundred and fifty years old; and
> (III) was normally discovered as a result of scientific excavation, clandestine or accidental digging, or exploration on land or under water; and

(ii) no object may be considered to be an object of ethnological interest unless such object is –
  (I) the product of a tribal or nonindustrial society, and
  (II) important to the cultural heritage of a people because of its distinctive characteristics, comparative rarity, or its contribution to the knowledge of the origins, development, or history of that people.

(19 U.S.C. §2601(2))

As O'Keefe has noted, these definitions significantly curtail the potential applicability of the CPIA (O'Keefe 2007, 111). For example, objects from sites of the historic or Colonial periods in North America and from historic shipwrecks will not qualify as archaeological materials if they do not reach the 250-year threshold requirement.

A State Party initiates the process by submitting a request for a bilateral agreement to the United States through diplomatic channels. The request is referred to the Cultural Property Advisory Committee, which consists of eleven members appointed by the President – three are experts in archaeology or anthropology; three are experts in the international sale of archaeological, ethnological and other cultural property; two represent the museum community; and three represent the general public (19 U.S.C. §2605(b)). This Committee evaluates requests from States Parties for bilateral agreements and makes recommendations to the President (who has delegated this function to the Assistant Secretary of State for Educational and Cultural Affairs) as to whether the statutory criteria are satisfied. The delegated decision maker makes the actual determinations required by the CPIA and, if the criteria are satisfied, initiates negotiation of a bilateral agreement to impose import restrictions under Section 303 or may take emergency action under Section 304.

The statutory determinations required for a bilateral agreement are:

(A) that the cultural patrimony of the State Party is in jeopardy from the pillage of archaeological or ethnological materials of the State Party;

(B) that the State Party has taken measures consistent with the Convention to protect its cultural patrimony;

(C) that –
  (i) the application of the import restrictions . . . with respect to archaeological or ethnological material of the State Party, if applied in concert with similar restrictions implemented, or to be implemented within a reasonable period of time, by those nations (whether or not State Parties) individually having a significant import trade in such material, would be of substantial benefit in deterring a serious situation of pillage, and
  (ii) remedies less drastic than the application of the restrictions set forth in such section are not available; and

(D) that the application of the import restrictions . . . in the particular circumstances is consistent with the general interest of the international community in the interchange of cultural property among nations for scientific, cultural, and educational purposes.

(U.S.C. §2602 (a)(1))

While some elements of these determinations track the language of Article 9, other elements clearly impose additional obligations on a requesting State Party. Other provisions appear inconsistent. For example, in (A) the phrase "jeopardy from the pillage" is used, whereas in (C)(i), the phrase "serious situation of pillage" is used. The third determination, (C)(i), anticipates that the United States' actions will be taken within a concerted or multilateral context. The nature and extent of this concerted action is not, however, spelled out in the statute, although it clearly includes actions that are expected to be implemented within a reasonable time.

There is also an important exception to this concerted action requirement. The statute provides:

> [T]he President may enter into an agreement if he determines that a nation individually having a significant import trade in such material is not implementing, or is not likely to implement, similar restrictions, but –
>
> (A) such restrictions are not essential to deter a serious situation of pillage, and
> (B) the application of the import restrictions . . . in concert with similar restrictions implemented, or to be implemented, by other nations (whether or not State Parties) individually having a significant import trade in such material would be of substantial benefit in deterring a serious situation of pillage.
>
> *(19 U.S.C. §2602 (c)(2))*

Reading both the basic provision concerning the concerted action requirement and the exception together, it would seem that the United States can enter into a bilateral agreement even in the absence of concerted action when (1) the United States is the only country to have a significant import trade in the material being considered or (2) it is not essential to deterrence of the pillage for another nation with a significant import trade to impose import restrictions. In the second circumstance, it is sufficient if the United States' own action regarding import restrictions will be of substantial benefit.

A bilateral agreement may not last more than five years, but it may be renewed an indefinite number of times. The agreement with El Salvador has been renewed four times. The criterion for renewal is that the same conditions that originally justified the agreement still exist (19 U.S.C. § 2602(e)).

The CPIA allows the United States to impose import restrictions, without the negotiation of a bilateral agreement, in certain circumstances. This emergency provision is the implementation of the last part of Article 9, which calls on States Parties to take "provisional measures" to prevent irremediable injury while an agreement on more permanent measures is pending. This provision under the CPIA is available only if the other State Party has already submitted a request for a bilateral agreement with supporting documentation for the criteria necessary for both a bilateral agreement and emergency action. The CPIA describes three circumstances that constitute an "emergency condition:"

> The term "emergency condition" means, with respect to any archaeological or ethnological material of any State Party, that such material is –
>
> 1) a newly discovered type of material which is of importance for the understanding of the history of mankind and is in jeopardy from pillage, dismantling, dispersal, or fragmentation;
> 2) identifiable as coming from any site recognized to be of high cultural significance if such site is in jeopardy from pillage, dismantling, dispersal, or fragmentation which is, or threatens to be, of crisis proportions; or
> 3) a part of the remains of a particular culture or civilization, the record of which is in jeopardy from pillage, dismantling, dispersal, or fragmentation which is, or threatens to be, of crisis proportions;

> and application of the import restrictions . . . on a temporary basis would, in whole or in part, reduce the incentive for such pillage, dismantling, dispersal or fragmentation.
>
> *(19 U.S.C. §2603(a))*

Many of the prerequisites for a bilateral agreement are not found here, including the concerted action requirement. Those circumstances that constitute an emergency condition are defined fairly narrowly and precisely. Such import restrictions may last initially only five years; they may be renewed only one time for a maximum of three additional years, in contrast with a bilateral agreement, which can have an unlimited number of renewals.

The United States has bilateral agreements with only sixteen nations: Belize, Bolivia, Bulgaria, Cambodia, China, Colombia, Cyprus, Egypt, El Salvador, Guatemala, Hellenic Republic, Honduras, Italy, Mali, Nicaragua, and Peru. An agreement with Canada was in effect from 1997 to 2002. In several cases, import restrictions under the emergency provisions had been imposed for particular materials before the respective bilateral agreement was negotiated and finalized. These include, for example, Mayan artifacts from the Cara Sucia region of El Salvador; culturally significant archaeological objects from the Sipan Region of Peru, and Mayan artifacts from the Péten region of Guatemala.

The United States maintains permanent restrictions on the importation of cultural materials illegally removed from Iraq after August 1990 under the Emergency Protection for Iraqi Cultural Antiquities Act (EPIC), enacted in late 2004 (Sections 3001–03, P.L. 108–429). This legislation authorized the President to exercise his authority under the CPIA to prohibit import of designated archaeological and ethnological materials from Iraq. This legislation is notable for defining the archaeological and ethnological materials of Iraq in accord with United Nations Security Council Resolution 1483 of 2003 in place of the normal CPIA definitions of these types of materials. In addition, although these import restrictions were authorized under the emergency provisions of the CPIA, 19 U.S.C. §2603, the EPIC Act provided that Iraq did not need to first bring a request for a bilateral agreement and the import restrictions would last for an indefinite period of time. These import restrictions went into effect in April 2008. Under legislation modeled on the special Iraq legislation, comparable import restrictions were imposed on cultural materials illegally removed from Syria after March 2011, thus implementing US obligations under UN Security Council Resolution 2199 of 2015.

O'Keefe has pointed out that the process for requesting a bilateral agreement imposes burdens on a State Party that were not anticipated by the Convention itself, particularly as a nation must prepare a request for a bilateral agreement in order to seek import restrictions in an emergency situation (O'Keefe 2007, 112). Despite this burden, some of the world's poorest nations, including Mali, Bolivia, El Salvador, and Guatemala, have been successful in obtaining bilateral agreements with the United States. In light of the fact that many States Parties to the UNESCO Convention automatically grant reciprocal recognition of other States Parties' export restrictions on cultural property, bilateral agreements with sixteen States Parties, which represents less than 15 percent of the states with which the United States could have agreements, are not evidence of an overwhelming compliance with Article 9. However, it was a significant step taken by probably the world's largest art market nation before most of the art market nations were ready to join the Convention at all.

Import restrictions imposed pursuant to either of the CPIA provisions become effective upon publication of a notice in the Federal Register. The agreement includes a list of designated categories of archaeological or ethnological materials that represent types of objects, rather than specific objects, that are subject to import restriction. The Cultural

Heritage Center of the State Department's Bureau of Educational and Cultural Affairs maintains a website, http://eca.state.gov/cultural-heritage-center/cultural-property-protection, that provides information about the import restrictions, including a chart of all import restrictions by country with their effective dates and a database of available images that are illustrative of the designated categories of materials whose import is restricted.

An archaeological or ethnological object that falls into one of the designated categories may be imported into the United States if it is accompanied by an export license, 19 U.S.C. §2606(a), or if satisfactory evidence can be presented showing that the object left the country of origin more than ten years before the date of entry or on or before the date the import restriction went into effect, 19 U.S.C. § 2606(b). The Department of Homeland Security enforces compliance with the import restrictions. The only remedy available under the CPIA is civil forfeiture of the object (19 U.S.C. §2609). Once an object is forfeited, title to it transfers to the US government, which then returns the object to the other State Party.

In addition to the reasons for the agreement and the list of designated materials, the agreement typically contains other provisions, primarily in Article II. These concern mutual cooperation between the United States and the other country in the realm of cultural heritage preservation, the provision of technical assistance, and certain provisions that are specific to the particular country involved. For example, the original MOU with El Salvador included the expectation that the national museum would be rebuilt and this was done within the first term of the bilateral agreement. The MOU with Italy includes the expectation that Italy will make its best efforts to provide materials that belong to the designated categories on long-term loan to museums in the United States, consistent with current Italian legislation that makes long-term loans available for educational, research, and conservation purposes. In response, Italy has now extended the period for which artworks can be on loan to four years, renewable for an additional four years. While these Article II provisions express directions in which the relations between the two countries may develop concerning cultural heritage, these undertakings are not prerequisites to the extension of an MOU, as they are not requirements under the statutory determinations, although, in some cases, they may relate to the statutory determinations (Kouroupas 2010, 331–3).

An international legal regime that relies on individual nations raises certain difficulties. The boundaries of modern nations and ancient cultures, even indigenous communities, do not necessarily coincide. The Inca culture in South America, the Maya culture of Central America and the Roman culture of the Mediterranean and Europe are but a few examples of ancient cultures that span more than one modern nation's borders. While import restrictions that operated on a cultural, rather than modern nation-state, basis might be more effective, international conventions are state-to-state agreements and function on that basis.

The first reported decision discussing import restrictions imposed under a CPIA bilateral agreement concerned the importation of two Colonial period paintings from Peru. United States v. Eighteenth Century Peruvian Oil on Canvas Painting of the "Doble Trinidad" or "Sagrada Familia con Espiritu Santo y Dios Padre," and Seventeenth Century Peruvian Oil on Canvas Painting of "San Antonio de Padua" and "Santa Rosa de Lima," 597 F. Supp. 2d 618 (E.D. Va. 2009). The US–Peru agreement includes "[o]bjects that were used for religious evangelism among indigenous peoples" including paintings of the Colonial period (Archaeological and Ethnological Material from Peru, 62 Fed. Reg. 31,713 at 31,720 (Dep't of Treasury, June 11, 1997)). There was some question as to whether the paintings originated from Bolivia or from Peru, but as the same categories of ethnological objects were covered by the bilateral agreements with both countries, the court did not find it necessary to determine which country was the country of origin. This approach is limited, however, to the circumstance in which all of the likely modern countries of origin have a bilateral agreement with the United States covering the same categories of objects.

The only other reported decisions concerning the CPIA bilateral agreements involved a test case instigated by the Ancient Coin Collectors Guild (ACCG) to challenge the validity of import restrictions on ancient coins from Cyprus and from China. The ACCG arranged for the import in April 2009 through Baltimore, Maryland, of unprovenanced coins that fit the Cypriot and Chinese designated coin types. The District Court for the District of Maryland dismissed the ACCG's complaint, on the ground, among others, that neither the Department of State nor Customs and Border Patrol, a bureau of the Department of Homeland Security, had exceeded its authority under the CPIA (Ancient Coin Collectors Guild v. US Customs and Border Protection, Dep't of Homeland Security et al., 801 F. Supp. 2d 383 (D. Md. 2011)). The US Court of Appeals for the Fourth Circuit affirmed this decision, relying in part on the sensitive nature of the conduct of foreign affairs and Congress's delegation to the Executive of significant discretion in carrying out the CPIA (Ancient Coin Collectors Guild v. Customs and Border Protection, Dep't of Homeland Security et al., 698 F.3d 171 (4th Cir. 2012)). The Fourth Circuit also held that once the United States meets its burden of establishing that the object is of a type appearing on a designated list, the importer bears the burden of establishing that the object is eligible to be imported into the United States. The court concluded that "the importer need not document every movement of its articles since ancient times. It need demonstrate only that the articles left the country that has requested import restrictions before those restrictions went into effect or more than ten years before the date of import" (Id. at 183). This decision provides substantive guidance that no particular category of ancient artifacts, including ancient coins, is, by its nature, ineligible to be placed on a particular designated list. Litigation is ongoing to determine whether these particular coins are subject to forfeiture.

It is difficult to assess the number of restitutions of cultural objects seized and forfeited by the US government and returned to their country of origin as a result of bilateral agreements under the CPIA. The US government does not maintain comprehensive statistics and, while the Department of Homeland Security occasionally publishes press releases announcing restitutions, these often do not state the legal basis for the forfeiture. However, objects have been returned to several countries under the bilateral agreements including to Italy, Peru, Guatemala, and China.

Implementation by other market countries

While it took close to thirty years before other major market countries demonstrated interest in the 1970 UNESCO Convention, that situation began to change significantly in the late 1990s and early 2000s. In 1998, France joined the Convention and in 2002, two of the largest market nations (after the United States), the United Kingdom and Japan, became parties. These were soon joined by Sweden and Denmark; Switzerland joined in 2003 and Germany in 2007. The most recent European countries to join the Convention are Luxembourg and Austria. Several of these countries decided to ratify the Convention in response to the looting of archaeological sites and museums that occurred during and after the US-led invasion of Iraq in 2003. Switzerland was motivated, at least in part, by the discovery of large quantities of looted antiquities that had been stored in the freeport zone of Geneva airport by the Italian dealer Giacomo Medici. Finally, some countries joined in response to their analysis of the 1995 UNIDROIT Convention on Stolen and Illegally Exported Cultural Property. While examining this later convention, which was drafted to appeal to the European continental countries, these countries realized that its more onerous requirements were not acceptable, whereas the less precise requirements of the 1970 UNESCO Convention made it more attractive. A sufficient number of market nations have now ratified and implemented the Convention that it seems possible to create a typology of methods of implementation.

"Across-the-board" import restrictions: Implementation of Article 3

Most States Parties grant reciprocal recognition to the export restrictions of other nations when those export restrictions are promulgated as part of their implementation of the 1970 UNESCO Convention. This broad approach to the recognition of other States Parties' export controls implements Article 3 of the Convention, which states: "The import, export or transfer of ownership of cultural property effected contrary to the provisions adopted under this Convention by the States Parties thereto, shall be illicit." Article 6(b), which states that States Parties "undertake . . . to prohibit the exportation of cultural property from their territory unless accompanied by the . . . export certificate" described in Article 6(a), is also an integral part of a trade regulatory scheme. The implementation schemes of three nations, Australia, Canada, and Germany, are examined as examples of across-the-board import restrictions.

Australia

Australia enacted its implementing legislation, The Protection of Movable Cultural Heritage Act, in 1986 before becoming a State Party in 1989 and amended it in 2011. It is perhaps unique among nations that have ratified the 1970 Convention in that its import controls apply to all illegally exported cultural objects, regardless of whether the country of origin is a party to the 1970 Convention. The export control that was violated only needs to be a "law of that country relating to cultural property" (Section 14(1)). In addition, it does not matter when the object was illegally exported from its country of origin, so long as the import into Australia occurred after the effective date of the legislation. Such an object is subject to forfeiture. A person who knowingly violates the import prohibition commits an offence punishable by a fine not exceeding $100,000 or imprisonment not exceeding five years or both (Section 14(2)). Australia is reported to be considering strengthening its legislation in the wake of the scandals involving Australian museums that acquired sculptural pieces stolen from Hindu temples from the dealer Subhash Kapoor (Pearlman 2013).

Canada

In 1978, Canada enacted broad import and export regulations, pursuant to Articles 3 and 6(b) of the Convention, when it adopted the Cultural Property Export and Import Act (CPEIA), R.S.C. 1985, c. C-51 ff. The CPEIA establishes a system of controls on the export of cultural materials from Canada and serves an important function in preserving Canada's cultural heritage (Nafziger et al. 2010, 302–5). This legislation allows the establishment of a list of cultural materials whose export is subject to control through an export permit requirement.

With respect to import controls, the CPEIA applies to "foreign cultural property," defined as "any object that is specifically designated by [a reciprocating state] as being of importance for archaeology, prehistory, history, literature, art or science" (R.S.C. 1985, c. C-51, § 37(1)). The definition is thus similar to the 1970 Convention's definition of cultural property. One recurring theme in the implementing legislation of several market nations is the question of how the UNESCO Convention's definition of cultural property as property that is "specifically designated" is viewed. One court in Canada answered this question with respect to Canada's import controls, in R. v Yorke, by holding that the Bolivian Decree, which subjected the textiles at issue to export control, was in compliance with the designation requirement and therefore fit the CPEIA's definition of "foreign cultural property." The court understood the difficulty posed by a specific designation requirement, particularly as applied to the types of archaeological and ethnographic objects that were frequently undocumented before their illegal removal, stating:

> [T]he appellant's submission that, to "specifically designate" cultural property something more was required of Bolivia than what was specified in the Decree, is not tenable. It would not be possible for a nation to create an itemized list of every piece of property to be protected. The categories have been made clear in the Decree . . . and they apply to the items seized from the appellant. Likewise, the suggestion that the term "weavings" is somehow overly broad and fails to distinguish those "weavings" which are of cultural significance from those which are not, is not persuasive. The term "weavings" is one of common usage and the Decree distinguishes them from property of other types of manufacture. Ms. Bubba-Zamora testified about the weaving tradition in Bolivia. Textiles that are cultural property reveal valuable information regarding ethnic groups and their religious practices.
>
> *(R. v Yorke (1998), 166 N.S.R. (2d) at 150)*

This may be the only judicial interpretation of the specific designation requirement and how it can be satisfied.

A "reciprocating State" is a "foreign State that is a party to a cultural property agreement." The Act envisages the possibility that Canada will enter into bilateral and multilateral agreements "relating to the prevention of illicit international traffic in cultural property." While the Act does not specifically refer to the 1970 UNESCO Convention as one such agreement, it is clear that the Convention fits this definition and that the Act's provisions therefore apply to any nation that is a State Party.

The operative provisions of the Act are relatively straightforward, stating, "it is illegal to import into Canada any foreign cultural property that has been illegally exported from that reciprocating State" (R.S.C. 1985, c. C-51, § 37(2)). The import restrictions apply only to foreign cultural property illegally exported after the date on which a cultural property agreement comes into force in both Canada and the reciprocating state. The relevant date for Canada with respect to the 1970 Convention is 1978.

Two examples of attempted recoveries of cultural materials under the Canadian Act occurred relatively early in its history and, in both attempts, it could not be established that the cultural materials had left their country of origin after the date on which the CPEIA went into effect. One involved a shipment of antiquities from Egypt that was seized at Mirabel Airport near Montreal in 1989 (Walden 1995, 208–10). The Egyptian authorities presented evidence that the artifacts had been illegally excavated and smuggled out of Egypt but ultimately were not able to present proof that they had been taken out of Egypt after 1978. A similar episode occurred in the prosecution of a dealer for importing artifacts smuggled out of Nigeria (R. v Heller (1984), 30 A.L.R. (2d) 130 (Q.B.)). This case involved the attempted prosecution of a New York dealer who imported a Nok terracotta sculpture into Canada that had been illegally exported from Nigeria (Shyllon 2000, 221).

The actions that Canada has taken to implement the 1970 Convention are clearly increasing in number. O'Keefe stated that between 1978 and 2000, there were eleven requests for returns, seven of which were successful. Between 2000 and 2007, there were five returns, one each to Peru, Bolivia, and Egypt, and two to Colombia (O'Keefe 2007, 149). According to Canada's 2010 report to UNESCO on its implementation of the 1970 Convention, between 2007 and 2010, Canada returned 350 cultural objects to Bulgaria, China, Egypt, Mali, and Nigeria (Canada 2010, 3). However, the largest seizure and return of cultural artifacts by Canada occurred in 2011 and involved the restitution to Bulgaria of 21,000 cultural objects, including 18,000 ancient coins and other objects such as jewellery, Byzantine crosses, amulets, belt buckles, and bronze eagles (Crawford 2011; Office of the Minister of Canadian Heritage and Official Languages 2011).

It is a criminal offense to import or attempt to import cultural property in violation of the CPEIA (R.S.C. 1985, c. C-51, §§ 43 and 45). The maximum penalty is a fine in the amount of $25,000 and imprisonment for up to five years (R.S.C. 1985, c. C-51 § 45). There seems to have been only one conviction under this provision in a case involving a dealer who imported textiles from Bolivia (R. v Yorke, 166 N.S.R. (2d) 130 (1998)) (O'Keefe 2007, 152–3).

Germany

Germany enacted implementing legislation for the 1970 UNESCO Convention in 2007. Under this legislation, Germany did not allow the import of any illegally exported cultural objects that had been individually classified in an accessible inventory by the country of origin at least one year prior to removal (termed the "list principle"). In an attempt to take account of the difficulties of inventorying freshly looted archaeological objects, the country of origin was given one year from the time when it gains knowledge of the excavation to place archaeological objects in the inventory (Germany 2007).

It is widely recognized that this approach is not effective for confronting the problems of the looting of archaeological sites which, by definition, produces undocumented artifacts whose existence is generally unknown until they appear in a market country. In recognition of this limitation, in 2016 Germany amended its legislation to deal more effectively with this problem (Germany 2016). This legislation is, at least in part, a response to the widespread looting that is occurring in Middle Eastern countries, particularly in Iraq and Syria, and fulfils Germany's obligations under United Nations Security Council Resolution 2199 (2015).

The new legislation unifies German law with respect to export controls. Of greater relevance to this discussion are the new provisions for import of archaeological objects into Germany. Under this legislation, an importer must present documentation that the cultural property was legally exported if it left another State Party to the 1970 UNESCO Convention after 2007, the date of Germany's ratification of the Convention. This shifts the burden to the importer to present such documentation; in the absence of such documentation, the cultural property is considered to have been unlawfully removed (Federal Government Commissioner for Culture and the Media 2016, 7). The burden is further shifted onto the importer because the legislation creates a presumption that, in the absence of documentation that establishes otherwise, cultural objects were unlawfully exported from the relevant State Party after 2007. This requirement recognizes that most states require licenses for the export of cultural property and that this provision, moving from a list principle to a category principle, particularly helps to protect archaeological objects.

Bilateral agreements

Switzerland is the only State Party, in addition to the United States, that requires other States Parties to enter into supplementary agreements in order to implement the 1970 UNESCO Convention. Despite this superficial resemblance, the Swiss legislation differs from that of the United States in several important respects. The Swiss legislation imposes import restrictions on categories of cultural objects but implements Article 3 rather than, as in the case of the United States, Article 9. For this reason, it is not limited to the categories of archaeological and ethnological materials but, rather, may apply to all types of cultural property.

The Swiss implementing legislation, the Cultural Property Transfer Act (CPTA), took effect in June 2005 (Loi fédéral du 20 juin 2003 sur le transfert international des biens culturels). The Swiss legislation permits the Swiss Federal Council to enter into agreements with other nations that are party to the 1970 Convention to protect "cultural and foreign affairs interests and to secure cultural heritage" (CPTA, Article 7). The Swiss legislation defines "cultural property" as "significant property from a religious or universal standpoint for archaeology, prehistory, history, literature, arts or sciences belonging to the categories under Article 1 of the UNESCO Convention of 1970" (CPTA, Article 2(1)). Without explicitly stating this, the Swiss definition omits the mention of "specific designation" found in Article 1 of the Convention.

The agreements include a list of designated artifact types of cultural property that are listed by category. This allows the import of objects to be restricted even if they have not been documented before their illegal removal and, in this respect, the Swiss agreements are similar to those used by the United States. While the Swiss agreements are not restricted to archaeological and ethnological materials, they primarily relate to categories of archaeological objects recognized as being of significant importance for the cultural heritage of a state.

Unlike the US bilateral agreements, the Swiss agreements are of potentially unlimited duration and do not need to be renewed. This potential for indefinite duration arguably presents a greater deterrent effect than the US system in which an agreement must be reconsidered every five years and there is always the possibility, as in the case of Canada, that an agreement will not be extended and objects whose import is currently restricted may, in the near future, become available for unrestricted import. Most of the Swiss agreements are truly mutual in nature in that they call for recognition of Swiss regulations on the export of cultural property and each agreement has two designated lists of protected cultural properties – one list of Swiss cultural property and the second list for the cultural property of the state with which Switzerland has the agreement.

Requests for an agreement are not subject to review by a committee of private citizens but rather are directly negotiated by officials of the Swiss Ministry of Culture. The Federal Council can also take additional measures when a "State's cultural heritage [is] jeopardized by exceptional events" (CPTA, Article 8). Unlike the bilateral agreements under the CPTA that implement Article 3, emergency actions taken under Article 8 are viewed as implementing Article 9 of the Convention and must be for a limited amount of time. While specifying that such actions may be taken under Article 9 of the Convention, Article 8 of the CPTA is not clear as to whether such actions are limited to archaeological and ethnological materials.

Finally, the CPTA adds criminal provisions for the intentional or negligent illicit import of cultural property or incorrect declaration of cultural property during import or transit. The maximum penalty under the CPTA for intentional violation is a fine of 100,000 Swiss francs or imprisonment of up to one year; for negligent violation, the maximum fine is 20,000 Swiss francs. If the offender acts on a professional basis, the sanction is a fine of up to

200,000 Swiss francs or jail for up to two years (CPTA, Article 24). If the offender is subject to a greater penalty under a different provision, then the greater penalty can be imposed. The CPTA adopts higher duties of diligence for "persons active in the art trade and auctioning business" (CPTA, Article 16).

Switzerland has agreements in force with Italy (2008), Greece (2011), Colombia (2011), Egypt (2011), China (2014), Cyprus (2014), and Peru (2016). While there have not been any prosecutions under the CPTA, several artifacts have been returned to their country of origin, including Greece, Italy, Egypt, Turkey, Peru, and Lebanon, although some of these actions do not seem to have been taken pursuant to a bilateral agreement (Switzerland n.d.). A group of 32 artifacts were returned to Egypt in June 2015 pursuant to the bilateral agreement and in conjunction with a celebration to mark the tenth anniversary of the Swiss legislation (Al-Youm 2015).

The Swiss legislation, like the United States' legislation, has the drawback of not automatically applying to illegally exported cultural materials, in the absence of a bilateral agreement. In contrast, however, because the Swiss legislation allows the Federal Council to respond to crisis situations without the need for a request from the affected state, import restrictions can be imposed on an emergency basis under the Swiss implementation of Article 9 of the 1970 UNESCO Convention. In the case of Syria, this is the route that was adopted when the Swiss Federal Council acted in late 2014 to restrict the import of cultural materials illegally exported from Syria after the beginning of the rebellion in March of 2011 through its Order 946.231.172.7 (Switzerland 2014; Neuhaus 2015).

The Swiss legislation that implemented the 1970 UNESCO Convention also made other changes in Swiss law regulating the art market. Perhaps prime among these were changes in the good faith purchaser doctrine, which permitted a seller to transfer title to stolen property to a good faith purchaser and made Switzerland, in the past, a place where title to stolen and looted antiquities could be laundered. These changes have altered the applicability of the doctrine to acquisitions of art and cultural objects, making Switzerland less desirable as an intermediate market country. While other countries now serve the function of transit point, Switzerland still seems to host a robust art trade.

Influence of the 1995 UNIDROIT Convention: Hybrid approaches

At this point in time, several market nations have ratified both the 1970 UNESCO Convention and the 1995 UNIDROIT Convention on Stolen or Illegally Exported Cultural Objects (Prott 1997). These nations typically adopt implementing measures pursuant to both Conventions.[3] These measures seem to emphasize compliance with the UNIDROIT Convention, which is mandatory in its requirements for implementation. One distinguishing difference (among several) between the two Conventions is that the UNIDROIT Convention pertains to private international law and implementing legislation creates private rights of action for recovery of stolen and illegally exported cultural objects, whereas the 1970 Convention operates on a state-to-state basis.

An example of a nation ratifying both Conventions is New Zealand, which joined the 1995 UNIDROIT Convention in late 2006 and the 1970 UNESCO Convention in early 2007. Its comprehensive legislation, the Protected Objects Act, incorporates elements of both Conventions into its domestic law (New Zealand 2007). In addition to regulating the export of protected cultural objects from New Zealand, the legislation reflects Articles 3 and 7 of the 1970 Convention in prohibiting the import into New Zealand of unlawfully exported protected foreign objects (Section 10A). The definition of "protected foreign object" tracks the definition of cultural property used in the 1970 UNESCO and UNIDROIT Conventions (Section 2(1)). This legislation also allows reciprocating states to bring actions to recover stolen or illegally exported protected objects (Section 10B). However, some nations have ratified only the 1970 UNESCO Convention and yet have incorporated some particular principle or measure that is found in the UNIDROIT Convention. The Netherlands and the United Kingdom will be considered as examples of a hybrid approach.

The Netherlands

The Netherlands took what may be viewed as an explicit hybrid approach in its implementing legislation (Netherlands 2009a). The legislation focuses on implementing Article 3 of the 1970 UNESCO Convention, rather than Article 9, and, in its accompanying Explanatory Memorandum, the Netherlands explicitly rejected the view of the United States that Article 3 did not need to be implemented (Netherlands 2009b, 12). The legislation prohibits the import of cultural property that "(a) has been removed from the territory of a State Party in breach of the provisions adopted by that State Party in accordance with the objectives of the Convention in respect of the export of cultural property from that State Party or the transfer of ownership of cultural property; or (b) has been unlawfully appropriated in a State Party" (Section 3). The primary enforcement mechanism is through a private right of action for a foreign nation that wishes to recover its illegally exported or unlawfully appropriated cultural property, but Dutch officials are also authorized to take such materials into custody when there is suspicion that this provision has been violated, pending the filing of a claim by the foreign nation (Section 10).

The explanatory memorandum clarifies that unlawful appropriation includes unlawful excavation at archaeological sites (Netherlands 2009b, 16). The explanatory notes refer to the UNIDROIT Convention's Article 3(2), which equates unlawful excavation at an archaeological site with theft and states that "a cultural object which has been unlawfully excavated or lawfully excavated but unlawfully retained shall be considered stolen, when consistent with the law of the State where the excavation took place." The Dutch legislation thus takes a very broad view of what is required to implement the 1970 UNESCO Convention. While the Dutch legislation is similar to that of Canada and other nations following the broad model of implementation of the 1970 UNESCO Convention's Article 3, the explanatory notes specifically refer to the UNIDROIT Convention in the definition of stolen property as applied to illegally excavated archaeological material and thus should be considered to represent a hybrid model.

United Kingdom

One can suggest that the United Kingdom has taken something of a hybrid approach as well, incorporating the misappropriation definition from the UNIDROIT Convention. When the United Kingdom ratified the 1970 UNESCO Convention, it originally took the position that it did not need to enact implementing legislation. However, in 2003, it enacted new criminal legislation, the Dealing in Cultural Objects (Offences) Act 2003, although this was not characterized as a direct means of implementing the 1970 UNESCO Convention. This Act created a new offense for dealing in "tainted cultural objects" (Ch. 27). One commits this offense if he or she "dishonestly deals in a cultural object that is tainted, knowing or believing that the object is tainted" (Section 1, Subsec. 1).

The statute defines a "tainted object" under the following circumstances: "(2) A cultural object is tainted if, after the commencement of this Act – (a) a person removes the object in a case falling within subsection (4) or he excavates the object, and (b) the removal or excavation constitutes an offence" (Section 2, Subsec. 2). Subsection 4 refers to objects removed from "a building or structure of historical, architectural or archaeological interest" or from an excavation. For purposes of the statute, it does not matter whether the excavation or removal took place in the United Kingdom or in another country or whether the law violated is a domestic or foreign law (Section 2, Subsec. 3). These provisions are clearly based on Article 3(2) of the 1995 UNIDROIT Convention and, to that extent, the UK legislation bears a similarity to the Dutch legislation implementing the 1970 UNESCO Convention.

Although it was not enacted as a means of restricting the importation of cultural objects, the UK legislation has been used as a means of seizing "tainted objects" upon entry. The offense of dealing in tainted cultural objects includes the import or export of such objects, in which case Her Majesty's Customs and Excise is empowered by Section 4 to investigate the potential offense and to seize such objects as part of the investigation (United Kingdom, Department of Culture, Media and Sport, 9). Section 49(1)(b) of the Customs and Excise Management Act 1979 allows for the forfeiture of goods that are imported contrary to a statute, in this case the Dealing in Cultural Objects (Offences) Act. If forfeited, the goods would be returned to their country of origin. Since 2005, archaeological objects from Afghanistan, Iran, Greece, India and possibly other countries have been seized (Vigneron 2008, 262, 292–3, 295; Steel 2012). In a recent case, a statue from Libya, which was misdeclared upon import as to both value and country of origin, was ordered forfeited under the Customs and Excise Management Act (HM Revenue & Customs v. Riad Issa Mohamad Al Qassas, Westminster Magistrates Court (1 Sept. 2015)) (Mercer 2015).

"Specific Designation": Japan

Some nations have adopted far narrower views of the 1970 UNESCO Convention in that they require that objects whose recovery is sought to have been recorded or inventoried before they are stolen or illegally exported. This requirement is particularly problematic for regulating the trade in previously undocumented objects, specifically, archaeological artifacts and ethnological materials. The prime example of this approach is Japan. It is likely that Japan adopted this approach because the country itself maintains inventories of cultural objects and otherwise allows for free trade in objects that are not inventoried.

Japan has likely taken the most minimal approach to implementation of the 1970 UNESCO Convention among State Parties. Japan became a party to the Convention in 2002 and enacted the Law concerning Controls on the Illicit Export and Import of Cultural Property (O'Keefe 2007, 202). Despite its name, it implements exclusively Article 7(b) of the Convention by prohibiting import of "specified foreign cultural property." Article 2 defines as cultural property what each State Party designates in accordance with Article 1 of the 1970 UNESCO Convention and thus seems to give the Convention a broad interpretation (O'Keefe 2007, 124–5). This is negated, however, in that Articles 3 and 4 apply only to "specified foreign cultural property" defined as "cultural property that has been stolen from an institution stipulated in Article 7(b)(i) of the Convention." Japan's implementation therefore seems entirely inadequate to deal with the problem of looted and therefore undocumented archaeological and ethnographic objects, as well as with the realities of difficulties in providing lists of objects stolen from museums and other public collections (O'Keefe 2007, 124–8; Lee 2004, 12–13).

When the specific designation requirement of Article 1 is interpreted as requiring inventorying of specific objects, it places a significant burden on a nation attempting to recover illegally removed archaeological objects, which when looted from the ground are, by definition, previously undocumented and ethnographic objects, which, by their nature as part of an indigenous community, may not be inventoried. Cultural objects that are part of a more traditional collection, such as a museum, church or private collection, may also not be inventoried. While inventorying is a desirable goal as it reduces the incentive for theft and increases the likelihood of recovery, it is often not feasible to fully inventory all cultural objects, particularly in developing nations where computerized databases and other technology may not be easily accessible.

Conclusion

The 1970 UNESCO Convention has steadily received ratification by market nations over the past almost twenty years, in sharp contrast to the first twenty years of its existence. This phenomenon seems to be in response to two events. One is the particularly egregious example of looting of archaeological sites and museum collections that occurred in Iraq following the 2003 Iraq War and the current crises throughout the Middle East. The second, perhaps ironically, occurred in response to decisions not to ratify the 1995 UNIDROIT Convention, which, although drafted to respond to the concerns of the European continent civil law nations, was largely rejected by them because of its more exacting requirements.

In contrast, many of the countries of origin, which tend to be the victims of the desire to obtain archaeological objects in particular for sale on the international market, have expressed increasing dissatisfaction with the 1970 UNESCO Convention in its current form. One reason for this dissatisfaction is the non-retroactive nature of the Convention. While international conventions are almost universally non-retroactive, this feature of the 1970 Convention seems particularly problematic to the countries of origin because the Convention does not assist these nations in recovering cultural objects that were removed during the nineteenth and first half of the twentieth century, often as the result of colonialism. While there may be ethical, moral, and cultural reasons for returning such objects (or some of them), international conventions by their nature are not retroactive and this situation would not be alleviated through a new convention.

A more significant concern is the "specific designation" requirement of Article 1 of the 1970 UNESCO Convention and the role that it plays as an impediment, depending on the form of implementation taken by some market nations, to the recovery of looted archaeological objects and therefore reduction in demand for such objects. A new convention is not, however, needed to resolve this problem. What is needed is for market nations to follow the lead of the example set by Canada in defining the designation requirement in a way that requires only designation of categories and not of individual objects, or the example set by the Netherlands and the United Kingdom in incorporating the UNIDROIT Convention's definition of stolen object that includes illegally excavated objects into their own legislation. With the increasing awareness of the large-scale looting of archaeological sites in the Middle East and the mobilization of the international community around the destruction that is being wrought today, perhaps this is the time for the countries of origin to bring political and other forms of pressure to bear to achieve this goal, which would be of significant assistance in protecting the world's archaeological heritage.

Notes

1 All opinions expressed in these materials are those of the author and not necessarily those of the US Department of State or of the US government.

2 There are several stages by which a state becomes party to an international treaty or convention. The first stage is signature. A convention is generally open to signature for only a limited amount of time. Whether or not a state signs a convention, the state can still ratify or accede to it, following whatever process is required for that particular country. The United States Constitution, for example, requires approval by two-thirds of the Senate for ratification. A treaty or convention is not binding on a state until it completes the formal ratification process, but, by signing a convention, the state indicates its intention to ratify and is expected not to act in ways that are contrary to the goals and purpose of the convention.

3 Those States Parties that are also members of the European Union must enact legislation implementing the European Union provisions regulating the movement of cultural objects: the Council Directive on the return of cultural objects unlawfully removed from the territory of a Member State, Council Directive No. 93/7 of March 15, 1993, OJ L 74 of March 27, 1993, and Regulation on the export of cultural goods, Council Regulation (EEC) No. 3911/92 of December 9, 1992, codified with several amendments in Council Regulation (EC) 116/2009 of December 18, 2008 (OJ L 39 of February 10, 2009) on the export of cultural goods. Italy's Code of the Cultural and Landscape Heritage (Legislative Decree no. 42 of 01.22.04, in particular Articles 73–87) is an example of legislation implementing these European Union provisions.

Bibliography

Al-Youm, Al-Masry. 2015. "Egypt to Retrieve 32 Artifacts from Switzerland in June." *Egypt Independent* (May 7), available at: http://www.egyptindependent.com/news/egypt-retrieve-32-artifacts-switzerland-june.

Canada. 2010. Report by Canada [to UNESCO] on the application of the 1970 Convention on the Means of Prohibiting and Preventing the Illicit Import, Export and Transfer of Ownership of Cultural Property, available at: http://www.unesco.org/new/fileadmin/MULTIMEDIA/HQ/CLT/pdf/canada_2010-11natrep_1970_en.pdf.

Coggins, Clemency C. 1969. "Illicit Traffic of Pre-Columbian Antiquities." *Art Journal* 29: 94–114.

Crawford, A. 2011. "Canada returns Bulgarian stolen artefacts." *CBC News* (June 10), available at: http://www.cbc.ca/news/canada/story/2011/06/10/bulgaria-artifacts.html.

Federal Government Commissioner for Culture and the Media. 2016. Key aspects of the new Act on the Protection of Cultural Property in Germany, available at: https://www.bundesregierung.de/Content/DE/_Anlagen/BKM/2016/2016-09-23-kulturgutschutz-informationen-englisch.pdf?__blob=publicationFile&v=2.

Fujii, H. 2004. "Particulars of Japan's Accession to the 1970 UNESCO Convention and an Outstanding Problem." *Culture Without Context* 14, available at: http://www.mcdonald.cam.ac.uk/projects/iarc/culturewithoutcontext/issue14/fujii.htm.

Germany. 2016. Act on the Protection of Cultural Property of 6 August 2016.

Germany. 2007. Implementation Act of 18 April 2007, section 6(2), sentences 1–3. BGBl.I. Nr. 21 (May 23).

Kouroupas, Maria P. 2010. "Preservation of Cultural Heritage: A Tool of International Public Diplomacy," in *Cultural Heritage Issues: The Legacy of Conquest, Colonization, and Commerce* (James A. R. Nafziger and Ann M. Nicgorski, eds.), 325–334.

Lee, K-G. 2004. "An Overview of the Implementation of the 1970 Convention in Asia," available at: http://www.unesco.org/new/fileadmin/MULTIMEDIA/HQ/CLT/pdf/Lee_en.pdf.

Mercer, David. 2015. "£1.5m Ancient Greek Statue Looted from Libyan Heritage Site 'Must be Returned'." *Independent* (Sept. 1), available at: http://www.independent.co.uk/news/world/middle-east/15m-ancient-greek-statue-looted-from-libyan-heritage-site-must-be-returned-10481937.html.

Meyer, Karl E. 1977. *The Plundered Past*. New York: Athenaeum.

Miles, Margaret M. 2008. *Art as Plunder: The Ancient Origins of Debate about Cultural Property*. Cambridge: Cambridge University Press.

Nafziger, J. A. R., Paterson, R. K. and Renteln, A. D. 2010. *Cultural Law: International, Comparative, and Indigenous*. Cambridge: Cambridge University Press.

Netherlands. 2009a. 1970 UNESCO Convention on the Illicit Import, Export and Transfer of Ownership of Cultural Property (Implementation) Act (June 12), available at: http://www.wetten.nl.

Netherlands. 2009b. 1970 UNESCO Convention on the Illicit Import, Export and Transfer of Ownership of Cultural Property (Implementation) Act Explanatory Memorandum.

Neuhaus, Nina M. 2015. "Switzerland Limits Trade in Syrian Cultural Property." *Institute of Art and Law Blog*, available at: http://www.ial.uk.com/news/switzerland-limits-trade-in-syrian-cultural-property/.
New Zealand. 2007. Protected Objects Act 1975, as revised 2007, available at: http://www.legislation.govt.nz/act/public/1975/0041/latest/DLM432116.html.
Office of the Minister of Canadian Heritage and Official Languages. 2011. "Government of Canada Returns Its Largest Ever Seizure of Cultural Property to the Republic of Bulgaria". *Canadian Heritage*, available at: http://www.newswire.ca/en/story/815789/government-of-canada-returns-its-largest-ever-seizure-of-cultural-property-to-the-republic-of-bulgaria.
O'Keefe, Patrick J. 2007. *Commentary on the 1970 UNESCO Convention*. Builth Wells, UK: Institute of Art and Law.
Pearlman, Jonathan. 2013. "900-year-old Dancing Shiva to be Returned to India." *Daily Telegraph* (Dec. 6), available at: http://www.telegraph.co.uk/news/worldnews/australiaandthepacific/australia/10500620/900-year-old-dancing-Shiva-to-be-returned-to-India.html.
Prott, L. V. 1997. *Commentary on the UNIDROIT Convention*. Leicester: Institute of Art and Law.
Shyllon, Folarin. 2000. "The Recovery of Cultural Objects by African States through the UNESCO and UNIDROIT Conventions and the Role of Arbitration," available at http://www.UNIDROIT.org/English/publications/review/articles/2000-2-shyllon-e.pdf.
Steel, P. 2012. "Hundreds of Stolen Items Returned to Kabul." 112/09*Museums Journal* (Sept. 1), available at: http://www.museumsassociation.org/museums-journal/news/01092012-stolen-items-returned-to-kabul.
Switzerland. 2014. "Verordnung über Massnahmen gegenüber Syrien" (Dec. 17, revised April 22, 2015), available at: https://www.admin.ch/opc/de/classified-compilation/20121374/index.html.
Switzerland. 2015. "Bilateral agreements," available at: http://www.bak.admin.ch/kulturerbe/04371/04377/index.html?lang=en.
Switzerland Federal Office of Culture. n.d. Media Releases, available at: http://www.bak.admin.ch/kulturerbe/04371/04375/index.html?lang=en.
United Kingdom, Department of Culture, Media and Sport Cultural Property Unit. 2003. "Dealing in Tainted Cultural Objects – Guidance on the Dealing in Cultural Objects (Offences) Act 2003," available at: http://www.culture.gov.uk/images/publications/Dealincultural.pdf.
United States Senate. 1982. Senate Report 97–564 on Implementing Legislation for the Convention on the Means of Prohibiting and Preventing the Illicit Import, Export and Transfer of Ownership of Cultural Property. 97th Cong., 2d Sess. (1982), available at https://eca.state.gov/files/bureau/97-564.pdf.
Vigneron, S. 2008. Trafic illicite et restitution des biens culturels, Royaume Uni, in Protection de la propriété culturelle et circulation des biens culturels. *Étude de droit comparé Europe /Asie* (M. Cornu and J. Fromageau, eds.), available at: http://www.gip-recherche-justice.fr/IMG/pdf/173-RF-Cornu_Protection_propriete_culturelle.pdf.
Walden, D. A. 1995. "Canada's Cultural Property Export and Import Act: The Experience of Protecting Cultural Property." (Special Issue) *U.B.C.L. Rev*: 203–216.

5

PROTECTION NOT PREVENTION

The failure of public policy to prevent the looting and illegal trade of cultural property from the MENA region (1990–2015)

Neil Brodie

Introduction

The Soviet Union's withdrawal from Afghanistan in 1989 and its dissolution two years later in 1991 opened a power vacuum across the Middle East-North Africa (MENA) region that was filled by a tangled mess of international, proxy and civil wars still continuing in 2015. From Afghanistan in the east to Libya in the west, from Yemen in the south to Syria in the north, the fighting triggered a wave of looting, theft and destruction of cultural property that swept across the region. As country after country fell victim to civil disturbance and conflict, images of ransacked museums and cratered archaeological sites became an ever-present reality of news reporting. International public policy, designed in and intended for the pre-globalized world of the 1960s, failed utterly to achieve any kind of hold on the problem. By April 2015, when members of Daesh posted on the Internet a video of themselves using explosives to demolish part of the ninth-to eighth-century BC Neo-Assyrian site of Nimrud, the international community had been reduced to doing little more than uttering a collective wail of despair, seemingly faced with a choice of doing nothing or sending in the troops.

Throughout the period in question, cultural property was damaged and destroyed intentionally and unintentionally by military action, for reasons of religious or ethnic sectarianism, and perhaps even as propaganda. A large if not the major cause of damage, however, was theft from cultural institutions and illegal digging of archaeological sites to feed the voracious demand of the international market in cultural objects. The cultural and socioeconomic harms of this market and the illegal trade that feeds it are well known (Gill and Chippindale 1993; Mackenzie 2005; Brodie 2012). But the illegal trade is not something driven by the military necessity of armies or the fanaticism of ideologues. It is a commercial construct. Of all causes of damage to cultural property, it is to all appearances the one most open to control. And yet, during the period in question, it flourished. By the 2010s, the looting and theft of cultural objects in the MENA region had become entirely predictable – as each country in turn fell victim to conflict, its cultural property would be targeted for monetary profit. This very predictability of events encouraged a belief that international public policy was not working (Brodie 2015a; 2015b). It could not stop the illegal trade nor could it minimize the damage the trade was causing. Nothing had been learned from the experiences of Iraq, Jordan and Afghanistan in the 1990s and 2000s that could help prevent or ameliorate damage to cultural property in Syria, Egypt and Libya in the 2010s. Policy had become entrenched and was unresponsive. Policy makers seemed unable to adapt to changing circumstances.

This chapter shows how from 1990 to 2015 international public policy aimed at cultural property protection (CPP) proved inadequate because of its primary reliance on *protecting* cultural property from theft and looting at source, and its corresponding lack of any measures aimed at *preventing* theft and looting by reducing demand on the destination market. First, the chapter looks at how the principles of CPP developed through international law and its implementations. Next it examines how CPP also became subject to policy measures aimed at crime control and maintaining international security, producing an operational convergence that strengthened strategies and actions aimed at *in situ* protection. The eruption of Daesh onto the world stage in 2014 brutally exposed the shortcomings of CPP and the ongoing inability of policy makers to prevent the looting and theft of cultural property. Thus the chapter concludes with a brief consideration of policy making itself, showing how it is shaped by special interest groups (SIGs) with different though coinciding agendas aimed at the *in situ* protection of cultural sites and away from prevention through demand reduction.

Cultural property protection policy failure

International CPP policy derives legitimacy and direction from two international conventions: the 1954 Hague Convention for the Protection of Cultural Property in the Event of Armed Conflict (including its First and Second Protocols) and the 1970 UNESCO Convention on the Means of Prohibiting and Preventing the Illicit Import, Export and Transfer of Ownership of Cultural Property (as augmented by the 1995 UNIDROIT Convention on Stolen or Illegally Exported Cultural Objects). Operational policy constructed from principles and recommendations enshrined within these conventions aims at cultural site protection at source (broadly defined to include physical *in situ* protection alongside the necessary infrastructural support, together with trade control to prevent illegal export) and the recovery and return of stolen or otherwise illegally traded cultural objects (Hladik 2013: 17; Manacorda 2011: 17, 40–41; Planche 2013). This policy approach has been characterized summarily as one of 'protection and recovery' (Brodie 2015a; 2015b). But it is a product of the 1950s and 1960s. It could not have foreseen and was ill-prepared for the globalizing revolution in transport and communication that enabled the episodes of massive conflict-associated looting that came to afflict the MENA region from 1990 onwards.

There are two very practical reasons for the failure of the protection and recovery approach to CPP when faced by these changing global circumstances. First, the policy emphasis on protection at source is unrealistic. Because of the demands they place on available resources, protective measures can never offer long-term, comprehensive protection to cultural sites. Furthermore, they dissipate when needed most during periods of conflict, civil disturbance or economic recession or collapse. Second, the emphasis on recovery and return of a policy that is used if not intentionally designed to protect the cultural contexts of cultural objects is dubious. By the time a looted object is recovered, its historical or aesthetic value has been lessened, perhaps severely so, by the destruction of context caused by its theft, clandestine excavation and illegal trade. And while it is possible to understand the symbolic, emotional and moral importance attached to the repatriation of significant works of art, such as that of the Shiva Nataraja returned to India from the National Gallery of Australia in 2014

(Chan 2014), most returned objects are not of that quality and do not occasion the same reception.

The illegal trade in cultural objects, like any other illegal trade, is the product of demand on the destination market (Elia 1993; Naylor 2002: 11; Polk 2009: 14). There would be no illegal trade in cultural objects if there were no collectors, museums and scholars willing to engage with stolen and illegally traded material. Yet the protection and recovery approach to CPP makes no real provision for initiatives aimed at preventing trade by subduing demand or diminishing the attractive pull of the destination market. What is missing is an interrelated set of pragmatic initiatives aimed at creating a more inhospitable commercial environment by increasing levels of risk for all market participants (Polk 2009; Chappell and Polk 2011; Mackenzie 2011). The precise configuration of a demand reduction approach would depend upon the legal and political realities of individual jurisdictions. It might include practical advice and help for law enforcement or look towards more extensive campaigns of public education. But a central component would be the creation of an administrative or regulatory environment that would incentivize legal trade while at the same time penalizing activities that encourage illegal trade – a strategy of 'punishment and persuasion' (Braithwaite 1985). Working together with the already established CPP approach of protection and recovery, trade prevention through demand reduction would offer long-term, proactive relief from looting and illegal trade.

In view of the practical shortcomings of the protection and recovery approach to CPP, the following section examines more closely its genesis and operational modes. It describes the principles of protection and recovery as founded in international law, looking at the strengths and weaknesses of relevant international conventions and the operational priorities they have birthed, and suggests how implemented actions have struggled to achieve their required end of protecting cultural property from looting and theft.

Cultural property protection policy instruments and actions

The 1954 Hague Convention for the Protection of Cultural Property in the Event of Armed Conflict

The starting point for any discussion of CPP is the 1954 Hague Convention for the Protection of Cultural Property in the Event of Armed Conflict (which popularized use of the term 'cultural property') and its 1954 First and 1999 Second Protocols. They are the end product of a centuries-long succession of soft and hard international laws and conventions concerned to protect cultural property from damage, destruction and plunder in times of armed conflict (O'Keefe 2006). The Hague Convention was conceived from the start as an instrument to safeguard cultural property from the damaging effects of military action and therefore places unilateral obligations on States Parties to protect and refrain from damaging cultural property during armed conflict. In the aftermath of World War Two, however, with the example of Nazi misappropriations of art and cultural property still fresh in mind, it was also designed to prevent the belligerent sponsored or condoned theft and looting of cultural objects. Since 1996, implementation of the Hague Convention has been in the hands of the Blue Shield organizations.

The applicability of the Hague Convention to recent conflicts in the MENA region has been limited because major military powers such as the US and the UK have not been States Parties.[1] Even so, if these powers had acted in accordance with the Convention, it is doubtful whether its provisions would have done much to staunch illegal trade and discourage theft and looting. The main thrust of the Hague Convention is to protect cultural property from intentional or unintentional damage during military action. Although the Convention does require action to protect cultural property against looting and illegal trade, it is questionable as to what extent its protection is intended to extend outside any immediate area of military occupation. Thus Article 4(3) of the Convention places a duty on States Parties 'to prohibit, prevent and, if necessary, put a stop to any form of theft, pillage or misappropriation of, and any acts of vandalism directed against, cultural property.' Article 4(3) is elaborated and reinforced by Article 1(1) of the First Protocol, which requires States Parties 'to prevent the exportation, from a territory occupied by it during an armed conflict, of cultural property', but then Article 1(2–3) extends obligations beyond active belligerents, requiring each State Party 'to take into its custody cultural property imported into its territory either directly or indirectly from any occupied territory', and 'to return, at the close of hostilities, to the competent authorities of the territory previously occupied, cultural property which is in its territory'. Not surprisingly, as a founding legal text of CPP, the Hague Convention is a clear expression of protection and recovery demanding *in situ* protection of cultural sites, indirect protection of cultural sites through trade control, and the recovery and return of illegally traded cultural objects.

No matter what its beneficial effect for protecting cultural sites from damage caused directly or indirectly by military action, as regards illegal trade, the Hague Convention and its Protocols are weakened fatally by their overly restrictive focus on ground warfare between States Parties, which by the twenty-first century was anachronistic. The provisions against illegal trade do not apply to occupied territory where the occupying power is a non-state actor, such as the Taliban or Daesh (O'Keefe 2006: 98–99, 299–300). Nor is there any provision for suppressing looting and illegal trade consequent to aerial bombardment. Bombing campaigns aimed at degrading economic infrastructure cause massive disruption to civil society and have become a common feature of warfare in the MENA region, leading impoverished and displaced civilians to engage in theft and looting.

The Hague Convention and its Protocols apply only to situations of overt armed conflict, though much of the looting and illegal trade since 1990 has occurred in countries that were not openly at war but still suffering economically from its effects. Jordan, for example, though conducting airstrikes against Daesh in 2015, has otherwise successfully avoided being drawn into any other military action. Nevertheless, archaeological sites throughout Jordan have been badly damaged by illegal digging. Thus throughout most of the period in question, the MENA region could be considered in broad terms as a conflict zone, with its countries suffering to a greater or lesser extent from the economic dislocation, refugee migration, and political and religious violence set in motion by international wars in Iraq and Afghanistan and civil wars in Syria, Libya and Yemen. For countries not directly engaged in armed conflict, however, the Hague Convention would not apply. For these reasons of limited subscription and heavily circumscribed applicability, the Hague Convention and its Protocols have had in practical terms only limited material impact. Their main contribution has been in shaping CPP by their early promulgation of the protection and recovery approach.

The Blue Shield organizations

In 1996, practical implementation of the 1954 Hague Convention and its Protocols was placed in the hands of the newly constituted International Committee of the Blue Shield (ICBS), founded with the support of UNESCO and participation of its five associated NGOs as 'pillar organizations' – the International Council on Archives (ICA), the International

Council of Museums (ICOM), the International Federation of Library Associations and Institutions (IFLA), the International Council on Monuments and Sites (ICOMOS) and the Coordinating Council of Audiovisual Archives Associations (CCAAA). The ICBS was supplemented in 2006 by the Association of National Committees of Blue Shield (ANCBS), which was established to coordinate the work of newly established national committees. The mission of the Blue Shield organizations is 'to promote the protection of cultural property … against threats of all kinds and to intervene strategically with decision makers and relevant international organizations to prevent and to respond to natural and man made disasters' (Blue Shield n.d.)

The inclusion of 'natural disasters' in this mission statement is surprising. There is no requirement in the Hague Convention to offer CPP against natural disasters, and it seems likely that this mission extension reflects the overall mandate of the pillar organizations and the professional expertise and interests of their members to protect the fabric and integrity of cultural property placed in their charge. It keys in well with military imperatives to avoid damaging cultural property during combat. It also serves to highlight the fact that the Blue Shield organizations are not constrained by the actual text of the 1954 Hague Convention and its Protocols. In practice, however, this coincidence of concern about natural and man-made disasters means that Blue Shield has placed operational emphasis on *in situ* protection and post-disaster restoration of cultural sites (Wegener 2008: 171). Strategies aimed at preventing looting and theft focus upon offering cultural sites physical protection, by military forces or other means, even though the practical limitations of such protection are recognized (Kila 2015: 200–202). The Blue Shield mission makes no provision for taking preventative action by subduing demand and reducing the size of the destination market. Members of the Blue Shield organizations defend this decision not to engage in strategies aimed at demand reduction by claiming that looting and the illegal trade are not a concern of Blue Shield as they fall under the scope of the 1970 UNESCO Convention on the Means of Prohibiting and Preventing the Illicit Import, Export and Transfer of Ownership of Cultural Property.[2]

The 1970 UNESCO Convention on the Means of Prohibiting and Preventing the Illicit Import, Export and Transfer of Ownership of Cultural Property

Members of the Blue Shield organizations look towards policy grown out of the 1970 UNESCO Convention on the Means of Prohibiting and Preventing the Illicit Import, Export and Transfer of Ownership of Cultural Property for controlling the illegal trade in cultural objects out of the conflict-wrought MENA region. Their view is understandable. The UNESCO Convention was conceived and drafted with the problems of illegal trade in mind. Principles enshrined within the 1970 UNESCO Convention have, together with those of the 1954 Hague Convention's First Protocol, shaped the CPP policy approach of protection and recovery.

The Convention places a wide-ranging set of obligations on States Parties (O'Keefe 2007). Articles 5 and 6 are concerned with ensuring the appropriate legal, administrative, technical and other professional expertise to secure the *in situ* protection of cultural property and control over the export of cultural objects. In other words, they are concerned to establish an institutional regime of CPP within the national jurisdiction of each State Party. But the effective functioning of the envisaged institutions requires a healthy economy, secure government control of territory and a strong jurisdiction. Many of the MENA countries have in the past possessed or continue to possess the necessary institutions, but their effectiveness has been reduced, often severely, during periods of conflict or civil disturbance when economies are degraded and central government control of territory becomes withdrawn or contested. In Iraq, for example, a well-resourced Department of Antiquities was able to fulfil the requirements of Articles 5 and 6 until after the 1991 Gulf War when the imposition of UN sanctions and infliction of sporadic bombing campaigns compromised its integrity and operation. The damage caused to the country's economy was accompanied by a rash of museum thefts and an upturn in illegal digging of archaeological sites (Gibson 1997).

Articles 7 and 9 establish the requirements among States Parties for the recovery and return of illegally exported cultural objects. Article 7(b)(ii) formalizes recovery and return as a fundamental component of CPP. Articles 7(b)(i) and 9 emphasize the conceptualization of protection to include trade control. Article (9) requires diplomatic action and envisages bilateral or multilateral cooperative agreements between States Parties. Such bilateral agreements form the central operational action of the US implementation of the 1970 Convention with the 1983 Convention on Cultural Property Implementation Act. But in the absence of functioning diplomatic relations such actions are not possible in wartime. Normal intergovernmental communication does not always endure and will not extend to *de facto* though not internationally recognized regimes such as the Taliban and Daesh. (Nevertheless, in August 2016, the US acted unilaterally to place emergency import controls on Syrian cultural property.)

Article 10 *is* concerned with demand reduction, largely by means of public education, though by not specifying any exact measures the Article is vulnerable to minimal or evasive compliance. The UK government, for example, has never systematically engaged in raising public awareness of the problems attendant upon buying cultural objects from the MENA region. Article 10(a) requires each State Party to 'oblige antique dealers, subject to penal or administrative sanctions, to maintain a register recording the origin of each item of cultural property, names and addresses of the supplier, description and price of each item sold and to inform the purchaser of the cultural property of the export prohibition to which such property may be subject.' Again though, the requirement is weak, offering no guidance about appropriate oversight or inspection. In the UK, dealers in cultural objects have successfully argued that the requirement is met by the transactions register they must by law already maintain for Value Added Tax (sales tax) accounting purposes. These tax registers are open for inspection by tax officials with no expertise in CPP.

Thus the main body of the 1970 UNESCO Convention is primarily concerned to protect cultural property at source by developing the necessary institutional capacity and by discouraging illegal export through trade control, and also to encourage the recovery and return of stolen and illegally exported objects. The provisions of the Convention cannot be guaranteed in wartime or during longer periods of peacetime 'cold' political confrontation. During the period in question domestic and diplomatic actions conducted within the framework of the 1970 Convention aimed at protecting cultural property and preventing illegal trade of cultural objects were not always viable for the MENA region. In view of the ongoing cultural destruction, UNESCO was forced into adopting an international coordinating role, advising and enabling a series of targeted 'emergency actions'.

UNESCO emergency actions

The work of UNESCO since its foundation in 1946 has been fundamental in establishing and promoting the legal and normative contexts of CPP. But as a peacetime organization, it has neither the financial resources nor the institutional capacity to offer effective solutions to 'emergency' threats to cultural property such as those posed by the extreme 'spikes' of looting and illegal trade that have been seen in the MENA region since 1990. UNESCO itself has said as much. On 4 June 2015, the UNESCO programme specialist for CPP was quoted as saying 'We lack adequate technical and financial means. This is an emergency situation which is new for UNESCO, which is not a humanitarian agency and is not designed to respond to emergency crisis situations, so we are redefining our goals and strategy' (Reinl 2015).

Up until then, the response had been made through a series of emergency actions. Emergency actions are structured by the protection and recovery approach to CPP and are planned, organized and implemented to a lesser or greater extent under UNESCO guidance and with the facilitation of UNESCO offices (UNESCO 2014). They mobilize teams of experts to advise upon damage mitigation through such actions as documentation, capacity building and awareness raising in countries whose cultural sites are being damaged by direct action or by theft and illegal trade. Emergency actions have met with limited success because they are usually reactive, arriving too late to prevent serious damage, and continue to struggle in hostile circumstances with the implementation of measures aimed at protection and recovery. Another problem is that an emergency action's targeting of international assistance at cultural site protection in one country also leaves sites of other countries vulnerable.

On 21 October 2011, for example, UNESCO announced it had convened a meeting of experts to discuss strategies for safeguarding the cultural property of Libya in the 'aftermath of conflict' (UNESCO 2011). (The conflict in question was the one fought between February and October 2011 that resulted in the overthrow and death of Muammar Gaddafi.) In line with the protection and recovery approach to CPP, the main recommendations were aimed at securing Libyan cultural sites through physical protection and infrastructural support. As regards illegal trade, the only recommendation was 'To collect information on missing cultural objects from catalogues, archives, inventories, and disseminating it among concerned institutions (INTERPOL, etc.) and auction houses with a view to stopping their further illicit circulation and favoring their return.' The emphasis was placed on recovery, with no real provision for preventing looting and theft by reducing demand. By January 2015, with Libya again in the grip of civil war, the implementation of this UNESCO action plan had stalled and the country's cultural property was facing the threat of illegal trade and other causes of destruction (di Lernia 2015: 548–549). The weakness of a policy initiative aimed at achieving *in situ* protection was once more exposed, unable to function when needed most during conflict. The Libyan emergency action also wasted resources that might have been better spent on demand reduction, and in so doing have reduced the incentive to loot and trade cultural property from Libya, and from other countries in the MENA region, including Syria.

In March 2011, the civilian population of Syria started demonstrations against the governing regime of Bashar al-Assad that subsequently degenerated into civil war. It was not until 10–13 February 2013, nearly two years later, that UNESCO held a meeting in Amman specifically to address 'the issue of illicit trafficking' in Syria (UNESCO 2013). The plan agreed was for *in situ* protection. Physical protection was clearly not possible in this case, and so protection was to be achieved through awareness raising and capacity building. The only provision made for demand reduction was for UNESCO and 'other international organizations' to 'foster cooperation with countries where the market for illegal works of art is more active, and launch preventive actions in collaboration with their authorities.' This recommendation was hopelessly vague and compares unfavourably with the level of detail included in other recommendations. The UNESCO action plan was implemented on 1 March 2014 as the Emergency Safeguarding of the Syrian Heritage Project (ESSHP), supported for three years by $2.46 million of European Union (EU) funding. Again, the plan was reactive, established three years after the onset of civil unrest and war. It failed to bring the situation under control, and the appearance of Daesh as an international actor worsened the situation and embroiled Iraq, necessitating another emergency action. The funding allocated to the ESSHP was not available for CPP in other countries, for example Libya in 2015 when the political situation there started to deteriorate once more.

In view of the demonstrable shortcomings of established CPP policy, it was surprising that throughout the MENA region policy makers continued to support emergency actions aimed at protection and recovery, and did not consider alternative strategies aimed at demand reduction. One explanation is that, during the period in question, CPP had fallen within the scope of crime control and international security policy making. The preferred operational goals of these policies were broadly concordant with those already existing for CPP. There was no challenge to the protection and recovery approach and no inducement to search out new solutions.

The criminalization of the illegal trade in cultural property

In the globalized and deregulated world of transnational flows of money, people and goods, the organization and control of illegal trade and markets have become major sources of criminal profit (Aas 2007; Naím 2007; Naylor 2002; Shelley 2014). Transnational illegal trades are socially harmful and the illegal trade in cultural objects is no exception. Bribes, extortion payments and other illegal disbursements are unavailable for taxation. Consumer spending on illicit commodities diverts money away from the legal economy and reduces taxable income. State agencies are corrupted and fiscally compromised, causing a deterioration of social provision that impacts negatively upon the integrity of civil society and government legitimacy. Unaccountable 'dirty' money is made available for other illegal enterprises. Concern that globalization has allowed the transnational expansion of illegal trades prompted the adoption by the UN in November 2000 of the Convention Against Transnational Organized Crime. Article 2(a) of the convention defines an 'organized criminal group' as a

> structured group of three or more persons, existing for a period of time and acting in concert with the aim of committing one or more serious crimes or offences established in accordance with this Convention, in order to obtain, directly or indirectly, a financial or other material benefit.

By this definition, the illegal trade in cultural objects is an organized crime (Manacorda 2011; Campbell 2013; Dietzler 2013; Mackenzie and Davis 2014). Thus the problems caused by the trade can be and have been recast as a crime control issue. Cultural sites could be protected by preventing the organized criminal trade that damages them.

International policy for controlling organized crime has focused upon strengthening criminal justice deterrence, first by increasing the range of investigative tools and powers available for use by police and other law enforcement agencies in apprehending criminals, and second by diversifying the kind of punitive sanctions that might reduce incentives to commit crimes (Scherrer 2010: 59–65; Finckenauer 2011). Money laundering laws and offences in particular have been developed to stop offenders profiting from the proceeds of crime (Naylor 2002: 18; Levi 2003: 219–222). There has been a growing move towards forfeiture or confiscation of criminal proceeds and assets.

For the illegal trade in cultural objects, stronger law enforcement has been confounded by the secrecy of the trade, the evidential requirement of proving a crime committed in a foreign conflict zone, and the difficulty of securing effective police collaboration in countries suffering from conflict or civil disturbance. A fall-back option has been to seize material because of customs violations. In the USA, Immigration and Customs Enforcement (ICE) in the New York area has been particularly effective in this regard, recovering and returning quantities of material from several MENA countries, and convicting two dealers for offences relating to the smuggling of material out of MENA through Dubai (Bruer and Rosen 2016).[3]

Crime control through strong law enforcement should have an important part to play in dismantling the destination market and thus preventing damage to cultural property through diminishment of looting and illegal trade. But for reasons already described, its material impact is questionable. Convictions are rare, and it remains to be established whether the conviction and removal of criminals from the destination market actually reduces the volume of illegal trade, or whether trade simply reconfigures and continues undiminished. Neither of the two dealers convicted by ICE received a custodial sentence, and by 2015 both were back in business. The recourse to customs seizures brings crime control policy into close alignment with the return and recovery strand of CPP. The recovery and return of an illegally traded cultural object is also an exercise in asset forfeiture. But the criticisms of the return and recovery strand of CPP still apply. The material recovered is often (though not always) of variable quality, and the quantities seized are probably not enough to constitute a financial deterrent.[4] Monetary losses incurred through confiscations are likely to be factored into pricing and accepted as a cost of doing business. There is a developing understanding for illegal trades generally (Finckenauer 2011: 310; Scherrer 2010: 65), including the illegal trade in cultural objects (Chappell and Polk 2011: 106–111), that while strong law enforcement should be a necessary component of a successful crime control policy, by itself it is not enough – there needs to be a complementary strategy of crime prevention through demand reduction.

The securitization of the illegal trade in cultural objects

The 1989–1991 collapse of the Soviet bloc is generally believed to have opened new horizons for transnational organized crime. As borders opened, funds of previously Soviet-controlled capital passed out of public into private hands and then across the borders of newly post-Soviet countries, with a consequent weakening of governance and public order at home and a flow of dirty money abroad for investment in other criminal enterprises, especially ones in areas not subject to effective rule of law (Makarenko 2012: 15–16). Thus during the 1990s the threats posed by organized crime to civil society in the USA and Europe became 'othered', perceived as emanating from an alien criminal conspiracy aimed at subverting consumer markets in the developed world (Edwards and Gill 2003: 268). Organized crime was presented as a threat to national and international security (Woodiwiss 2003: 20). Working within this narrative, the operational goals of US-led international crime control policy started shifting towards suppressing the production of illegal commodities at source and interrupting their supply to the destination market.

The situation grew worse after the 9/11 attacks on the USA. The activities of transnational crime and terror groups became increasingly entangled with the appearance of 'hybrid' organizations and the creation of a global 'crime–terror nexus' (Makarenko 2012; Shelley 2014). Like criminals, 'terrorists' and insurgent militias are known to raise money through the organization and control of illegal trades, and to rely upon corrupt public and private actors to facilitate the movement and laundering of goods and money. The idea of a crime–terror nexus reaffirms the view that crime control is an issue of national or international security

(Edwards and Gill 2003: 269; Naylor 2002: 42). Such is the case with the illegal trade in cultural objects, because of the increasingly visible link with criminal and militia funding. As early as 1996 it was being reported in Afghanistan that Mujahideen and Taliban militia groups were actively digging up artifacts for sale or levying a tax on the sale of artifacts (Brodie 2009: 50–51). Similar though largely unconfirmed reports were made from Iraq after the 2003 Coalition invasion (Brodie 2011). By 2013 militia groups in Syria were said to be selling artifacts to buy weapons and the issue came to more broad public attention in 2014 with extensive reporting of the profits that Daesh was reputedly making from the trade (Al-Azm et al. 2014).

For the international community, the narrative of threatened security informed Security Council Resolution (UNSCR) 2199, which in February 2015 placed trade controls on Syrian cultural objects and reaffirmed trade controls on Iraqi cultural objects. Aimed primarily at degrading economic support for Daesh and Jabhat al-Nusra (JAN), for cultural property it 'noted with concern' in Article 16:

> that ISIL [Daesh], ANF [JAN] and other individuals, groups, undertakings and entities associated with Al-Qaida, are generating income from engaging directly or indirectly in the looting and smuggling of cultural heritage items from archaeological sites, museums, libraries, archives, and other sites in Iraq and Syria, which is being used to support their recruitment efforts and strengthen their operational capability to organize and carry out terrorist attacks.
>
> *(UN Security Council 2015)*

Its proposed remedy in Article 17 was:

> that all Member States shall take appropriate steps to prevent the trade in Iraqi and Syrian cultural property . . . illegally removed from Iraq since 6 August 1990 and from Syria since 15 March 2011, including by prohibiting cross-border trade in such items, thereby allowing for their eventual safe return to the Iraqi and Syrian people.
>
> *(UN Security Council 2015)*

Again, the intention was to offer protection at source by means of trade control and secure the recovery and 'eventual safe return' of illegally traded objects.

The UNSCR 2199 trade controls reflected CPP policy, but were enacted within a broader security-related initiative to reduce the economies of the terrorist organizations Daesh and JAN. Their effectiveness is questionable. They are open to the same set of criticisms as UNESCO emergency actions. They are reactive, coming too late to prevent serious damage. There is no recognition of the practical problems of discriminating between material illegally exported before or after the stated date thresholds.[5] They are country-specific and thus difficult to enforce when archaeological cultures spread across the borders of more than one modern state. Trade controls generally have enjoyed limited success because of porous borders. Within the MENA region itself, the many long land and sea frontiers are difficult to police, particularly during times of conflict or civil disturbance. Outside the MENA region, things are not much better. With only limited customs inspections of shipping containers, airline luggage and mailed parcels, it is only occasionally that any illegally traded cultural objects are intercepted. In the general celebration that greeted the announcement of UNSCR 2199, no one stopped to reflect why the trade in Iraqi objects was still a problem in 2015 when trade controls had first been introduced by UNSCR 661 in August 1990.

Thus by 2015 there was operational convergence between CPP, crime control and international security policies. Customs seizures and trade controls were intended to interrupt supply to the destination market, thereby reducing the incentive to loot and steal at source. There was no operational imperative or practical provision in any of the policies to reduce destination market demand. There was no understanding that emergency actions and trade controls always arrive too late and are constrained by their focus on a single country. For protection to be proactive, it requires prevention that is global in application. The trade needs to be diminished and the incentive to steal or loot already reduced before any episode of conflict or civil disturbance, whenever and wherever it may occur in the world. Demand reduction is key.

The endgame: Daesh and the destruction of cultural property

In March 2013, Daesh seized control of the regional capital of Raqqa in eastern Syria. Reports began to leak out of the theft of objects from Raqqa museum and of 'large scale' (Cockburn 2014) or 'massive' (Lamb 2014) looting of archaeological sites. Then, in June 2014, Daesh burst into media prominence with the rout of the Iraqi army at Mosul and the occupation of a large part of western Iraq. A newspaper article reported on the capture and analysis by Iraqi intelligence of computer memory sticks containing information about Daesh finances. It seemed to make the alarming claim that Daesh had made $36 million from the sale of cultural objects from one area of Syria alone (Chulov 2014). From what is known of the financial structure of the trade in cultural objects, the claim is not a very likely one. Prices multiply many times over as objects pass from source to the destination market (Brodie 2014: 34–35). For Daesh to be making $36 million from the sale of objects obtained from one area of Syria would have implied a destination market for Syrian cultural property valued in billions of dollars. In July 2014, the $36 million figure was rendered even less believable by news that Daesh profits were derived from taxing the excavation and trade of cultural objects (Al-Azm et al. 2014). That being the case, then the $36 million taken by Daesh as tax would be only a small part of the total value of what by extrapolation would then be a totally unbelievable multi-billion-dollar trade.

This figure of $36 million was never corroborated (or discounted) by independent examination of the memory sticks (Hardy 2014), and so should be considered questionable at best.[6] Nevertheless, despite the uncertainties and unrealities surrounding the figure, traditional and social media and increasingly the political establishment seized upon the idea that Daesh was profiting from the looting and trade of cultural objects to the tune of millions of dollars annually (e.g. Abhyankar 2014; Drennan 2014; Howard et al 2014; FATF 2015: 16, 37). These speculative and probably inflated assessments of the monetary value of the trade to Daesh were not being made by uninformed reporters in newspapers, but by respected members of the political, military and cultural heritage establishments – the kind of people who have the ear of the policy makers. They seemed to be overlooking the fact that on 23 October 2014 the US Treasury Department had published the text of a speech made by David Cohn about the financing of Daesh (Cohen 2014). He believed Daesh was largely self-financing, raising money through oil sales, kidnapping for ransom, and extortion or taxation of businesses in areas under its control. He made no mention of cultural property. By this time, however, the media coverage was writing itself. The story was 'trade makes millions for ISIS' (e.g. Hall 2015; Crowcroft 2015), and the millions were being used to further human suffering. The illegal trade in cultural objects had passed from being a crime against culture to a crime against humanity.

On 14 May 2014, the US Department of State announced that it had designated Daesh and JAN as Foreign Terrorist Organizations (USA 2014). A few months later, on 22 November 2014, working with this new terrorist ordering of the Syrian conflict and media perceptions of a multi-million-dollar trade, US Secretary of State John Kerry spoke on the issue of threats to Syrian and Iraqi cultural property at the Metropolitan Museum of Art in New York City (Kerry 2014). After declaring that 'Ancient treasures in Iraq and in Syria have now become the casualties of continuing warfare and looting. And no one group has done more to put our shared cultural heritage in the gun sights than ISIL,' he went on to describe the US response. The US was providing or increasing funding for the American Schools of Oriental Research to document the condition of cultural sites in Syria and Iraq, for the training in Iraq of Iraqi conservation experts, and for the National Science Foundation in partnership with the American Association for the Advancement of Science to monitor the destruction of cultural sites in Syria. Thus by May 2015, for the US government, the illegal trade in cultural objects from Iraq and Syria had become well entrenched as an issue of national security and in consequence substantial funding was being made available for initiatives aimed at documenting and tackling the problem at source. Kerry signally failed to consider or acknowledge that demand on the destination market might be exerting a causal attraction or to announce federal funding for any project that might look towards prevention by reducing market demand.

While privately doubting the exaggerated reporting of Daesh profits, some cultural heritage and law enforcement professionals thought the securitization of CPP to be a positive step forward as it attracted political attention and increased funding for countermeasures.[7] Unfortunately, the funding was for source-directed projects of a type that had been shown in the past to be inappropriate for the task at hand. Funding was also supplied only for projects concerning Iraq and Syria. Nothing was offered for other countries whose cultural property was being stolen or destroyed by groups not officially categorized as posing a terrorist threat. In May 2015, despite the UNESCO emergency actions and UNSCR 2199, it was reported that the looting of cultural sites in Syria was on the increase (Al-Azm 2015; Casana 2015). By then, too, Daesh was looking towards cultural property not as something to be sold, but as something to be destroyed.

Daesh had been systematically destroying Shia and Sufi shrines in occupied areas of Syria and Iraq without much international reaction until in March 2015 social and conventional media lit up with outrage at the Internet release of a video showing Daesh personnel destroying exhibits in Mosul museum, Iraq. Another barrage of condemnation followed when on 4 April 2015 Daesh posted a video showing men using pickaxes and hammers to attack statues and architectural reliefs at the first- to third-century AD site of Hatra in Iraq. On 11 April 2015, another Daesh video showed the explosive demolition of the Northwest Palace of the ninth- to eighth-century BC Neo-Assyrian site of Nimrud in Iraq. For a brief moment in time, CPP teetered on the edge of militarization. Iraq's minister of culture asked for US-led airstrikes on Daesh militia seen approaching other cultural sites (Barnard 2015). Italy's minister of culture called for the creation of a UN peacekeeping force that would be able to intervene and defend cultural sites (Scammell 2015). These calls for military action were repeated more widely through social media. Though resisted by the US and other powers with operational forces in the region, the move for militarization of CPP formed the logical endpoint of a policy momentum developing through criminalization and then securitization.

The motives and motivations of Daesh for their markedly visual destructions of ancient, pre-Islamic cultural sites became the subject of much speculation. Perhaps the destructions were associated with a larger campaign of commercial looting, whereby smaller objects were sold on the market and larger objects and structures were destroyed (Chulov 2015). Perhaps they were part of a strategy of cultural cleansing, designed to eradicate the identity and memory of non-Sunni communities and to weaken their historical attachments to territory (Jiyad 2015). They might have been intended to draw in foreign forces for a prophesied apocalyptic military showdown (Chulov 2015). But perhaps in reality they were expressions of iconoclasm. The attributions of universal cultural value to ancient remains by the 1954 Hague Convention and the 1970 UNESCO Convention may have prompted the Daesh destructions as an iconoclastic reaction to the perceived 'worship' of false idols in their secular temples (museums), perhaps enabling Daesh to argue also that the international community values cultural property more than human life (Colla 2015). Daesh itself, through its English-language mouthpiece magazine *Dabiq*, claimed to have destroyed the 'idols' because of the admiration shown to them by unbelievers, and celebrated the 'rage' of the unbelievers occasioned by their destruction. The article in *Dabiq* was written after the damaging attacks on the Mosul museum and associated media coverage but before the demolition of Nimrud. Perhaps the media outcry that followed the March Mosul video prompted the later destructions (Jones 2015).

The possibility that Daesh might make ideological, propaganda or psychological use of cultural property was not unexpected. Scholars and officials inside Iraq had been warning anybody who would listen as early as October 2013 about the likely danger of publicizing any link between Daesh and cultural property.[8] In Libya, a senior scholar argued likewise, asking for the media to keep 'a lower profile' (Kingsley 2015). Their warnings fell on deaf ears. The security narrative had politicized cultural property. The failure to control illegal trade before 2014 had left fertile ground for media sensationalism and loud, strident and factually aberrant assertions of the monetary and cultural value of cultural property. These hysterical and impotent outbursts may only have helped convince Daesh of the cultural, emotional or political importance of cultural property to the international community, and thus of the potential use of violent and declarative destruction as a psychological weapon of terror, aimed either at those it wished to confront, those it wished to subdue or those it wished to recruit (Stern and Berger 2015: 198–218).

Conclusion: Policy and policy making

By 2015, CPP had become entwined with crime control and international security, yet it had still failed to achieve any kind of decisive hold on the problem of looting and theft of cultural property. Policy makers had been unable to go beyond protection and recovery to offer anything new, and policy making itself seemed locked in a vicious cycle of repetition. Policy making, rather than policy, looked to be at issue, unreflecting and seemingly incapable of learning from past experience. Yet policy making in this field is a poorly understood process. The route from looting and theft in Syria to UNSCR 2199, for example, is a difficult one to follow. Doubtless there were back-channel representations, consultations and negotiations, and a concern on the part of policy makers to be seen to be doing something in response to heightened public concern. The people involved must know what happened. But there is no full and detailed description of the process that is open to critical analysis.

What is more open to consideration is the constitution and role of special interest groups (SIGs) in policy formation. Each SIG comprises a community with a commonality of interest and purpose, held together discursively by a shared conceptual vocabulary. A SIG is a source of expert advice but also of advocacy. Members of SIGs are often called upon in an advisory capacity by UNESCO, the UN Security Council and national governments. They are expected to provide objective advice from the standpoint of their professional expertise, but such advice is inevitably directed by their concerns and the nature of their expertise. Thus SIGs are biased towards offering preferred solutions to discursively framed problems. In many domains this is a healthy process, as multiple viewpoints allow for more fertile policy making. For CPP, however, this looks not to be happening. Instead, there are at least five different SIGs working in unintended synergy to drive policy in an unproductive direction, away from anything that might promote prevention and towards more interventions aimed at protection and recovery. The SIGs in question are the military, cultural heritage experts, security experts, domestic and expatriate actors of individual MENA countries, and the 'demand community' – the collectors, dealers, museum curators and university academics that constitute demand on the destination market.

The military

Since the public outcry that greeted the plunder of the Iraq National Museum and other cultural institutions in 2003 and the accompanying looting of archaeological sites, the armed forces of NATO and maybe other countries have become sensitized to the issue of CPP. In the first place, it is simply bad publicity for the armed forces of a country and by extension the country itself to be portrayed as 'cultural barbarians' when damaging or failing to protect cultural sites in conflict areas. But military planners have begun to recognize that avoiding damage to cultural sites during active combat can act as a 'force-multiplier' by not unnecessarily antagonizing the local population (Stone 2013: 170). Thus military planners have come to appreciate the political and strategic benefits of securing *in situ* protection of cultural property during wartime. They have no reason, however, to take account of the destination market, which is a civilian domain outside their competence and remit.

Cultural heritage experts

This SIG comprises a large and diverse community of conservators, architects, art historians, archaeologists, lawyers, museum curators and university academics. They act on their own behalf or through the agency of their professional organizations or NGOs. For its emergency actions, UNESCO seeks partnerships and consultations with appropriate cultural heritage experts and leans heavily for advice and support upon the UNESCO associated NGOs (ICA, ICOM, IFLA, ICOMOS, CCAAA). The expertise available within these NGOs and among cultural heritage experts more generally is relevant largely for the protection, documentation, conservation, restoration and reconstruction of cultural property. ICOM is the only organization with any active expertise as regards the illegal trade in cultural objects. When individual cultural heritage experts are consulted for emergency actions, they are invariably selected for their experience of working in the country in question. Cultural heritage experts are not usually interested or even aware of what is happening on the destination market and have no understanding of its organization and operation.

Security experts

This SIG comprises a small and poorly defined community of academics, retired military personnel and other commentators who are primarily concerned with issues of national or global security. They are only concerned with CPP insofar as it is regarded as a security issue, and aimed at denial of support for terrorist groups.

Domestic and expatriate actors

The government agents and private citizens of countries engaged in conflict usually have a vested interest in protecting the cultural property of their home countries, as well as in securing more general humanitarian assistance. They are politically, personally and emotionally committed to the wellbeing of their home countries. They act through diplomatic channels, the offices of UNESCO, or through their own personal and professional networks to mobilize private, public and political support for intervention in their home countries. Arguing for policies that would divert material support away from source towards measures aimed at reducing destination demand would be incompatible with their domestic commitment.

Demand community

This SIG comprises wealthy collectors allied with senior academics and museum curators and directors. They deny any functional relationship between demand and supply. Together, they form a powerful constituency that is able to rebuff criticism of their actions and deflect policy interventions away from what they consider to be unwarranted interference with their own interests and practice in constituting demand, and towards tackling the problem at source.

There is a very real possibility that UNESCO emergency actions and associated initiatives such as UNSCR trade controls conform in intent and content to the interests of these SIGs, each with its own reasons for directing policy towards offering protection and recovery. These SIGs possess neither the inclination nor the expertise to offer anything different.

The inflexibility of CPP in the hands of SIGs provides a good example of path-dependency (Klein and Marmor 2006: 902), where policy making is constrained by the limitations of long-vested, structuring interests and an inherited operational toolkit. Working against that unforgiving grain, it is difficult to create space for more creative rethinks of what might be possible, desirable or productive. By 2015 however, UNESCO was beginning to show an interest in market reduction (Prott 2011). Paragraphs 50 and 51 of the 2015 operational guidelines for the implementation of the 1970 Convention offered a way forward when they expanded upon Article 5(e) of the Convention which states that each State Party should establish 'for the benefit of those concerned (curators, collectors, antique dealers, etc.) rules in conformity with the ethical principles set forth in this Convention; and taking steps to ensure the observance of those rules.' Paragraphs 50 and 51 of the guidelines suggested that these rules should be developed regionally, nationally and internationally, and apply to a broader range of actors than originally specified, including additionally anthropologists, archaeologists, conservators, restorers and other relevant professional staff. They also recommended elements of compulsion and incentive, very much in line with the market reduction approach of punishment and persuasion, though absent from the original text of the Convention (UNESCO 2015: 13). It remains to be seen how the broader policy making community and its SIGs will react to this potentially productive departure for CPP.

Acknowledgements

The writing of this chapter was supported by the European Research Council under the European Union's Seventh Framework Programme (FP7/2007–2013)/European Research Council Grant agreement no. 283873 GTICO.

Notes

1 The US ratified the Convention but not its protocols in 2009.
2 Several Blue Shield members have made this claim independently in private conversations with the author. The Director of Programs and Partnerships of ICOM, one of the five pillar organizations, made the claim publicly in December 2014 at a conference where the author was in attendance.
3 ICE showed the application of strong law enforcement to best effect in its pursuit of Asian art dealer Subhash Kapoor. By 2015, Operation Hidden Idol had achieved three convictions and recovered 2,622 south and southeast Asian cultural objects from Kapoor's business premises in the New York area (Mashberg 2015). Kapoor himself was under arrest in India.
4 It is not well reported, but transit countries in the MENA region such as Turkey, Jordan and Lebanon have been seizing large quantities of material, much more than the countries of the destination market. Lebanon, for example, reported 46 seizures of material from Syria during the three years 2012–2014 (Seif 2015).
5 The UNSCR date thresholds ignored export controls established by Iraqi national law in 1936 and Syrian national law in 1963.
6 In May 2015 US special forces recovered documents showing that between 6 December 2014 and 26 March 2015 Daesh collected $265,000 through a 20 per cent tax on the trade in cultural objects, suggesting a total monetary value for the taxed trade of approximately $1.3 million for four months (Keller 2015).
7 Observations made by several individuals in conversation with the author.
8 An Iraqi culture ministry official warned the author about the possibility at a conference in September 2013, and again in 2014. A similar view was reported in the press (Bowley 2014).

Bibliography

Aas, Katja F. 2007. *Globalisation and Crime*. London: Sage.

Abhyankar, Rajendra. 2014. 'Syrian "Blood Antiquities" Proliferate Urgent Need for an International Agreement'. *World Post*, 11 March 2014. Electronic document, http://www.huffingtonpost.com/rajendra-abhyankar/syrian-blood-antiquities-_b_6095248.html (accessed 7 June 2015).

Al-Azm, Amr. 2015. 'The Pillaging of Syria's Cultural Heritage'. *Middle East Institute*, 22 May 2015. Electronic document, http://www.mei.edu/content/at/pillaging-syrias-cultural-heritage? (accessed 30 May 2015).

Al-Azm, Amr, Salam Al-Kuntar, and Brian I. Daniels. 2014. 'ISIS' Antiquities Sideline'. *New York Times*, 2 September 2014.

Bailey, Martin and Melanie Gerlis. 2013. 'Guilty Plea Over Antiquities'. *Art Newspaper* 249, 10 September 2013.

Barnard, Anne. 2015. 'Race in Iraq and Syria to Record and Shield Art Falling to ISIS'. *New York Times*, 8 March 2015.

Blue Shield. (n.d). 'International Committee of the Blue Shield (ICBS)'. US Committee of the Shield website. http://uscbs.org/international-affiliates.html (accessed 13 June 2015).

Bowley, Graham. 2014. 'Antiquities Lost, Casualties of War'. *New York Times*, 3 October 2014.

Braithwaite, John. 1985. *To Punish or Persuade: Enforcement of Coal Mine Safety*. Albany: State University of New York Press.

Brodie, Neil. 2009. 'Consensual Relations? Academic Involvement in the Illegal Trade in Ancient Manuscripts'. In *Criminology and Archaeology: Studies in Looted Antiquities*, edited by Simon Mackenzie and Penny Green, 41–58. Oxford: Hart.

Brodie, Neil. 2011. 'Scholarship and Insurgency? The Study and Trade of Iraqi Antiquities'. In Illicit Traffic of Cultural Objects: Law, Ethics, and the Realities. An Institute of Advanced Studies Workshop, 4–5 August. Perth: University of Western Australia. http://traffickingculture.org/publications/brodie-neil-2011-scholarship-and-insurgency-the-study-and-trade-of-iraqi-antiquities-in-illicit-traffic-of-cultural-objects-law-ethics-and-the-realities-an-institute-of-advanced-studies-works/ (accessed 30 May 2015).

Brodie, Neil. 2012. 'Uncovering the Antiquities Market'. In *The Oxford Handbook of Public Archaeology*, edited by Robin Skeates, Carol McDavid and John Carman, 230–252. Oxford: Oxford University Press.

Brodie, Neil. 2014. 'The Antiquities Market: It's All in a Price'. *Heritage and Society* 7(1): 32–46.

Brodie, Neil. 2015a. 'Syria and its Regional Neighbors: A Case of Cultural Property Protection Policy Failure?' *International Journal of Cultural Property* 22: 317–335.

Brodie, Neil. 2015b. 'Why is No One Talking About Libya's Cultural Destruction?' *Near Eastern Archaeology* 78(3): 212–217.
Bruer, Wesley and Alexander Rosen. 2016. 'The Fed's Real-Life Indiana Jones'. *CNN*, 3 June 2016. http://edition.cnn.com/2016/06/03/politics/hsi-indiana-jones-homeland-security-investigations/ (accessed 20 June 2016).
Campbell, Peter B. 2013. 'The Illicit Antiquities Trade as a Transnational Criminal Network: Characterizing and Anticipating Trafficking of Cultural Heritage'. *International Journal of Cultural Property* 20: 113–153.
Casana, Jesse. 2015. 'Satellite Imagery-Based Analysis of Archaeological Looting in Syria'. *Near Eastern Archaeology* 78(3): 142–152.
Chan, Gabrielle. 2014. 'Stolen Indian Statue, Shiva Nataraja, To Go Home During Tony Abbott Visit'. *Guardian*, 5 September 2014.
Chappell, Duncan and Kenneth Polk. 2011. 'Unravelling the "Cordata": Just How Organised is the International Traffic in Cultural Objects?' In *Crime in the Art and Antiquities World: Illegal Trafficking in Cultural Property*, edited by Stefano Manacorda and Duncan Chappell, 99–116. New York: Springer.
Chulov, Martin. 2014. 'How an Arrest in Iraq Revealed Isis's $2bn Jihadist Network'. *Guardian*, 15 June 2014.
Chulov, Martin. 2015. 'A Sledgehammer to Civilisation: Islamic State's War on Culture'. *Guardian*, 7 April 2015.
Cockburn, Patrick. 2014. 'The Destruction of the Idols: Syria's Patrimony at Risk from Extremists'. *Independent*, 11 February 2014.
Cohen, David S. 2014. 'Remarks of Under Secretary for Terrorism and Financial Intelligence David S. Cohen at The Carnegie Endowment For International Peace, "Attacking ISIL's Financial Foundation"'. 23 October 2014. Electronic document, https://www.treasury.gov/press-center/press-releases/Pages/jl2672.aspx (accessed 8 June 2015).
Colla, Elliot. 2015. 'On the Iconoclasm of ISIS'. 5 March 2015. Blog post, http://www.elliottcolla.com/blog/2015/3/5/on-the-iconoclasm-of-isis (accessed 8 June 2015).
Crowcroft, Orlando. 2015. 'ISIS: Islamic State's War on History and the Multimillion Dollar Global Antiquities Trade'. *International Business Times*, 13 April 2015. http://www.ibtimes.co.uk/isis-islamic-states-war-history-multimillion-dollar-global-antiquities-trade-1496177 (accessed 13 June 2015).
Dietzler, Jessica. 2013. 'On "Organized Crime" in the Illicit Antiquities Trade: Moving Beyond the Definitional Debate'. *Trends in Organized Crime* 16: 329–342.
di Lernia, Savino. 2015. 'Save Libyan Archaeology'. *Nature* 517, 29 January 2015: 547–549.
Drennan, Justine. 2014. 'The Black-Market Battleground'. *Foreign Policy*, 17 October 2014. http://foreignpolicy.com/2014/10/17/the-black-market-battleground/ (accessed 8 June 2015).
Edwards, Adam and Peter Gill. 2003. 'After Transnational Organised Crime? The Politics of Public Safety'. In *Transnational Organised Crime: Perspectives on Global Security*, edited by Adam Edwards and Peter Gill, 264–281. London: Routledge.
Elia, Ricardo J. 1993. 'A Seductive and Troubling Work'. *Archaeology* 46(1): 64–69.
FATF. 2015. *Financing of the Terrorist Organisation Islamic State in Iraq and the Levant (ISIL)*. Paris: Financial Action Task Force. http://www.fatf-gafi.org/topics/methodsandtrends/documents/financing-of-terrorist-organisation-isil.html (8 June 2015).
Finckenauer, James. 2011. 'Organised Crime'. In *Oxford Handbook of Crime and Public Policy*, edited by Michael Tonry, 304–324. Oxford: Oxford University Press.
Gibson, McGuire. 1997. 'The Loss of Archaeological Context and the Illegal Trade in Mesopotamian Antiquities'. *Culture Without Context* 1: 6–8.
Gill, David W. J. and Christopher Chippindale. 1993. 'Material and Intellectual Consequences of Esteem for Cycladic Figures'. *American Journal of Archaeology* 97: 601–659.
Hall, John. 2015. 'The ISIS Smugglers Making up to $1million per Item Selling Ancient Antiquities Looted from the Rubble of Syria'. *Daily Mail*, 17 February 2015.
Hardy, Sam. 2014. 'German Media Investigation Does Not Disprove Islamic State Antiquities Trafficking, May Corroborate It and its $36m Income'. Blog post, https://conflictantiquities.wordpress.com/2014/11/28/germany-iraq-syria-islamic-state-antiquities-looting-intelligence-corroboration/ (8 June 2015).
Hladik, Jan. 2013. 'The UNESCO Conventions on the Protection of Cultural Property'. In *Culture and Development: Stop the Illicit Traffic of Cultural Property*, edited by Herman van Hooff, 14–18. Havana: UNESCO.
Howard, Russell D., Jonathan Prohov and Marc Elliott. 2014. 'Opinion: How ISIS Funds Terror Through Black Market Antiquities Trade'. *USNI News*, 27 October 2014. http://news.usni.org/2014/10/27/isis-funds-terror-black-market-antiquities-trade (accessed 8 June 2015).

Jiyad, Sajad. 2015. 'Why is ISIS Destroying Iraq's Cultural Heritage'. *Daily Star*, 10 April 2015.

Jones, Christopher. 2015. 'What Is ISIS' Media Strategy'. 22 April 2015. Blog post, https://gatesofnineveh.wordpress.com/2015/04/22/what-is-isis-media-strategy/ (accessed 8 June 2015).

Keller, Andrew. 2015. 'Documenting ISIL's Antiquities Trafficking: The Looting and Destruction of Iraqi and Syrian Cultural Heritage: What We Know and What Can Be Done'. 29 September 2015. Electronic document, http://www.state.gov/e/eb/rls/rm/2015/247610.htm (accessed 17 November 2016).

Kerry, John. 2014. 'Remarks at Threats to Cultural Heritage in Iraq and Syria Event'. 22 September 2014. Electronic document, http://www.state.gov/secretary/remarks/2014/09/231992.htm (accessed 8 June 2015).

Kila, Joris D. 2015. 'From Crimes Against Art to Crimes Against Cultural Property: New Perspectives and Dimensions in Art Crime'. In *Cultural Property Crime: An Overview and Analysis of Contemporary Perspectives and Trends*, edited by Joris D. Kila and Marc Balcells, 167–205. Leiden: Brill.

Kingsley, Patrick. 2015. 'ISIS Vandalism has Libya Fearing for its Cultural Treasures'. *Observer*, 7 March 2015.

Klein, Rudolf and Theodore Marmor. 2006. 'Reflections on Policy Analysis: Putting it Together Again'. In *Oxford Handbook of Public Policy*, edited by Michael Moran, Martin Rein and Robert E. Goodin, 746–770. Oxford: Oxford University Press.

Lamb, Franklin. 2014. 'Raqqa is Being Slaughtered Silently'. *Scoop*, 10 May 2014. http://www.scoop.co.nz/stories/HL1405/S00084/raqqa-is-being-slaughtered-silently.htm (accessed 13 June 2014).

Levi, Michael. 2003. 'Criminal Asset-Stripping: Confiscating the Proceeds of Crime in England and Wales'. In *Transnational Organised Crime: Perspectives on Global Security*, edited by Adam Edwards and Peter Gill, 212–226. London: Routledge.

Mackenzie, Simon. 2005. *Going, Going, Gone: Regulating the Market in Illicit Antiquities*. Leicester: Institute of Art and Law.

Mackenzie, Simon. 2011. 'The Market as Criminal and Criminals in the Market: Reducing Opportunities for Organised Crime in the International Antiquities Market'. In *Crime in the Art and Antiquities World: Illegal Trafficking in Cultural Property*, edited by Stefano Manacorda and Duncan Chappell, 69–86. New York: Springer.

Mackenzie, Simon and Tess Davis. 2014. 'Temple Looting in Cambodia: Anatomy of a Statue Trafficking Network'. *British Journal of Criminology* 54: 722–740.

Makarenko, Tamara 2012. *Europe's Crime–Terror Nexus: Links Between Terrorist and Organized Crime Groups in the European Union*. Brussels: European Parliament Policy Department C, Citizens' Rights and Constitutional Affairs.

Manacorda, Stefano. 2011. 'Criminal Law Protection of Cultural Heritage: An International Perspective'. In *Crime in the Art and Antiquities World: Illegal Trafficking in Cultural Property*, edited by Stefano Manacorda and Duncan Chappell, 17–50. New York: Springer.

Mashberg, Tom. 2015. 'New York Authorities Seek Custody of Stolen Artifacts Worth Over $100 Million'. *New York Times*, 14 April 2015.

Naím, Moisés. 2007. *Illicit*. London: Arrow.

Naylor, R. Thomas. 2002. *Wages of Crime: Black Markets, Illegal Finance, and the Underworld Economy*. Ithaca, NY: Cornell University Press.

O'Keefe, Patrick. 2007. *Commentary on the 1970 UNESCO Convention*. Leicester: Institute of Art and Law.

O'Keefe, Roger. 2006. *The Protection of Cultural Property in Armed Conflict*. Cambridge: Cambridge University Press.

Planche, Edouard. 2013. 'The 1970 Convention'. In *Culture and Development: Stop the Illicit Traffic of Cultural Property*, edited by Herman van Hooff, 20–22. Havana: UNESCO.

Polk, Kenneth. 2009. 'Whither Criminology in the Study of the Traffic in Illicit Antiquities?' In *Criminology and Archaeology: Studies in Looted Antiquities*, edited by Simon Mackenzie and Penny Green, 13–28. Oxford: Hart.

Prott, Lyndel. 2011. 'Strengths and Weaknesses of the 1970 Convention: An Evaluation 40 Years After its Adoption'. Background paper, http://www.unesco.org/new/fileadmin/MULTIMEDIA/FIELD/Brussels/pdf/strengths%20and%20weaknesses%20of%20the1970%20convention.pdf (accessed 20 June 2016).

Reinl, James. 2015. 'UN Unable to Stop IS Relic-Smuggling from Iraq and Syria'. *Middle East Eye*, 4 June 2015, http://www.middleeasteye.net/news/un-unable-stop-relic-smuggling-iraq-and-syria-2015625246 (accessed 8 June 2015).

Seif, Assad. 2015. 'Illicit Traffic in Cultural Property in Lebanon'. In *Countering Illicit Traffic in Cultural Goods*, edited by France Desmarrais. Paris: ICOM.

Scammell, Rosie. 2015. 'Create UN Military Unit to Protect Ancient Sites from ISIS, says Italy'. *Guardian*, 19 March 2015.

Scherrer, Amandine. 2010. 'International Policy Discourses on Transnational Organised Crime: The Role of International Expertise'. In *Defining and Defying Organised Crime*, edited by Felia Allum, Francesca Longo, Daniela Irrera and Panos A. Kostakos, 55–68. London: Routledge.

Shelley, Louise I. 2014. *Dirty Entanglements: Corruption, Crime and Terrorism*. Cambridge: Cambridge University Press.

Stern, Jessica and J. M. Berger. 2015. *ISIS: The State of Terror*. London: William Collins.

Stone, Peter. 2013. 'A Four-Tier Approach to the Protection of Cultural Property in the Event of Armed Conflict'. *Antiquity* 87: 166–177.

UNESCO. 2011. International Meeting of Experts on the Cultural Heritage of Libya. 21 October 2011. Paris: UNESCO. Electronic document, http://www.unesco.org/new/fileadmin/MULTIMEDIA/FIELD/Brussels/pdf/Recommendations%2021oct-approved-final.pdf (accessed 13 June 2015).

UNESCO. 2013. 'Regional Training on Syrian Cultural Heritage: Addressing the Issue of Illicit Trafficking'. 10–13 February 2013. Amman: UNESCO. Electronic document, http://www.unesco.org/new/fileadmin/MULTIMEDIA/FIELD/Amman/pdf/20130322_Report_Syria_workshop_FINAL_01.pdf (accessed 13 June 2015).

UNESCO. 2014. 'UNESCO Strengthens Action to Safeguard Cultural Heritage Under Attack'. 12 August 2014. Electronic document, http://whc.unesco.org/en/news/1176/ (accessed 13 June 2015).

UNESCO. 2015. 'Operational Guidelines for the Implementation of the Convention on the Means of Prohibiting and Preventing the Illicit Import, Export and Transfer of Ownership of Cultural Property'. Electronic document, http://www.unesco.org/new/fileadmin/MULTIMEDIA/HQ/CLT/pdf/OPERATIONAL_GUIDELINES_EN_FINAL_FINAL.pdf (accessed 13 June 2015).

UN General Assembly. 2015. 'Resolution 69/196'. Adopted by the General Assembly on 18 December 2014. Electronic document, https://www.unodc.org/documents/organized-crime/trafficking_in_cultural/RES-681-86/A_RES_69_196_E.pdf (accessed 13 June 2015).

UN Security Council. 2015. 'Resolution 2199 (2015)'. Electronic document, http://www.securitycouncilreport.org/atf/cf/%7B65BFCF9B-6D27-4E9C-8CD3-CF6E4FF96FF9%7D/s_res_2199.pdf (accessed 13 June 2015).

USA. 2014. 'Terrorist Designations of Groups Operating in Syria'. Press release, US Department of State, 14 May 2014. http://www.state.gov/r/pa/prs/ps/2014/05/226067.htm (accessed 13 June 2015).

Wegener, Corine. 2008. 'Assignment Blue Shield'. In *Antiquities Under Siege: Cultural Heritage Protection After the Iraq War*, edited by Lawrence Rothfield, 163–174. Lanham: AltaMira.

Woodiwiss, Mike. 2003. 'Transnational Organized Crime: The Global Reach of an American Concept'. In *Transnational Organised Crime: Perspectives on Global Security*, edited by Adam Edwards and Peter Gill, 13–27. London: Routledge.

6

A PARADOX OF CULTURAL PROPERTY

NAGPRA and (dis)possession

Susan Benton

> We believe that they have a heart, they have a mind of their own. They're alive.
> They're active. That's how hard we believe in those objects.
> They're the ones that are giving us the opportunity to do our obligations.
>
> *Wilton Kooyahoema[1] (Benton Bruning 2013:265)*

> I wanted a rattle and moccasins.
> And then the collecting bug seized me and I was lost.
>
> *George Gustav Heye[2] (Mason 1958:11)*

Cultural objects compel and inspire. They can empower and engage those who value them as manifestations of long-enduring beliefs. They can intrigue and seduce those who see them as exotic collectibles. Strong and contrasting opinions shape the tumultuous dynamics of claims to cultural property.

What is "cultural property"? What associated rights and obligations should society recognize? It has been argued that the concept of cultural property is inherently paradoxical. "Cultural property is contradictory in the very pairing of its core concepts. Property is fixed, possessed, controlled by its owner, and alienable. Culture is none of those things" (Mezey 2007:2005). Efforts to address cultural property concerns raise complex and often conflicting notions of what objects we value, why we value them, and how they should be dealt with throughout time.

At the largest scale of inquiry, multinational coalitions engage in efforts to articulate and manage humankind's global cultural legacy. The 1954 Hague Convention speaks to the cultural heritage of "every people" as it trumpets a global call for protection of cultural sites and objects during armed conflict (Hague 1954: preamble). The 1970 UNESCO Convention declares that "cultural property constitutes one of the basic elements of civilization and national culture, and that its true value can be appreciated only in relation to the fullest possible information regarding its origin, history and traditional setting." The UNESCO Convention further calls for countries to be "increasingly alive to the moral obligations to respect [their] own cultural heritage and that of all nations" and to manage their collections according to "universally recognized moral principles" (UNESCO 1970: preamble).

While it may be tempting to look for universal values in the search for solutions to dilemmas involving cultural property, no single value system can be articulated and accepted by all stakeholders. The United Nations, despite its use of universalist language, acknowledged in its *2007 Declaration on the Rights of Indigenous Peoples* that Indigenous peoples, while equal to all others, have suffered historical injustices that compel particular attention and redress. Cultural property is one area of concern to which the Declaration speaks:

> Indigenous peoples have the right to practice and revitalize their cultural traditions and customs. This includes the right to maintain, protect and develop the past, present and future manifestations of their cultures, such as archaeological and historical sites, artefacts, designs, ceremonies, technologies and visual and performing arts and literature.
>
> States shall provide redress through effective mechanisms, which may include restitution, developed in conjunction with Indigenous peoples, with respect to their cultural, intellectual, religious and spiritual property taken without their free, prior and informed consent or in violation of their laws, traditions and customs.
>
> *(UN 2007: Article 11)*

The Declaration reflects the culmination of twenty-five years of focus by the United Nations on historical injustices inflicted on Indigenous peoples.[3] Despite its powerful language, however, the Declaration is not a legally binding instrument. Its power only lies in its potential to influence national legislation supportive of Indigenous interests.

In the late twentieth century, the United States enacted legislation seeking to provide a mechanism through which Native American tribes can recover human remains and important cultural items that were removed from their places and peoples of origin without consent. NAGPRA is a leap forward in terms of national efforts to acknowledge some of the myriad traumas and injustices inflicted on Native peoples. At the same time, however, it is constricted by its own language and by the realities of bureaucracy and clashing worldviews that linger and continue to dampen the force of Native voices who seek just resolution of historical wrongs through repossession and control over their cultural legacy.

NAGPRA: A national attempt to address Indigenous cultural dispossession

The Native American Graves Protection and Repatriation Act (NAGPRA) endeavors to redress some of the historical injustices inflicted on the cultural heritage of Indigenous people in the United States. NAGPRA was adopted in 1990, seventeen years prior to the United Nations' adoption of its Declaration. The enactment of NAGPRA followed close to a century of national cultural preservation laws that began in 1906 with the Antiquities Act and include notable legislation such as the 1966 National Historic Preservation Act (NHPA) and the 1979 Archaeological Resources Protection Act (ARPA). The NHPA focuses on the federal government's role in preserving sites and structures with historical value to society in general, while ARPA focuses on the scientific excavation, curation, and study of items, including human remains, characterized as "archaeological resources." In contrast, NAGPRA is the first US law to attempt to place Indigenous priorities explicitly at the forefront of cultural property decision-making, at least as they relate to public collections and Indigenous burial sites.

During most of the twentieth century, archaeological concerns took precedence in developing laws and policies affecting the excavation of burials and the collection of Native American objects. The research community valued Native American cultural objects in large part for what they might tell non-Native people about the country's pre-contact past. Remains and objects were to be preserved and kept available indefinitely for study in order to educate the larger populace about Native cultures. Traditional Western policies toward historic preservation and curation did not accommodate conflicting Indigenous practices, such as those intending some objects, such as Yup'ik masks or Zuni *Ahayu:da* (war gods), to succumb to the natural elements (Dubin 2001:30–31).

Increasing contact between Native and non-Native people spurred marketplace demand for items from Native cultures. Although some objects began to be mass-produced in response to the collecting hunger of the early marketplace, demand also continued for rare, "authentic" collectibles. The Indian Arts and Crafts Act was enacted in the early twentieth century to focus on authenticity; it required that objects held out as Native-American must have been created by a Native American craftsperson. One of the goals of this legislation was to stimulate and protect the market for authentic Indian-made objects and stop non-Native made material being passed off as Native (Dubin 2001:31). As was often the case throughout the larger arts marketplace, however, questions about authenticity were of ongoing interest to the collecting world, which wanted items "made by Indians," preferably reflecting pre-contact, ritual, or cultural practices, while questions about the appropriateness of the items' sources, such as burials or sacred sites, were rarely raised. In the last decades of the twentieth century, many stakeholders, including Indigenous communities, museums, scholars, and others, increasingly voiced concerns about larger historical, legal, political, and cultural contexts from which objects have been allowed to circulate through the marketplace and make their way into public and private collections (Greenfield 1995:xiii).

Perspectives about the legal, ethical, and moral appropriateness of excavating, studying, collecting, and displaying cultural objects vary widely among present-day peoples who prioritize their values in different ways. Heritage laws in the United States have evolved in ways that only partially address the variability of heritage values held by constituent groups: repatriation versus preservation; confidentiality versus shared knowledge; ownership versus custodianship. Notable cultural property disputes in other contexts, such as those surrounding the removal of the Parthenon ("Elgin") Marbles from Greece,[4] highlight the intensity and, at times, intransigence of those on contrary sides of struggles to control the fates of ancient objects. As legal structures and opinions pertaining to the protection and management of cultural heritage continue to evolve, we continue to face daunting challenges in our efforts to establish social priorities and strike balances among those with conflicting value systems.

It is important to understand the scope and limitations of NAGPRA's role in mediating interests in cultural items. NAGPRA is United States federal legislation applicable nationwide to Native American human remains, funerary objects, sacred objects, and objects of cultural patrimony – as defined in the law – that are held in federally funded institutions or removed from federal or tribal lands since the statute's enactment. It does not apply to all Native American cultural objects, and it requires federal recognition for an Indigenous group to have decision-making authority about such objects or about human remains with which it may claim affiliation. NAGPRA imposes certain processes, such as mandated consultation, by which decisions must be made to resolve the disposition status of the human remains and cultural items at issue.

NAGPRA mandates that museums and federal agencies, in consultation with federally recognized Native American tribes, assess the cultural identities of Indigenous groups and the extent to which they relate to earlier groups from which human remains and other cultural objects derive. This mandate triggered widespread interest and focus on questions about the nature of archaeological research and its impacts on Native American descendant groups.[5] The prompt explosion of literature on the relations between archaeologists and Native Americans in the repatriation era confirms the imperative for the archaeological community to involve itself proactively in the ongoing debates involving cultural affiliation. One group of archaeologists declared that "[t]he nature of archaeology in the twenty-first century depends on the outcome of debates currently raging in the discipline, as 'people without history' strive to reclaim their pasts" (McIntosh et al. 1996).

The enactment of NAGPRA was a watershed event in the history of Americanist archaeology (Lovis et al. 2004). By bringing together archaeologists, curators, and Native American groups – at times solely through the force of law – and by reallocating rights and obligations pertaining to large swaths of the archaeological record, NAGPRA has profoundly reshaped the ways in which scholars, descendant communities, and the public access, research, interpret, and manage the material remains of the American past (Ferguson et al. 2000). NAGPRA's forced consultations and reallocations of decision-making authority triggered collisions of archaeological and Native American approaches to articulating cultural identities and acknowledging connections between present and past peoples (Thomas 2000). Yet in the wake of NAGPRA's mandated consultations and negotiations, some stakeholders have been finding ways to transcend their differences and willingly pursue collaborative research efforts. Such efforts are reshaping theoretical and methodological approaches to exploring and interpreting aspects of the human past (Mills et al. 2008). The growth of archaeological practices that are informed by Indigenous perspectives and interests reflects important changes in why and how scholarly research is conducted in this realm.[6]

NAGPRA is also seen by many as important human rights legislation that provides Native American peoples with voice and power previously unavailable to them as they seek to care for their ancestors and for sacred and ceremonial objects. The displacement of people and objects over the centuries since European arrival has been immense, playing out through forced relocation, excavation of graves, removal of bodies from battlefields for scientific research, and collection of objects. NAGPRA provides important, albeit limited, power for Native American groups to shift control and apply their own value systems to decisions about how graves, human remains, and important cultural items are cared for.

Since NAGPRA's enactment, many positive relationships have been forged between archaeologists and tribes as a result of the increased number of collaborations (Swidler et al. 1997; Zimmerman et al. 2003). At the same time, scholarly and public debates have continued about the validity and importance of competing interests related to the scientific study of human remains and culturally sensitive objects. A rich mosaic of publications has explored various perspectives on archaeologist–tribal relations and the handling of human remains.[7]

Scientific, tribal, and other approaches to understanding cultural links to the past are reflected in the diversity of ways that people assert control over the material remains of the past. None of these diverse viewpoints will necessarily find its direct correlative in NAGPRA. The statute's purpose in assessing cultural affiliation is limited to its goal of resolving the particular matters addressed by the statute itself. It does not endeavor to explain links between the present and the past in terms that satisfy Native American or scientific views; instead, NAGPRA establishes processes to resolve claims for control over particular Native American remains and cultural items.

From a legal standpoint, NAGPRA has reshaped rights and liabilities of the scientific and cultural communities by empowering certain Native American groups to take primacy in decision-making authority over the fate of human remains and cultural items in museum, agency, and university collections. It recasts ideas about evidence admissible in court by allowing consideration of information that might appear to fall outside the rules related to hearsay, such as oral tradition and folklore,[8] and to allow people to be qualified in court as experts who may not hold the traditional educational credentials often expected by the legal system.

NAGPRA has also turned some ideas about scientific freedom on their head in some significant respects. Prior to the twentieth century, researchers and explorers throughout the United States effectively had free rein to excavate, study, and build collections of Native American human remains and items. Throughout the twentieth century, the United States had laws in place that have generally favored the interests of the scholarly community, supporting the excavation, investigation, study, collection, interpretation, and curation of cultural objects. Scholars often pursued those interests with total or significant disregard of the perspectives or wishes of descendant communities. NAGPRA restructured the power dynamics between Native Americans and archaeologists, by decreasing the volume of materials available for research while simultaneously increasing the level of interaction between these groups.

NAGPRA in action

A legal tool designed to resolve some conflicts can perform like a scalpel, precisely targeting the problem area and removing the source of pain. However, when designed with an eye to resolving deep cultural conflicts, such as those embedded in repatriation, a legal tool may, instead, feel like bludgeon. In practice, NAGPRA has led to the return of thousands of Native American human remains and cultural items. Some tribes and institutions have developed innovative, collaborative curation methodologies for many more that remain in public collections. Yet deep concerns remain, and the repatriation journey is far from complete. Amid the flurry of publications, formal notices, and public debates, the voices of Native American individuals dealing with the actual business of repatriation have often gone unheard. Beyond the boundaries of the law's definitions, directives, and processes, Native American individuals and communities experience the realities of trying to find, identify, and resolve the fates of their ancestors and valued objects. For instance, just locating ancestors across the vast museum/university matrix offers one daunting challenge; negotiating for their return presents another.

NAGPRA's repatriation process, as set forth in the law, begins with an institutional inventory of cultural items in curation and ends with the transfer of possession or control to a culturally affiliated Indian tribe. The formal process, however, represents a limited stretch of road on a much longer journey for tribes. Tribal members involved in issues of repatriation struggle with the realities that led to institutional curation of the remains of their ancestors and valued cultural objects. They confront the difficult emotional and cultural challenges involved in the identification and consultation process, when they must discuss and analyze details of how human remains and burial items came to be removed from their resting places, studied by scientists, displayed as art objects, sold on the marketplace as collectibles, and stored in boxes on basement shelves. They witness their sacred objects being handled in ways that are anathema to their religious beliefs.

When items are ultimately identified as culturally affiliated with a tribe, tribal representatives face additional cultural and personal hurdles: determining and carrying out appropriate disposition decisions for the items. Conversations with Native American experts who have taken on the responsibility of dealing with repatriation have revealed a complex mosaic of issues that touch the communities and individuals involved. Theresa Pasqual, former director of the Acoma Historic Preservation Office, noted that complicated realities underpin legal efforts to resolve historical injustices:

> Okay, here's an institution, here's a research facility. Do the inventory, do the documents, this is the process to follow. . . . We have to move them through the NAGPRA process, but we've never addressed those underlying issues of what got those remains there . . . We have to start looking at these other problems, and how to start addressing those underlying issues.
>
> *(Benton Bruning 2013:263).*

Ms. Pasqual's comment highlights the distinction between dealing with physical remains and objects themselves, which NAGPRA addresses, and dealing with the difficult historical realities that led to the disturbance of burials and the removal of individuals and sacred objects for purposes contrary to the deepest interests of their communities. NAGPRA is not designed to tackle the many wrenching underlying questions of how such items came to be treated as appropriate for purchase and collection. Much of the international arts marketplace continues to ignore or deny the legitimacy of such questions; collectors still seek rare objects deriving from "exotic" origins.[9] In recent years, several art auctions held in Paris, France, have sold important cultural items taken from tribal communities in the US. The items, considered sacred deities to their origin communities, were sold as Katsina "masks" over the passionate and public objections of tribal representatives and other supporters prior to and at the auctions.

The scientific community has also wrestled with challenges to its claim of authority to study human remains, as reflected in the protracted lawsuit by scientists against the US government over control of ancient remains known as "Kennewick Man." The scientists asserted, and the court agreed, that evidence was insufficient to legally prove the Native American ancestry of the remains for purposes of applying NAGPRA.[10] The Kennewick Man case highlighted the difficulties of drafting laws and regulations that clearly and adequately address the rights and obligations of all parties involved.

Debates triggered by NAGPRA reach beyond its legal confines to many different legal, political, and philosophical realms. Perhaps changes should be made to clarify or modify the statute or its regulations, to more accurately interpret or implement those provisions, or to bring public expectations into better alignment with the law. David Hurst Thomas summed things up concisely: "NAGPRA remains a very murky piece of legislation, and clarifying it will be a bumpy political process" (Thomas 2000:275).

What is in store for those continuing their engagement with NAGPRA? Disputes still rage and differing worldviews continue to clash as parties debate notions of rights, responsibilities, ownership, and stewardship. NAGPRA addresses specific issues and processes, but it cannot resolve all the substantive and emotional tensions that stretch well beyond the four corners of the legislation, tensions involving larger issues of cultural autonomy, civil rights, human rights, and sovereignty. NAGPRA is not a panacea for the myriad concerns of Indigenous peoples, scholars, and the public relating to protection, study, access, and control over Native American cultural objects. Perhaps it is at least a step toward greater autonomy for Native Americans seeking to assert their own value systems in the caretaking of cultural objects.

Key concepts in the law

A few important concepts lie at the crux of many debates about the benefits and detriments of NAGPRA. Definitions of "sacred object," "cultural patrimony," and "cultural affiliation" create a means to systematize determinations of which items qualify for repatriation and which groups qualify to claim them. At the same time, the definitions create tensions due to varying understandings and beliefs about what constitutes sacredness, cultural importance, and group relatedness. In an effort to delineate situations where repatriation is mandated, the law provides definitions that have proven to be problematic both in identifying which items qualify for repatriation and who is entitled to claim control over them.

The requirement that a tribe "prove" that a cultural item qualifies for repatriation raises concerns about the proprietary nature of certain knowledge. Disclosure of culturally sensitive information can sever the link between information and its value to the community. Only through the control of certain knowledge elements by particular individuals or groups does some traditional knowledge maintain its vitality as an active asset of the community. By requiring disclosure of the bases upon which an object meets the definition of "sacred" or "patrimony," NAGPRA arguably presses Indigenous groups to violate their own values by requiring them to "make their case" through disclosure of information that will allow outsiders to determine whether they will recognize their NAGPRA-based claims and acknowledge their shared identity with human remains and cultural items at issue. As explained by Octavius Seowtewa, leader of the Galaxy Medicine Society at Zuni,

> A lot of problems stem from giving esoteric information about who we really are. Some of that information has been used against the tribes. Some of that information was not supposed to have been given out. Some of this information is putting tribes against each other, and that is one of the few things that need to be changed in NAGPRA.
>
> *(Benton Bruning 2013:246).*

As the law was being drafted, concerns about access to culturally sensitive information led to a change in language that reduced the NAGPRA Review Committee's right of access to such information from "full and free"[11] to "reasonable."[12] Left unanswered, however, is the question of what is "reasonable" and whose judgement should prevail in making such a decision.

Complexities involving claims for sacred objects and objects of cultural patrimony extend beyond issues of confidentiality. Determining sacredness for NAGPRA's purpose is fraught with concerns about proof. The law requires analysis of whether the objects were, and still are, necessary for use by traditional religious leaders. Debates continue over which parties should be recognized as proper authorities to speak to this designation. As noted by Mr. Seowtewa in his comment expressing concern about the negative impacts that may result from disclosure of esoteric information, many Native Americans have expressed concerns about having to reveal confidential information to outsiders in order to "prove" the sacredness of objects. Claims for objects on the basis of cultural patrimony involve questions of whether objects were owned individually or communally when first transferred from tribal hands and whether the transferor had tribal authority to act on behalf of the group. Culturally diverse concepts of property ownership and custodianship, and questions about rights and obligations associated with possession, have led to debates over whether, for example, a Navajo singer's widow had proper authority to sell ritual objects,[13] or whether the sale of masks by individual members of the White Mountain Apache tribe in the early twentieth century should ever be considered voluntary in light of the pervasiveness of harsh conditions under which the Apache people were living at the time (NAGPRA Review Committee 2006). Again, questions about how collections came to be made, and the very difficult conditions that led to significant cultural items leaving communities, remain outside the purview of NAGPRA. Like many pieces of legislation however, these 'pre' issues often return and are embedded in the very negotiations themselves. NAGPRA triggers discussions about rights of possession but leaves open the means by which tribal claimants must prove their claims.

Under NAGPRA, an Indian tribe or Native Hawaiian organization with the closest cultural affiliation to an item is entitled to control its ultimate disposition. Cultural affiliation is defined as "a relationship of shared group identity which can be *reasonably traced* historically or prehistorically between a present day Indian tribe or Native Hawaiian organization and an identifiable earlier group." In order to prove a claim of cultural affiliation, the statute identifies a wide range of acceptable evidence – geography, biology, archaeology, anthropology, linguistics, kinship, folklore, oral tradition, and history – as well as "other relevant information or expert opinion" (NAGPRA Section 7(a)(4)). Once cultural affiliation is determined, the affiliated group is empowered to determine what disposition is appropriate for the item, be it return to the claimant group, ongoing curation, reburial, or otherwise.

Yet again, there are complexities embedded in legal mandates to "reasonably trace" relationships between present-day peoples and past groups. This mandate invokes concepts of identity anchored in the past and continuing into the present. It also reaffirms tensions embedded within the larger recognition process, in that only federally recognized tribes can make use and make claims under NAGPRA. This leaves non-federally recognized tribes without a legal means of redress for their similarly situated ancestors and items of cultural significance.

Group identity is a cultural construct, a conceptualization shared by those within the group who, by the nature of their particular perspectives, see themselves as connected to each other in a culturally distinct manner from those outside the group. Because of federal conditions for formal recognition, group identity has also become a legal construct. In order to operationalize a group's identity when dealing in contexts such as NAGPRA's consultation and repatriation processes, non-Native stakeholders, such as museums, universities and federal agencies, must accept that group's assertion of identity. Perspectives about shared group identities may connect one contemporary group to the past as well as to other contemporary groups through shared conceptions of ancestry. This can complicate NAGPRA's implementation, which assumes one affiliated or "most closely affiliated" tribe.[14]

Indigenous perspectives of identity and affiliation may hinge on ancestral relationships to a place or a landscape, shared symbolic systems, paradigms of explanation about origins and migrations, and other factors. Shared group identity is not a precisely constituted concept, but is rather a bundle of concepts and understandings that includes a plethora of meaningful social elements such as traditional knowledge, landscapes, specific places, histories, material objects, lineage ties, and symbolic representations. NAGPRA has little room to take in this complex of social considerations and relationships around cultural materials that are the very subject of this law.

Legislative history: Negotiation and compromise

Prior to NAGPRA's passage, tribal representatives and scholars from across the nation testified to Congress about the need for federal legislation to combat two primary concerns. The first was the continued excavation of Indigenous graves, driven by disparate motives such as scholarly research, a vocational interest in discovering artifacts, or looting of objects to satisfy a market hungry for ancient and authentic Native American goods. The second was the vast number of Native American human remains accumulated in institutional collections, many of which came from legally sanctioned excavations or removals.

This testimony and related efforts triggered calls for legislation to provide a mechanism for the return of the remains and related funerary objects to tribal descendants (Senate Report

1990:3). The 1868 Surgeon General's order to Army field officers to collect and send Indian skeletons to Washington, DC for scientific study is a notorious example of the type of action that contributed to the growth of some institutional collections (House Report 1990:9). The Senate Select Committee on Indian Affairs commiserated with tribal leaders who expressed concerns that museums and federal agencies had not historically conducted meaningful inquiry into the circumstances by which donors or sellers had acquired items. Concern over the continued growth of a black market trade in Native American funerary and ceremonial objects also played a part in Congress's decision to support the law (Senate Report 1990:5).

A few notable events in the complex history preceding NAGPRA's enactment help illustrate the impetus for its ultimate passage. In the 1970s, following negotiations over the return of several skulls of Modoc tribal members to their descendants, the Smithsonian Institution adopted its first departmental policy on repatriation. That policy authorized the Institution to return named individuals to their identifiable descendants. In the 1980s, the policy was expanded to allow for repatriation of human remains and associated funerary objects "that could be culturally linked to extant Native American groups, going well beyond descendants of named individuals" (Ortner 1994:12). Those efforts culminated in the passage of the National Museum of the American Indian Act of 1989, which continues to govern the Smithsonian's repatriation obligations and played a significant role in paving the way for NAGPRA's enactment one year later. The separate governance of the Smithsonian's repatriation activities under the NMAIA, however, has been the subject of some criticism, in part due to the lack of a requirement to report its activities to Congress (GAO Report 2011:27) and the lack of an appeals process for the Institution's decisions about cultural affiliation (GAO Report 2011:29).

NAGPRA's passage was also preceded by intensive efforts to explore and understand the balance of interests at stake in handling Native American human remains and objects. In 1988, the Senate Select Committee on Indian Affairs conducted a hearing on possible legislation to establish a repatriation process for human remains. Action was postponed in acquiescence to several witness requests that museums and Native American communities first have the opportunity to discuss the subject (House Report 1989:13). In 1989, the Heard Museum in Phoenix, Arizona, hosted a year-long dialogue on museum–Native American relationships. The resulting report, issued on February 28, 1990, still failed to take decisive action on resolving the fate of human remains in collections, reflecting that these issues were far from resolved when the law was enacted. Nonetheless, the report expressly acknowledged the legitimate interests of all stakeholders and called for legislation respecting Native American human rights while also valuing scientific study and education (House Report 1989:14):

> The panel recommended that all resolutions be governed by respect for the human rights of Native Americans and the value of scientific study and education. The majority believed that "Respect for Native human rights is the paramount principle that should govern resolution of the issue when a claim is made . . . " The Panel was split on what to do about human remains which are not culturally identifiable. Some maintained that a system should be developed for repatriation while others believed that the scientific and educational needs should predominate. The report strongly supported dialogue between museums and Indian tribes during all aspects of both the acquisition of sensitive materials, and repatriation requests. The Panel concluded that Federal legislation on this matter was needed; the panel itself was unable to reach consensus on how to address this challenging issue.

Despite the urging of the 1989 Heard Museum panel in its call for federal legislation, Congress did not establish a process in the statute for addressing culturally unidentifiable remains. Instead, it delegated to the NAGPRA Review Committee the responsibility for "compiling an inventory of culturally unidentifiable human remains that are in the possession or control of each Federal agency and museum and recommending specific actions for developing a process for such remains" (NAGPRA Section 8(c)(5)). It took twenty years for regulations to be adopted relating to the disposition of culturally unidentifiable human remains (NAGPRA Regulations 10.11) and the resulting regulations, effective as of May 14, 2010, were hotly debated and challenged in various ways by various stakeholders, as parties argued for the prompt burial of all curated remains while others advocated ongoing research, some of whom wanted to pursue cultural affiliation ties and others of whom wanted to continue pursuing other research goals. It has been argued that "the new rule effectively undermines NAGPRA's core principles. By treating culturally unaffiliated remains as one monolithic category, the new rule discounts Native American rights, mistreats remains, and disenfranchises Native American groups from controlling their own cultural identities" (Birkhold 2011:2048). Other perspectives see the designation of remains as "unidentifiable" as a way for institutions to justify holding onto their collections (see Gould this volume).

Amid strong opinions and protracted debates, many stakeholders in the tribal, museum, and scientific communities did work diligently to achieve legislation that, even if not perfect, would be acceptable to a broad spectrum of stakeholders. It is a complicated matter to develop broadly acceptable protocols and processes for accessing, controlling, and managing interests in important cultural objects such as those subject to NAGPRA, particularly when parties hold radically different and often conflicting worldviews about such matters. Earlier legislation did little to encourage substantive negotiation over the control and ownership of cultural objects. With the advent of NAGPRA, the negotiating table was set, and, like it or not, the parties were required to sit together and work through the delineated process. Many have found the process to be complicated, time-consuming, financially draining, and conceptually challenging. Although NAGPRA's passage was applauded by many as a historic step forward in redressing wrongs inflicted on Indigenous peoples of the US, the law has also been challenged as a mandated process rife with financial, administrative, and cultural difficulties, with the hardships largely falling upon Native peoples.

As repatriation efforts have unfolded, Native American participants have been starkly "reminded of the nature of our existence within the American political landscape … A Native American person who wishes to work in repatriation frequently walks a tightrope between what she believes to be true and what she can demonstrate archaeologically" (Lippert 2008: 120–121; Gould this volume). Tensions created by the dissonance between knowledge systems and processes is an undeniable aspect of the important work of repatriation, particularly for Native American scholars who seek to co-exist amid clashing worldviews about involvement with, and investigation of, Indigenous culture as well as the place of history within legislative intentions.

The historical realities leading to NAGPRA's enactment have very deep roots, reaching back to the earliest days of contact between Indigenous peoples and Europeans. It is impossible to ignore those realities, colonial violence, and cultural wounds suffered over the course of close to 500 years of interaction. Exacerbating the situation are inconsistencies and conflicting values reflected in laws and policies as developed and amended over time. NAGPRA re-opened this past in explicit ways, and some argue that it is a necessary part of the healing process. Its requirements that tribes demonstrate the importance of objects according to legal definitions and provide evidence that they can "reasonably" trace identity connections create tensions that fold into the complex process of repatriation. This is because what might be culturally important does not necessarily correspond to the categorical terms as articulated in legislative definitions. Standards established and justified under Western legal and scientific viewpoints as the *a priori* point of departure can produce immense burdens for tribes seeking to satisfy those standards in order to recover their ancestors and sacred objects.

Despite the many challenges involved in assessing cultural affiliation, museums, universities, and tribes across the country continue to explore innovative and diverse ways of managing and caring for culturally sensitive objects. For example, the Smithsonian Institution's National Museum of Natural History has developed a "Traditional Care Policy Statement" to assist tribes and curators in developing appropriate procedures for storing and treating sensitive items that remain curated at the museum (NMNH 2005).

There are several examples of museums working with Indigenous groups to build ongoing relationships stemming from their initial interactions under NAGPRA and working together to rethink the role of the museum as a place where Indigenous voices and perspectives can be experienced. Emily Moore, in her article "Propatriation: Possibilities for Art after NAGPRA," highlights Harvard's Peabody Museum, which, for close to a century, had displayed a Tlingit totem pole that had been taken from a village in 1899. After the Peabody returned the totem pole pursuant to a claim under NAGPRA, Tlingit peoples gave the museum a cedar log to enable it to commission a new pole to be carved by a Tlingit master carver, Nathan Jackson. Tlingit members dedicated the new pole at a commemorative event held at the museum in 2001 (Moore 2010). In recent years, the American Museum of Natural History has collaborated with various tribes in an effort to enable them to reconnect with objects and to include tribal perspectives in the development of related curation and exhibition policies (Graham and Murphy 2010).

Legal definitions and mandated consultations, while created in a good faith effort to pursue laudable goals, often fall far short of enabling Native American stakeholders to truly resolve concerns about the appropriate disposition of important cultural items. Continuing debates over whether human remains are Native American, whether objects are sacred or of shared group significance, and whether tribes share identities with earlier groups all emphasize the inherent difficulties involved in efforts to reach agreement about such matters. However, these debates can find new points of clarification when efforts towards better understanding continue, as the more recent scholarship affirming the Native American origin of the Kennewick Man has revealed (see Meltzer 2015).

Indigenous perspectives

During in-depth discussions with cultural resource advisors from Acoma, Hopi, and Zuni Pueblos as part of my dissertation research (Benton Bruning 2013), Pueblo representatives discussed their experiences with and perspectives about NAGPRA. These discussions further developed conversations begun during an earlier multi-year collaborative project involving potential connections of these communities to a site known as Chaves-Hummingbird Pueblo in the Rio Puerco Valley of central New Mexico (Adler and Benton Bruning 2007), where NAGPRA concepts informed the dialog about cultural affiliation.

In our discussions, the most pressing NAGPRA issues identified by the advisors were the power of definitions, institutional inconsistencies in carrying out NAGPRA's processes, resource limitations, unexpected complications, and emotional impacts on tribal representatives involved in carrying out NAGPRA on behalf of their communities. The balance of this chapter addresses these perspectives.

The power of definitions

Any single description of what makes an object sacred, given the multitude of belief systems and practices, will fail to include many objects considered sacred by many tribal peoples. Determining whether an object should be recognized as sacred within the meaning of the law is a difficult process. NAGPRA's definition sets limits on what will be recognized as sacred for repatriation purposes, but this does not necessarily conform to the views of tribal members who are responsible for caring for objects of spiritual importance. The legal definition only includes ceremonial objects that are currently needed by traditional religious leaders to carry out their religious practices. This definition thus excludes objects that are not created for ceremonial use and objects that once may have been used ceremonially but are no longer needed in that capacity, whether or not they continue to have ongoing sacredness to the community from which they derive.

The definition of "cultural patrimony" also creates concern and confusion, with its presumption that objects considered to be culturally significant at a group level must, therefore, be group "owned" rather than the property of an individual. The concept of private property in US law, which presumes that the individual owner has the unrestricted right to dispose of an object, does not necessarily correlate with tribal understandings of ownership and stewardship of culturally important objects.

Octavius Seowtewa, a cultural resources expert from Zuni Pueblo, illustrated the challenge of conveying the sometimes-complex nature of a tribe's relationship with a cultural item, which transcends mere questions of property ownership:

> There is a kilt in the Brooklyn Museum. It stated that, "the individual dancer came up to me and gave me this kilt after the performance show." This is not true. The right information is that the item is a sacred object used in a ceremony; it belongs to an individual but it can be borrowed from a family member or another kiva group to be used in a ceremony. It is an item of cultural patrimony, right? It belongs to an individual but it can be used by a group as a whole. That's where cultural patrimony needs to be re-defined. Because this one little example would make it harder for the legal experts to really define true ownership. I do own something, but my nephews can come in and borrow it. Or some people that I don't even know; if they know that I have something they can use for dances, they can come in and borrow it. . . . There are different avenues to cultural patrimony.
>
> *(Benton Bruning 2013:228)*

The definition of "cultural affiliation" is broadly worded and can include many ways of describing how groups share a traceable identity through time and space. The scope of inclusion – for instance which groups are related to other groups – can be the subject of much debate when parties involved disagree and seek to sway others to agree with their particular interpretation. Mr. Seowtewa reflected on the struggles to interpret defined terms in the law:

> If the definitions of things were simplified, it would make it a lot easier for ordinary people, especially the traditional leaders. We didn't have the luxury of going to law school; we don't understand the "whereas" and all that. If it were simplified with regular language that traditional leaders could understand, it would be beneficial. With NAGPRA, every year it seems like it's getting harder to read, because the

> intent has been manipulated to suit individuals. It's not – the way I look at it, it's not helping the tribes' dealings with federal agencies. It's getting to be a lot harder, just trying to identify items of cultural patrimony, sacred items, cultural affiliation. All these have to be dealt with just for one little item. If the wording is not right and if it is something that we hold dear or sacred to us, we can't get it back, because we didn't know how to apply it. They're trying to get more information about why we hold it sacred.
>
> *(Benton Bruning 2013:230)*

It can be daunting for tribal representatives to effectively discuss important cultural matters within the confines of mandated NAGPRA definitions. Tribes have their own understandings about their historical relatedness to other tribes. This manifests in cultural details such as ceremonial practices but also manifests in temporal details connecting people to places over time. It is a matter of time as well as place; an assessment of aboriginal land occupancy for the purposes of assessing cultural affiliation should always include an analysis of which tribal group(s) arrived at a place and departed from a place at which time(s). However, NAGPRA processes often focus on geographical connections without sufficient regard to the timeframes during which various groups engaged with a particular area. Thus, there is a concern that all groups who interacted within a geographical location may be treated as sharing cultural affiliation with cultural items found at that place, regardless of when a particular group may have arrived or departed. This concern arose notably during multi-tribal consultations about affiliation with Chaco Canyon in New Mexico, which is an immensely important cultural site for many Indigenous groups in the American Southwest.[15]

Institutional inconsistencies

The customized approaches developed by different institutions to carry out their repatriation responsibilities create difficulties for tribes seeking to work effectively to carry out their overarching goals. Each consultation process is unique and can raise new challenges. Issues discussed and resolved with one institution must be addressed from the beginning again when the conversation moves to another institution. It can take extensive time, effort, and resources to work on a tribe-by-tribe basis to examine and discuss cultural items. However, trying to shortcut that process can do a great disservice to individual tribes who may wish to analyze and discuss their views with the institution privately, rather than, for example, being asked to participate in group meetings in an effort to expedite the process, as happened in the Chaco Canyon affiliation process. Collections vary in scale, scope, and complexity. Consequently, the consultation process may vary as well, with different collections requiring different levels of engagement between tribal and institutional representatives.

Tribal representatives thus must navigate the complexities of each institution's customized approach to analyzing cultural items and assessing potential cultural affiliation. Because NAGPRA empowers institutions, not tribes, to make the initial determinations about cultural affiliation, the justifications for these determinations will vary from institution to institution. This process places tribes in a challenging position of having to respond to the methodologies and conclusions of others, rather than establishing their own bases for consultation and cultural affiliation determinations.

All parties involved with NAGPRA have had to learn how to consult with each other effectively. Over time, many institutions have honed their approaches and customized the ways that they work with individual tribes. The time and effort it takes to do effective inventories and consultations are also considerable. The complex realities of establishing and carrying out processes for returning objects to tribes became apparent as institutions and tribes began the actual process of researching and documenting collections, developing appropriate and effective means of communicating with each other, and learning about ways in which objects are valued in different contexts.

Pressure to complete the NAGPRA process heated up as the National NAGPRA Office began acting on the penalties provision of NAGPRA and assessing civil penalties against museums found to have failed to comply with their consultation and inventory obligations. The impact on tribes of the threat of penalties against museums has been two-fold: it can be beneficial to press institutions to carry out their responsibilities without undue delay, while it can be detrimental if museums rush through the process for the sake of completion (and avoidance of civil penalties), rather than continuing efforts to work with tribes in a thorough manner that respects the timing needs of tribal representatives and leaders as they find the best ways of addressing repatriation within their communities.

For many tribes, the reburial of human remains stands apart from other aspects of repatriation. Attempts to resolve all aspects of repatriation during a single phase of consultation have led to consternation among tribal consultants, who often focused on reburial as the most pressing matter to deal with. Discussions about whether objects qualified as sacred or cultural patrimony, while of high importance to tribes, often were delayed while tribal representatives focused their available time, energy, and resources on efforts to secure reburial of ancestors. The unique bundle of emotional, cultural, and political concerns involved in tribal efforts to deal with the concept and realities of curated human remains requires its own time and space for resolution and healing; NAGPRA's processes seem ill-suited to address those needs.

While great efforts have been made and continue to be made to resolve the fates of human remains identified as ancestral to contemporary groups, contentious debates have flared over the concept of "culturally unidentifiable" human remains. Remains have been designated as culturally unidentifiable because of a lack of accepted evidence demonstrating shared group identity with a present-day, federally recognized tribal group. The idea of any human remains being designated as "unidentifiable" suggests that no amount of effort can result in the identification of a cultural group to which such remains are related, despite the reality that the designation might be due to a lack of federal recognition or the inability of tribal representatives to pursue full consultation with all the institutions holding human remains given their limited time and funding for these tasks.

To further complicate matters, the Department of the Interior adopted regulations setting deadlines by which institutions were required to assemble a list of culturally unidentifiable human remains and provide that list to the National NAGPRA Office for inclusion on a public database, which then became subject to new disposition processes established under NAGPRA regulations adopted long after enactment of the original legislation. As a result, human remains that, given more time and effort, might be identified as related to a particular cultural group are at risk of being handled as unidentifiable and removed from the possibility of later tribal affiliation if disposition under the regulatory scheme occurs before there is an opportunity to make such an identification.

Resource limitations

Every step in the NAGPRA process takes effort, time, and resources. Tribes, like institutions, must allocate human and financial resources to enable them to participate in each phase of the repatriation process, which involves preparing and reviewing inventories, coordinating and carrying out consultations, traveling to institutions to assess remains and items, and carrying out actual repatriation to the tribes. The National NAGPRA program provides grants to assist with some aspects of repatriation, but the reality of what is needed to participate fully and effectively in the repatriation process is daunting. There has been widespread concern about the lack of resources available to assist parties in carrying out the letter and spirit of the law. During a 2009 congressional hearing on the status of NAGPRA's implementation, representatives of tribal, institutional, and organizational groups involved in repatriation sent a resounding message to Congress highlighting the disparity between resources and ongoing needs.

Staffing at tribal offices is an ongoing dilemma due to lack of funds. As noted by Octavius Seowtewa, "Some of the paperwork piles up until it comes to a point where 'It's too late now'" (Benton Bruning 2013:252). Theresa Pasqual lamented the effect of funding limitations on the Acoma tribe's ability to engage in NAGPRA's process: "You want them to be part of the process, but you're not increasing the funding, so you're still putting them at a disadvantage and they can't participate in the process" (Benton Bruning 2013:253). When agreement on repatriation is reached, time and expense is involved to appropriately prepare items for their return, travel with them, and complete repatriation ceremonies. Tribes, museums, and the National NAGPRA Review Committee have all called for more funding to assist with NAGPRA.

Unexpected complications

As part of now-defunct museum preservation protocols, some cultural objects have been treated with arsenic or other toxic substances while in curation in an effort to preserve and protect them from pest infestation. The handling of contaminated objects and re-introducing them into communities through repatriation has created unanticipated danger for tribal members. The National Park Service has warned that "[t]he potential for pesticide residue remaining on collection objects is very high. Objects with such residues pose a health risk to curatorial staff and to the public. . . . " (NPS 2001). When speaking about this complication, Leigh Kuwanwisiwma, head of the Hopi Cultural Preservation Office, lamented that the Arizona Poison Control Center once argued that a heavily contaminated Katsina figure should not be brought back to the reservation, creating a conundrum for those charged with the responsibility to care for their people and their objects. "[P]art of the problem is, we don't know how to dispose of them. To throw it away would be like giving a death penalty to a fellow brother" (Fausset 2002).

Emotional impacts

Repatriation is, at one level, a legally mandated administrative process by which the possession and control of objects are transferred back into tribal hands. At another level, it is a legal mandate that can potentially disrupt the professional lives of archaeologists and museum professionals by diminishing opportunities for research, curation, and display. At a much deeper level, repatriation is an intensely difficult and emotional experience for individual Native Americans vested by their communities with the responsibility to carry out the process. Historical realities that led to institutional possession, curation, and scientific study of Native American cultural items can be extremely tragic, offensive, and heart wrenching for individuals to come to terms with. NAGPRA requires individuals to confront those realities as they witness the bones and precious objects of their ancestors in museum storage facilities, university basements, or on public display; as they help to find a way to resolve the fates of those persons and objects; and as they work with their communities to try to heal from the impacts of repatriation.

Individual and collective responsibilities to care for cultural items and places permeate Puebloan societies. Migration routes, ancestral burial sites, sacred objects – these foci of custodianship responsibilities arise within and well beyond questions about repatriation. Individuals within Puebloan communities may be vested with responsibility to protect sites, to care for and properly use cultural objects, and to try to recover the remains of their ancestors and cultural items that were removed from their communities over time. The emotional impact of bearing these responsibilities can be high. As parties carry out their administrative activities during the repatriation process, those outside the tribal communities may not be aware of the ongoing emotional impact that these obligations may have on individuals charged with their care and protection.

Behind the veils of legal language and administrative process lie many complicated, disturbing, and vitally important revelations, decisions, and actions. The process of dealing with human remains has clearly been the most emotionally difficult for tribal representatives, but funerary objects, sacred objects, and objects of cultural patrimony each carry the weight of history, loss, and (sometimes) recovery. Tribal leaders carrying out repatriation obligations carry a heavy burden. Theresa Pasqual shared personal reflections on the toll that repatriation can take:

> Because of the cultural parameters that exist around NAGPRA remains, it's like there's not an outlet for some of the most, even the most harsh NAGPRA projects that we've come into. We have one right now on the books that we haven't tackled, and we're just beginning discussion. But it's . . . just heads. It's just heads. For me, personally, to watch these cultural leaders, these men, how do they deal with that emotionally? How do they . . . Because, even if it's unspoken, it's that history, you're constantly reliving it. I also find myself, even in my role, knowing how challenging those things can be, almost in a way that a woman does, from a motherly approach, to try and protect them from that emotional burden as much as possible. Because it's not like these men go home and talk about all the things that they've encountered, and it takes a toll. But, this one in particular, that's probably why it hasn't moved in the way that we would like it to, because it's a tough one. It's just heads. That's all it is. And to know they were being used for scientific research. And that, in all likelihood, there will probably never be a point where you will find the rest of the body. How do you explain that?
>
> *(Benton Bruning 2013:257)*

Conclusion

Well beyond the legal confines of NAGPRA, Native communities continue to deal with the heavy impacts on their people and culture from the losses – and the returns – of their disinterred ancestors and dispossessed cultural objects. The concept of cultural property, embodying a paradoxical combination of possession and identity, reflects the complexities inherent in NAGPRA. The worldviews of Wilton Kooyahoema and George Gustave Heye, as reflected in their statements at the opening of this chapter, may be irreconcilable. However, there is growing recognition within the United States and throughout the international community that the historical disrespect and injustices suffered by Indigenous peoples should no longer be tolerated. As stated in the United Nations' Declaration on the Rights of Indigenous Peoples, there is an "urgent need to respect and promote the inherent rights of Indigenous peoples." As part of that growing recognition, efforts to address cultural property concerns should focus more deeply and meaningfully on aspects of culture understandings and caretaking obligations emanating from the communities of origin themselves.

A long and tumultuous history of colonization in the United States led to pervasive dispossession of Indigenous ancestors and cultural objects. NAGPRA endeavors to address some of these wrongs and shift possession and control back to the communities of origin. It is not, however, a panacea for the damage that has been wrought upon those communities. In implementation, NAGPRA has proven to be riddled with challenges that are being tackled with varying levels of success through the painstaking efforts of many involved in the processes. Even when the administrative aspects of repatriation are completed, the weight and responsibilities of the experience linger on. A paradox of cultural property lies in the disparate notions of dynamic culture and static property interests. NAGPRA provides yet another paradox: the offer of repossession set against yet another suite of mandates requiring Indigenous communities to satisfy the expectations of outsiders in order to bring ancestors and culturally potent items home again.

Notes

1 Wilton Kooyahoema is a member of the Hopi tribe, located in Arizona, US.

2 George Gustav Heye was an avid private collector who, through his foundation, established the initial collections of the Smithsonian Institution and served as Director of the Museum of the American Indian. See http://nmai.si.edu/explore/collections/history/.

3 See the report by UN Special Rapporteur, Mr. José Martinez, "Study of the Problem of Discrimination Against Indigenous Populations," 1981–1983: https://www.un.org/development/desa/Indigenous peoples/publications/martinez-cobo-study.html (accessed 27 March 2017).

4 For varying perspectives on the status of the Parthenon Marbles, see Hitchens 1997 and Merryman 1985.

5 For a sampling of thoughtful scholarship on the subject, see Dongoske 2000; Dongoske et al. 1997; Duff et al. 2008; Echo-Hawk 1997; Fine-Dare 2002; Goldstein and Kintigh 2000; Thomas 2000; Lippert 1997; Lovis et al. 2004; Owsley and Jantz 2001; Pyburn 2003; Swidler et al. 1997; Trope and Echo-Hawk 2000; Tsosie 1997; Whiteley 2002.

6 See Smith and Wobst (eds.) 2005.

7 See, for example, Brown 2003; Dongoske et al. 2000; Evers and Toelken 2001; Fine-Dare 2002; Fluehr-Lobban 2003; Mihesuah 2000; Richman and Forsyth 2004; Swidler et al. 1997; Watkins 2000; Zimmerman et al. 2003.

8 See NAGPRA Section 7(a)4.

9 See media reports of the sales: http://www.reuters.com/article/us-france-auction-masks-idUSKBN0OR1DG20150611 (accessed 27 March 2017).

10 See Bruning 2006 and Thomas 2000 for discussions of the case and its implications.

11 US House of Representatives House Report 5237, Version 1, Section 7e (1990).

12 NAGPRA Section 8f.

13 See US v. Corrow, 119 F.2d 796 (10th Cir. 1997), confirming the criminal conviction of a non-Indian artifact trader for attempting to sell items qualifying as Navajo cultural patrimony in violation of NAGPRA. One issue was whether the items, Navajo Yei B'Chei, were individually owned by the family of the haatali (religious singer) who used them during life and were therefore transferable to Corrow by his widow, or whether they were communally owned by the tribe such that they would fall under NAGPRA. Navajo witnesses differed in their perspectives about the ownership or custodianship status of the items.

14 See NAGPRA Section 7(e).

15 The dispute over group consultations involving cultural affiliation with Chaco Canyon is discussed in the minutes of the NAGPRA Review Committee Meeting held May 3–5, 1999. http://www.nps.gov/nagpra/REVIEW/meetings/RMS017.PDF (accessed 27 March 2017).

Bibliography

Adler, Michael and Susan Benton Bruning. 2007. "Navigating the Fluidity of Social Identity: Collaborative Research into Cultural Affiliation in the American Southwest." In *Collaboration in Archaeological Practice*. Walnut Creek, CA: AltaMira Press.

Antiquities Act of 1906, 34 Stat. 225, 16 United States Code, 431–433.

Archaeological Resources Protection Act (ARPA). 1979. Public Law, 96–95. 16 United States Code Section 470aa–470mm.

Benton Bruning, Susan. 2013. "Exploring Culture in Shared Spaces: Integrating Research on Western Pueblo Identities and Affiliations in the Repatriation Era." PhD dissertation, on file at Southern Methodist University.

Birkhold, Matthew H. 2011. "Tipping NAGPRA's Balancing Act: The Inequitable Disposition of 'Culturally Unidentified' Human Remains Under NAGPRA's New Provision." National Native American Law Students Association (NALSA) 10th Annual Student Writing Competition Winner, 246–296.

Brown, Michael. 2003. *Who Owns Native American Culture?* Cambridge, MA: Harvard University Press.

Bruning, Susan. 2006. "Complex Legal Legacies: NAGPRA, Scientific Study, and Kennewick Man." *American Antiquity* 71(3): 501–521.

Dongoske, Kurt E. 2000. "NAGPRA: A New Beginning, Not an End, for Osteological Analysis – A Hopi Perspective." In *Repatriation Reader: Who Owns American Indian Remains?* edited by Devon A. Mihesuah, 282–291. Lincoln: University of Nebraska Press.

Dongoske, Kurt E., Mark Aldenderfer, and Karen Doehmer. 2000. *Working Together: Native Americans and Archaeologists*. Washington, DC: SAR Press.

Dongoske, Kurt E., Michael Yeatts, Roger Anyon, and T. J. Ferguson. 1997. "Archaeological Cultures and Cultural Affiliation: Hopi and Zuni Perspectives in the American Southwest." *American Antiquity* 62(4): 600–608.

Dubin, Margaret. 2001. *Native America Collected: The Culture of the Art World*. Albuquerque: University of New Mexico Press.

Duff, Andrew, T. J. Ferguson, Susan Bruning, and Peter Whiteley. 2008. "Collaborative Research in a Living Landscape: Pueblo Land, Culture, and History in West-Central New Mexico." *Archaeology Southwest* 22(1): 1–25.

Echo-Hawk, Roger. 1997. "Forging a New Ancient History for Native America." In *Native Americans and Archaeologists: Stepping Stones to Common Ground*, edited by Nina Swidler, Kurt Dongoske, Roger Anyon, and Alan Downer, 88–102. Walnut Creek, CA: AltaMira Press.

Evers, Larry and Barre Toelken (eds.). 2001. *Native American Oral Traditions: Collaboration and Interpretation*. Logan: Utah State University Press.

Fausset, Richard. 2002. "Indians Face Dilemma of Toxic Relics: Antiquities – Preservative Substances used by Early Curators Raise Health and Religious Questions for Tribes Seeking the Return of their Sacred Items." *Los Angeles Times*, September 1. Accessed at: http://articles.latimes.com/2002/sep/01/local/me-native1 (accessed 27 March 2017).

Ferguson, T. J., Roger Anyon, and Edmund J. Ladd. 2000. "Repatriation at the Pueblo of Zuni: Diverse Solutions to Complex Problems." In *Repatriation Reader: Who Owns American Indian Remains?* edited by Devon A. Mihesuah, 282–291. Lincoln: University of Nebraska Press.

Fine-Dare, Kathleen. 2002. *Grave Injustice: The American Indian Movement and NAGPRA*. Lincoln: University of Nebraska Press.

Fluehr-Lobban, Carolyn. 2003. *Ethics and the Profession of Archaeology*. Walnut Creek, CA: AltaMira Press.

Goldstein, Lynne, and Keith Kintigh, 2000. "Ethics and the Reburial Controversy." In *Repatriation Reader: Who Owns American Indian Remains?* edited by Devon A. Mihesuah, 180–189. Lincoln: University of Nebraska Press.

Government Accountability Office (GAO) of the United States. 2011. Report on the Smithsonian Institution. GAO-11.515, May 25.

Graham, Martha, and Nell Murphy. 2010. "NAGPRA at 20: Museum Collections and Reconnections." *Museum Anthropology* 33(2): 105–124.

Greenfield, Jeannette. 1995. *The Return of Cultural Treasures*. Cambridge: Cambridge University Press.

Hague. 1954. Hague Convention for the Protection of Cultural Property in the Event of Armed Conflict.

Hitchens, Christopher. 1997. *The Elgin Marbles: Should They Be Returned to Greece?* London: Verso Books.

House Report. 1989. House Report 101–877, United States House of Representatives.

House Report. 1990. House Report 5237, Version 1, United States House of Representatives.

Indian Arts and Crafts Act, Public Law 74–355. 1935. 25 United States Code 305 et seq.
Kakaliouras, Ann M. 2012. "An Anthropology of Repatriation: Contemporary Physical Anthropological and Native American Ontologies of Practice." *Current Anthropology* 53(5): S210–S221.
Lippert, Dorothy. 1997. "In Front of the Mirror: Native Americans and Academic Archaeology." In *Stepping Stones to Common Ground*, edited by Nina Swidler, Kurt E. Dongoske, Roger Anyon, and Alan S. Downer, 120–127. Walnut Creek, CA: AltaMira Press.
Lippert, Dorothy. 2008. "Not the End, Not the Middle, But the Beginning: Repatriation as a Transformative Mechanism for Archaeologists and Indigenous Peoples." In *Collaboration in Archaeological Practice*, edited by Chip Colwell-Chantaphonh and T. J. Ferguson, 119–130. Walnut Creek, CA: AltaMira Press.
Lovis, W. A., Keith W. Kintigh, Vincas P. Steponaitis, and Lynne G. Goldstein. 2004. "Archaeological Perspectives on the NAGPRA: Underlying Principles, Legislative History, and Current Issues." In *Legal Perspectives on Cultural Resources*, edited by Jennifer P. Richman and Marion P. Forsyth, 165–184. Walnut Creek, CA: AltaMira Press.
McIntosh, R., S. Keech McIntosh, and T. Togola. 1996. "People Without History." In *Archaeological Ethics*, edited by Karen D. Vitelli, 185–197. Walnut Creek, CA: AltaMira Press.
Mason, J. Alden. 1958. "George G. Heye, 1884–1957." Leaflets of the Museum of the American Indian, Heye Foundation 6(11).
Meltzer, David. 2015. "Kennewick Man: Coming to Closure." *Antiquity* 89(348).
Merryman, John Henry. 1985. "Thinking About the Elgin Marbles." *Michigan Law Review* 83(8): 1880–1923.
Mezey, Naomi. 2007. "The Paradoxes of Cultural Property." *Columbia Law Review* 107: 2004–2046.
Mihesuah, Devon A. (ed.) 2000. *Repatriation Reader: Who Owns American Indian Remains?* Lincoln: University of Nebraska Press.
Mills, Barbara, Mark Altaha, John R. Welch, and T. J. Ferguson. 2008. "Field Schools without Trowels: Teaching Archaeological Ethics and Heritage Preservation in a Collaborative Context." In *Collaborating at the Trowel's Edge: Teaching and Learning in Indigenous Archaeology*, edited by Stephen W. Silliman, 5–49. Tucson: University of Arizona Press.
Moore, Emily. 2010. "Propriation: Possibilities for Art after NAGPRA." *Museum Anthropology* 33(2): 125–136.
NAGPRA Review Committee. 2006. Meeting Minutes. November 3–4, 2006. Accessed at: http://www.nps.gov/nagpra/ (accessed 27 March 2017).
National Historic Preservation Act (NHPA). 1966. Public Law 89–665, 16 United States Code 470 et seq.
National Museum of the American Indian Act (NMAIA). 1989. Public Law 101–185. 20 United States Code 80q.
National Museum of Natural History (NMNH). 2005. "The Management of Culturally Sensitive Collections of the Department of Anthropology." Smithsonian Institution Policy and Procedures Guidelines. Accessed at: http://www.nmnh.si.edu/anthrp/repatriation/pdf/tcpst.pdf (accessed 27 March 2017).
National Park Service (NPS). 2001. "Chronology of Pesticides Used to on National Park Service Collections." *NPS Conserve O Gram* 2(16). Accessed at: http://www.cr.nps.gov/museum/publications/con serveogram/02-16.pdf (accessed 27 March 2017).
Native American Graves Protection and Repatriation Act (NAGPRA). 1990. Public Law 101–601; 25 United States Code 3001 et seq.
Ortner, Donald J. 1994. "Scientific Policy and Public Interest: Perspectives on the Larsen Bay Repatriation Case." In *Reckoning with the Dead: The Larsen Bay Repatriation and the Smithsonian Institution*, edited by Tamara L. Bray and Thomas W. Killion, 10–14. Washington, DC: Smithsonian Institution.
Owsley, Douglas W. and Richard L. Jantz. 2001. "Archaeological Politics and Public Interest in Paleoamerican Studies: Lessons from Gordon Creek Woman and Kennewick Man." *American Antiquity* 66(4): 565–584.
Pyburn, K. Anne. 2003. "Archaeology for a New Millennium: The Rules of Engagement." In *Archaeologists and Local Communities: Partners in Exploring the Past*, edited by Linda Derry and Maureen Malloy, 167–184. Washington, DC: SAR Press.
Richman, Jennifer R. and Marion P. Forsyth. 2004. *Legal Perspectives on Cultural Resources*. Walnut Creek, CA: AltaMira Press.
Senate Select Committee on Indian Affairs. 1990. United States Senate Report 101–473.
Smith, Claire and H. Martin Wobst (eds.). 2005. *Indigenous Archaeologies: Decolonising Theory and Practice*. Oxford: Routledge.
Swidler, Nina, Kurt Dongoske, Roger Anyon, and Alan Downer (eds.). 1997. *Stepping Stones to Common Ground*. Walnut Creek, CA: AltaMira Press.

Thomas, David Hurst. 2000. *Skull Wars: Kennewick Man, Archaeology, and the Battle for Native American Identity*. Minneapolis: University of Minnesota Press.

Trope, Jack F. and Walter R. Echo-Hawk. 2000. "The Native American Graves Protection and Repatriation Act: Background and Legislative History." In *Repatriation Reader: Who Owns American Indian Remains?* edited by Devon A. Mihesuah. Lincoln: University of Nebraska Press.

Tsosie, Rebecca. 1997. "Indigenous Peoples' Claims to Cultural Property: A Legal Perspective." *Museum Anthropology* 21(3): 5–11.

United Nations (UN). 2007. Declaration on the Rights of Indigenous Peoples.

United Nations Education, Scientific and Cultural Organization (UNESCO). 1970. Convention on the Means of Prohibiting and Preventing the Illicit Import, Export and Transfer of Ownership of Cultural Property.

Watkins, Joe. 2000. *Indigenous Archaeology: American Indian Values and Scientific Practice*. Walnut Creek, CA: AltaMira Press.

Whiteley, Peter. 2002. "Archaeology and Oral Tradition: The Scientific Importance of Dialog." *Amerian Antiquity* 67(3): 405–415.

Zimmerman, Larry J., Karen D. Vitelli, and Julie Hollowell-Zimmer (eds.). 2003. *Ethical Issues in Archaeology*. Walnut Creek, CA: AltaMira Press.

PART II

Museums, archives and communities

Jane Anderson and Haidy Geismar

Cultural institutions like museums and archives are critical sites for shaping debates and discourses around cultural property. This is not only in relation to collections and the varying questions about the accumulation and assemblage of cultural 'things', but also within the very politics of museum display and representation. Questions about who gets to speak for and on behalf of a community are now central to cultural property discussions. In these contexts, there has been a strategic movement away from a zero-sum question of ownership, expanding the discourse into cultural rights, entitlements, ethics and responsibility. Critics however might see this shift as reinforcing the boundaries of ownership and its consequences for the production of knowledge and the practice of cultural representation. The conversation about cultural property that intersects with museums raises important issues around public trust, memory and authority. It encourages reflexivity upon our understanding of the power of objects, the ongoing resonance of their exchange histories and various routes of circulation, and the relationships that give them meaning.

Community is as slippery a term as any and its use as a general descriptor has the danger of erasing the very real political differences and historical experiences that exist within any grouping named as such. As Raymond Williams observed and more recently Bennett, Grossberg and Morris have elaborated, community is a 'keyword' in our vocabulary of culture and society, but it requires increased specification and care when being used in order to offset false equivalences (Williams 1976; Bennett et al. 2005). Karp, Kreamer and Levine offer the idea of community as deeply experienced encounters where "cultures, identities and skills are acquired and used" (Karp et al. 1992: 4). We might also add here how important place, memory and time are for expanding this idea of community and how a sense of group belonging enables individuals to also conceptualise identity. What experiences make up any community, and how identity across and within a social grouping is produced through moments of openness and closure, also suggest that a community is never a fixed entity. Community is always in processes of development and change.

This section explores the multiple ways that museums and archives and the communities from which institutional collections originated inform and mutually work to determine ideas of cultural property in relation to these collections. Especially in the past two decades, the extension of curatorial and other authority to groups of people outside the museum walls has become pivotal to institutional futures. This process has not only brought ideas and ideals of community into being; it has also enabled engagement with peoples who have not only been marginalised and excluded from institutions but also of whose belongings these institutions have become owners, stewards, guardians and caretakers. The necessity of these engagements has broken apart traditional ideas and language of 'objects' and 'property' and has also been central in redirecting understanding of historical power relations in the transit of cultural properties, in both tangible and intangible forms.

James Clifford's development of Mary Louise Pratt's conception of a contact zone (Pratt 1991; Clifford 1997) articulates the museum and archive as sites of engagement between institutions and communities inflected by these histories and power dynamics. There has been a recent backlash against the secondary appropriation of the idea of a contact zone within museum practice as a way to authorize and celebrate new kinds of participation and collaboration (e.g. Gere 1997; Bennett 2013). Recent critics have argued that the formulation of the 'contact zone' is neocolonial (Boast 2011) as it ignores power differentials that make the contact moment possible and becomes another burden of representation for Native peoples who, through the opening up of the museum, are charged with saving the institution's reputation (Mithlo 2004). In the chapters assembled here, Fred Myers and Aaron Fox both offer a close analysis of the multiple relationships and movements of cultural property that can occur between community, institutions and between individual collectors. Both trace these movements through the production of film and audio, forms not traditionally considered cultural property but now very much part of a cultural property spectrum. Rae Gould and Jennifer Kramer make visible the shifting lines of responsibility and care in response to the extreme sensitivities of the US federal legislation governing the return of Native American human remains, or ancestors, and in the transformation of meaning that can be bestowed onto items that have deep First Nation histories. These two chapters speak to the complex layers of mistrust and misunderstanding that continue to condition relationships between Indigenous communities and institutions demonstrating the ongoing legacies of settler colonialism. George Nicholas draws on a range of examples to explore the question of why the tangible always trumps the intangible in cultural property policy in Canada.

The diverse and rich repatriation literature of the past 20 years has opened understanding about the multiple relationships of meaning and memory that are embedded within cultural property as very particular belongings and items of embodiment. More than 20 years after the passing of NAGPRA the landscape has changed dramatically – there has been an almost universal outlawing of treating human remains as collections like any other. Similarly, the obligation to consult has also become mainstream in the curation of many ethnographic collections. The politics of repatriation, including what that really means at a legislative, institutional and community level and what histories of colonial violence it evokes, are the subject of Rae Gould's chapter. With specialized experience as both a NAGPRA co-ordinator within a university context working on repatriation and a member of the Nipmuc Nation in Massachusetts, Gould unravels what it takes to commit to the return of Native American human remains and how much institutional will matters in this process. In this Gould is very clear: the point and project of NAGPRA is assuring the safe and complete return to Native communities of their ancestors who were wrongly taken from graves and burial sites across the country. This unique violence and disruption has its base within colonial logics of supremacy and the use of science in support of this. The very language that Gould deploys here, renaming human remains as ancestors, for instance, does very important work in de-objectifying and pointing to the strategic erasure of Native standpoints and protocols about respect for the dead. Specifically focusing on one part of the legislation pertaining to the new provision, Section 10.11, developed for the dispossession of culturally unidentifiable human remains, Gould argues how this provision within the law has worked to support institutional agendas that position the return of ancestors to their communities of origin as secondary concerns.

As Gould's chapter illustrates how legal categories are adapted and interpreted to serve specific purposes, Kramer similarly points to the multiple relationships of looking and seeing Native works within institutions. Using the example of the loan agreement put in place between the Seattle Art Museum and the Denver Museum in a wager over the 2014 Super Bowl that led to the loan of artwork considered significant to each institution, Kramer explores how cultural property can be full of investments and misplaced meaning. In an account of the various possible routes of circulation of cultural property, the Raven Mask of the Nuxalk community is transformed from community cultural property into a different kind of spectacle. In this 'looking relations', or how we see and how we create relationships through shared experiences of looking, are critical. As Kramer states, 'When non-Native viewers impose their own meaning onto manifestations of Nuxalk culture, historically unequal power relations between Native and non-Native people become further accentuated.'

In turn, the debates about repatriation have become nuanced in the context of the explosion of digital media and other new forms of collecting. A 2011 conference at the Smithsonian, *After the Return* (see Bell, Christen and Turin 2012), interrogated the meaning of repatriation in the light of new media practices and collections. Participants at the conference engaged with how the boundaries of collections, and the possibilities of their experiential presence in communities (as well as communities being brought into the museum), had increased massively (see also Silverman 2015 and Harrison et al. 2013). At the same time, there continues to be a fervent resistance to the status of collections as property and the power relations that this perpetuates. At the above conference, Jim Enote, the Director of the A:shiwi A:wan Museum, made an impassioned plea to not forget that the return of digitized collections to communities is not the same as repatriation (Boast and Enote 2013).

With regard to the complex ways in which different media activate questions about ownership and entitlement of collections, Fred Myers' chapter underscores the way that film and other indexical images work to establish relationships and other effects in the world. This chapter tracks the initial making and subsequent return of visual recordings made of the Pintupi, an Aboriginal group in central Australia, in the early 1970s as they encounter and negotiate new living conditions in established governmental settlements. Myers' account offers a unique position; he was there when the film footage was originally made and he is intimately involved in the collaboration and negotiation that leads to the making of *Remembering Yayai* that utilizes this footage in 2015. Through this positioning, Myers is able to explore the different tensions and ambivalences in cross-cultural negotiations of rights and representation. The archive as the repository for the original footage and the conditions of authorial control that remain relatively fixed within that space adds an additional layer of complexity to the negotiations required from a community standpoint. Myers' piece highlights how ownership and collaboration pivot on each other in the process of making representations and negotiating the complexities of cultural property. This chapter offers itself as a rich ethnography of cultural property, illustrating just how it can function as a marker of identity and difference.

In Aaron Fox's chapter, the archive is also a site of investigation and analysis but at a different register. Here the focus is on tracing the multiple hidden alliances and relationships that led to the making of a significant ethnographic music archive, the Laura Boulton Collection, at Columbia University's Department of Ethnomusicology. In this account we are afforded insight into what might be understood as the archive of the archive – the documentary trail that once uncovered reveals myriad interpersonal motivations and strategic manoeuvring. What we learn from Fox is that the making of an archive, of a collection, is never assured and is haphazard at best, and the representation of it as whole and complete is a fiction that serves very particular interests. This chapter is about how the archive itself emerges as cultural property. Thus in bringing it to life, and the way one person's archive goes on to live in the world – who it engages, who it reaches out to – demonstrates how cultural property activates its own forms of agency.

The final chapter by George Nicholas offers a reflection upon the multiple cultural positions that inform, condition and also limit understandings of cultural property. Nicholas makes the argument that cultural property is an essentially inseparable aspect of heritage. In doing so he draws largely from the multi-year interdisciplinary project in Canada that he directed, *Intellectual Property Issues in Cultural Heritage*. This project allowed for various investigations and interventions into ideas of heritage, property, ownership and responsibilities to and for tangible and intangible cultural property. The breadth of this work and the examples used in this chapter highlight the range of issues facing communities in the translation of their material and immaterial culture and cultural expressions into dominant languages of cultural property and possession.

Together these chapters work to highlight how the figure of cultural property is involved in activating and producing a variety of relationships between communities and institutions like archives and museums. These engagements turn upon colonial histories of collecting and documentation and the multiple lives that this material has gone on to have. The varied meaning that it can mobilize depends upon who is looking, who is accessing and who it is indexing and referencing. These chapters also point to the unique moments that underpin the making of cultural property as well as the temporal dimensions that continue to inform its circulation and its characterization. Cultural property is not only many things to many people; it is also used strategically to mark specific moments and events, and thus it too becomes an active agent in the making of identity and in the calibrations of cultural difference.

Bibliography

Bell, Joshua A., Kimberly A. Christen, and Mark Turin. 2013. "Introduction: After the Return." *Museum Anthropology Review* 7(1–2): 1–21.

Bennett, Tony. 2013. "The 'Shuffle of Things' and the Distribution of Agency." In Rodney Harrison, Sarah Byrne and Anne Clarke (eds.), *Reassembling the Collection: Ethnographic Museums and Indigenous Agency*. Santa Fe: School for Advanced Research.

Bennett, Tony, Lawrence Grossburg and Meaghan Morris. 2005. *New Keywords: A Revised Vocabulary of Culture and Society*. London: Blackwell Publishing.

Boast, Robin. 2011. "Neocolonial Collaboration: Museum as Contact Zone Revisited." *Museum Anthropology* 34(1): 56–70.

Boast, Robin, and Jim Enote. 2012. "Virtual Repatriation: It Is Neither Virtual nor Repatriation." In *Heritage in the Context of Globalization*, Vol. 8. Springer Briefs in Archaeology. New York: Springer New York.

Clifford, James. 1997. *Routes: Travel and Translation in the Late Twentieth Century*. Cambridge, MA: Harvard University Press.

Harrison, Rodney, Sarah Byrne and Anne Clarke. (eds.) 2013. *Reassembling the Collection: Ethnographic Museums and Indigenous Agency*. Santa Fe: School for Advanced Research.

Karp, Ivan, Christine Kreamer and Steven Levine. 1992. *Museums and Communities: The Politics of Public Culture*. Washington, DC: Smithsonian Institution.

Mithlo, Nancy M. 2004. "Red Man's Burden. The Politics of Inclusion in Museum Settings." *American Indian Quarterly* 28(3–4): 743–763.
Pratt, Mary Louise. 1991. "Arts of the Contact Zone." *Profession*, 33–40.
Silverman, Raymond. (ed.) 2015. *Museum as Process: Translating Local and Global Knowledges*. London: Routledge.
Williams, Raymond. 1976. *Keywords: A Vocabulary of Culture and Society*. London: Oxford Press.

7
NAGPRA, CUI AND INSTITUTIONAL WILL

D. Rae Gould

Introduction

Having been engaged in the Native American Graves Protection and Repatriation Act (NAGPRA) for several decades – both as a tribal representative and a museum/institution representative – I have seen different sides and practices of this US law. I have witnessed examples of both how the law can work and result in repatriation, and how it can be used to retain what some museum professionals and scientists feel are "evidence" or "material culture" needed to further our collective understanding of the human past. Even when officially acting as a museum representative at a major university implementing NAGPRA, I was also always a representative for my tribe[1] and the tribal peoples we engaged with in repatriation efforts. I cannot separate these as distinct responsibilities because NAGPRA's goal is, first and foremost, to repatriate ancestors, funerary objects, sacred objects and objects of cultural patrimony to tribes they are related to.[2]

A simple choice of language – that we referenced Native American human remains as ancestors – suggests that at institutions like the University of Massachusetts Amherst a shift was required in how the important issues, practices and physical "objects" are understood, and in relation to the critical and legal debates that still surround NAGPRA. Transitioning from language focused on objects, property and the decontextualized term "human remains" to a working understanding that we were now stewards of tribes' ancestors re-situates the ongoing relationships to ancestors that exists at every institution with NAGPRA responsibilities. This language also forces reflection on the harm created in the taking of these ancestors (and other NAGPRA-sensitive collections) and for the generations of tribal members affected by these actions. Through NAGPRA we can only try to amend some of this harm and hope to offer some piece of the healing process. What I came to realize through working to repatriate ancestors and belongings, though, was that the circle is never really closed, even though I worked hard to achieve that. Other institutions, unfortunately, may never achieve this shift or work to close the circle, as they continue to work under what I term a "retentive philosophy" of owning and keeping ancestors and objects.

By the time I began my position at UMass, the institution had developed what I term the "institutional will" to *want* to comply with not only the law, but also the spirit of the law in the most genuine way; the end goal always focused on repatriation and return of ancestors and items to tribes. Much of the development of institutional will at this university was due to a "changing of the guards" resulting from retirements of older faculty members, hiring younger and Native faculty members with different ideals and ethics reflective of trends in academia, and increased engagement of Native graduate students, in addition to increased pressure from tribes to more fully comply with the law and achieve repatriation. For other institutions, however, the internationalist perspective that knowledge and cultural property belong to all and should be controlled by those who "know best" with resources to "protect" these – versus the nationalist perspective emphasizing the rights of specific populations to control their cultural heritage and the human remains and objects associated with that (Merryman 1986) – continues to fuel fierce exchanges with no immediate end in sight.

This chapter discusses one of the major issues in the US repatriation process: the practice of institutions categorizing ancestors as CUI, or "culturally unidentifiable," to resist repatriation to the rightful tribes. The CUI designation is used to impede repatriation of ancestors, as it can be arbitrarily applied[3] and hides the politics of an institution resistant to NAGPRA. Next I provide several case studies that demonstrate how institutional will has developed within many museums and universities, while others continue to practice retentive and more "internationalist" philosophies and resist repatriation of both human remains and funerary objects, clearly contrary to the human rights component intended within the spirit of NAGPRA. Such institutions maintain ideological positions that the benefits of science and knowledge outweigh the rights of tribes to repatriate ancestors and items; in essence, the issue is one of control. The institutions discussed in this chapter with retentive philosophies are continuing colonialist and paternalistic practices based on racism, disrespect and a sense of entitlement that continues to plague museums and institutions rooted in Euroamerican ideals of supremacy that have dominated politics, laws, economics, and social and race relations for centuries.

This chapter offers an analysis of the (all too common) rhetoric institutions and individuals use regarding their support of NAGPRA against the actual practices they engage in. It compares the concepts of institutional will to really comply with the law (in spirit *and* in practice) against the reality and practice of having retentive philosophies, i.e. keeping ancestors at the institution. Using a well-known institution as the primary case study, this chapter identifies a specific mechanism within NAGPRA that allows institutions and museums to maintain a veneer of compliance without actually addressing the purpose of the law: returning ancestors to tribes. One institution – Harvard University – is representational in this practice because it posits itself as a leader in repatriation, as seen in the examples provided. Unfortunately, Harvard and several others mentioned below have used the rhetoric of compliance with NAGPRA, but it is an empty rhetoric as it is not being followed in practice. As many tribes know, weaknesses in the law can be used as a gateway to non-compliance for institutions with retentive philosophies. While the *appearance* of institutional will is publicly performed, a closer look at the actual operation and practice of some institutions reveals a façade that fractures under scrutiny. Using select case studies, this chapter offers a model of how to see through this façade. As Mashpee Wampanoag representative Ramona Peters has noted, if museums and institutions with retentive philosophies are exposed, perhaps they will change their positions. This chapter attempts to address the issue of museums and institutions failing to fulfill their legal and affirmative duties to consult and repatriate.

The chapter begins by providing a brief history of the Native American Graves Protection and Repatriation Act (US 43 CFR Part 10), then highlights key components related to culturally unidentifiable (CUI) human remains, and provides case studies of both positive and negative interpretations of culturally unidentifiable remains. It also addresses some of the impediments (such as museums determining cultural affiliation) and best practices (such as museums hiring Native Americans) NAGPRA practitioners have outlined recently. Although NAGPRA is a complex law, changing through practice – and through the continued input of Native Americans, archaeologists, museum professionals and other academics and collectors – the discussions remain centered on a simple perspective: museums and institutions can be defined as having the institutional will to do the right thing and seek repatriation, or as having a retentive philosophy borne out of colonialist philosophies which privilege science over the return to tribes of their ancestors. There is no middle ground in this centuries-long battle for the tribes that have waited far too long for the return of ancestors and items that sit on the shelves and in the vaults of museums that purport to "protect" America's history for us.

A brief overview of NAGPRA

Enacted in 1990, the Native American Graves Protection and Repatriation Act is a federal law applying to tribes, federal agencies and museums (including institutions) in the United States; it has no legal effect on international repatriations or claims by US tribes to ancestors or objects in other countries (although it can work as a model for how non-US institutions could pursue repatriation). The National NAGPRA website (http://www.nps.gov/nagpra/) is very user-friendly and provides information for understanding the law, including a glossary of terms and explanations for those working for both museums/institutions and tribes; it's often a starting point for those just learning about the law as well as an often-used resource for many who have worked with the law for years.

Briefly, the law is intended to provide a "process for museums and Federal agencies to return . . . Native American . . . human remains, funerary objects, sacred objects, or objects of cultural patrimony to lineal descendants, and culturally affiliated Indian tribes and Native Hawaiian organizations." The law also now includes provisions for repatriating "unclaimed and culturally unidentifiable Native American cultural items" (discussed further below) (http://www.nps.gov/nagpra/FAQ/INDEX.HTM#What_is_NAGPRA). Cultural affiliation is central to the process and is a documented connection between human remains and/or objects and a modern-day tribe (or tribes) by a preponderance of evidence standard; tribes are defined as being federally recognized by the Bureau of Indian Affairs (BIA), in addition to Native Hawaiian Organizations (NHOs). A NAGPRA Review Committee aids in monitoring the process and facilitating resolutions of disputes that arise concerning repatriation (usually between tribes and museums failing to work within the spirit of the law), with meetings held twice yearly and open to the public. While a detailed explanation of the law is not possible in this chapter, extended explanations and discussions can be found in Fine Dare (2002), Thomas (2000), Mihesuah (2009) and other articles and publications such as *Mending the Circle* (http://www.repatriationfoundation.org/mtc.html), in addition to the NAGPRA website.

All federal agencies must comply with NAGPRA, while the Smithsonian Institution is required to repatriate under a separate law passed a year before NAGPRA (National Museum of the American Indian Act of 1989, 20 USC 80q, Public Law 101–185). Also, any museum or institution with Native American collections and receiving federal funds must comply with NAGPRA and are all defined as "museums" under the Act. Educational institutions such as UMass Amherst, Harvard University, University of Michigan and Indiana University – all discussed in this chapter – are considered museums subject to the law because they receive federal funding and have human remains or objects of Native American origin.

As may be immediately obvious, a number of issues can already be identified within these parameters. First, the law only applies to museums and institutions receiving federal funding and therefore not to local historical societies and museums or private individuals that don't receive funding but possess Native American collections. Nothing prevents them from engaging in a repatriation process and, in fact, repatriation can sometimes be less onerous outside of NAGPRA, but no federal law compels them to engage in NAGPRA (unless federal land is involved).

A second issue that plagues the repatriation process is that institutions do not always have resources to comply, even if they have the institutional will. Documenting human remains and objects acquired or excavated decades or centuries ago – and often without the detailed information collected in modern times – can be extremely time consuming and research intensive. Once knowledge is gained about remains and objects, submitting inventories (of human remains and associated funerary objects) and summaries (of potential unassociated funerary objects, sacred objects and objects of cultural patrimony) to National NAGPRA and to tribes from across the country and Native Hawaiian organizations requires time, staff and additional resources. And all of this needs to (or *should*) be completed in consultation with those most likely to have an interest in the remains or objects. Identifying these tribes and NHOs sometimes cannot even begin until the history and provenience is known, if possible. When this knowledge cannot be gained due to time-consuming research and resources required to identify all collections, human remains and associated funerary objects (AFOs) are categorized as CUI. Some museums use the CUI categorization, though, to avoid complying with the law, a main focus of this chapter.

Beyond these barriers, some institutions engage in research and regard human remains as scientific resources to study (despite the 27-year-old federal law in place) even if they have been in storage for decades or centuries with little prior interest in their scientific value. For some scientists, such as Douglas Owsley of the Smithsonian's Museum of Natural History and others, returning human remains is like burning books, resulting in loss of valuable knowledge to both scientists and Native people (Peck and Seaborn 1998). In this more internationalist perspective, scientists remain the knowledge authorities and continue to decide for Native Americans what information is valuable and how best to treat (and study) their ancestors. Sonya Atalay, as a member of the NAGPRA Review Committee, recently noted, "Universities are in the business of researching. And . . . they have benefitted from having these collections in their possession. They're in the business of educating students, and students work directly with these collections" (National NAGPRA 2015, V1: 176). Scientists and institutions that continue these practices are teaching the next generation retentive philosophies based on regarding ancestors as scientific specimens and are, in essence, disregarding federal law aimed at reclassifying human remains as ancestors rather than as objects of scientific study.

On the tribal level significant hurdles for engaging with NAGPRA often exist as well. Like institutions, tribes also do not always have sufficient resources; they need to investigate locations and curation history of hundreds of thousands of ancestors and objects, consult with museums and institutions that are sometimes hundreds of miles away, and seek repatriation. And if the museum or institution lacks the institutional will to support information exchange, travel costs and time required to complete consultations, the ancestors continue to sit on shelves. Grants from National NAGPRA can help support these efforts and are available to both tribes and institutions, but funding is limited and the grants are competitive. Often tribes don't have the trained grant writers large institutions like Harvard University do and institutions are awarded the grants over the tribes, but the grant funds do not always result in repatriation (again, if the institution has a retentive philosophy). So most tribes must absorb the financial burden of repatriation work, one of the reasons so many cases take years or decades to complete. And non-federally recognized tribes have the extra burden that, technically, museums and institutions only *have* to consult with federally recognized tribes. Ancestors (and other NAGPRA items) connected to non-federally recognized tribes (like the Nipmuc Nation) are automatically classified as CUI, providing yet another opportunity for institutions to retain them.

One of the most contested issues with NAGPRA is that of cultural affiliation determination, discussed extensively in this chapter. Most agree that NAGPRA[4] was (and still is) a compromise. According to the law, museums and institutions determine cultural affiliation, creating an inventory of human remains and associated funerary objects *in consultation with* tribes or NHOs (25 USC 3003(b); 43 CFR 10.9(b)) through a "good faith effort." Even after consultations – or too often without – ancestors are categorized as culturally unidentifiable, and defined as "cultural items" for which no culturally affiliated present-day Indian tribe or NHO can be determined (43 CFR 10.9 (d)(2)). It is clear in reading the regulations that consultation is the heart of the law and the means to successful repatriation, the goal of the law. Museums and institutions are technically responsible for initiating consultation and the National NAGPRA website hosts a database of all inventories submitted, for both ancestors categorized as culturally affiliated and as CUI (http://www.nps.gov/nagpra/onlinedb/index.htm).

At the heart of cultural affiliation determination lies the battle to define what and who is Native American. The Kennewick Man case, for example, resulted in a protracted struggle between scientists and tribes from the Northwest to decide whether an individual almost 10,000 years old inadvertently discovered on the bank of the Columbia River in Kennewick, Washington, could still be considered as "Native American" and connected to modern-day tribes. The political implications of an ancestor being too old to be considered Native American have reverberated deeply and at great cost to tribes seeking to repatriate other ancient ancestors and items. The Kennewick Man case (the focus of Thomas 2000) provided further incentive for institutions like Harvard University to deny cultural affiliation based on remains being "too old." This is the focus of the discussion below.

Defining "CUI" ancestors

After 27 years of practice and application, NAGPRA has profoundly changed the ways archaeology is conducted in the United States. Some of these changes include: 1) how Native peoples and archaeologists interact and share knowledge, 2) how cultural knowledge, continuity and property are defined and examined by archaeologists, and 3) the ways archaeologists and anthropologists understand connections between so-called "prehistoric" and contemporary Native peoples. Defining pre-Contact ancestors and artifacts as CUI is a result of the language in the law itself and is used to continue a long history of colonization and historical erasure of Native American peoples; it privileges a certain type of authority to make that designation at the expense of other authorities, often Native, who might offer an alternative view.

The basic definition of CUI is that human remains and associated funerary objects cannot be affiliated through a preponderance of evidence to a modern-day tribe, tribes or NHO. With no universal application of the definition of cultural affiliation,[5] case by case decisions are made within each federal agency, museum and institution. Even with precedents set by earlier repatriations, institutions with retentive philosophies still make their own cultural affiliation determinations based on their understandings of the past (examples are provided below). Additionally, if ancestors or items can be connected to a tribe but that tribe is not federally recognized, they are defined as CUI (as noted above). Connections to a documented historic tribe no longer extant (such as the Massachusett Indians in Massachusetts) would also result in a CUI categorization, as would insufficient evidence of an "identifiable earlier group" ("We don't know who that group was") and connections to a present-day tribe. While the law provides for a wide range of interpretation to help achieve repatriations if a desire to culturally affiliate exists, it also leaves open many possibilities for defining ancestors as CUI.

For the purposes of the legislation, determining cultural affiliation involves using up to ten lines of evidence, all having equal weight: geography, kinship, biology, archaeology, anthropology, linguistics, folklore, oral tradition, history and other (see endnote 5). Equal weight means that one line of evidence (such as archaeology or biology) is not considered more valid or informative than another (such as kinship or oral tradition). In theory, tribal knowledge of history, culture and connections in the past known through oral tradition and kinship ties has just as much weight for determining cultural affiliation as information provided by non-tribal archaeologists or anthropologists in written or documented form. Cultural affiliation is established when the preponderance of the evidence (more than 50 percent certainty),[6] based on any of the lines, leads to *reasonably tracing* connections between past and present-day groups. A museum or institution can also use a legal threshold of "reasonable belief" for cultural affiliation, meaning even less than 50 percent certainty to determine cultural affiliation repatriation. In contrast, other legal levels of evidence (in addition to preponderance of the evidence) are clear and convincing evidence (65–75 percent certainty) and reasonable doubt (85–95 percent certainty).[7] In legal terms, the threshold for determining cultural affiliation (determined by the museum or institution) is low and "scientific certainty" is definitely not required, and in practice, institutional will to culturally affiliate, using just one line of evidence and choosing to broadly interpret evidence, leads to repatriation. Yet, if a museum does not have institutional will, the burden of proof to demonstrate cultural affiliation lies with tribes, with their often limited resources.

Even with institutional will, available information at times does not support determining cultural affiliation. Sometimes absolutely no information about the original location (or provenience) of ancestors or items exists and it is not possible to determine which modern-day tribes are connected to them. Sometimes museums and institutions want to disclose that they have human remains or objects in their possession they are seeking to repatriate and list publicly on the National NAGPRA database as CUI while consulting to determine cultural affiliation. The University of Massachusetts Amherst took this approach and then changed the cultural affiliation once consultations were complete. Sometimes tribes engaged in consultations indicate that while they are willing to receive ancestors and items, they feel uncomfortable claiming full cultural affiliation if they cannot clearly demonstrate a connection, even if an institution supports a cultural affiliation determination. All of these are valid reasons to categorize ancestors or items as CUI and are done within the spirit of NAGPRA toward achieving repatriation. And not being able to determine cultural affiliation does not mean repatriation cannot occur (see below).

Too often, though, a museum wants to claim CUI due to "no temporal link" to modern-day tribes to avoid repatriation, as with Harvard University. Several case studies presented below reveal how the designation of CUI becomes a deliberate strategy that has worked for museums with retentive philosophies and no intention of repatriating certain parts of their collections.

For museums and institutions with institutional will, the addition of part 10.11 of the NAGPRA regulations effective May 2010 (Disposition of Culturally Unidentifiable Native American Human Remains, often referred to as 10.11 or the CUI Rule) provides a way to achieve repatriation despite lack of cultural affiliation. The heart of this rule relies on the geographic line of evidence to make connections between ancestors and items and modern-day tribes and NHOs. Tribes and NHOs may request repatriation of human remains and associated funerary objects previously removed from their modern-day tribal lands or aboriginal territories. Aboriginal occupancy can be documented by:

- a final judgment of the Indian Claims Commission (ICC) or United States Court of Claims;
- a treaty or treaties;
- an Act of Congress;
- or an Executive Order (43 CFR 10.11(b)(ii)).

Moreover, according to the legislation, "A museum or federal agency official must initiate consultation regarding the disposition of culturally unidentifiable human remains and associated funerary objects within 90 days of a request from a tribe or NHO." The rule is more detailed and can be found in its full text in the Federal Register publication (75 FR 12403, Mar.15, 2010).

As with the original 1990 Act however, the addition of 10.11 was another compromise for Native Americans. For example, in implementing 10.11, museums *must* consult and repatriate human remains but only *may* repatriate associated funerary objects. For many tribes, receiving the remains of ancestors without the objects buried with them is not an option, so museums with retentive philosophies have yet another way to avoid repatriation even with an established process for returning CUI ancestors.[8]

Clay Dumont (2011) has addressed some of the controversies surrounding the CUI rule and what he refers to as scientific "happy talk" that seeks to explain the development of NAGPRA and 10.11. In their retelling of history, archaeologists and others supported the passing of NAGPRA, which was written to "strike a balance" between scientists and Native people as a compromise where both sides could be equal. According to this narrative, the law adds to a long-standing "respectful" collaboration that has existed between both groups. The passing of 10.11, therefore, undermines the original intent of the law and gets in the way of people working together because it interferes with the collaborative process (theoretically) already present. In other words, according to this narrative, there was nothing wrong with the status quo of how cultural affiliation was being determined (which gave museums and institutions a clear advantage).

A more accurate narrative provided by Dumont is that once it became clear to everyone that NAGPRA would pass, the goal of those with retentive philosophies became to thwart the ability to determine cultural affiliation. Rule 10.11 is controversial because a legal process of repatriating CUI ancestors removes an exit strategy used by museums and institutions with retentive philosophies to comply with NAGPRA. As Dumont notes, the rule "leaves little doubt that the National NAGPRA Program and the secretary of the interior view the purpose of NAGPRA legislation as the return of Native dead [including those classified as CUI] to Native peoples" (2011: 5). The controversy surrounding 10.11 demonstrates that cultural affiliation continues to be a contested "zone" and, therefore, an excellent place for an exit strategy based on either inconclusive evidence, competing evidence, "confusion" or just lack of will.

Harvard University has provided a prime example of this strategy, as detailed in the case studies below. Although Dumont celebrates May 2010 as marking a "significant victory in the centuries-long struggle . . . to protect [Native] dead and their funerary objects," he also acknowledges the rule is "far from perfect" (2011: 5), as would many others engaged in NAGPRA. In 2011, an estimated 120,000 Native American ancestors remained in federally funded institutions (Dumont 2011: 5), due to either being categorized as CUI or simply lack of compliance with NAGPRA. The real victory – the complete return of all ancestors and items – 27 years after the passing of NAGPRA is yet to arise on the horizon. The case studies presented in the following section demonstrate how, several years after implementation of 10.11, institutional will – rather than law or amendments – remains the key factor in determining whether or not repatriation occurs.

Institutional will and retentive philosophy: Examples from Indian Country

The concept of "institutional will" (having the desire and will to achieve repatriation) developed for me after over 15 years of working with NAGPRA, both as a tribal representative and for an institution (UMass Amherst). I watched the university I first developed a relationship with through consultations to repatriate ancestors develop the genuine desire and will to comply with the law over this period. The institution and the people who worked for it believed that the return of ancestors and Native American items was the only ethical and responsible position, and worked hard to make that happen. Only after knowing that they had institutional will to repatriate could I see myself being part of the faculty and team that implemented NAGPRA on behalf of the university. I served as Repatriation Coordinator for UMass from 2010 to 2014 in the first full-time position dedicated to NAGPRA at the university. Creating this position was itself evidence of a desire to return ancestors and items. During this same 15-year period, I engaged in consultations with several institutions on behalf of my tribe, including Harvard University's Peabody Museum of Archaeology and Ethnology, and encountered first-hand the opposite concept: what I call a "retentive philosophy" (resistance to comply with NAGPRA and a desire to retain collections because they are viewed as scientific specimens). Examples of these concepts are shared below through interactions different tribes engaged in the NAGPRA process have had with museums or institutions. The primary example of an institution with a retentive philosophy shared in this chapter is Harvard University, and several case studies demonstrate how this institution repeatedly retains Native American ancestors and items from tribes across the country. Although the institution presents itself as a leader in working with tribes and in repatriation through public statements made at NAGPRA Review Committee meetings[9] and in other public settings, this façade is clearly visible when details of the exchanges staff responsible for NAGPRA compliance have with tribes are revealed, or in the language staff use to discuss their repatriation work.

For example, tribes from Massachusetts have directly encountered Harvard's retentive philosophy through consultations over the years. During an April 2013 consultation with the Nipmuc Nation regarding CUI ancestors, museum representatives at Harvard informed tribal members (including myself) that their CUI determinations are based on temporal evidence, indicating that ancestors and objects older than 2,000 years lacked the "shared group identity" key to cultural affiliation. When asked what the "evidence" for this arbitrary division was, they were not able to clearly articulate it to the satisfaction of the tribal representatives (also well-versed in the historical and archaeological literature, in addition to tribal knowledge of southern New England). Demonstrating preponderance of the evidence to prove cultural affiliation thus became the burden of the tribe, although the institution appeared sincere in its attempts to comply with NAGPRA by consulting with a non-federally recognized tribe. The result of the consultation was Harvard University suggesting the tribe submit "additional documentation" to demonstrate cultural affiliation.

Since New England tribes lost much of their land by the eighteenth century, aboriginal land (recognized through an ICC claim, US Court of Claims, treaties, an Act of Congress or an executive order)[10] – the basis of CUI repatriations through 10.11 – does not apply in most cases. The nineteenth-century reservations established for more western tribes also do not exist in this area, although a number of tribes established reservations through land claims and federal acknowledgement in the later twentieth century. Previous consultations with the Wampanoag Repatriation Confederation resulted in similar conversations regarding ancestors from Massachusetts. For this institution, consultations function as a specific means to claim it has "fulfilled" its obligation to complete the *process* required to be in compliance with NAGPRA. These consultations are not, then, genuine consultations. They are mono-directional and the power to say what the evidence is and what it means clearly rests with the institution. Relying solely on meeting the obligations for the process, but not advancing the claims any further, is an example of not operating within the spirit of the law. Without institutional will, the goal of NAGPRA (actual repatriation) will usually not be achieved.

Other tribes from different areas of the country have had similar experiences with Harvard, despite precedent repatriations with other museums for ancestors or items from the same areas or even sites. These cases are becoming well-known for those engaged in NAGPRA who work together and share knowledge of museums and institutions with retentive philosophies. Some of these issues are publicly recorded at the bi-annual National NAGPRA Review Committee meetings, with minutes available on the NAGPRA website (see, for example, the March 2015 meeting minutes at http://www.nps.gov/nagpra/).

During an April 2014 Harvard University consultation, MACPRA (Michigan Anishinaabek Cultural Preservation and Repatriation Alliance) tribes visited the university for consultations toward repatriating human remains and artifacts. As part of the visit, the tribes requested a public dialogue in the form of an evening roundtable, which was well-attended and provided a glimpse into the nature of museum–tribal consultations at Harvard. Patricia Capone (Director of Repatriation and Research Services and Museum Curator at Harvard's Peabody Museum of Archaeology and Ethnology) said the museum's focus was on learning and gaining a better understanding of its collections, and that "intentionality" is important.[11] To underscore the focus of Harvard's "intentionality," NAGPRA Coordinator Sandra Dong showed the film "Full Circle," a chronicle of the museum's repatriation of a totem pole to Alaska. The backdrop behind the screen was a display of Northwest Coast masks, most likely objects of cultural patrimony. While a nice public performance of "intent" and good will, the feel-good film focused on the return of the totem pole juxtaposed against NAGPRA-sensitive objects most tribes might not want on display was telling for anyone observational in the audience, or who knew Harvard's retentive philosophy.

Dong reiterated Capone's sentiment that NAGPRA offers an opportunity to learn from different people and provides a perspective on American history. Capone explained her initial interest in NAGPRA when it was passed in 1990, and how when she began at Harvard University that became an "inquisitiveness," in addition to an interest in colonialism and physical representations. She added it was a "privilege" to be part of "the process" and work with people on NAGPRA. Neither Capone nor Dong (the museum's primary NAGPRA representatives) mentioned actual repatriation of human remains or objects to tribes as the goal (or even *a* goal) of their work during this opportunity of dialogue with the tribes and public. When combined with the experiences tribes have had with the museum's resistance to repatriate, it is clear that a retentive philosophy guides both the rhetoric and the actions of Harvard's repatriation representatives.

In contrast, MACPRA representatives Shannon Martin and Sonya Atalay discussed repatriation not in the context of colonialism or research used by Harvard representatives, but as an opportunity to be good ancestors themselves and to right some of the wrongs that have occurred through this human rights law. Martin, Director of the Saginaw Chippewa Ziibiwing Center of Anishinabe Culture and Lifeways, described the reinterment part of repatriation as a recommitment ceremony (versus a reburial) as the ancestors and objects are being recommitted to the earth[12] and, I would add, the commitment of these tribal members to continue this work reaffirmed with each repatriation effort they undertake.

As part of these discussions, Harvard representatives were asked how they determine if ancestors are CUI and how consultations that are supposed to be part of the cultural affiliation determination (such as with the Michigan tribes) inform that. Capone responded that they follow the process outlined in the law and the steps, all of which are based on an examination of readily available evidence and consultation, and that in some cases "there are conflicts." Martin added that some of these determinations are made through master narratives,[13] echoing Clay Dumont's assessment noted above.

After three days of consultation, the Michigan tribes were informed by Harvard's "experts" that the ancestors and objects could not be culturally affiliated, despite evidence presented by the tribes demonstrating knowledge of the ancestors and associated artifacts. Perhaps foretelling this result, Shannon Martin shared at the roundtable an example of an effective process they utilized to force repatriation in Michigan. Storming a University of Michigan Board of Regents meeting was a powerful and effective turning point for that institution, which had also maintained a retentive philosophy. This approach resulted in Michigan transforming from "stonewalling" to actively engaging in repatriation of both human remains and objects. In essence, the tribes forced the development of an institutional will now firmly entrenched in Michigan's philosophy regarding NAGPRA. Just as importantly, addressing the university's regents – a powerful decision-making center of the institution – alerted them to the university's responsibilities under federal law *and* that staff were making decisions resulting in non-compliance, which they may not have been aware of. A similar approach with other institutions harboring retentive philosophies may be just as effective.

Although Harvard University repeatedly presents itself as an institution in the forefront of repatriation in public comments at NAGPRA Review Committee meetings and other settings, it continues to hold one of the largest and broadest collections subject to NAGPRA. At the Spring 2015 NAGPRA Review Committee meeting, Capone provided an update on the university's NAGPRA implementation, noting it had "committed significant resources and attention over many years to implement NAGPRA and to cultivate the relationships necessary to this effort." She also noted how the museum has "partnered with Native American communities and other institutions across the United States toward mutual goals of education and research . . . [and] considers the experience to be a privilege. The process has benefited each of [the institution's] missions of education, research and developing relationships with Indigenous communities and scholars" (National NAGPRA 2015, V1: 183–4).

"Implementation" of NAGPRA at Harvard University – decades after enactment of the Act – includes "continu[ing] to refine policies and procedures for sensitive collections and to strive for improved approaches to expanding accessibility to Native American communities whether through NAGPRA or other means . . . [and] respond[ing] to frequent informational inquiries from students or other interested parties," according to Capone. She also noted that the museum is "grateful for the consultations of NAGPRA and collaborations beyond that have so broadly benefited the institution, and . . . [led] to new ways of understanding through the NAGPRA process" (National NAGPRA 2015, V1: 184–5). In this rhetoric, as at the public setting with the Michigan tribes, no mention of actually returning ancestors or items to tribes was made.

But, to further demonstrate its "significant commitment" to NAGPRA, in Spring of 2015 "a display on NAGPRA in part responding to these interests" opened at the museum and has been "a museum priority," according to Capone. What has clearly *not* been a priority for Harvard University is the return of ancestors and items to Native American tribes. A museum display such as this continues a public rhetoric of compliance, while the reality as demonstrated through completed repatriations demonstrates a significant gulf in what is being said and what is actually being done. Nevertheless, Harvard has pointed out that over the past year the museum had welcomed six in-person NAGPRA consultation visits and hundreds of other exchanges by phone or email with tribes across the country (National NAGPRA 2015, V1: 184–5). Nipmuc representatives experienced one of these in-person consultations with Harvard University in 2013 (noted above), with the same result as the MACPRA representatives: Harvard University "experts" informing the tribes that no cultural affiliation exists between the ancestors they hold and modern-day tribes. Consultations, like museum displays on NAGPRA, become another layer of the façade supporting the rhetoric and appearance of NAGPRA compliance, in essence a strategy to work within a law with weaknesses that allow non-compliance by savvy practitioners.

Other tribes have had similar experiences with Harvard. A few years ago the Wabanaki Intertribal Repatriation Committee claimed ancient remains from Maine, which the university denied with no explanation of why the evidence was not accepted. Bonnie Newsom, Penobscot representative, has stated that "there needs to be a process whereby if a tribe has made a claim, denied or not, [they] have some role in the work . . . done on those remains until the [affiliation] issue is resolved . . . if . . . an institution . . . continue[s] to do study . . . that's ethically wrong until we have an opportunity to present more information or clear up the reasons why we were denied those remains" (National NAGPRA 2015, V1: 206–7). In another claim by the Wabanaki dating to 2011, letters to eight institutions with remains and objects from Maine resulted in one institution denying the claim (Harvard University), again with no explanation of why the evidence was insufficient for cultural affiliation. While Harvard (holding the human remains) denied the Wabanaki claim, the R. S. Peabody in Andover, Mass. (holding the funerary objects) affirmed cultural affiliation and is moving toward repatriation (National NAGPRA 2015, V2: 201–2). Minutes of NAGPRA Review Committee meetings over the past few years document how other tribes across the country continue to experience resistance from Harvard University and similar institutions with retentive philosophies.

Another institution still developing institutional will is Indiana University. The university only began an official NAGPRA "project" in 2013, yet federal grant funds (in the form of an National Science Foundation (NSF) grant) were awarded to this institution, which is just now, after two decades, making progress on a collection that includes thousands of individuals, mostly still classified as CUI.[14] The NSF grant project focuses on how "practicing archaeologists and bioanthropologists prepare future professionals to handle ethical issues raised by NAGPRA . . . using a collegium workshop format" (National NAGPRA 2014, V1: 220). The project will also create a website that will act as a "dynamic hub" for visitors to retrieve information (such as talks or course and media materials) related to repatriation. For tribes, time could be better spent on actually doing the work of NAGPRA: consultations leading to repatriation. Like so many other institutions, Indiana University had not consulted with tribes before categorizing ancestors as CUI (National NAGPRA 2015, V2: 215–16). In 2015, the university was awarded a consultation grant for over $46,000, which it plans to use for consultation with at least 10 tribes,[15] indicating that a shift may be happening at that institution after decades of non-compliance. Indiana has publicly expressed a desire and objective to establish lines of communication that will facilitate returning "ancestral remains and funerary objects . . . to appropriate tribal communities" (National NAGPRA 2014, V1: 222) and only time will tell if it has developed genuine institutional will.

Harvard University, University of Michigan and Indiana University are far from the only institutions across the country that have had retentive philosophies or used the designation of CUI to avoid repatriation. As of 2015, almost 18,000 ancestors and over 150,000 associated funerary objects were classified as unidentifiable or unaffiliated, where museums and institutions have not completed (or demonstrated completion of) consultations with tribes that could lead to affiliation and repatriation (National NAGPRA 2015, V1: 48).

There are certainly times when classifying ancestors as CUI is the appropriate (and desired) path, and what tribes prefer, as noted above. For example, UMass Amherst developed institutional will to complete a number of repatriations, partly as a result of conversations with tribes in New England needing the university to fulfill its obligation both to the law and to the communities it worked with. Tribal people from the region have long-standing relationships with the university, contributing to Native Studies courses as guest speakers, attending annual symposia, powwows and other events, and attending as students. Yet the contradiction loomed that while this collaborative relationship existed, the university continued to hold almost 100 ancestors from the area identified as CUI because they were not readily affiliated with any *federally* recognized tribes, but from an area most closely associated with non-extant and non-federally recognized tribes. Thus identifying these ancestors as CUI was appropriate and indicated the institution's commitment to acknowledging the continued presence of the non-extant and non-recognized tribes and continued relationships to the ancestors. This example also demonstrates how any institution can choose to acknowledge, consult with and repatriate to non-federally recognized tribes; nothing in NAGPRA bars that from happening and a process is clearly laid out in the regulations.

Between 2010 and 2014, UMass published five Notices of Inventory Completion (NICs), plus two between 2004 and 2010. The institution initially inventoried some ancestors as CUI on the NAGPRA database to make the information public and then consult with tribes regarding their wishes to either culturally affiliate or have the ancestors remain CUI. UMass's approach has been to consult broadly, and culturally affiliate if possible and *if* that is the wish of tribes.

Both University of Michigan and University of Massachusetts, and now Indiana University, developed institutional will following pressure from tribes to not only engage in the *process* of NAGPRA, but to do so in the *spirit* of the law, with the goal of actual repatriation. These institutions have become examples of positive institutional will over the past decade and now work with tribes to return ancestors and items to the people and homelands they belong to. Other institutions, such as Harvard University, have continued colonial logics that originally governed the collection and theft of ancestors; the need to keep these as university property is tied to ideas of their objective and isolated nature as human remains with scientific value, rather than as ancestors with active relationships to present-day tribes. Even well into the twenty-first century changing philosophies at certain institutions has proven difficult. Only with legal or public pressure will they likely develop the institutional will to repatriate Native American ancestors and items that rightfully belong to tribes.

For example, California tribes have been very vocal about the need for institutions in that state to comply with NAGPRA, and are being heard. In 2014 the University of California, Davis hired Megon Noble as the first full-time staff member dedicated exclusively to NAGPRA compliance. The university – which has approximately 300 sets of remains from 62 sites and 12,000 funerary objects – has made "a conscious decision to embrace both the letter and the spirit of the law with the recent development of the[ir] NAGPRA program" (National NAGPRA 2015, V2: 187), according to Noble. Noble has a reputation for embracing NAGPRA and the spirit of the law, so the university's decision to hire her is a strong indicator that they intend to repatriate and their words are not just rhetoric.

Impediments and best practices

One of the greatest challenges to the success of NAGPRA is the control museum and institution officials have over the process (mainly, deciding cultural affiliation), and other impediments result in tens of thousands of ancestors still not repatriated. Some of these were discussed at recent NAGPRA Review Committee meetings. Lack of sufficient investigations by National NAGPRA has allowed retentive philosophies to persevere. The law allows for the Secretary of the Interior to assess civil penalties against museums that fail to comply with the requirements of the law, but complaints must first be initiated (usually by tribes) with National NAGPRA. The process and the enumeration of different ways museums fail to comply are in the NAGPRA regulations (Section 10.12), but lack of an investigator during some periods over the past decade (due to lack of government funding) has led to a backlog of cases not investigated for several years. In a five-month period in the 2014–15 fiscal year, NAGPRA received three written allegations of museums failing to comply and one Notice of Museum Failure to Comply was recorded. One Review Committee member suggested that investigations be a public process, as it is an area where transparency would be valuable to both tribes and museums (National NAGPRA 2015, V1: 34–5). Presently, only when investigations are completed are results published by NAGPRA. Even Review Committee members are not informed of on-going investigations and some take well over a year, once they make it to the top of the backlog list. Yet some still believe that forcing investigations of non-compliant institutions and museums has merit. Mashpee Wampanoag representative Ramona Peters recently commented: "I want to encourage tribes who are having these problems to use . . . civil penalties. We were successful . . . Without museums actually paying the fees [civil penalties], there's no deterrent really . . . they would be more inclined to comply with the law if we actually used or sharpened the teeth of the law" (National NAGPRA 2015, V1: 71–2).

Ryan Wheeler, Director of the Robert S. Peabody Museum in Andover, Massachusetts, described one impediment to his institution's efforts toward repatriation: the issue of split collections. Historically some institutions kept funerary objects and sent remains to other institutions, or remains of the same individuals or from the same site were split between institutions. For example, the Pecos, New Mexico, collection was split between the Andover Peabody and Harvard Peabody museums, and "the institutions have divergent ideas about the application of the Act," on cultural affiliation, to be exact (able or *wanting* to culturally affiliate), and the misuse of CUI. Harvard possesses the human remains and refuses to culturally affiliate, while Andover Peabody has chosen to culturally affiliate funerary materials from the same site. This case, in particular, highlights how a lack of institutional will, as at Harvard and others with similar split collections, remains an impediment to repatriation

(National NAGPRA 2015, V2: 176). Many tribes will wait until they can repatriate all of the material to complete the transfer and reinterment processes.

Another impediment is remains that have been culturally affiliated but not yet listed in Notices of Inventory Completion (the final step in a museum, institution or federal agency's legal obligation before final transfer to tribes). As of early 2015, over 3,000 human remains had been culturally affiliated in lists given to National NAGPRA but not yet repatriated. And a number of museums did not provide any evidence of consulting with tribes or NHOs while developing their CUI inventories, technically not complying with the law.

Ultimately, responsibility for delays in completing the process of repatriation lies not with National NAGPRA; the burden is on museums and institutions to draft and submit notices for publication, then return ancestors and items. As Ramona Peters (who has worked on repatriation since before the law was enacted) noted, deterrents such as civil penalties only work if they are exercised, and tribes need to know which the resistant museums are in order to push for investigations and penalties to be enforced (National NAGPRA 2015, V1: 72). The need for both more investigations and more public knowledge of those investigations clearly exists, especially with institutions with retentive philosophies such as Harvard. For tribes with a one- or two-person office managing both Tribal Historic Preservation and NAGPRA duties, resources and manpower don't always exist to challenge institutions, and formal investigations by National NAGPRA can take several years to complete.

While these and many other impediments to repatriation remain, a number of solutions and best practices developed over the past few decades do help respond to them. Penobscot representative Bonnie Newsom recently expressed a common frustration of many tribes: "decision-making authority relative to cultural affiliation determinations rests with the individuals in positions of power in these institutions . . . We never gave away our rights to care for our ancestral remains or to manage our cultural heritage. I find it extremely unjust that others have taken those rights and responsibilities away from us and that the NAGPRA process perpetuates that by giving non-Native entities decision-making authority about the care of our ancestral remains and cultural heritage" (National NAGPRA 2015, V2: 203). One possible solution, suggested by Review Committee member Steve Titla, is for museums and institutions to employ more Native people in decision-making positions (National NAGPRA 2015, V2: 206). The institutions that have done this (such as UMass) demonstrate institutional will beyond seeking collaborations that benefit the institution "toward mutual goals of education and research," and/or "new ways of understanding through the NAGPRA process," as Harvard University has stated its goals and foci to be (National NAGPRA 2015, V1: 183–5). After over two decades of NAGPRA, the goal of *every* museum and institution – especially those that present themselves as at the forefront of the field – can be nothing other than *achieving* repatriation. The goal of NAGPRA is not education, research, new ways of understanding or developing policies and procedures, although these certainly are often part of the process; the goal of NAGPRA is repatriation. But, as Steve Titla expressed it, decisions made by "museums sometimes are not logical, and they are made by non-Natives" (National NAGPRA 2015, V2: 207–8).

And for federal agencies still in control or possession of thousands of ancestors some solutions to the impediments and barriers they face include clarifying definitions in the regulations, requiring museums, institutions and other non-federal repositories (holding collections belonging to agencies) to report on their collections to agencies, and agencies having authority to request information from repositories (National NAGPRA 2015, V1: 176–7). Funding is always an impediment to overcome. Ramona Peters has stated that repatriation is "meaningful . . . [and] important. It's our human rights being exercised, and it needs to be better supported by the federal government" (National NAGPRA 2015, V1: 73). Most other tribes would agree.

The Colville, Umatilla, Yakama, Nez Perce and Wanapum tribes have offered several ideas to increase compliance and best practices for consultation, curation and repatriation. For example, knowing which museums have received federal funds and thus are required to comply with the law but have not, would be helpful. No clear understanding of the extent of unaccounted-for Native American remains that could be repatriated under NAGPRA exists. Updated contact lists for key tribal personnel would assist museums, institutions and agencies, who should understand that they cannot dictate who participates in consultations. Consultations can include more than one tribe and non-federally recognized tribes. Tribes appreciate honesty, and consultations should include policy and decision makers who can provide answers and assurances. Consultations should also begin early in a relationship and may not, in fact, have an end; they should be held as often as needed and take as long as needed. Effective consultations build relationships that continue after a project or a repatriation is complete (National NAGPRA 2015, V2: 100–2).

These tribes also offer best practices for curation and management of ancestors and objects, noting first that curation should be respectful for both ancestors and their living descendants and that policies and procedures regarding care and access should involve potentially affiliated tribes. Policies regarding requests for information and research, in particular, should be created with tribes and not solely by institutions and agencies. Best practices for physical transfers include: open communication with everyone involved, providing support for both the museum or agency and tribes, and keeping the best interests of the ancestors and objects in mind (such as location and long-term protection) (National NAGPRA 2015, V2: 102–3).

Concluding remarks

These best practices remind us that beyond the legal obligations museums, institutions and federal agencies in the United States have to comply with the Native American Graves Protection and Repatriation Act, they also have a *moral* obligation to satisfy what is clearly human rights law designed to correct at least some of the offenses committed against Native Americans over the past 500 years. These offenses include genocidal atrocities resulting in the deaths and subjugation of millions over the centuries, and storage and display of ancestors and items by the dominant non-Native culture. Many tribes still face too many obstacles and resistance to repatriation of their ancestors, and funerary, sacred and cultural patrimony objects from museums and institutions that have yet to develop institutional will. At this juncture, we no longer need to ask if and how NAGPRA works. The pertinent question is: How can we create institutional will when an institution or museum refuses to repatriate? Different tribes have used several options: initiating an investigation through National NAGPRA (and hoping it is completed in a reasonable time); requesting a Finding of Fact by the NAGPRA Review Committee regarding details of a case; for the Michigan tribes, storming a board of regents meeting to make them aware of non-compliance at their institution; and using the media and public support to turn the tide.

My experiences working both within and with museums and institutions have been mixed. While the university I worked for developed the institutional will to embrace its responsibilities, others I interacted with to either facilitate repatriation or as a consulting party (with Harvard University) demonstrate that many museums have a long way to go. Harvard University, as one example, often claims "no temporal link" exists between ancestors and modern-day tribes, classifying human remains and objects as CUI even when precedent cases for cultural affiliation exist. When asked during a consultation why they would want to retain human remains or objects, the university's response was, "Well, we are a museum."[16]

This statement clearly defines what the "intentionality" of Harvard University is. As of February 2015, the university had listed on the NAGPRA databases 1,083 culturally affiliated individuals plus 4,067 AFOs, originally published and then updated between 1994 and 2015. Some of these will have been repatriated but it's unknown from the database how many remain at the institution. Beyond that, Harvard has listed 7,048 individuals as CUI, plus 14,473 AFOs, supporting the fact that designating ancestors as CUI is a practice for this institution.[17] While some of these ancestors and items may have little to no provenience, others were taken from specific and known locations that modern-day tribes have clearly expressed cultural ties to. And this list does not include other NAGPRA-sensitive items at the institution (unassociated funerary objects, objects of cultural patrimony and sacred objects) not captured in these databases and only traceable in summary letters the institution may have sent to individual tribes. Many of these NAGPRA items are ethnographic objects (like the Northwest Coast masks noted above) valued by museums like Harvard for artistic and educational value.

This chapter has discussed a key issue in the repatriation process – the practice of institutions categorizing ancestors and items as CUI, or "culturally unidentifiable" – and shared case studies demonstrating how institutional will is changing among some museums and universities, while others continue to practice retentive philosophies and resist repatriation. This philosophy is clearly against the human rights component intended with the spirit of NAGPRA, and using the CUI category is clearly a conscious strategy employed by some institutions to retain ancestors and items subject to NAGPRA. Museums, institutions and federal agencies receiving federal funds and thus subject to NAGPRA have an *affirmative duty* to actively participate in repatriation of Native American remains and objects through consultation with tribes and Native Hawaiian organizations, including previously culturally unidentifiable ancestors through the addition of 10.11 of the NAGPRA regulations in 2010.

As noted in the beginning of this chapter, NAGPRA is a diverse, complex and contested law changing through practice, and through the input of Native Americans, archaeologists, museum professionals and other academics, and collectors. More than anything, though, NAGPRA is Indian Law and Human Rights Law, clearly created to right some of the wrongs that have occurred, as Sonya Atalay noted (personal communication, April 2014). What this chapter encourages is focusing on what we do have the power to change: institutional will. While some valid reasons remain for classifying Native American ancestors as CUI – such as no provenience information, to share information until consultations are complete, or because tribes prefer the CUI designation – this is a designation that should be used only in certain circumstances, and *in consultation* with tribes. According to the law, ancestors connected to non-federally recognized tribes or tribes no longer extant are also considered CUI. Non-Native control of the process, though, often obfuscates both the process and intent of the law.

Ramona Peters has noted that, "for museums in this country that receive federal money, if . . . their names are out there as people who are doing something shameful, then maybe they wouldn't do it" (National NAGPRA 2015, V1: 72–3). This chapter has attempted to respond to this call, but on a limited basis. Too many museums and institutions continue to fail at fulfilling their legal and affirmative duties to consult and repatriate. Without developing institutional will – through either a change of philosophy within or by being "encouraged" through legal processes like investigations by National NAGPRA – impediments will continue to prevent ancestors and items from going home.

The Wampanoag Repatriation Confederation had repatriated 522 ancestors as of Spring 2015, noting it was a long and difficult process to achieve. Ramona Peters has considered these difficulties as primarily involving resistance from museums. After decades she grapples with trying to understand: "I think we're talking about three worlds here, the one where the ancestors walk and they walk in ours and they walk in the museums, and then there is us, the present day walking with the DNA of thousands of years, and then there are people who came here, whose ancestors are from another world, another land, but yet their worldview creates a resistance to cooperating in a good way" (National NAGPRA 2015, V1: 67–8). These remain the core issues surrounding NAGPRA, classifying ancestors as CUI, and the clear need for more institutions to develop the institutional will to achieve the objective of this law: repatriation.

Notes

1 Nipmuc Nation of Massachusetts.

2 For definitions of these terms, see the glossary on the National NAGPRA website at http://www.nps.gov/nagpra/TRAINING/ GLOSSARY.HTM.

3 One of weaknesses of NAGPRA is that cultural affiliation is determined by museums and institutions, and many tribes must "prove" connections to ancestors. Harvard University, for example, claims that ancestors older than 2,000 years cannot be culturally affiliated with modern-day Indian tribes, while other institutions clearly recognize connections between older ancestors and modern-day tribes.

4 Citations for the Native American Graves Protection and Repatriation Act: 25 USC 3001 et seq. [Nov. 16, 1990], codified in: 43 CFR 10.

5 Cultural affiliation is defined as: "A relationship of shared group identity which can be reasonably traced historically or prehistorically between a present-day Indian tribe or Native Hawaiian organization and an identifiable earlier group (25 USC 3001 (2)). Cultural affiliation is established when the preponderance of the evidence – based on geographical, kinship, biological, archeological, linguistic, folklore, oral tradition, historical evidence, or other information or expert opinion – reasonably leads to such a conclusion" (43 CFR 10.2 (e)).

6 Defined as: "As standard of proof in civil cases, is evidence which is of greater weight or more convincing than the evidence which is offered in opposition to it; that is, evidence which as a whole shows that the fact sought to be proved is more probable than not" (*Black's Law Dictionary*, 6th edition; http://www.nps.gov/nagpra/TRAINING/GLOSSARY.HTM) (accessed 27 March 2017).

7 Sherry Hutt, personal communication, NAGPRA Training, Oct. 2010.

8 The final rule publication and comments associated with the finalization of rule 10.11 are in the Federal Register, Vol. 75, No. 49, https://www.gpo.gov/fdsys/pkg/FR-2010-03-15/pdf/2010-5283.pdf (accessed 27 March 2017).

9 See meeting minutes transcriptions at https://irma.nps.gov/DataStore/Reference/Profile/2193294 (accessed 27 March 2017).

10 43 CFR 10.6 (a)(2)(iii)

11 Personal communication at the April 2014 public roundtable.

12 Personal communication at the April 2014 public roundtable.

13 Personal communication at the April 2014 public roundtable.

14 As of February 2016 Indiana University reported through the NAGPRA database possession of 75 individuals and 396 AFOs culturally affiliated, plus 5,270 individuals and 9,783 AFOs as CUI (including some excavated in the late 1980s and 1990, the year NAGPRA was passed).

15 http://viewpoints.iu.edu/policy-briefings/2015/08/10/iu-awarded-consultation-grant-for-native-american-graves-protection-and-repatriation-act/ (accessed 27 March 2017).

16 Patricia Capone, personal communication, April 2013.

17 Some of the CUI listings have been recategorized as culturally affiliated but remain on the CUI listing for record keeping and documenting the transition from CUI to culturally affiliated. Even with some overlap possible for Harvard University, the number of CUI ancestors and AFOs in that institution's possession is exceedingly high.

Bibliography

American Indian Ritual Object Repatriation Foundation. 1995. *Mending the Circle: A Native American Repatriation Guide*. New York: American Indian Ritual Object Repatriation Foundation. Available at: www.repatriationfoundation.org.

Dumont, Jr., Clay W. 2011. Contesting Scientists' Narrations of NAGPRA's Legislative History: Rule 10.11 and the Recovery of "Culturally Identifiable" Ancestors. *Wicazo Sa Review* (Spring), pp. 5–41.

Fine Dare, Kathleen. 2002. *Grave Injustice: The American Indian Repatriation Movement and NAGPRA*. Lincoln, NE: University of Nebraska Press.

Merryman, John Henry. 1986. Two Ways of Thinking about Cultural Property. *American Journal of International Law*, Vol. 80, No. 4, pp. 831–853.

Mihesuah, Devon Abbott, ed. 2009. *Repatriation Reader: Who Owns American Indian Remains?* Lincoln, NE: University of Nebraska Press.

National NAGPRA. 2014. Minutes and Transcripts for the 53rd Review Committee Meeting. Washington, DC, Nov. 20–21, V1 & V2.

National NAGPRA. 2015. Minutes and Transcripts for the 55th Review Committee Meeting. Amherst, MA, March 3–4, V1 & V2.

Peck, Danielle and Alex Seaborn. 1998. *Bones of Contention: Native American Archaeology*. Princeton, NJ: Films for the Humanities and Sciences.

Thomas, David Hurst. 2000. *Skull Wars: Kennewick Man, Archaeology, and the Battle for Native Identity*. New York: Basic Books.

8

BETTING ON THE RAVEN

Ethical relationality and Nuxalk cultural property

Jennifer Kramer

Section one: The wager of the Nuxalk raven forehead mask

In this chapter, I explore the tensions between understandings of cultural property and cultural exchange as they have emerged on the Northwest Coast of Canada and the USA at a moment of media-focused attention and the resulting renegotiation of relations between a First Nation in British Columbia and a metropolitan art museum.

On January 26, 2014, the Seattle Art Museum (SAM) and the Denver Art Museum (DAM) announced a friendly wager on the outcome of Super Bowl 2014 between the Denver Broncos (Figure 8.1) and the Seattle Seahawks (Figure 8.2). Following in the footsteps of other light-hearted bets between cities over major competitive events, each museum chose an artwork from their collection to represent their respective football team's mascot. SAM Director Kimberly Rorschach explained to the press: "There's an emotional connection

Figure 8.1 The Denver Broncos logo.
Source: Courtesy of the Denver Broncos Football Club.

Figure 8.2 The Seattle Seahawks logo is a registered trademark of Football Northwest LLC.
Source: Courtesy of the Seattle Seahawks Football Club.

Figure 8.3 Frederic Remington, *The Broncho Buster*. 1895, bronze, 23¼ inches. Denver Art Museum Collection: The Roath Collection, 2013.91.
Source: Photo © Denver Art Museum.

Figure 8.4 Forehead Mask of Raven, Nuxalk, ca. 1880, alder, red cedar bark, copper, pins, paint, 4⅛ x 5⅛ inches. Seattle Art Museum, Gift of John H. Hauberg, 91.1.71.
Source: Paul Macapia.

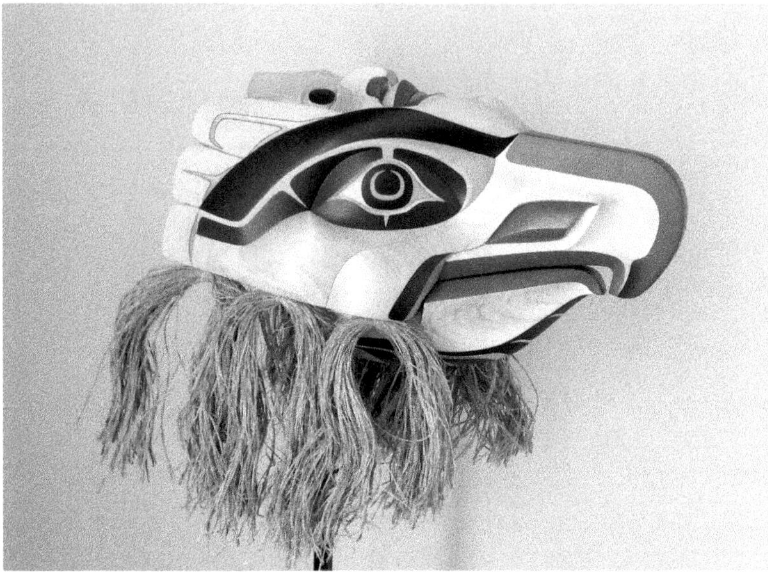

Figure 8.5 Seahawk mask by Nuxalk carver Latham Mack, 2016. Medium: Alder, red cedar bark. Size: L 19⅜ x W 12⅜ x H 11¾ inches (excl. cedar bark).
Source: Image courtesy of Latham Mack.

to art, like there can be for sports" (quoted in CBC News January 27, 2014). The bet stated that whichever city's football team lost the big game, their waged artwork would go on loan for three months to the winning city, displayed in the winning city's museum, with expenses paid by the losing city's museum. The museums considered this a cultural exchange.

DAM selected a Frederic Remington 1895 bronze sculpture called "The Broncho Buster" (Figure 8.3) and SAM selected a circa 1880 forehead mask in the shape of a raven's head from the Nuxalk people of Bella Coola, British Columbia, Canada (Figure 8.4). SAM Curator of Native American Art, Barbara Brotherton chose this particular piece (# 91.1.71) because she considered it an "absolutely stunning masterpiece from our collection" (pers. comm. January 28, 2014). SAM Director Rorschach further explicated: "We know that the Seahawks logo is based loosely on Northwest Coast Native American design. It just seemed natural to choose one of our great works that is of a bird reminiscent of that logo" (quoted in CBC News January 28, 2014).

Clearly, both museums were responding to the loyalty of sports fans by selecting artworks that visually reflected the teams' mascots. DAM Director Christoph Heinrich said "the fever surrounding Super Bowl Sunday is an opportunity for both cities to show off what makes them special, on and off the field" (quoted in CBC News January 29, 2014). Since each artwork was meant to represent the city in which it was located, aesthetically valued pieces were chosen to materialize municipal pride and to tangibly evoke sports prowess. Possessing in one's collection a "masterpiece," judged to be such by "the art-culture system" (Clifford 1988:223), was being held up as proof of strong identity.

DAM released a press statement explaining its art selection: "The bronze horse symbolizes the spirit and tenacity of the Wild West. Popular from the time of its creation, The Broncho Buster stands today as an icon of the region and is thought of as the first action bronze of a western hero" (quoted in Hendrick January 27, 2014). SAM too justified its choice by interpreting visual characteristics of the Nuxalk raven forehead mask as aggressive competitor:

"The open mouth suggests the ferocity of this bird of prey, possibly a supernatural 'man-eater'"[1] (quoted in Hendrick January 27, 2014).

This latter reading took artistic (and cultural) license when it playfully suggested a bellicose meaning (echoing United States football's traditional "trash talk") that did not reflect Nuxalk sacred and ceremonial functions of the mask as transmitter of inheritance and conveyer of social identity. Moreover, the museum knew this mask's cultural meaning was not that of a "man-eater" because Brotherton had written this description for the museum's on-line catalogue record in 2011: "This elegant depiction of Raven carved in the skillful Nuxalk style was the property of a high-ranking man or woman who was a member of the *Sisawk* society, sometimes referred to as the society of chiefs. The dancer's regalia were associated with a special name, songs, and dance movements that were passed down and validated during potlatches" (SAM on-line collection website).

SAM unwittingly promoted "looking relations" (Townsend-Gault 2004:189; Baloy 2014:221, 253) when it read the surface of the mask as a sports metaphor, inadvertently blocking the non-Native viewer from understanding both the original (and ongoing) use of this type of mask in Nuxalk culture and the colonial history that allowed for its cultural alienation through collection and museum display (Cole 1985; Townsend-Gault, Kramer and Ki-ke-in 2013). As both Charlotte Townsend-Gault and Natalie Baloy have explicated, "looking relations" are superficial because they allow spectators to see only a beautiful facade but also have powerful effect because they hide the real relations arising from settler-colonial injustices imposed on Native people. Pressures from Canada's Indian act, missionization, residential schools, and other assimilative techniques enabled Native material culture to be collected as artifact or art and owned within a Western legal definition by institutions or private collectors. Thus, when non-Native viewers impose their own meaning onto a material manifestation of Nuxalk culture, historically unequal power relations between Native and non-Native people become further accentuated. Looking relations can present an image of exchange that in fact masks a much more zero-sum end-game with regards to the ownership of cultural items.

On April 7, 2012, SAM Curator Barbara Brotherton upon invitation had attended the potlatch of Nuxalk Hereditary Chief Anuspuxals (Jeffrey Snow) in Bella Coola.[2] She went specifically to consult with the Nuxalk about the eight Nuxalk masks in the SAM collection. During this potlatch she had "floor time" to present photographs of these masks to the community and to ask the chiefs and those in attendance for information that would help the museum better care for, display, and interpret their cultural heritage. These large-scale photographs circulated and then were left with the Nuxalk chiefs. The museum hoped to learn more about their specific meaning and culturally appropriate protocol for their presentation, but at that time did not receive feedback about the Nuxalk raven forehead mask from the community. Upon reflection, Brotherton noted: "Had I had some direct information (which I was actively seeking and publicly asking for) this mask would have never been chosen for the Seattle–Denver cultural exchange" (Brotherton pers. comm. April 25, 2016).

Given this experience, it would be facile to reproach the museum for objectification of Nuxalk culture. Nonetheless, the mask has routinely been classified in typical museum terminology in exhibit label and published catalogue by accession number, materials, date, and measurements (see Holm 1995:182) and in art language as a "masterpiece" owned by the museum. Suggesting the mask could be considered a man-eating bird is sensationalist and understandably could lead to Nuxalk feelings of decontextualization, misrepresentation, and exoticization. Many Nuxalk did feel that a sacred mask used ceremonially to pass on social identity should not be used as a bet for a sports competition and expressed their opinions and indignations on social media sites, encapsulated by this tweet from NuxalkNation.org under the hashtag "decolonize": "Nuxalk masks are sacred ceremonial items, not simply 'art' display pieces" (January 28, 2014). Numerous bloggers and on-line commentators interpreted SAM's actions as trivializing, disrespectful, and potentially demeaning of Nuxalk culture, although some took a more Western "possessive individualism" approach (see Macpherson 1962):

> When I create a piece of art and give or sell it to someone else they . . . can do whatever they wish with it regardless of what I think. . . . A culture stands or falls on its own ability to be relevant without the need for outside compliance or validation.
>
> *(CBC News January 28, 2014, accessed on June 19, 2014)*

Others, such as the author of the following comment, take an ironic and naturalizing attitude: "Hi Spain, yes it is the BC Guy's Museum, I am going to let my buddy borrow my Picasso that I legally own, just letting you know" (CBC News January 28, 2014, accessed on June 19, 2014). How quickly the Internet filled with personal reactions and emotional responses shows the potency of this debate and belies a tawdry or reductive analysis.

The Nuxalk, like many, first heard about this wager through news and social media. Circulating rumors offering inaccurate information gave some members of the Nuxalk Nation the impression that this bet (like one made in a casino for example) could result in a permanent transfer of ownership between SAM and DAM. A Victoria-based journalist contacted the Nuxalk Administration and asked for a statement from elected Nuxalk Chief Councilor, Wally Webber. As Chief Webber happened to be in Vancouver on other business, his response was videotaped in the CBC studios. Snxakila (Clyde Tallio), recognized speaker for the Nuxalk Hereditary Chiefs, thinks that: "The news reporter was fishing for a story and must have fed [Wally Webber] a bunch of lies to get a reaction" (pers. comm. January 28, 2014). Snxakila stated this because he believes Chief Webber wasn't given all of the facts of the cultural exchange and was purposefully put on the spot in order to create emotional tension by insinuating cultural appropriation by SAM toward the Nuxalk Nation.

Chief Councilor Webber was actually quite circumspect in his reaction after hearing that an important piece of his community's cultural heritage was being offered in a sports wager without obtaining the permission of the Nation or giving the courtesy of an advanced warning. In an interview with CBC News, Webber states:

> They informed the Broncos about it and they've never contacted us. If they're not going to respect what they have of ours, send it back to us where it will be looked after right. . . . They call it a man-eating raven. It is not that. It's a high-ranking mask for the chiefs' sacred dances, and to see it being used this way in a bet is not very kosher with us.
>
> *(January 28, 2014)*

Nuxalk encounters with British colonialism and Canadian assimilation can justifiably be understood as a successive, cumulative, and extensive history of appropriation (i.e. theft of land, resources, people, children, material culture, and cultural knowledge[3]) that warrants a far more defensive statement than Chief Webber gave. His considered response most likely derives from previous experiences with museums that strengthened connections with the Nuxalk.

Changing relations between Indigenous people and museums

The end of the twentieth and beginning of the twenty-first century has progressively witnessed Indigenous people working with and within cultural institutions to exert authority over the care, display, and interpretation of their material heritage. Increasingly, museums understand that objects in their collections still have ongoing connections to communities from whence they originated. It is now more common for museums to strive to respectfully recognize active relations between people and their cultural property with explicit museum mandates of access and knowledge sharing (e.g. Peers and Brown 2003; Carr-Locke 2015; Geismar 2013; Krmpotich and Peers 2013; Lonetree 2012; McCarthy 2011). Some institutions have begun to develop different consultative and collaborative protocols and co-management processes dependent on the collections they house, the communities with which they regularly engage, and the political structures of the nation-state in which they sit. For example, Te Papa Tangarewa, the national museum of Aotearoa New Zealand embraces the governing policy of biculturalism and the right of Maori communities to care and manage their taonga (treasures) in accordance with their tikanga (custom) (McCarthy 2011:114–15; see Tapsell this volume).[4]

The growing museum perspective of stewardship or guardianship of objects in collections affirms originating communities' inalienable bonds to these objects, and is gradually replacing the market-driven idea of legal ownership complicit with the ability of museums to alienate. In Canada, museums are more frequently recognizing their responsibility to serve as guardians rather than owners of property (Phillips 2011). At the Museum of Anthropology (MOA) at the University of British Columbia (UBC) in Vancouver, we are committed to making the museum more welcoming and open to originating communities whom we believe are our primary stakeholders. Our successful renewal project launched in 2010, "A Partnership of Peoples: New Infrastructure for Collaborative Research" (Museum of Anthropology 2000), intends to ensure MOA is a place for reciprocal research and collaborative projects. There exists a developing trust that these relationships can be mutually beneficial. At MOA this is borne out in the increase in co-curated exhibitions (such as the three-sited exhibition "c̓əsnaʔəm: the city before the city," a collaboration between the Musqueam First Nation, the Museum of Vancouver, and MOA), the rise in the number of Indigenous artists who utilize the collections we house for their artistic inspiration and cultural research (Kramer 2015b), and the enlarging circle of Indigenous people who borrow historical or contemporary museum objects for ceremony at home.

Further, some anthropologists consider the term "cultural property"[5] (meant to acknowledge originating communities' connections) a potential barrier to the ancestral agency of objects and their crucial position in social relationality (Busse 2008; Geismar 2008; Herle 2008). As a result, at MOA, we consider the material culture we hold as "belongings" rather than cultural property, especially in our relationship to the Coast Salish Musqueam people on whose traditional, ancestral, and unceded territory the museum and university sit. As Musqueam community member and co-curator of MOA's "c̓əsnaʔəm: the city before the city" exhibition Jordan Wilson explains:

> While our belongings . . . may not always be owned by the Musqueam community in a Western legal sense, "belongings" references a different sense of ownership, one that is continuous and unbroken. And when we speak about belongings, we are speaking about more than physical items; we are speaking about our history, where we come from, and who we are today.
>
> *(Wilson 2016)*

The use of the term "belongings" is a tactic to recognize cultural values and the multiplicity of ways of knowing the world, and acknowledges the right of people to self-represent and self-define. Belongings in museums have Indigenous owners but can also be stewarded outside Indigenous communities. In understanding that MOA is only a steward of the physical object, not owner of the intangible authority materialized by the object, the museum endeavors to consult with Indigenous communities and the specific rights' holders about the appropriate storage, display, or loan of their belongings (Kramer 2015a; Clifford 2013).

Chief Councilor Wally Webber would certainly have been aware of the various ways that MOA has worked with the Nuxalk Nation on a number of consultative and collaborative projects.[6] Webber's critical response and the resulting negative publicity could have been minimized if SAM had included the Nuxalk Nation in its decision to select mask #91.1.71 to represent Seattle. This was a situation of differing cultural protocols that resulted in missed opportunities. According to CBC News reportage, "SAM Director Rorschach said she understood the Nuxalk Nation's concerns, but pointed out the exchange was only temporary and not a transfer of ownership. She said it is common to lend pieces without consultation" (January 28, 2014).[7] Due to long-established museum protocol and European-derived logics of property, the museum did not contemplate asking the Nuxalk Nation permission to use their cultural patrimony in a sports bet. From SAM's perspective, loaning objects from the museum's collection does not require external consultation with a community of origin as this action is not considered a change of ownership. Since SAM believed it had the prerogative as legal owner to decide the mask's use, it did not occur to the museum staff that celebrating the mask for its aesthetic achievement could be perceived as a loss to, or even a derogation of, Nuxalk culture.

Even those not familiar with Native Northwest Coast cultures or carving styles can recognize the delicacy of this raven's rendering and sense that it is imbued with some sort of power. The missing communication in this cross-cultural gaffe is that Western aesthetics are not necessarily commensurate with sacred Native spirituality, regardless of how both systems share transcendence as a value. "These sorts of misunderstanding are in part due to the fact that the appropriate use of an idea, image or object is governed by the cultural protocols and worldview of a particular group, and what might be acceptable use of cultural heritage by one group may be viewed as unacceptable by another" (La Salle and IPinCH 2013). As Chief Councilor Webber succinctly stated: "You have to understand the culture before you start doing stuff" (quoted in CBC News January 28, 2014). In this situation, if SAM had followed Nuxalk protocol that respects cultural stewardship and sought permission to bet the raven forehead mask, then cross-cultural exchange, knowledge sharing, and reciprocal relations might have resulted.

It is evident that Western laws of ownership and Native systems of stewardship and cultural property are varying value systems that in this situation were not in sync. Anthropologist Cara Krmpotich responds: "Super Bowl bet aside, it seems like a dissonance in how property is thought about. SAM is taking a property approach that they own it, therefore they can loan it as desired. The Nuxalk chief [Wally Webber] is taking a more inalienable approach – they may not legally own it, but how it is stewarded still matters" (Facebook quote January 31, 2014). Townsend-Gault (2013:972) describes the resulting effect as "[t]he tension created as distinct regimes of validation ricochet off each other."

Nuxalk property laws were and are different: hereditary chiefs steward tangible and intangible cultural heritage (i.e. masks, totem poles, talking sticks, rattles, songs, dances, and origin stories) for the extended families they represent (see Kramer 2006, 2013; McIlwraith 1948 [1992]: Vol. I, pp. 166–7, 179). While Nuxalk material culture may be sold, the Nuxalk maintain their rights to own or "belong to" the intangible inheritance or prerogative materialized in the object (Kramer 2006:60–1; Krmpotich 2010:172). Even though this mask was probably sold out of Nuxalk hands and, from a European-derived property system, alienated from the Nuxalk as a commodity and legally coming into SAM's possession through a donation, the Nuxalk consider themselves inalienably connected with it.[8]

The museum did further damage to its potential relationship with this First Nation by not informing them about this mask's new position in the public eye. If SAM had asked permission before wagering this mask, it would have received information about its sacred meaning for the Nuxalk. Given time to reflect, the Nuxalk might have felt that it was a compliment to the aesthetic strength and power of their culture that of all the artworks in SAM's collection this one had been selected to represent the city of Seattle. Moreover, this could have been an excellent platform for the tiny 1,500 person Nuxalk Nation from the central Northwest Coast of Canada to become globally known and get their concerns heard by millions of Super Bowl-viewing football fans.

One unexpected outcome of this misunderstanding was that the Nuxalk Nation (a relatively recent unity that self-identified in the 1980s (Kramer 2006:25)) took baby steps in returning to their traditional governance structure by recognizing the decision-making powers of hereditary chiefs. It is a move (back) toward Nuxalk hereditary chiefs' stewarding tangible and intangible cultural heritage for their people. Interestingly, quite often Indigenous communities articulate material culture in museum collections as their cultural patrimony in order to tactically mobilize museum objects as proof of pre-colonial imagined sovereignty (Clifford 2013:18; Kramer 2006). When elected Chief Councilor (but also coincidentally Hereditary Chief Snxiluulha) Wally Webber was asked what he would have said if the museum had come to him and asked permission to use this mask, he replied: "To me, it is up to all the hereditary chiefs and elders back home. We would meet back home and then we would make a decision" (CBC News January 28, 2014). As Snxakila (Tallio) explained to Brotherton during a phone conversation: "It is the hereditary chiefs' job to take care of people's spirituality. . . . The chiefs own these things [such as masks] and care for them on behalf of their members. . . . Our goal at home is for museums to work with hereditary chiefs" (pers. comm. February 18, 2014).

One way to think about this encounter of varying value systems (enflamed by media maelstrom) is as a crucible and a catalyst that launched Nuxalk sovereigntists to reassert their traditional governance system. In this light, the raven forehead mask became abstracted into a symbol representing all Nuxalk cultural heritage in need of de-colonization. Previously (Kramer 2004, 2006), I have identified this rhetorical declaration as an act of "figurative repatriation." In this case, "a Nuxalk claim of ownership is established by means of feeling connected, taking responsibility for, and controlling the uses of a cultural object without legally owning it. Thus, the mask metaphorically returned to its origins even though, physically, it remains in a foreign place, far from 'home'" (Kramer 2006:88). Strategically "figurative repatriation requires interactive spaces outside of Native territory so that messages of Native control and ownership can be heard, seen, and witnessed by non-Native audiences" (Kramer 2006:96). In this sense, the media publicity served as the foreign place for Nuxalk identity-assertion.

A reclaiming of control has occurred even when the actual mask has not returned to Nuxalk ownership. While the media mistakenly called the elected Nuxalk Administration for an official authorial response instead of the Nuxalk hereditary chiefs, the community came together to agree that situations involving their cultural heritage and sacred ceremonies were the jurisdiction of hereditary chiefs who stewarded these cultural belongings in the name of their extended families. Contemporary protocol has now been established that divides the elected chief councilor and council's responsibilities from those of the hereditary chiefs. Snxakila (Tallio) informed me that in the future the Nuxalk hereditary chiefs will be meeting as a group to make decisions that relate to cultural heritage, territory, and sovereignty (pers. comm. February 18, 2014).

To its credit, once SAM learned that the Nuxalk Nation did not approve of the raven forehead mask being part of a sports wager, it publicly announced that it had withdrawn the mask from the wager and replaced it with Tsuji Kako's 1901 "Sound of Waves," a six-paneled Japanese screen depicting an eagle, which also bears an uncanny likeness to the Seahawk logo.[9]

What was meant foremost to be an opportunity for cultural exchange between the cities of Seattle and Denver had the potential to become another type of cultural exchange between an art museum and a First Nation. This story can certainly be told as dueling value systems of aesthetics/art and sacredness/spirituality and incommensurate Indigenous and European-derived ways of thinking about property, resulting in accusations of cultural appropriation and disrespect, trivialization of sacred ceremony and the objectification of culture. However, I would like to suggest an alternative reading. This meeting of meaning systems has the potential to turn "looking relations" into reciprocal relations – what Dwayne Donald calls "ethical relationality" – "an ecological understanding of human relationality that does not deny difference, but rather seeks to understand more deeply how our different histories and experiences position us in relation to each other" (2012:93, 103, quoted in Baloy 2014:29).

The Seattle Art Museum swiftly responded to its cross-cultural mistake in order to realign its relationship with the Nuxalk to one of shared esteem. "We have the greatest respect for the Nuxalk's art and culture and intended the forehead mask to be a cultural exchange with the Denver region," Rorschach said (quoted in Lederman January 29, 2014). Nuxalk Hereditary Chief Lhlalyam (Charles Nelson) stated: "I feel much better that the wager's not happening, definitely . . . It gives me comfort. [The mask] is being shown the respect that it needs" (quoted in Drews 2014). As Krmpotich aptly observes for the Haida (but it applies to the Nuxalk as well): "Respect is contingent on knowing who you are as an individual, but also in knowing that your identity is largely determined by your relations, and the interdependence of persons, families and communities" (2010:166). The staff at SAM are learning to think about respect in this manner.

Reciprocal relations are based on mutual respect and grow strong through attempts to understand different cultures' value systems. Being open to the flow of variable meanings and interpretations leads to a more productive cultural exchange. Snxakila (Tallio) seeks to turn Nuxalk cultural heritage in museums from "retired pieces – a tribute to a way of life that doesn't exist" (pers. comm. February 18, 2014) into practicing, living objects that work to engender social relations, both back in Bella Coola and between the Nuxalk and the rest of the world. "These objects are vessels between ancestors and people today . . . [They are] used to get our positions in the community," he said (pers. comm. February 18, 2014). Tangible cultural heritage, such as the raven forehead mask, can also become vessels to bridge relations between museums and First Nations, non-Native and Native people.

Section two: Resetting relations

Nuxalk Hereditary Chief Lhlalyam (Charles Nelson) stated to the press: "We want to take this as a lesson and learn from this mistake, build from here and start creating a relationship. . . . We just don't have that relationship with the museum yet" (quoted in Drews 2014). In order to correct this embarrassing and public miscommunication and hopefully reset their relations with the Nuxalk, SAM Director Rorschach phoned Chief Wally Webber to apologize.[10] She admitted that SAM had made a mistake in not asking for Nuxalk permission in advance. She offered to bring the raven forehead mask to Bella Coola for a visit and conveyed that the museum was open to discussions of repatriation as a potential outcome. Curator Brotherton commented to the author: "We are making plans to bring the mask to Bella Coola . . . It will be nice to have this concluded in a positive way and to go forward with good understanding" (pers. comm. August 13, 2014). Clearly, the museum desired to realign its relations with the Nuxalk and hoped physically bringing the mask home, whether for a visit or permanently, would be part of a process of "ethical relationality" – a continuing journey toward reciprocal relationship building.

It is worth highlighting here that federally funded museums in the United States have a legal duty under the Native American Graves Protection and Repatriation Act of 1990 (Public Law 101–601; 25 USC 3001–3013) to repatriate Native American "cultural items" defined as human remains, funerary objects, sacred objects, and objects of cultural patrimony to lineal descendants, Indian tribes, and Native Hawaiian organizations. However, this law does not extend to Indigenous peoples outside the USA. Thus, SAM was offering to act above and beyond the legislated requirements in order to remedy relations.

Although the Nuxalk Nation did not rule out the possibility of repatriation in the future, Snxakila (Tallio) told the author that they were not ready to receive this mask because they did not have an appropriate place to care for it (pers. comm. February 18, 2014). He envisions a Nuxalk storehouse connected to a Nuxalk big house where ceremonial work would occur. Alternative to a Western-style museum, material heritage in the storehouse would be available to Nuxalk ceremonial initiates and artists to study for spiritual inspiration and aesthetic stimulation. They would not be "on display" in a visual sense, but instead would be cared for as embodied ancestors necessitating respect.

In place of repatriation negotiations, SAM staff moved swiftly to bring the mask to Bella Coola to demonstrate their earnest desire for reciprocal relations. They were invited to bring the raven forehead mask to a potlatch hosted by Nuxalk Hereditary Chief Lhlalyam on September 27–28, 2014. Barbara Brotherton brought SAM conservator Elizabeth Brown into dialogue with Nuxalk hereditary chiefs to ensure that packing and conservation work done to stabilize the mask for its long journey was culturally appropriate and permissible.

Brotherton and Brown drove the mask to Bella Coola by car since the size of the mask crated under SAM's art shipping requirements would be too big to fit into the small-scale airplanes that regularly flew into the Bella Coola Valley. This trip took three days: Seattle to Vancouver, Vancouver to Williams Lake, and William's Lake to Bella Coola with Director Rorschach flying in to meet them. When the mask arrived in Bella Coola on September 26, it was immediately taken to the basement of a local church, unpacked and shown to members of the community. Nuxalk came to see the mask that had created such a furor in the media and now temporarily united the rural Native community of Bella Coola with the urban art museum of Seattle.

Initially, the Nuxalk considered bringing the raven forehead mask back into active use by having it fulfill its *Sisawk* (chiefly society) functions to be danced during a potlatch. The Nuxalk spoke with SAM conservator Elizabeth Brown to learn more about the current condition of the mask and determine whether work should be done before it travelled and how it should be conveyed. Brown sent images of the mask and it was decided that she would make a small repair to a crack for travel and the Nuxalk would make any other repairs they felt necessary after they examined it in person. The final decision on its stability was left up to Nuxalk visual inspection and so the museum staff did not know whether the mask would be danced when it arrived in Bella Coola. Upon seeing the mask in the church basement, the Nuxalk collectively decided that the mask was too fragile to be danced, but were still pleased to present it to the community during the potlatch.

Imperative to everyone was the intention to replicate the mask. This would allow the raven forehead mask to continue its social and ceremonial work and would emphasize that the Nuxalk value a mask for the ancestral prerogatives it materializes, and not for its age or patina. In fact, traditionally, if a mask became worn or unsafe to dance then it would be retired and replaced, and this custom is ongoing in Bella Coola today. Thus, a mask's intangible worth can be reproduced in a serial manner repeatedly. However, honouring the raven forehead mask as both an ancestral link and as a visiting dignitary at Hereditary Chief Lhlalyam's potlatch suggests the Nuxalk have also absorbed some of the Western preservationist reverence for objects with history. Or perhaps this demonstrates Nuxalk understanding of what can be accomplished by figurative repatriation?

Hereditary Chief and artist Ximximlayc (Robert "Skip" Saunders) offered to carve the copy. SAM sent him measurements, drawings, and photos of the mask from many angles including three-dimensional scans so he could carve the copy in time for the upcoming Lhlalyam potlatch. Even so, Chief Ximximlayc was surprised upon seeing the raven forehead mask as to how much smaller it was than the replica he had made (Tallio pers. comm. May 21, 2016). Evidently, the experience of viewing the mask in person and holding it cannot be replaced by other means (Bunn-Marcuse 2015; Kramer 2016, 2015b).

On September 27, the SAM representatives were honoured guests at the Chief Lhlalyam potlatch. Rorschach, Brotherton, and Brown were called onto the floor and publicly thanked for bringing the raven forehead mask home for a visit, while the mask itself watched over these social events.[11] On the second day of the potlatch, the mask was held by Head Hereditary Chief Sixilaaxayc (Noel Pootlass), blessed by Elder and Potlatch Speaker Skwyayc (Karen Anderson), while Nuxalk hereditary chiefs Chief Snuxyaltwa (Deric Snow), Chief Q'umulhla (Rhonda Schooner Sandoval), Chief Nanus (Mike Tallio), Chief Snxaluulhla (Wally Webber), and Chief Lhlalyam (Charles Nelson) witnessed. Skwyayc prayed over the mask, spread eagles' down on it, and sang to it. Following this respectful recognition, carver Chief Ximximlayc (Skip Saunders) brought out the replica mask he made so they could be blessed together. Afterwards, he danced the raven forehead mask that he had carved.

At one point, the youth were called onto the sacred floor where the potlatch work was being done. Carver Lyle Mack held the mask in his hands and had the opportunity to inspect it up close, thereby gaining artistic inspiration and spiritual connection from physical proximity to his ancestor's carving depicting chiefly rights manifested in cedar. As many Nuxalk commented: "It's so wonderful that this has come back to us! The young people can learn from it and our carvers can learn from it" (pers. comm. from Barbara Brotherton October 20, 2014). Touching and viewing this mask surely energized Lyle Mack and other Nuxalk artists to continue to create for ceremonial use in the community and for sale in the fine art market.

By the end of the weekend-long potlatch filled with social and spiritual work, the recently carved Nuxalk raven forehead mask faced its inspirational ancestor, the historical raven forehead mask from the SAM collection. Displayed face-to-face, they emitted sacred and aesthetic power so that potlatch guests affirmed the ongoing connections between contemporary and ancestral chiefs and the long line of hereditary artists who are recognized by the Nuxalk as "the hands of the family."

Once the potlatch attendees had all been gifted with presents for witnessing the ceremonial work accomplished, Brotherton and Brown turned around and drove the raven forehead mask out of the Bella Coola Valley and to the Seattle Art Museum where it is back on display as masterwork 91.1.71. However, the museum has changed how it thinks about and stewards this mask. SAM has instituted a process for asking the Nuxalk Chiefs' permission if a loan or photographic reproduction is requested for this cultural property. When the author sought copyright permission to publish an image of this raven forehead mask, which by United States Law is outside copyright protection due to it being 75 years beyond the death of its maker (assumed because it is believed that the mask's creation dates to the 1880s), I was asked to obtain permission from the Nuxalk Nation. This protocol enacts a different kind of legal jurisdiction, one that makes this book chapter part of the process of recognition of Nuxalk ownership of their belongings. This too is part of the building of ethical relationality.

In conclusion, when the Nuxalk raven forehead mask went home (even if only for a visit) a ceremonial act of figurative repatriation transpired, witnessed by the representatives of the Seattle Art Museum. As I have stated elsewhere:

> Figurative repatriation can only be accomplished on foreign terrain – that of the museum or other transcultural, public spaces of display. This strategic act requires the presence of non-Native audiences to ensure that messages of Native control and ownership can be heard, seen, and witnessed by non-Native people. Thus, refutation of non-Native ownership of Native cultural objects is found in interactive spaces that are sites for the creation of empowering social relations.
>
> *(Kramer 2006:120).*

In this sense, the Nuxalk gym where the potlatch was held in Bella Coola became a transcultural, public space of display. And within this interactive space, the mask was respectfully recognized as a Nuxalk belonging, and a creator of ethical relationality.

This case study details how one mask can be family treasure, First Nations cultural property, and museum masterpiece; it can manifest chiefly power and has the potential to amplify city pride in the skill of its sports team. While the visual can be mobilized politically, looking relations can be changed to ethical relations. The Nuxalk Nation uphold their sovereign cultural rights and will maintain the mask's social and political roles by dancing its descendant version in future potlatches. In this manner, Nuxalk hereditary chiefs continue to fulfill their sacred functions within the community. Further, new relations of solidarity and cultural understanding have been born between the Seattle Art Museum and the Nuxalk Nation.

Postscript

On September 26, 2016, Nuxalk artist Latham Mack shared images on Instagram of a Nuxalk-style Seahawk mask that he had recently carved (Figure 8.5), labelled "Seahawk mask!" with a celebratory and energetic exclamation point. Mack posted: "After I did some research on the [SAM/DAM] bet I wanted to carve a Nuxalk style Seahawk mask. It wasn't until I saw the transformation mask depicting an Eagle from the Kwakwaka'wakw tribe where the Seahawks logo originated from, inspiring me to create my own version of the Seattle Seahawks latest logo. The face on top of the Seahawk's head represents a football player" (Mack 2016).

Hinting at some of his motivations and goals in making his Nuxalk version of a mask representing the Seattle Seahawk logo, Mack followed the image with the telling hashtag descriptions: "#nuxalksculpture #sculpture #fineart #thesecretweaponisout #multifigure #raiseyourstandards #seahawk #osprey #fierce #fresh #northwestcoastart #Nusq'lst #lathammack." (Nusq'lst is where the Mack family are from in the Bella Coola Valley.) Through the creation of this mask and its public display on Facebook I think that Mack is making a statement about what a Seahawk would actually look like if carved by a Nuxalk artist. Mack is asserting his authority to know what Nuxalk carving is and how it should be deployed.

He is not only engaging with and responding dynamically to the mistaken representation of the SAM Nuxalk raven forehead mask as an inspiration for the Seattle Seahawk logo, but also actively taking back control of the representation of Nuxalk identity from museums and others. Clearly, this is an action that can be read as a movement toward reciprocal relationality but on Nuxalk terms.

Acknowledgments

Stutwinitscw (Thank you): Karen Anderson, Barbara Brotherton, Elizabeth Brown, Lyle Mack, Katie Bunn-Marcuse, Megan Moody, Charles Nelson, Noel Pootlass, Kimberly Rorschach, Clyde Tallio, Wally Webber, Robin Wright, the Burke Museum of Natural History and Culture, the Museum of Anthropology at the University of British Columbia, the Nuxalk Nation, and the Seattle Art Museum. I especially appreciate Barbara Brotherton, Elizabeth Brown, Megan Moody, Clyde Tallio, and Wally Webber for reading earlier versions of this article and providing me with corrective feedback.

Thank you to the Intellectual Property Issues in Cultural Heritage: Theory, Practice, Policy, Ethics Project (IPinCH) that spurred me to write an initial account of this research for the *IPinCH Digest* in June 2014.

A sincere thank you to Haidy Geismar and Jane Anderson for the helpful editorial advice and encouragement as I revised this chapter.

Notes

1 Someone in the Seattle Art Museum's marketing division must have written this publicity release (potentially a Seattle Seahawks football fan), because it was not a quote from curator Barbara Brotherton, nor had she approved this description of the Nuxalk raven forehead mask.

2 Barbara Brotherton met Chief Anuspuxals (Jeffrey Snow) when collaborating with the Museum of Anthropology (MOA) at the University of British Columbia (UBC) on a small exhibition curated by the author's UBC "Museum Practice and Curatorship" students in consultation with members of the Nuxalk Nation. Titled "Together Again: Nuxalk Faces of the Sky," the exhibition opened on April 5, 2012, at MOA and reunited two parts of a nineteenth-century Nuxalk celestial mask that had been separated at some point between 1920 and 1958, resulting in the internal face mask bought by MOA in 1963 from the Campbell River Historical Association (# A8367) and the external corona (with the addition of a different internal Nuxalk face mask) donated to the Seattle Art Museum (SAM) in 1976 (# 91.1.95). The exhibition subsequently traveled to SAM for display between December 5, 2012, and June 23, 2013, before the two masks were divided again and returned to their separate museums.

3 In my ethnography of the Nuxalk, *Switchbacks: Art, Ownership, and Nuxalk National Identity*, I have a chapter called "The History of Bella Coola: A History of Theft" where I discuss the "theft of resources such as timber and fish (due to DIA policies and the Department of Fisheries and Oceans allocations); theft of people (due to European disease-induced population decline); theft of children (due to residential schools); theft of material art and objects (due to anthropologists and other collectors); and finally, theft of cultural knowledge (due to missionization, the anti-potlatch law, and anthropology)" (Kramer 2006:23).

4 In Aotearoa, New Zealand, with the government's adoption of the policy of biculturalism in the late 1980s, the creation of the Museum of New Zealand Te Papa Tangarewa (Te Papa) in 1992, and the 2005 Te Papa Mana Taonga Policy that "affirms and acknowledges the spiritual and cultural connections of the people to taonga or treasures" (McCarthy 2011:115). In 2009, the then-CEO of Te Papa, Dr Seddon Bennington explained the importance of recognizing the museum as a guardian rather than an owner of Maori taonga. "Guardianship, known in Maori as kaitiakitanga acknowledges both the rights and responsibilities of the museum and other owners in the care of collections [at Te Papa]" (Geismar 2008:115).

5 Anthropologist Mark Busse expands on this point: "Cultural property is an infelicitous phrase . . . [because of] its inherent commercial connotation. Anglo-American concepts of property, which increasingly dominate international treatments of property are, of course, closely related to and deeply

embedded in concepts of markets, commodities, and private property. To use the language of property is to use the language of the market and to unquestionably assume a person's right of alienation and right to profit through the transacting of property" (Busse 2008:193).

6 I have worked with Nuxalk Hereditary Chiefs, elected band councilors, cultural teachers, language speakers, and artists on numerous research projects over the past twenty years. Since becoming one of the curators responsible for the Pacific Northwest collections at MOA, I have collaborated with various Nuxalk experts on the re-organization of Nuxalk belongings in the new visible storage galleries called "Multiversity: Ways of Knowing," which opened in January 2010 (Kramer 2015a), the student-curated exhibition "Together Again: Nuxalk Faces of the Sky" in April 2012, and a Nuxalk Film Festival and Dance performance in September 2012, as well as ongoing research relationships with Snxakila (Clyde Tallio) tracking Nuxalk artistic styles in museum collections.

7 While this is accurate for art museums in the United States of America, in New Zealand and Canada the loaning of Indigenous objects between museums for exhibition without community consultation is starting to be questioned. The forward-thinking Laboratory of Archaeology (LOA), a teaching and research institute at UBC that holds archaeological materials from British Columbia, states for its loan policy: "The LOA will present requests for loans to the applicable First Nations for their consideration. Both LOA and the First Nations groups must approve a loan" (accessed June 14, 2016, http://anth.ubc.ca/research/laboratory-of-archaeology/loans-of-artifacts-for-exhibition/).

8 No one living in Bella Coola remembers this specific raven forehead mask; therefore it probably left the Nuxalk Nation long ago, but how is not known. There are certainly known examples of Nuxalk regalia sold outside the community, sometimes by their Nuxalk recognized owner/guardian and sometimes by someone who did not have the Nuxalk right to sell (see Kramer 2004, 2006; Cole 1985). There are also references to regalia being taken without permission either from someone's home, from a cache of masks in the woods, or from burial sites. Tracing back the mask's provenance, SAM received the Nuxalk raven forehead mask in 1991 as part of a large donation of Native Northwest Coast objects from John H. Hauberg, an art patron and SAM board member. He purchased this mask from Michael Johnson, a notorious Seattle art dealer. Johnson claimed that he acquired the Nuxalk raven forehead mask in the early 1970s, but probably not directly from Bella Coola because a number of elders told Barbara Brotherton that they do not remember it ever being in the community (pers. comm. October 20, 2014).

9 Robin K. Wright of the University of Washington Burke Museum of Natural History and Culture researched the Native Northwest Coast mask that actually did serve as inspiration for the designers of the Seattle Seahawks logo in 1976. It is a nineteenth-century Kwakwa̱ka̱'wakw transformation mask of eagle/human in the collection of the Hudson Museum at the University of Maine. Satisfyingly, the museum crowd-sourced the funds with generous support from Bekins Northwest, "the official mover of the Seattle Seahawks," to bring this transformation mask to the Burke Museum where it was aptly displayed in the exhibition "Here and Now: Native Artists Inspired" (November 22, 2014–July 27, 2015) curated by Kathryn Bunn-Marcuse. Upon its arrival in Seattle, it played centre stage to a Burke Museum press event celebrating the Seattle Seahawks' push for the Super Bowl, which was successful (Burke Museum 2015; Morris 2015; Wright 2014a, 2014b).

10 The SAM director should have called the Nuxalk hereditary chiefs to apologize to them as the wronged party and, in this way, recognize them as the authority in this matter, but fortunately elected Chief Councilor Wally Webber was also Hereditary Chief Snxiluulha, so Rorschach inadvertently respected the re-establishment of traditional protocol.

11 Interestingly, the Nuxalk chose to perch the mask during the potlatch on top of its acid-free packing materials prepared by the SAM conservation staff for its travel, but this decision was not one required by the conservator or the Seattle Art Museum. This action suggests an absorption by the Nuxalk of the aura of value ascribed to heritage items and the correlative protection of the historical material object as befitting conservation and museological guidelines.

Bibliography

Baloy, Natalie. 2014. "Spectacle, Spectrality, and the Everyday: Contemporary Settler Colonial Politics, Aboriginal Alterity, and Ex/Inclusive Spaces in Vancouver." PhD Thesis, Anthropology. Vancouver, BC: University of British Columbia.

Brotherton, Barbara. 2011. Seattle Art Museum On-Line Catalog.

Bunn-Marcuse, Kathryn. 2015. "Here and Now: Native Artists Inspired." Paper delivered at the Native American Art Studies Association. Santa Fe, October 2.

Burke Museum. 2014. "Mask that Inspired Seattle Seahawks Logo on Display at Burke Museum." Burke Museum Blog, November 18. http://www.burkemuseum.org/press/mask-inspired-seattle-seahawks-logo-display-burke-museum (accessed 27 March 2017).

Busse, Mark. 2008. "Museums and the Things in Them Should Be Alive." *International Journal of Cultural Property* 15(Spring): 189–200.

Carr-Locke, Sarah. 2015. "Indigenous Heritage and Public Museums: Exploring Collaboration and Exhibition in Canada and the United States." PhD in Archaeology. Burnaby, BC: Simon Fraser University.

CBC News. 2014a. "Super Bowl Wager of Native Mask Upsets BC First Nation." *The Canadian Associated Press*, January 28. http://www.cbc.ca/news/canada/british-columbia/super-bowl-wager-of-native-mask-upsets-b-c-first-nation-1.2513950 (accessed 27 March 2017).

CBC News. 2014b. "Super Bowl Wager Pits Seattle, Denver Art Museum." *The Canadian Associated Press*, January 29. http://www.cbc.ca/m/touch/arts/story/1.2515673 (accessed 27 March 2017).

Clifford, James. 1988. "On Collecting Art and Culture" in *The Predicament of Culture: Twentieth Century Ethnography, Literature and Art*, 215–252. Cambridge, MA: Harvard University Press.

Clifford, James. 2013. *Returns: Becoming Indigenous in the 21st Century*. Cambridge, MA: Harvard University Press.

Cole, Douglas. 1985. *Captured Heritage: The Scramble for Northwest Coast Artifacts*. Norman: University of Oklahoma Press.

Donald, Dwayne. 2012. "Forts, Colonial Frontier Logics, and Aboriginal-Canadian Relations: Imagining Decolonizing Educational Philosophies in Canadian Contexts" in *Decolonizing Philosophies of Education*. Ali A. Abdi (ed.), 91–111. Rotterdam, The Netherlands: Sense Publishers.

Drews, Kevin. 2014. "At BC First Nation's Request, Seattle Art Museum Pulls Mask from Super Bowl Bet." *The Canadian Press*, January 29. http://www.ctvnews.ca/canada/at-b-c-first-nation-s-request-seattle-art-museum-pulls-mask-from-super-bowl-bet-1.1662026 (accessed 27 March 2017).

Geismar, Haidy. 2008. "Cultural Property, Museums, and the Pacific: Reframing the Debates." *International Journal of Cultural Property* 15(Spring): 109–122.

Geismar, Haidy. 2013. *Treasured Possessions: Indigenous Interventions into Cultural and Intellectual Property*. Durham, NC and London: Duke University Press.

Hendrick, Thomas. 2014. "Seattle, Denver Art Museums Bet Artwork on Super Bowl." *KWGN*, January 27. http://kwgn.com/2014/01/27/seattle-denver-art-museums-bet-artwork-on-super-bowl/ (accessed 27 March 2017).

Herle, Anita. 2008. "Relational Objects: Connecting People and Things Through Pasifika Styles." *International Journal of Cultural Property* 15(Spring): 159–179.

Holm, Bill. 1995. *The Spirit Within: Northwest Coast Native Art from the John H. Hauberg Collection*. Seattle, WA: Seattle Art Museum.

Kramer, Jennifer. 2004. "Figurative Repatriation: First Nations 'Artist-Warriors' Recover, Reclaim and Return Cultural Property through Self-definition." *Journal of Material Culture* 9(2): 161–182.

Kramer, Jennifer. 2006. *Switchbacks: Art, Ownership, and Nuxalk National Identity*. Vancouver, BC: UBC Press.

Kramer, Jennifer. 2013. "'Fighting with Property': The Double-edged Character of Ownership" in *Native Art of the Northwest Coast: A History of Changing Ideas*. Charlotte Townsend-Gault, Jennifer Kramer and Ki-ke-in (eds.), 720–756. Vancouver, BC: UBC Press.

Kramer, Jennifer. 2014. "Appropriation (?) of the Month: The Bet of the Broncho and the Raven." *IPinCH (Intellectual Property Issues in Cultural Heritage: Theory, Practice, Policy, Ethics) Digest*, June 19. www.sfu.ca/ipinch/outputs/blog.

Kramer, Jennifer. 2015a. "Möbius Museology: Curating and Critiquing the Multiversity Galleries at the UBC Museum of Anthropology" in *Museum Transformations: Art, Culture, History. Volume 4: The International Handbook of Museum Studies*. Annie E. Coombes and Ruth B. Phillips (eds.), 489–510. Oxford: Wiley-Blackwell Press.

Kramer, Jennifer. 2015b. "Flinching and Other Acts of Decolonization and Globalization in the Contemporary Ethnographic Museum." Paper delivered at the American Anthropological Association Meetings, Denver, CO, November 20.

Kramer, Jennifer. 2016. "Blowing the Whistles: Imagining Kimsquit through Nuxalk and Heiltsuk Collections at the Smithsonian's National Museum of the American Indian." Paper delivered at the Society for Applied Anthropology Conference, Vancouver, BC, March 30.

Krmpotich, Cara. 2014, January 31. On Facebook, Jennifer Kramer's personal page. Retrieved January 28, 2014 from: http://www.facebook.com/jennifer.kramer.718 [post date January 28, 2014] (accessed 27 March 2017).

Krmpotich, Cara. 2010. "Remembering and Repatriation: The Production of Kinship, Memory and Respect." *Journal of Material Culture* 15(2): 157–179.

Krmpotich, Cara, Laura Peers et al. 2013. *This is Our Life: Haida Material Heritage and Changing Museum Practice.* Vancouver, BC: UBC Press.

La Salle, Marina and the IPinCH Cultural Commodification Working Group. 2013. "Appropriation and Commodification of Cultural Heritage: Ethical & IP Issues to Consider." IPinCH Fact Sheet, unpublished manuscript.

Lederman, Marsha. 2014. "Canadian First Nation Rules Super Bowl Bet Involving Sacred Mask Offside." *The Globe and Mail,* January 29. http://cached.newslookup.com/cached.php?ref_id=123&siteid=2115&id=4625649&t=1391012991 (accessed 27 March 2017).

Lonetree, Amy. 2012. *Decolonizing Museums: Representing Native America in National and Tribal Museums.* Chapel Hill: University of North Carolina Press.

McCarthy, Conal. 2011. *Museums and Maori: Heritage Professionals, Indigenous Collections, Current Practice.* Walnut Creek, CA: Left Coast Press.

McIlwraith, T.F. 1948 [1992]. *The Bella Coola Indians,* 2nd edition. 2 Volumes. Toronto, Buffalo, NY and London: University of Toronto Press.

Macpherson, C. B. 1962. *The Political Theory of Possessive Individualism.* Oxford: Clarendon Press.

Mack, Latham. 2016. Instagram posted September 26, 2016 seen on Facebook, accessed on November 29, 2016: https://www.facebook.com/hashtag/multifigure?source=feed_text&story_id=10154743489641202&pnref=story (accessed 27 March 2017).

Morris, Cathy. 2015. "Origin of the Seahawks Logo: The Story Unfolds." Burke Museum Blog, January 27. http://burkemuseum.blogspot.ca/2015/01/the-origin-of-seahawks-logo-story.html#.Vw_i1HBPKc8 (accessed 27 March 2017).

Museum of Anthropology. 2000. "A Partnership of Peoples: A New Infrastructure for Collaborative Research at the University of British Columbia's Museum of Anthropology." Canadian Foundation for Innovation Grant Application.

Nuxalk.Nation.org [NuxalkNation]. 2014. Nuxalk masks are sacred ceremonial items, not simply "art" display pieces. #decolonize [Tweet]. Access date: January 28, 2014 [Tweet no longer active online as of December 1, 2016].

Peers, Laura and Alison K. Brown. 2003. *Museums and Source Communities: A Routledge Reader.* London: Routledge Press.

Phillips, Ruth B. 2011. *Museum Pieces: Toward the Indigenization of Canadian Museums.* Montreal and Kingston, Ont.: McGill-Queens University Press.

Townsend-Gault, Charlotte. 2004. "Circulating Aboriginality." *Journal of Material Culture* 9(2): 183–202.

Townsend-Gault, Charlotte. 2013. "The Material and the Immaterial across Borders" in *Native Art of the Northwest Coast: A History of Changing Ideas.* Charlotte Townsend-Gault, Jennifer Kramer and Ki-ke-in (eds.), 963–994. Vancouver, BC: UBC Press.

Townsend-Gault, Charlotte, Charlotte, Kramer, Jennifer, and Ki-ke-in (eds.). 2013. *Native Art of the Northwest Coast: A History of Changing Ideas.* Vancouver, BC: UBC Press.

Wilson, Jordan. 2016. "'Belongings' in 'c̓əsnaʔəm: the city before the city'." *IPinCH Digest,* January 27. http://www.sfu.ca/ipinch/outputs/blog/citybeforecitybelongings (accessed 27 March 2017).

Wright, Robin K. 2014a. "Introducing the Mask that Inspired the Seattle Seahawks Logo." Burke Museum Blog, January 28. http://burkemuseum.blogspot.ca/2014/01/in-search-of-true-inspiration-for.html#.Vw_kBHBPKc8 (accessed 27 March 2017).

Wright, Robin K. 2014b. "Mask that Inspired the Seahawks Logo Discovered in Maine Museum." Burke Museum Blog, February 20. http://burkemuseum.blogspot.ca/2014/02/mask-that-likely-inspired-seahawks-logo.html#.Vw_jfnBPKc8 (accessed 27 March 2017).

Personal communications

Kramer, Jennifer. 2014. Personal communication with Snxakila (Clyde Tallio), January 28.

Kramer, Jennifer. 2014. Personal communication by phone with Barbara Brotherton, January 28.

Kramer, Jennifer, Barbara Brotherton, and Snxakila (Clyde Tallio). 2014. Three-way phone conversation, February 18.

Kramer, Jennifer. 2014. Personal communication by email with Barbara Brotherton, August 13.

Kramer, Jennifer. 2014. Personal communication by phone with Barbara Brotherton, October 20.

Kramer, Jennifer. 2016. Personal communication by email with Barbara Brotherton, April 25.

Kramer, Jennifer. 2016. Personal communication with Snxakila (Clyde Tallio), May 21.

9

WHOSE STORY IS THIS?

Complexities and complicities of using archival footage

Fred Myers

Introduction

Ideas about ownership and collaboration are two axes in the process of making representations and negotiating the complexities of cultural property when working with Aboriginal people and their archives. Based on my previous work on images and cultural property in Western Desert Aboriginal communities and broader work on materiality (Myers 1988, 2004, 2014), I am particularly interested in how film and other indexical images work to establish relationships and other effects in the world. Concepts of property – as cultural or intellectual property – are, in this sense, efforts to articulate, specify, and determine some of these relationships and effects. If objects, in the widest sense, are promiscuous in the entanglements they can inhabit or produce, to follow Thomas (1989), I am interested here in the limitations of the attempts to contain these flows. In the discussion that follows, the particular material properties of film objects are crucial.

In this chapter, I present an account of the relationships established, evoked, negotiated, and abrogated in the course of a project of "repatriating"[1] film footage to an Indigenous Australian community, a project that led to the making of an archive-based documentary that stitches together and brings into visibility several distinct but related trajectories and personal histories. I offer this essay as a case study, illuminating the vexed and unstable intersections of relationships and rights in the production of visual representations of an Indigenous Australian history. I will trace (1) the "making" of a filmic representation at a particular point in time, both in Australia and in the history of the role film plays, and (2) the repatriation or return of this material to source communities and the very distinct conditions that make this possible. My goal is to understand the motivations of different players at multiple locations along the cultural property spectrum and how they shape this project's outcome.

There are two stories to be told here. One is the story of the production of what is now an archive of film footage shot in an Indigenous community in 1974, and what that means and continues to mean to the Pintupi people whose families were its subject. This includes their relationships to each other as well as to the filmmaker, Ian Dunlop, and to myself, an anthropologist who served as a translator and advisor during the filming and who has continued to work with these people since then. The other story concerns what is very evident in the film, namely the Australian governmental interventions into Indigenous life, meant to manage its Aboriginal populations. This "context" is what placed Dunlop in the position of producing the footage to begin with, but governmentality is a context that changes throughout the history of the footage, informing ongoing attempts to control the footage and its life as an object within an archive.[2] Owing to space constraints, this chapter largely focuses on the first of these two stories.

Commonwealth film

My story begins, at least for our purposes, in the early 1970s in the remote Pintupi[3] outstation of Yayayi, 180 miles west of Alice Springs, where I began my research as a PhD student in anthropology, at age 25, in July 1973. But the relationships shaping this project, which are also embedded in a history of filmmaking in Australia, go back to the 1950s and the career of Ian Dunlop, who was a director in Australia's Commonwealth Film Unit.[4] Part of a broader modernist project to document Australia and its progress to the Australian nation in 1957, Dunlop was sent to the Giles Weather Station in remote Western Australia to make "a film about the establishment of a remote weather station" (Deveson and Dunlop 2012). While his focus was Australia's scientific establishment at work in this remote location (the film was eventually called *Balloons and Spinifex*),[5] Dunlop was very taken with the surrounding environment and especially the evidence of independent-living foraging families out beyond the weather station. He could see the smoke from their fires off in the distance and resolved to return and make a film that he imagined as a "day in the life of a nomadic family" (Dunlop 1979:117; see also Deveson and Dunlop 2012). Eventually, he was able to persuade his superiors, and the Commonwealth Film Unit,[6] to allow him to carry out this project. The resulting work, *Desert People* (1967) was an extraordinary, award-winning masterpiece. Dunlop shot numerous rolls of color slide film in documentation for the Australian Institute of Aboriginal Studies, which paid for the trip. Among those he met on that trip was Minyina (Yanyatjarri) Tjampitjinpa and ten years later Dunlop decided he wanted to follow up with these people, to make a film about what had happened in their lives since settlement at Papunya. In 1974, the Pintupi people, who had first come east to Papunya and Haasts Bluff, were living at the small community of Yayayi in the Northern Territory. This is where Dunlop came to talk to them about filming their lives.

Stage 1: Self-determination and rights in representation

Yayayi was a fairly remote place, with only a windmill and tank providing water for about 300 Pintupi-speaking people who had moved there as a breakaway "outstation" in order to escape the larger government-operated, multi-language group settlement of Papunya – which they experienced as overcrowded and riven by conflict, and in which they were considered and sometimes ridiculed as less civilized (see Myers 1986). Not the first such attempt on the part of these migrants from the west to form their own distinct community, this move from Papunya occurred under the favorable policies of the Labor Government of Prime Minister Gough Whitlam, putting into practice its emphasis on "Aboriginal self-determination." Those known as "the Pintupi" had become visible to the Australian public earlier, through the much publicized patrols to contact them "in the bush" in the early 1960s (Long 1964a, 1964b) and some sensationalist accounts of their discovery by the famous anthropologist Donald Thomson (1962). Their move to Yayayi in May 1973 gained some national attention as Aboriginal activists pressured health officials to provide services at the new outstation (Myers 2016). By 1973, there was some support for the movement of small populations away from the large government-administered settlements that had been created as centers of assimilation and sedentarization. This was part of a new order for the Department of Aboriginal Affairs.

It was less than a year after this move to Yayayi that Ian Dunlop arrived in the community to discuss making a film about the Pintupi people he had met in 1964. As a young PhD student, I had been doing research at Yayayi for several months and was becoming reasonably fluent in Pintupi and familiar with the people there. Following his experience at making film with Yolngu at Yirrkala, where he collaborated with anthropologists Nancy Williams and Howard Morphy, Dunlop asked me to help with translation, and later consultation, about making the film. My experience at Yayayi had already made me wary of the responsibility of representation, of seeming to tell other people's stories.[7] And I had heard a number of angry criticisms from Aboriginal people of unsatisfactory or disappointing filmmaking projects (insufficient money, inappropriate nudity, transgression of ritual protocols). Moreoever, especially for many of the older people at Yayayi, there was a general reluctance about having one's image taken. Nonetheless, I admired Dunlop's earlier work and appreciated both his sincerity and the possible significance of what he proposed. I agreed to help, but I did so on behalf of the Yayayi Community Council, as it was known, and with their blessing. In this way, I thought, I was not to be directly a part of the film team. I imagined that the film enterprise (any film enterprise) had a potential for tensions and problems that I wanted to avoid.

I agreed to be an advisor, and in this role, I translated for Dunlop when he presented his proposal to the Yayayi Council. A number of the Pintupi at Yayayi remembered Dunlop from the 1964 meeting in the Pollock Hills of Western Australia, when he had been ascribed the subsection classification of Tjampitjinpa. Some of them knew the people with whom he had worked on *Desert People*. These associations eased his connection at Yayayi. With this background of trust, the community agreed to filming – with the commitment from Film Australia of $200 per week to the Yayayi Community Council. It was also agreed that there would be no filming of ritual activity. By 1974, despite early participation in a program of salvage ethnographic filming,[8] the Pintupi, like most Western Desert people, had decided to refuse recording of men's ritual life and had asked to withdraw earlier films from public circulation.[9] What was proposed in 1974 was different – a documentary about community life – and the Council agreed to allow the filming. In this agreement, nowhere written down but in line with the emerging expectations of consultation associated with the policy of Aboriginal self-determination, there was a specific assertion of Pintupi rights – local community rights – over the filming activity, over what could and could not be filmed, and Ian made it clear he would not impose the camera on people who wished to be left out.

As Ian Bryson (2002) has recorded, ethnographic film practice in Australia was changing at this time. Dunlop had himself begun to work in a collaborative manner[10] with Yolngu people in what became the Yirrkala Film Project, incorporating – for example – their ideas of what he should film (see Deveson and Dunlop 2012).[11] Dunlop was sensitive to the rights of the local community to allow or refuse permission to film, in line with the emerging policies of the federal Department of Aborginal Affairs embracing Aboriginal "self-determination" and local control of who could even visit communities. I do not remember there being any discussion at the time about rights to the material or of the necessity of any consultations in subsequent editing or production of the film. The presumption was that the footage would belong to Film Australia, although as "author," Dunlop always insisted that his assent would be necessary for any usage. He adamantly resisted the usage of his material as "stock" footage without his agreement.

Dunlop arrived back at Yayayi in early June 1974, with a crew of two men and two 4-wheel-drive vehicles.[12] The crew camped with tents and trunks at Yayayi for nearly a month and shot some 26 reels of 16mm color sync footage. Dunlop was fortunate to record a number of distinctive events at one of the first independent outstations in the context of self-determination. These included the visit to Yayayi of the Executive Officer of the relatively new Aboriginal Arts Board, transactions over the sale of acrylic paintings with the manager of the Papunya Tula Artists company, and meetings of the elected Village Council. The crew moved pretty freely and comfortably around the community, focusing on those people and families who were accepting of their presence and avoiding those who were reluctant.

Subsequently, in May of 1975, I travelled to Sydney with two Pintupi men (Freddy West Tjakamarra and George Yapa Tjangala) as translators and commentators to document the many hours of footage with Dunlop at his house. This was audio recorded and eventually transcribed. The resulting documentation added something like fifteen double-sided audio-cassettes of 90 minutes each to the material recorded at Yayayi and constituted an emerging archive.

In the end, however, nothing happened. Dunlop never made a film from the material. This was the first time he had shot his own footage, and he was dissatisfied with his camera work. Further, he was unable to find what he thought was a satisfactory organizing principle for the film.[13] The footage and documentation remained with him at Film Australia until his retirement in 1987, at which time it was lodged (along with other Film Australia material) at the Australian National Archives.

Retake: Engaging in repatriaton

As no edited version was made, we never had the opportunity to show this material back to Pintupi people, who by 1981 had moved back to their own country, at the communities of Kintore, Northern Territory, and later Kiwirrkura, Western Australia. The footage was available as a 16mm workprint, and had only been developed after shooting at Yayayi had finished and the crew had returned. Later, it was too costly to transfer the material to another medium in order to take it back.

As the changing technology of video recording had made sync sound and small cameras possible, so did the rapidly changing technology of the digital age offer new possibilities. In 2005, the National Archives of Australia transferred the footage to VHS tape, old technology by this time but thought perhaps to be the best medium for returning footage to an Aboriginal community. Aboriginal people in Central Australia were quite familiar with tape and more experienced about film material generally; they had been watching videos and even making informal recordings with portable video cameras since the late 1980s. Ian and I had remained in contact as friends as we had the idea to "repatriate" the film by bringing it back to show it and to see what people thought of it. By 2006, and with the blessing of the Australian Archive – which was committed to such "repatriation" – I brought a digitized version of the footage back and showed it to the community at Kiwirrkura.[14]

Showing such "old" footage brought up the issue of Indigenous cultural protocol that needed to be addressed. The footage – now over 30 years old – contained images of people who were deceased. In earlier years, and certainly in 1974, extending to film and photography, the traditional taboo on the names and images of the deceased would have meant showing such footage was unacceptable. By 2006, the local protocol on images of the deceased was no longer as important to a younger generation who were leaders in the community, and in many desert communities, people actively wanted to see their relatives and themselves on film.[15] They had no photographic record of their own of that crucial period. But ideas about cultural knowledge and secrecy are complex and unstable. I knew many people wanted to see this footage, and they had invited me to come show it to them, but they hadn't actually seen it. What if there was something offensive or problematic that we hadn't foreseen?

To be certain the footage was acceptable for screening to the Pintupi public at Kiwirrkura, I arranged to show all of it first to the resident head Councillor, Jimmy Brown Tjampitjinpa (himself a former resident of Yayayi, although not there during the filming in 1974). Jimmy asserted his authority as the person who should make this determination. He clearly enjoyed watching it, and told us it was suitable for the public viewing we planned. Indeed, he helped arrange for us to have the "town hall" in which to show it.[16] As a consultation, the answer was clear. Not only was it okay to show images of the deceased, but also there was nothing of a ritual or esoteric nature that could not be seen by everyone.

However, a screening is not simply a formal occasion of agreement or refusal and it could not be only a consultation with Jimmy Brown. This was my first trip to Kiwirrkura since 1988, and I had many old friends and acquaintances, some of my very closest friends from the 1970s, to see and explain why I was there. The screening was for me an engagement with old friends, and their reactions, their knowledge of why we were there, were important. In order to find out something about the "community" response, this screening could not take place without some preparation and conversation, some renewed connection with my friends from the past. It was with them that I wanted to share this experience. When I arrived, the day was filled with conversations that connected me to the situation of the present, who had passed away, who had had children, and where my friends were. Nonetheless, during the two nights of public screening at Kiwirrkura, I was worried. In a world of shifting protocols and introduced media forms, as well as the distributed nature of rights over images, unanimity or consensus is unpredictable: some elders might be disturbed by an image or disagree on principle that they had not (yet) been personally consulted (see also Myers 2004, 2014). However, to my relief, the reception was joyous and positive, with obvious pleasure expressed at the sight and sound of beloved family members who had passed away. The conversations on the following days reinforced this sense, with requests for copies of the video and images I might have of themselves and relatives. One young woman said the film made her feel proud, seeing her relatives happy and healthy. At nearby Kintore, when I returned from Kiwirrkura, I was unable to have a public screening, but a small-scale viewing with Marlene Nampitjinpa Spencer (who had been a teenager in the film footage and would later be the narrator of our film) and her family gathered around my laptop computer was even more encouraging about the local desire to have this material. Again, there were requests for copies.

With the agreement of the National Archives, which was supportive of our project,[17] I left copies of the material with the clinic at Kiwirrkura, where the nurse (the beloved, now deceased, Annie Dixon) agreed to hold it for the community so it would not be lost, and the images would not become available to unauthorized persons. Not long afterwards, Sister Annie (as nurses are called in Australia) called and spoke to Lisa Stefanoff, an Australian anthropologist and former student who had assisted me on the trip to Kiwirrkura:

> She [Annie Dixon] wanted to send us images of people watching the film in the past weeks. Bobby [West] left soon after we did and gave the tapes[18] to Annie for safekeeping. The clinic has apparently become an all-day, all-evening cinema ever since. I could hear it playing as we talked – amazing to feel connected back to that place through this sonic relay. People are apparently watching the tapes over and

> over and over with hardly a quiet moment between, wanting to borrow them for home viewing too. Annie's being strict and not letting the tapes leave her care. I told her that Ian has started the process with Film Australia to get permission for multiple copies to be available to families. She's not 100% sure but she thinks that one of the men is doing a thank you painting for Ian at the moment.
>
> *(Lisa Stefanoff, email June 27, 2006)*

Not only did Annie report that people were watching it constantly, but she was very impressed that they were noticeably commenting on the healthy status of those they saw in the film.

How to mobilize an archive

This initial interest left us with several problems: how to make the film material *available* and *useful to* the Pintupi communities. At the simplest level, how could we assure local people continued access to this archival material, and in what form? Moreover, what did they want to do with it? And who had rights to it?[19]

This last question was not necessarily a question that a filmmaker would have raised in 1974, despite the emergence of Aboriginal self-determination. But with this archival material, the uncertain future of the footage as an object in the National Archive, and the national questions about Indigenous intellectual and cultural property that had become prominent, it seemed the relevant question to ask.[20]

In 2008, partly because of the experiences of screenings in Kintore and Kiwirrkura, a collaboration between Ian Dunlop, Peter Thorley (a curator at the National Museum of Australia who had been a school teacher-linguist at Kintore in 1988),[21] Pip Deveson (Dunlop's editor and research assistant, now at the ANU), and myself at NYU began. Our first step was to secure a small grant to digitize and color correct the original 16mm footage. However, the intent was never simply to make a film or to restore it, but it was linked to an idea of sustaining the footage as Pintupi "heritage" and assuring Pintupi access to that heritage – through a partnership with an institution of some stability, namely the NMA. The hope was to build a partnership with an ongoing institution that would be committed to sustaining Pintupi heritage, so they could know where it was and have it reproduced if necessary.[22]

Practically, the next step was to get the footage in shape. Travelling to Sydney, Dunlop and Deveson oversaw the digitization and color correction of the material, representing – as we understood it – Dunlop's continued authorial ownership of the footage he had shot and his continued interest in making a film with it. We received a further research grant to document, with contemporary Pintupi descendants of those in the footage, retrospective understandings of the film and the early outstation at Yayayi itself.[23]

Is there a film?

Over the next three years, we conducted interviews and consultations with both Pintupi and whites who were present at Yayayi in 1974. The most extensive consultations took place with two sets of Pintupi interlocutors – in Canberra the following year, with two elder women leaders, Irene Nangala and Monica Robinson Nangala,[24] and at Kiwirrkura after that, with two men, Bobby West Tjupurrula and Jimmy Brown Tjampitjinpa. These were the "Pintupi Dialogues" we had mainly intended in titling our research grant that way.

In these consultations, all recorded as we watched and discussed footage, the Pintupi consultants consistently identified four themes: (1) the significance of relatives, (2) the health of the people, (3) the strong leadership indicated by meetings in the community as how the elders "spoke strong" and "looked after" people, and (4) sharing or exchange. "People will want to see the kangaroo hunts [that were filmed]," Irene said, "to see their family." On the busy activity of making artifacts, of much interest to Dunlop, Irene remembered, "They used to make artifacts every day. [Referring to that time at Yayayi as well as during the filming.] So many!" Watching the exchanges and conversations of their elders, Irene and Monica remarked more than once, "Those were happy men!" And their pleasure at the familiar foibles of their relatives was always near the surface of their responses: at the image of one of the young men, sitting on a flour drum and holding himself in a careful posture, they laughed, jokingly, at his apparent self-regard: "Handsome man!" Hearing the figure of $5 mentioned, they commented on the different understandings of money from the perspective of the present: "They think this is a lot of money." They saw in the footage a better time than their present, in some ways, as closer to the ideals of their culture, and as an example of the self-direction – "doing things for themselves" – through which Pintupi had been able to return to their homelands in the Western Desert. Significantly, some of the consultants drew specific attention to their own current roles as leaders in the community as being modelled on the actions of their senior relatives in the film.

These interviews were largely for research purposes, for documentation, and it was not clear until nearly the end of this process that a film might come out of it. This only transpired in 2013, when Deveson and I finally recorded an interview with Marlene Nampitjinpa Spencer, a senior community leader who had been a lively young teenager at the time of Dunlop's original filming. Her interview was extraordinary – drawing out and reiterating in dramatic and captivating fashion what we had learned from other consultants. We had discovered a pretty consistent set of frameworks that accounted for what people saw in the footage. At this point, the question was what we might do with this.

We thought the film footage was very strong and many people who viewed it – Indigenous Australian and otherwise – also felt it had direct value. Of course, many Pintupi people were most interested in seeing themselves and their relatives in it. For them, any editing that might remove any of these images would be less than desirable.[25] But others – Indigenous and others for whom this isn't precisely their own history, and more general viewers – also saw something important in the footage in the ways that people carried themselves, the authority of their bearing, their humor, and so on. For myself, I was convinced that the film material, because of its long takes and sync sound, could invite viewers into the intimate world of daily life in a remote community and in that, allow for a more realistic comprehension of self-determination as a "life project" (Blaser 2004), illuminating the pace and forms of self-organization and conversation among people. These themes resonated, I believe, with those articulated by the Pintupi consultants.

In reflecting on the process in 2012, in Canberra, I formulated my thoughts as we recorded ourselves in the documentation project. For me, the presence and availability of this footage was quite amazing because it has many kinds of significance for the kinds of stories that we could tell about Pintupi and Aboriginal life from it. One part of its significance is as a record of what I call a kind of "Indigenous sociality," of the style of everyday life, of how people actually communicate and engage with each other in intimate and other ways, how they express their "relatedness" as *walytja* (see Myers 1986). Another significance is its value in the context of the political present, corresponding to the Northern Territory Intervention and broader shifts in Australian federal policies, where there has been so much questioning of the policies of "self-determination" and various kinds of Aboriginal policy ("self-management," etc.).[26] Because this was one of the very first outstations that were supported by the newly elected, transformative Labor government of Gough Whitlam and its new policies of Aboriginal self-determination, the Yayayi footage is an extraordinary record of this early history – of something of how life was lived there. Many people are confident they know everything there is to know about what these small remote communities were like. Actually, however, few people really know much of life in this early period. And the footage is, to a considerable extent, an *independent* record. It is a recording that one can unpack and discuss what was happening. One can see government officials visiting, from the Aboriginal Arts Board or bringing pay packets to the community; one can see the conversations that take place, the misunderstandings, the understandings, the communications that are occurring. The footage is valuable to open up conversations about what people wanted, what they thought was happening with "self-determination" there. This is what Blaser (2004) meant by the concept of "life project," as opposed to some simple cultural essentialism: the mixed and entangled relationship between an indigenous community as it pursues its own ends within the constraints and opportunities that surround it. This is all happening in the film material. Finally, it is an incredible record for Papunya Tula Artists – the Aboriginal-owned cooperative in which the acrylic painting movement began (see Bardon and Bardon 2004; Johnson 2010; Myers 2002). In the Yayayi footage, one can see senior men painting in the isolated painting camp beside the creek; you can see and hear the men talking, discussing things with each other; one can see the documentation of a painting, and a visit from the Aboriginal Arts Board. These are early moments of the articulation between Aboriginal painting and the government institutions that were supporting it, nurturing it through grants and marketing. It is possible to see a great deal about the history of Aboriginal people in these small communities as they are engaging with the government, as they are developing their own futures in whatever ways possible.

These are reasons why I wanted to make this available for the descendants of the people who had lived at Yayayi, people living at Kintore and Kiwirrkura now, to talk about their past and their history and maybe to evoke memory that we could then record. What did they think about what was happening at that time? This was a way to elicit their memories and possibly archive a range of responses from people who were there that they could draw on themselves in thinking about where they had been and where they were going.

Making the film: Collaboration in principle and practice

We had imagined initially that editing a shorter film out of the archival material would be directly collaborative, expecting or hoping for participation in an actual editing process. The research consultations and interviews also included extensive interviews recorded with all the non-Indigenous people who appear in the footage. We didn't have a script or structure for a film from the footage, a film that would incorporate the multiple perspectives and themes articulated by the Pintupi consultants and the others we interviewed. In fact, none of the Pintupi consultants seemed to imagine this sort of version, in conceiving a film that would communicate their perspectives along with those of outsiders, to a broader audience. This is a difference, perhaps, in working with people who do not have an idiom or practice of talking about old photos and other images. Early on, for example, I showed a scene of Yayayi in which my friend Bobby West's mother was sitting in the family camp with his younger brother. Both mother and brother are now deceased, and I was concerned how this might affect Bobby, what he would say. His mother had died at the hands of his father, in an unfortunate act of violence at night when Bobby was a young man, and his brother had died from petrol sniffing. His response was unexpectedly in reference to something else entirely: "That's my dog, there. Really strong one!" Whatever his feelings, they were not expressed at that moment.

Nonetheless, it became clear that scenes in the film could evoke memories and stories. When the Aboriginal Arts Board visits Yayayi, at the very beginning of Dunlop's stay and an important scene in the final film, the Pintupi painting men have a rather tense discussion with Peter Fannin, the Papunya Tula Arts advisor then, about the prospects of their getting a vehicle. Fannin has to tell them that the larger community of Papunya will get a vehicle first, but that later they will put in a grant for another, which Bob Edwards supports. As we screened this scene in 2011, at Kiwirrkura, Bobby West was not particularly interested in the politics and competitions of that earlier moment. Rather, he remembered Peter Fannin as his teacher at Papunya and that he used to take the kids swimming at Yalkipi, a waterhole not far from the large settlement. And he commented on the vehicle that Papunya Tula subsequently obtained for Yayayi and how it took Bobby to Balgo Hills Mission later that year, where he met some of his long-separated family (see below). As in this example, the film footage was most commonly linked to very specific personal memories and relationships. Bobby – like Irene and Monica – was impressed with the meetings that were recorded in which the men engaged with the problems facing the community. There is a scene in which the head councillor, Shorty Bruno, admonishes a gathering of men at a meeting after a bout of drunkenness and violence, "Don't bring grog into the community. If you do, drink it in your own camp; don't give it to anybody." His comment relates very directly to the circumstances of self-determination that we wanted to document. He recognizes their serious efforts to address the problems, and that is what drew Bobby's attention: "At least they talked about things and sorted them out" (Bobby West, at Kiwirrkura, Oct. 23, 2010).

By 2014, when we consulted with Bobby further, this time about the completed film (entitled *Remembering Yayayi*) with Marlene as the narrator, his comments brought these themes even more directly into focus. I will discuss them further below. Here, I simply want to point out how much this film is understood in light of the Pintupi pursuit of autonomy, self-direction – "doing things for themselves."

What we had from all these interviews and responses, at this point, were themes, discussions. The consultants were interested in the footage, but they had no suggestions of any further steps we might take. They wanted the film to be available, copies for themselves or somehow in the community. But the non-Indigenous participants in this – especially Pip, Ian, and I – were trying to figure out how to make these dialogues, these understandings of the socialities of self-determination, available to those who did not speak Pintupi, did not know everyone in the footage, and who were not likely to wade through 10 hours of footage.

What could collaboration be if we didn't have an editing partner? From the perspective of the present, I think we had a poor understanding of what collaboration or partnership could be. There wasn't a Pintupi editor with whom to work. In fact, it seems that they were content with having us make a version, following their insights, and for them to approve or disapprove.[27] We didn't have the kind of interviews and film material that could hold the footage together. None of our consultants had taken on the task of explaining or narrating. It wasn't until Deveson and I were able to film with Marlene Nampitjinpa Spencer that we had the prospect of a film, rather than an archival compilation.

I had first shown Marlene the footage on my initial trip to Kintore in 2006, in a laptop screening with her family. Her animated response at the time was part of what made it seem worth pursuing the project. But Marlene was and is a busy person, a leader in her

Figure 9.1 Marlene Nampitjinpa Spencer watching archival footage with relatives in Kintore, NT, in 2006.
Source: Photo Fred Myers.

community and spokesperson for health organizations (at first for the Pintupi Homelands Health Service and more recently for the Western Desert Dialysis Project). We weren't able to film with her until 2013. Coordinating Marlene's time in Alice Springs with mine and Deveson's was necessary for the interview, and by this point, we began to think of the Dialysis Project, known more colloquially as "the Purple House" (because of the color of the house in which the project was housed), as another partner in the film project. It is an institution that embodies Pintupi, and Aboriginal, political concerns and self-direction.[28]

Marlene's commentary was recorded in a hotel room in one day. It brought out an inner life of the film, gave concrete form to the relationships on the screen, maintained a perspective on the film events as a past that she treasured, and illuminated the value of these rare visual archives for contemporary populations who have little access to their own history. As with Bobby West, the images provoked memories: her little brother, Jacky (who died young from petrol sniffing), she remembered laughingly: "He always used to follow me like that." The old ladies near her mother's camp, she laughed, are "all inside the tent, hiding from the camera. At night they sleep there, might be a thousand people, this way and that."

Marlene wanted the recording to succeed. She faced the camera, and Pip behind it, with confidence and was comfortable allowing the discussion to follow the footage, opening up to the discussion of her own life. She spoke in both Pintupi and English, turning from me (in Pintupi, largely) to Deveson (partly translating or repeating what she said). Remarkably, in retrospect, reflecting on the footage and that time led her to focus on the importance of her father's example, of working for (the) people, of leadership. Bobby had similarly, in conversation with me while we were discussing the film, made connections between the example of his father (Freddy West) and other senior men who had taught him and his responsibilities for leadership and caring for his people. The past, or more specifically this past, a memory of it stimulated by the footage, was bringing these current leaders in their communities to find the model for active political agency in that earlier period. Was this a legacy of Pintupi self-determination?

The next day, Marlene had arranged for me to visit the Purple House. Shortly after I got there, a bus arrived with some of the patients and visitors who were in town. Marlene pointed to a large woman who knew me from Yayayi days but whom I did not immediately recognize as Kayu Napangarti. Napangarti threw her arms around me in a greeting of pleasure, and that morning, I began to recognize how many of my old friends and acqaintances had come to make the Purple House part of their existence. The path from the bush to settlement, from the Western Desert, to Yayayi, to Kintore was ending up in renal failure and dialysis for many. It became clearer what Pintupi saw in the healthy bodies of the footage from 1974, and also that the footage should be linked in some way to this project.

From the moment we recorded this interview, Deveson and I thought we had a thread on which we could draw the Yayayi footage together. The organizing framework would be the themes that all the consultants had identified, but Marlene's emotional responses to different scenes, her identification of people and interpretation of what was being done and spoken would allow an audience to share in her memories. Moreover, the arc of the interview, which gradually led to her contemplation of the deaths of her senior relatives, brought her to consideration of what had passed, of her own memories and loss.[29] We asked her to start by telling us the story of how she got to Yayayi, to Papunya, when she was a little girl. We wanted her to situate her response to the footage in her own knowledge of living at Yayayi in 1974. She responded by identifying herself as follows, "My name is Marlene Nampitjinpa, and I was born in Western Australia, at Kiwirrkura, in 1959. I'm going to try and tell this story, about history. Old days story." She told the camera that when the original footage was being shot, people weren't really familiar with cameras, that they didn't have images of themselves. She discussed how her family had lived when she was a small child, and how they had come to Papunya and subsequently why Pintupi had moved to Yayayi.[30]

Marlene's interview ended very emotionally, with her acknowledgement of the deaths of her relatives, her sense of them as being alive in the images but all gone. "Parara," she recalled, "my favorite cousin. All gone." Why have they died, too early, she asks? "Should be there, all these men. Why they gone too early?" She ponders the health issues, familiar to her from her career as a health worker and spokesperson. With tears streaming, she draws herself together and faces the camera to say, "This is my story. Because it really touched me this video. I knew all the men, all the women, the people when I was a young girl in Yayayi." From her joy and pleasure at seeing the living images of herself and her family to her grief at their loss, the film shows something of the value such archival materials have for Indigenous people as well as illuminating the lives of people in a remote community in the early period of self-determination. Seeing the footage, she told us, "make me happy. It touches my heart. *Kurrunparni pungu* [struck my spirit]." She remembered seeing the footage for the first time, when I showed it to her at Kintore in 2006, and she commented, "We didn't have pictures of our own people, their voices." We believed we could make the film.

It fell to Deveson, the camera person and editor, to pull the footage and the interview into a film over the following five months. We had rough translations from my 1975 work in Sydney with Freddy West and George Yapa, and also the commentary of the four consultants in 2010 and 2011. This was a huge task, with 10 hours of Yayayi footage alone, besides the other material and interview with Marlene. But as her editing began to identify particular scenes, Deveson and I, and sometimes with Thorley's help, coordinated in producing accurate and careful translations of the Pintupi speech in each scene. This was particularly significant to me; I saw the flow of everyday life around the exchange of banter, teasing, food, and oratory as a vital contribution of the original footage – essential to understanding the familiar sociality of Pintupi people that has generally been inaccessible to outsiders. This editing work took place in Canberra, with Ian participating at times with Deveson, occasional visits by Thorley, and with communication by email and skype between Canberra and New York. Eventually, we had a rough cut, which Deveson sent to me, and for which I provided further translations and clarifications.

One more stage of preparation remained. The unedited original footage had been screening regularly, if not continuously, in Kintore and Kiwirrkura as well as Alice Springs (in the dialysis treatment rooms at the Purple House). Because of this acceptance and constant exposure, and after consultation along the way, we were somewhat assured that the film material was acceptable. Marlene saw the actual edited film version when she visited Canberra in 2013 for health meetings, and was shown the film by Deveson. She announced herself happy with it.

We felt we still needed to be sure that we had final approval from community leaders, especially from men because of the inclusion of what is a public moment in the *Tingarri* ceremonies at Yayayi. In this scene, young men who have been secluded for later stages of ritual instruction in ceremonies known as *Tingarri* are brought out into the community behind a barrier of leaves and branches held by senior men to obscure their being seen. Dunlop had been permitted to film this public event, and it had been screening regularly in community viewings, but we wanted to be certain about it.

I was still unable to travel for a consultation in the communities, which in the best of circumstances I would have preferred to undertake myself, personally and in Pintupi. However, we were able to send a copy of the DVD to Alice Springs for a consultation that would draw on the support of our partner institution, Papunya Tula Artists. A friend and colleague, Luke Scholes, who had formerly worked closely with senior Pintupi men at Papunya Tula Artists, was working at the Purple House (where the footage was watched, in any case).[31] We asked Luke, who knew Bobby West well, to show him the film edit and see if it was acceptable.[32] Given the difficulties of finding time with Bobby, a much travelled and serially involved leader at Kiwirrkura and Papunya Tula Artists, this took a while. Eventually he was able to see it.

Luke Scholes reported carefully on his consultation with Bobby:

> First and foremost, Bobby loved the film. I have the feeling that he was genuinely affected by the film also; he echoed a lot of what Marlene had to say throughout. He thought it was a wonderful record of that time and that he was very happy that the footage exists.
>
> The only thing Bobby raised as a small concern was Marlene's comments about the section of the film that shows the boys coming out of the bush. Bobby commented that it was "*Tingarri* Business, not *Tjilkatja*." "Like University," he said. "Learning how to sing the *Tingarri*." "She didn't know, so she shouldn't say, should be quiet." I then asked if anything needed to be done about this section of the film and he said, yes, it should be taken out. I got the feeling that [for] Bobby … this was to protect Marlene in a way.
>
> The rest of the film he thoroughly enjoyed.
>
> *(Luke Scholes email, Feb. 25, 2014a)*[33]

We followed up on this concern. What changes does he want us to make? In return email, Luke wrote as follows:

> I can't recall exactly Marlene's comment regarding that part. I think it was something very innocuous like: "All the young men, coming back from business" and Bobby thinks she is suggesting that she was privy to some aspect of the type of ceremonies being performed. I think Bobby thinks it is unwise for Marlene to appear to have knowledge on [this], which Bobby thinks her comment implies. Therefore he believes that [the] small comment that Marlene makes should be removed. Again, Bobby didn't make a big deal of it, maybe just distancing Marlene from the male domain. He did suggest she should not say anything "because she doesn't know" (the exact nature of the business being performed) and therefore Tjapanangka [i.e. Myers] should take that bit out.
>
> *(Luke Scholes email 2, Feb. 25, 2014b).*

What is at issue here is a familiar concern in Indigenous Australia, namely the gender segregation of ritual/esoteric knowledge.[34] Bobby was asking that some small edits be made in the film to make certain that it was clear that Marlene was not speaking inappropriately about "men's business" when she narrated the scene in which we show the movement of *Tingarri* novices into the camp. The offending portion, we realized, was a comment Marlene had made about "when they grab the boys and take them to the bush." Now omitted from her commentary, this could seem to be a reference to male initiation proper (*Tjilkatja*), and not the more publicly open *Tingarri* ceremonies and performances – which Bobby likens to "University" (see Myers 1986, on different categories of ritual and performance). There is an important parallel here in the distinction between *Tingarri* and more focused male initiation: when Papunya painters were criticized for revealing restricted material in their paintings in 1971–1972, they decided to restrict themselves to the public portions of *Tingarri* stories, a category of Ancestral activity that they determined to be acceptable for limited revelation.[35] It would be inappropriate, even transgressive, for a woman to speak of or even to imply knowledge of men's initiatory rituals. Thus, the narration of the film had to avoid such implication.[36]

There was diplomacy of other sorts involved in this consultation as well. Bobby had been an immense support in every stage of supporting the project, and perhaps my own closest friend in the Pintupi community. Ideally, he might have been the narrator, but what we had on camera militated for other choices. Therefore, we had wanted to explain to him how it was that the film came to be edited around the narrative and figure of Marlene, and none of the other consultants. The edits became even more important, however, as it was necessary to avoid a violation of rights Pintupi men shared with others in these ceremonies.

When those edits were done, we sent the final version back out to Alice Springs to seek approval not only from Bobby again, but also from the Indigenous governing board of the Western Desert Dialysis Project, mainly made up of senior Pintupi women. The group included Marlene, but also Irene Nangala who had been one of the initial consultants and supporters of the project. The governing board approved it, and were confident to allow its being shown at Kintore as part of the public celebration of the Purple House's Tenth Anniversary, on September 25, 2014. The only objection was that people in the film were sometimes heard swearing, which a few thought indecorous, but they were swept aside, apparently, by Marlene's enthusiasm. The women supported the screening. It screened at Kintore without any difficulty, making the first public screening in the community itself.

Circulation: Authors and other owners

More or less at the same time, we submitted the film to the Margaret Mead Film and Video Festival at the American Museum of Natural History in New York, one of the premier ethnographic film venues. Moving beyond a community screening, for which the terms of our use were clear, we needed to get permission to do so from the National Film and Sound Archives (NFSA). Since Dunlop was one of the directors and the footage under consideration had been shot by him while working at Film Australia, we had assumed we would have the rights to use it in a film.

To Dunlop's consternation and our surprise, however, this was not the view of the NFSA. Formally and officially, they held copyright to the footage that had been shot by Dunlop, as it was a product of Film Australia (which later became Screen Australia) and Dunlop had been an employee. Thus, these materials became the property of this government archive. Therefore, if we were to proceed with a film, we would have to pay licensing fees (fees per second used) for use of the footage. There were approximately 40 minutes used. While they were willing to discount the fee, in light of the fact that this was educational work and even further because we had contributed over $10,000 to digitize and color correct the footage, we were left with the prospect of paying more than $10,000 further.

Subsequently, Dunlop remembered that he had a memorandum of understanding developed upon his retirement in 1987 that gave him permission to continue working on his film projects. While the Yayayi project had not been specifically named in this document, in the first meeting with the NFSA he had neglected to mention this agreement.[37] Through a letter of protest (really, indignation) that Dunlop sent to the head of the NFSA, our concerns reached the highest level, but at this time, we could make no further progress. This still left a considerable sum to be paid for the rights to show the film at film festivals world-wide. At standard rates, the rights for licensing the material for a DVD for distribution, even by an educational institution, would be around $50,000.[38] Pressed for time, and against Dunlop's wishes, we used funds from our research grant to pay the discounted license fees we had been offered for film festival screenings alone ($12,960) so the film could be shown at the Margaret Mead Film Festival – and subsequently at other festivals.

As the footage moved from the documentation project and community participation to a new stage of being, a new use, the NFSA added an additional condition – they required proof of "the community's" agreement to have the footage used in our film.[39] While this followed the laudable protocol of many government organizations to recognize Indigenous cultural property rights in their images, since we had been working closely with Pintupi consultants, and with the agreements of our own Human Subjects protocols (through the Australian National University) and with an Indigenous organization (Papunya Tula Artists), we had a layering of consent for the project. While the NFSA required some form of "community" approval, it was really unclear what this "consent agreement" would look like. We were somewhat taken aback when the NFSA put forward a rather different model of consultation developed in a recent history project with the historian Professor Ann McGrath.[40] It set a consent process that was impossible for us to meet as we could hardly backtrack to develop our project retroactively to follow the new model set forth. We felt that from the first, our project had been done in consultation. What was needed, now, and from the largely institutional and bureaucratic side of things, was for a "community" council to sign off literally, and on paper. Unfortunately, by 2014, these councils did not exist – casualties both of the controversial NTER and also of the reorganization of communities into larger entities, the "shires." However, the staff at the NFSA were agreeable to accepting a letter from Bobby West, who wrote his approval as a senior man and representative of Kiwirrkura:

> My name is Bobby West Tjupurrula. My father and many other of my family appear in the film "Remembering Yayayi." I was a consultant on the project, when I was chairperson of the Kiwirrkura Community and gave comments and advice on much of it, I have approved the final version with one small change that I requested.
>
> We have been working with Fred Myers and Pip Deveson on the video from 1974 since 2006, and we are all so happy to see our mothers and fathers again and to show them to our kids.
>
> Sincerely,
>
> Bobby West Tjupurrula
>
> *(Letter to National Film and Sound Archives, June 2, 2014)*

It was reassuring to me that, in sending his letter of approval Bobby said that "he thought it was important that we can all see this film" (Luke Scholes email, June 2, 2014c).[41]

The NFSA also required the permission of Papunya Tula Artists as they were listed as the contact for permissions for Yayayi footage.[42]

However, the problems of licensing fees and negotiations around them were not over. There remained some surprises for us in the response of the National Film and Sound Archives and their sense of proprietary ownership over the footage itself.

In 2014, the NFSA quoted license fees of over $100,000 for rights to use the archival footage in television. We had imagined that the relatively new National Indigenous Television channel (NITV)[43] might be interested in screening this film, as it spoke to many Indigenous concerns about "Aboriginal self-determination" and the continued pressure for "assimilation," but also it represented a situation – of relatively traditional people, speaking their own language – in an Aboriginal history that many Indigenous people might imagine their ancestors to have lived. If this seemed a plausible and productive outcome, the proposed fees foreclosed it. The NFSA approach at that time treated *Remembering Yayayi* as simply a usage of their archival property. They respected that the footage was a form of cultural property of the Pintupi communities, registered by the requirement of their agreement to usages. That is, no one could use this footage without such agreement. However, the NFSA claimed ultimate copyright as represented by licensing fees for various usages. Despite Dunlop's insistence that his understanding with Film Australia, which had preceded the existence of the footage in NFSA vaults, allowed him to continue to work on and make films from his prior work, the NFSA view was that this understanding referred only to the specifically named projects in his retirement agreement. Informal knowledge suggests that the advent of significant licensing fees in projects of an educational (vs commercial) value was relatively recent and probably a consequence of the governmental restructuring of the archives and reduction of support.[44]

The conversations between members of our project and representatives of the archive were not productive, and at times seemed very much at cross-purposes. By 2015, however, the Australian National University legal counsel took up the case. We realized that, as the host of our research grant and by its agreement in setting up that relationship, the ANU (itself a government institution) was at least one of the "owners" of the work we were producing. Deputy University Counsel Rachel Vance made the argument, successfully it seems, for "a solution that allows the wider release of the film which has only been possible to create as a result of the significant and considerable contributions to the Work (and the derivative works) by Ian Dunlop, FA (NFSA), Pip Deveson, ANU, NMA, Papunya Tula Artists and the ARC" (letter of June 17, 2015 to Adam Flynn at NFSA). Vance's letter draws attention to the multiple parties who have been involved in producing the film, contributing in various ways (financial and otherwise), and a history of connection to it. Dunlop's initial "authorial" rights have an important place in this discussion. Indeed, as Jane Anderson (2013:230) has pointed out crucially in regard to the formation of archives themselves more generally, "authorship is an integral component for understanding how archives are constituted, how they distribute certain kinds of authority, and how they circulate meaning." "Authorship" has cultural significance in the organization of this archive. Thus, the legal counsel points out that "Ian Dunlop remained and continues to be the expert on this material [the footage] and to this day when the FA Collection Film Library has a request to use some of Ian's ethnographic footage they nearly always refer it to him for his opinion and advice (fee-free)" (Anderson 2013). But, in recognition of what have emerged as further conditions of archival rights, so also she argues for the significance of the consent of Papunya Tula Artists and the elders of the Pintupi communities to use the footage and their encouragement of its being accessible to them and to the public. On the other hand, NFSA has not contributed to what she calls "the Work."

These are arguments for waiving the license fees, based on the agreement FA granted in 1987 and 1988. However, they also represent a case for the changing and complex relationships that are justly embodied in the film, especially as "Neither Ian Dunlop nor ANU intend to commercially exploit the film but want it to be accessible to a wider audience than can be reached through film festivals or non-commercial screening" (Vance 2015; Anderson 2013)

Screenings

Our initial licensing agreement with NFSA allowed us to show *Remembering Yayayi* in film festivals worldwide. The first such screening was the Margaret Mead Film Festival at the American Museum of Natural History in New York. By this point, we had decided that the film – as a projection of Pintupi history – should not be used simply as a representation, but rather that it should and could be used to put forward Pintupi contemporary aspirations – as an intimation of their aspirations for self-determination and to help bring attention and support for the Dialysis Project, with which Marlene and Irene were closely associated. Since that project has made its goal the support of people's relationship to place as a basis for a cultural future, it seemed the proper location of the film screening. For the screening, our research grant budget allowed us to bring Marlene to represent the film and also to make the connection to the Dialysis Project.

The screening in New York was a great success. On October 24, 2014, Marlene sat in the front of the theater, beside Pip and me. As the screen lit up with her image at the start, she began to talk back to the film – just as she had when I showed her the footage on my laptop in 2006. Her laughter at herself speaking, her commentary in English and Pintupi, freed the New York audience to enjoy the humor and pathos in the film. When it was over, we handed the microphone to her for the short question and answer period, and she spoke – in English – about the health issues of people in Central Australia. As she said then, she had this role because she could overcome her shyness.

The next screening was the official launch of the film in Australia, at the National Museum of Australia, April 10, 2015. The NMA was a partner in the project, so this was the logical place to show the film, and Thorley arranged for the film to be shown there with the explicit goal of linking it to the museum's acquisition of a "dialysis chair" for its collection as an important component of a planned exhibition about Aboriginal health. This was an attempt to mobilize the film to benefit the Pintupi communities – giving them visibility for their health cause as well as their concerns about their security in homeland communities. We hoped that they would be able to use the opportunity to recruit support for the Dialysis Project, drawing both on the audience for the film and the proximity of government agencies they could meet on their visit.

The response to the film was moving, again mobilized by Marlene's extrafilmic commentary. In the Q&A that followed, both Marlene and Monica spoke about the film and the situation of health in the desert communities. However, the most crucial moment was the commentary by the CEO of the Dialysis Project, Sarah Brown, as she linked the film to the current situation. By April 2015, with remote communities directly under attack from the Federal Government her comments pointed to the importance of some kind of self-determination for health, and she reminded the audience that the Dialysis Project was a Pintupi initiative. They had lobbied government for help, wanting to have treatment centers in their remote homeland communities so the older people could remain on their country and close to their kin; such proximity is important to their health, and also important to the transmission of cultural knowledge to the next generations. The Dialysis Project, she told the audience, is not a government project; Pintupi people did it themselves.[45] Just as they had moved to Kintore through their own initiative (and really to Yayayi), so the Dialysis Project was a part of that history of doing things for themselves.

That the film could be a platform for these discussions, and materially so by providing an occasion on which the situation of Indigenous people in remote communities was made visible, seemed appropriate. The question one expects to hear about making a film for which the audience is outsiders is "what value does it have for the local people themselves?" From the initial response of viewers at Kiwirrkura about the health of their relatives back then, to their recognition of the leadership of their elders in the film, to the current threat to remote communities, the existence and form of the film had significance for them.

Subsequently, the film has been accepted to three major ethnographic film festivals,[46] but these screenings will not have the presence of Marlene or other Pintupi interlocutors. The distances are great and the costs too high.

Memories

Continued and repeated dialogues at all stages of the development of this film have been a productive means of consultation. Over time, we have learned more about the effect of the film for Pintupi viewers, its connections to their memories of that time and the ways they look back to that time from the present. This excerpt from an email from Luke Scholes detailing more extensive and very important commentary from Bobby West, shows, in significant ways, how this footage is and has been processed. His comments lead him to a broad reflection on the costs and tensions of leadership:

> I thought I would just record everything Bobby spoke about for your interest. . . . Bobby asked how old Ian was and if Ian had a son? [He] Commented that Jeff Stead[47] is now living in Melbourne.
>
> During the section of the film where a second car is to be purchased for Yayayi, Bobby remembered that the second car was a yellow Landrover which was driven

> to Balgo for business. He thought that at this time there were no Pintupi who could drive, so Snowy Tjampitjinpa and Linda Syddick's husband drove them. He also commented that George Maxwell Tjampitjinpa, Donald Tjapaltjarri, Riley Rowe and Ronnie Tjampitjinpa were the first Pintupi to learn to drive.
>
> Bobby had a lot to say about the old man sitting in the humpy, Kulitu, Joe Young's father, who I am sure you recognized. He was a cripple who could only walk sometimes due to a badly wounded leg. John Bennett had speared him in a dispute regarding the unfair distribution of meat. Bobby was amazed to hear his voice during the arrival of the business mob shouting instructions with his typically prominent voice.
>
> Bobby commented on the practice of young initiates bringing back "toy" weapons for the younger children that they had fashioned during their time in the bush. He mentioned that Malpa Jackson, Ray James and one of the Bruno boys were a part of that group of boys going through business. He commented that Ray not long after this was taken to Yuendumu to attend more business but ran away and set off for Yayayi again only to be tracked down by the old men. Bobby said he was still a boy at this stage and so stayed away from this business while it was on. He stayed with Ginger Tjakamarra and Wintjiya, Long Jack also.
>
> Bobby made special mention of Shorty Bruno, saying he thought Shorty was a tremendous leader of the Yayayi community. He said other people were jealous of Yayayi and how well it was run. He said Ronnie was also one of the bosses there but was not well respected or trusted due to his "me, me" attitude and his like for a drink.
>
> He told the story of the group of jealous men from Haasts Bluff and Papunya who travelled to Yayayi and offered to take Shorty hunting. They all went hunting together and shot many kangaroo, but then the men shot and killed Shorty. Using magic they brought him back to life and sent him back to the community where he quickly became sick and died.
>
> Toward the end of the film, Bobby lamented the greed that has engulfed [names a community]. This was partly in response to the wonderful images of the families sharing the marlu [kangaroo] which Bobby audibly responded to. He said that back in those days everyone shared the spoils of the hunt and everything else they had. He named almost every prominent member of the [community], and said he thought they were not like the old people sharing their money, food and cars. They only thought of themselves. . . .
>
> *(Luke Scholes email, Feb. 25, 2014a)*

Scholes notes that Bobby's comments were made at a time in which new arrangements for mining royalties were being signed which excluded many people who had thought of themselves as relatives.

Bobby's reflections are exactly what we had hoped to hear during the earlier primary consultations, at Kiwirrkura and Canberra, but memories and reactions emerged more piece-meal. Talking to Luke, in conversations subsequent to those he had with me, Bobby reiterated and extended the story forward from the footage of the painters' request for a vehicle to his own memories of the yellow Landrover they later obtained and used to visit Balgo and recreate ties among disparate Western Desert relatives. On a darker note, possibly, Bobby was prompted to talk about the Yayayi leader Shorty Bruno's death by my question to Marlene about her father's death. He went beyond his earlier, somewhat truncated praise for Yayayi's leadership in sorting things out in meetings. While Marlene had dropped her head to the table at my question about where he died, Bobby thought back to suspicions Pintupi had about the death of a leader, the result of jealousy at his standing and at Yayayi's success. I had heard this story, whispered from time to time, from my own history and visits. I was surprised to hear it surface like this, but it shares with much of the commentary we heard – about the strength of the older people, their leadership in establishing an independent Pintupi community and the model of responsibility they created for the next generation – for people like Bobby and Marlene.

Still, for a film that presents the early moments of Aboriginal self-determination, a political project engaged with the Australian state and a colonial heritage, it is disconcerting to have the story told in local parlance – jealousy, sorcery, death.

Conclusion

> Unless there is a feeling of ownership on the part of the [Australian Indigenous] people you are working with, the effort simply cannot be sustained, because it is a huge effort in ways that are quite unnatural for them culturally. Filmmaking is almost the opposite of anything that can work in their culture. It is completely hierarchical generally, and they work entirely by consensus. It's also rigidly scheduled and that's not how they work at all.
>
> *(Rolf de Heer, Myers Interview about Charlie's Country, recorded New York City, June 6, 2015).*

In discussing the complexities of filmmaking with an Aboriginal community, in the quotation with which I head this conclusion, the noted Australian filmmaker Rolf de Heer drew attention most directly to the contradiction between the hierarchical organization of commercial filmmaking and the emphasis on consensus in Indigenous practice. Indeed, I began this chapter with this sense of the obstacles or challenges that lie in wait for those who might want to engage ethically and properly with people who have very different relationships to film material and to develop a project of "returning" to them material that is of historical and personal interest. The object of my consideration has been a body of material that is itself embedded in a history of distinctive moments, practices, and institutions (governmental, local). The rights and duties it reflects and within which it exists have been changing, not only as Indigenous rights to their own images have become more forcefully articulated and recognized by (in this case) Australian governmental archives and protocols, but also as technology has made these objects available to viewing and possession in new ways. These circumstances require renewed attention to the properties of archival material and archival material as a form of property. The existence of the footage is critical, but the question is much more than who owns the footage, and while that becomes important later, the process shows a real shift in thinking about ownership of the visual image.

I have followed the processes in which a body of film footage is produced in 1974, becomes an archival object, is brought back to the community, becomes an object of reflection, and eventually becomes the basis from which a film is made – as a movement through various regimes of property. I explain the initial reasoning behind the production of the film footage by Ian Dunlop, the happenstance reasons why it never really came to anything in terms of a final production when Dunlop made it, and the way in which the material has continued to be remembered and desired because of what it contains and what kind of place Yayayi (the community of filming) was. Finally, I try to show how it came into life as a whole because of the collaboration and investment of many parties. The time for making that "whole" had to emerge temporally and socially, an important dimension of collaboration and the lives that something we might call "cultural property" has.

The process I am describing here is framed by the conundrum of the very idea of "cultural property" itself, a concept derived from forms of Western law that suggest a stable concrete object whose provenance can be determined conclusively. Despite its attractiveness and value in defending or asserting Indigenous rights to their own cultural knowledge, it is difficult to use such a concept to describe the fluid, relational and constantly changing ways in which Aboriginal ideas of protocol and custodianship continue to be negotiated in ongoing activity. This is the problem, in my view, with efforts to establish an acceptable framework of guidelines such as the various, laudable "ICIP" – Indigenous Cultural Intellectual Property – protocols. They are premised on a very limited idea of what can happen in circumstances of cultural flow. One might simply consider the way in which the taboo on images of the deceased has changed over the generation of the film's existence.

Current protocols that attempt to specify cultural property in Indigenous representation (such as Janke 2002) suffer from imagining these forms in terms that ignore, restrict, or deny the complexity of the entanglements inhabited by the materialities of culture. Protocols may, for example, impose a stability that imagines an endpoint of negotiation. In the case of intercultural film projects such as the one I have discussed, this includes everything from retrieving archival material to the temporalities of production and the negotiations of circulation. In the discussion of the complexities of filmmaking with an Aboriginal community which I use to start this section, Rolf de Heer draws attention most directly to the contradiction between the hierarchical organization of commercial filmmaking and the emphasis on consensus in Indigenous practice.

The issues are not restricted to Indigenous protocols. I remember that my own access – right to research with – the Yayayi archive through the National Archive depended on being an authorized researcher via support from Dunlop – acknowledging his rights as the "author" of the material. Indeed, if one recognizes the collective nature of filmmaking as Howard Becker (1982) does in his famous *Artworlds*, one sees the articulation or delineation of rights and identities in a "film" reflected in contracts and credits, sometimes disputed, but clearly an attempt to determine accountabilities, authorship, and so on – the relationships objectified – in a product.

"Collaboration" and "consultation" are both terms now commonly extended to discussions of culture-making that involves multiple parties and especially parties that have different rights, different forms of power, and different technological or skill capacities in representing the stories and lives of human beings (see also Anderson and Montenegro in this volume). Both terms are ethically charged, but perhaps inadequate to characterize the complexities of the relationships to which they guide us. There are two central points I want to make. The first is that the processes in which these practices are carried out are neither seamless nor effortlessly consensual. The second is that film, as a distinctive form of cultural property, is not something that is simply "owned." Rather, this "property" is a foundation for social relationships. The processes of collaboration and consultation make it a platform on which a variety of relationships are established and produced.

In a very generative essay on property, the anthropologist Marilyn Strathern has written insightfully about the way in which property may specify a particular moment for objects in relational flow: "Ownership gathers things momentarily to a point by locating them in the owner, halting endless dissemination, effecting an identity" (1999:177). Strathern directs us away from overly stable conceptions of "property." Whatever usage they have come to have in the emerging protocols of "cultural property," it seems that the practice of property in

Western law does not simply fall back on such stabilities. In the final argument put forward by the ANU legal counsel, it was impressive to see that every form of relationship was drawn into the attempt to articulate what is at stake in this new hybrid object, *Remembering Yayayi*. This dispute, if we can call it that in formal terms, will, in the end, produce a final outcome, a determination – namely, the waiver of license fees that allows us to screen the film and distribute it non-commercially on DVD and free-to air TV. But what we see is not a simple, straightforward application of rules, but a negotiated recognition of identities and relationships, responsibilities, around the object. Presumably also settled by such a determination might be accountability for effects of the film – for example, if there are objections to portions of it being screened. Emotional harm?

Finally, I must speak to what I see as the most fundamental dimension of the mobilization of this film material in collaboration. The question that was hanging over the project was what value it might have for those identified with the film subjects. For whom does the question of Pintupi autonomy and health in 1974 matter and in what ways? In that sense, the context for this project lies in the governmental threats of closing remote Indigenous communities, a threat that actually includes the Pintupi community of Kiwirrkura since the funding in Western Australia is most directly threatened. But this specific threat exists as part of a growing push toward forms of assimilation and away from support for cultural futures that the previous Prime Minister Tony Abbott called "lifestyle choices." Remote dialysis, the immediate mission of the Western Desert Dialysis project, understands Indigenous health in Central Australia, contrastingly, as linked to being "on country," to sustaining the transmission of culture between generations by having the elderly renal patients close to their families and country. To mobilize the film in this context, for example, by screening on national television or regional screenings, allows Pintupi socialities and desires to be shared and to speak in the space that currently engulfs them.

Acknowledgements

The research on which this chapter is based was supported by grants from the Australian Institute of Aboriginal and Torres Strait Islander Studies (2009) and an Australia Research Council Linkage Grant (2010–2013), as well as support from the National Museum of Australia. This chapter is much indebted to many people, as is the story told. I want to thank my colleagues Ian Dunlop, Pip Deveson, Peter Thorley, and Nic Peterson for their many contributions, collegiality, and ideas. Especially, I thank Bobby West, Jimmy Brown Tjampitjinpa, Marlene Nampitjinpa Spencer, Monica Robinson, Irene Nangala for their support, insight, and patience. Thanks especially to Papunya Tula Artists for sponsoring the project. I thank Paul Sweeney and Luke Scholes, at Papunya Tula, for their support of the project, of getting out into the Kintore and Kiwirrkura communities, and for various consultations along the way. Thanks also to Sarah Brown and the Western Desert Dialysis Project for support and for helping define a future for this project. Thanks to the numerous interviewees we pestered in this process: Jeremy Long, Bob Edwards, Jeff Stead, Peter Fannin, Terry Parry, Ken and Leslie Hansen, Dick Kimber. And thanks to Carolyn Cann for helping find some of the materials we consulted in developing the archive of the project. Finally, thanks to Faye Ginsburg, Jane Anderson, and Haidy Geismar for reading and discussing this chapter with me and helping to make it come about – and especially to Jane for a Herculean effort to edit the chapter down to size.

Notes

1 I realize there is considerable debate about whether returning digital material to a community is "repatriation." Here I am using the term in a colloquial sense as we were using it to discuss more generally a return to the Pintupi communities of video material shot with them but which they had not seen. The extent to which it would be repatriated in any more formal sense was itself a question we had.

2 I am indebted to Jane Anderson for this way of teasing apart the complex story in these terms.

3 Pintupi is one of the many dialects of the broader Western Desert language family. The people referred to as Pintupi are Western Desert people who came eastward toward missions and settlements on the eastern edge of the desert, to Hermannsburg, Haasts Bluff, and later Papunya, from the 1930s to the 1960s. In moving from the desert eastward, they settled – or became sedentarized – in communities that relied partly on food and resources from outside and aimed at their protection and later their assimilation toward the Anglo-Australian norm. See Myers (1986).

4 The Commonwealth Film Unit was originally established in 1945 as the Australian National Film Board to produce documentary films dealing with matters of national Australia.

5 Dunlop, I. and Gray, J. 1958. *Balloons and Spinifex*. Australian Commonwealth Film Unit, Lindfield, NSW.

6 Renamed Film Australia in 1973.

7 See Myers (2006).

8 See Bryson (2002). The resulting films of this project, directed by Roger Sandall, were *Pintupi Revisit Yaru* and *Pintupi Revisit Yumari*.

9 Discussions of the restrictions on filming ceremony and the specific events – or transgressions – that brought these concerns into play can be found in Bryson (2002) and Myers (2015).

10 Deveson (2012) writes that "Dunlop had gone to Yirrkala [in 1970] wanting to adopt a new approach to his filming with people – and wanting to establish a real collaboration with Yolngu."

11 Dunlop's ideas about ethnographic filmmaking were evolving at this time, both through his own engagements with people, through the growing availability of lighter cameras, sync sound and color film, and through a growing awareness of ethnographic film work elsewhere – of Jean Rouch, Robert Gardner, Colin Young in 1966 and Tim Asch and David MacDougall in 1972 (Deveson 2012).

12 Sound operator Es Giddy and backup camera operator Jon Rhodes.

13 The activities of ethnography and filmmaking were not always easily coordinated. The sheer technical and physical requirements of getting the camera and sound recording set up, getting a decent angle to capture activity, asking people to continue what they were doing or to do it again so they could get it right – all of these materialities of filmmaking were in conflict with my own rather less constrained activities. Especially, since Pintupi communities are rather unstructured, and unplanned, the project of filming in them is often at odds with their pace and flow.

14 I went alone. Dunlop had been planning to accompany me on the trip, but only a few weeks before we were to leave, he broke his leg badly in a fall, and was unable to travel. My former student Lisa Stefanoff and Basil Schild joined me on the visit to Kiwirrkura and helped record the events there.

15 In 1973 and 1974, at Yayayi, Pintupi people would sometimes come across – or ask to see – a book with photographs of themselves or their relatives. The older people would often slam a book closed, or put it down, if they came across the image of someone who was deceased. They certainly would not speak their name, and would whisper to me some terms to identify them. Younger people would, even then, be interested to see.

16 Jimmy Brown pre-screened the footage attentively, quietly clicking his tongue at moments that struck him, responding to scenes. Jimmy was one of the "old Pintupi," people who had come in from the bush before 1960, and he regarded the "new Pintupi" with a certain kind of nostalgia, relatives but people who were still "bush" people. At the long sequence of Yanyatjarri Tjampitjinpa making boomerangs, he commented, "He's a happy man. Everybody likes to be around him. Always happy." At another point, when Freddy West was butchering and sharing a kangaroo he cooked, Jimmy remembered, "He was a very kind man" (Myers field notes Monday May 29, 2006).

17 Louise Curham, Project Officer, Film Preservation at the National Archives was very helpful in the project, allowing access and reproduction of materials.

18 While the email refers to "tapes," it was actually copies of the DVD that we left at Kiwirrkura. As will become clear, my close friend Bobby West Tjupurrula was one of the principal consultants and supporters of the whole project.

19 The fields of power and interest around this footage have been even more complex than I can discuss within the narrative confines of this chapter. The trip to Kiwirrkura to screen the film required crossing into Western Australia and engaging with the Ngaanyatjarra Land Council that represents Kiwirrkura as well as the Central Land Council that represents Kintore. This required negotiating another set of relationships and jurisdictions, not to speak of personal animosities and jealousies.
20 As a side note, I should say that the film material had already achieved usefulness. When the Indigenously owned painting cooperative Papunya Tula Artists celebrated the building of a new studio at Kintore in 2007, they invited me to show some of the archival footage to connect the early days of Papunya Tula (at Yayayi) with the present. At the screening, the Pintupi descendants of those in the footage were interested, even enthusiastic, about this material. Later, in 2007 the National Museum of Australia held an exhibition of Pintupi paintings, "Pintupi Painting: Out of the Desert," focused on work of the mid-1970s. I suggested to Vivien Johnson, the guest curator, that she consult with Ian Dunlop about using some of the footage involving the painters. Ian's long-time collaborator, Pip Deveson, was contracted to make a one-off, 20-minute film for display within the exhibition. The film was translated and entitled *Pintupi Painters at Yayayi*. This proved to be a huge success. The audience in the small theatre (within the exhibition) was never less than half full, with standing room only on the final weekend.
21 Peter Thorley has been an important part of the repatriation and documentation project, in the processes of consultation and later in the screening at the National Museum. As Partner Investigator of the ARC grant, he was the link to the National Museum. Thorley was a curator at the National Museum in 2008, but his link to the project is based on his history as a teacher-linguist at the Pintupi community of Kintore in 1988. Not only did he speak Pintupi-Luritja quite well, he was very close as a colleague with two Pintupi women educators, Irene Nangala and Monica Robinson Nangala – the two women we asked to be consultants on the project, because of their interest in Pintupi history, their concern that this be part of local education, and their skills as cultural translators.
22 In my visit to Central Australia in 2006, I had discussions with then-Media Officer at the Central Land Council, Jane Hodgson, and also some communication with the Ngaanyatjarra Media Centre as locations for holding or sharing the footage as "Pintupi heritage." Neither really had the resources or capacities to do so effectively.
23 This grant was from the Australian Institute of Aboriginal and Torres Strait Islander Studies (AIATSIS). The AIATSIS grant allowed us to work with two Pintupi consultants in Canberra for a week in 2010, and two others at Kiwirrkura in 2011, sessions we recorded and documented for the archive that we expected to produce for the footage, as documents of Pintupi history.
24 Monica and Irene were leaders at Kintore. They had considerable experience as teachers in the Kintore school and through that had participated in the development of the ideology of Pintupi self-determination, of "holding the community" (see Keeffe 1992; Folds 2001).
25 For this reason, a set of three DVDs, with menus that made major sequences easily accessible, were prepared and distributed to people who had requested copies through Papunya Tula.
26 The Northern Territory Intervention, officially known as the Northern Territory Emergency Response Act 2007, was a controversial Federal response to reports of rampant child sexual abuse and dysfunction in Aboriginal communities in the Northern Territory and a significant movement away from policies of self-determination. For a sense of these debates, readers might consult Altman and Hinkson (2007). Two of the key antagonists of the self-determination policy and support for homeland communities have been Helen Hughes (2007) and Gary Johns (2001).
27 I am not the only person to experience this. Even Indigenous colleagues, curators for example, have suggested that collaboration may take place through this kind of initiation and response. Certainly, it seems unrealistic to expect one's partners to have the kind of aesthetic and technical frameworks to construct the edited version of a film – at least not without some kind of training.
28 It was, itself, the result of Pintupi initiative for remote dialysis, funded by an art auction and supported in part by proceeds from Papunya Tula Artists.
29 In contrast, the dialogue with Bobby has been sporadic, or better, punctuated in time – less narratively coordinated.
30 This material has been used in a second film Deveson has edited, *Marlene's Story*, which will be a "special feature" with the main film.
31 Scholes was an ideal choice to do this consultation. He has had extensive experience with Pintupi men, both as a field officer at Papunya Tula Artists, and also through his involvement with consultation issues while he was an assistant curator at the National Gallery of Victoria during the "*Tjukurrtjanu:*

Origins of Western Desert Art" exhibition in 2011 which had involved important considerations of what could and could not be seen by a general public. For discussion of this, see Myers (2011: ix-xi).

32 Bobby, as chairman of Papunya Tula Artists, had been familiar with some of the issues surrounding the exhibition of restricted imagery and had been an important consultant on the question of how to exhibit (or not) some of the early collection of Papunya Tula paintings at the Museum and Art Galleries of the Northern Territory.

33 Luke's email included more extensive and very important commentary from Bobby, showing in significant ways how this footage is and has been processed. I will return to these later in the chapter.

34 See Myers (2014).

35 See Myers (2002, 2014, 2015).

36 Deveson made those editing changes, and given the comfort with which footage had been accepted for public screening over the past several years, along with its approval for screening by Jimmy Brown in 2006, we felt we had support to go forward with a new edit.

37 This MOU between Dunlop and Film Australia was "A Policy for the Future Custody and Use of Ethnographic Film Collection produced by Ian Dunlop for Film Australia between 1962 and 1996."

38 Initially, we were told that the licensing fees for worldwide distribution would be between $50,000 and $140,000.

39 A previous contract with the NFSA had been for use of the material in academic research which would also constitute "Fair Dealing" under the Australian Copyright Act.

40 See http://www.deepeninghistories.anu.edu.au/protocols-for-indigenous-research/ (accessed August 12, 2015). The conditions of this project were radically different from those that led to the existence and histories of our archive.

41 I discuss elsewhere Bobby's concerns about the film earlier in this process.

42 We got this letter of support from Papunya Tula Artists:

> Papunya Tula Ltd is a company that is owned by the Pintupi people of Kintore and Kiwikurra.
>
> We have been working with Professor Fred Myers since 1974 when Ian Dunlop filmed him and our parents and grandparents at Yayayi. We are very happy with the film, "Remembering Yayayi," that Professor Myers and Pip Deveson have made with that old film. They have consulted us at every stage of making the film including showing us the final version.
>
> We want to be able to have copies for the community and for Professor Myers and Pip Deveson to be able to show it to other people. We want people to know about how our parents and grandparents were living.
>
> *(letter from Paul Sweeney, Manager, June 23, 2014)*

43 The National Indigenous Television channel (NITV) was originally funded as a nationwide Indigenous television service by the Australian government in 2005, launched in 2007 and was originally only carried by cable and satellite providers. In 2012 SBS (Special Broadcasting Service, one of Australia's public broadcasting services dedicated to multilingual and multicultural programming) took over the management and operation of NITV and the network was re-launched as a free-to-air channel.

44 Most of the people with whom I spoke offered their opinion that these fees, and the application of them, were a response to severe budgetary cuts made to Screen Australia and the National Archives, including the National Film and Sound Archives.

45 Lacking help from the government, but rather with support from Papunya Tula and the Australian Aboriginal art world, the first dialysis machine and treatment center was acquired with proceeds from an art auction at the Art Gallery of New South Wales that accompanied the retrospective exhibition of Papunya art, "Papunya Tula: Genesis and Genius," curated by Hetti Perkins.

46 These festivals were the Royal Anthropological Institute Film Festival, in Bristol, England, June 2015; the Nordic Anthropological Film Association Festival in Warsaw, Poland, September 2015; and the Jean Rouch International Film Festival, Paris, France, November 2015.

47 Jeff Stead was community adviser at Yayayi in 1974, a position he held as a field officer with the Department of Aboriginal Affairs. Stead, with whom Deveson and I conducted a separate interview in 2011, appears several times in the film footage.

Bibliography

Altman, Jon and Melinda Hinkson, eds. 2007. *Coercive Reconciliation: Stabilise, Normalise, Exit Aboriginal Australia*. Melbourne: Arena Publications.
Anderson, Jane. 2013. Anxieties of Authorship in the Colonial Archive. In Cynthia Chris and David Gerstner, eds. *Media Authorship*. New York: Routledge, pp. 229–246.
Bardon, Geoffrey and James Bardon. 2004. *Papunya: A Place Made After the Story*. Melbourne: Miegunyah Press.
Becker, Howard. 1982. *Artworlds*. Berkeley: University of California Press.
Blaser, Mario. 2004. Life Projects: Indigenous People's Agency and Development. In M. Blaser, H. Feit and G. McRae, eds. *In the Way of Development: Indigenous Peoples, Life Projects and Globalization*. London: Zed Books, pp. 26–44.
Bryson, Ian. 2002. *Bringing to Light: A History of Ethnographic Filmmaking at the Australian Institute of Aboriginal and Torres Strait Islander Studies*. Canberra: Aboriginal Studies Press.
de Heer, Rolf. Public interview about *Charlie's Country*, recorded June 6, 2015. New York City.
Deveson, Philippa and Ian Dunlop. 2012. The Ethnographic Filmmaking of Ian Dunlop in a Decade of Change. *Humanities Research* 18(1): 21.
Dunlop, Ian. 1979. Ethnographic Filmmaking in Australia: The First Seventy Years (1898–1968). *Studies in Visual Communication* 9(1): 11–18.
Folds, Ralph. 2001. *Crossed Purposes: The Pintupi and Australia's Indigenous Policy*. Sydney: UNSW Press.
Hughes, Helen. 2007. *Lands of Shame: Aboriginal and Torres Strait Islander "Homelands" in Transition*. Sydney: Centre for Independent Studies.
Johns, Gary. 2001. *Waking up to Dreamtime*. Singapore: Media Masters.
Johnson, Vivien. 2010. *Once Upon a Time in Papunya*. Sydney: UNSW Press.
James, Diana. 2014. For Shame, Nicolas Rothwell. *Crikey*, March 31. http://blogs.crikey.com.au/northern/2014/03/31/why-nicolas-rothwell-should-be-ashamed/. Accessed March 31, 2014.
Janke, Terri. 2002. *Visual Cultures, Protocols for Producing Indigenous Australian Visual Art and Craft*. Strawberry Hills, NSW: Aboriginal and Torres Strait Islander Arts Board Australia Council.
Keeffe, Kevin. 1992. *From the Centre to the City: Aboriginal Education, Culture and Power*. Canberra: Aboriginal Studies Press.
Lockwood, Douglas. 1964. *The Lizard Eaters*. Melbourne: Cassell Australia.
Long, J. P. M. 1964a. The Pintubi Patrols: Welfare Work with Desert Aborigines. *Australian Territories* 4 (5): 43–48.
Long, J. P. M. 1964b. The Pintubi Patrols: Welfare Work with Desert Aborigines. *Australian Territories*, 4(6): 24–35.
Myers, Fred. 1986. *Pintupi Country, Pintupi Self: Sentiment, Place and Politics among Western Desert Aborigines*. Canberra and Washington, DC: Australian Institute of Aboriginal Studies and Smithsonian Institution Press.
Myers, Fred. 1988. Burning the Truck and Holding the Country: Forms of Property, Time, and the Negotiation of Identity among Pintupi Aborigines. In T. Ingold, D. Riches, and J. Woodburn, eds. *Hunter-Gatherers, II: Property, Power and Ideology*. London: Berg Publishing, pp. 52–74.
Myers, Fred. 2002. *Painting Culture: The Making of an Aboriginal High Art*. Durham, NC: Duke University Press.
Myers, Fred. 2004. Ontologies of the Image and Economies of Exchange. *American Ethnologist* 31(1): 1–16.
Myers, Fred. 2006. We Are Not Alone: Anthropology in a World of Others. Key Informants in the History of Anthropology. *Ethnos* 71(2): 233–264
Myers, Fred. 2011. Translating Indigenous Protocol. In P. Batty and J. Ryan, eds. *Tjukurrtjanu: Origins of Western Desert Art*. Melbourne: National Gallery of Victoria, pp. ix–xi.
Myers, Fred. 2014. Showing Too Much or Too Little: Predicaments of Painting Indigenous Presence in Central Australia. In G. Penny and L. Graham, eds. *Performing Indigeneity*. Lincoln, NE: University of Nebraska Press, pp. 351–389.
Myers, Fred. 2015. Paintings, Publics and Protocols: The Early Paintings from Papunya. *Material Culture Review/Revue de la Culture Materielle* 79: 78–91.
Myers, Fred. 2016. History, Memory and the Politics of Self-Determination in an Early Outstation. In N. Peterson and F. Myers, eds. *Experiments in Self-Determination Histories of the Outstation Movement in Australia*. Canberra: ANU Press.
Peterson, Nicolas and Fred Myers, eds. 2016. *Experiments in Self-Determination Histories of the Outstation Movement in Australia*. Canberra: ANU Press.

Pinney, Christopher and Nicolas Peterson, eds. 2003. *Photography's Other Histories*. Durham, NC: Duke University Press.
Rothwell, Nicolas. 2014. Songlines Project Sparks Indigenous Culture War. *The Weekend Australian*, March 22.
Ryan, Judith and Phillip Batty, eds. 2011. *Tjukurrtjanu: Origins of Western Desert Art*. Melbourne: National Gallery of Victoria.
Scholes, Luke. 2014a. Personal communication. Email, 25 February 2014.
Scholes, Luke. 2014b. Personal communication. Email, 25 February 2014.
Scholes, Luke. 2014c. Personal communication. Email, 2 June 2014.
Stefanoff, Lisa. 2006. Personal communication. Email, 27 June 2006.
Strathern, Marilyn. 1999. *Property, Substance, and Effect: Anthropological Essays on Persons and Things*. London: Athlone Press.
Thomson, Donald. 1962. The Bindibu Expedition: Exploration among the Desert Aborigines of Western Australia: I. The Approach. *Geographical Journal* 128(1): 1–14.
Vance, Rachel. 2015. Letter to Adam Flynn at National Film and Sound Archives. 17 June 2015.
West, Bobby. 2014. Letter to National Film and Sound Archives of Australia. 2 June 2014.

Filmography

Desert People. Dir. Ian Dunlop. Film Australia. Lindfield, NSW. 1967
Balloons and Spinifex. Dir. Ian Dunlop and J. Gray. Australian Commonwealth Film Unit. Linfield, NSW. 1958.
Pintubi Revisit Yumari. Dir. Roger Sandall. Australian Institute of Aboriginal Studies. 1970.
Pintubi Revisit Yaru-Yaru. Dir. Roger Sandall. Australian Institute of Aboriginal Studies. 1972.

10

THE ARCHIVE OF THE ARCHIVE

The secret history of the Laura Boulton Collection

Aaron Fox

Introduction

Professional archivists of ethnographic collections[1] assume ethical responsibility for the management of "records," both in the objectified sense of documents, sound recordings, images, digital files, or artifacts, and in the ideational sense of the contents, meanings, and creative intentions those records may encode. Archivists also manage, in increasingly self-conscious ways, the *rights* of others to access, to study, to publish, to circulate, to remake, to destroy, and to benefit from the objective and ideational contents of the archive, but within structures not merely of our own design and bound to a very troubled history that produced the archives we manage. Certainly when we work in public or public-facing private institutions, we are bound by explicit canons of compliance policy and broad canons of privileged access.[2] And in many aspects of our job, we conceive of ourselves, and our institutions, as bound by the law, or rather, by many different laws and systems of legal understanding and interpretation, which refutes any notion of "the" law's uniformity or rationality.

Controlling access to documents under (direct or indirect) legal authority from the state is inherent in the very idea of the archive as a modern bureaucratic institution. The power of the archive's invocation of a neutral territoriality and a linear temporality lies, as in Derrida's famous formulation (1996), in the possession of documents that "speak the law." But such documents, while found in archives, may not always be found among the documents for which our archives exist to provide controlled access in the interests of preservation, which means they may not be found at all by those wondering "why does this institution own this stuff and get to say who uses it?" These other records are not the primary objects of preservation or access we hold, nor are they typically conceived of as what archivists call "metadata" for those objects, although in this chapter that is exactly how I will propose we view them: as metadata for the archive itself.

Rather than being accessible to users of the archive, such records are frequently to be found in the files of the institution's General Counsel, or in a locked cabinet in the archive Director's office. They are the legal documents, and associated communications, that constitute the archive's sovereignty. "The Archive," as it turns out, has an archive of its own, which in turn has an archive, and so on *ad infinitum*. Archiving documents of cultural history is an inherently recursive project, and such recursivity is the source of the archive's power to define the reality it represents. Archiving is a generative activity; it always produces more documents than it purports to preserve and protect. And some of those documents, are contracts and opinions and memoranda drawn up by (and for) lawyers, administrators, donors, and collectors sometimes in ways that have profound implications for a critique of the ethnographic archive as a neutral institution, or even a legitimate one.

In recent years, archivists working in academic and museum-based settings and especially those charged with managing collections of materials identified as products of Indigenous communities have been compelled to pay increasingly critical attention to the management of the explicit and potential rights (of access, interpretation, and profit) inherent in the documents or objects in our collections, and not (just) to the media or objects or ideas they contain. This has put us in the position of *restricting* access more vigorously than our predecessors did, at the same time as we have sought to open up access or "repatriation" to "stakeholders" (a revealing current term of art in the trade) who have previously had little access to these collections, both through our own direct outreach and via online catalogs and databases that can open the archive to searches by anyone on earth.

But archivists of Indigenous cultural heritage and property are in a position somewhat at odds with the politics of "open access" championed by a broader community of information science and archiving in public-facing and publicly funded private and non-profit institutions. Many archivists and librarians working in university or museum settings, especially, have lately embraced an ideological commitment to providing "open access" to formerly restricted collections, concerned about the hastening commercial privatization of the commons and compelled by the power of knowledge to reach the entire globe in digital form at a low cost.

Among open access advocates, a rights regime dominated by profit-making interests is seen as *the* primary hegemonic power. In resisting this the archive serves the public good by removing economic and other barriers to the open and non-discriminatory circulation of knowledge produced, especially, through public investment. The handling of fragile physical materials has become a trivial burden in an era of high-resolution digital copies and technologies of mediation that allow for immediate global circulation of something that might have taken an intercontinental journey to view or hear only 30 years ago. The utopian vision of everyone having access to everything – the opening of the archive – has a powerful force among professionals in archive management, and I am not immune to its charms.

But the more utopian visions of open access also entail a throwing up of hands at historical facts and political realities that will not be so easily converted to archival objects of contemplation, and not just from those who profit economically from keeping the price of knowledge high. Those of us who are gatekeepers to ethnographic archives containing documents of formerly colonized people, and of Indigenous or Aboriginal people and communities in particular, have lately been driven by the opposite ambition. We wonder if we might somehow reduce access, further restrict unfettered circulation of things that have been allowed to leak out of archives for decades, limit or control digital circulation, and enforce archive policies and interpret questions of legality not only as representatives of science or our employing institutions – as keepers of an asset for research – but as advocates for the cultural rights and sensibilities and feelings of Indigenous people. In this position we have become agents for these interests in the archive within our institutional and disciplinary settings. We also caution our institutions in their refined concern with legality over decades of archive building. These institutions have in fact put themselves in a position of something that shades over into *illegality*, registering and protecting claims of institutional "ownership" that cannot withstand a rational process of legal "discovery," and that remain vulnerable to future litigation as a result.

Many archivists of ethnographic collections of Indigenous provenance have meanwhile embraced a critical practice centered on the "repatriation" of documents and objects from the collections we manage to the communities from which they were extracted. Although the word is fraught with ambiguity, it presents a prospect enhanced by the rise of digital technology that has severely eroded what were once major technical barriers to more widespread access to sound archives. The global digital public sphere, for all its proven capacity to abet the informal, indiscriminate, and "illegal" circulation of documents such as recordings, also provides far greater potential for the serendipitous discovery of archival collections of interest by descendants of people whose voices and images are represented in ethnographic archives, and a low-cost and high-utility medium for not only delivering repatriated documents to their stakeholders or subjecting them to communal interpretation, but retaining them as archival resources for "research" and community-based institutional and scholarly collaboration as well.

This approach to the archive as a social justice project, evinced by a growing number of repatriation projects and an increase in grant support for them[3], is especially seductive for the media archivist dealing with sounds, images, films or videos, or textual documents as primary archival objects. For when conceived of as "merely" a document that can be reproduced and distributed easily, the sonic (or filmic or photographic or textual) archival object is considered (typically) as format-independent and replicable, presenting no significant or apparent barriers (in practical terms of economic cost and technical expertise) to archive–community reciprocity mediated via digital reproduction. This approach however, centered on repatriation as a form of compensation for appropriation and very belated reciprocity to Indigenous people for helping us build our disciplines by sharing their culture with our predecessors, perpetuates and naturalizes a *structural legitimation* of the alienation of rights inherent in the manner in which our archives were assembled and aggregated over the course of the twentieth century in the first place.

And here it is worthwhile to pause over the ease with which disciplines that have been involved in producing these archives have rationalized their practices as disinterested science about – *or* interested advocacy for – Indigenous people, in particular. The ethnographic archive of Indigenous cultural expressions has a particular and fraught centrality in the history of anthropological (and ethnomusicological and museological) disciplines, which can frankly be said to *directly* owe their existence to the genocide of Indigenous people by European colonists and their successor settler-colonial nation-states. A North American ethnographic archivist working in an institutional context today cannot escape being the lineal professional descendant of predecessors whose work was funded and publicly engaged with primarily for the purposes of rationally administering the containment and assimilation of militarily defeated Native populations. The archive can thus be seen as a site of intelligence gathering and surveillance casting traditional cultures and contemporary Indigenous people as "vanishing" remnants of a distant collective past suitable for salvage, appropriation, and nostalgia, amounting to a denial of the living continuity and modernity of the peoples thus represented, and glossing over historical accountability for complicity in the marginalization of Indigenous communities. (Anderson 2005; Deloria 2004; Kreps 2013; Morse 2012)

From the perspective of the formerly colonized community or the modern Indigenous subject, ethnographic archives are all too easy to see as *war memorials* built by the victors, as well as treasure troves of meaningful patrimony. When vast historical territories become a few inches on a shelf, when the tapes on those shelves are in a language that no one can translate, when someone has commercially released that recording for money, or sold it as a "collection" to a university, the archive is a metonym for a larger loss, and not just a site of preservation and recovery. From engaging many times in recent years with the descendants of people whose voices fill the tapes that line the shelves of my own office space, I know that such encounters are routinely and simultaneously ecstatic and traumatic. The tears that often flow on a listener's first encounter with an ancestor's distant, barely audible voice are never simply tears of joy.

Archivists base their professional ethics on the assertion that they serve the interests of other people, a diverse public. Of course the identity of this public can be, and has been, understood in diverse ways, related fundamentally to a shifting and complex calculus of legitimacy (are you a "credentialed scholar?"), authenticity ("do you represent the tribal government?"), and power ("might you wish to fund our operations or my research?"). Imagining this public and their interests is a primary focus for the archivist. Doing so in the present entails critically thinking about the relationships between the explicit institutional archival mission to preserve a record of the past, and the deep historical *complicity* of that mission in legitimating the elimination or marginalization of certain people from that past, their descendants' exclusion from participation in determining the meaning of the past in the present, and their communities' rights to reclaim or re-interpret the treasures we claim to be holding safely for the future.

My arguments in this chapter also demand that I say explicitly that many of us make good livings managing ethnographic archives, and that my talk of complicity is not just addressed to a general "archivist" subject. I thus include *myself* when invoking the terms "archivist" and "anthropologist." Acknowledging our personal complicity in the structures I criticize here is necessary, even (especially) if we approach such work with an intention to decolonize our professions, to recognize emergent historical claims to the archive, or to right what we have come to see as the ethical and technical failures (and in some cases, even the crimes) of our predecessors.

For the remainder of this chapter, I will turn to a more concrete and narrow exercise: an analysis of a series of documents in which the "ownership" of a collection of field recordings I now manage, made by a single collector over a 30-year period in the mid-twentieth century, was asserted, defined, specified, claimed, transferred, sold, resold, divided up, and dispersed: the archive of the archive. The broader history of these documents and their assertions is vastly beyond my scope here, although I will try to address it prospectively.

My focus will be on a series of transactions and representations that came well after the sounds of Indigenous performers that are now "owned" by Columbia University were first inscribed on acetate or aluminum discs or ferrous-oxide coated reel-to-reel tapes, or more recently on CDs and hard drives and cloud-storage backup servers. This is one piece – albeit an important one for thinking past the metanarratives I described above – of a holistic critical historical analysis that must invoke the multiple temporalities and geographies that intersect in the ethnographic archive. A complex unfolding of related events, practices, and agencies produced (and continue to produce) the modern ethnomusicological sound archive.[4]

I am concerned primarily with the phase of the cycle during which a single collector's work, much of it conducted in "drive by" fashion, among people of whom she had little real knowledge, wound up dignified with a high-priced sale and became an institutional research collection at one of the world's leading universities. Specifically, I am interested in *contracts* that defined the boundaries of the object being "purchased," and the arguments produced that continued to reshape those boundaries in the mountains of memoranda, minutes, and personal correspondence that produced those contracts.

My aim is to show here how Laura Boulton's recordings were *constituted as a collection, and thence as "non-profit" intellectual property* through a messy process from which many people and institutions have benefited. Moreover many other agendas and goals and desires that shaped this conversion of Boulton's recordings to "The Laura Boulton Collection of Traditional and Liturgical Music, in the Center for Ethnomusicology, within the Department of Music, at Columbia University in the City of New York" were left unstated, justified rhetorically by an appeal to the ethnographic archive as having self-evident scholarly and publicity value, and to the intentions of a "non-profit" enterprise as an Ivy League university as above suspicion. Virtually no person or institution involved in the construction of the "Laura Boulton Collection," over a period of many decades, at Columbia and other institutions alike, and not excepting Boulton herself, ever approached the constitution of the "Laura Boulton Collection" without a personal agenda unrelated to the contents of the archive, and in most cases unrelated to the value of the archive for the stated purpose of its creation, disinterested scientific research and teaching.

The archive of the archive: Documenting the documentarians

Since 2003, I have been the institutional gatekeeper[5] of the Laura Boulton Collection of Traditional and Liturgical Music (hereafter LBCTLM, or just "The Boulton Collection," as it is widely but confusingly known, given the existence of different, if overlapping, "Boulton collections" at two other institutions). The Boulton Collection is an archive of several thousand hours of recordings housed in Columbia University's Center for Ethnomusicology, in the form of reel-to-reel tape copies of original master discs now at the Library of Congress (on "permanent loan" from Columbia), and in the form of hard drives full of digital data on my office desk, and existing in a nearly (but not perfectly) duplicate set of tapes at Indiana University's Archives of Traditional Music, to which Boulton left her estate, including her personal tape copy of her collection.

Boulton, born Laura Craytor in 1899 in Ohio, and educated to the BA in Music at Denison College, had parlayed an amateur interest in recording what she thought of as "primitive" and "ancient" music into a wide-ranging career as a public intellectual, author, filmmaker, and lecturer – or as she later memorably described herself, a "Music Hunter" (Boulton 1969). She traveled widely and recorded, filmed, and photographed in dozens of Indigenous communities. She wrote and spoke with commanding assurance about a wide range of cultures she had encountered, but possessed very little anthropological expertise.

She was a fine performer, however, with a theatrical bearing in person and in prose, and something of a mid-century self-made American type. She had a strong ability to project herself heroically into dramatic stories of life among the "primitives," to draw recognizably stereotyped (if often affectionately patronizing) caricatures of Indigenous people with her descriptions, and to deploy other tropes and conventions of mid-century American travel writing, film, and photography, then still a male-dominated enterprise in which she stood out as a woman.

Boulton was many things, a public intellectual, a travel writer and filmmaker, and performer, but she was not an academic. Her correspondence[6] reveals that she was generally resentful of the economic and prestige-earning success of her academic counterparts in the music-collecting business, but barely interested in their more theoretical questions about why different cultures had different musics and what musical styles might reveal about those cultures' values and histories that other idioms of expression might not. Her haphazard methods, her limited theoretical understandings of cultural difference and change, her constant need to scrabble for funding or lecturing gigs by flattering rather than challenging the prejudices of her sponsors and audiences, her willingness to speculate and confabulate to emphasize her own importance and her bravery in obtaining her recordings, all prevented her from engaging in more than facile ways with the developing field of academic ethnomusicology. This is despite having extensive contact with its pioneering practitioners from the early 1930s and onward.[7] Her commitments were to breadth over depth, to comparison over ethnography, to rigid distinctions between traditional and modern cultural practices, and for the explanation of human cultural difference and "primitive" cultures in broadly evolutionary and natural historical terms.

To the extent that her work had a scholarly basis, it was the late nineteenth-century *Vergleichende Musikwissenschaft* of Erich M. Von Hornbostel and Carl Stumpf, centered as that paradigm was on developing and analyzing the ethnographic archive in service of comparative, evolutionist, and naturalistic psychological explanations for cultural difference (Christensen 1991; Reed 1993). Comparative musicology proposed to examine the relationship between cultural difference and differences in formal elements of musical style, in search of a non-linguistic approach to the question of the universality (or non-universality) of the human mind. Psychological dispositions specific to (racialized) cultural groups were thought to be uniquely discoverable through the decontextualized technical and transcription-based analysis of variations in musical style. These views were already anachronistic, at the level of scholarly theories of cultural and musical difference, by the time Boulton began her recording career in the 1930s.

But despite corresponding with many figures in academic anthropology, folklore, and ethnomusicology, Boulton had little knowledge of the scholarship they were producing, or the way the function of sound archives was changing as ethnomusicology became institutionalized within American university music departments during the 1950s and 60s. And indeed, the comparativist and evolutionist framework invoked in Boulton's rhetoric was sustained in the academic setting of the 1960s, when her engagement with Columbia occurred. The academic institutionalization of ethnomusicology within music departments (rather than anthropology departments) ensured its continuing relevance to the discipline's legitimacy in the Eurocentric and score-fetishizing American musical academy.

Beginning in the early 1950s, Boulton had begun to seek out academic employment to work on her collection. From her correspondence it is clear that she had also begun to think of the products of her collecting work as an economic asset under her ownership as intellectual property even earlier. Her communication with several attorneys in the 1940s begun as she proceeded to produce commercial recordings and sign royalty agreements with Folkways Records (and other publishers) throughout the 1950s. The important point here is that the conception of these recordings as an intellectual property asset was in Boulton's mind *during* the period of her most prolific recording efforts.

By the early 1960s, entering her sixth decade, Boulton had become less able to travel the world with her gear and retinue, and was palpably tired of the constant hustle to raise funds and find supporters. Having accumulated a hoard of recordings, photographs, films, books, musical instruments, and notes from her travels, and having tasted the success of monetizing recordings for Folkways Records, while also keenly observing the remarkable emergence of ethnomusicology as a discipline in the booming Cold War US academy, Boulton looked for a "patron" whose support could bring this material together and secure her legacy, fame – and retirement.

PhD programs in ethnomusicology were created at UCLA, Wesleyan University, and Indiana University (with many others following quickly) in the early and mid-1960s, each centered on a comparative sound archive as a primary program asset and a necessity for the training of ethnomusicologists for research. Despite the cultural relativist trajectory of the fledgling subdiscipline, it asserted continuity with the comparative paradigm of Von

Hornbostel, especially at the level of methods, emphasizing the importance, for training graduate students at least, of transcribing diverse styles of music from archival recordings as a primary research technique. The persistent emphasis on comparison, music transcription and analysis, and scientific archive building, remained as a European influence on the American discipline well into the last years of the last century, reflecting an intertwined and sometimes fraught relationship between "anthropological" and "musicological" emphases within the field that persists to this day.[8]

Much of this dynamic, in which the colonial ethnomusicological research archive was centrally figured and constructed as an essential asset for a forward-looking program of music research, is owed to the pioneering discipline-building influence of Hungarian ethnomusicologist and anthropologist George Herzog (1901–1983). Herzog, a student of both Von Hornbostel and Boas, pursued a career-long goal of replicating the Berliner Phonogramm-Archiv in the United States (Christensen 1991), beginning at Columbia and Yale during the 1930s and 40s, and later fully realized with his efforts to found the Archives of Traditional Music at Indiana University (hereafter, IUATM) beginning in the late 1940s. The IUATM would in fact go on to become the pre-eminent ethnomusicological archive in North America, and a vitally important institution for the discipline.[9]

By the early 1960s, Boulton (who had recorded under Herzog's supervision in 1933) was shopping her "collection," which she often represented as including instruments, photos, films, and books as well as recordings, with her services as curator hopefully attached, to various universities and wealthy friends in search of a sinecure. She had also begun a romantic involvement with the wealthy and recently widowed New York architect and painter Julian Clarence Levi (1874–1971), then the oldest living alumnus of Columbia University's undergraduate College.

It was due to Levi's significant financial influence on Columbia – and in turn to Boulton's significant emotional influence on Levi – that "The Boulton Collection" became for the first time recognized as a single entity, a unitary bundle of diverse yet somehow comparable objects, with uniform underlying property rights belonging to the recordist, that could thus be purchased from the recordist as a "collection," which is to say as *her intellectual property*.

The courtship of Laura Boulton

The LBCTLM was formally constituted as a research archive belonging to Columbia University in a purchase agreement with the collector first executed by all parties in June 1962, with a date of sale set in 1964 (first January, later extended to March). Boulton and her collection were initially to be under the aegis of the Columbia Libraries, and remained so until late 1964. The Center for Ethnomusicological Studies (later Center for Studies in Ethnomusicology, then Center for Ethnomusicology), with Boulton as its inaugural curator, was subsequently constituted as the institutional home of the collection within the Department of Music in February 1965 by a (second) vote of the senior faculty of the Department.

The story of Columbia's pursuit of the collection – or rather of Levi's money by means of the collection – unfolds over several years, beginning with a 1962 agreement that the University would acquire Boulton's collection including:

> "notes concerning it and all [her] right, title, and interest [and] a transcription of [her] notes describing each recording in the collection to the satisfaction of Columbia University" for the price of "$5,000 of February 15 and August 15 of each year during [her] lifetime"
>
> *(Letter from Stanley Salmen to Laura Boulton, June 14, 1962 [IUATM, CE 029a-b])*

The sale was announced in advance of the signing of the agreement in the *New York Times*, on May 23, 1963, referring to the $150,000 purchase price, in the name of the late Alice Fries Levi, as a "gift to the Music Department" of a collection containing "over 15,000 selections." The final sale agreement, executed in June, also provided Boulton with an unsalaried appointment. Instead, she was separately compensated from the purchase of her collection with Levi's money, invested in an annuity for her and with the title "Curator" of what was then being called "The Laura Boulton Collection of Traditional and Exotic Music." The initial date of transfer of ownership was set as January 1, 1964, at which point the University Libraries expected Boulton to complete work cataloging the "collection" thus enumerated and then to assimilate the collection into the library system's holdings.

During the intervening 18 months, Boulton was to be compensated with $1,000 a month (around $8,000 in 2015 dollars)[10] for her "consulting services" and a "lease" of the collection by the University. The eventual transfer was then postponed, to March of 1964, in a revised letter of agreement which specifically states that Boulton would "transfer title" to the recordings at that time. This revision was necessary after Boulton failed to meet the January deadline which also meant she was paid for 21 months of consulting. The letter, from Salmen, stated that the University "understand[s] from you that you are the owner of the collection of recorded music described by you as the Laura Boulton Collection of Traditional and Exotic [*sic*] Music. This letter will express the agreement of the Trustees of the . . . University . . . [to] purchase your collection, and your agreement to sell your collection together with any notes concerning it and all your right, title, and interest thereto," before going on to reiterate the same financial terms as the earlier agreement (Letter from Salmen to Boulton, Jan. 17, 1964 [IUATM, CE059a-b]).

In the intervening two years, during which the collection was "leased" from Boulton by Columbia, Boulton was initially placed under the supervision of the Columbia University Libraries. She chafed at oversight from professional librarians, who showed little respect for her amateurism either. Boulton's ambition was to establish a Center to house the collection and form a base for her own work. Evidently she also saw this as a way to maintain control over the collection after it ceased being her legal property. Her initial location in the Libraries (not the Music Department) quickly and predictably generated conflict that threatened the entire enterprise she envisioned.

By as early as late 1963, Boulton and Levi put pressure on the University administration to move her appointment fully into the Department of Music. Here she had a nominal ally in Prof. William Rhodes, who was interested in building a graduate program in ethnomusicology and was shrewd enough to see an angle in the courting of Levi on behalf of the administration. This was a view he shared with Prof. Jack Beeson, who was Acting Chair of the Music Department in 1963–1964.[11] The Music Department's senior faculty however initially resisted absorbing the Boulton enterprise, largely out of concern over Boulton's amateurism and Levi's heavy-handed influence. But in early 1965, Levi proposed to the administration and the Department that they revisit the question of a separate Center within the Music Department. In a new twist, Levi would offer full financial support with a second major gift, while the proposed Center could develop plans to seek external foundation funding and pursue new acquisitions for its archives.

On February 16, 1965, Prof. William Mitchell persuaded his senior colleagues to vote in support of the Center, after Levi committed a significant additional amount of funding to the enterprise, now to be called "The Center for Ethnomusicological Studies" with a planned affiliated graduate program. This was the Department's main local interest in the acquisition which was to be governed very strictly by a committee of faculty. Rhodes and Mitchell persuaded their colleagues that the situation could be controlled and bring many new assets into the Department, both directly from Levi and indirectly from the administration.

In summary, and as I have described elsewhere in further detail (Fox 2014), this sequence of events – the purchase of a "research collection" from Boulton, and the subsequent negotiations that led to the establishment of a special Center in the Department of Music (the oldest and among the most distinguished such departments in the US) – was a pretext understood by all parties as focused on satisfying a wealthy alumnus. Administrators and faculty members, despite their misgivings about the scholarly value of the project, allowed this alumnus to purchase the Laura Boulton Collection on behalf of the University, with the proceeds from the sale going to Ms. Boulton. Levi's money – what he spent up front on the collection and in subsequent years greasing the skids at Columbia to install Boulton as Curator of a new Center (around $250,000 between 1962 and 1970),[12] and the much larger sum he eventually left the University when he died in 1971 ($4.8 million)[13] – created the motivation and the institutional political context in which Boulton's collection could become an "archive." From the outset of these discussions it was imagined as an "asset" and an investment with very little regard to its contents.

The strategy for the University was in having the archive as an archive. It was not very interested in what it contained as such an archive was increasingly irrelevant to the enterprise of ethnomusicology as it had taken shape by the late 1960s which centered around ethnographic field research rather than archival analysis. But the archive's acquisition would nonetheless establish Columbia's foothold in the emerging discipline.

The University's administration was seeking to profit to the tune of millions of dollars from flattering Mr. Levi, and looking for a partner in doing so. The Music Department was willing to go along for a cut of the eventual action that would fund the creation of a new PhD program in ethnomusicology for which the Center and the Boulton Collection were projected as key assets. Clarence Levi was primarily interested in helping Boulton achieve the recognition she sought. As Boulton wrote in a grandiose 1963 essay entitled "I Search for Ancient Music," and published in *Columns*, the journal of the Friends of Columbia's Libraries, as an accompaniment to an announcement of Columbia's initial acquisition of the Laura Boulton Collection:

> When I began, there was no word for the specialization which I chose, but now if you look in a new dictionary, you may find the term "Ethnomusicologist." My interest has been, and still is, centered in people and their music; not just to analyse the music, but to see how it functions in their lives, the role it plays in work, in worship, and in every emotional aspect of society, primitive and exotic. My collection, said to be one of the largest private ones of its kind, has become invaluable to students in all parts of the world, because there is so much music and documented information in it which can never be recorded again.
>
> *(Boulton 1963:13)*

Laura Boulton craved legitimation commensurate with her self-aggrandizing view of her work. Nearly everyone involved in the history of Boulton's relationship with Columbia, with the exception of Boulton and Levi themselves, saw Ms. Boulton as an amateur collector at best, and a theatrical fraud at worst, peddling what Columbia faculty member and ethnomusicologist Nicholas England (a prominent scholar of West African music) called a "travelogue through exotica" in a disparaging private memo to his colleagues on the senior faculty prior to their February 1965 meeting to vote on whether to accept Boulton and her new Center in exchange for Levi's money.[14]

England (and pioneering sociomusicologist Paul Henry Lang) were the lone dissenting voices on the faculty. England's senior colleagues supported the administration out of their own interest in gaining the resources needed for a graduate program in his discipline. For this they all agreed to a fiction: that this collector's "travelogue" was a systematic academic "archive" produced by an expert on musics which could be transformed into an asset worthy of Columbia University and sufficient to make Columbia competitive in the emergent sub-discipline of ethnomusicology. Of course, this involved projecting, successfully as it turned out, what would happen once Levi died and his major bequest came in. The Oct. 14 1971 edition of the *New York Times* called it "one of the largest gifts in the University's history."

It is perhaps unsurprising, but nonetheless worthy of note, that in the voluminous meta-archive of letters, memoranda, proposals, draft contracts, fundraising plans and appeals, and meeting minutes related to this phase of Columbia's acquisition and consolidation of the Laura Boulton Collection as a scholarly research archive, there is *not one single mention* of the people whose voices are recorded in the Collection, or their descendants, as either stake-holders or beneficiaries of the Collection. They remain an utterly voiceless abstraction to all of the parties engaged in this process, including Boulton herself. Indeed, they were irrelevant to the whole enterprise.

After 1965: Determining the meaning of ownership

For lack of space, I can only briefly rehearse the next phase of the consolidation of the Laura Boulton Collection as intellectual property, and its dispersal. Boulton installed herself in the new Center in the Music Department beginning in 1965, titled as the Curator, then Director, then Curator Emeritus (after she reached the mandatory retirement age in 1970) of the Center. She toiled for several years annotating the collection, publicizing the Center, lobbying for budgetary resources, and devoting most of her energies to writing an autobiography based on her extensive review of her field notes and material titled *The Music Hunter* (1969). But Boulton had a personality that agitated others which produced frequent conflicts with faculty members, and led eventually to the University bringing in (at England's suggestion) a consultant to inventory the Collection, assess whether its contents matched Boulton's representations of it during the sale, and examine her archival practice. The person brought in to do this was Prof. Dieter Christensen, a trained archivist who had worked under Von Hornbostel's student Marius Schneider at the Berliner Phonogramm-Archiv.

Christensen applied his professional perspective to the situation and asserted that Boulton was alienating (or withholding) significant parts of the collection she had represented as included in the sale. She had structured the sale in increments for tax purposes which allowed her to postpone the transfer of her instruments, photographs, and books. The report also suggested that Boulton's skills as a recordist, archivist, and amateur ethnomusicologist were inadequate to the job she occupied. It also acknowledged that Columbia had no facilities for proper preservation of the original acetate and aluminum discs, let alone for adding new acquisitions to the archives. The report questioned Boulton's frequent public representations of the Collection as a world-class archive by comparing the Collection unfavorably with competing institutions' holdings and challenging many of the objective representations Boulton had made about the Collection's contents. In a cover letter to the report, addressed to Beeson, Christensen scathingly concluded that "any change in the structure and function of the Collection can be implemented only in the absence of Dr. Boulton . . . because any qualified ethnomusicologist would find it hard to attempt this task in her presence" (Center for Ethnomusicology Administrative Files, Document 027a-c, submitted January 22, 1971).

Christensen's 1971 report, held in the private files of the Center for Ethnomusicology, which limits its accessibility, recommended the University hire an academically trained, professorial rank archivist if it had any hopes of converting this asset into the basis for a solid graduate program in ethnomusicology. Unsurprisingly, and again illustrative of the competing agendas of all parties in the making of this archive, Christensen himself presented the ideal candidate. The report and the denigration of Boulton served very particular interests and it is hard to know if Boulton was quite as incompetent as she was made out to be by these men of privilege intent on deposing her. In 1972 within a year of the report and following the 1971 death of Clarence Levi and his nearly $5 million bequest to the University, Christensen was hired with tenure and Boulton was forced to depart. She left for retirement in Arizona, where she nursed, perhaps understandably, a grudge against Columbia University that would be posthumously expressed in the disbursal of her estate.

In the intervening thirty years, Christensen led the development of a PhD program in ethnomusicology and devoted considerable efforts to organizing, growing, and modernizing the Boulton Collection, pursuing new acquisitions and a systematic cataloging strategy and then a systematic digitization strategy in the late 1990s and early 2000s. But most importantly, he convinced the University that the value of the Boulton Collection lay not in the physical recordings, but in their content as the University's intellectual property. This followed directly the same logic that Boulton had leveraged – that the recordings constituted her intellectual property, which was alienable, an asset that could be sold. This inspired two further inflections in the status of Boulton's recordings.

In correspondence between March and May of 1973, with Associate Provost Robert Brookhart, Christensen discussed a plan to transfer the original master discs in the Boulton Collection to the Library of Congress. This transfer had been initiated prior to her leaving by Boulton as the Curator of the collection, although she lacked official authorization. Although he was brought in following a damaging report that raised questions about Boulton's legitimacy as a curator, surprisingly Christensen fully concurred with the planned transfer. He wrote to Brookhart explaining that "the value [of the Collection] resides in the recorded information, not in the physical carrier of the information," and emphasizing that while the materials would be on "permanent loan" to the Library of Congress, "the University retains all rights etc. in the recordings." He further added that "the material value of the discs is negligible once the information has been duplicated" (Christensen to Assoc. Provost Brookhart, May 8, 1973, held in the Center for Ethnomusicology's private files).

The Library of Congress's Archive of Folk Song, under Director Alan Jabbour, had different ideas. They resisted Columbia's terms of ownership, understanding that this constituted a restriction on the users of the materials at the Library. When Christensen advised Brookhart, in March of 1973, to insist on the University's maintenance of intellectual property rights following the proposed transfer, Boulton responded to Brookhart's inquiry about maintaining the University's ownership rights by saying she did not recognize the authority of the Music Department over the management of her collection. Indeed, it is possible to detect a subtext in the documents of this period that the Department, Christensen, and the administration were actively colluding to make Boulton's continued involvement with Columbia, even as Director Emeritus, intolerable.

Jabbour eventually accepted the deposit under the stipulation, as written by Christensen, that the recordings would remain "the property of the Trustees of CU under the supervision of the Curator of the Laura Boulton Collection in the Department of Music," and that the

Library of Congress would make high-quality tape duplicates of the collection, including one for the collector and two for the University (Draft Agreement between CU and LoC, May 1, 1973 [Center for Ethnomusicology Private Files, 035a-e]).

In June of 1973, final agreement between Boulton, Columbia University and the Library of Congress was reached. Boulton agreed to cease her involvement with Columbia's management of her recordings, and took much of her original collection with her, but not taking the copyright in it. In a letter of agreement she signed with Brookhart, she agreed to end her relationship with Columbia, and to the following stipulation concerning the ownership of her Collection:

> The Collector recognizes that the University owns all right, title and interest, including the copyright, in the Laura Boulton Collection of Traditional and Liturgical Music, consisting of original recordings (tapes, discs, wax cylinders) purchased by the University by agreements dated June 14 1962 and Jan. 27, 1964.
>
> *(Brookhart to Boulton, June 6, 1973; [IUATM; CE 036])*

This agreement sharply reduced the original 1962 terms of sale to include only Boulton's actual field recordings excluding the roughly 200 tracks she had already published commercially on 11 albums released through Folkways Records in the 1950s, and no other parts of her archival collection. It also granted Boulton exclusive rights to use the recordings for her own activities, including publication, with due credit given to Columbia, and provided "no action is taken that shall diminish the university's rights, including the copyright." In a very controlling stipulation the University stated that it required the Library of Congress to inform Columbia even if "a person wishes to publish *on* material in the Boulton Collection" and agreed that it will refer such persons to Boulton for consultation as well. The agreement specifically stipulated that it terminated "with the death of the collector" and that "no rights under this agreement shall accrue to [the collector's] heirs, executors, administrators, assigns, or successors."

This document would seem, bearing Boulton's signature as it does, to end the matter of ownership. But in fact, it did not do so. Boulton created a personal foundation to hold her assets in her last years, to be administered after her death by her long-time assistant, Shirley Porter. However, at the time, in 1973, this seemed to close the matter from Columbia's point of view. Christensen took over as Director of the Center, the master recordings went to Washington, DC, where they were duplicated on to several sets of 7.5ips ¼" reel-to-reel tapes, two of which went to Columbia University, and one to Laura Boulton herself under the terms of the agreement of June 8, 1973, which stipulated: "It is agreed that Columbia University shall retain all rights to the [Boulton] Collection, including exclusive rights to publication of verbatim transcription of speech and music contained therein" (Draft Agreement, June 1, 1973 [IUATM; CE 035d]).

I pause to note that this is a remarkable assertion of rights for a purportedly scholarly archive, prohibiting not only the duplication of recordings without permission, but even proscribing the transcription and analysis of their contents. The University literally retained the right to prevent *quotation* from the recordings, which is an assertion of ownership of the underlying intellectual property on the recording, and quite a different matter from prohibiting the publication and sale of copies of the recording as such. As indefensible as it might be, Columbia's 1973 contractual understanding with a branch of the United States Government was that the University in fact owned the *underlying compositions* encoded on easily duplicated recordings, by virtue of having bought the recordings from their recordist.

After Boulton: The Indiana Agreement and the end of ownership

To bring my story forward nearly to the present, briefly, when Boulton died in Arizona in October 1980, she was in possession of a complete tape copy of the recordings "owned" by Columbia, supplied to her by the Library of Congress under the terms of its 1973 agreement with Columbia. She also retained many musical instruments, thousands of books and hundreds of photographs, and many thousands of items of correspondence and documentation of her work and life – she was an obsessive collector, not only of music, but of every record and document of her own doings. Her assets, including money from the sale of her recordings to Columbia, were left in trust to the Laura Boulton Foundation. Shirley Porter diligently carried out Boulton's intention to deliver all of her materials to the Indiana University Archives of Traditional Music then under the direction of the most eminent pioneer in ethical management of ethnomusicological archives, Anthony Seeger. To this day, IUATM receives royalty payments from the sale of her Folkways (now Smithsonian Folkways) Records albums, a modest amount that is of little consequence to a major research university, but that nonetheless has never found its way to the descendants or communities of the people she recorded.

Nevertheless, because Columbia asserted its ongoing ownership over the portion of the Boulton Collection which Columbia had duly purchased in 1962–1964, and to which it had retained rights in the permanent loan to the Library of Congress in 1973, and because Boulton's personal collection included her copy of the same recordings, Indiana University and Columbia University have had to come to an agreement about future use of and access to those recordings at IUATM. According to Columbia and its legal counsel the majority constitute Columbia's intellectual property which they became the day Columbia purchased them as a "collection" in 1962. These negotiations have produced their own documentary trail, which again reflects individual (Seeger's and Christensen's) and generationally distinct views of the nature of traditional music as intellectual property (Christensen 2002; Seeger 2001). The negotiations resulted eventually in a key document that remains the template for relations between the institutions that now hold Boulton's recordings. In an "Instrument of Gift" executed on January 22, 1990, between the Boulton Foundation, the Trustees of Indiana University, and the Library of Congress, Boulton's "Tape Collection," bequeathed with her Foundation's assets to Indiana University, is described as a separate entity from the "Laura Boulton Collection" at Columbia and the Library of Congress, even though there is extremely substantial overlap between the two sets. It sets elaborate but generous rules concerning access, use, and commercial licensing for the Tape Collection at Indiana University (a public institution with a mandate to serve all citizens of its state equally, which applies to library access of all sorts). The Instrument of Gift specifically "transfers title to the intellectual and intangible property . . . and to the physical possession of the originals" of the collection from the Foundation (which arguably holds no such title, Boulton having sold it to Columbia in 1962, for many of the recordings). The agreement goes on to transfer all of Boulton's remaining master recordings (which however do not overlap the Columbia set) to the Library of Congress, which in turn disclaims specifically in its portion of the agreement that its acceptance of the gift of the physical tapes "shall be construed as a conclusive determination by the Library that the University and/or the Foundation do in fact possess such literary property . . . in these materials." While this may have been boilerplate language, it is remarkable for being the *very first instance* where a lawyer involved in a transaction around this collection expressed any doubt whatsoever about the legitimacy of the collector's initial claim to the intellectual property rights they contained. And still, at this point, no party had yet raised any concern with the interests of the participants in these recordings and their descendants (although Seeger would shortly go on to become a champion of such interests as the Director of Smithsonian Folkways Records).

Christensen, on behalf of Columbia University, initially objected strenuously to this agreement as Shirley Porter began to work it out with IUATM in the late 1980s. In a series of letters with Seeger, also held in the private files of the Center for Ethnomusicology, Christensen asserts Columbia's ongoing claim to original intellectual property rights, and Columbia's ability to impose terms on the *publication* of these materials, if not on the access policies of its fellow archiving institutions. In subsequent years, archivists at all three institutions would come to accept an informal arrangement whereby IUATM or the Library of Congress would contact Christensen to authorize what were the very few scholarly uses of the Boulton materials that led to any sort of publication.

The agreement was tested in 1994, when Smithsonian Folkways (then headed by Seeger) sought Columbia's permission to include Navajo songs Boulton had recorded in 1933 and 1940, in Chicago and in New Mexico and Arizona, on a lavishly produced CD. Christensen agreed to license the songs at no charge, noting that the recording was being curated by the two leading ethnomusicological specialists on Navajo music and had certain educational value, with Columbia given due credit in the CD's insert booklet. It has since been invoked several more times for small projects using the archive. But it remains mostly a vaguely recalled structure, and until my own repatriation work with the Boulton archive began, very little scholarly interest was attracted to the Boulton materials during the 1980s or 1990s.

Conclusion

A few years later, it was that CD of Navajo songs which ended up triggering the recognition of the voice of Pablo Wellito, a celebrated Navajo healer, by his granddaughter and great-granddaughters in 2002. The liner notes in the CD led one of those great-granddaughters to the door of my office, as the newly installed Director of the Center for Ethnomusicology. That experience, in my first months in charge of the Laura Boulton Collection, initially set me on the agenda of repatriating the collection, which is the next phase of the tale I have been relating here.

Initially inspired by the idea that Columbia's ownership of the recordings as intellectual property meant that Columbia could also in fact *return* rights, or devolve its ownership to communities of origin, I soon learned that the law provides weak possibilities for challenges to its paradigm in such domains. Columbia's "ownership" of these recordings rested, firstly, on its simple possession of the recordings and its power to aggregate funding, and secondly on a series of fictions about the importance, value, and conditions of production of the Boulton Collection, and thirdly and most profoundly, on a hunger for funding and an obsequiousness before wealth that had prominent scholars and administrators checking their professional and intellectual standards at a wealthy donor's door. I have discovered that any attempt to interrogate these "rights" yet again can cause them to crumble to brittle bits like an old acetate disc. I have learned that partner institutions have their own understandings of the agreements, of the law and their own legally mandated missions.

A critical perspective on such collections and archives starts by questioning the legitimacy of the archive's claims to ownership of culture. It proceeds to show how the materials in these collections were not transformed into private intellectual property for any reasons related to the stewardship of their contents, and certainly not with any consideration of the interests of their real creators and those people's descendants and communities. Instead, they were transformed into intellectual property to create economic value, in exactly the same process that commercial recording companies and publishers have used to mine oral traditions. Their status as intellectual property in Western terms allowed collectors like Boulton to legally alienate traditional cultural expressions from their original contexts.

Through community-based and directed work, of which "repatriation" is only an initial step, a growing number of archivists and scholars, of whom an increasing number identify as Indigenous, are at least now trying to discover *who* "really" owns these sounds and ideas. This has entailed critical examination of the legal principles and theories of property rights under which any particular assertion of ownership might be made, whether as a general phenomenology of cultural mediation, or as a hegemonic intention to appropriate a particular expression, or as a way of absolving ourselves of the responsibilities that come with assumption of rights.

The laws of intellectual property have rarely, if ever, been available as an instrument of justice for Indigenous musicians and their communities except in occasional tokenistic ways, whether rights under those laws are exercised by commercial or non-profit or scientific interests. Intellectual property law has, instead, primarily been an instrument of appropriation and theft, and not only in the immediate sense, but in the perpetuation of stereotypes of Indigenous people and cultures as in need of protection under laws that have rarely served their interests, no less than our predecessors talked about their cultures as something that could be salvaged for science (Anderson and Christen 2013). Moving forward into an era of honesty about the colonial archive's deeper history, and being similarly honest about the motivations and realities of "non-profit" activities purportedly serving the public good, are necessary correctives if the archive is to become a site for the advancement of social justice.

I have argued here, in the context of a complex tale of the creation and subsequent transformation of one particular collection of traditional music, that ethnomusicological sound archives are the products of dense and tangled histories of personalities, agendas, interests, constraints, and shifting legal and ethical frameworks surrounding such entities. As these factors accumulate over time, and come into conflict, they in turn change the meaning of the archive itself, and the possibilities for its use for research, teaching, remembrance, and cultural revival. Such histories are often undetectable in the presentation of archival objects themselves, instead remaining submerged in the documentation that constitutes any given archive as a legally defined entity, and in the memories and actions of a diverse range of participants – an "archive of the archive" that recedes from view as time passes, or that requires extraordinary levels of access and research effort to recover. In addition to the ethical critique advanced in this chapter, the practical implication of my argument is that it is incumbent on contemporary sound archivists to make such efforts, and to publicize their findings, so that future users of such collections can understand the full context in which the meaning and significance of any given archive's contents has been institutionalized.

Acknowledgments

For assistance with the Laura Boulton papers at Indiana University's Archive of Traditional Music, and other documents related to the Indiana/Columbia relationship, I thank Daniel Reed, Alan Burdette, Marilyn Graf, and Suzanne Mudge. For conversations salient to my arguments here, I am also especially grateful to Lauren Amsterdam, Emily Clark, Dieter Christensen, Kenneth Crews, Steven Feld, Robin R. R. Gray, Susan Lepselter, Amanda Minks, Marti Newland, Ana Maria Ochoa, Trevor Reed, Chie Sakakibara, Anthony Seeger, and the elders, leaders, and members (too numerous to list here) of the communities where the Center for Ethnomusicology has participated in repatriation projects since 2003. I regret that I can no longer thank the late Jack Beeson and Shirley Porter, both of whom told me things they didn't have to reveal in the interest of truth. For painstaking work analyzing and cataloging hundreds of documents, I thank Catherine Mullen, Rachel Meirs, Lauren Amsterdam, and Hannah Rose Baker. For editorial comments on this chapter, I thank Jane Anderson and Ryan O'Byrne. I gratefully acknowledge support for research reported on in this chapter from the United States National Science Foundation Arctic Social Sciences Program and from Columbia University.

Notes

1 I will speak here of "archivists" in general, but with primary focus on those of us who manage university- or museum-based collections of media that purport to be "documents" of Indigenous and other "traditional" cultures, and an even more specific attention to the curation of ethnomusicological sound recordings in such settings. I will try to make the sense of the term clear in context, but there are significant differences in the politics and phenomenologies of the archive that pertain to audio-visual materials, text documents, singular physical artifacts, and human remains "collected" from Indigenous communities or lands, all of which are aggregated in museums and archives. In particular, the reproducibility of media would seem to contrast with the discrete singularity of an artifact or human remains. The categorical error involved in this common misperception of both the politics and the phenomenology of music recordings, films, photographs, and text documents (the mistaking of map for territory, in classic logical terms, and in actual historical terms to which it is related, map-making being a primary technology or colonial territoriality) is in many ways the subject of this chapter, the point of which is that "the law" (with respect to intellectual property) *constructs* myriad and changeable distinctions between maps and territories with a sovereign agency that is rooted in the assumption of historical privilege. Maps are indexes and icons of territories, both metonymically and metaphorically representing territory. But they become territories themselves over time in the archive.

2 And yet, as in all bureaucratic contexts, the personal power that can be exercised at the margins is far more substantial for its ability to invoke or bypass structural obstacles encoded in instruments of formal governance such as explicit access policies.

3 This includes my own public support from the US National Science Foundation.

4 To list only the highlights, such an account would need to attend to the *longue durée* of the colonial project; to the unfolding of multiple logics of elimination to justify the removal and genocide of Native people; to the conversion of the genocidal project from a military to an administrative one under rubrics of assimilation and forced educational and religious deculturation; to the history of recording of Native people by amateurs and commercial interests; to the professionalization of that practice as folklore, ethnomusicology, and commercial music prospecting; to the development of the scholarly sound archive as a pillar of the ethnomusicological project within the academy; to the sale, appropriation, and exhibition of recordings from within the archive; to the digital transformation of audio storage, manipulation, circulation, and mediation; and to the large-scale contemporary effort among archivists of my generation to "repatriate" these recordings.

5 As Director of Columbia University's Center for Ethnomusicology 2003–2008 and currently, and as the Center's archivist in the interim.

6 Boulton carefully preserved her extensive correspondence between the late 1920s and the end of her life; this documentation is housed at the Indiana University Archive of Traditional Music.

7 It is of course true that just being a woman was a significant obstacle to an academic career path in anthropology or ethnomusicology in the mid-twentieth century. In fact, "song-catching" – amateur field recording of traditional or Indigenous musics in a purportedly systematic way – was frequently the alternative path for women with an interest in comparative musicology in the first decades of recording technology's practical existence. However, several of Boulton's female contemporaries – most notably Frances Densmore and Helen Roberts – managed to move between public and academic worlds on the basis of similar projects (see Rakhonen 2003).

8 Indeed, it was the strategic decisions taken by Mantle Hood, Bruno Nettl, and even the anthropologists Alan Merriam and David McAllester to align the emergent discipline of American ethnomusicology with deeply Eurocentric departments of music rather than with cultural anthropology. In seeking kinship with archival music historians and analytic music theorists whose singular focus was Western art

music, ethnomusicologists were compelled to legitimize their ethnographic practice as rooted in European music scholarship, by emphasizing that they too had an archive, a canon, and an analytic technique, and placed high value on the literate representation of musical sound through a foregrounding of music transcription as a central method.

9 For an important and extended consideration of Herzog's role in building the IUATM (and American ethnomusicology around the maintenance of the colonial sound archive), see Reed (1993).

10 Around $8,000 a month in 2015 inflation-adjusted dollars, or around $95,000 per year, around the current base salary for a newly hired Associate Professor, for comparison's sake.

11 I interviewed Prof. Beeson personally about this history in 2004.

12 My estimate of $250,000 is based on $150,000 as the purchase price of the collection in the form of an annuity for Ms. Boulton (that would eventually pay out – at $10,000 a year – at least $200,000 over the remainder of her lifetime, equivalent to around $400,000 in inflation-adjusted dollars). It also includes a $60,000 payment for the operations of the new Center used to soften the Department's senior faculty who opposed the new Center, and smaller amounts paid out by Levi during the late 1960s to support the Center.

13 At the time, this was the largest individual gift ever made to Columbia, roughly equal to a $30 million gift in 2015.

14 Boulton's sour relationship with the libraries had led her to prevail upon Levi to intervene, and he did so with both threats and incentives, offering a substantial additional sum to the Music Department ($60,000, or roughly $500,000 in inflation-adjusted 2015 terms) as start-up funding that would benefit the entire department, and intimating that more would soon follow.

Bibliography

Anderson, Jane. 2005. "Indigenous Knowledge, Intellectual Property, Libraries, and Archives: Crises of Access, Control and Future Utility." *Australian Academic and Research Libraries* 36(2): 83–94.

Anderson, Jane. 2013. "Anxieties of Authorship in the Colonial Archive" in *Media Authorship*, C. Chris and D. Gerstner, eds. New York: Routledge, pp. 229–246.

Anderson, Jane, and Kim Christen. 2013. "'Chuck a Copyright on It:' Dilemmas of Digital Return and the Possibilities for Traditional Knowledge Licenses and Labels." *Museum Anthropology Review* 7(1/2): 105–126.

Boulton, Laura. 1963. "I Search for Ancient Music." *Columbia Library Columns* 12(2): 13–22.

Boulton, Laura. 1969. *The Music Hunter: The Autobiography of a Career*. New York: Doubleday.

Christensen, Dieter. 1973. Unpublished letter to Associate Provost Brookhart, May 8. Columbia University Center for Ethnomusicology Administrative Files.

Christensen, Dieter. 1991. "Erich M. Von Hornbostel, Carl Stumpf, and the Institutionalization of Comparative Musicology" in *Comparative Musicology and the Anthropology of Music: Essays on the History of Ethnomusicology*, Bruno Nettl and Philip V. Bohlman, eds. Chicago: University of Chicago Press.

Christensen, Dieter. 2002. "Berlin Phonogramm-Archiv: The First 100 Years." Music Archiving in the World: Papers Presented at the Conference on the Occasion of the 100th Anniversary of the Berlin Phonogramm-Archiv. VWB, Verlag für Wissenschaft und Bildung.

Deloria, Philip J. 2004. *Indians in Unexpected Places*. Lawrence: University Press of Kansas.

Derrida, Jacques. 1996. *Archive Fever: A Freudian Impression*. Chicago: University of Chicago Press.

Feld, Steven. 1994. "From Schizophonia to Schismogenesis: The Discourses and Practices of World Music and World Beat" in *Music Grooves: Essays and Dialogues*, Charles Keil and Steven Feld, eds. Chicago: University of Chicago Press, pp. 257–289.

Feld, Steven. 1996. "Pygmy POP. A Genealogy of Schizophonic Mimesis." *Yearbook for Traditional Music* 28: 1–35.

Feld, Steven. 2000. "A Sweet Lullaby for World Music." *Public Culture* 12(1): 145–171.

Fox, Aaron A. 2014. "Repatriation as Re-Animation Through Reciprocity" in *The Cambridge History of World Music: Vol. 1 (North America)*, P. Bohlman, ed. Cambridge: Cambridge University Press.

Hopi Cultural Preservation Office. 2013. "Hopi and Zuni Songs Return Home." Hopi Tumalhoymuy Tutuveniam, September 2013. https://hopimusic.files.wordpress.com/2013/09/htt-september-2013.pdf (accessed 27 March 2017).

Gray, Robin R. R. 2015. "Ts'msyen Revolution: The Poetics and Politics of Reclaiming." PhD Dissertation, Anthropology. The University of Massachusetts, Amherst.

Kreps, Christina. 2013. *Liberating Culture: Cross-Cultural Perspectives on Museums, Curation, and Heritage Preservation*. New York: Routledge.

McMillan, Robert. 1991. "Ethnology and the NFB: The Laura Boulton Mysteries." *Canadian Journal of Film Studies* 1(2): 67–82.

Morse, Bradford W. 2012. "Indigenous Human Rights and Knowledge in Archives, Museums, and Libraries: Some International Perspectives with Specific Reference to New Zealand and Canada." *Archival Science* 12(2):113–140.

Rahkonen, Carl. 2003. "The Real Song Catchers: American Women Pioneers of Ethnomusicology." Paper presented at the Music Library Association, Women's Music Round Table, Austin, Texas, February 14. http://www.people.iup.edu/rahkonen/WP/real_song_catchers.htm (accessed 27 March 2017).

Reed, Daniel. 1993. "The Innovator and the Primitives: George Herzog in Historical Perspective." *Folklore Forum* 26(1/2): 69–92.

Reed, Trevor. 2009. "Returning Hopi Voices: Toward a Model for Community-Partnered Repatriation of Archived Traditional Music." MA Thesis. Teachers College, Columbia University, New York.

Reed, Trevor. 2013. "KUYI Hopi Radio Interviews Zuni Elders about Repatriated Songs." Hopi Music Repatriation Project. https://hopimusic.wordpress.com (accessed 27 March 2017).

Sakakibara, Chie. 2009. "'No Whale, No Music': Iñupiaq Drumming and Global Warming." *Polar Record* 45(235): 289–303.

Salmen, Stanley. 1964. Unpublished letter to Laura Boulton, January 17. Held in Laura Boulton Papers, Indiana University Archives of Traditional Music, Bloomington, IN.

Seeger, Anthony. 2001. "Intellectual Property and Audiovisual Archives and Collections" in *Folk Heritage Collections in Crisis*. Washington, DC: Council on Library and Information Resources. http://www.clir.org/pubs/reports/pub96/contents.html/contents.html (accessed 27 March 2017).

Taylor, Timothy D. 2003. "A Riddle Wrapped in a Mystery: Transnational Music Sampling and Enigma's Return to Innocence" in *Music and Technoculture*, R. Lysloff and L. Gay, eds. Middletown, CT: Wesleyan University Press, pp. 64–92.

Wolfe, Patrick. 2006. "Settler Colonialism and the Elimination of the Native." *Journal of Genocide Research* 8(4): 387–409.

Zemp, Hugo. 1996. "The/An Ethnomusicologist and the Record Business." *Yearbook for Traditional Music* 28: 36–56.

11

TOUCHING THE INTANGIBLE

Reconsidering material culture in the realm of Indigenous cultural property research

George P. Nicholas

Introduction

Why does the tangible always trump the intangible in discussions of cultural property?[1] How has this affected the evaluation and protection of ancient or culturally significant objects and places from the perspective of heritage holders and heritage managers – seldom the same people? And how do local values direct decisions regarding cultural property, heritage research, and preservation policies? Over the past 25 years or so, such questions have been explored by archaeologists and others who seek new knowledge of past lifeways; by members of descendant communities, especially Indigenous ones for whom connections to the past mean much more than artifacts on display; and by policy makers charged with the protection of cultural heritage. This has contributed to a rich academic discourse but with too few on-the-ground results due largely to the profound power imbalances that persist in so-called settler countries (e.g. Australia, Canada, the United States), and the unwillingness or inability of those involved to effect real change in the heritage realm. This has resulted is outstanding concerns about ethics, intercultural relations, and dispute resolution.

This imbalance is as much about epistemology as it is about the politics of knowledge. In the Western world, archaeology has long been viewed as the most robust of the various approaches to identifying and interpreting the story of humanity's development and its great diversity, focused as it is on material culture – the physical expressions of past human behavior extending back into antiquity. Over the past 50 years, a suite of theoretical tools and technological advances has provided the means to learn about ancient peoples with astonishing detail. Given these advances, and poised as they are between science and the humanities, archaeologists have often taken on the mantle of official stewards of the past.

In recent decades, however, archaeology has been taken to task from both within and outside the discipline as to what it was, or was not, doing. By the 1980s there were calls from some factions to move away from the generalizing, explanatory goals of the neo-evolutionary orientation that dominated archaeology since the 1960s (see O'Brien et al. 2005), to a more relativistic position that emphasized meaning and questioned, amongst other things, the authority of archaeological interpretation (e.g. Hodder et al. 1995). Within settler countries, this latter focus was coincident with strident calls from Indigenous peoples[2] for participation in research on or affecting their heritage, and its management, as well as for relinquishing authoritative positions that depend upon specific worldviews (e.g. Davidson et al. 1995; Deloria 1967; Nicholas and Andrews 1997; Swidler et al. 1997). These issues were also playing out within the larger context of anthropology (see Harking 2010), as they continue to do today. For its part, archaeology responded with a significant broadening, both in theory and practice, including considerable attention being paid to the concerns of descendant communities (Atalay et al. 2014; Lydon and Rizvi 2010; Nicholas 2014; Smith and Wobst 2005).

Much has thus been accomplished to make archaeology more responsible, representative, and relevant in terms of community engagement or orientation (e.g. Lyons 2013; Skeates et al. 2010). But there are some significant hurdles in extending these goals to heritage management.[3] This is because management decisions are influenced by who controls, has access to, and benefits from cultural property, both tangible and intangible, as well as by who has the right or controls the representation of these issues. The emphasis on "evidence" in site interpretation and evaluation (see Chapman and Wylie 2015) has foregrounded material culture as the aspect of heritage that requires consideration and preservation, yet physical expressions of heritage may be less important than their intangible aspects to some heritage holders.

Importantly, while these topics elicit much discussion and contention in archaeology and other realms of heritage-related research (e.g. Bell and Paterson 2009; Kuprecht 2014; Riley 2004), they are also being debated by local and national governments and agencies, by organizations such as the International Council of Museums and by such international organizations as WIPO and the United Nations (e.g. Maina 2011; Srinivas 2012). Prominent here are demands by Indigenous peoples for more meaningful participation in decisions affecting their heritage and livelihood, the need to move from "consultation" to "partnership" or "consent," and for professional organizations and government agencies to lessen their control over other peoples' heritage.[4] Furthermore, while Indigenous cultural property, both tangible and intangible, should be afforded protection under existing state, provincial, or federal law, this has had only limited success (Battiste and Henderson 2000; Bell and Paterson 2009; Kuprecht 2014; Riley 2004).

In this chapter I argue that the emphasis on material culture (i.e. things) has skewed our understanding of "heritage" and what should be preserved, particularly in the context of Indigenous cultural property. This has had a significant impact upon Indigenous peoples worldwide, and been detrimental to their identity and wellbeing, as well as limiting the benefits they have received from research into their heritage.

I begin with a brief look at how cultural property is acknowledged differently by international conventions and local (i.e. provincial) heritage policies in Canada. This sets the stage for an examination of differences between Western and Indigenous perspectives on cultural property, and then of the subsequent challenges for protecting Indigenous heritage. Next I discuss some of the responses, synergies, and alternative strategies that have arisen in response through a range of examples drawn from the IPinCH Project, an international initiative that addresses intellectual property issues affecting Indigenous peoples. I conclude with a consideration of the responsibilities that come with engaging with other people's cultural property, and the decisions that each of us must make in that regard.

Many of the examples provided are drawn from Canada, and the majority of those from British Columbia due to unresolved heritage concerns in the province. I intentionally provide a wide variety of examples, rather than a smaller number of in-detail studies, to more effectively illustrate the breadth of concerns that require attention.

Heritage as material bound

In both common use and the realm of heritage management, "cultural property" is most often construed as something physical; this is clearly reflected in the Hague Convention for the Protection of Cultural Property[5] (1954):

> The term "cultural property" shall cover, irrespective of origin or ownership:
>
> (a) movable or immovable property of great importance to the cultural heritage of every people, such as monuments of architecture, art or history, whether religious or secular; archaeological sites; groups of buildings which, as a whole, are of historical or artistic interest; works of art; manuscripts, books and other objects of artistic, historical or archaeological interest; as well as scientific collections and important collections of books or archives or of reproductions of the property defined above;
> (b) buildings whose main and effective purpose is to preserve or exhibit the movable cultural property defined in sub-paragraph (a) such as museums, large libraries and depositories of archives, and refuges intended to shelter, in the event of armed conflict, the movable cultural property defined in sub-paragraph (a);
> (c) centers containing a large amount of cultural property as defined in sub-paragraphs (a) and (b), to be known as "centers containing monuments."

A similar orientation has also been reflected in US heritage legislation: "In amending the National Historic Preservation Act of 1966, the 96th Congress realized that the existing Historic Preservation Program fails to provide clear coverage for the full range of cultural resources in the United States. Historic properties are the sole type of resource specified for protection and benefits. When not embodied in a structure or site, intangible elements of our cultural heritage fall outside the scope of this law" (Loomis 1983: iii).

The emphasis on the tangible expressions in the realm of heritage – objects, structures, and places – is understandable. Within archaeology and related contexts, it is the material culture record that is used to identify, evaluate, and preserve or mitigate impact on heritage "resources" considered "significant" (Hardesty and Little 2009). Such assessments emphasize scientific values, albeit with some attention to historical, religious, and local values as well.

But cultural property, defined in this manner, is but one dimension of the much broader concept of "heritage," which I define as the objects, places, knowledge, customs, practices, plants, stories, songs, and designs that define or contribute to a person's or group's identity, history, worldview, and wellbeing. Although intangible aspects are recognized in heritage policies (e.g. as intellectual property [WIPO] and as intangible cultural heritage), "artifacts" and "sites" are still the primary referent in archaeological practice and heritage management due to the necessity of "evidence" in scientific reasoning, as well as in upholding the legal obligations of heritage policies. As one example, the Heritage Conservation Act (1996) of British Columbia (Canada) includes this provision[6]:

> (2) Except as authorized by a permit issued under section 12 or 14, or an order issued under section 14, a person must not do any of the following:
>
> (a) damage, desecrate or alter a Provincial heritage site or a Provincial heritage object or remove from a Provincial heritage site or Provincial heritage object any heritage *object or material* that constitutes part of the site or object;

(b) damage, desecrate or alter a burial place that has historical or archaeological value or remove *human remains* or any heritage *object* from a burial place that has historical or archaeological value;
(c) damage, alter, cover or move an aboriginal *rock painting* or aboriginal rock *carving* that has historical or archaeological value;
(d) damage, excavate, dig in or alter, or remove any heritage *object* from a site that contains *artifacts, features, materials or other physical evidence* of human habitation or use before 1846. . . . [emphasis added].

Definitions provided include:

> "heritage object" means, whether designated or not, personal property that has heritage value to British Columbia, a community or an aboriginal people;
> "heritage site" means, whether designated or not, land, including land covered by water, that has heritage value to British Columbia, a community or an aboriginal people;
> "heritage value" means the historical, cultural, aesthetic, scientific or educational worth or usefulness of a site or object.

The Heritage Conservation Act is potentially a powerful piece of legislation, and one that includes provisions to accommodate First Nations interests, including concerns about the protection of sacred sites, ancestral grounds, and other aspects of heritage that may have little or no material culture (still) associated with them.[7] Again, however, the emphasis of physical remains, and more generally the limited accommodation of First Nations heritage values, including spiritual or sacred places, has continued to be problematic in British Columbia and indeed in settler countries worldwide due to land claims, sovereignty claims, and a host of other unresolved issues.[8] While there is nominally protection for intangible heritage, there is also a disconnect in Canada and elsewhere between state or provincial legislation and what is called for by UNESCO's Convention for the Safeguarding of Intangible Cultural Heritage (2003), which includes this definition (in Article 2(1)):

> The "intangible cultural heritage" means the practices, representations, expressions, knowledge, skills – as well as the instruments, objects, artefacts and cultural spaces associated therewith – that communities, groups and, in some cases, individuals recognize as part of their cultural heritage. This intangible cultural heritage, transmitted from generation to generation, is constantly recreated by communities and groups in response to their environment, their interaction with nature and their history, and provides them with a sense of identity and continuity, thus promoting respect for cultural diversity and human creativity. . . .

Notably, the convention is strongly oriented to *contemporary* heritage expressions, with no explicit reference to the presence or expression of intangible heritage in non-modern (e.g. archaeological) contexts despite the mention of their continuance through generations.

Even when concerted effort is made to seek fuller acknowledgement of intangible cultural property, significant tensions persist between the dominant society and Indigenous peoples within settler countries regarding land claims, reburial and repatriation, DNA research, research ethics, protection of burial grounds and sacred places, and so on (e.g. Nicholas et al. 2015). This reflects, in part, the limited congruence between legislation designed explicitly to protect the material dimensions of heritage, and international conventions and other efforts seeking to acknowledge and protect intangible heritage. Indigenous peoples continue to have limited participation in matters concerning their heritage, which has a vital role in their identity, worldview, and wellbeing. While this is very much an issue of law and participation, it also has a significant bearing on how "cultural property" and "heritage" are defined and implemented in practice, and also on the degree to which intangible cultural property is acknowledged – a topic explored in the next section.

When cultural property is immaterial

Despite the fact that anthropology strives to appreciate the diversity that comprises humankind, there has nonetheless been the tendency to interpret that diversity through a Western lens of understanding – a perspective shaped by an empiricist rationality that developed during the Enlightenment and skewed by the power relations that continue to inflect the production of knowledge in universities. The result is that while many will acknowledge that a mountain is sacred to a certain group, for example, they tend to be satisfied only when there is some physical evidence of religious practice associated with it, particularly in the context of land claims, resource extraction, or land development. This focus on tangible "proof" continues to haunt the application of heritage policies in the Americas and other settler countries, where the vast majority of the archaeological and early historic record is associated with Indigenous cultures but under the control of the state.

While there is no one "pan-Indian" worldview – and I am cautious about essentializing here – significant differences do exist between Western and Indigenous societies, and their respective knowledge systems, in terms of worldview, ecological relations, modes of explanation, conceptions of time, and so on. Heather Harris (Cree-Métis) notes that "the universe [and everything in it] is alive, has power, will and intelligence" (2005: 35), where familiar Western dichotomies – natural/supernatural; nature/culture – may be absent or at least different, and the past, present, and future may be self-referential. Thus ancestral beings may be part of this existence, not another dimension; ownership of objects, songs or stories, even places may be communal, not individual; landscape features may be living beings (see Brady et al. 2016). Such factors have substantial implications for how cultural property was and is defined and enacted in daily life (it may be animate, for example).

Recognizing the nature of indigenous worldviews, heritage, and knowledge systems is thus essential to making sense of contemporary claims around Indigenous cultural property (see Augustine 1997; Bruchac 2014; Riley 2004). My position follows that of Bell and Napoleon (2008: 6–7), who note that "The very terms 'culture,' 'property,' and 'ownership' are Western legal, social, economic, and political constructs that are imposed on First Nations. . . . However, to varying degrees and within specific contexts these terms are still incomprehensible (i.e. no equivalent concept in First Nations languages), inappropriate (i.e. disrespectful of First Nations concepts), or inadequate (i.e. too narrow)." This is why I view cultural property as an essentially inseparable aspect of heritage.

The notion of property as "something owned" is of course not exclusively a Western notion. Within Indigenous societies, individuals, families, clans, and other entities could and did possess not only objects, but also places, songs, stories, and much more. With these came types of immediate but also intergenerational attachments, responsibilities, and entitlements perhaps unfamiliar to Western understanding. As one example, Brian Noble has explored the contrasting notions of "owning as property" vs. "owning as belonging" within and between Canadian First Nations: "The phrase 'owning as property' describes a system that emphasizes property as a commodity capable of individual ownership and alienation for the purposes of resource use and wealth maximization. In contrast, 'owning as belonging' places greater emphasis on transactions that strengthen relationships of respect and responsibility between people and what they regard as 'cultural property'" (2008: 465).

Likewise, the division of property into "tangible" and "intangible" forms may be unfamiliar, indeed even artificial or unnatural when applied to Indigenous contexts. Objects, even if ancient, may be seen not as *reflections* of past lives but as vessels that contain some essence of those lives; rock art images may *embody* ancestral beings. Ancient objects are often important touchstones of history, family heirlooms that connect generations. One such heirloom is held by Joanne Coombes Brown, who is Carrier Cheslatta Nation (British Columbia) – a *chundoo lat'ooz-a-tut' chjooth*, which is an inner-bark scraper commonly used by Carrier people to obtain cambium. This one was made by Cheslatta Chief Louie for his wife, who gave it to her daughter, Lottie (Louie) Jack, who in turn gave it to her daughter, Christine Jack, Joanne's mother: "As a child I didn't know that its presence reminded her of days gone by, and of a lifestyle that would be lost in our next generation. . . . It represented the nuanced smells and tastes of so many spring days, complete with those noises the earth makes only at that time of year. It reminded her of her grandfather, and she remembered her grandmother using this tool."

An additional connection between object and identity is brought forward by Jordan Wilson (2016) in his discussion of nomenclature concerning the ancestral Musqueam village of *c̓əsnaʔəm* in what is today Vancouver, British Columbia. He makes a compelling argument to use the Musqueam name (vs. "Marpole Midden") and "belongings" (vs. "artifacts") because this "reinforces the ongoing connection our community has to both place and the things taken from it." Indeed, this simple shift in words is remarkably effective in forcing one to personalize the past (see Carcross-Tagish First Nation et al. 2016 and Spector 1993 for additional examples).

More generally, a distinct concept of "heritage" may be absent in many Indigenous societies since what it represents is entwined with all other facets of people's lives. As one Yukon First Nations member notes about heritage, "It's everything that makes us who we are" (Carcross-Tagish First Nation et al. 2016: 30). The knowledge that shapes and guides each person's life is learned, earned, shared, and cared for, often hand-in-hand through objects or places. Likewise, for the Mistissini Cree of northern Quebec, material expressions of heritage, such as traditional technology, have an active role in healing and wellbeing (Guindon 2015). Their concept of *maamaahtaaukaschihtaau* ("resourcefulness") "encapsulates the complex relationships existing between the ideational and material constituents of what Westerners know as technology" (p. 80). This is exemplified by the Mistissini's integration but also reworking of Euro-Canadian technology into their traditional lifeways.

For some Indigenous peoples, not only may things be considered animate, but so too is heritage – that is, so-called heritage objects need to be used and relations with heritage places need to be maintained and nourished. The culturally appropriate care of objects of Indigenous patrimony in some museums, which may include storing some items separately, and the burning of sweet grass, or smudging, at least nominally acknowledges the living aspects of the objects kept there. In fact, this practice has in recent years become part of museum curatorial practices[9] where ceremonial objects may be housed in a museum, but are "checked out" by community members as needed (Peers and Brown 2003). Heritage objects may thus continue to have a role – a life – within their respective communities.

Finally, expressions of heritage may be at one integral unto themselves but also part of something larger. For the Mi'kmaq, a named place on the landscape where Gloscap's dogs were transformed into a rocky outcrop (Sable 2011) is also part of a constellation of stories that are an historical record, a connection to (still-present) ancestors, and a touchstone of identity. In the case of ancestral remains, there may be no perceived difference between a bone fragment or preserved hair or even DNA sample and the person whole. In this case, what might be casually termed an artifact, a scientific specimen, or cultural property is actually a person.

It is evident in each of these cases that cultural property is not just "things." While one's engagement with the world may be grounded through its material culture, it is always filtered through the society's collective knowledge, experiences, traditions, social obligations, and origin stories that both shape and reflect what people do, and why. Thus, there is fundamentally no difference between the place and the stories and knowledge that location holds, or between an object and the historical continuity it may exude or the social obligations it may convey. This in turn requires that the archaeological (or other) analyses of such cultural property, and the "management" of such heritage (including determination of significance), impose great responsibility on outsiders who engage with other people's heritage and all that it represents.

Challenges associated with Indigenous cultural property

Clearly archaeologists and others who are the gatekeepers and managers of heritage objects, places, and information need a better understanding of the cultural systems they represent – and the nature of cultural property therein. Coupled with its emphasis on empirical observation, evidence, and explanation, archaeology's quest for new knowledge of what it is to be human is relentless and seemingly boundless (i.e. no topics should be off limits). While archaeology has broadened substantially to address the needs of Indigenous peoples (see Nicholas 2014 for a review), such efforts have translated unevenly into general practice, especially in heritage management. Despite court rulings that now give weight to oral histories in archaeological site assessment and land claims, the burden of proof effectively remains on material culture. Indeed, there seems to be implicit mistrust of the value and legitimacy of non-tangible material as a legitimate source of data or "truth." In some cases, Indigenous groups[10] have successfully turned to archaeological data to demonstrate continuity of land use in land title cases. However, oral histories, traditional knowledge, and other forms of evidence are often suspect, whether in specific legal cases like *Delgamuukw vs. British Columbia* (Culhane 1997) or the Hindmarsh Island case in Australia (Bell 1998) for instance, or more generally (Mason 2006).

Not surprisingly, descendant communities, especially Indigenous peoples, have major concerns relating to how their cultural property is treated by others, especially when used in inappropriate, unwelcome, or harmful ways. Examples here include: modern and ancient DNA research (Pullman and Nicholas 2011; TallBear 2013); control of, benefits of, access to, and protection of heritage objects, places and information (Bell and Paterson 2009); efforts to repatriate cultural patrimony and human remains, and the information derived from those (Kuprecht 2014); inappropriate display of sacred objects; and the selective acceptance of traditional knowledge (Isaac 2011; Nicholas and Markey 2014). In addition, virtually all elements of indigenous heritage, traditional knowledge, and cultural objects and sites have long been viewed as part of the public domain, free for the taking and enjoyment of others.

Here I briefly highlight two examples of special challenges relating to different types of Indigenous heritage: the proper care of cultural property; and identifying and respecting the sacred. Each has practical, ethical, and legal dimensions. While the examples are drawn from North America, comparable examples occur widely.

Proper care of cultural property

How should Indigenous heritage items be cared for when removed from their cultural context and kept by others elsewhere? For the Zuni of the American Southwest, proper care of the *Ahayu:da* (carved wooden figures, considered animate beings, residing on mountaintop shrines) is to let them return to the elements when their active life is over (Merrill et al. 1993), while for museum curators and conservators it is to keep them in climate-controlled rooms with the goal of preserving them indefinitely. These are two diametrically opposed modes of care and obligation.

In the age of technological (and increasingly digital) reproducibility (e.g. Ahmed et al. 2014), there are also challenges associated with "replicas." For example, Gwyneira Isaac's (2011) study of the intangible aspects of Zuni cultural patrimony reveals that replicas of ceremonial items may be fundamentally no different from the original item, even when made by non-Zuni, and may be animate or filled with power. This has led to concerns about who has access to Zuni knowledge, and about its appropriation and misuse. On the other hand, the use of reproductive technologies can also be used to protect Indigenous cultural property. This is illustrated by a recent collaboration between the Tlingit and the Smithsonian Institution (Hollinger et al. 2013) which used 3D digitization and reproductive technologies to make copies of important but old and fragile sacred items that could fulfill both community needs and the mandate of the museum; Tlingit oversight not only ensured no threats to the integrity of the pieces, but provided added value. While very promising, such collaborations require a considerable investment of time and resources; there are also many technical and ethical issues associated with the digitization of cultural property (Boast and Enote 2013; Brown and Nicholas 2012; Christen 2006; Ngata et al. 2012).

Identifying and respecting the sacred

Among the greatest concerns that Indigenous peoples have are threats to sacred sites, cemeteries, and other places of religious or historical significance to them. Part of the problem is that, as cultural property, heritage places may be of types unfamiliar to outsiders (e.g. ancestors transformed into rock) or may lack an archaeological (i.e. material evidence) component.[11] Objects can be under threat if not treated properly (according to Indigenous protocols) or not identified as sacred by museum staff. Likewise, objects that are recognized for their archaeological value, such as a carved stone figures, may in fact be considered animate and must be treated differently, even if not considered sacred. In the case of one such being, the Sto:lo in British Columbia believe that "T'xwelátse is a man. He was turned to stone but he is still alive" (Sto:lo Nation 2012: 15). Most archaeologists and heritage managers have little experience with what is literally, in this case, "living heritage."

Another challenge is also that not all information about cultural property is appropriate to share. Indigenous groups are often reluctant or unwilling to identify sacred places, for various reasons such as protection of the site or other cultural protocols, which can be a challenge for heritage managers. As Arvid Charlie, a Hul'qumi'num elder (British Columbia), states:

> There's nothing really written down about our sacred things, our sacred ways, sacred areas. We've been brought to question that. Well, other people have said, "Well, you guys must have not very many important sites that's why it's not recorded." You know, when we're trying to look at some . . . or something about sacred sites. The answer from our home area is: those things that are really sacred,

> no one is allowed access to. We didn't share it. We don't share it with just anybody. It was good for that day – we kept our heritage, our culture – but today that almost works against us.
>
> *(cited in McLay et al. 2008: 151)*

Finally, even when heritage sites and objects are protected by law, misunderstanding about the nature of cultural property remains problematic. In the recent Grace Islet controversy in British Columbia, a property owner, acting legally under the provisions of the Heritage Conservation Act (cited earlier), began construction of a house on a small island that had at least 16 recorded burial cairns, literally building on top of/around several. This technically left the "archaeological component" of the burial ground intact, but was clearly inappropriate and caused considerable harm to local First Nations until construction was permanently stopped in early 2015 (Nicholas et al. 2015). Part of the problem is that Indigenous and Euro-Canadian burial grounds are treated differently under the law (pre-1846, they an archaeological site; post-1846, a cemetery). In addition, the landowner received compensation of $5.45 million, of which $840,000 was for the property itself, and $4.6 million for "losses suffered." As I've noted elsewhere, "What has been conspicuously absent, however, has been *any* consideration given to the local First Nations – not for lost "enjoyment" but for the harm, "losses suffered" from the impact of disturbance of historic places they consider sacred or otherwise vital" (Nicholas 2017).

In each of these cases, there are fundamental differences between Western and Indigenous conceptions of "property." Some objects are animate. Ancestors are part of *this* existence, a notion outside the realm of Western understanding. Understanding cultural beliefs is thus vital to how Indigenous heritage, and all it means, is conceived by outsiders/heritage managers/researchers. It is the responsibility of those charged with caring for or otherwise managing other people's cultural property to enfold such understanding into the practice of heritage curation and management. While there are provisions for recognizing and protecting intangible property in heritage legislation in North America (e.g. Guest 1996; McJohn 2005), they are applied or interpreted inconsistently.

Good practices with (other people's) cultural property

There are today a variety of practices being employed around the world that engage with cultural property in ways that foreground community values, interests, and needs. These provide both examples of, and incentive for, the integration of Indigenous conceptions of property into museum curation, heritage management, and archaeological practice. In some cases these values emanate from the community and are directed only to the community (e.g. Mukurtu, a digital content management system developed with the Warumungu Aboriginal community [Australia], explicitly designed to suit the protocols of Indigenous communities around the organization and accessibility of esoteric knowledge[12]); in other cases they provide opportunities for information sharing and collaborative exploration, interpretation, and protection of cultural property with those outside the community (e.g. the Reciprocal Research Network, an innovative partnership between the Musqueam Indian Band, the Sto:lo Nation and Sto:lo Tribal Council, the U'mista Cultural Society, and the University of British Columbia's Museum of Anthropology to facilitate reciprocal and collaborative research).[13] There are also initiatives developed by non-Indigenous partners intended to support community needs, which may also provide "added value" to traditional forms of heritage research (i.e. those with scientific or historical orientation).

Here I provide a set of examples of approaches to cultural property that (a) directly benefit the heritage holders, (b) reveal new ways of thinking about, and doing, heritage management, and (c) are each situated in an understanding of cultural property/heritage in which the tangible and intangible aspects are indivisible. These are all drawn from the Intellectual Property Issues in Cultural Heritage (IPinCH) Project (2008–2016).[14] This was an international research collaboration providing research, knowledge, and resources assisting academic scholars, descendant communities and others in negotiating equitable terms of cultural heritage research and policies. The team included more than 50 archaeologists, anthropologists, museum and cultural tourism specialists, lawyers, ethicists, and others, along with 25 partner organizations, and more than 100 Associate members and student participants. Since 2008, IPinCH worked to explore the diverse values that underlie attitudes, decisions and actions to facilitate fair and ethical exchanges of knowledge relating to cultural heritage, especially that of Indigenous peoples. IPinCH sought to ensure that communities, not academics, are the primary beneficiaries of the research conducted – a challenging proposition for any university-based initiative.

IPinCH engaged locally and at national or international levels to address Indigenous heritage needs while also working to better understand conceptions of heritage, to improve university research ethics, and research practices, and also influence heritage policies and their implementation. Efforts in each realm are briefly outlined below.

Insights into Indigenous intellectual/cultural property rights

Worldwide, concerns have arisen over the nature of culture, property, knowledge, and rights of Indigenous peoples. Frequently, these reflect a failure to recognize the important roles that customary and informal legal systems continue to play in Indigenous societies, as relating to land, traditional knowledge, and ancestral objects and places. A series of IPinCH-funded community-based studies[15] provided opportunities to learn about local conceptions of ownership and rights. For example, the Yukon First Nations initiative sought understandings of heritage values of three of its members: Champagne & Aishihik First Nations, the Carcross-Tagish First Nation and the Ta'an Kwach'än Council:

> Although participants identified various forms of art and cultural expression as holding significant cultural importance, these "things" alone do not constitute the value. Rather, it is the relationships – the experiences and the stories attached to them – that establish their significance. While a physical item itself can have some inherent value, the process of sharing traditional knowledge derived from it, and the aggregate of experience shared between people, is often attributed higher significance.
>
> *(Carcross-Tagish First Nation et al. 2016: 53)*

In British Columbia, the Secwepemc Territorial Authority project began with the premise that Secwepemc Peoples' have economic, political, and legal authority within their territory. For community participants, heritage "takes in the political and economic relations, your spiritual relations, your practices, your laws, morals and ways on the land, all those kinds of things" (Noble et al. 2016). What is evident from these and the other community initiatives is that both "heritage" and "heritage objects" tend to be linked to multi-faced notions of stewardship, responsibility, spirituality, and relationships. Indeed, for Yukon First Nations, "the heritage value of an object is not necessarily related to its age, rarity, or uniqueness, but rather it is determined largely on the basis of connection to community" (Carcross-Tagish First Nation et al. 2016: 68).

Community needs

The funding provided to the community-directed initiatives worldwide helped to address local concerns about a variety of issues affecting cultural property. For example, the Moriori of the Chatham Islands, New Zealand developed a cultural database for traditional knowledge, a management plan based on Moriori aspirations and *tikane* (cultural protocols and obligations) to protect a sacred grove of *rakau momori* (living tree carvings), and ethical protocols and guidelines for research and fieldwork (Thorpe et al. 2015); in the Canadian Arctic, the Inuvialuit repatriated information from objects in museum collections far away and established new education programs; the Sto:lo (British Columbia) developed guidelines for research on ancestral human remains that enable generating knowledge within a mutually acceptable framework of authority, control, and use; and in Kyrgyzstan, a series of sustainable, culturally appropriate, and community-embedded projects address the preservation and educational use of cultural property, including in cultural tourism.

Research ethics

IPinCH itself became a case study in alternative research ethics and practice in terms of giving communities complete control over the research process. This revealed significant tensions between the project, university policies, and funding agencies. Some of the community projects literally took years to have the funding and ethics application approved, pointing to the need for revising university policies. To aid that process, and to share lessons learned, IPinCH hosted a national research ethics conference, "Working Better Together"[16] in 2015 that brought together scholars, practitioners, students, administrators, and policy makers of diverse cultural and professional backgrounds from across Canada to explore what it means to work collaboratively in Indigenous research.

Heritage management

In late 2014, in response to the continuing construction on the Grace Islet burial ground (noted above), a group of IPinCH team members developed the *Declaration on the Safeguarding of Indigenous Ancestral Burial Grounds as Sacred Sites and Cultural Landscapes.*[17] The declaration states the importance of recognizing and protecting Indigenous ancestral burial sites and calls on all levels of government to work together to ensure such sites are not subject to alteration or damage. It is also a reminder to all parties, including both non-Indigenous governments and researchers, of their *existing* legal and ethical obligations with respect to First Nations sacred sites on which human remains of cultural and spiritual significance are interred. Here as elsewhere, cultural property represents the tangible and intangible aspects of people's lives, a concept that many in Western society need assistance in learning to recognize and respect.

Public education

Another important IPinCH goal was to educate and provide resources to Indigenous communities, heritage practitioners, policy makers, and the general public to enable them to better understand and make informed decisions about cultural property. This included symposia and workshops on such topics as "Cultural Commodification, Indigenous Peoples, and Self-Determination," and "DNA and Indigeneity: The Changing Role of Genetics in Indigenous Rights, Tribal Belonging, and Repatriation." To date, IPinCH has produced

96 videos, in addition to fact sheets, teaching resources, and academic publications. One important output from the Commodifications workshop was the recently published booklet, *Think Before You Appropriate: Things to Know and Questions to Ask in Order to Avoid Misappropriating Indigenous Cultural Heritage. A Guide for Creators and Designers.*[18]

What these and other endeavors demonstrate is that collaborative projects and community-driven projects enhance not hinder understandings of cultural property. This may help to confront the conundrum of heritage management, which has most often been informed by values and goals divorced from the communities whose heritage it is. No less important is challenging the notion that indigenous heritage is public domain. As IPinCH has hopefully demonstrated, enabling community-based or collaborative research practices and promoting a "some rights reserved" model to cultural property and the knowledge it conveys may help to avoid many of the issues outlined earlier.

Not unwrapping the sacred bundle

For the most part, Indigenous peoples are genuinely interested in what archaeology and other research practices can reveal about their cultural property and past lifeways, as well as what ethnographies have captured of traditional customs prior to the impact of colonialism. Indigenous groups are actively involved in archaeology, traditional knowledge recording, and even studies of ancient human remains (Nicholas 2010; Solomon and Thorpe 2012). However serious concerns loom large when research results reveal or threaten information that is not meant to be shared, or cause cultural, spiritual, or economic harm. More broadly, there is potentially much at stake regarding academic/scientific vs. community access and ownership of knowledge, restrictive vs. inclusive modes of resolution, the rights of knowledge holders vs. knowledge users, and legal vs. customary definitions of intellectual property, as well as the legal and ethical challenges of new technologies (e.g. digital repositories) and research initiatives.

The case of "sacred bundles" thus provides an important point of reference in terms of ethical issues vs. scientific knowledge in regards to cultural property. Secret ceremonies, hidden ritual objects, sacred bundles – all represent aspects of cultural property that, for Western scholars, beg for discovery, description, and analysis, but for others are recognized as off limits.

What are sacred bundles? These are literally bundles of objects, most often associated with Indigenous societies in the Americas (but having counterparts elsewhere), that possess great spiritual power, and thus require great care and responsibility by those authorized to possess or use them. From the perspective of Western science, these bundles provide opportunities for new knowledge about Indigenous belief systems. Thus, Margaret Brown Vega's (2015) study of sacred bundles from Chile points to the value that analysis of such objects may have, as does Timothy Pauketat's (2013) broader study of how such objects inform understandings of agency in ancient religious practices. And yet from an insider's perspective, those revelations would be disastrous. Traditionally, Aboriginal peoples in Australia, for example, even accidentally encountering what was restricted, could be met with harsh penalties or death (Berndt and Berndt 1992).[19]

Such spiritually powerful cultural property demands careful consideration, including meaningful discussions with those whose heritage is represented. Should these bundles be opened? There are new technologies that provide opportunities for non-invasive research. In the case of a Pawnee sacred family bundle donated to a museum, X-raying it provided an acceptable means to learn of its contents, although it is perhaps surprising who wanted it opened and examined after it had been donated to the Kansas State Historical Society:

> What that next step could be, however, became a source of debate. The donor had given permission to open the bundle, examine the contents, and undertake necessary conservation action. But do scientists have the right to invade a sacred item such as this bundle because of a possible need for conservation and a scientific quest for information, and should these concerns outweigh the issue of sacredness to the Pawnee and other Native American peoples?
>
> *(Good 1989: 5).*

I now raise two important questions about cultural property in the context of the issues brought forward in this chapter. Should we consider not unwrapping the "sacred bundle" of the cultural property values, knowledge, and history that descendant communities wish to keep private or at least control? Can we accept that there are some things that we should not know; and if so, is our existing knowledge of the world threatened or lessened? Respecting this notion of cultural privacy, as it were, is difficult for scholars who are used to having the freedom to pursue any research avenue, let alone the current state of almost instant gratification of networked knowledge access. Yet acknowledging the wishes of descendant communities can often yield unexpected rewards as trust and respect are earned.

I am not suggesting that we stop doing archaeology or research on heritage objects and sites. But I do contend that we must recognize that aspects of Indigenous cultural property often fall outside our familiar frame of reference. What follows is a set of observations that may provide some guidance.

Heritage research for whose sake?

Heritage research has typically been oriented to scientific goals or the refinement of history, with material culture being both the touchstone to, and evidence of, ancient lives. Archaeologists, ethnoarchaeologists, and ethnographers have long worked with local communities to directly observe activities, ask questions, and otherwise glean knowledge of that society. This has greatly enriched anthropology's understanding of the human condition at both large (i.e. generalizing) and local (i.e. identifying diversity) levels. Yet these efforts, which are dependent upon local knowledge, have done little to benefit the descendant communities. Even those approaches oriented to *meaning*, such as phenomenology, are primarily directed to an archaeological audience. One could argue that this represents a type of appropriation of Indigenous knowledge.

There have been efforts to turn this around, generally within the context of postcolonial, critical, Marxist, and Indigenous archaeologies.[20] These theoretical streams acknowledge that heritage holders/descendant communities should have decision-making roles in how their heritage is cared for and preserved, and be the primary beneficiaries of research on or use of their heritage. Many of the examples in the previous section reflect these goals. Some of the familiar elements of ethnographic research can be reformulated to foreground community needs while still yielding new understandings that benefit outside researchers (e.g. Castañeda and Matthews 2008; Edgeworth 2006; Hamilakis and Anagnostopoulos 2009). These can provide more nuanced definitions or approaches to heritage – and the meaning(s) of cultural property – that benefit everyone.

A necessary tension

Anthropologists and anthropologically oriented archaeologists are caught between a commitment to understanding the world, past and present, as fully as possible on the one hand, and respecting the customs, values, and customary laws of the living peoples with whom we work, on the other. Do we foreground the collection, analysis, and curation of cultural property as vestiges of shared human heritage to fulfill scientific needs or public interest? Or do we respect the wishes, needs, and concerns of descendant communities for whom the cultural property may be a vital part of their heritage? These are not always at odds. I explore this situation briefly, not from the usual position of power sharing in heritage decisions, but by relating to what researchers/anthropologists can and should know about values embedded in cultural property.

Indigenous spirituality is one of the most problematic areas of archaeological research that seems tantalizingly out of reach, but an important goal, nevertheless (e.g. Bloch 2014; Hall 1997; Pauketat 2013). But it is an area of great sensitivity and privacy for Indigenous peoples as it is integrally connected to identity, wellbeing, and relationships and responsibilities to a living world.[21] As one Yukon elder states, "It's that real sense of spiritual connection. I don't know where it comes from, but it's part of who we are. Our ancestors are here, you know. You look up the hill there at the gravesite, those are all our ancestors up there. They are here with us today" (Carcross-Tagish First Nation et al. 2016: 37).

There is much to consider about mutual understandings in this realm:

> Spiritualism is a part of indigenous life that most archaeologists reference but few unpack. . . .The concept is applied with three purposes. First, it highlights a cultural arena of historical significance that is contrasted with materialist approaches, although its use acts more like a container for complex ideas than a window into them. Second, it is a placeholder for culturally specific forms of rationality that differ from archaeological expectations based on neo-classic economics (here, spirituality has agency to chart history in unexpected ways). Third, it is a philosophical framework that orients the values and epistemologies in indigenous history. In the majority of cases however, the spiritual content of history is unexplored by archaeologists, serving instead more . . . as a critique of archaeology than an analysis of the history of Indigenous peoples.
>
> *(Martindale and Nicholas 2014: 457)*

Relative to these three points, we can see that the quest for fuller recognition of how knowledge of the original (and current) role of objects or places of spiritual importance is also situated within a suite of political, interpretive, and philosophical positions. This situates all of us – Indigenous or Western – in the awkward position of determining how we can learn about unfamiliar belief systems and rationalities without intruding (further) into business that is not ours. Such tensions should be welcomed as they tend to force action and, in this case, may drive respectful and mutually rewarding conversations about cultural property.

Moving beyond the tangible

As noted above, archaeological research and heritage management are heavily based upon material culture. From a Western perspective, *things* remain the measure of consequence; tangible property continues to the "real" thing. This is ironic as no material culture – no artifact or site – has any meaning without the values that are ascribed to it (Geismar 2013: 2; Nicholas and Hollowell 2007; see also Carman 2005; Waterton and Smith 2009). Consequently, when we are dealing with someone else's cultural property, not having full knowledge or understanding of the cultural context or meaning of what is represented has significant implications.

Beyond finding the means to attain such understanding we also need to consider how we conceive of cultural property at a more fundamental level. In their study of how a Neolithic tomb in England has been interpreted, Chris Fowler and Oliver Harris (2015) make an astute observation of materiality that resonates strongly with the challenges I have outlined. Informed by what they refer to as the new materialism, they refer to (heritage) objects or places not as singular entities but rather as "ever changing *bundles of relations*, to emphasise the way they are constantly fluid and in flux. This has helped overcome an older view of material things simply as inert objects, brought to life only through human agency" (2015: 128, emphasis added).[22]

Such a view has considerable merit in acknowledging that different knowledge systems intersect at the nexus of cultural property, and resonates strongly with perspectives shared by Indigenous peoples (see examples above). Within Indigenous cultural property, those artifacts *do* reflect technological advances, population movement, and evolutionary change as read into them by archaeologists, as much as they reflect the different meanings that Indigenous peoples themselves see in them. Both sets of values and knowledges are present at once; while we may not be able to observe each at the same time,[23] it's not one without the other. A similar position is advanced by Fowler and Harris: "We cannot understand the complexity of the 'world of materials' . . . if we insist that only one mode of analysis is appropriate: modulating between modes – continually reconfiguring phenomena in varying ways – is vital to exploring what things are and can be" (2015: 144–145).

For Indigenous peoples, attaining respect for and protection of cultural property is not an academic exercise in alternative epistemologies, but a pressing need. Their heritage is under constant threat of destruction, appropriation, and commodification. All peoples have a cultural legacy worthy of respect and protection, but in colonial contexts, Indigenous peoples have historically had little control over their own affairs.

Conclusions

Treasured possessions, objects of cultural patrimony, ancient artifacts, traditional knowledge, names, intellectual property, ancestral human remains, animate objects, relationships – these and more are expressions of Indigenous cultural property. Collectively, they express or constitute the history, identity, and values of peoples whose lifeways and worldview may be fundamentally different from those of the dominant society now occupying their traditional lands. Whether in the Americas, Africa, the Pacific, or elsewhere, Indigenous peoples and their heritage have contributed much to Western science, foodways, art, and entertainment, but with little control over, or benefits from such uses.

In this chapter I have examined some of the challenges of caring for indigenous cultural property in the realm of heritage studies. Implicit in this discussion is the need for a fuller understanding of what "heritage" is in different cultural contexts and, importantly, a recognition that in some cases the physical expressions of heritage may be less important to the heritage holders than their intangible aspects. This has presented considerable challenges to protecting Indigenous heritage objects and sites even when protected by law. Overcoming these challenges is not impossible but does require a willingness to think outside the box (of Western values). To develop effective, equitable, and meaningful ways to acknowledge and protect heritage objects, places, and information – whether our own or anyone else's – local values and understandings must be sought out (Hollowell and Nicholas 2009). Whether we speak of "cultural property" or "heritage," ultimately we are dealing with the essence of who people are – and that is something that deserves great care and respect.

Acknowledgements

I thank Haidy Geismar and Jane Anderson for their invitation to develop this chapter, and Sarah Carr-Locke, Catherine Bell, Julie Hollowell, Kelly Bannister, John Welch, Joanne Brown, Alison Brown, Ian Lilley, George Smith, Joe Watkins, Robert Hershey, and Laurajane Smith for ideas, resources, and otherwise assisting with its completion.

Notes

1 Throughout this chapter I use "cultural property" and "cultural heritage" more or less as synonyms, with the latter more encompassing within Indigenous contexts for reasons outlined here (also see Bell and Napoleon 2008; Prott and O'Keefe 1992). I purposefully shy away from the more nuanced or legal aspects of "property" here as defined and applied in Western law and heritage practices, which emphasize material objects (i.e. things).

2 Referring to so-called Fourth World and/or formerly disempowered, or disenfranchised, or colonized peoples who are "marginal or dominated by the states that claim jurisdiction over them" (Maybury-Lewis 2002: 7).

3 Here I distinguish between "archaeology" and "heritage". Archaeology is the study of (past) human behavior through material culture; it is largely focused on the tangible. Heritage, on the other hand, I define as the values and meanings ascribed to or associated with objects and places.

4 For Canada, the legitimacy of such claims is illustrated by a series of landmark court decisions that acknowledge the historic imposition of colonial interests upon First Nations, and seek to provide an alternative framework: in the *Delgamuukw v British Columbia* decision (1997), the Supreme Court of British Columbia recognized the legitimacy of oral histories in land claims, while in *Tsilhqot'in Nation v British Columbia* (2014) the Supreme Court of Canada established Tsilhqot'in land title. While both cases are ostensibly about sovereignty and heritage, there are strong economic forces involved as well.

5 http://portal.unesco.org/en/ev.php-URL_ID=13637&URL_DO=DO_TOPIC&URL_SECTION=201.html (accessed 27 March 2017).

6 http://www.bclaws.ca/Recon/document/ID/freeside/00_96187_01#section13 (accessed 27 March 2017).

7 Michael Klassen (2013: 61) notes: "First Nations are often strong advocates of [the Act], and many recognize its potential for protecting their heritage," given it "has provisions for designating specific 'heritage sites' (potentially including 'traditional use,' ceremonial, or sacred sites)." However, there has been much frustration with efforts to achieve this due to the province's apparent unwillingness to find "solutions to deal with issues arising out of the *HCA* or protecting First Nations sacred/cultural sites ..." (p. 68).

8 There are significant similarities and differences between these countries, in terms of the history of colonization, and its effects upon and responses by Indigenous peoples; Miller (2003) provides an insightful review. There are also differences in heritage policies; in Canada, federal heritage policies are limited, with most responsibilities at the provincial or territorial level. In the United States, there is strong federal legislation for heritage matters, as well as legislative acts that protect Native American interests, including the Native American Graves Protection and Repatriation Act (1990) and the American Indian Religious Freedom Act (1978). Australian heritage is covered by both federal and state or territory laws.

9 Not all museums are able or willing to accommodate such needs (see Brown 2014: 30).

10 In fact, the number of Indigenous individuals who are archaeologists or who are employed in the realm of heritage research/management has been steadily growing worldwide (Nicholas 2010). The notion of archaeologists vs. Indigenous peoples is increasingly artificial and inaccurate.

11 Named places or features of the landscape, which represent where important events took place, are not the equivalent to the names Western societies arbitrarily assign. In the Northwest Territory (Canada),

place-name recording is considered an important aspect of heritage management (http://www.pwnhc.ca/cultural-places/geographic-names/) (accessed 27 March 2017).

12 http://mukurtu.org/about/.nm (accessed 27 March 2017).

13 https://www.rrncommunity.org (accessed 27 March 2017).

14 www.sfu.ca/ipinch. (accessed 27 March 2017).

15 Fifteen such projects were funded by IPinCH, taking place in Canada, the United States, Australia, New Zealand, Kyrgyzstan, and elsewhere. In each case, community values and needs were foregrounded in a ground-up research process; studies were identified by and co-designed with the community, which benefited directly; the community reviewed research products and data to determine what information could be shared, and retained full control of the project. Information on these and the other community projects, including final reports, videos, and other materials, is available at: http://www.sfu.ca/ipinch/project-components/community-based-initiatives. (accessed 27 March 2017).

16 http://www.sfu.ca/ipinch/events/ipinch-events/working-better-together-conference-indigenous-research-ethics/ (accessed 27 March 2017).

17 www.sfu.ca/ipinch/resources/declarations/ancestral-burial-grounds (accessed 27 March 2017).

18 http://www.sfu.ca/ipinch/resources/teaching-resources/think-before-you-appropriate/ (accessed 27 March 2017).

19 This recognition continues today; while at a conference in 2008, I witnessed an Aboriginal man state during a presentation on northern Australian rock art that he "could be killed" for having seen what he was, by custom, not supposed to see of certain images from his territory that had been shown there.

20 See McNiven (2016) for recent review.

21 See Brown (2003); Owen (2008); Nicholas and Wylie (2012) for examples of how Indigenous spiritualism has been appropriated or used in unwelcome or inappropriate ways.

22 As I've noted elsewhere, "Ultimately heritage is not about things; it is about relationships and what these things mean to people" (Nicholas 2015).

23 Fowler and Harris also reference the notion of interdeterminancy, where one can measure either a particle's position or momentum, but not both. This resonates also with Karl Heider's study of the Japanese tea ceremony, where specific actions can be viewed versus the overall milieu, but not both at the same time.

References

Ahmed, Namir, Michael Carter, and Neal Ferris. 2014. Sustainable Archaeology through Progressive Assembly 3D Digitization. *Digital Imaging* 46(1): 137–154.

Atalay, Sonya, Lee Clauss, Randall McGuire, and John Welch (editors). 2014. *Transforming Archaeology: Activist Practices and Prospects*. Left Coast Press, Walnut Creek, CA.

Augustine, Stephen J. 1997. Traditional Aboriginal Knowledge and Science versus Occidental Science. Report for the Biodiversity Convention Office of Environment, Canada.

Battiste, Marie, and James Youngblood Henderson. 2000. *Protecting Knowledge and Heritage: A Global Challenge*. Purich Publishing, Saskatoon, Canada.

Bell, Catherine, and Val Napoleon. 2008. Introduction. In *First Nations Cultural Heritage and Law: Case Studies, Voices, and Perspectives*, edited by Catherine Bell and Val Napoleon, pp. 1–30. UBC Press, Vancouver.

Bell, Catherine, and Robert Paterson (editors). 2009. *Protection of First Nations Cultural Heritage: Laws, Policy, and Reform*. UBC Press, Vancouver.

Bell, Diane. 1998. *Ngarrindjeri Wurruwarrin: A World That Is, Was, and Will Be*. Spinifex Press, North Melbourne.

Berndt, Ronald M., and Catherine H. Berndt. 1992. *The World of First Australians: Traditional Aboriginal Life: Past and Present*. Aboriginal Studies Press, Canberra.

Bloch, Lee J. 2014. The Unthinkable and the Unseen: Community Archaeology and Decolonizing Social Imagination at Okeeheepkee, or the Lake Jackson Site. *Archaeologies* 10(1): 70–106.

Boast, Robin, and Jim Enote. 2013. Virtual Repatriation: It is Neither Virtual nor Repatriation. In *Heritage in the Context of Globalization: Europe and the Americas*, edited by Peter Biehl and Christopher Prescott, pp. 103–116. Springer, New York.

Brady, Liam M., John J. Bradley, and Amanda J. Kearney. 2016. Negotiating Yanyuwa Rock Art: Relational and Affectual Experiences in the Southwest Gulf of Carpentaria, Northern Australia. *Current Anthropology* 57(1): 28–52.

Brown, Alison K. 2014. *First Nations, Museums, Narrations: Stories of the 1929 Franklin Motor Expedition to the Canadian Prairies*. UBC Press, Vancouver.

Brown, Deidre, and George P. Nicholas. 2012. Protecting Indigenous Cultural Property in the Age of Digital Democracy: Institutional and Communal Responses to Canadian First Nations and Maori Heritage Concerns. *Journal of Material Culture* 17(3): 307–324.

Brown, Michael. 2003. *Who Owns Native Culture?* Harvard University Press, Cambridge, MA.

Bruchac, Margaret. 2014. Indigenous Knowledge and Traditional Knowledge. In *Encyclopedia of Global Archaeology*, edited by Claire Smith, pp. 3814–3824. Springer Science and Business Media, New York.

Carman, John. 2005. *Against Cultural Property: Archaeological Heritage and Ownership*. Duckworth, London.

Carcross-Tagish First Nation, Champagne & Aishihik First Nations, Ta'an Kwach'an Council, Tr'ondek Hwech'in First Nation, Sheila Greer, and Catherine Bell. 2016. *Yukon First Nations Heritage Values and Resource Management: Perspectives from Four Yukon First Nations*. IPinCH Project website.

Castañeda, Quetzil, and Christopher N. Matthews. 2008. *Ethnographic Archaeologies: Reflections on Stakeholders and Archaeological Practices*. AltaMira Press, Lanham, MD.

Chapman, Robert, and Alison Wylie (editors). 2015. *Material Culture as Evidence: Best Practices and Exemplary Cases in Archaeology*. Routledge, New York.

Christen, Kimberly. 2006. "Ara Irititja": Protecting the Past, Accessing the Future – Indigenous Memories in a Digital Age. *Museum Anthropology* 29: 56–60.

Culhane, Dara. 1997. *The Pleasure of the Crown: Anthropology, Law and First Nations*. Talonbooks, Burnaby, BC.

Davidson, Ian, C. Lovell-Jones, and R. Bancroft. 1995. *Archaeologists and Aborigines Working Together*. University of New England Press, Armidale, NSW.

Deloria, Vine, Jr. 1967. *Custer Died for Your Sins: An Indian Manifesto*. University of Oklahoma Press, Norman.

Edgeworth, Matt. 2006. *Ethnographies of Archaeological Practice: Cultural Encounters, Material Transformations*. AltaMira Press, Lanham, MD.

Fowler, Chris, and Oliver J. T. Harris. 2015. Enduring Relations: Exploring a Paradox of New Materialism. *Journal of Material Culture* 20(2): 127–148.

Geismar, Haidy. 2013. *Treasured Possessions: Indigenous Interventions into Cultural and Intellectual Property*. Duke University Press, Durham, NC and London.

Geismar, Haidy. 2015. Anthropology and Heritage Regimes. *Annual Review of Anthropology* 44: 71–85.

Good, Diane L. 1989. *Birds, Beads and Bells: Remote Sensing of a Pawnee Sacred Bundle*. Kansas State Historical Society Anthropological Series 15. Kansas Historical Society, Topeka.

Graham, Laurie, and Stephen McJohn. 2005. Indigenous Peoples and Intellectual Property. *Washington University Journal of Law and Policy* 19: 313–337. http://openscholarship.wustl.edu/law_journal_law_policy/vol19/iss1/16.

Guest, Richard. 1996. Intellectual Property Rights and Native American Tribes. *American Indian Law Review* 20(1): 111–139.

Guindon, François (in collaboration with the Neeposh family). 2015. Technology, Material Culture and the Well-Being of Aboriginal Peoples of Canada. *Journal of Material Culture* 20(1): 77–97.

Hall, Robert. 1997. *An Archaeology of the Soul: North American Indian Belief and Ritual*. University of Illinois Press, Ubana.

Hamilakis, Yannis, and Aris Anagnostopoulos (editors). 2009. Archaeological Ethnographies (Special Issue). *Public Archaeology* 8(2–3): 63–317.

Hardesty, Donald L., and Barbara Little. 2009. *Assessing Site Significance: A Guide for Archaeologists and Historians*. AltaMira Press, Lanham, MD.

Harking, Michael E. 2010. Uncommon Ground: Holism and the Future of Anthropology. *Reviews in Anthropology* 39: 25–45.

Harris, Heather. 2005. Indigenous Worldviews and Ways of Knowing as Theoretical and Methodological Foundations for Archaeological Research. In *Indigenous Archaeologies: Decolonizing Theory and Practice*, edited by Claire Smith and H. Martin Wobst, pp. 33–41. Routledge, New York.

Hodder, Ian, Michael Shanks, Alexandra Alexandri, Victor Buchli, John Carman, Jonathan Last, and Gavin Lucas (editors). 1995. *Interpreting Archaeology: Finding Meaning in the Past*. Routledge, New York.

Hollinger, R. Eric, Edwell John, Jr., Harold Jacobs, Lora Moran-Collins, Carolyn Thome, Jonathan Zastrow, Adam Metallo, Günter Waibel, and Vince Rossi. 2013. Tlingit–Smithsonian Collaborations with 3D Digitization of Cultural Objects. *Museum Anthropology Review* 1(1/2): 201–253.

Hollowell, Julie, and George Nicholas. 2009. Using Ethnographic Methods to Articulate Community-Based Conceptions of Cultural Heritage Management. *Public Archaeology* 8(2/3): 141–160.

Isaac, Gwyneira. 2011. Whose Idea Was This?: Museums, Replicas, and the Reproduction of Knowledge. *Current Anthropology* 52(2): 211–233.

Klassen, Michael A. 2013. Indigenous Heritage Stewardship and the Transformation of Archaeological Practice: Two Case Studies from the Mid-Fraser Region of British Columbia. Ph.D. Dissertation, Department of Archaeology. Simon Fraser University, Burnaby, BC.

Kuprecht, Karolina. 2014. *Indigenous People's Cultural Property Claims: Repatriation and Beyond*. Springer, New York and London.

Loomis, Ormond (coordinator). 1983. *Cultural Conservation: The Protection of Cultural Heritage in the United States*. American Folklife Center, Library of Congress, and National Park Service, Department of the Interior.

Lydon, Jane, and Uzma Rizvi (editors). 2010. *Handbook of Postcolonial Archaeologies*. Left Coast Press, Walnut Creek, CA.

Lyons, Natasha. 2013. *Where the Wind Blows Us: Practicing Critical Community Archaeology in the Canadian North*. University of Arizona Press, Tucson.

McLay, Eric, Kelly Bannister, Leah Joe, Brian Thom, and George Nicholas. 2008. A'lhut tu tet Sul'h-weentst "Respecting the Ancestors": Understanding Hul'qumi'num Heritage Laws and Concerns for Protection of Archaeological Heritage. In *First Nations Cultural Heritage and Law: Cases Studies, Voices and Perspectives*, edited by Catherine Bell and Val Napoleon, pp. 158–202. UBC Press, Vancouver.

McNiven, Ian. 2016. Theoretical Challenges of Indigenous Archaeology: Setting an Agenda. *American Antiquity* 81(1): 27–41.

Maina, Charles Kamau. 2011. Power Relations in the Traditional Knowledge Debate: A Critical Analysis of Forums. *International Journal of Cultural Property* 18: 143–178.

Martindale, Andrew, and George Nicholas. 2014. Wayfinding: Archaeology as Federated Knowledge. *Canadian Journal of Archaeology* 38(2): 434–465.

Mason, Ronald J. 2006. *Inconstant Companions: Archaeology and North American Indian Oral Traditions*. University of Alabama Press, Tuscaloosa.

Maybury-Lewis, David. 2002. *Indigenous Peoples, Ethnic Groups, and the State*. Allyn and Bacon, Boston.

Merrill, W. L., E. J. Ladd, and T. J. Ferguson. 1993. The Return of the "Ahayu:da": Lessons for Repatriation from Zuni Pueblo and the Smithsonian Institution. *Current Anthropology* 34(5): 523–568.

Miller, Bruce G. 2003. *Invisible Indigenes: The Politics of Nonrecognition*. University of Nebraska Press, Lincoln.

Ngata, Wayne, Hera Ngata-Gibson, and Amiria Salmond. 2012. Te Ataakura: Digital Taonga and Cultural Innovation. *Journal of Material Culture* 17: 229–244.

Nicholas, George P. (editor). 2010. *Being and Becoming Indigenous Archaeologists*. Left Coast Press, Walnut Creek, CA.

Nicholas, George P. 2014. Indigenous Archaeology ("Archaeology, Indigenous"). In *Oxford Bibliography of Anthropology*, edited by J. L. Jackson. Oxford University Press, Oxford.

Nicholas, George P. 2015. Why Heritage is Not Just About "Things." TEDx talk: https://www.youtube.com/watch?v=HbPLXTJwVMY&list=PLjMPDTlr8hYk3cIx-Xa00FR3uAde6VnK6.

Nicholas, George P. 2017. Culture, Rights, Indigeneity, and Intervention: Addressing Inequality in Indigenous Heritage Protection and Control. In *Archaeologies of "Us" and "Them" – Debating the Ethics and Politics of Ethnicity and Indigeneity in Archaeology and Heritage Discourse*, edited by C. Hillerdal, A. Karlström, and C.-G. Ojala, pp. 199–216. Routledge, London and New York.

Nicholas, George P., and Thomas D. Andrews (editors). 1997. *At a Crossroads: Archaeology and First Peoples in Canada*. SFU Archaeology Press, Burnaby, CA.

Nicholas, George P., and Julie Hollowell. 2007. Ethical Challenges to a Postcolonial Archaeology. In *Archaeology and Capitalism: From Ethics to Politics*, edited by Y. Hamilakas and P. Duke, pp. 59–82. Left Coast Press, Walnut Creek, CA.

Nicholas, George P., and Nola M. Markey. 2014. Traditional Knowledge, Archaeological Evidence, and Other Ways of Knowing. In *Material Culture as Evidence: Best Practices and Exemplary Cases in Archaeology*, edited by R. Chapman and A. Wylie, pp. 287–307. Routledge, New York.

Nicholas, George P., and Alison Wylie. 2012. "Do Not Do Unto Others. . .": Cultural Misrecognition and the Harms of Appropriation in an Open-Source World. In *Appropriating the Past: Philosophical Perspectives on Archaeological Practice*, edited by Robin Coningham and Geoffrey Scarre, pp. 195–221. Cambridge University Press, Cambridge and New York.

Nicholas, George P., Brian Egan, Kelly Bannister, and Emily Benson. 2015. Intervention as a Strategy in Protecting Indigenous Cultural Heritage. *The SAA Archaeological Record* 15(4): 41–47.

Noble, Brian. 2008. Owning as Belonging/Owning as Property: The Crisis of Power and Respect in First Nations Heritage Transactions with Canada. In *First Nations Cultural Heritage and Law: Case Studies, Voices, and Perspectives*, edited by Catherine Bell and Val Napoleon, pp. 465–488. UBC Press, Vancouver.

Noble, Brian, Arthur Manual, and Emma Feltes. 2016. Secwepemc Territorial Authority Honoring Secwepemc Land and Knowledges, Laws as Peoples' Heritage. IPinCH Project.

O'Brien, Michael J., R. Lee Lyman, and Michael B. Schiffer. 2005. *Archaeology as a Process: Processualism and its Progeny*. University of Utah Press, Salt Lake City.

Owen, Suzanne. 2008. *The Appropriation of Native American Spirituality*. Continuum, London and New York.

Pauketat, Timothy R. 2013. *An Archaeology of the Cosmos: Rethinking Agency and Religion in Ancient America*. Routledge, New York.

Peacock, Celmara, David Collett, and Linda Baulch. 2015. Assessing Stories before Sites: Identifying the Tangible from the Intangible. *International Journal of Heritage Studies* 21(10): 962–982.

Peers, Laura, and Alison K. Brown (editors). 2003. *Museums and Source Communities: A Routledge Reader*. Routledge, New York.

Prott, Lyndel V., and Patrick J. O'Keefe. 1992. "Cultural Heritage" or "Cultural Property." *International Journal of Cultural Property* 1(2): 307–320.

Pullman, Daryl, and George Nicholas. 2011. Intellectual Property and the Ethical/Legal Status of Human DNA: The (Ir)Relevance of Context. *Inuit Studies* 35(1/2): 146–164.

Riley, Mary (editor). 2004. *Indigenous Intellectual Property Rights: Legal Obstacles and Innovative Solutions*. AltaMira Press, Walnut Grove, CA.

Sable, T. 2011. Legends as Maps. In *Ta'n Wetapeksi'k: Understanding from Where We Come*, edited by T. Bernard, L. M. Rosenmeier, and S. Farrell. Eastern Woodland Publishing, Truro, NS.

Schaepe, David M., Susan Rowley, Stó:lō Xyolhmet S'olhetawtxw Sq'éq'ip (Stó:lō House of Respect Committee) Members, with Darlene Weston, and Mike Richards. 2015. *The Journey Home – Guiding Intangible Knowledge Production in the Analysis of Ancestral Remains*.

Skeates, Robin, Carol McDavid, and John Carman. 2012. *The Oxford Handbook of Public Archaeology*. Oxford University Press, Oxford.

Smith, Claire, and H. Martin Wobst. 2005. *Indigenous Archaeologies: Decolonizing Theory and Practice*. Routledge, New York.

Solomon, Maui, and Susan Thorpe. 2012. Taonga Moriori: Recording and Revival. *Journal of Material Culture* 17(3): 245–263.

Spector, Janet. 1993. *What this Awl Means: Feminist Archaeology at a Wahpeton Dakota Village*. Minnesota Historical Society Press, St. Paul.

Srinivas, Krishna Ravi. 2012. Protecting Traditional Knowledge Holder's Interests and Preventing Misappropriation – Traditional Knowledge Commons and Biocultural Protocols: Necessary but Not Sufficient. *International Journal of Cultural Property* 19: 401–422.

Sto:lo Nation and Sto:lo Research and Resource Management Centre. 2012. Man Turned to Stone: T'swelåtse. Chilliwack, British Columbia.

Swidler, Nina, Kurt E. Dongoske, Roger Anyon, and Alan S. Downer (editors). 1997. *Native Americans and Archaeologists: Stepping Stones to Common Ground*. AltaMira Press, Walnut Grove, CA.

TallBear, Kim. 2013. *Native American DNA: Tribal Belonging and the False Promise of Genetic Science*. University of Minnesota Press, Minneapolis.

Thorpe, Susan, and Maui Solomon. 2015. Moriori Cultural Data Base: IPinCH Case Study Final Report. Hokoteki Moriori Trust and IPinCH Project.

Vega, Margaret Brown. 2015. Ritual Practices and Wrapped Objects: Unpacking Prehispanic Andean Sacred Bundles. *Journal of Material Culture* (published Oct. 2015).

Waterton, Emma, and Laurajane Smith. 2009. There Is No Such Thing as Heritage. In *Taking Archaeology Out of Heritage*, edited by Emma Waterton and Laurajane Smith, pp. 10–27. Cambridge Scholars Publishing, Cambridge.

Wilson, Jordan. 2015. Belongings in "c̓əsnaʔəm: the city before the city." IPinCH website: http://www.sfu.ca/ipinch/outputs/blog/citybeforecitybelongings%20.

PART III

Local histories

Jane Anderson and Haidy Geismar

In this section we present a global perspective on cultural property by illuminating its very local histories. As described in the Introduction, discourses and legal framings of cultural property emerged in Europe and were exported around the world through colonial empires. Law was not just a vital form of colonial governance, it was also a form of cultural colonization, defining and privileging colonial values, using key legal categories (like property for instance) as a way of shaping colonial subjectivities, erasing local values and political systems and even suppressing local languages. However, despite the totalizing aim of the colonial project, it was impossible to entirely eradicate cultural and political systems of meaning and governance (Deloria 1969; Comaroff and Comaroff 1991, 1997; Chatergee 1994; Mamdani 1996; Merry 2000; Dirks 2001; Stoler 1995, 2003). In turn, a Eurocentric focus on this colonial period obscures both local histories in the negotiation of colonial logics and power as well as processes of empire building in other parts of the world (Mignolo 2011; Byrd 2011; Geismar 2013). The four chapters here are presented to provincialize the dominant narrative of cultural property that comes largely from European contexts and draws our attention to the need for alternative accounts of cultural property that have their origin in other parts of the world (Anzuldúa 1987; Chakrabarty 2000).

As we argued in the Introduction, although cultural property has its antecedents in early Renaissance and Enlightenment histories in Europe, its current usage and politics is a product of modernity, specifically from the 1870s onwards, with particular international engagement and consensus building in the mid- to late twentieth century. As a distinctly modern figure then, cultural property is made and remade through the politics, economics, global designs and relationships of state and non-state parties during this period. But not all of these move in the same direction or with the same influence. Here we want to redirect and refocus by considering alternative non-European state engagements with cultural property.

In his work unravelling the persistent forms of colonialism woven into our globalized present, Walter Mignolo argues that there are three types of critiques of modernity. The first, postmodernity, is internal to the history of Europe and as such functions as a Eurocentric critique even though its reach is global. The other two types (dewesternization and decoloniality) emerged from "non-European histories entangled with western modernity" (2011: xii), and whilst they now also reach into multiple sites, they derive from very particular experiences of modernity. In pointing to the differentiated standpoints for current critiques of modernity, Mignolo is pointing to the significance of locality in shaping forms of knowledge production. In conversation with theorists like Jean and John Comaroff, Arturo Escobar and Jodi Byrd, Mignolo helps us reframe the question to ask: how might the geopolitics of knowing cultural property shift if we change the direction of the gaze (Escobar 2008; Mignolo 2000, 2011; Comaroff and Comaroff 2012; Byrd 2011)?

In her chapter, Sandra Rozental considers the interface between international discourses of cultural property and the hybrid conception of 'patrimonio', which emerged in Mexico as a particular synthesis of Spanish colonialism and an indigenously inflected Mexican nationalism. She teases apart the language of 'patrimonio' and how this has been strategically mobilized by the Mexican state in the production of a national identity that incorporates a pre-Hispanic past. In demonstrating this point, Rozental looks at both the language and logic of Mexican cultural property legislation alongside a very specific example of the taking of a pre-Hispanic artifact from the town of Coatlinchan for public display in the National Museum. This cooption of the Indigenous by the nation, to generate a state identity that is Indigenous, not necessarily in solidarity with the politics of local communities, but in terms of the meta-Indigenous category produced for the international community, is a common story – reflected in contributions in this volume from Australia, New Zealand and the United States. Rozental illustrates why it is important to look to the ways in which cultural property discourse is translated into local idioms and to understand the history and resonance of terms like 'patrimonio'. Local histories of cultural property signify the multivalence and hybridity that is built into the category from the beginning. This becomes more evident if we look carefully at the way it is adopted, reframed and re-positioned within non European nation-states in the present day.

Shu-li Wang and Michael Rowlands' chapter considers the shifts in the politics of cultural property from a Chinese perspective. The heritage boom in China over the past 25 years has led to a significant increase in the number of museums built and heritage sites established, as well as a surge of new collecting and arts markets. Initiated through changing ideologies around private property, Wang and Rowlands argue that this expansion of the heritage and museum industry has been encouraged by the state as part of a pursuit of the production of collective memory and as efforts towards very specific patriotic education in an era of rapid globalizing change. Cultural property here is being used as a tool to secure a sense of internal collectivity that reaches back into a long dynastic history of meaning-making about what it is to be Chinese. Consequently there are very specific cultural references and points of departure, but in the present it is also being successfully merged with dominant UNESCO categories and definitions. With this translation from a Chinese context into the international bureaucratic framing, there is a transformation in the meaning of cultural property that is occurring for the Chinese art market and also for the future shape of Chinese collective memory.

Morag Kersel's chapter asks whether artifacts are the common heritage of humankind or whether specific communities or nations have proprietary rights to this material. By presenting an overview of her research in the Middle East, Kersel juxtaposes the dynamic of the movement of objects across the region, with the more statist and static language of UNESCO. Kersel rightly identifies the tensions that exist in local understandings of exchange and that version which is embodied in UNESCO conventions. Kersel's own project tracks sets of pots and basalt bowls distributed globally through an innovative exchange from the Bab adh Dhra' tomb in Jordon, and exposes the unruliness of object movements across state borders through the market, as well as through archaeological and museum exchanges. Kersel cautions us to read UNESCO and other cultural property legislation as a policy of movement as much as restriction, which both advocates for a regulated but important flow of objects, and limits that flow within the boundaries of states. In this way, the capacity of objects to truly be 'cultural ambassadors and messengers' has limits.

Boatema Boateng also takes up the question of the capacity for state adaptation and adoption of international policy frameworks, in particular by considering the colonial histories of intellectual property law and copyright. Boateng is interested in exposing the cultural entanglements of intellectual property law and the powerful transformation of African ideas of culture, creativity, individual ownership, authorship and possession that came through the colonial importation of this body of law. Intellectual property law is intimately bound up with histories of empire and colonization, and Boateng's work is a welcome addition to the increasing attention to colonial copyright and the different experiences of its implementation, co-development and appropriation in non-European contexts (see Bently 2007; Anderson 2009). Boateng argues that the European conceptions of history and time, which placed Africans outside both, continue to affect how this European body of law operates. Illustrating this point in the context of Ghana, Boateng makes the poignant point that even through the experiences of decolonization and independence, this colonial legal structure, as incompatible and inadequate as it was and remains, has been very difficult to shift and change. This has had significant consequences for how an independent Ghana conceptualizes its ideas of culture, its properties and its ownership.

In all these chapters, UNESCO and its conventions and bureaucracy function as a certain 'centre' that is increasingly being destabilized. Localizing cultural property does not necessarily mean taking UNESCO out of the frame. Instead UNESCO is being dislodged as the primary locus of knowledge production. How cultural property has been made in non-European contexts and the various efforts to decolonize that concept (which is also a feature of other chapters in this volume) remains a critical project for the future of cultural property. What these chapters illustrate and also grapple with, is how, even in the local histories, a globalized category of cultural property continues to maintain considerable power to effect and produce new forms of global nationalism which depend upon very specific ideas of culture.

Bibliography

Anderson, Jane E. 2009. *Law, Knowledge, Culture: The Production of Indigenous Knowledge in Intellectual Property Law*. Cheltenham, UK: Edward Elgar.

Anzuldúa, Gloria. 1987. *Borderlands/La Frontera: The New Metiza*. San Francisco, CA: Aunt Lute Books.

Bently, Lionel. 2007. "Copyright, Translations and Relations between Britain and India in the Nineteenth and Early Twentieth Centuries." *Chicago Kent Law Review* 82(3): 1181–1240.

Byrd, Jodi. 2011. *The Transit of Empire: Indigenous Critiques of Colonialism*. Minneapolis: University of Minnesota Press.

Chakrabarty, Dipesh. 2000. *Provincializing Europe: Postcolonial Thought and Historical Difference*. Princeton, NJ: Princeton University Press.

Chattergee, Partha. 1994. *The Nation and Its Fragments: Colonial and Postcolonial Histories*. Princeton, NJ: Princeton University Press.

Comaroff, Jean, and John Comaroff. 1991. *Of Revelation and Revolution: Christianity, Colonialism and Consciousness in South Africa (Volume One)*. Chicago: University of Chicago Press.

Comaroff, Jean, and John Comaroff. 2012. *Theory from the South: Or, How Euro America is Evolving Towards Africa*. Boulder, CO: Paradigm Publishers.

Comaroff, John, and Jean Comaroff. 1997. *Of Revelation and Revolution: Christianity, Colonialism and Consciousness in South Africa (Volume Two)*. Chicago: University of Chicago Press.

Deloria, Vine, 1969. *Custer Died for Your Sins*. New York: Macmillan.

Dirks, Nicholas. 2001. *Castes of Mind: Colonialism and the Making of Modern India*. Princeton, NJ: Princeton University Press.

Escobar, Arturo. 2008. *Territories of Difference: Place, Movements, Life, Redes*. Durham, NC: Duke University Press.
Geismar, Haidy. 2013. *Treasured Possessions: Indigenous Interventions into Cultural and Intellectual Property*. Durham, NC: Duke University Press.
Mamdani, Mahmood. 1996. *Citizen and Subject: Contemporary Africa and the Legacy of Late Colonialism*. Princeton, NJ: Princeton University Press.
Merry, Sally. 2000. *Colonizing Hawaii: The Cultural Power of Law*. Princeton, NJ: Princeton University Press.
Mignolo, Walter. 2000. *Local Histories/Global Designs: Coloniality, Subaltern Knowledges and Border Thinking*. Princeton, NJ: Princeton University Press.
Mignolo, Walter. 2011. *The Darker Side of Western Modernity: Global Futures and Decolonial Options*. Durham, NC: Duke University Press.
Stoler, Ann Laura. 1995. *Race and the Education of Desire: Foucault's History of Sexuality and the Colonial Order of Things*. Durham, NC: Duke University Press.
Stoler, Ann Laura. 2003. *Carnal Knowledge and Imperial Power: Race and the Intimate in Colonial Rule*. Berkeley: University of California Press.

12

ON THE NATURE OF PATRIMONIO

"Cultural property" in Mexican contexts

Sandra Rozental

Introduction

In January 2010, Mexico's National Institute of Anthropology and History (INAH) threatened to sue Starbucks for using images of pre-Hispanic artefacts and monuments on promotional materials designed for the Mexican market. In a radio interview, the INAH spokesperson, Julio Castrejón,[1] stated that Starbucks' use of the images of the Aztec Calendar Stone and the Teotihuacan Moon Pyramid on a set of mugs was a "scandal," given that the corporation had not asked for the appropriate permissions, or paid royalties to reproduce objects belonging to Mexico's patrimony or *patrimonio*, framed as the nation's "cultural property." Although the use of the images on the mugs was not seen as desecrating Mexico's ancient heritage – a punishable offense under federal law – the INAH argued that these things belonged to the Mexican people and, therefore, any commercial use or reproduction was subject to state regulation, approval, and compensation.

The Spanish term patrimonio condenses both its English equivalents "heritage" and "inheritance" while also indexing the patriarchal power relations that have historically ensured the existence of the Mexican state. "Patrimonio," therefore, does different kinds of work than "heritage" or "inheritance" because it is also made up of the "pater" of "patria" and, thus, implies the Mexican state's political sovereignty over certain lands and their assets, as well as over its citizens (Lomnitz 2001: 9–11). Patrimonio legislation regulates ancient artefacts and monuments, as well as other kinds of matter found in the subsoil like oil, water, and mineral ores, as public property that cannot be owned by individual or collective bodies other than the Mexican state. These materials, formerly the property of the Spanish king who based the colonial project on the exploitation of subsoil resources, are considered the enduring, timeless, and inalienable substances that sustain the Mexican national project (Azuela 2011). However, under Mexican law, not all substances that make up national patrimonio are treated equally: unlike oil or minerals, pre-Hispanic remains are considered "inalienable possessions" (Weiner 1992). Because their retention is crucial to national culture, these objects cannot ever be exchanged, not even by the Mexican state.[2]

In most policy documents and public discourse, much like in the 2010 Starbucks case, the Mexican state's patrimonio claims have been translated as "cultural property" or "cultural heritage" following UNESCO guidelines and the language of prominent international cases calling for the repatriation of objects from international museums and collections. In the early 1980s, for example, Mexico negotiated the restitution of a set of Teotihuacan murals bequeathed to the Fine Arts Museum of San Francisco by a private collector upon his death through appeals to the ethics of returning Mexico's "cultural property" to its citizens (Seligman 1999; Berrin 1988). More recently, the INAH mobilized the language of "repatriation of national cultural property" to secure the return of early colonial manuscripts from the Bible Society Collection in the United Kingdom to Mexico's National Anthropology Museum as part of the Institute's seventieth-anniversary celebrations.[3]

Whereas the Mexican government has appealed to the category of "cultural property" in cases where multinational corporations have used images of artefacts considered patrimonio without the necessary permissions or compensations, as well as to demand the return of artefacts illegitimately appropriated by foreign states, international museums, and private collectors, the language of cultural property is almost non-existent within Mexico to describe specific communities' or groups' claims to objects and sites. As Castrejón admitted in the 2010 interview cited above, many establishments, companies, towns, collective bodies, and private persons make use of ancient sites, objects, and their likenesses.[4] This diversity of appropriations is in fact fostered by the ways in which patrimonio works as a kind of public property that belongs to all Mexicans alike, even though, by law, the sole body responsible for administering, caring for, and enforcing property rights over patrimonial things is the Mexican state. As Jane Anderson has argued, law is a rich field of study because it is far less stable and consistent than it is often believed to be (2009). As I will show, in Mexico, the ambiguities and contradictions of patrimonio laws, namely with regard to how these laws establish distinctions between "nature" and "culture," in fact produce complicated and overlapping claims to ancient sites and artefacts.

Unlike in many settler-colonial contexts where distinct indigenous sovereignties have been formally recognized and can, thus, use legal frameworks to claim rights and require the repatriation of significant objects (Fforde, Hubert and Turnbull 2002; Fine-Dare 2002; Myers 2004; Turnbull and Pickering 2010; Geismar 2013), in Mexico, such claims are complicated by the state's appropriation of indigeneity, and specifically of pre-Hispanic indigenous material culture, as the tangible inheritance of all Mexicans. Unlike Aboriginal reserves in Canada, Native nations in the United States, and semi-autonomous Aboriginal lands in Australia, in Mexico there are no separate sovereignties, indigenous or otherwise, recognized by Mexican law, that could legally claim objects or monuments defined as national property or patrimonio. All Mexicans, regardless of their ethnic identity, linguistic group, way of life, or religious affiliation, are by law considered to share a common ancestry, rooted equally in the country's indigenous and Spanish colonial legacies. Indigenous artefacts from the pre-Hispanic past are, therefore, legally owned, administered, and managed by the Mexican state as the entire nation's property and collective cultural legacy. As such, the Mexican state has the power to expropriate monuments and remove artefacts from local contexts in favor of their exhibition as patrimonio in public institutions. In turn, specific communities have mobilized practices and appealed to idioms outside national legal registers to sustain their claims on territories, sites, and objects they consider key components of local history and community identification (Castañeda 2009; Liffman 2011; Morehart 2012).

In this chapter, I show how the Mexican regime of patrimonio denies the possibility of idioms of cultural property on national soil by legally separating artefacts and monuments as "culture" from the lands where they are found, as well from their social and environmental contexts. In law and in practice, the regime of patrimonio assumes the existence of clear-cut boundaries between nature and culture by detaching objects considered the tangible instantiations of national "culture" from their locations and source communities. Through this legal extrication that does not necessarily represent the actual entanglements of objects and sites, the state denies actors' local claims, property rights, and other kinds of attachments to ancient indigenous material culture.

This legal bind has led to cases of property disputes over pre-Hispanic artefacts and sites that have been well documented since the beginning of archaeological practice in the nineteenth century and continue to this day. Perhaps the most famous and conflict-laden example concerns the site and ruins of Chichen Itzá in the Yucatán Peninsula. The site, recently declared one of the new Seven Wonders of the World, was privately owned for much of its history and has been subject to conflicting claims since the early twentieth century (Castañeda 1996; Breglia 2006). Only a few years ago, the state government of Yucatán purchased the site as a major profit-generating tourist attraction. The sites of Teotihuacan in the Central Valley and of Cholula in Puebla have also attracted much media attention as residents have been fighting government-sponsored commercial initiatives and development projects seeking to transform land associated to the sites into a Walmart in the case of Teotihuacan, and a series of public infrastructure projects, namely highways and overpasses, in Puebla. These cases have all been very controversial because the state's legal responsibility to protect patrimonial objects and sites is embedded in a long history of nation-making. In these cases, however, the state is complicit with capitalist enterprises seeking to commercialize patrimonio.

Patrimony as national property and as a central feature of nationalism based on a kind of Western "possessive individualism" has been the subject of both anthropological and legal studies (Handler 1988; Merryman 1986, 1989) and of literatures that have explored what "having" or "owning" culture entails (Brown 2003, 2004). More recent work has been done to analyse what the limits of cultural property and heritage might look like in contemporary contexts (Dent 2009; Forsyth 2010; Coombe and Lewis 2011; Collins 2015; Kaltmeier and Rufer 2016).[5] Following Rosemary Coombe's argument that cultural property laws and practices are always simultaneously prohibiting, constitutive, and enabling of alternative agendas (1998, 2009), I look at the effects of patrimonio in Mexican contexts as a paradox: both as a body of laws and a set of practices that claim certain objects, sites, and substances as the public property and collective "cultural" inheritance of all Mexicans, and, at the same time, as the sole property of the Mexican state that can consequently dispossess specific communities and cordon sites off from local contexts in favor of the nation.

I show how the history of Mexico's legislation regarding pre-Hispanic artefacts and de facto claims to such vestiges by a variety of social actors and collectivities – including the Mexican state – complicate the translation and the assumed equivalence between "cultural property" and patrimonio. As Katherine Verdery and Caroline Humphrey state in the introduction to their edited volume *Property in Question*, the use of the language of property in cultural property cases implies a "politics of recognition" that assumes a unity between a people and things that has in turn been mobilized in postcolonial contexts to reclaim objects illegitimately removed from indigenous and other communities (2004: 7). Yet, in Mexico, pre-Hispanic objects are considered the material instantiations of national identity and have been legally construed as the tangible inheritance of the Mexican people as a whole, regardless of historical, regional and local differences, largely ignoring competing claims to artefacts.

I focus on the town of San Miguel Coatlinchan, famous for the forced removal of a colossal pre-Hispanic stone carving in the 1960s and its relocation to the National

Anthropology Museum as national patrimonio, to ethnographically illustrate how Mexican patrimonio in fact differs significantly from conventional understandings of "cultural property," thereby urging us to think critically about the latter's appropriateness as a global category. Coatlinchan is a town located in Mexico City's ever-growing eastern periphery. In the current Mexican political and legal context, its residents cannot use property law to assert their claims over pre-Hispanic artefacts, or over their territories. Nevertheless, *Tlacuaches*,[6] as the town residents are known in the area, claim those rights through patrimonio and the affective and ecological ties that they have historically sustained with ancient material culture found on their lands. Teasing out the competing claims that emerged following the monolith's removal as patrimonio, I show how objects from Mexico's past that have been legally produced as the nation's "cultural property," that is, as separate, authentic, and singular artefacts that are intrinsically linked to the nation, are in fact bound to, and embedded in, landscapes, social worlds, and ecological relationships that exceed their designation not just as national property, but as a kind of property located in a distinct realm referred to as "culture."

How pre-Hispanic remains became the "cultural" property of the nation

Historians of Mexico have shown that pre-Hispanic ruins have not always been claimed as Mexico's national heritage, or been subject to laws framing ancient indigenous monuments and artefacts as the inalienable property of the nation (Brading 1985; López Caballero 2008; Bueno 2010, 2016). Patrimonio legislation has evolved over time to produce pre-Hispanic material

Figure 12.1 The Coatlinchan monolith at the National Anthropology Museum's entrance.
Source: Photo by Sandra Rozental, 2011.

culture as intrinsically linked to national identity, crafting a relatively recent separation between these material remains imagined as having "cultural" value and other kinds of patrimonial things, substances, and places legally defined as "nature" or "natural" kinds of resources.

During colonial times and well into the eighteenth century, New Spain's elites were keen on adopting metropolitan traditions through the use of Spanish-style dress, religion, and forms of cultural production. Pre-Hispanic objects were largely destroyed out of fear of indigenous idolatry, although some were collected and studied as curiosities (Achim forthcoming). It was not until the nineteenth century that New Spain creoles began to use indigenous legacies to justify their secession from Spain and legitimate their claims to their New World territories (Brading 1991). Yet, the designation of pre-Hispanic material culture as legally defined national heritage would take place much later in the nineteenth century (Tenorio 1996), and consolidate in the first decades of the twentieth century in the aftermath of the Mexican Revolution (Brading 1988, 2001).

The changing status of pre-Hispanic materials can be traced through the various legal configurations and developing protocols for managing these objects. The first laws that controlled pre-Hispanic vestiges were drafted in the wake of the early nineteenth-century fascination with antiquities. At the same time as the ruins of ancient Greek and Roman civilizations were being excavated in Europe, Mexico's ancient artefacts became scientific specimens and valuable collectibles. Following Mexican Independence in 1821, the first republican legislation to protect ancient monuments was drafted in 1827. These laws were created not so much to care for these objects as inherently tied to national identity, but to control their export and lucrative markets on an international scale, alongside raw materials like gold and silver ore and cochineal that had before been considered the Spanish king's patrimony and were the main sources of the empire's economic prosperity (Lombardo de Ruiz 1988; Cottom 2008).

Legal scholar Norma Rojas Delgadillo argues that the separation between "natural" and "cultural" patrimonio was consolidated only in the first decades of the twentieth century as pre-Hispanic vestiges became the inalienable possessions of the Mexican nation (2006). Following the Mexican Revolution, in 1914, the Law on the Conservation of Historical and Artistic Monuments and Areas of Natural Beauty was the first to systematically claim the state's ownership and responsibility over patrimonio as intrinsically linked to national identity. In 1916, the Law on the Conservation of Historical and Artistic Monuments, Buildings, Churches and Objects gave further authority to the state by giving it the power to expropriate monuments and objects deemed of national significance from private hands and from other collectivities such as corporate towns. These laws, however, did not contain specifications regarding the land monuments and objects were found in, or any other kind of natural formation that ruins might be associated with. The case of the Chichen Itzá cenote, a body of water that was dredged at the turn of the twentieth century by Edward H. Thompson, the owner of the land the site was located on, to extract pre-Hispanic objects, led to a legal battle that lasted several decades precisely because the cenote was considered a natural formation, rather than a man-made part of the ancient Maya city (Coggins and Ladd 1992; Lerner 2001). Patrimonio laws, thus, created tensions and property disputes because they imagined a fixed distinction between "natural" formations and "cultural" productions that did not account for the ambiguous status of many sites located on specific territories.

In the 1930s, state control over pre-Hispanic artefacts was reinforced via new laws that made monuments as well as certain landscapes and "areas of natural beauty" of "public interest" given their historical, archaeological, or aesthetic value (Rojas Delgadillo 2006; Cottom 2008: 207–213). These laws really emphasized the public quality of certain monuments and artefacts that were by then key to the national project. The state's role was then to make these sites and artefacts accessible to all Mexicans through their transfer and display in public institutions such as museums or their securing inside INAH-run archaeological sites.

In the 1970s, Mexico strengthened the separation between "natural" and "cultural" patrimonio by signing the 1970 UNESCO Convention on the Means of Prohibiting the Illicit Import, Export and Transfer of Ownership of Cultural Property and the 1972 UNESCO Convention Concerning the Protection of the World Cultural and Natural Heritage. These international protocols furthered the separation of "cultural" heritage from other kinds of "natural" and "biological" heritage through their distinct definitions in Articles 1 and 2 of the 1972 UNESCO Convention.[7] These definitions were adopted by Mexican legislators, separating Mexico's "cultural" and "natural" heritage, and the government bodies responsible for each. Article 73 of the Constitution subsequently placed cultural property under the jurisdiction of "cultural" bodies such as the Ministry of Education, the INAH and other educational institutions, whereas "natural" patrimony became the responsibility of the Ministry of Healthcare and Assistance in charge of safeguarding Mexico's environment.[8]

Mexico's participation in instruments of international law was not legally binding, but rather part of a broader strategy to position the country and its culture on a world stage. Through travelling exhibitions and pavilions designed to promote Mexico at International Exhibitions and World's Fairs, as well as the staging of the 1968 Olympics in Mexico City, the Mexican government sought to transform the image of Mexico as a modern, yet culturally singular destination, a place where state-of the art infrastructure met the indigenous exotic (Kuri 2003; Zolov 2004; Castañeda 2014; Cruz Porchini 2016). In the translation from UNESCO conventions to state legislation, cultural property and national heritage came to be conflated in Mexican patrimonio. Translation, in this case, is not a rendering-equivalent, but rather, a local adaptation, a forging-into-being of a genre of legislation that would help produce Mexico as a worthy and respectful player on a world stage.

Today, Article 27 of the Mexican Constitution is the main legal body that regulates national patrimonio understood as land, water, mineral ores, and oil, and "natural wealth" such as forests and national parks, although the latter are subject to many ambiguities and irregularities (Azuela 2011). Other legislation protects tangible and intangible patrimonio cast as having "cultural value" or as central to the production and reproduction of "national identity." Article 73, section XXV of the Mexican Constitution makes Congress responsible for safeguarding monuments of archaeological, historical, or artistic value, in collaboration with state, municipal and local authorities and institutions. The federal government, however, has jurisdiction over these other instances. Indeed, in contemporary legislation, pre-Hispanic vestiges continue to exist as "cultural" matter in need of protection, conservation, and display by the Mexican state, the sole owner and body responsible for caring for and preserving patrimonio. Legally, the INAH can regulate and authorize ancient artefacts' travel to temporary exhibitions to promote Mexican culture abroad, can receive payments for the use of images and even authorize "official reproductions" of monuments, buildings, and sites, but cannot sanction these objects' sale or exchange given their legal status as the inalienable and tangible "cultural" instantiations of the nation. Cultural property has, thus, legally been produced as separate from other kinds of patrimonio treated as natural resources and assets that, like oil, are public property, but whose exchange and resulting profits are key to sustaining the nation economically.

Who owns Mexico's ancient past?

As the INAH spokesperson stated in the 2010 interview regarding the Starbucks case, regulating patrimonio is extremely difficult in Mexico. In the interview, Castrejón mentions the vast number of stalls, restaurants, shops, and hotels all over the country that call themselves after a pre-Hispanic site or people, or use images of iconic artefacts as logos on T-shirts and other merchandise. He emphasized this legal conundrum through a spatial metaphor: "We can only pursue cases where national icons are denigrated. If the law was applied more strictly, we would need several states or at least one whole state to lock everyone away!"[9] Despite this admission and the fact that the INAH treats most cases where images of pre-Hispanic objects are used as omissions rather than criminal acts, and therefore, hardly ever enforces the state's property rights over patrimonio on Mexican soil, the Federal Law for Artistic, Archaeological and Historical Zones and Monuments does criminalize the excavation, possession, and sale of pre-Hispanic materials by any actor that is not affiliated to, or authorized by, the INAH. If taken on without the proper permits, such acts are legally pursued as looting or as illegal trafficking and are subject to prison sentences and heavy fines (Cottom 2008).

Following the appropriate registry and documentation of collections with the INAH, private collectors and other local heritage institutions ranging from state to community museums that cannot legally own pre-Hispanic artefacts can, however, be designated as their custodians. To be eligible for this status, these entities must report their collections to the INAH, have them catalogued, and sign a legally binding contract whereby the INAH grants them custodianship over national property for a set time period, under rigorously enforced display and conservation conditions.

Given the state's sole ownership and sovereignty over pre-Hispanic materials, since the end of the nineteenth century, monuments and artefacts have been subject to expropriations and transferred to Mexico City's museums as the only legitimate place for storing the nation's cultural property. Historian Christina Bueno has discussed these processes as "forging patrimonio" in reference to anthropologist Manuel Gamio's famous book for national consolidation through centralised government published in the wake of the Mexican Revolution, *Forjando Patria* (1916). In this book, Gamio, a student of Franz Boas, championed the use of "culture" and the disciplines of anthropology and archaeology as techniques of government deployed to create a mestizo nation (Brading 1988; Kouri 2010). Gamio's revolutionary nationalism was built on the foundations of Mexico's ancient indigenous heritage, but premised on the modernization of contemporary indigenous populations resulting in a homogeneous national culture. For Bueno (2016), one of the ways the project of national consolidation was made tangible was through the seizing and transfer of pre-Hispanic artefacts from all over the country to its political and cultural center in Mexico City. Since then, the Mexican state has actively appealed to patrimonio laws to legitimize its appropriation and expropriation of artefacts and monuments from communities, as well as from private persons, criminalizing any other kind of property relation and attachment. Despite state efforts to regulate patrimonio, its paradoxical standing as both public property belonging to everyone and the sole property of the Mexican state, as well as its legal severance from local and environmental contexts, has led to ambiguities and oftentimes fraught claims over ancient sites and artefacts.

Making patrimonio in Coatlinchan

San Miguel Coatlinchan, a relatively small town 35 miles east of Mexico City, became well known in the late nineteenth century following the unearthing of a 167-ton pre-Hispanic carving on its lands, identified as the ancient rain deity Tlaloc.[10] The figure, to this day the largest single stone carving found on the American continent, lay in a ravine a few miles away from the town's center. These lands belonged to a hacienda that was later expropriated by the Mexican state following the Revolution and given to Coatlinchan as a communal land grant or *ejido* in the 1930s. Having been a small agricultural and corporate town for centuries, soon after the archaeological discovery Coatlinchan became a tourist destination for day-trippers visiting Mexico City's surroundings. Engineers studied the possibility of moving the carving to its assumed rightful place as part of Mexico's iconic patrimonio collections in Mexico City, but due to its enormous weight, struggled to find the technological means to move the massive monument. Until 1964, the carving remained in Coatlinchan, as an important landmark, visited by national and foreign tourists who contributed to the local economy by purchasing food, tipping guides, and buying figurines and archaeological fragments from town residents.

In the 1960s, as the Cold War unfolded, pitting liberal and socialist political philosophies and economic models against one another, Mexico sought to position itself as a modern yet unique nation through a combination of cultural promotion and technological innovation. In this context, the then president of Mexico, Adolfo López Mateos, approved one of the most ambitious cultural projects in recent Latin American history: the construction of a new state-of-the-art National Anthropology Museum to house Mexico's patrimonio. The museum was designed as a mirror to reflect back to the Mexican people an image of national identity and cultural cohesion based on a unity in diversity model. The consolidation of regional differences into a single narrative stressed national unity and homogeneity by incorporating indigenous groups – both past and present – to the national project. Even as the directing narratives celebrated Mexico's rich and diverse indigenous cultures and civilizations, the museum flattened the country's diversity by emphasizing a core sameness shared by all Mexicans.

Figure 12.2 Political cartoon by Car titled "Al alcance del pueblo or At the people's reach" published the day after the National Anthropology Museum opened to the public.

Source: *El Universal*, Thursday September 17, 1964.

In the museum, this narrative was carefully crafted in the building's architecture culminating in Mexico's Central Valley and in the entire nation's assumed pre-Hispanic heritage. In the museum's design, Mexico's pre-Hispanic cultures were (and still are) exhibited in the lower-level galleries according to regional civilizations that all led to a central gallery devoted to the Aztecs of central Mexico. On the second floor, each regional pre-Hispanic civilization is mirrored by a contemporary indigenous culture-area represented through ethnographic collections and dioramas. The central gallery is the only one that does not have a second-floor counterpart, architecturally stressing that the heirs to Mexico's Aztec heritage are all Mexicans. This Aztec-centric nationalism placed the civilization that ruled central Mexico just before the Spanish conquest as the legitimate ancestors of all Mexicans, rather than as a specific group that inhabited only a small part of Mexico's territory during a very specific time period, and that was also known for its colonial appropriation of other pre-Hispanic cultures and people (Garcia Canclini 1990; Errington 1993).

The Coatlinchan stone carving, both because of its size and proximity to Mexico's geographic center, was chosen as the central feature for the museum, originally imagined as the building's pillar in the middle of the main courtyard, and eventually positioned as its emblematic monument on Reforma, one of the city's main avenues. When the museum plans were being drafted in the early 1960s, INAH representatives, museum staff, and engineers were sent to Coatlinchan to survey whether the carving was attached to bedrock. Once they demonstrated that the carving was a bounded mass separate from the earth in which it lay, it could be re-imagined as a distinct object that belonged to the nation as patrimonio.[11] As I explained above, Mexican law constructed artefacts and monuments as separate from the lands in which they are located. However, if an object is attached to bedrock, similarly to the Chichen Itzá cenote that was legally defined as a natural formation, it is considered a geological feature and cannot be severed or removed from the site. This is one of the premises that both then and now legally defines the difference between a monument or object of "cultural" or "historic" significance and "natural" patrimonio. Once the Coatlinchan monolith was determined to be a distinct object, it became alienable from Coatlinchan but inalienable from Mexico. Consequently, state authorities devised an engineering project to weigh, lift and transport the statue to the newly built museum in 1964.

Given that the carving was legally established as an item of national cultural property, it could appear surprising that government officials went to Coatlinchan to negotiate the monolith's removal with local authorities. Yet, historians of Mexican post-revolutionary authoritarian politics have shown that negotiation was central to the governing tactics of the ruling party, the Partido Revolucionario Institucional (PRI), that involved corporatism and cooptation (Gillingham and Smith 2014). Traces of these negotiations between government bodies and Coatlinchan residents linger to this day. Before his death in 2013, Pedro Ramírez Vázquez, the architect in charge of the museum project, reminisced about having gone to a town assembly to convince town representatives that the carving was a national treasure and, therefore, had to be taken to the National Anthropology Museum where both Mexicans and foreigners could admire it.[12] Don Pedro, an elderly man in Coatlinchan jealously keeps a copy of a contract signed by the municipal and state authorities and Coatlinchan's representatives in 1963 that states that the "idol" would be given to the museum in exchange for a highway, a school, a medical center, and two wells. The carving here becomes an object of exchange between Coatlinchan residents (represented by those who signed the contract) and the Mexican state. For both parties, the

Figure 12.3 The monolith's transfer.
Source: Photo courtesy of the Pedro Ramírez Vázquez Archive, April 16, 1964.

exchange indexed a pathway to further modernization for Mexico: for the state, the centralization, control and display of its cultural wealth; for the town, the establishment of infrastructure that would contribute to social mobility, economic growth, and community well-being.[13] And yet, the paradox remains: the state dispossessed a community of an ancient artefact that was significant, perhaps on other terms, to its members, in the service of the greater project of producing a national culture.

The monolith's significance to Coatlinchan's residents can be measured by the fact that, despite the negotiations and agreements to exchange the monolith for state infrastructure, several Tlacuaches decided to sabotage the carving's transfer on the night before the engineers were scheduled to take it away. They stormed the site, destroyed the structures built to lift the heavy stone onto the vehicle that would transport it to the museum, and stole the engineers' dynamite. The army was called in the next day to suppress the rebellion and the town was put under military siege. Three months later, having rebuilt all the contraptions that town residents had destroyed, the carving was forcefully removed from Coatlinchan and eventually erected in front of the museum where it stands to this day as a public monument in the middle of a circular fountain.

At the time, the Mexican press reported on Tlacuaches' efforts to stop the transfer, explaining the town's attachment to the monolith based on their misplaced belief in its supernatural rain-making powers. The uprising was explained, not as a property dispute, but as being fuelled by ancient superstitions that had survived into the mid-twentieth century. For example, the bi-monthly journal *Impacto*, reported: "The angered residents of Coatlinchan were prepared to stop the transfer of the gigantic idol that represents the god Tlaloc armed with stones and mallets . . . [They say that] 'If they take it away, it will stop

Figure 12.4 Close-up of comic strip, *Una deidad en el asfalto*.
Source: Una deidad en el asfalto, Editorial Novaro/SEP, October 1964, p. 19.

raining here; our crops will be lost. We cannot allow them to remove it!'" (1964: 24–26). A few months after the transfer, the Mexican government, through the sponsorship of the Ministry of Education, even published a comic book *Una Deidad en el Asfalto* that gave a similar version of events. In one of the strips above, an army officer is depicted trying to convince locals to "stop acting like pagans" given that the "idol" has merely "archaeological value." Meanwhile, the town priest is shown patiently reminding his congregation that "archaeological monuments belong to the nation, not to a specific town" (1964).

Only one newspaper, *La Prensa*, seems to have hinted that the town's uprising was sparked by town residents' attachment to the stone as an integral part of their community, its territory, and livelihood. One of their reporters interviewed two elders, Jesús Ortíz Galicia, 83 and Juan Campos Hernández, 79, both natives of Coatlinchan who "had known" the *Piedra de los Tecomates*, as the monolith was known in the area, since their childhood. The reporter included the conversation with the two men:

REPORTER: Do you think that if they take Tlaloc away it will stop raining?
ELDERS: No sir, the one who gives us bread, water and life is in heaven.
REPORTER: Why then are you opposed to the monolith's transfer?
ELDERS: We all love the place where we have always lived. We have become fond of and attached to our surroundings. And so, we became accustomed to seeing and loving Tlaloc. Also, people come to see him and this is good for the town since it is poorer and poorer every day.

*(*La Prensa *1964a)*

The Mexico City journalist concluded that for the elders, "the monolith is something that cannot be separated from the village. They don't think of themselves as idolaters, but would just like everything to remain the same" (ibid.). This report acknowledged the local value of the stone, both as part of the landscape of Coatlinchan residents' lives, and as objectifying the potential for tourism revenue.

The monolith-as-contested-property was featured a second time in the same newspaper, a few days later, during the official unveiling of the monument in Mexico City where a representative from Coatlinchan, Salomon Romero, was quoted saying:

> This object was taken by government orders because it is part of national property and in my town, there has been a misunderstanding by individuals misguided in orientation and culture . . . We must thank the Tlaloc monolith for all the benefits it has brought from the bottom of our Mexican hearts: we now have a school, a shrine to scholarship for our children of today and tomorrow. We must know, *compañeros*, that if we want our nation (*patria*) to be great, it will only happen if we create a cultured, moral and civic sentiment for it.
>
> (La Prensa *1964b: 22)*

In this quote, Salomon Romero represents himself and his community as having sacrificed their local claims to Tlaloc for the good of the state; his words render the stone the vehicle that produces Coatlinchan's belonging to the modern nation.

The reporter from *La Prensa* also quoted the then Minister of Education, Jaime Torres Bodet, thanking the residents of Coatlinchan's who "eloquently bore witness to the deep human sentiment of national unity in Mexico." Following Salomon Romero's speech, Torres Bodet addressed the people of Coatlinchan:

> From the place where [the monolith] lay dormant for centuries, [you] decided to accompany your eminent neighbour all the way to Chapultepec, not so as to bid it farewell, since he will continue to be yours, as well as of all Mexicans, but to publicly show the civic and understanding spirit with which you have allied yourselves with President López Mateos' government project, animated by the purpose of gifting an appropriate object worthy of the grandeur of the magnificent collections of the National Museum of Anthropology.
>
> (La Prensa *1964b: 22)*

These quotes demonstrate that patrimonio had to be produced; Tlaloc became national cultural property via the exertion of Mexican sovereignty over local claims to the statue's significance.

In her ethnography of archaeological sites in Yucatán, Lisa Breglia has shown how patrimonio is a property regime founded on ambivalence given that pre-Hispanic monuments and sites are legally produced as both "everyone's and nobody's at once" (2006). Looking at patrimonio through the extraction and exchange of mineral ores in Guanajuato, Elizabeth Ferry analyzes this alleged paradox by looking at patrimonio as an idiom that allows for the reproduction of collectivities, including, but not exclusively, the Mexican nation. In her account, based on Annette Weiner's interest in inalienable possessions as forms of "keeping while giving" (1992), Ferry shows that patrimonio is "not ours alone" because it is contested and claimed by several overlapping, oftentimes conflicting, collectivities (2005). In Coatlinchan, the state's claim over pre-Hispanic ruins as national property activated and consolidated community value in the stone, its dramatic removal forcing the articulation of the monolith as a source of community belonging and wellbeing, as well as social and biological reproduction.

Figure 12.5 The monolith captured and being erected as a monument in front of the National Anthropology Museum.
Source: Photo courtesy of the Pedro Ramírez Vázquez Archive.

Material ecologies of patrimonio

Whereas Tlacuaches' reactions to the dispossession of the monolith by the Mexican state in the 1960s can be interpreted as a dispute over the appropriate place and legitimate ownership of a bounded object, contemporary practices point to patrimonio as much more than a field of contested property. Following Mexico's transition to neoliberal governance, free trade, and multiculturalism in the 1990s, claims to the pre-Hispanic past and its material remains have become even more fraught. In 1992, constitutional reforms dismantled corporate forms of landed property that communities could before count on to maintain the inalienability of their lands and territories. Only archaeological sites and monuments remain as inalienable kinds of property recognized by Mexican law and allegedly protected by the state from urbanization and development projects. In this context, indigenous communities are using indigeneity, and internationally recognized idioms of indigenous cultural property, to appeal to UNESCO and other international organizations to declare their lands and sacred landscapes world heritage sites (Liffman 2011). Establishing some form of continuity with the indigenous past through archaeological remains has become a way for communities to guarantee their claims to territories increasingly coveted by state-funded development projects and multinational companies looking for land, raw materials and natural resources.

Coatlinchan is no exception. Located so close to Mexico City, what was once a small agricultural village has increasingly become part of the seemingly unending urban sprawl. Construction companies and multinational development projects see much potential and profit in the region. The most notorious of these projects is the New Mexico City International Airport. Since its announcement in the early 2000s, the airport project has detonated land disputes and even armed resistance from the towns whose lands are going to be affected. The region has, meanwhile, become subject to urbanization and real estate projects. For example, the next-door town to Coatlinchan, Chimalhuacan, was organized, much like Coatlinchan, around large extensions of communal arable land and forests until the mid-1990s, when it was transformed into an outer suburb of the capital – now home to thousands of state-subsidized low-income houses. Unlike Chimalhuacan, Coatlinchan has managed to retain its lands, although many of its residents complain that some of their neighbors are selling their *ejido* plots, leading to the construction of new neighborhoods where there were once only *milpas* or maize fields. Thus, Tlacuaches constantly feel the threat of the city's expansion and speak pessimistically about the future of their town and its territories.

In this menacing context, the stone sculpture that was removed from Coatlinchan over fifty years ago is re-emerging, despite its physical absence, as a marker of community belonging and territoriality. The town itself is peppered with its images and replicas of all sizes, in private homes, communal offices, schools, and public squares. The building that houses the civic officials' headquarters, for example, bears a mural painted in the early 2000s with a large representation of the monolith standing next to the phrase: "We are history, we make history." In 2007, a life-size poured-concrete replica of the carving was built on Coatlinchan's main square by the municipal government and placed standing inside a fountain, imitating the display of the pre-Hispanic monolith as it has stood on Reforma since 1964. I have elsewhere shown how the monolith's replicas, or "replica mass" to use George Kubler's phrasing (1962), tap into an older tradition of iteration and itinerancy of saint images that were the main identifying indices of territoriality and community belonging in many Mexican towns in the past (Rozental 2014).[14] The emergence of replicas in Coatlinchan point to the transformation of the stone into an index doing similar kinds of work as saint images as a result of its transfer from Coatlinchan to the National Anthropology Museum in Mexico City. The rendering of the carving as patrimonio – involving its relocation from a peripheral community and instantiation in a central museum – produced the absent stone as a kind of treasure, an index and guarantee of community belonging and recognition that can always be found buried under the town's territory.[15]

During one of my visits to her store in 2010, Josefina, a woman in her 60s who sells stationery and gifts, expressed a sentiment that I heard often during my conversations with Tlacuaches: "you know, even though they took away the stone and it now stands in Mexico City, it is still ours, it never really left Coatlinchan." The prominence of reproductions, and Tlacuaches' enduring sense that the aura of the stone is still present in Coatlinchan despite its physical absence, point to absence itself as a generative force. In this context, patrimonio produced national cultural property, but also gave rise to these local disruptions. Rather than being an alternative way in which communities can make claims upon encompassing legal regimes or seek recognition through transnational bodies such as UNESCO, the case of the Coatlinchan carving demonstrates that in Mexico, cultural property is mobilized by the state in the production of a national identity that incorporates – via expropriation from local contexts – the pre-Hispanic past. Yet, in the wake of dispossession, Tlacuaches maintain a sense of local distinction by producing meaning from the stone's absence.

In fact, in Coatlinchan, the missing monolith continues to be related to forms of social organization, environmental plenty and even rain, destabilizing the object's boundedness as a distinct item of property merely related to cultural reproduction, that is, an object that can be removed, relocated, and perhaps someday returned. In Coatlinchan today, the ancient carving and other artefacts from the pre-Hispanic past are not unique, authentic, separate, and severable objects, but rather inextricable components of processes of both social and biological reproduction. Unlike the laws that sever and alienate cultural productions from land and environmental milieus, townspeople's narratives and practices blur the boundaries between nature and culture. Ancient artefacts are key actors within intertwined and interconnected ecological relations that make them essential not just to the town's "culture" and identity, but transform them into resources and forms of materialization that are central to the town's enduring existence, to its residents' claims over their territories, its natural resources, and even to the conditions for life itself (Rozental 2016b).[16]

Figure 12.6 The monolith *in situ* in Coatlinchan in 1963.
Source: Photo courtesy of the Pedro Ramírez Vázquez Archive.

In the 1960s, the media used Coatlinchan residents' insistence that without the monolith, drought would decimate the region to cast Tlacuaches as superstitious and ignorant Indians who believed in the stone deity's rain-making powers. Town residents were rendered incapable of appreciating the carving as part of the nation's secular patrimonio, as well as resistant to the Mexican state's progress-oriented policies. Although at the time many Tlacuaches, like those foregrounded in the *La Prensa* articles mentioned above, denied that the carving was somehow associated to water or had any supernatural powers as an ancient deity, town residents today stress that rainfall has in fact decreased astonishingly since the monolith was removed in 1964. Tlacuaches explain that, prior to the monolith's removal, they were perhaps poor, but they could harvest maize, grains, squash, and beans to survive on their own lands. They had fruit trees and gardens that provided them with fresh and varied foods. Once the stone was removed, it stopped raining and their lands became barren; even the springs that supplied them with drinking water dried up. Following the area's decreasing water supply and resulting agricultural shifts, the stone's removal is considered by most Tlacuaches not as a loss of cultural property, but as an ecological watershed that transformed their environment, livelihoods, and overall well-being dramatically.

For example, these new climatic conditions have led certain plants, trees, and mushrooms that used to be common in the area to become scarce and even disappear. Many of the town's older residents tell stories about their childhood visits to the ravine where the monolith lay, known alternatively by the stone's name as "Tecomates" or as the *Paraje de la Piedra* (the stone's spot). They recall the place as a green, lush landscape even during the dry season that turns the rest of their territory into dust. They remember nostalgically how they used to organize school outings and picnics around or even on the stone. In their memories, the site containing the carving becomes a lasting symbol of Coatlinchan's dwindling fertility and wealth in natural resources.

Doña Luz, a woman in her mid-80s, told me about a plant known, like the stone, as "Tecomate," that grew in the ravine. This plant bore fruit used to cure respiratory problems and to prevent miscarriages. Yet, it mysteriously disappeared from Coatlinchan around the same time as the carving was taken to the capital. Flora, a woman in her late-90s, also associated the monolith's removal with changes in Coatlinchan's ecosystem. She recalled how she would go to the *Paraje de la Piedra* to gather mushrooms and medicinal herbs when the rains were just starting. But now, none of these things grow there anymore. Within these elders' recollections, the stone was connected to a local ecosystem that included the stone, but also plants, grass, mushrooms, and herbs used both for food and for local healing practices, and thus, linked to town residents' bodies and their sustenance. It was this ecosystem that was profoundly disrupted by the stone's removal.

The ecological and meteorological consequences of the monolith's removal are in turn experienced by town residents as thwarting Coatlinchan's wealth in pre-Hispanic artefacts that used to be common in the town's arable lands. Tlacuaches often speak of their childhood collecting adventures, gathering figurines (*ídolos*) and potsherds (*tepalcates*) to sell to tourists who visited the site on weekends. "They were so plentiful," Marcelo, a man in his 40s, once told me, "that we didn't think we needed to keep them as anything special." It was during the rainy season that these fragments emerged and became visible for town residents who used to spend most of their days tilling the soil. Tlacuaches now not only lament that since the carving was removed, the rains have stopped and they have had to find new sources of livelihood, but also worry that *ídolos* and *tepalcates* that previously emerged from the soil with moisture, almost like organic matter, are now so scarce. Given their new status as rare finds, instead of selling pre-Hispanic figures to visitors (very few tourists still visit Coatlinchan and ask to go see where the Tlaloc monolith once lay), Tlacuaches are collecting them and, as Agustín, a man in his 40s, told me, "keeping them safe" in their homes. For Tlacuaches, removing these objects from circulation after decades of having actively participated in their exchange materializes their status as inalienable patrimonio, while simultaneously connecting them to present-day claims over land and natural resources in a region recently overtaken by intensive urbanization, drought and economic hardship.

Conclusions

Heritage scholars have, over the past few decades, written about the alternative uses of heritage by local communities and other social actors whose attachment to artefacts, monuments and landscapes exist parallel to their jurisdiction as "national property" (Herzfeld 1991; Jones 2005) and to what Laurajane Smith discussed as "authorized heritage discourse" (2006). In Coatlinchan, such uses and appropriations are not necessarily contesting state laws and practices that claim objects and monuments from the pre-Hispanic past as national patrimonio and, thus, as the state's property. Tlacuaches have no legal recourse to claim the stone currently in Mexico City. Because the monolith is officially produced as national patrimonio, there is no legal basis to petition the state and its heritage institutions for any special kind of rights to the object, or for its return to Coatlinchan. In fact, rather than recognition, compensation, reparation, or repatriation, in legal terms, Tlacuaches could be subject to sanctions for reproducing an object that belongs to the state. Town residents' claims on pre-Hispanic artefacts, and especially on the monolithic carving that was removed from their lands in the 1960s, therefore, exist parallel to these objects' legal production as authentic, separate, and bounded things that belong to the nation.

As this ethnographic case shows, Mexican patrimonio produces a kind of national cultural property, mobilizing culture as an asset of a state seeking to assert its role on a global stage – not a resource for specific communities in need of recognition. By emphasizing a clear-cut distinction between nature and culture, patrimonio laws in fact sever objects considered cultural productions from their locations, as well as from their social and environmental milieus. These objects are produced as national heirlooms that belong both to all Mexicans, and at the same time, can only be owned and controlled by the Mexican state as the nation's inalienable cultural property. Like in the 2010 Starbucks case mentioned in the introduction, the Mexican state claims its rights over these artefacts and their representations as national "cultural property" vis-à-vis foreign actors including international museums and multinational corporations. Yet, on Mexican soil, these objects cannot be claimed by any locally specific actor, and are even expropriated and removed from source communities as national heritage. Despite the laws and practices that define pre-Hispanic artefacts and sites as the nation's cultural property, in the wake of state-making efforts through processes of dispossession, the residents of Coatlinchan are making sense of the statue in its absence. Through their narratives and practices, they are actively weaving these artefacts back into Coatlinchan's landscape and ecology, despite their physical absence, or even perhaps, because of it.

Acknowledgements

Research for this chapter was made possible by the Wenner-Gren Foundation and the American Council of Learned Societies/Andrew W. Mellon Foundation. I conducted fieldwork in Coatlinchan for 14 months from 2008 to 2009, and have since recurrently returned for short-term stays. I am grateful to Haidy Geismar and Jane Anderson for their invitation to contribute to this reader, as well as to Miruna Achim, Alejandra Leal, Matthew H. Robb, and Sabra Thorner for their comments on drafts of this text. I would also like to thank the members of the seminar Nación y Alteridad, and especially Antonio Azuela, whose comments during a workshop helped me refine my arguments. All translations are mine unless otherwise noted.

Notes

1 The full interview is available on *W Radio*'s website: http://www.wradio.com.mx/escucha/archivo_de_audio/julio-castrejon-director-de-medios-del-inah-tazas-de-starbucks-usan-imagenes-prehispanicas/20100108/oir/935475.aspx (accessed January 2016).

2 Although the word "patrimoine" is used in French-speaking contexts to refer to heritage objects and sites, "patrimony" is seldom used in English.

3 A commemorative exhibition celebrated the repatriation of Mexico's cultural property following the complicated negotiations that led the INAH to purchase the Chimalpahin Codex at auction in 2014. For more on this case see Martínez Baracs (2015) and http://www.codicechimalpahin.inah.gob.mx/ (accessed January 2016).

4 Mary Ellen Miller, Khristaan Villela and Matthew H. Robb show the many ways in which the image of the Aztec Calendar Stone has been used since the object's excavation in 1790. They argue that these "afterlives" make this specific monument not only one of Mexico's most ubiquitous and iconic artefacts, but also one of the most famous objects in world archaeology (2010).

5 See also the introduction and excellent collection of essays on heritage and processes of reproduction and replication that appeared in the dossier "Matters of Patrimony" in the *Journal of Latin American and Caribbean Anthropology* (Rozental, Collins and Ramsey 2016).

6 Residents from the various towns in the area have similar nicknames. *Tlacuaches* – translated in English as opossums – became Coatlinchan's residents' nickname because these animals were common in their territory. The animal's fame for its abilities to deceive predators, and its status as an endemic species to the Americas, is the subject of great pride for Coatlinchan's residents.

7 In the Convention, Article 1 states: "For the purposes of this Convention, the following shall be considered as 'cultural heritage:' monuments: architectural works, works of monumental sculpture and painting, elements or structures of an archaeological nature, inscriptions, cave dwellings and combinations of features, which are of outstanding universal value from the point of view of history, art or science; groups of buildings: groups of separate or connected buildings which, because of their architecture, their homogeneity or their place in the landscape, are of outstanding universal value from the point of view of history, art or science; sites: works of man or the combined works of nature and man, and areas including archaeological sites which are of outstanding universal value from the historical, aesthetic, ethnological or anthropological point of view." Article 2 then explains: "the following shall be considered as 'natural heritage:' natural features consisting of physical and biological formations or groups of such formations, which are of outstanding universal value from the aesthetic or scientific point of view; geological and physiographical formations and precisely delineated areas which constitute the habitat of threatened species of animals and plants of outstanding universal value from the point of view of science or conservation; natural sites or precisely delineated natural areas of outstanding universal value from the point of view of science, conservation or natural beauty." See UNESCO website http://whc.unesco.org/en/conventiontext/ (accessed July 2015).

8 In 1994, the responsibility for Mexico's "natural" patrimonio was transferred to the newly created Ministry of the Environment, Natural Resources and Fishing, which in 2000 became the Ministry of the Environment and Natural Resources.

9 Mexico is a federation divided into 32 states. In the quote, Castrejón is alluding to these states as distinct territorial entities.

10 Since the nineteenth century and to this day, scholars of ancient Mexico and archaeologists have argued over the sculpture's possible identity within the pre-Hispanic pantheon. Whereas some believe it represents Tlaloc, the Aztec male rain deity, others believe it represents Chalchihuiltícue, Tlaloc's female counterpart.

11 Documents in the National Anthropology Museum archive show that a group of museum designers were sent to Coatlinchan to determine whether or not the stone was a separate and, therefore, severable, monument. This was confirmed by Mario Vázquez, one of the head museum designers at the time (personal communication).
12 Interview with author, 2010.
13 The validity of the contract has been questioned by many Tlacuaches who say the members of the assembly, many at the time illiterate peasants, were duped by the government into signing a contract without having been briefed on its contents.
14 See also the documentary *The Absent Stone* (2013) by Sandra Rozental and Jesse Lerner for a visual representation of Coatlinchan's multiple replicas.
15 For a discussion on the uses of idioms of treasure and treasure hunting to describe practices around town patrimonio in Coatlinchan, see Rozental (2016a).
16 I am using "ecology" thinking of Gregory Bateson's writings refining social life as co-constitutive and interdependent systems made up of individuals, societies, organisms, and ecosystems (1972).

Bibliography

Achim, Miruna. Forthcoming. *From Idols to Antiquity: Forging the National Museum of Mexico 1825–1867*. Lincoln: Nebraska University Press.

Anderson, Jane E. 2009. *Law, Knowledge, Culture: The Production of Indigenous Knowledge in Intellectual Property Law*. Cheltenham, UK: Edward Elgar Publishing.

Azuela, Antonio. 2011. "Property in the Post-Post-Revolution: Notes on the Crisis of the Constitutional Idea of Property in Contemporary Mexico." *Texas Law Review* 89: 1915–1926.

Bateson, Gregory. 1972. *Steps to an Ecology of Mind: Collected Essays in Anthropology, Psychiatry, Evolution, and Epistemology*. Chicago: University of Chicago Press.

Berrin, Kathleen, ed. 1988. *Feathered Serpents and Flowering Trees: Reconstructing the Murals of Teotihuacan*. San Francisco; Seattle: Fine Arts Museums of San Francisco; University of Washington Press.

Brading, David A. 1985. *The Origins of Mexican Nationalism*. Cambridge: Cambridge Centre of Latin American Studies.

Brading, David A. 1988. "Manuel Gamio and Official Indigenismo in Mexico." *Bulletin of Latin American Research* 7: 75–89.

Brading, David A. 1991. *The First America: The Spanish Monarchy, Creole Patriots and the Liberal State 1492–1866*. Cambridge: Cambridge University Press.

Brading, David A. 2001. "Monuments and Nationalism in Modern Mexico." *Nations and Nationalism* 7(4): 521–531.

Breglia, Lisa C. 2006. *Monumental Ambivalence: The Politics of Heritage*. Austin: University of Texas Press.

Brown, Michael F. 2003. *Who Owns Native Culture?* Cambridge, MA: Harvard University Press.

Brown, Michael F. 2004. "Heritage as Property." In *Property in Question: Value Transformation in the Global Economy*, edited by Katherine Verdery and Caroline Humphrey. Oxford: Berg.

Bueno, Christina. 2016. *The Pursuit of Ruins: Archaeology, History, and the Making of Modern Mexico*. Albuquerque: University of New Mexico Press.

Bueno, Christina. 2010. "Forjando Patrimonio: The Making of Archaeological Patrimony in Porfirian Mexico." *Hispanic American Historical Review* 90(2): 215–245.

Castañeda, Luis. 2014. *Spectacular Mexico*. Minneapolis: University of Minnesota Press.

Castañeda, Quetzil E. 1996. *In the Museum of Maya Cultures*. Minneapolis: University of Minnesota Press.

Castañeda, Quetzil E. 2009. "Heritage and Indigeneity: Transformations in the Politics of Tourism." In *Cultural Tourism in Latin America: The Politics of Space and Imagery*, edited by Jan M. Baud and Johanna Louisa Ypeij. Boston: Brill, pp. 263–296.

Coggins, Clemency Chase, and C. Ladd. 1992. "Artifacts from the Cenote of Sacrifice, Chichen Itza, Yucatan." *Memoirs of the Peabody Museum of Archaeology and Ethnology* 10(3).

Collins, John F. 2015. *Revolt of the Saints: Memory and Redemption in the Twilight of Brazilian Racial Democracy*. Durham, NC: Duke University Press.

Coombe, Rosemary J. 1998. *The Cultural Life of Intellectual Properties: Authorship, Appropriation, and the Law*. Durham: Duke University Press.

Coombe, Rosemary J. 2009. "The Expanding Purview of Cultural Properties and Their Politics." *Annual Review of Law and Social Science* 5: 393–412.
Coombe, Rosemary J., and Melissa F. Baird. 2015. "The Limits of Heritage: Corporate Interests and Cultural Rights on Resource Frontiers." In *A Companion to Heritage Studies*, edited by William Logan, Mairead Nic Craith, and Ullrich Kockel. Chichester: Wiley Blackwell, pp. 337–354.
Cottom, Bolfy. 2008. *Nación, patrimonio cultural y legislación: los debates parlamentarios y la construcción del marco jurídico federal sobre monumentos en México, siglo XX.* Mexico City: Miguel Angel Porrúa.
Cruz Porchini, Dafne. 2016. *Arte, propaganda Y diplomacia cultural a finales del Cardenismo, 1937–1940.* Mexico City: Secretaria de Relaciones Exteriores.
Dent, Alexander. 2009. *River of Tears: Country Music, Memory, and Modernity in Brazil.* Durham, NC: Duke University Press.
Errington, Shelly. 1993. "Progressivist Stories and the Pre-Columbian Past: Notes on Mexico and the United States." In *Collecting the Pre-Columbian Past*, edited by Elizabeth Boone. Washington, DC: Dumbarton Oaks, pp. 209–249.
Ferry, Elizabeth Emma. 2005. *Not Ours Alone: Patrimony, Value, and Collectivity in Contemporary Mexico.* New York: Columbia University Press.
Fforde, Cressida, Jane Hubert, and Paul Turnbull. 2002. *The Dead and Their Possessions: Repatriation in Principle, Policy and Practice.* London: Routledge.
Fine-Dare, Kathleen S. 2002. *Grave Injustice: The American Indian Repatriation Movement and NAGPRA.* Lincoln: University of Nebraska Press.
Forsyth, Miranda. 2012. "Lifting the Lid on 'The Community': Who Has the Right to Control Access to Traditional Knowledge and Expressions of Culture?" *International Journal of Cultural Property* 19(1): 1–31.
Gamio, Manuel. 1916. *Forjando Patria: Pro-Nacionalismo.* Mexico City: Porrúa Hermanos.
García Canclini, Néstor. 1990. *Culturas Híbridas. Estrategias para Entrar y Salir de la Modernidad.* Mexico City: Grijalbo.
Geismar, Haidy. 2013. *Treasured Possessions: Indigenous Interventions into Cultural and Intellectual Property.* Durham, NC: Duke University Press.
Gillingham, Paul, and Benjamin Smith, eds. 2014. *Dictablanda: Politics, Work, and Culture in Mexico, 1938–1968.* Durham, NC: Duke University Press.
Handler, Richard. 1988. *Nationalism and the Politics of Culture in Quebec.* Madison: University of Wisconsin Press.
Herzfeld, Michael. 1991. *A Place in History: Social and Monumental Time in a Cretan Town.* Princeton, NJ: Princeton University Press.
Impacto. 1964. "En defensa de su dios Tlaloc, se amotina el pueblo de Coatlinchan," 731.4, de marzo: pp. 24–25.
Jones, Siân. 2005."That Stone was Born Here and That's Where It Belongs: Hilton of Cadboll and the Negotiation of Identity, Ownership and Belonging." In *Able Minds and Practiced Hands: Scotland's Early Medieval Sculpture in the 21st Century*, edited by S. Foster and M. Cross. Society for Medieval Archaeology Monograph 23: 37–53.
Kaltmeier, Olaf, and Mario Rufer, eds. 2016. *Entangled Heritages: Postcolonial Perspectives on the Uses of the Past in Latin America.* London: Routledge.
Kouri, Emilio. 2010. "Manuel Gamio y el indigenismo de la Revolución Mexicana." In *Historia de los intelectuales en América Latina: Los avatares de la "ciudad letrada" en el siglo XX*, edited by Carlos Altamirano. Buenos Aires: Katz Editores.
Kubler, George. 1962. *The Shape of Time: Remarks on the History of Things.* New Haven, CT: Yale University Press.
Kuri, Ariel Rodríguez. 2003. "Hacia México 68. Pedro Ramírez Vázquez y el Proyecto Olímpico." *Secuencia* 56: 035.
La Prensa. 1964a. "Coatlinchan despidió al ídolo," 19 Feburary: p. 22.
La Prensa. 1964b. "Coatlinchan decidido a conservar su Tlaloc," 24 February: p. 7.
Lerner, Jesse. 2001. "Thompson en el cenote sagrado." *Alquimia* 13 (Sept.–Dec.): 23–26.
Liffman, Paul M. 2011. *Huichol Territory and the Mexican Nation: Indigenous Ritual, Land Conflict, and Sovereignty Claims.* Tucson: University of Arizona Press.
Lombardo De Ruíz, Sonia. 1988. *Antecedentes de las Leyes Sobre Monumentos.* Mexico City: Instituto Nacional de Antropología e Historia.
Lomnitz, Claudio. 2001. *Deep Mexico, Silent Mexico: An Anthropology of Nationalism.* Milwaukee: University of Minnesota Press.

López Caballero, Paula. 2008. "Which Heritage for Which Heirs? The Pre-Columbian Past and the Colonial Legacy in the National History of Mexico." *Social Anthropology* 16(3): 329–345.
Martínez Baracs, Rodrigo. 2015. "Manuscritos mexicanos peregrinos." *Letras Libres*, February: 88–90.
Merryman, John Henry. 1986. "Two Ways of Thinking about Cultural Property." *American Journal of International Law* 80(4): 831–853.
Merryman, John Henry. 1989. "The Public Interest in Cultural Property." *California Law Review* 77(2): 339–364.
Morehart, Christopher T. 2012. "What if the Aztec Empire Never Existed? The Prerequisites of Empire and the Politics of Plausible Alternative Histories." *American Anthropologist* 114(2): 267–281.
Myers, Fred. 2004. "Ontologies of the Image and Economies of Exchange." *American Ethnologist* 31(1): 5–20.
Rojas Delgadillo, Norma. 2006. "Cultural Property Legislation in Mexico: Past, Present and Future." In *Art and Cultural Heritage: Law, Policy, and Practice*, edited by Barbara T. Hoffman. Cambridge: Cambridge University Press.
Rozental, Sandra. 2014. "Stone Replicas: The Iteration and Itinerancy of Mexican Patrimonio." *Journal of Latin American and Caribbean Anthropology* 19(2): 331–356.
Rozental, Sandra. 2016a. "Unearthing Patrimonio: Treasure and Collectivity in San Miguel Coatlinchan." In *Entangled Heritages: Postcolonial Perspectives on the Uses of the Past in Latin America*, edited by Olaf Kaltmeier and Mario Rufer. London: Routledge: 137–152.
Rozental, Sandra. 2016b."In the Wake of Mexican Patrimonio: Material Ecologies in San Miguel Coatlinchan." *Anthropological Quarterly* 89(1): 157–196.
Rozental, Sandra and Jesse Lerner. 2013. *The Absent Stone*. Film. 82 mins.
Rozental, Sandra, John F. Collins, and Jason Ramsey. 2016. "Matters of Patrimony: Anthropological Theory and the Materiality of Replication in Contemporary Latin America." *Journal of Latin American and Caribbean Anthropology* 21(1): 7–18.
Seligman, Thomas K. 1999. "The Murals of Teotihuacán: A Case Study of Negotiated Restitution." In *The Ethics of Collecting Cultural Property: Whose Culture?*, edited by Phyllis Mauch Messenger. Albuquerque: University of New Mexico Press: 73–84.
Smith, Laurajane. 2006. *Uses of Heritage*. London: Routledge.
Tenorio, Mauricio. 1996. *Mexico at the World's Fairs: Crafting a Modern Nation*. Berkeley: University of California Press.
Turnbull, Paul, and Michael Pickering, eds. 2010. *The Long Way Home: The Meaning and Values of Repatriation*. New York and Oxford: Berghahn Books.
Una Deidad en el Asfalto. 1964. Aventuras de la Vida Real, Editorial Novaro-SEP.
Verdery, Katherine and Caroline Humphrey, eds. 2004. *Property in Question: Value Transformation in the Global Economy*. Oxford: Berg.
Weiner, Annette B. 1992. *Inalienable Possessions: The Paradox of Keeping-While-Giving*. Berkeley: University of California Press.
Zolov, Eric. 2004. "Showcasing the 'Land of Tomorrow:' Mexico and the 1968 Olympics." *The Americas* 61(2): 159–188.

13

MAKING AND UNMAKING HERITAGE VALUE IN CHINA

Shu-Li Wang and Michael Rowlands

Since the 1990s China has experienced a heritage boom, developing an increasing number of museum and heritage sites. It is estimated that 100 museums have been built each year and the number has increased from 717 in 1985 to 3,800 in 2014 (National Bureau of Statistics of China 2014; Alberge 2014). Accompanied by a surge of cultural entrepreneurs, there is also an increased interest in private art collecting and art markets (which were once banned), resulting in the establishment of numerous private museums in the post-Mao China. Wealthy cities such as Xi'an and Chengdu each claim to have made themselves a "museum city", setting the goal of building a hundred private museums in five years. This important social phenomenon reflects the legalization of private property and the ownership of heritage in China's reformed market. Indeed, this expansion of the heritage and museum industry has been encouraged by the state as part of a pursuit of collective memory and patriotic education in an era of rapid change (The State Council 2016). In post-Mao China, rapid urbanization, mass migrations and unprecedented social and economic transformations have triggered a sense of identity crisis, loss, anxiety and nostalgia (Anagnost 1997; Madsen 2014). Cultural property and its display have become a kind of technology of governance for managing social transformation and social tensions as the state pursues its vision of civilization and quality (Oakes 2013; Wang 2016). As Anagnost has stated, "with the collapse of a Marxist vision of history, we see a 'fevered' search for a national subjectivity that can restore a sense of historical agency to China in terms which are in some ways a striking departure from the Maoist era but which are in other ways strangely continuous with it" (Anagnost 1997: 8).[1] China's historical past and heritage that were once considered an impediment to China's search for modernity were re-interpreted with new sources of national pride.

Museums work to provide a platform for China's continuation of tradition and heritage while claiming to embrace a distinctive future. But this recent expansion of the museum and heritage industry in China is not unconnected to neoliberalism with the rise of consumer markets and the spread of capitalism with Chinese characteristics. Of vital importance has been the appropriation of an international cultural property and heritage discourse, realized in China by the country's fervent participation, since 1987, in UNESCO's World Heritage listing, with China now boasting the second largest number of the World Heritage Sites. Therefore, one has to situate the current picture of a museum and heritage industry in China within the wider framework of a state-led nationalism on the one hand and cultural entrepreneurship under the impact of a market economy on the other hand, both embedded and propelled by a global heritage discourse.

Making heritage value

This chapter is about re-conceptualizing value for cultural heritage and property within a museum context in China. The principal contrast we draw with Western concepts of heritage value, which emphasize general interpretations of authenticity and ownership, derives from the need of Han Chinese people to connect to ancestors and ancestral pasts in terms of respect and remembrance (e.g. Freedman 1966, 1979; Feuchtwang 1992). While historians have focused on the continuity of, albeit a Han-centered, historiography, we argue that the continuity of Chinese civilization as a totality, and the notion of "Chinese-ness," are disseminated by a shared cultural symbolism and material heritage flowing down an indigenous idea of the "river of history."[2] This distinctive concept of the ancestral ownership and possession of heritage value is manifested through making and remaking heritage materials from the past, identifying emblems of tradition and ancestry and bringing them somehow into the continuous present experience of Chinese people. The Chinese notion of authenticity is thus about connecting to the past, and heritage value that lies in the preservation of the past for collective ownership. We argue that the European notion of exclusive ownership does not apply to the case of Imperial China and contemporary practice, as is shown by the contradiction between the state's adoption of the international legal discourse of intellectual property rights and patent law, and a collective concept of heritage as possession and reproduction at the local level.

By referencing "Chinese" in this account, we focus on the social imaginary of Han Chinese people. As Steven Harrell noted, Han Chinese people have, for centuries if not millennia, been cultivating and educating non-Han "barbarians" (Harrell 1995) through various civilizing projects which "is a kind of interaction between peoples, in which one group, the civilizing centre, interacts with other groups (the peripheral peoples) in terms of a particular kind of inequality" (1995: 4). The Han Chinese situated at the center of a Han worldview claim to originate a superior level of civilization and to be able to educate ethnic peripheral peoples with Confucian teaching and moral ideology. The distinction between Han and non-Han ethnicity does not lie in blood or kinship relation but lies in the degree of assimilating Confucius values. In a similar vein, the concept of China as an empire is a *Tianxia* (天下), meaning all under heaven, concept where the world order is open to diffusion and the Emperor or equivalent is situated at the core (Levenson 1967). Given all the obvious political and economic transformations during the twentieth century in China, we would argue that the basic ideology of *Tianxia* has been sustained, albeit transformed into a new form of civilizing project. Indeed, as argued by Wang (2013, 2016), international heritage discourse has been internalized in various ongoing state civilizing projects in post-Mao China.

The state also has been using international heritage discourse that has been promoted by UNESCO through various heritage conventions and nominating World Heritage Sites as a means by which to include and assimilate the culture and heritage of ethnic minorities into a dominant national discourse. International heritage discourse is adopted in China as a means to link a distinctive idea of past to a path to modernization and the presentation of itself as the civilizational center of East Asia. This was shown by China's vivid participation of heritage projects in Angkor Wat and the Silk Road. As was made clear in the opening ceremony of the Beijing Olympics, the government in China does not regard itself as "ruling" in the same sense as a Western-style modern nation state. Governmentality is performed like Geertz's concept of "theatre state" or Tambiah writing on galactic polities (Geertz 1981; Tambiah 1977) by performing cultural tradition and history as a mythical time extending from the origins of imperial time to the present. A long-term cosmological continuity encompassing capacity for political and economic transformation is envisaged, allowing for periodic ruptures and revitalization as in the attack on the "four olds" of the Cultural Revolution (1966–1976).

In China, the practice and conservation of cultural heritage in the legal sense,[3] and the establishment of public museums in institutional settings, only came into practice in the early twentieth century as China was transitioning from an imperial to a republican system (Wang 2017). Discourses around heritage making have been reinforced by UNESCO's World Heritage Program, which has become part of the idea of the "heritage industry" (Hewison 1987; Lowenthal 1985; Smith 2006; Harrison 2016). The top-down "UNESCOization" (Berliner 2012) of heritage is also a modern concept dovetailing with cultural "property" and ownership in an exclusive legal sense which has been incorporated into heritage conventions in China. This has been exemplified by the massive expansion of museums and heritage sites within a unified idea of China, and is juxtaposed against a broad range of heritage values that have guided practice since imperial times on the ground. The modern concept that China is a state has been reinforced by the UNESCO heritage program where the state assumes the legal mandate to protect, to manage and to speak for the heritage properties within its own territory, including ethnic minorities.

In this chapter, we argue that firstly the political and ideological notions of nation states absorbed in late Imperial China[4] result in different attitudes towards heritage and museums, as well as different notions of authenticity and possession. In Imperial China (221 BCE–1911 CE), the authority of the emperors was "legitimized by their kinship status within the ruling clan, and the ruled were often viewed as the 'children' of the rulers" (Lu 2014: 212). For example, the authority of the Three Dynasties (c. 2100–220 BCE) was based on an extended patrilineal kinship and its power needed to be legitimized through ancestral worship and rituals (Chang 1981). This political system was re-assured by Confucianism, which emphasized filial piety throughout the imperial period. As such, the Empire and the People were both considered as children belonging of the Emperor. Unlike China, in Europe, ancient states were organized in administrative bureaucracies and their authorities were developed through transcending kinship relations (Lavenda and Schultz 2007, cited in Lu 2014: 211–212). The modern nation state (1911–) was defined with clear boundaries of polity and bureaucracy, and sovereignty based on monarchic/aristocratic or democratic principles that retained the Roman judicial ideal of interregnum or territorial integrity based on the legitimate use of force. However, during the imperial period China was identified by the term *Zhongguo* (中國) – which means Middle Kingdom, and which, as the Chinese-language name for modern China, was conceptualized as being situated as the cosmological center of the world. The territoriality of the Empire was a relational concept justifying the infinite extension of the political center and frontier. Peripheral localities were linked to the center through bureaucracy and taxes, a tribute system and ritual practices (Feuchtwang 1992; Elman 2000), as well as through reproduction and mimicry of material forms.

Secondly, as we will encounter in the next section, throughout history, making, remaking and appropriation of heritage objects has been considered part of the tradition in the production and appreciation of heritage objects. This ontological difference in the significance and status of particular items labeled as "cultural heritage" began to shift with the introduction of European conservation practices and museum systems to China in the early twentieth century, and with World Heritage discourse in the 1970s (Hevia 2001; Madsen 2014). For example, Hevia (2001; also in Labadi and Long 2010) describes how the heritage site of

Chengde, which was built by an ethnic group, was used by the Chinese government as a symbol of the harmonious integration of ethnic groups into China. While state sovereignty is the legally responsible body for World Heritage nomination, this heritage nomination mechanism has registered the state as the primary legal custodian of all the heritage properties within its territorial region.

Thirdly, though China does have a long history of collecting antiquities that can be dated back to the Zhou dynasty (*c.*1046–256 BCE), when it comes to systematic institutional display and performance, Chinese museological theories and practices are very much influenced by European practices. The European idea of heritage as property, the concept of which is linked to the birth of the nation state, is materialized through visual display (Anderson 1991) and experimented through using visual technologies, as elaborated by Bennett's discussion of the exhibitionary complex (1995). In Imperial China, objects collected were not for public display. Heritage was conceptualized as a collective responsibility to preserve and store objects within ancestral halls, temples or imperial shrines for very specific kinds of viewing and consumption. The value of heritage was held and cultivated by family lineages. Collections were viewed as signs of political power, wealth, social status or cultural capital, rather than in the context of emerging public cultures. These different notions of heritage, cultural property and material culture have continued to be practiced in the present and somehow mixed with the contemporary capitalist economy and with the objectification of modern legal definitions of property rights.

We start by exploring traditional Han Chinese art practices using archaeological data, historical accounts and ethnographic research to examine ever-evolving ideas around the value of making, collecting, exhibiting and negotiating cultural property in China. This has resulted in a very particular image of a "continuous" past that somehow "always" contained the values of the Chinese nation. Secondly, we present a cultural account of the changing role of relics, *wenwu* (文物), and of personhood in shaping Chinese nationalism, historiography and perceptions of time. Moreover, our analysis goes on to examine the emergence of the contemporary Chinese art market, which correlates with the (private) museum and heritage boom, and which, through practices of collecting and exhibiting, is linked to discourses of Confucian ideals of philanthropy, as well as to distinctions in taste and identity (cf. Bourdieu 1984). Lastly, we argue that in China, the process of making cultural property into a form of value that can be articulated, appropriated and even cultivated, blurs the boundaries between subject and object. We intend to examine how the heritage discourse in China has challenged the European epistemology that separates subject and object/material and immaterial, for instance which has resulted in a tension within UNESCO between tangible and intangible heritage. We also explore how this discourse challenges the notion of authenticity. In other words, we approach questions of how China's heritage discourse is negotiated within international cultural property regimes, and what degree of prominence they have in the ways that local Chinese museums and private collectors alike position themselves.

Making, remaking and collecting material heritage

In China the idea of the physical value of "authenticity" through the preservation of object forms was not a significant value in imperial times. Moreover, because the significance of heritage lay in its broader cultural value, replicas were considered as "not only a way to prolong the object's life, but also to improve its qualities" (Varutti 2008: 101). This concern for the ongoing life of heritage also exists in other East Asian cultures. For instance, the most eminent example in international heritage discourse is the Ise Grand Shinto temple in Japan.

The ritual reconstruction of the timber temple, which occurs every 20 years, has challenged Eurocentric heritage practices and provoked debate regarding the meaning of authenticity in conservation practice that favored stable and fixed materiality that was the focus of preservation and maintenance. The practice of rebuilding and hence continuous and deliberate renewal is in contrast to the majority of World Heritage Sites and has posed several challenges to UNESCO's World Heritage Convention, resulting in the 1994 Nara Document on Authenticity. This document drafted during the conference held in Nara, Japan in 1994 legitimizes heritage practices of periodic dismantling, rebuilding, repairing and re-assembling of wooden heritage. The renewals of buildings are considered to be opportunities for change rather than replication, as is the case in East Asian countries. As Rowlands (2005: 280) points out, "a 'Western' philosophy of 'restoration' is deployed primarily as an expatriate exegesis on the value of particular sites, buildings and objects as repositories of cultural capital." For example, the classic guidelines for the conservation of heritage are based on the Athens Charter (1933) and the Venice Charter (1964), which were originally developed for the conservation of stone monuments in Greece and Italy, respectively.

The practice of making reproductions of portable heritage has had a long history in China. Generations of artists copied ancient masters as part of their artistic training (So 2008). This has resulted in numerous copies of bronzes, paintings, calligraphies, etc. among the heritage material of the Chinese art world. Li Ling (2005) uses the term "*shuogu zhujin* (鑠古鑄今)" to describe this phenomenon, which refers to recasting antiquity towards the making of the present.[5] Evidence of a preoccupation with preserving or more accurately copying past materials with an attention to difference in China is supported by archaeological data and imperial collections. As early as the last centuries BCE, ancient Chinese society was already aware of its antiquity (Rawson 2004; So 2008; von Falkenhausen 2013). For example, at the archaeological site of Anyang Yinxu (*c.* 14th – 11th century BCE), Late Shang-period jade objects excavated from the tomb of Fuhao stylistically mimic works of temporally diverse origins, including the fourth-millennium BCE Hongshan culture or the third-millennium BCE Shijiahe culture in Hebei (von Falkenhausen 2013: 43). Some of these had been reworked into Shang-style pieces (*c.* sixteenth through eleventh century BCE) and some remained in their ancient styles. As noted by von Falkenhausen, "a concern with ancestral figures both remote and recent is pervasively attested in Shang civilization, the notion that material relics from the past enjoyed a special prestige does not seem far-fetched" (2013: 46). Moreover, ritual bronzes produced in Late Shang emulated Middle Shang or even earlier styles. The past was remembered by creating links to the visual signature of prominent ancestors. This archaizing imitation of artworks has continued and been a prominent feature of Chinese arts (von Falkenhausen 2013).

During the Shang and Western Zhou (1046–771 BCE) dynasties, bronze vessels were used by the ruling elites in religious rituals and as symbols of a clan's political role. Bronzes used in the ritual worship of ancestors were kept in ancestral temples above ground to be used by clan members until they were buried with their owners. In addition, bronze vessels had been used to signify an individual's status. For example, an emperor (*tianzi*) was buried with nine bronzes, a general (*zhuhou*) with seven, a *dafu* (official) with five, a *shi* (scholar) with three, and *Shi* (a lower-class scholar) with one. Moreover, items of material heritage such as ritual utensils were intentionally reproduced and linked to the social and political status, historical pedigree and cultural heritage of their owners. As So has suggested, "the underlying impetus for these archaic revivals appears to be essentially political" (2008: 32). During the Western Zhou period, ritual bronzes were inscribed with the phrase *Zizisunsun young bao young* (子子孫孫永寶用), meaning they were intended to be kept and used forever by descendants. Bronze vessels preserved in ancestral temples had been the primary model for bronze casters. Records have shown that Han dynasty (206 BCE–220 CE) and later tombs have also occasionally yielded older bronzes (So 2008). Archaeological findings suggest that during the Eastern Zhou dynasty (770–221 BCE), when resources were scarce due to a long period of warfare, sometimes bronzes were melted down to cast other articles (So 2008: 5–6). It was believed that new bronze vessels retained the power of the one they came from. It is also unlikely that the bronzes would have been produced from the same moulds, as the decorated Shang and Western Zhou moulds were smashed to pieces to release the finished bronze (So 2008: 10). Instead we have the "animistic" theme that the material and/or the forms of older objects contain a spirit force that can be transmitted through the act of remaking. Where inscriptions survive, transmission of a more ancestral spirit form is indicated and becomes the major source of responsibility to the past. Acts of keeping and copying serve the same function of displaying ancestral piety. It is notable that this did not result in exactly the same objects being made. This is not only because clay moulds were destroyed after use; objects made in later generations consciously copied archaic styles, but with deliberate variation to create new forms but retain a connection to the past forms.

There are also other types of imitation that infuse Chinese definitions of cultural property and art in direct contrast to the paradigms of European art history.[6] Chinese scholars were fascinated by objects with inscriptions that were believed to carry the historical record and value of the past. Since the Tang dynasty (618–906 CE) scholars undertook field trips in search of stone inscriptions. (Even today in museums, objects with inscriptions or collections that include inscriptions are in high-profile places and in art markets are sold at higher prices). For example, today the price of oracle bones[7] depends not on the size but on the characters carried on them. Rubbing as an important collecting practice was recorded as early as the Five Dynasties period (907–960 CE). As a new artistic style, rubbings emerged from a focus wherein inscriptions or patterns on stone stelae, monuments or bronzes were inked and pressed to paper. Rubbings were not conceived as simple "copies"; instead, the skill with which they were reproduced was itself appreciated as original artistic expression. When *Jinshixue* (金石學, the study of metal and stone) became popular during the Song dynasty (960–1279 CE), more rubbings of bronzes, monuments or engraved stelae were made. Thus, a connoisseurship of rubbings developed that was itself appreciated and led to them being collected as historical relics, both for their own aesthetic value and to be used as models for calligraphic practice (Wu 2003; von Falkenhausen 2013: 39). Making rubbings remains a contemporary practice. The techniques of rubbing require training to acquire, and highly skilled practitioners may be considered masters. Even today, specialist artisans of rubbings are trained and hired at major museums or archaeological field stations in China. During Wang's fieldwork[8] in museums in China, she met Mr Guo, who in 2013 was an antiquities keeper at the Forbidden City in Beijing, was trained as a master of rubbing and made rubbings of the stored objects on site. Ms Sanniu was a helper at the archaeological field station of Anyang Yinxu; she was also selected to learn rubbings and was instructed to make them for the bronzes excavated at the site. There are also positions for masters making rubbings at all national museums and archaeological stations in China, as well as in the National Palace Museum in Taipei, Taiwan, where collections were taken from China during the civil war in the 1940s to justify the Nationalists' claims to represent China over the Communists, and to claim a continuous presence of Chinese civilization in Taiwan. Although museums and archaeological departments have hired practitioners using "Western" methods of conserving objects, the production of rubbings as a means of preserving historical records is considered to be the traditional way of keeping the past present not only in museums within China but also in museums in Chinese diasporic regions such as Taiwan. It is interesting to note that there are no rubbings made for non-Han objects.

Learning through emulation, imitation and copying have therefore long been a tradition in the Chinese art world. The imitation of ancient styles had become a guiding ideal of literati and scholar-officials by late Imperial China. Already from the sixth century, when art historian Xie He published "Six Principles of Chinese Painting," it became established that "transmission by copying" should be one of the key skills in the learning of painting. Imitation here is different from copying or forsaking innovation in the European idea. In China, imitating calligraphy and paintings was intended to "bring out the spiritual essence of the ancients" (von Falkenhausen 2013: 43). For example, during the Tang dynasty, the idea of partaking in the spiritual essence of another individual was represented in that person's written traces, much in the way one becomes one with the Buddha in Indian religious practice by meditating in front of a statue portraying him. Moreover, upon mastering earlier styles it was expected that an artisan's individual style would emerge, forming a smooth extension out of the past. The imitation is considered as another work of art and is also considered to contain characteristics of the imitator. Craig Clunas (2004a: 36) describes how a fifteenth-century calligrapher Wen Zhengming honored his master by following these art practices, seeing them as the "perfect balance between the transmission of ancient models and the formation of his own style" and this reflects a chain of cultural transmission. Wen Fong (1962: 103, cited in Tam 2014:87) identifies four traditions in studying replicas of paintings and calligraphies – *mu* (摹, to trace), *lin* (臨, to copy), *fang* (仿, to imitate), and *tsao* (造, to invent). In Chinese paintings, for example, having multiple versions is common and one can expect there to be multiple versions of great works (Tam 2014). Apart from the portable heritages, classical canons of literature were traditionally among the artistic forms that were re-interpreted and re-written in several versions, and the creative reproduction of masterpieces was welcomed. During the imperial period, Chinese philosophy had been developed based on interpretation and adding footnotes to the ancient canons, and these different versions of interpretations became canons themselves (Huang 2007).

In the sense that copying past work is considered a means of perfecting a skill, emulation was considered honorable, and a tribute to the past and to past masters. It should be noted, though, that exact replication was not the objective because "a good fake is not just about making copies of existing pieces – of which an over-supply will render the efforts of the forger ineffective – but rather about creating something unique and beautiful in the style and spirit of the original" (von Falkenhausen 2013: 12). This understanding of materiality in Imperial China not only breaks with the European notion of authenticity but also breaks with the distinction between tangible and intangible materials. Artisanship is not measured by "originality" or "creativity" but by ability to approach ancestral ties/histories and respect for tradition.

In China the idea of "fake," "authenticity" or "authorship" does not exist in the same way that they have been developed within a European context.[9] Copied objects in China are seen as original if they are created to bring an old style and maintain the spirit/essence into the new, whereas in the European context, in an age of mechnical reproduction, the essence of a work of art is associated with its originality and uniqueness and copies are thought to have lost that aura (Benjamin 1969). There is no issue over "rights" to copy and recopy heritage materials in China. Instead, the transmission of rights to inscriptions and other forms belonging to lineages, groups and emperors is symbolic of a respect for ancestry, and for connections to the past and tradition. The absence of a concept of the "fake" in Chinese art during the imperial era has resulted in a contradiction in the contemporary discourse of patent rights and intellectual property rights in both worldwide intellectual property discourse and in the Chinese context. For example, the numerous *shanzhai* (山寨) – meaning fake or copied – products in contemporary China cannot simply be explained as a profit-oriented economic behavior. As shown by contemporary ethnographic researches by Tinari (2010) and Wong (2013), at Dafen village, where painters are (re)producing the paintings of Van Gogh and selling them around the world, the painters are not considered to be "copying" but performing an act of adaptation and innovation. We argue that in China, where there is no idea of ownership to the exclusion of others, artistic, and collecting, practices have blurred the boundary between fake and authentic in the arts world.

Collecting practice as self-cultivation

Shoucang (收藏), collecting or collection in Chinese, means to keep (or to reserve) and hide when used as a verb, and storage or hidden objects as a noun. We argue that there is a relationship between person, object and thing through collecting and copying practices in China. In fact, collecting/copying is considered to be a way of cultivating oneself and becoming a morally better person, as well as perpetuating heritage in the present. Collecting has been recognized as a means of legitimizing the right to rule and responsibility to obey oneself, and the act of emulation has been practiced throughout Chinese history. Moreover, objects have been used to justify one's political or hierarchical position in the ritual system since ancient times, and the practice of collecting has been considered to cultivate one's mind since the Song dynasty.

Among artistically valuable objects collected, calligraphy was placed at the top of the hierarchy. Von Falkenhausen discusses the concept of *wen* (文), literate or writing, and historiography in China. Writing is not merely functional but, just like painting, is also appreciated for its aesthetic qualities. In Chinese thought, as illustrated vividly by Yen (2005), handwriting can be taken as a reflection of a person's inner self and an important means of self-cultivation and self-expression. Calligraphy has therefore played an important role in Chinese art history. It is possible to cultivate oneself through imitating and practicing the calligraphy of a morally exemplary person (von Falkenhausen 2013: 42; Bai 2013: 392). Similarly, writings and inscriptions were considered as a link to the past in the ancient Chinese ancestral cult (von Falkenhausen 2013). In imperial times, calligraphy as handwriting was interwoven with the notion of personhood. In other words, we can conclude that writing and calligraphy, associated with *wen* (literate), were "highly empowered cultural form[s] through which power is articulated, social relations lubricated, deep knowledge extracted and one's relationship with the world is interpreted, ultimately indicating and formulating Chinese personhood" (Yen 2005: i).

The Confucian idiom *gewu* (格物), to study the nature of things or to investigate things, is understood as a way of augmenting one's virtue. *Wu* could be interpreted as nature or objects. The practice of *gewu* was propagated by scholar-officials in the Song period in order to become a Confucian moral person. *Gewu zizhi* (格物致知), to study the nature of things to attain truth, forms the Confucian foundation for personal morality, and has been the subject of interpretation by many scholars over the course of Chinese history. In this sense, Song scholars did not merely learn from the textual canons; material objects provided other paths to knowledge. Aesthetically pleasing objects were believed to turn the owner into a morally better person. This is very likely to suggest that when a philosophical school that promoted *gewu* flourished, so did private collecting and a flourishing of the antiquities market during this period (Wang 2017).

To sum up this section, firstly, collecting practices are believed to be linked to self-cultivation, forms of knowledge production and legacy building that links to the past. Secondly, collections themselves are believed to change their materiality and status through collecting practice. Lastly, not only is collection linked to improved social status, the cultivation of collections is also considered to be the cultivation of one's morality. It is often expressed by contemporary collectors in China that their actions are directed more to ideals of self-promotion and family distinction than they are to the idea of collecting as kind of investment.

The history of collecting and the concept of *wenwu*

The Chinese term for antiquities or relics is *wenwu*. *Wen* translates as literate, books, civilian or Confucian doctrine, and *wu* refers to things or objects. In China, the term *wenwu* first appeared in the *Chronicle of Zuo*, written in the fourth century BCE, in which it referred to the ritual system in the imperial court and the maintenance of a hierarchical relationship among people; however, the term later emerged to refer to objects that were used in the ritual system to maintain the permanence of social relationship. Early dynastic meanings of *wenwu* objects, such as jade and bronzes, were held to justify the political power of the Emperor. It was not until the Tang and Song dynasties (seventh through thirteenth centuries) that, as the study of antiquities became more popular among intellectual-officials, the meaning of *wenwu* was expanded to cover ancient objects. By the twentieth century the term could be used to describe any object made by human hands that was of historical or aesthetic significance – a broad substitute for cultural property (Wang 2017).

During the Northern Song period (960–1127), the study of *Jinshi* (the study of metal and stone) became popular. Scholars studied objects to understand the historical past. For example, in Imperial China, collections were politically, religiously and socially symbolic, and were normally in the hands of nobles or officials. Since the Tang and Song dynasties, because of the surge of private collecting and markets, collections were also in the hands of private connoisseurs and intellectuals. As such, *wenwu* were no longer limited to bronzes and jades of the ancient period, but later also included paintings, calligraphies, porcelains, etc. Moreover, *wenwu* were associated with the power, authority and political status of the empire and its officials. Since the Shang dynasty, bronze vessels had been used by the ruling elites to signify their religious rituals and political roles. Later on, since the Song dynasty, *wenwu* were more related to aesthetic values, wealth and social prestige that are similar to those of modern times, and were also in the hands of connoisseurs such as intellectuals. Moreover, Song officials collected ancient things as tools to learn about the past. With private collections flourishing during the Ming and Qing dynasties (fourteenth through twentieth centuries), *wenwu* were therefore not only symbols of imperial glory but for the appreciation of the public at large. By the Ming and Qing dynasties, *wenwu* had been replaced by the terms *guwan* (古玩, ancient playthings) and *gudong* (古董, ancient treasures or ancient curios). Use of the terms *gudong* and *guwan* may be an indicator that collections and collecting flourished in Ming and Qing society. During the republican era, use of the term *guwu* (古物, ancient objects) was widely adopted; *gu* means antique and *guwu* refers to anything from the past.

Bai has used the term *cultural hierarchy* as an operational concept used to rank collectible items (2013: 392). In Bai's (2013: 392) study of late-Qing official-collectors, he pointed out that among collectibles, metal and stone objects with inscriptions were the most highly valued, after which came calligraphy and paintings, while textiles and other artworks had the least value. Unlike European paradigms, which deem fine art the most valuable, bronzes bearing place inscriptions were considered to be of the highest scholarly value (Bai 2013:

394), and the hierarchy from bronzes to textiles is retained in the logic of museum display in China today as in both the National Museum of Chinese History in Beijing and the National Palace Museum in Taipei. Using the term *wenwu* emphasizes the essential cultural value of heritage materials, while the shift to terms such as *gudong* or *guwan* has represented a shift toward the commodity aspects of heritage value. Moreover, it is possible to suggest that in Imperial China the Chinese attitude toward *wenwu* was more concerned with their roles in justifying the past whilst the Europeans focused more on the symbolic meanings of art expressions and aesthetic values of objects.

During the late Qing period, there was a break with China's historical past, during which Chinese intellectuals became fascinated with Western technology and imperial power, and with re-examining Chinese tradition. The increasing cultural contact and exposures to the outside world in the late Qing period had led to the introduction of the European practices of heritage conservation and a European form of museums that present not only collections, but that also showcase China itself by displaying antiquities once hidden away in storage (Wang 2017). These were proposed by Chinese scholarly officials and European missionaries. For example, scholar-officials Kang Youwei (1858–1927) and Zhang Qian (1853–1926) had proposed the establishment of museum systems that resembled those of Western civilization and symbolized advancement. In addition, scholar Wang Guowei (1877–1927) called attention to a need to distinguish the property rights of the imperial household and the state when the last Emperor Puyi, who abdicated in 1911, then lived off the sale of the imperial collections from the Forbidden City. He had questioned what "national" cultural heritage is about (Aisin-Gioro 1986). Secondly, it was also the war-torn era when major Chinese antiquities were looted by foreign invaders; the prevention of "national" heritage being lost abroad had been widely called for. This period witnessed the transformation of cultural heritage from imperial collections to national cultural heritage, and to the idea of public ownership of cultural property, much in the way such processes occurred with the establishment of other nation states (e.g. Anderson 1991). National museums displayed imperial collections as well as archaeological findings. In 1914 *Guwu chenlie suo* (Display Room of Antiquities) was opened. In 1925, the imperial collection in the Forbidden City was opened to the public for the first time (Wang 2017). It was an era that witnessed the birth of Chinese archaeology with major excavations organized by Academia Sinica searching for the "origin" of Chinese civilization and the first capitals of China in places like Xiaxian and Anyang Yinxu. As such, in this period, heritage and museums began to be associated with Western civilization, science and technology and were considered a means for China's path towards modernization.

The 1930 Law on the Preservation of Ancient Objects was passed by the Nationalist government in response to concerns over the imminent threat of losing Chinese cultural heritage abroad by the invasion of imperial powers and serious lootings. This was China's first formal regulation concerning cultural artifacts. State sovereignty was declared in territorial claims of the nation state, breaking with the traditional *tianxia* concept that gave definition to national heritage in the legal sense. The current state is now the legal heritage protector of all properties within its territorial boundary, including those of ethnic minorities. Moreover, this law used the term *guwu* (anything from the past); at around the same time, the term *wenwu* also reappeared. The shift from *wenwu* to *guwu* in the Ming and Qing dynasties had loosened the definition of heritage to anything from the past; however, the shift back from *guwu* to *wenwu* during the Republican era secularized the concept of heritage. Since the establishment of the People's Republic of China in 1949, the term *wenwu* has been used officially in all government documents, and refers to any historical remains made before 1795. Conversely, *gudong* and *guwan* refer to objects in private collections and instead of historical significances, their economic value is emphasized. According to Wang Cheng-Hua (2010), in the early twentieth century (a time of political crisis in the Qing court and of the invasion of colonial powers), *wenwu* became contextualized as the accumulation of national learning (*guoxue*, 國學), representing China as a whole and narrating a lineal Chinese history. However, in Mao's era, a rupture appeared whereby *wenwu* or cultural relics were redefined as museum objects having the scientific value necessary to document each stage in social evolution. For example, at the National Museum of Chinese History in Beijing the Chinese dynastic past was redefined into several stages for Marxist evolutionary ideology and archaeological materials were used to quantify the progress of historical periods (Wang 2017). But during the Cultural Revolution Chairman Mao and Premier Zhou asked the Red Guard to protect the museums because precious antiquities justifying the continuity of Chinese history were stored inside. However, collections held in private hands and heritage sites were largely destroyed by the Red Guard (Liu 2013). This ideological link between art and politics had also been made over the course of Imperial Chinese history. Each new ruler took custodianship of antiquities of previous rulers and then commissioned new works based on the models of the past. For those treasures lost abroad, *wenwu* became imbued with symbolic meaning supporting the construction of a discourse of national humiliation through which Chinese citizens were meant to learn lessons of colonial invasion. During the communist era (1949–1980s), antiquities relating to the imperial past were considered as "old" and remains of feudal superstition and were largely attacked by the Red Guard. Those holding collections were considered class enemies of the common people; private ownership and art markets were banned.

It was not until the 1980s with the economic reform and the state's participation in the UNESCO heritage listing that the imperial past has been re-valued and private collecting is possible. In 1982 (revised in 1991 and 2002), the state first issued the Law of the People's Republic of China on Protection of Cultural Relics. During this period, a new term, *yichan* (遺產) (heritage), appeared. It originally referred to inherited property but came to be associated with historical remains, objects and architecture, and now includes intangible heritage. The term is often used together with *wenhua* (culture), to give *wenhua yichan*. Subsequently, various amendments have expanded and adjusted the meaning of heritage in accordance with UNESCO definitions, widening the meaning from tangible to include intangible heritage, from object to include landscape, and from cultural sites to include natural sites. While the 1930 law only focused on Han Chinese cultural heritage, the 2002 revision included more vernacular heritage. Moreover, the introduction of the idea of intangible heritage to China in 2004 was intended explicitly to celebrate, and include, cultures of ethnic groups. In addition, the concept of the eco-museum was introduced to China in the late 1990s and was established in the area of Guizhou, Yunnan where major ethnic minorities were located. As Madsen (2014) noted, the state now presents itself as a protector of China's diverse heritage that links everyday life to an imagined 5,000 years of glorious Chinese tradition.

The art market and private museum boom in contemporary China

In 2009, two bronzes depicting the heads of a rabbit and a rat from the Summer Palace in Beijing, which had been taken by British and French troops in 1860 during the Second Opium War, were put up for auction at a Christie's sale in Paris. These had been displayed originally as part of a series of twelve bronze animal heads on the palace fountain. The auction caused huge debates in China and tensions between Christie's and the Chinese government, which had asked the auction house to halt the sale and to return the objects to China. Cai Mingchao, a Chinese bidder, successfully thwarted the sale to a person outside China by submitting the winning bid of 15 million euros, then refusing payment. Mr Cai later cited a patriotic motivation, claiming that "many of us just want these Chinese treasures to come home" (Zhang 2009). "I believe that any Chinese person would stand up at that moment. I am making an effort to fulfil my own responsibilities . . . It's just the chance happened to come to me" (Zhang 2009).

While private ownership was not recognized during the Mao era, the recognition of private property rights in 2007 Property Law of the People's Republic of China has resulted in an explosion of antiquities collecting as well as state-led museum-building and heritage-making projects. Curio shops, antiquities markets, private museums and auction houses are doing business in big cities like Beijing, Shanghai, Chengdu, Xi'an and Guangzhou. The theme of national humiliation through the loss of important heritage to the West in the 19th century has been emphasized by the state that the people of China must act as trustees of their traditions and cultural heritage. It is now common for Chinese collectors to buy Chinese treasures around the world, then to repatriate them. In international art markets, Chinese buyers differ from most in their focus on bidding for Chinese arts. Take the Christie's autumn 2010 sale for instance. 85% of the lots for Chinese art were sold to buyers from Greater China (China, Hong Kong, Macao and Taiwan) (Wang 2012: 151). National museums are negotiating with museums abroad for the return of Chinese treasures, and even competing to outbid each other (Wang 2012: 28). Chinese diasporas are also buying reproductions of Qing-style furniture to decorate their homes in Europe and elsewhere.

With the strong patriotic motivation that all cultural property should return to China, Chinese buyers do not hesitate to buy back looted antiquities, and objects from ancient tombs, archaeological sites and museum collections. Many of these illegally obtained objects have been smuggled overseas and re-sold in Hong Kong via legal auction houses. The Chinese authorities then make claims for their restitution to the mainland (Wang 2012: 32). Moreover, it is interesting to note that objects excavated from tombs are usually treated negatively, and disturbing the burial sites of the dead is considered inauspicious. Chinese collectors did not buy bronzes or funerary wares in the old times because they were ritual vessels that had been buried in tombs (Wang 2012: 48). However, at a sale at the Sackler auction house, "several of the top bronze vessels were purchased by Chinese dealers to be returned to China, suggesting that the drive to repatriate China's 'lost' cultural heritage is no longer exclusive to the popular art categories, but covered the entire spectrum of Chinese material culture" (Wang 2012:48).

The Chinese state and the Chinese nouveau riche have also actively entered the market for relics both locally and abroad to contribute to state museums. As of 2003 the Forbidden City had "acquired a total of 223,506 new works, of which 20,000 were donations from individuals and 324 were classified as Class One cultural relics. Donations were also made by foreigners" (Wang 2012: 107–108). Among these donors, for example, Geng Baochang, the prominent porcelain scholar and Jingdezhen's last commissioner of porcelain, donated a significant collection of family porcelains (Wang 2012: 107, 151). Indeed, cultural repatriation is a main impetus driving the collecting of art among Chinese people. Our ethnography in Quanzhou shows that there has been a tendency among Chinese migrants to return objects and images to original ancestral temples as they have intangible relationship from where they came.

In 2011, we visited three private, local-initiative heritage projects in southwestern China. Mr Fan Jianchuan, founder of the Jianchuan Museum complex in Anren, claimed he would donate the entire museum complex to the nation after he died because he wanted to contribute something positive to it. Surprisingly, the founders of all three identified their actions as a means of glorifying and honouring the nation; they took historical objects as the material record of history, and imbued their collection activities with moral reasoning. They identified their efforts, which are part of a cultural repatriation trend, as patriotic crusades on behalf of the nation. One cannot simply compare the private museum boom in China to those in Europe or the United States. In China, our research into private museums and collections pointed to founders' individual patriotic ideals connecting museums and the notion of heritage as transmitting value to the future, to the national good and philanthropy, as well as taste and identity. The establishment of private museums is encouraged by local governments as part of their development plans; they are also included in the state's patriotic education system as a means of connecting the Chinese people to their heritage.[10] As a result, museum content is highly censored by governments. It is noteworthy that all museums' contents have to be reviewed by the propaganda departments or publicity departments at national, provincial or municipal levels. While Chinese billionaires may participate in the global art market to buy back Chinese art works to donate to China's museums, private museum projects demonstrate a similar commitment to honor their pasts through filial attachment to place and cultural practice. In a sense, this is not so different from a more general concern with the influence and power of intellectuals in public life in China. Whilst the Western ideal of the public intellectual meets various levels of fulfillment, in China there is a much greater awareness that the Confucian ideal of the scholar is both edifying and critical. The world renouncer role of the scholar extends back to the birth of Confucianism as part of the Axial Age phenomenon (Jaspers 2011) but more widely is associated with both contemporary popular Daoist and Chinese Buddhist philosophies (Chau 2011; Feuchtwang 1992)

Collecting practices as a symbol of taste and class in contemporary China

There is an idiom in Chinese – *shengshi shoucang, luanshi huangjin* (盛世收藏，亂世黃金) – which means "Collect [antiquities] in good times, [buy] gold in troubled times." Traditionally wealthy families have prized the possession of antiquities, and today, this idiom also captures the contemporary arts boom in China, with the trend of collection correlating with the perceived affluence of the current period. Behind the booming art market, it is interesting to note that a growing number of nouveau riches in the reform era use arts and artifacts to increase their prestige, and this is helping to drive the boom. These nouveaux riches are sometimes called *baofahu* (暴發戶), a negatively connoted term typifying overnight success and a propensity to spread money around lavishly. The term implies a lack of culture, which one may try to counteract by collecting antiquities to demonstrate cultural taste. Antique collecting has become a means of displaying prestige among rich elites. Many wealthy Chinese people now regard art as a portfolio, as well as a way to represent their status. "If I want to be not just a millionaire but someone who plays with the big boys, I'd better be someone who collects art" (Zhang 2009). As the market for investment in China is still limited – although the economy is opening up – wealthy Chinese businessmen also consider art as an investment, making antiquities a liquid asset and their collection an act of patriotism among the nouveau riche. China now has the largest number of billionaires in the world, and they are using that wealth to "reclaim parts of Chinese history from Western collectors" (Pogrebin 2011). Chinese businessmen are now buying Chinese collections as an investment, as a symbol of their good taste, and to show their patriotism to China.

When people collect antiquities for *yang xing* (養性) (self-improvement) this is for complex reasons of investment, self-cultivation, and a desire to exhibit aesthetic appreciation. For instance, Mr Chang who has opened antiquities shops around Anyang mentioned that the major part of his business was with the government. Governors gifted each other cultural objects as a sign of their good taste. He once told us that people who collect are understood as *you wenhua* (有文化), meaning "people with culture". As a collector who joined weekend classes offered by the Chinese Academy of Social Science in Shanghai mentioned, "having a lot of money is not enough to be a rich person, one needs to have money as well as have 'taste'." During our fieldwork in China, we encountered numerous collectors. They mentioned that it is not enough to be rich, people need also to demonstrate they are cultured, and collecting was a way to show this.[11] This argument can find parallels in Grant's description of gift giving in Soviet economies and Ssorin-Chaikov (2013) on the making of gifts to Soviet leaders.

Yet the collection and appreciation of art and cultural artifacts is, in large part, also drawn from the belief that people have to respect their elders and ancestors, and to be reverent to things, and this continues to be seen in the art acquisitions made by Chinese nouveaux riches today. In a sense, loyalty to one's country and family plays a major part in art acquisition, as does the importance of looking back on China's history as one of the great empires of the world. Such pride is instrumental in understanding how the Chinese appreciate their own art and culture, which, in turn, stimulates buyers to acquire artefacts.

Collection, collecting and collectors

In China, cultivating collections depends on in part on the person/thing/object relationship, and is different from the Western idea of relics/amulets/talisman that connotes the capacity of objects to heal and cure, to perform miracles. While in traditional practice collectors are cultivated through objects collected, as exemplified by the *gewu* practice mentioned above; the value of material heritage can be transformed and cultivated through constant interaction with collectors. As time goes by, the collections become part of the collectors. Among these objects are tea-pots, jades, literati walnuts, stones, etc. For example, *yang hu* (養壺), meaning cultivating a tea pot through constant care and by using it with high class tea makes the culture of the tea pot better, is commonly practiced by ordinary tea drinkers. Jade can also be cultivated by wearing it (*yang yu*, 養玉); it is believed that jade comes to carry the spirit, *qi*, of the wearer. Hsieh (2016) described how literati walnut collecting in contemporary China is nurtured through collectors' skillful attentiveness – through massaging (*rou*, 揉), kneading (*nie*, 捻), and pinching (*za*, 榨) (Lu 2006). The bodily practices, such as developing the skills of holding, swirling, rubbing and sounding are part of collecting practice of heritage materials. As Hsieh (2016) described it, the older the walnuts, the more valuable they become in the art market. On the other hand, the mindset of collectors themselves can also be cultivated and transformed through collecting practices. For instance, the market itself radically influences collectors and what they collect. Other anthropological studies have also shown how bodily practices can change mind and achieve higher hierarchical status (Yan 2008; Yu 2009). For example, Chinese *kung fu* (功夫) practitioners and monks found that they believe they are cultivating mind and morality through the bodily practices (Yan 2008). As such, a supreme *kung fu* practitioner is also perceived to be a morally better master. Yu (2009) researched *zen qi* (禪七) in Taiwan, showing that Buddhist followers seek to improve their minds through meditation and *zen* practices and vice versa. In other words, collectors vs. collections, human agents vs. things, or subjects vs. objects, are mutually constitutive in the processes of collecting or the interaction of objects vs. subject. In this sense, the heritage value of both collectors and collections are transformed and can be obtained.

In China, material objects from the past are not merely taken as curiosities, scientific specimens, religiously charged relics or treasures; instead, objects are associated with personhood and moreover, with personal virtue. Lin (2008, 2015) has explored the materialization of deity statues in Chinese religion. The different natures of materials mediate distinct kinds of divine power. Chang (2015) described the artistic appropriation and copying of deity Mazu's statues in China and Taiwan showing how the locals intend to link with the center through material standardization. In addition to deity statues, ancestral tablets (*shenzupai*, 神祖牌) are believed to carry the spirits of those dead whose names are inscribed on them. There are two parts to the ritual included in ancestor worship, namely worship of ancestral tablets at home or in ancestral halls, and worship at grave sites. Cloth tombs (*yiguanzhong*, 衣冠塚) are buried tombs containing the used clothes or utensils of the dead. The spirits of the ancestors are considered to reside in the material, and they are revered as representations of the ancestors themselves. These examples have challenged the Western epistemology, which intends to separate subject and object or mind and body, and which has resulted in the differentiation of tangible and intangible heritage. While in China, as the cases shown above an historical relic has a spiritual or even moral dimension, and thus carries a spiritually significant agency. Moreover, heritage materials can be cultivated and their values can be transformed through collecting practices. Heritage materials are thus transmitted as forms of power.

Concluding remarks

We have presented how Han Chinese people try to make respectful connections with their pasts through practices that have made and remade collective ideas of ancestral identity. "In the Confucian tradition, such impulses associate the act of donation with surrendering ancestral substance to the cosmological center, and are ultimately associated with an ancestral notion of gaining immortality not by remembrance but by the fusing of substances" (Thompson 1988, cited in Evans and Rowlands 2014: 282). The value of material objects and displays in their projects derives not from their materiality per se, but in their materialization of cultural, emotional and, we argue, kin, ethnic and regional ties rooted in identification with historical past that linking past and future. The significance of portable im/material heritage is located not only in the material itself but also in the memory and practices that mediate between material worlds and humans/non-humans. Heritage values transmitted through material culture are located in techniques of calligraphy and painting, in the methods of displaying jades, porcelains, bronzes and textiles, in the aesthetic appreciation of forms, and in the Confucian philosophy that approaches the ideal person. Moreover, they shed light on the epistemological understanding of heritage in China where notions of authenticity and the separation of subjects and objects do not have a clear-cut definition and may even, at times, not exist.

These long term transformations in heritage value have imported both paradox and ambiguity into cultural property discourse in China. At the state level, China has ratified various UNESCO conventions and followed UNESCO's definition of heritage into its existing legal sense of heritage conservation. The changing roles and definition of *wenwu* over time has meant that the Chinese government eventually agreed with the UNESCO definition of heritage as expressed in the 2002 Law of the People's Republic of China on the Protection of Cultural Relics in China. However, numerous paradoxes and local methods of heritage practices occurred on the ground, when combining Chinese heritage value with local and diverse Han and non-Han historical understandings that are beyond and sometimes contradict UNESCO and other official definitions. The traditional Chinese discourse on *wenwu* has blurred the boundaries of singular authorship, authenticity and fake, collection and collectors, subjects and objects. These ambiguities are made visible in the hierarchies of value presented and displayed by objects and collections in national museums, by the creators of private museums claiming heritage with patriotic motivation and historical values, as well as the explosion of antiquities markets and the incentives of individual collectors that links collecting practices to patriotic motivation, taste and class as well self-cultivation.

Acknowledgements

The authors would like to acknowledge Prof Mingming Wang, Dr Nicole T. C. Chiang and Ms Chao-hui Tu for their commenting on the earlier draft of this chapter. For conducting this research Shu-Li Wang would like to thank the generous funding support from the project "Time in Intercultural Context," directed by Prof. Dr. Maarten E.R.G.N. Jansen (Faculty of Archaeology, Leiden University, the Netherlands), which has received funding from the European Union's Seventh Framework Program (FP7/2007–2013) under grant agreement n° 295434.

Notes

1 Similarly, as Pierra Nora explored for the case of France, "the acceleration of history" and the modernist posture towards the past after the French revolution brought the role of monumental heritage to the fore as medium for collective remembering. He referred to *lieux de memoire*, sites of memory, because there were no longer *milieux de memoire*, real environments of memory (1989:7).
2 Even though Imperial China experienced many dynastic power shifts, and despite two periods of rule, the Yuan and Qing dynasties were by non-Han Chinese.
3 The 1930 Law on the Preservation of Ancient Objects.
4 The conceptualization of China as an empire is still very much influenced the political discourse in contemporary China.
5 Rawson identified three activities associated with archaism: "antiquarianism (the practice of collecting and studying antiquities)", "re-production", and "archaism (a new style based on the past)" (1995:22–27). Von Falkenhausen (2013) used the term "antiquarian mentality" to describe how it was normal for authorities in pre-imperial China to be engaged in remaking material heritage such as past ritual bronzes and jades.
6 In fact, before the 19th century, the concept of art as we understand it today did not exist in China, neither did it exist in Europe before the 18th century (Clunas 2004b). The Chinese term for art, *yishu (藝術)*, was defined as human activities performed with skills that included skills in performing rites, music, archery, charioting, calligraphy, divination and mathematics. It was not until 19th century that in the Complete Library of the Four Treasuries complied by emperor Qianlong, in the category of "*Yishu*," treatises on music, chess and seal carving are included alongside books on paintings and calligraphy (Chiang 2014:3–5).
7 Oracle Bones are pieces of animal bones or shells which were used originally in divination in ancient China, especially during the Shang dynasty.
8 Since 2009, Dr Wang has conducted fieldwork in museums, World Heritage sites and archaeological stations in Anyang, Chengdu and Xi'an in China.
9 For issues surrounding "fakes" in Chinese art world, *The Orientations* magazine published a special issue on the subject in November/December 2015 (vol. 46 No.8).
10 The number of museums has also been growing in a dramatic rate. Both museums and heritage sites have been promoted by the state as "bases of patriotic education" since the early 1990s. As of 2008 all public museums (except archaeological parks) are free to the public.
11 Prof Michael Rowlands has been participating in heritage projects in Southwest of China and Fujian. Since 2009 Dr Shu-Li Wang has been doing ethnographic research in archaeological museums and World Heritage sites in Anyang, Chengdu and Xi'an. In 2011 both authors did fieldwork in Chengdu and Yunnan to observe the private heritage projects in China.

Bibliography

AFP. 2011. "Chinese Boost Prices in World's Auction Houses." *Independent*. Accessed 10 July 2015. http://www.independent.co.uk/life-style/chinese-boost-prices-in-worlds-auction-houses-2198558.html.

Aisin-Gioro, Puyi. 1986. *From Emperor to Citizen: The Autobiography of Aisin-Gioro Puyi*, translated by W. J. F. Jenner. Beijing: Foreign Languages Press.
Alberge, Dalya. 2014. "China's Wealthy Building New Museums to Display the Country's Treasures." *Financial Times*. Accessed 10 July 2015. http://www.ft.com/cms/s/0/5002360a-f632-11e3-a038-00144feabdc0.html#axzz478Ux9Ggb.
Anagnost, Ann S. 1997. *National Past-Times: Narrative, Representation, and Power in Modern China*. Durham, NC: Duke University Press.
Anderson, Benedict. 1991. *Imagined Communities: Reflections on the Origin and Spread of Nationalism*. New York and London: Verso.
Appadurai, A. 2015. "Mediants, Materiality, Normativity." *Public Culture* 27(2): 221–237.
Bai, Q. 2013. "Antiquarianism in a Time of Crisis: On the Collecting Practices of Late-Qing Government Officials, 1861–1911." In *World Antiquarianism. Comparative Perspectives*, edited by A. Schnapp, 386–403. Los Angeles: The Getty Research Institute.
Benjamin, Walter. 1969. "The Work of Art in the Age of Mechanical Reproduction." In *Illuminations: Essays and Reflections*, edited by Hannah Arendt. New York: Schocken Books.
Bennett, Tony. 1995. *The Birth of the Museum*. London: Routledge.
Berliner, D. 2012. Multiple Nostalgias: The Fabric of Heritage in Luang Prabang. *Royal Anthropological Institute* 18: 769–786.
Bourdieu, Pierre. 1984. "The Aristocracy of Culture." In *Distinction: A Social Critique of the Judgement of Taste*. New York: Routledge.
Callahan, William A. 2004. "National Insecurities: Humiliation, Salvation, and Chinese Nationalism." *Alternatives: Global, Local, Political* 29(2): 199–218.
Chang, Hsun. 2015. "The Statue of Mazu, Appropriation, and the Discussion on Watson's Concept of 'Standardization.'" *Journal of Archaeology and Anthropology* 82: 5–26.
Chang, K.C. 1981. "Archaeology and Chinese Historiography." *World Archaeology* 13(2): 156–169.
Chau, Adam Yuet, ed. 2011. *Religion in Contemporary China: Revitalization and Innovation*. Oxon and New York: Routledge.
Chiang, Nicole T.C. 2014. "Redefining an Imperial Collection: Problems of Modern Impositions and Interpretations." *Journal of Art Historiography* 10: 1–22.
Clunas, Craig. 2004a. *Elegant Debts: The Social Art of Wen Zhengming, 1470–1559*. London: Reaktion Books.
Clunas, Craig. 2004b. *Superfluous Things: Material Culture and Social Status in Early Modern China*. Honolulu: University of Hawaii Press.
Ebrey, Patricia Buckley. 2008. *Accumulating Culture: The Collections of Emperor Huizong*. Seattle: University of Washington Press.
Elman, B. 2000. *A Cultural History of Civil Examinations in Late Imperial China*. Berkeley and Los Angeles: University of California Press.
Evans, Harriet, and Michael Rowlands. 2014. "Reconceptualising Heritage in China: Museums, Development and the Shifting Dynamics of Power." In *Museums, Heritage and International Development*, edited by Paul Basu and Wayne Modest. London: Routledge.
Feuchtwang, Stephan. 1992. *The Imperial Metaphor: Popular Religion in China*. London and New York: Routledge.
Freedman, Maurice. 1966. *Chinese Lineage and Society: Fukien and Kwangtung*. London: University of London, The Athlon Press.
Gaskell, Ivan. 2012. "Spilt Ink: Aesthetic Globalization and Contemporary Chinese Art." *British Journal of Aesthetics* 52(1): 1–16.
Geertz, Clifford. 1981. *Negara: The Theatre State in Nineteenth-Century Bali*. Princeton, NJ: Princeton University Press.
Harrell, Stevan. 1995. "Civilizing Projects and the Reaction to Them." In *Cultural Encounters on China's Ethnic Frontiers*, edited by Stevan Harrell. Seattle: University of Washington Press.
Harrison, R. 2016. *Heritage: Critical Approaches*. London and New York:Routledge.
Hevia, James L. 2001. "World Heritage, National Culture, and the Restoration of Chengde." *Positions* 9 (1): 219–243.
Hewison, Robert. 1987. *The Heritage Industry: Britain in a Climate of Decline*. London: Methuen Publishing Ltd.
Hobsbawm, Eric, and Terence Ranger. 1983. *The Invention of Tradition*. New York: Cambridge University Press.

Hsieh, I-Yi. 2016. "Nuts: Beijing Folklore Connoisseurship in the Age of Heritage Construction." *Asian Anthropology* 15(1): 52–67.
Huang, Chun-Chieh. 2007. "The Defining Character of Chinese Historical Thinking." *History and Theory* 46(2): 180–188.
ICOMOS. 1931. "Athens Charter for the Restoration of Historic Monuments." ICOMOS. Accessed 20 Sep 2012. www.icomos.org/en/charters-and-texts.
ICOMOS. 1964. "International Charter for the Conservation and Restoration of Monuments and Sites (The Venice Charter)." ICOMOS. Accessed 20 Sep 2012. www.icomos.org/en/charters-and-texts.
Jaspers, Karl. 2011(1949). *The Origin and Goal of History*. London: Routledge.
Kopytoff, I. 1988. "The Cultural Biography of Things." In *The Social Life of Things. Commodities in Cultural Perspective*, edited by A. Appadurai. Cambridge: Cambridge University Press, pp. 64–91.
Labadi, Sophia, and Colin Long, eds. 2010. *Heritage and Globalisation, Key Issues in Cultural Heritage*. Abingdon: Routledge.
Latour, Bruno. 1996. "On Interobjectivity." *Mind, Culture, and Activity* 3(4): 228–245.
Levenson, Joseph Richmond. 1967. "The Province, the Nation, and the World: The Problem of Chinese Identity." In *Approaches to Modern Chinese History*, edited by Rhoads Murphey and Mary Clabaugh Wright. Berkeley: University of California Press.
Lowenthal, D. 1985. *The Past Is A Foreign Country*. Cambridge: Cambridge University Press.
Li, L. 2005. *Recasting Antiquity*. Hong Kong: The Chinese University of Hong Kong.
Lin, Wei-ping. 2008. "Conceptualizing Gods through Statues: A Study of Personalization and Localization in Taiwan." *Asian Anthropology* 8: 1–30.
Lin, Wei-ping. 2015. *Materializing Magic Power: Chinese Popular Religion in Villages and Cities*. Cambridge: Harvard University Asia Center.
Liu, Jianmei. 2013. "Work on the Protection of Cultural Heritage in the 1970s. (20世纪70年代前后中国文物保护工作述略)." *Modern China* 4(20): 47–55.
Lu, Tracey L-D. 2014. *Museums in China: Power, Politics and Identities*. Oxford and New York: Routledge.
Lu, XiaoRong. 2006. *On Walnuts (核桃卢谈核桃)*. Beijing:Wenwu Publication.
Madsen, Richard. 2014. "From Socialist Ideology to Cultural Heritage: the Changing Basis of Legitimacy in the People's Republic of China." *Anthropology & Medicine* 21(1): 58–70.
National Bureau of Statistics of China. 2014. "National Bureau of Statistics of China 2013." China Statistics Press. Accessed 10 July 2015. http://www.stats.gov.cn/tjsj/ndsj/2014/indexch.htm.
National People's Congress. 1982. Law of the People's Republic of China on Protection of Cultural Relics. Edited by National People's Congress, Beijing.
National People's Congress. 2002. Law of the People's Republic of China on Protection of Cultural Relics (2002 Amendment). Edited by National People's Congress, Beijing.
National People's Congress. 2007. Property Law of the People's Republic of China. Edited by 5th session of the Tenth National People's Congress, Beijing.
Nora, Pierra. 1989. Between Memory and History: *Les Lieux de Memoire*. *Representations*(Special Issue: Memory and Counter-Memory)26:7–24.
Oakes, Tim. 2013. "Heritage as Improvement: Cultural Display and Contested Governance in Rural China." *Modern China* 39(4): 380–407.
Progrebin, Robin. 2011. "China's New Cultural Revolution: A Surge in Art Collecting." *The New York Times*, September 6, 2011. http://www.nytimes.com/2011/09/07/arts/chinese-art-collectors-prove-to-be-a-new-market-force.html.
Rawson, Jessica. 2004. "Novelties in Antiquarian Revivals: The Case of the Chinese Bronzes." *The National Palace Museum Research Quarterly* 22(1): 1–34.
Rowlands, Mike. 2005. "A Materialist Approach to Materiality." In *Materiality*, edited by Daniel Miller, 72–87. Durham, NC: Duke University Press.
Schnapp, A. 2013. "Introduction: The Roots of Antiquarianism." In *World Antiquarianism. Comparative Perspectives*, edited by A. Schnapp. California: The Getty Research Institute.
Skinner, William, ed. 1979. *The Study of Chinese Society: Essays by Maurice Freedman*. Stanford, CA: Stanford University Press.
Smith, L. 2006. *Uses of Heritage*. Oxon: Routledge.
Ssorin-Chaikov, Nikolai. 2013. "Gift/Knowledge Relations at the Exhibition of Gifts to Soviet Leaders." *Laboratorium: Russian Review of Social Research* 5(2): 166–192.
State Council. 2016. "On the Improvement of the Work of Heritage Conservation. (国务院关于进一步加强文物工作的指导意见)." Edited by People's Republic of China, The State Council in Beijing.

So, J. F. 2008. "Antiques in Antiquity: Early Chinese Looks at the Past." *Journal of Chinese Studies* 48: 1–34.

Tam, Karen. 2014. "Dolce & Banana, A Shanzhai Creator's Manual: Production and Consumption of Fake in Contemporary Chinese Art Practices." In *The Changing Landscape of China's Consumerism*, edited by Alison Hulme. Oxford: Chandos Publishing.

Tambiah, Stanley J. 1977. "The Galactic Polity: The Structure of Traditional Kongdoms in Southeast Asia." *Annals New York Academy of Sciences* 293: 69–97.

Tinari, Philip. 2010. "Original Copies: The Dafen Oil Painting Village." In *The Craft Reader*, edited by Glenn Adamson, 297–302. Oxford: Berg Publishers.

Tsing, Anna Lowenhaupt. 2004. *Friction: An Ethnography of Global Connection.* Princeton, NJ: Princeton University Press.

Varutti, Marzia. 2008. "Which Museum for What China? Museums, Objects and the Politics of Representation in the Post-Mao Transition (1976–2007)." Ph.D., Docteur en Etudes du Développement, Université de Genève.

Von Falkenhausen, L. 2013. "Antiquarianism in East Asia: A Preliminary Overview." In *World Antiquarianism. Comparative Perspectives*, edited by A. Schnapp, 35–66. Los Angeles: The Getty Research Institute.

Wang, A. 2012. *Chinese Antiquities. An Introduction to the Art Market.* London: Lund Humphries.

Wang, Cheng-Hua. 2010. "The Qing Imperial Collection, Circa 1905–1925: National Humiliation, Heritage Preservation and Exhibition Culture." In *Reinventing the Past: Archaism and Antiquarianism in Chinese Art and Visual Culture*, edited by Hung Wu. Chicago: University of Chicago Press.

Wang, Shu-Li 2013. "The Politics of China's Cultural Heritage on Display – Yinxu Archaeological Park in the Making." Ph.D. thesis in Anthropology. University College London.

Wang, Shu-Li. 2016. "Civilization and the Transformation of Xiaotun Village at China's Yinxu Archaeological Site." In *World Heritage on the Ground: Ethnographic Perspectives*, edited by Beliner, D. and Baumman, C., 171–192. New York and Oxford: Berghahn.

Wang, Shu-Li. 2017. "Exhibiting the Nation: Cultural Flows, Transnational Exchanges and the Development of Museums in Japan and China in the Early Twentieth Century." In *Eurasian Encounters: Museums, Missions and Modernities*, edited by C. Stolte and Y.Y. Kikuchi. Amsterdam: Amsterdam University Press.

Wong, Winnie Won Yin. 2013. *Van Gogh on Demand: China and the Readymade.* Chicago: University of Chicago Press.

Wu, Hung. 1995. *Monumentality in Early Chinese Art and Architecture.* Stanford, CA: Stanford University Press.

Wu, Hung. 2003. "On Rubbings – Their Materiality and Historicity." In *Writing and Materiality in China*, edited by Judith Zeitlin and Lydia Liu, 29–72. Cambridge: Harvard University East Asian Publication.

Yan, Xuecheng. 2008. "Is Daoism Cultural? A Study of Daoist Cultivation." *Journal of Zhongzheng University* 11.

Yeh, Y. 2005. *Calligraphy and Power in Contemporary Chinese Society.* London and New York: Routledge.

Yu, Shuenn-Der. 2009. "Introduction: Bodily Cultivation as a Mode of Learning." *Taiwan Journal of Anthropology* 7(2): 3–12.

Zhang, L. 2009. "Patriotic Bidder Thwarts Relics' Sale." *China Daily.* Accessed 10 July 2015. http://www.chinadaily.com.cn/cndy/2009-03/03/content_7528047.htm.

14

OBJECT MOVEMENT

UNESCO, language, and the exchange of Middle Eastern artifacts

Morag M. Kersel

In September 2012, The University of Pennsylvania Museum of Archaeology and Anthropology (Penn Museum) loaned to Turkey a collection of 24 gold jewelry pieces, dating to ca. 2400 BCE. Legally purchased on the antiquities market in 1966 by the Penn Museum, the jewelry was sold with no known associated archaeological findspot although the pieces are similar to others recovered from Troy, an archaeological site in modern Turkey (Rose, 2016, 2017). Immediately following the acquisition, Penn Museum curator George Bass studied the collection remarking on the difficulty of pinpointing an original find spot for the artifacts (Bass, 1966, 1970) of the "international style", exhibiting characteristics of both Greek and Near Eastern jewelry of the mid-to-late third millennium BCE, Bass (1966, 1970) noted similarities with the Early Bronze Age jewelry of Troy (northwest Turkey), Poliochni on Lemnos (Greece), and Ur (southern Iraq) (Rose, 2017: 88). This inability to determine an initial archaeological context ultimately resulted in *The Pennsylvania Declaration* (Rose, 2017: 88), in which the "curators, board of managers, and director of the University of Pennsylvania Museum of Archaeology and Anthropology voted unanimously to purchase no antiquities in the future unless their place of origin and legality of export is *certain*" (*The Pennsylvania Declaration* 1970 [emphasis mine]). With this bold statement the Penn Museum became the first institution to take up such a position on the acquisition of undocumented materials by a museum.

Some 40 years later, with new technology, Ernst Pernicka of the University of Tubingen analyzed the soil found lodged inside one of the "Troy Gold" gold pendants leading him to conclude that the particle's composition was consistent with the soil in the Trojan plain (Rose, 2017; UPENN Press Release, 2012).After learning of results of the soil analysis the Turkish Ministry of Culture and Tourism contacted the Penn Museum regarding the potential repatriation of the gold to Turkey (UPENN Press Release, 2012). After a series of conversations between the University of Pennsylvania and the Turkish Ministry of Culture and Tourism a final decision was made on the disposition of the gold; it would be loaned to Turkey, indefinitely. The Williams Director of the Penn Museum Julian Siggers clarified the indefinite loan arrangement by stating that despite the new findings by Pernicka, there remained a lack of substantial evidence for the archaeological context of the collection – an argument could still be made for an original findspot in Greece or the Near East (Avril, 2012; Velioglu, Bandle, and Renold, 2013). In exchange for the gold Turkey agreed to facilitate the loan of artifacts to the Penn Museum for future exhibitions (Rose, 2017: 89). Additionally, according to Rose (2017: 89), all-important permits for University of Pennsylvania researchers to carry out excavation and survey in Turkey were offered in return for the "Troy Gold". The movement of the "Troy Gold" from the United States to Turkey through an indefinite loan allows the Penn Museum to retain ownership of the artifacts, while Turkey in taking physical possession of the material can determine the disposition of their cultural heritage (Rose, 2016, 2017).

Interestingly, there was little comment on the claim of the Penn Museum to retain legal title to the material. In the opinion of most the 1966 purchase date appears to be central to any discussion surrounding "ownership": 1966 predates the entry into force of the 1970 UNESCO *Convention on the Means of Prohibiting and Preventing the Illicit Import, Export and Transfer of Ownership of Cultural Property* (1970 UNESCO Convention) in 1972. The 1970 UNESCO Convention is the customary law most often acknowledged in debates over ownership. Even though Turkey has had a national ownership law in place since 1906 (Çelik, 2016; Özel, 2005, 2010) or one could argue as early as 1869 under the Ottoman Empire (see Çelik, 2016; Kersel, 2008, 2010; Özel, 2005, 2010), the general consensus was that the 1966 good faith purchase of the artifacts by the Penn Museum was legal. This case study in the movement of artifacts prompted disagreement and ongoing discussion between various international and professional communities, as well within academic circles. The Penn Museum director Siggers supported the movement of the "Troy Gold" back to Turkey stating: "We have a strong, long-standing partnership with Turkey, in which *cultural exchange* and *cultural understanding* are of paramount importance. In light of this history and our recent scientific testing, this agreement is right and appropriate" (UPENN Press Release, 2012 [emphasis mine]). Others did not agree. Responding to the proposed movement of the "Troy Gold" Pernicka expressed his concerns: "This will create problems for other museums because Turkish authorities will see this as a way to regain their culture heritage" (Wu, 2012). The positions of Siggers and Pernicka epitomize the long-standing debate over the movement of objects: cultural nationalists vs. cultural internationalists (Bauer, 2007; Merryman, 1986, 1996, 2005). This particular incident also encapsulates other issues associated with the movement of material: ownership, national identities, museum acquisitions, scientific inquiry, documentation, the legal antiquities market, and the legacy of colonialism.

Art and artifacts can be very effective communicators of cultural traditions and artistic inspiration fundamental to the intellectual and spiritual development of humanity. Forcefully articulated by Paul Bator (1983, pp. 30–31) is the notion of the object as envoy: "Art is a good ambassador. It stimulates interest in, *understanding* of, and *admiration* for a country" (emphasis mine). In order for objects to act as diplomatic agents, messengers, or representatives of states or cultures, movement of the object is usually involved. At times this movement is positive with the consent of the country of origin, while at other times the movement is negative – clandestine, suspect, and unauthorized. The movement of objects may appear to be singularly positive, but some nations, cultures, or individuals do not wish to participate in this exchange, instead preferring objects to remain within the confines of their borders, institutions, and even homes. There is also an on-going tension between the physical transfer of artifacts and their preservation and protection: with increasing movement the potential damage to cultural objects intensifies. These conflicting desires in tandem with the conceivable physical harm to artifacts has resulted in a need for the control of movement in the form of local, national, and international conventions, policies, and laws – some endeavors favoring the unfettered interchange of items and some enacting restrictive policies intent on virtually halting all transfer. Resulting in what Bauer (2007) refers to as a maelstrom of ownership theories, property laws, and export/import policies and controls, now besieging the material heritage of humankind. In order for an object to act as an ambassador *sensu* Bator (1983), there has to be a consensus on what moves, why it moves, where it moves, and how it moves. Are artifacts the "cultural heritage of mankind" (1954 UNESCO language) or does the material belong to individuals, nations, or states as might be interpreted in the language of the 1970 UNESCO Convention? The following relocates the discussion beyond the polarizing and entrenched conversations surrounding the binary stance on the movement of objects. An examination of the language in various UNESCO cultural heritage documents, focusing on examples from the Middle East, shows how artifacts are imagined as emissaries acting on behalf of nations, epochs, sites, or people, and allows for a consideration of the broader movement of objects.

The language of UNESCO and movement

Disagreement over movement raises several significant factors regarding the global exchange of cultural material. First, there is a need for the creation of a universal system of protection, with agreed upon principles, rules, and procedures established by an international organization and adopted by national administrations; second, the establishment of international norms, which address concerns regarding the positive and the negative elements associated with the circulation of cultural items; third, the increasing legal and illegal demand (institutional and individual) for cultural objects, the legacy of colonial enterprises, and a desire to fulfill the ideal of access for all will need to be taken into account when considering movement (Casini, 2011). The United Nations Educational, Scientific, and Cultural Organization (UNESCO) is the perceived authority on all things pertaining to cultural heritage and though often laudable, the efforts of UNESCO in regulating the movement of art and artifacts are not without their detractors, problems, and limitations (see De Cesari, 2010; Di Giovine, 2008; Meskell, 2012, 2014; Pearlstein, 2014; Singh, 2011).

Initial UNESCO efforts

One of the first instances where UNESCO took on the issue of the movement of cultural objects was in 1950, just after the establishment of the organization with the *UNESCO Agreement on the Importation of Educational, Scientific, and Cultural Materials* (1950 UNESCO Agreement). The Preamble urges co-operation between nations in all branches of intellectual activity, including "the *exchange of* publications, *objects of artistic and scientific interest* and other materials of information" and provides further that the Organization shall "collaborate in the work of advancing the *mutual knowledge and understanding of peoples. . . .* " (1950 UNESCO Agreement, Preamble [emphasis mine]). Daniels (2012) suggests that the 1950 UNESCO Agreement was intended to promote cultural exchange, not economic trade, resulting in a framework which made it possible the movement of "antiques over 100 years old" (1950 UNESCO Agreement, Annex B). Embedded in the language of the 1950 UNESCO Agreement are the terms "exchange" and "mutual knowledge and understanding of peoples" phrases used with consistency in later UNESCO documents (and echoed by more recent advocates like Bator and Siggers) aimed at authorizing the movement of objects for the purposes of education, relationship building, and engendering goodwill across the globe.

The passage of the *Hague Convention for the Protection of Cultural Property in the Event of Armed Conflict* (1954 Hague Convention) in 1954 was an international effort in reaction to the widespread looting and theft of cultural items that occurred during and after World War II. Many of the provisions in this document were fairly limited in regards to the movement of artifacts, instead focused on the exportation and seizure of material during periods of occupation and the subsequent repatriation of cultural materials once hostilities ceased (1954 Hague Convention). For the purposes of a discussion centered on movement, one notable aspect of the 1954 Hague Convention is in the Preamble, which declares that cultural property was not simply for the use and benefit of the country from which it came, but of importance to "the cultural heritage of mankind" (1954 Hague Convention Preamble). Podesta (2008) suggests that the inclusion of this statement in the 1954 Hague Convention was not a reflection of the framers' underlying contention that all countries should share equally in cultural history; the choice of language may simply have been a strategy to discourage the destruction of one country's relics by a citizen of another country during times of conflict by blatantly appealing to a common "European" ancestry (Podesta, 2008, p. 468). This initial underpinning of a common and revered "European" heritage recurs in later UNESCO Conventions and Recommendations and has been the focus of critiques on the Eurocentric and Western-focused nature of UNESCO and its programs (De Cesari, 2010; Di Giovine, 2008; Duedahl, 2011; Meskell, 2012, 2014; Prott, 2005; Singh, 2011; Wong, 2008).

Following the 1954 Hague Convention, UNESCO advanced two significant recommendations aimed at the movement of cultural items, adopted by several State Parties. The first, the 1956 *Recommendation on International Principles Applicable to Archaeological Excavations* (1956 UNESCO Recommendation), which, among other things, urged museums to take "all necessary measures" to "ascertain that there is no reason to believe that [archaeological] objects have been procured by clandestine excavation, theft or any other [illicit] method," further recommended that museums and excavators lend assistance in recovering any objects improperly removed from excavations (O'Keefe, 2000, p. 11). The introduction of the 1956 UNESCO Recommendation also invokes the language of movement and diplomacy: "Convinced that the feelings aroused by the contemplation and study of works of the past do much to *foster mutual understanding between nations*, and that it is therefore highly desirable to secure international co-operation with regard to them and to further, in every possible way, the fulfillment of their social mission" (1956 UNESCO Recommendation [emphasis mine]) – ancient objects with a mission to act as global ambassador on behalf of the nation from where they originate. Section 23(c and e) of the 1956 UNESCO Recommendation proposes that nations might allocate objects (including those deemed duplicate) to foreign excavators, to scientific institutions, and for museum exchanges, further accentuating the desirability of movement (see Brodie, 2004; Kersel, 2015a, 2015b; Leventhal and Daniels, 2013 for further discussion of duplicate material).

In signing on to the various UNESCO documents nations tacitly support the idea of a common heritage, although perhaps not always in agreement on whose heritage is the common element. The 1950 UNESCO Agreement, the 1954 Hague Convention, and the 1956 UNESCO Recommendation all use diplomatic language to encourage the movement of this common heritage, employing terms like exchange, cooperation, mutual understanding – all supporting the movement of archaeological artifacts. In the post-colonial Middle East of the 1950s, burgeoning with nascent nation states, these UNESCO efforts were also aimed at leveling the playing field with the West, with the intention of eliminating the colonial legacy of "West knows best." Objects of great importance were being uncovered in the Middle East and the museums, institutions, and individuals of the West had much interest in gaining access to this shared past. Middle Eastern nations were intent in using those same objects to strengthen nationalistic ties to the land and their heritage (see Abdi, 2001; Abu El-Haj, 2001; Bernhardsson, 2005; Çelik, 2016; Colla, 2007; Corbett, 2015; Miles, 2009; Reid, 2002; Shaw,

2003), setting up a situation of competing desires for the same sets of artifacts and monuments. Acting as mediator the language in the UNESCO documents advanced a scenario in which the archaeologically rich nations of the Middle East were encouraged to "exchange, share, and cooperate" with the West in order to foster "mutual understanding" but often with little or no benefits to the countries of origin. Inevitably there was escalating tension over the movement of cultural material resulting in increased instances of theft and a growing black market in the illegal movement of antiquities. Resistance to the one-way movement of artifacts from the newly established Middle Eastern states to the former colonial powers in the West is well documented (Abdi, 2001; Bernhardsson, 2005; Colla, 2007; Corbett, 2015; Goode, 2007; Reid, 2002; Shaw, 2003), although membership in UNESCO and the ratification of the various conventions and agreements provided the Western imprimatur that nascent states eagerly sought (see Kersel, 2008, 2010). This dichotomy buttressed the cultural internationalist vs. cultural national template for future considerations on the movement of objects.

The second stage of UNESCO, movement, and diplomacy

Recognizing that the trade in illegal artifacts was continuing unabated and that archaeological sites across the globe were under threat due to the problem of illegal excavation, the 1964 *Recommendation on the Means of Prohibiting and Preventing the Illicit Export, Import and Transfer of Ownership of Cultural Property* (1964 UNESCO Recommendation) provided ethical guidelines for countries of origin and acquiring institutions to work together to protect threatened cultural property. The 1964 UNESCO Recommendation urged individual nations to protect the cultural heritage within their borders because "cultural property constitutes a basic element of civilization and national culture, and that familiarity with it leads to *understanding and mutual appreciation* among nations" (emphasis mine), using the same language of diplomacy to reaffirm the power of objects to act as ambassadors. While advocating for the legitimate exchange of material through loan, the 1964 UNESCO Recommendation placed greater emphasis on individual state responsibilities and rights in protecting the cultural heritage of mankind, acknowledging the tension between those countries with sought-after archaeological material and those countries seeking the artifacts. The 1964 UNESCO Recommendation essentially paved the way for the *Convention on the Means of Prohibiting and Preventing the Illicit Import, Export and Transfer of Ownership of Cultural Property* (1970 UNESCO Convention), which highlighted the need for states to work together to curb the problem of illicit export, urging them to adopt the provisions that would result from such a convention (Podesta, 2008, p. 467).

The 1970 UNESCO Convention endeavored to stem the illegal movement of artifacts by encouraging nations to create systems for tracking and recording artifacts, while at the same time requiring nations to assist in the return of such relics. Reports by Coggins (1969, 1972) and Meyer (1973) catalogued the staggering rates of looting of archaeological sites and the unregulated movement of antiquities, which encouraged nations to adopt the 1970 UNESCO Convention. Under the 1970 UNESCO Convention "exchange" should be jointly agreed to and the acquisition of materials by collectors (institutional and individual) should be of documented, legally available material. It also encouraged international efforts to protect the landscapes and artifacts of countries under serious threat. Prott (2005) suggests that perhaps an impetus for the 1970 UNESCO Convention was to stem the very apparent flow of objects from less-developed nations to collectors, usually with a much higher per capita income and from the West. This imbalance resulted in an unequal exchange that reinforced notions of cultural imperialism, rather than an equal partnership (see Kersel and Luke, 2015). In response to this one-way movement, countries enacted national ownership laws in an attempt to protect what they conceived as their cultural heritage and to control the movement of material, eschewing the "cultural heritage of humankind" diplomatic language of UNESCO. The legislative legacies of the Ottoman Empire and the French and British Mandates resulted in many of the emerging Middle Eastern states having national cultural heritage laws in place well before the 1970 UNESCO Convention (see Bernhardsson, 2005; Bisheh, 2001; Çelik, 2016; Colla, 2007; Goode, 2007; Kersel, 2008, 2010; Reid, 2002; Özel, 2010). Earlier in the century countries like Egypt, Iran, Iraq, Jordan, and Turkey all passed legislation in order to keep their cultural heritage within their borders although with varying degrees of in-country financial and logistical support, resulting in differential protection and monitoring of archaeological sites and monuments.

The 1976 UNESCO *Recommendation Concerning the International Exchange of Cultural Property* (1976 UNESCO Recommendation) included the following language:

> [T]he circulation of cultural property . . . is a *powerful means of promoting mutual understanding and appreciation among nations*. . . . [A] systematic policy of *exchanges* among cultural institutions, by which each would part with its surplus items in return for objects that it lacked, would not only be enriching to all parties but would also lead to a better use of the international community's cultural heritage which is the sum of all the national heritages.
>
> *(1976 UNESCO Recommendation [emphasis mine])*

At first glance the language in the 1970 UNESCO Convention and in the 1976 UNESCO Recommendation may appear to support the belief that the international movement of cultural objects, rather than something to be discouraged or grudgingly tolerated, serves desirable ends and should be encouraged (Bator, 1983, pp. 30–31). The original intent of these recommendations was not to nurture commercial enterprise but to promote educational exchange between governments through a public forum (museums and/or academic institutions): the international access to knowledge through the exchange of cultural material between countries. The following case study illustrates how tomb groups from the Early Bronze Age (*c.* 3600–2000 BCE) site of Bab adh Dhra' embodying the exchange language of UNESCO were moved from Jordan to other nations in order to foster knowledge, to generate goodwill, and to increase interest in the modern and ancient Middle East.

Object movement: Bab adh Dhra', Jordan

In the 1960s in response to reports of looting in Jordan and witnessing an increase in Early Bronze Age (EBA) artifacts for sale in the Jerusalem antiquities shops, Paul Lapp (then director of the W. F. Albright Institute for Archaeological Research in Jerusalem) excavated a number of tombs at the site of Bab adh Dhra' under the auspices of the American School of Oriental Research (ASOR) (Kersel, 2015a). Lapp recovered thousands of pots and other artifacts from the various shaft tombs and charnel houses (Lapp, 1966). Unfortunately, before publishing the results of his excavations Lapp died unexpectedly in a swimming accident off the coast of Cyprus in 1970, resulting in a state of uncertainty for the Bad adh Dhra' material in storage (Kersel, 2015a). In the 1970s R. Thomas Schaub and Walter Rast wanted to return to Bab adh Dhra' in order to undertake further excavations of the site. In order to secure permission from the Jordanian Department of Antiquities, the earlier material from the Lapp project had to studied, published, and curated (Kersel, 2015a)

The storage and publication dilemmas associated with the EBA pots led the Jordanian Department of Antiquities and ASOR (the Lapp excavation sponsors) to come up with an innovative initiative. Tomb groups from Bab adh Dhra' would be distributed to interested ASOR member academic institutions for the purposes of display and education (Nancy Lapp to Adnan Hadidi, the director of the Jordanian Department of Antiquities, 1 August 1977, Bab adh Dhra' file, American Schools of Oriental Research Archives). The tomb groups would also be made available to R. Thomas Schaub and Walter Rast who were charged with the publication of the Lapp excavations. "For the government of Jordan the underpinning rationale for the movement of these tombs groups was to increase interest in Jordanian archaeology and to encourage cooperative archaeological efforts between the United States and Jordan" (Kersel, 2015a, p. 50). The objects were to act as ambassadors on behalf of Jordan – once people saw the pots, they would be drawn to visit or to start excavations in the country in collaboration with Jordanian colleagues (Kersel, 2015a, 2015b).

> A total of 1,186 pots and 10 basalt bowls were distributed to 24 institutions in Australia, Canada, and the United States. Generating almost $14,000 in income, proceeds from the pot allocation were used for future publications and excavation at Bab adh Dhra', small projects conducted by the American Center of Oriental Research (the American archaeological research institution based in Amman), and other ASOR initiatives. The movement of tomb groups to educational institutions guaranteed that Jordanian archaeological material was readily available for study, that it could be viewed publicly so that people might become inspired to visit Jordan having experienced its material culture. The controlled exchange of tomb groups allowed the Jordanians to decide how and where their cultural heritage was displayed in the public domain rather than in individual homes, adding to the potential production of archaeological knowledge. It was thought that the opportunity afforded to educational institutions to access this material at a reasonable cost, with the imprimatur of the Jordanian government, might also decrease the demand for archaeological artifacts from the market (illegal or legal), thus protecting the threatened archaeological landscapes of Jordan.
>
> *(Kersel, 2015a, p. 51)*

Only 1 of the 24 institutions that received an initial set of ceramics requested a refund from ASOR and this was due to a misunderstanding over suitability for a proposed exhibit:

> We are, in fact, not happy with the pottery we received. Hardly any of it is intrinsically "displayable", either because of its fragmentary state or its lack of artistic or even craftsmanly interest. Furthermore, most of it is of the *miniature variety*. What we received is totally different from what the advertisement – with its photograph of full-sized, complete, and some decorated vessels – led us to expect. Frankly, we feel deceived and wonder if those 15 institutions requesting groups who were unsuccessful in their quest for a tomb group aren't the fortunate ones after all.
>
> *(Letter from George Dales, Curator of Near Eastern Archaeology at the Lowie Museum, University of California at Berkeley to Nancy Lapp, September 23, 1977, Bab adh Dhra' file, American Schools of Oriental Research Archives (ASOR))*

Disappointed with miniatures George Dales, curator at the Lowie Museum, returned the Charnel House A8 tomb group, which was then redistributed to Andrews University where it remains to this day. In a recent email exchange with the curator of the material Constance Gaines stated that Andrews University, which has had an ongoing program of archaeology in Jordan for decades, is pleased to have the tomb group and uses it often in teaching and for public display.

Archival evidence and recent ethnographic interviews (carried out under approved Ethical Review Board Protocols) indicate that those directly involved with the Bab adh Dhra' tomb group exchange were and still are satisfied with the arrangement. Representatives from the Jordanian Department of Antiquities acknowledge that while unconventional in approach the tomb group distribution scheme had the desired effects of freeing up much needed storage space, increasing interest in the archaeology of Jordan, and providing educational opportunities for study of this period of the Jordanian past. Recently, Bab adh Dhra' excavator R. Thomas Schaub recalled that the tomb group distribution allowed for further excavation and study at Bab adh Dhra' in addition to supporting the publication of the Paul Lapp excavations (Schaub and Rast, 1989).

In 1981, Nancy Lapp followed up on each of the tomb groups confirming that, with one exception (the Lowie Museum), they were all still located in their original institutions, and all of the groups were still displayed and available for study. Currently the interdisciplinary *Follow the Pots Project* (http://followthepotsproject.org/) is attempting to trace the current location of the tomb groups. Of the 24 groups, 12 have been tracked, all of which are in their original 1970s locations. One is still on public display. The original incentive for the tomb group circulation, as educational tools and as ambassadors on behalf of the government of Jordan, continues until today (Nancy Lapp to ASOR Representatives of Institutional Members, December 26, 1977, N. Lapp correspondence). An additional element of the *Follow the Pots Project* is an examination of the historic and current demand for these ceramic vessels. Did the exchange of the tomb groups create a desire for individuals to "own" a piece of the past? Interviews with local and foreign purchasers of EBA ceramics in the legal market are being conducted in order to assess the impact of the tomb group distribution on consumer demand. This case study brings to life much of the original intent of the various UNESCO documents, which emphasize both the protection of cultural heritage and a shared notion of positive exchange, with the goals of knowledge production and access to the Jordanian past outside the state borders.

In the initial stages of drafting the 1970 UNESCO Convention and the 1976 UNESCO Recommendation, the framers were not so concerned with eliminating the circulation or interchange of cultural material, but were focused on mitigating the loss of cultural heritage through archaeological site destruction and the influence of market forces whereby artifacts disappeared into private collections, never again to be seen. UNESCO's effort aimed at promoting a shared universal heritage (the cultural heritage of mankind, increasing the knowledge of the civilization of man, promotion of mutual understanding and appreciation among nations) acted as a platform for dialogue and cooperation with the common purpose of protecting the past. The Jordanian tomb group program embodied these goals in the past and in the present through a negotiated agreement between cultural internationalists and cultural nationalists, a rare occurrence in the debate over the movement of objects.

To move or not to move: Cultural internationalists and cultural nationalists

For better or for worse, the 1970 UNESCO Convention established a dualistic system – those states with cultural items and those states that desire cultural items – creating an Us vs. Them scenario in which each side has to grapple with certain sets of parameters designed to protect cultural resources. This clash was explicit in the influential work of Stanford law professor John Merryman (1986), who coined the terms cultural internationalists and cultural nationalists to describe the oppositional factions associated with the movement of cultural material. These labels carry with them a number of preconceptions and associations – both positive and negative. Cultural nationalism often conjures up adverse connotations, misunderstood by some as a purely emotional appeal by archaeologically rich nations that wish to reclaim and retain all of the items they view as rightfully theirs; while cultural internationalism is viewed as masking the true intention of market nations that wish to obtain the cultural property of other nations and cultures for their own interests (Sheng, 2008, p. 60). Cultural internationalists and cultural nationalists agree on basic principles associated with the material past: the preservation and protection of artifacts are important and the looting, theft, and the destruction of archaeological sites are undesirable effects. But these positions are often divided over in-country retention, repatriation, and the movement of objects.

This twofold model is hugely reductionist and overly simplistic. It avoids the basic premise advanced by the 1954 Hague Convention – each person makes a contribution to the culture of the world. It does not take into consideration "intra-nationalists," a term introduced by Watkins (2005) to describe various nations (specifically referring to First Nations). Coombe (1993, pp. 260–261) has also taken exception to Merryman's (1986) labels, claiming that he equates nationhood with statehood and is not prepared to recognize the existence of more than one nation within a sovereign state. Nor does this dichotomous classification take into consideration the viewpoint typically held among anthropologists, archaeologists, and ethnographers, which places primary emphasis on the contextual information associated with cultural objects, highlighting the acquisition of information about the human past through relationships and proper scientific documentation (Brodie, 2003). This position has been forcefully argued by many (Fincham, 2009; Handler, 1992; Luke and Kersel, 2013; Posner, 2007), who maintain that in order to have meaning objects must be surrounded by other objects, by words, by architecture, by the remnants of human activity.

The cultural nationalist discourse generally held among archaeologically rich nations (those providing the artifacts) is preservationist and emphasizes the relationship between cultural objects and national identity, culture, and history. The notion of nationalism is based on the principle of national sovereignty, which emphasizes a nation's control over all people, things, and conduct within its territory. A core premise of the cultural nationalist position is that objects surviving from the past belong to and represent the nation (Coombe, 1993; Watkins, 2005). These objects form a constituent part of the national identity and therefore objects should stay within territorial borders. Objects in the global arena should be repatriated in order that the country may be whole again: even though the modern borders bear little or no resemblance to those of ancient nations and states. A criticism often leveled at the cultural nationalist position is the failure to recognize that other nations benefit from exposure to the culture and heritage of archaeologically rich nations – the value of an object as ambassador in a foreign museum. Branding them retentionists, James Cuno (2008, p. 19) claims "The nationalist retentionist cultural property laws conspire against our appreciation of the nature of culture as mongrel, overlapping, and a dynamic force of uniting rather than dividing humankind;" objects on the move and in locations other than their place of origin bring us closer together, allowing for greater understanding of different cultures.

Cultural internationalism, typically characterized by market nations (those buying the artifacts) de-emphasizes nationalism and is critical of retentionism (Anglin, 2008; Cuno, 2008). Cultural internationalists believe that artifacts should be free to circulate throughout the world in order to enrich the lives of all people. Supporters assert that the best way to protect and preserve archaeological resources is to allow them to be traded freely on the open market rather than forcing artifacts underground into a black market. Criticisms leveled at this position typically invoke the legacy of colonialism: unauthorized appropriations and theft from cultural institutions that predate the establishment of UNESCO and its universal norms, values, and laws of national ownership. Others claim that cultural internationalists perpetuate the idea that archaeologically rich nations are "unable" to care for their cultural heritage (Prott, 2005). Private collectors, who successfully acquire objects and who may believe that they are "saving" objects (see Kersel, 2006, 2014; Thompson, 2016), do not always provide open access, instead preferring to care for their items in the privacy of their own homes. Contra to the underlying principles of the various UNESCO documents, these privately held objects do not participate in exchanges, instead performing as personal cabinets of curiosity.

While opinion is divided on whether objects should move, they in fact do move – both legally and illegally as they are passed between individuals, enter networks, cross borders, often evading law enforcement. How do objects move?

How objects move

"[T]he circulation of cultural property … is a powerful means of promoting mutual understanding and appreciation among nations" (1976 UNESCO Recommendation); "[C]o-operation between nations … including the exchange of objects … will advance mutual knowledge and understanding of peoples" (1950 UNESCO Agreement); "Contemplation of works of the past foster mutual understanding between nations" (1956 UNESCO Recommendation) – the language of UNESCO is explicit in advocating for the exchange of objects for the purposes of knowledge production, mutual understanding, building good relations between nation states. Clearly there is a common theme in the UNESCO language, which advocates for moment, albeit movement regulated and under mutually agreed-upon principles and circumstances. If the basic premise is that the movement of objects is beneficial, how does movement occur?

Legal markets

In an effort to allow objects to move, some nations have enacted laws that allow for a legal trade in antiquities. Particular states have control over which artifacts enter the market, often profiting from the sale of the material economically, either through direct sales or through dealer licensing schemes. Cultural internationalists have argued that a licensed trade in antiquities is the embodiment of the language of UNESCO, encouraging the transfer of artifacts, which allows them to act as ambassadors on behalf of their countries of origin. The notion of fostering a legal market is perhaps the defining difference between cultural internationalism and cultural nationalism. Cultural nationalists believe that cultural property should never be the subject of legitimate trade. Cultural internationalists claim that the various UNESCO Agreements, Conventions, and Recommendations encourage the movement of cultural material (Anglin, 2008; Hoffman, 2010; Watkins, 2005) and the best way to control movement is through a legally sanctioned, licensed trade. The cultural internationalist position firmly believes that international trade (the legal market) is inherently desirable and they support the notion that most artifacts are redundant (see Brodie, 2004; Kersel, 2015a; Leventhal and Daniels, 2013 for discussions on whether artifacts are ever redundant), lacking special archaeological significance or cultural importance for the archaeologically rich nation (those countries with archaeological resources) and therefore available for transfer and exchange. While 1976 UNESCO Recommendation does not expressly use the term redundant, the euphemism "surplus items" does appear in the Recommendation.

"[E]ach [State Party] would part with its *surplus items* in return for objects that it lacked" (emphasis mine), implying that there are items in archaeologically rich nations that could be exchanged. The terminology used – duplicate, excess, redundant, and surplus – designates a portion of the material culture of a nation as insignificant and available to enter the marketplace without deleterious consequence to the cultural heritage of archaeologically rich nations and that such material meets the individual and institutional demand for objects (see Brodie, 2004; Leventhal and Daniels, 2013).

In one of the most balanced accounts of the schism over the movement of cultural items, Bauer (2007) draws attention to the fact that all sides in the debates regarding the antiquities trade and the problem of looting make certain assumptions that they regard as unquestionable truths about the trade. Cultural nationalists base much of their thinking about movement on the premise that the trade can be completely eradicated. And cultural internationalists make ludicrous assertions that demand for antiquities has no effect on the archaeological landscape or the theft from cultural institutions (Bauer, 2007, p. 698). Coming to a consensus on the trade involves moving beyond these long-held notions regarding the positive and negative movement of material, which may include a provision for a legal, well-monitored market.

Arguments championing the sale of this material have been made by a variety of supporters of the legal trade in antiquities. Merryman (1996, p. 29) suggests that the sale of surplus items is the medium through which the archaeologically rich nation can most efficiently generate meaningful income. At the same time these objects act as effective envoys, conveying the artistic and intellectual mastery of the originating state. The excess income could be used for a variety of purposes including archaeology, conservation, and oversight of heritage management, as demonstrated with the exchange of the tomb groups from Bab adh Dhra' – the financial proceeds were used to fund further excavations at the site and the publication of earlier investigations. Some (Anglin, 2008; Cuno, 2008; Hoffman, 2010; Merryman, 1996; Pearlstein, 1996) argue that museums, collectors, and dealers who have been supplied by the legal market are more likely to conform to other aspects of national cultural heritage legislation and may be more disposed to repatriate items of contention.

Opposing this position are those who believe that cultural material should not be bought and sold in the marketplace because market demand encourages the looting of archaeological sites, even if there are "surplus" items available for valid purchase. In his discussion of redundant material, Brodie (2004, pp. 86–87) asserts: "from an archaeological perspective the term 'redundant' is problematic." Differentiating between the art world where stylistically indistinguishable pieces are considered surplus or redundant and the world of archaeology where minute points of dissimilarity might reveal important facts about ancient exchange, production, and trade (Brodie, 2004, p. 86) stresses that the designation of the term redundant to material is fraught with difficulties. In support of the cultural international position rumors abound that archaeologically rich nations everywhere have store rooms filled with identical, culturally insignificant material that they do not know what to do with, cannot care for, and have locked away in musty, damp conditions that are harmful to the objects (see Kersel, 2015a, 2015b). It is unlikely that the high-end sales – individuals and institutions – are interested in a run of the mill duplicate pot. Nor will museums be enthusiastic about acquiring objects that bear the label "duplicate," "excess," or "surplus". The motivation for most collectors is rarity, beauty, and a host of other factors (Kersel, 2014; Thompson, 2016). The question of whether a legal market facilitates positive movement (a nationally sanctioned exchange of material, which satisfies the consumer) is the focus of ongoing inquiry into the legal antiquities market in Israel.

Object movement: The legal market for antiquities in Israel

Every day it is possible for visitors to the Old City of Jerusalem or to Tel Aviv or to Jaffa to buy an artifact and take it home. The legal trade in antiquities in Israel is a legacy of earlier Ottoman legislation and British Mandate Ordinances that made provisions for the legal movement of archaeological material within the region in order to meet the demand for objects from the Holy Land (see Kersel, 2008, 2010, 2014). Promoted and endorsed by luminary collectors like Teddy Kolleck and Moshe Dayan, the legalized trade became enshrined in the antiquities law of Israel enacted in 1978. The Antiquities Law 5738–1978 vests the ownership of cultural heritage found after the benchmark date of 1978 in the State of Israel. At the same time, the law establishes a legal trade in antiquities: it is legal to buy and sell artifacts from collections (private, museums, and existing shop inventories) established before the Antiquities Law of 1978. After that date, all newly discovered antiquities are the property of the state. There are between 30 and 40 licensed dealers throughout the country from where collectors (individual and institutional) can legally purchase their objects. Ongoing ethnographic interviews confirm many collectors of Near Eastern material echo the rationales for early archaeological practice in the region – a desire to establish a connection to the land and the past through the material remains. Collectors attempt to recreate history through the purchase of artifacts (Kersel, 2011, 2014). Israel benefits (monetarily and diplomatically) from the demand for Holy Land objects: a simple oil lamp can act as a cultural ambassador on behalf of Israel, as a connection to a person or place from the Bible, or as a souvenir. Purchasers benefit emotionally, intellectually, and physically from their lawful purchase of a Holy Land antiquity (see Kersel, 2014).

Individual collectors who participate in the legal market for antiquities have myriad motivations for making purchases, sometimes based on their religious affiliation, their personal history, or a traditional practice. Through ethnographic research with visitors to the region it is clear that Evangelical Christians buy different artifacts from Muslims or Jews or non-religious visitors. In a recent exchange (July 2015) in a licensed shop three individuals wanted to buy coins. The dealer asked if they had a particular time period, place, or event they wished to be associated with the coins. One of the individuals stated he wanted something "from the time of Jesus – a coin that Jesus might have touched." The tourist left the shop with a widow's mite, one of the most popular items in the antiquities market. The mite, minted as early as 103 BCE and referenced in the New Testament, was the smallest denomination of coin used only in the province of Judaea, appealing to buyers who want something that could originate from the Holy Land. The mites are highly desirable as mementoes of a trip and the associated biblical story of Jesus, the widow, and temple offerings (Mark 12: 41–44). There are thousands of these coins legitimately available for sale.

While a legal market may facilitate the legitimate movement of redundant or surplus material with the permission of the state, there is also ample opportunity for illegally acquired artifacts to enter the legal market (see Kersel, 2006, 2014). Whatever the collector's motivation – financial, faith-based, individual memento, institutional, or simply an objet d'art for the mantel – there is little doubt that collecting contributes to the destruction of the archaeological landscape, theft from museums and religious institutions, and the ongoing loss of knowledge and access to the past (see Kersel, 2006, 2014; Mackenzie and Davis, 2014). These illegal elements result in what can only be considered contrary to the UNESCO principles of exchange, fostering mutual understanding, and the safeguarding of cultural heritage. The legal market authorizes the movement of material but often with undesirable consequences. The result is negative movement – purloined artifacts, crossing borders illegally, and being laundered at some point in their journey from the ground to the consumer (Kersel, 2006).

The long-term loan of objects between nations may provide an alternative to sales in the legal market. As the name suggests, this endeavor enables countries of origin to loan archaeological materials to institutions (and more rarely to individuals) for the purposes of display, education, research, or personal enjoyment. Long-term loan arrangements may have the added benefit for the archaeologically rich nation in that there is a financial transaction associated with the material on loan (Kersel, 2015a). Long-term loans might generate significant revenue for the country of origin that could be used to fund further excavation, additional storage facilities, artifact conservation, or museum displays. Loaning nations have experienced the benefit of traveling exhibits. Egypt, for example, earned in excess of $13 million USD for its national coffers with the exhibition *Quest* (Warring, 2005). Financial incentives might encourage the movement of objects in a long-term loan scenario.

Long-term loans: "Troy Gold" on the move

The recent long-term (or indefinite) loan of the "Troy Gold" from the University of Pennsylvania Museum of Archaeology and Anthropology to the Government of Turkey is an excellent example of objects on the move and the embodiment of UNESCO language related to the "cultural heritage of mankind" and the exchange of objects. The Government of Turkey will place the "Troy Gold" on display in a new museum planned for the archaeological site of Troy, allowing the citizens of Turkey to access their plundered past, while at the same time increasing tourism to the area (Rose, 2016, 2017). In "exchange" in February 2016 the Penn Museum received more than 120 artifacts on loan from Turkish museums in Ankara, Anatalya, Gordion, and Istanbul (Sy, 2016). *The Golden Age of Midas* exhibit, a collaborative effort between the Penn Museum and the Republic of Turkey, is the direct result of the language of exchange and the encouragement of positive movement in the various UNESCO documents illustrating the possibilities for mutual respect and understanding, knowledge development, and goodwill between nations mediated by objects. In addition to the loan of archaeological material for display purposes, researchers at the University of Pennsylvania (Penn) have also benefited from a pledge for increased collaboration between Penn and Turkey, including support for future archaeological investigations through the issuing of excavation permits (Avril, 2012). The movement of archaeological material from the Penn Museum to Turkey on long-term loan in exchange for the loan of Turkish objects for display at the Penn Museum is the manifestation of UNESCO language writ large – moving objects is a good thing, everyone benefits.

This legacy of movement in the Middle East is the result of earlier Ottoman legislative efforts that insisted that archaeological finds from the Empire should be transferred to the national museum in Istanbul (Bahrani, Çelik, and Eldem, 2011; Çelik, 2011, 2016; Kersel, 2008, 2010; Özel, 2010; Shaw, 2003). These efforts were in direct response to the high-profile removal of valuable archaeological artifacts and monuments (Roosevelt and Luke, 2006, p. 181) by Western explorers and archaeologists in the region. Permits for excavation and the export of artifacts were required of foreign investigators but the regulations set forth by the Empire were often ignored. This resulted in the establishment of laws intended to stem the outward movement of material from the borders of the Empire (Shaw, 2003, pp. 73–74; Shoup, 2008, p. 115).

This long history of cultural heritage preservation and protection law beginning with Islamic jurisprudence prior to the 1869 decree regulating antiquities (see Çelik, 2016; Özel, 2010) was aimed at finding a balance between knowledge production and tourism with looting and exploitation of its cultural resources (Betley, 2013). The earlier legislative efforts of 1869, 1874, 1884, and 1906 established fundamental concepts, which formed the basis for future legislative efforts not only in Turkey but also in the former territories of the Ottoman Empire, the modern Middle Eastern countries of Egypt, Jordan, Israel, and Palestine among others (see Kersel, 2008, 2010). The common tenet in each example of law aimed at protecting cultural heritage is the establishment of a blanket state-ownership claim over all moveable and immoveable cultural properties (Betley, 2013; Çelik, 2016; Özel, 2005, 2010). These national ownership laws afforded newly established nations additional control over the movement of objects through stricter export controls, at the same time as providing greater oversight over foreign research projects through a permitting process and the dissolution of the practice of *partage* (the division of finds from archaeological projects – see Kersel, 2015a). In many of the nascent states there was interest in leveraging archaeological excavations as evidence for nationalist claims, which bolstered the need for greater control over the material culture recovered as a result of investigations. The nationalization of cultural patrimonies was a reaction to the imperialism of the eighteenth and nineteenth centuries (see Kersel and Luke, 2015) and a product of the political realities of the twentieth century. The rise of the retentionism of cultural nationalism and its attendant policies and laws is an outcome of the ransacking of the monuments of less well-developed countries by entities from the West in the years leading up to statehood (Brodkey, 2009, p. 329). It is not surprising that there is a divide over the movement of objects and that an international body in the form of UNESCO stepped in to adjudicate movement.

Moving objects, language, and UNESCO

Ratification of international conventions, signing of bilateral treaties, and the marshaling of resources to protect and recover artifacts all demonstrate concern and respect for the cultural property of nations. Carrying out this mandate means that UNESCO, "the only UN agency specifically mandated with the responsibility for promoting creativity and safeguarding the world's diverse cultural heritage" (UNESCO, Mission Statement), is intimately involved with the adoption of a multi-layered set of agreed-upon norms, ranging from international treaties and conventions to operational policies and mutual agreements. Terms and phrases are deliberately chosen – "the cultural heritage of mankind," "increasing the knowledge of the civilization of man," the "promotion of mutual understanding and appreciation among nations," "surplus objects, exchange, interchange, and circulation" – but can be interpreted differently and directly reflect the historical moments in which they were drafted. Effective international oversight of the movement of antiquities requires the intervention of a number of actors, with UNESCO playing the unique role of *objective* overseer and mediator between those who support movement and those who do not.

A key issue in legal and policy debates surrounding cultural material is one of ownership: are artifacts the universal common heritage of mankind or do specific communities or nations have proprietary rights to their own objects? Whereas the agency's 1954 Hague Convention defines cultural material as the universal heritage of mankind, its 1970 UNESCO Convention regards cultural objects as a heritage that is particular to the cultural identity of a given nation. The contradictions inherent in UNESCO language make consensus over policy, programs, and movement of cultural artifacts often difficult to achieve. An overemphasis on national cultural heritage may result in the isolation of artifacts. Conversely, the overemphasis on the cultural heritage of humankind may result in the extraction of important national cultural pieces or the alienation of a culture from its material remains. Fortunately, resolving this controversy may be achieved through balanced views (Bauer, 2007; Kremer and Wilkening, 2010) that support collaborative solutions aimed at accessibility and preservation – mutually beneficial partnerships aimed at lessening pillage and the illegal movement of artifacts. The best channels for promoting practical solutions for movement may be outside the formal legal frameworks of governments, through informal networks of experts and institutions, the development of joint research projects, and international exchanges through long-term loans and traveling exhibitions.

Recent loans, repatriations, and cooperative agreements regarding cultural heritage reinforce this positive trend in overcoming the prevailing "Us vs. Them" scenario. Objects make excellent ambassadors, and the language of various UNESCO Conventions and Recommendations supports this notion; the challenge now is arriving at mutually agreed-upon programs and policies, which facilitate the movement of objects.

Acknowledgements

I offer my thanks to Haidy Geismar and Jane Anderson for the invitation to participate in this volume and for their insightful comments on earlier drafts of this chapter. I am grateful to Monther al-Jamhawi, Director General of the Department of Antiquities, Jordan, for continued support of this research. Many thanks to Brian Daniels and Richard Leventhal for the invitation to present an earlier version of this chapter at the "World Heritage Now" conference at the University of Pennsylvania, September 2012. This work would not be possible without the efforts of Meredith Chesson and R. Thomas Schaub of the Expedition to the Dead Sea Plain Project of the University of Notre Dame. This chapter is dedicated to Tom Schaub (1933–2015).

Bibliography

Primary sources

ASOR. Archival documents, American Schools of Oriental Research, Bab edh Dhra' Correspondence.

Lapp, N. Archival documents, N. Lapp Correspondence.

UNESCO. (1950) Agreement on the Importance of Educational, Scientific, and Cultural Materials. Paris, UNESCO.

UNESCO. (1954) Hague Convention for the Protection of Cultural Property in the Event of Armed Conflict.

UNESCO. (1956) Recommendation on International Principles Applicable to Archaeological Excavations.

UNESCO. (1964) Recommendation on the Means of Prohibiting and Preventing the Illicit Export, Import and Transfer of Ownership of Cultural Property.

UNESCO. (1970) Convention on the Means of Prohibiting and Preventing the Illicit Import, Export and Transfer of Ownership of Cultural Property.

UNESCO. (1976) Recommendation Concerning the International Exchange of Cultural Property. Adopted 26 November 1976.

UNESCO. (2015). UNESCO Mission Statement. [Online] Available from: http://en.unesco.org/about-us/introducing-unesco [Accessed May 25th, 2015].

Secondary sources

Abdi, K. (2001) Nationalism, Politics, and the Development of Archaeology in Iran. *American Journal of Archaeology* 105(1): 51–76.

Abu El-Haj, N. (2001) *Facts on the Ground. Archaeological Practice and Territorial Self-Fashioning in Israeli Society*. Chicago: University of Chicago Press.

Anglin, R. (2008) The World Heritage List: Bridging the Cultural Property Nationalism-Internationalism Divide. *Yale Journal of Law and the Humanities* 20(2): 241–275.

Avril, T. (2012) Penn Museum Lends Possibly Plundered Items to Turkey. *Philadelphia Inquirer*, September 7. [Online] Available from: http://articles.philly.com/2012-09-07/news/33651449_1_penn-museum-penn-s-museum-turkish-minister [Accessed January 15, 2016].

Bahrani, Z., Çelik, Z. and Eldem, E. (2011) Introduction: Archaeology and Empire. In Bahrani, Z, Çelik, Z., and Eldem, E. (eds.), *Scramble for the Past: A Story of Archaeology in the Ottoman Empire, 1753–1914*, pp. 1–45. Istanbul: SALT.

Bass, G. (1966) Troy and Ur. Gold Links Between Two Ancient Capitals. *Expedition* (Summer): 26–39.

Bass, G. (1970) A Hoard of Trojan and Sumerian Jewelry. *American Journal of Archaeology* 74(1970): 335–341.

Bator, P. (1983) *The International Trade in Art*. Chicago: University of Chicago Press.

Bauer, A. A. (2007) New Ways of Thinking About Cultural Property: A Critical Appraisal of Antiquities Trade Debates. *Fordham International Law Journal* 31(3): 690–723.

Bernhardsson, M. T. (2005) *Reclaiming a Plundered Past. Archaeology and Nation Building in Modern Iraq*. Austin: University of Texas Press.

Betley, M. (2013). The Historical Foundations of Cultural Heritage Law: Turkey. MA Thesis, Master of Arts Program in the Social Sciences, the University of Chicago.

Bisheh, G. (2001) One Damn Illicit Excavation After Another: The Destruction of the Archaeological Heritage of Jordan. In Brodie, N., Doole, J., and Renfrew, A. C. (eds.), *Trade in Illicit Antiquities: The Destruction of the World's Archaeological Heritage*, pp. 115–118. Cambridge, UK: McDonald Institute for Archaeological Research.

Brodie, N. (2003) Stolen History: Looting and Illicit Trade. *Museum International* 55: 10–22.

Brodie, N. (2004) Export Deregulation and the Illicit Trade in Archaeological Material. In Richman, J. R., and Forsyth, M. P. (eds.), *Legal Perspectives on Cultural Resources, Heritage Resources Management Series*, pp. 85–99. Walnut Creek, CA: AltaMira Press.

Brodkey, A. K. (2009) The Failure of the Nationalization of Cultural Patrimonies. In Merryman, J. H. (ed.), *Thinking about the Elgin Marbles: Critical Essays on Cultural Property, Art, and Law*, pp. 329–331. The Netherlands: Kluwer Law International.

Casini, L. (2011) "Italian Hours": The Globalization of Cultural Property Law. *International Journal of Constitutional Law* 9(2): 369–393.

Çelik, Z. (2011) Defining Empire's Patrimony: Late Ottoman Perceptions of Antiquities. In Bahrani, Z, Çelik, Z., and Eldem, E. (eds.), *Scramble for the Past: A Story of Archaeology in the Ottoman Empire, 1753–1914*, pp. 443–479. Istanbul: SALT.

Çelik, Z. (2016) *About Antiquities: Politics of Archaeology in the Ottoman Empire*. Austin: University of Texas Press.

Coggins, C. (1969) Illicit Traffic of Pre-Columbian Antiquities. *Art Journal* 29: 94–98.

Coggins, C. (1972) Archaeology and the Art Market. *Science* 175: 263–266.

Colla, E. (2007) *Conflicted Antiquities: Egyptology, Egyptomania, Egyptian Modernity*. Durham, NC: Duke University Press.

Coombe, R. (1993) The Properties of Culture and the Politics of Possessing Identity: Native Claims in the Cultural Appropriation Controversy. *Canadian Journal of Law and Jurisprudence* 6(2): 249–285.

Corbett, E. D. (2015) *Competitive Archaeology in Jordan: Narrating Identity from the Ottomans to the Hashemites*. Austin: University of Texas Press.

Cuno, J. (2008) *Who Owns Antiquity? Museums and the Battle Over Our Ancient Heritage*. Princeton, NJ: Princeton University Press.

Daniels, B. (2012) Reconfiguring the Museum: The Development of UNESCO's Museum Policies. Paper presented at World Heritage Now: Evaluating the Past, Present, and Future of UNESCO's Cultural Policy Program. University of Pennsylvania, September 2012.

De Cesari, C. (2010) Creative Heritage: Palestinian Heritage NGOs and Defiant Arts of Government. *American Anthropologist* 112(4): 625–637.

Di Giovine, M. A. (2008) *The Heritage-scape. UNESCO, World Heritage, and Tourism*. New York: Lexington Books.

Duedahl, P. (2011) Selling Mankind: UNESCO and the Invention of Global History, 1945–1976. *Journal of World History* 22(1): 101–133.

Fincham, D. (2009) The Fundamental Importance of Archaeological Context. In Charney, N. (ed.), *Art and Crime: Exploring the Dark Side of the Art World*, 1–12. Westport: Greenwood Publishing.

Goode, J. (2007) *Negotiating for the Past: Archaeology, Nationalism and Diplomacy in the Middle East, 1919–1941.* Austin: University of Texas Press.

Handler, R. (1992) On Valuing of Museum Objects. *Museum Anthropology* 16: 21–28.

Hoffman, M. R. (2010) Cultural Pragmatism: A New Approach to the International Movement of Antiquities. *Iowa Law Review* 95: 665–694.

Kersel, M. M. (2006) License to Sell: The Trade in Antiquities in Israel. PhD Dissertation, Department of Archaeology, University of Cambridge.

Kersel, M. M. (2008) The Trade in Palestinian Antiquities. *Jerusalem Quarterly Winter* 33: 21–38.

Kersel, M. M. (2010) The Changing Legal Landscape for Middle Eastern Archaeology in the Colonial Era, 1800–1930. In Emberling, G. (ed.), *Pioneers to the Past: American Archaeologists in the Middle East, 1919–1920*, pp. 85–90. Oriental Institute Museum Publications 30. Chicago: Oriental Institute.

Kersel, M. M. (2011) The Lure of Ancient Artifacts. *The Bible and Interpretation: In My View – Opinion*, November 16. [Online] Available from: http://www.bibleinterp.com/opeds/ker358016.shtml [Accessed February 16, 2016].

Kersel, M. M. (2014) The Lure of the Artefact? The Effects of Acquiring Eastern Mediterranean Material Culture. In Knapp, A. B. and van Dommelen, P. (eds.), *The Cambridge Prehistory of the Bronze and Iron Age Mediterranean*, pp. 367–378. New York: Cambridge University Press.

Kersel, M. M. (2015a) Storage Wars. Solving the Archaeological Curation Crisis? *Journal of Eastern Mediterranean Archaeology and Heritage Studies* 3(1): 42–55.

Kersel, M. M. (2015b) Rejoinder: An Issue of Ethics? Curation and the Obligations of Archaeology. *Journal of Eastern Mediterranean Archaeology and Heritage Studies* 3(1): 77–80.

Kersel, M. M. and Luke, C. (2015) Civil Societies? Heritage Diplomacy and Neo-Imperialism. In Meskell, L. (ed.), *Global Heritage: A Reader*, pp. 70–93. London: Wiley-Blackwell.

Kremer, M. and Wilkening, T. (2010) Protecting Antiquities: A Role for Long-Term Leases? Research Paper 1114, Department of Economics, University of Melbourne. [Online] Available from: http://www.economics.unimelb.edu.au/downloads/wp/wp10/1114.pdf [Accessed December 3, 2015].

Lapp, P. W. (1966) The Cemetery at Bab edh Dhra'. *Archaeology* 19: 104–111.

Leventhal, R. M. and Daniels, B. I. (2013) "Orphaned Objects", Ethical Standards, and the Acquisition of Antiquities. *DePaul Journal of Art, Technology, & Intellectual Property Law* 23(2): 339–361.

Luke, C. and Kersel, M. M. (2013) *US Cultural Diplomacy and Archaeology: Soft Power, Hard Heritage*. New York: Routledge.

Mackenzie, S. and Davis, T. (2014) Temple Looting in Cambodia. Anatomy of a Statue Trafficking Network. *British Journal of Criminology* 54(5): 722–740.

Merryman, J. H. (1986) Two Ways of Thinking About Cultural Property. *American Journal of International Law* 80(4): 831–853.

Merryman, J. H. (1996) A Licit International Trade in Cultural Objects. In Briat, M. and Freedberg, J. A. (eds.), *Legal Aspects of International Trade in Art, Vol. V: International Sales of Works of Art*, pp. 3–46. The Hague: Kluwer Law International.

Merryman, J. H. (2005) Cultural Property Internationalism. *International Journal of Cultural Property* 12(1): 11–39.

Meskell, L. (2012) The Rush to Inscribe: Reflections on the 35th Session of the World Heritage Committee, UNESCO Paris, 2011. *Journal of Field Archaeology* 37(2): 145–151.

Meskell, L. (2014) States of Conservation: Protection, Politics, and Pacting within UNESCO's World Heritage Committee. *Anthropological Quarterly* 87(1): 217–243.

Meyer, K. (1973) *The Plundered Past. The Traffic in Art Treasures*. New York: Athenaeum.

Miles, M. M. (2009) *Art as Plunder. The Ancient Origins of Debate about Cultural Property*. Cambridge: Cambridge University Press.

O'Keefe, P. (2000) *Commentary on the UNESCO 1970 Convention on Illicit Traffic*. London: Institute of Art Law.

Özel, S. (2005) The Protection of Cultural Properties in Turkey. In Schneider, E., and Schneider, R. M. (eds.), *Cultural Property Protection: Istanbul Conference, Summer 2004*. Berlin: Berliner Wissenschafts-Verlag GmbH.

Özel, S. (2010) Under the Turkish Blanket Legislation: The Recovery of Cultural Property Removed from Turkey. *International Journal of Legal Information* 38(2): 177–184.

Pearlstein, W. J. (1996) Claims for the Repatriation of Cultural Property: Prospects for a Managed Antiquities Market. *Law and Policy in International Business* 28(1): 123–150.

Pearlstein, W. J. (2014) White Paper: A Proposal to Reform US Law and Policy Relating to the International Exchange of Cultural Property. *Cardozo Arts & Entertainment* 32(3): 561–650.

Podesta, J. M. (2008) Saving Culture, but Passing the Buck: How the 1970 UNESCO Convention Undermines its Goals by Unduly Targeting Market Nations. *Cardozo Journal of International and Comparative Law* 16(2): 457–491.

Posner, E. A. (2007) The International Protection of Cultural Property: Some Skeptical Observations. *Chicago Journal of International Law* 8(1). Article 12. [Online] Available from: http://chicagounbound.uchicago.edu/cjil/vol8/iss1/12. [Accessed April 14, 2015].

Prott, L. V. (2005) The International Movement of Cultural Objects. *International Journal of Cultural Property* 12(2): 225–248.

Reid, D. M. (2002) *Whose Pharaohs? Archaeology, Museums, and Egyptian National Identity from Napoleon to World War I.* Berkeley: University of California Press.

Roosevelt, C. H. and Luke, C. (2006) Looting Lydia: The Destruction of an Archaeological Landscape in Western Turkey. In Brodie, N., Kersel, M. M., Luke, C., and Tubb, K. (eds.), *Archaeology, Cultural Heritage and the Antiquities Trade*, pp. 173–187. Gainesville: University Press of Florida.

Rose, B. (2016) Archaeology, Museums and War in the 21st Century. Keynote address at *Collaborative Futures for Museum Collections: Antiquities, Provenance, and Cultural Heritage.* October 16, Menil Collection, Houston, TX.

Rose, B. (2017). Beyond the UNESCO Convention: The Case of the Troy Gold in the Penn Museum. *Journal of Eastern Mediterranean Archaeology and Heritage Studies* 5(1): 87–91.

Schaub, R. T. and Rast, W. (1989) *Bāb edh-Dhrā': Excavations in the Cemetery Directed by Paul W. Lapp (1965–67).* Winona Lake, IN: Published for the American Schools of Oriental Research by Eisenbrauns.

Shaw, W. M. K. (2003) *Possessors and Possessed. Museums, Archaeology, and the Visualization of History in the Late Ottoman Empire.* Berkeley: University of California Press.

Sheng, G. (2008) International Protection of Cultural Property: Some Preliminary Issues and the Role of International Conventions. *Singapore Year Book of International Law* 12: 57–79.

Shoup, D. (2008) Monuments, Materiality, and Meaning in the Classical Archaeology of Anatolia. PhD Dissertation, Department of Classical Art and Archaeology, University of Michigan.

Singh, J. P. (2011) *United Nations Educational, Scientific, and Cultural Organization (UNESCO): Creating Norms for a Complex World (Global Institutions).* New York: Routledge.

Sy, A. (2016) Penn Museum Celebrates Life and Myth of King Midas. *The Daily Pennsylvanian*, February 16. [Online] Available from: http://www.thedp.com/article/2016/02/penn-museum-king-midas-exhibit. [Accessed February 16, 2016].

The Pennsylvania Declaration. (1980) Decision of Curators of the University Museum University of Pennsylvania, April 1, 1970, Expedition 22/3. [Online] Available from: http://www.penn.museum/documents/publications/expedition/PDFs/22-3/The%20Pennsylvania.pdf [Accessed April 6, 2013].

Thompson, E. (2016) *Possession: The Curious History of Private Collectors.* New Haven: Yale University Press.

University of Pennsylvania Museum of Archaeology and Anthropology. (2012) Penn Museum Strengthens Partnership with Turkey, Agrees to Indefinite Term Loan of Troy Gold. Press Release, September 4. [Online] Available from: http://www.penn.museum/press-releases/887-penn-museum-strengthens-partnership-with-turkey,-agrees-to-indefinite-term-loan-of-troy-gold.html [Accessed May 13, 2015].

Velioglu, E., Bandle, A. L. and Renold, M-Á. (2013) Case Troy Gold – Turkey and the University of Pennsylvania Museum of Archaeology and Anthropology. Platform ArThemis, Art-Law Centre, University of Geneva. [Online] Available from: http://unige.ch/art-adr [Accessed May 4, 2015].

Warring, J. (2005) Underground Debates: The Fundamental Differences of Opinion that Thwart UNESCO's Progress in Fighting the Illicit Trade in Cultural Property. *Emory International Law Review* 19(1): 227–303.

Watkins, J. (2005) Cultural Nationalists, Internationalists, and "Intra-nationalists": Who's Right and Whose Right? *International Journal of Cultural Property* 12(1): 78–94.

Wong, L. E. (2008) Relocating East and West: UNESCO's Major Project on the Mutual Appreciation of Eastern and Western Cultural Values. *Journal of World History* 19(3): 349–374.

Wu, H. (2012) Turkish "Troy Gold" at Penn Museum Stirs up Controversy. *The Daily Pennsylvanian*, September 12. [Online] Available from: http://www.thedp.com/article/2012/09/turkish-troy-gold-at-penn-museum-stirs-up-controversy [Accessed December 15, 2014].

15

CULTURES OF PROPERTY

African cultures in intellectual and cultural property regimes

Boatema Boateng

Introduction

In protecting culture, intellectual property (IP) laws appear to stand apart from culture. However, cultural and legal scholars have shown that IP laws are in fact cultural in reflecting very particular ideas about what kinds of work can be protected legally (Coombe, 1998; Oguamanam, 2004; Boateng, 2011a and b; Anderson, 2013). As a result, and as critical scholars of IP law have shown, such laws operate unequally towards different kinds of knowledge and culture (Boyle, 1996; Posey & Dutfield, 1996; Aoki, 1998; Coombe, 1998; McLeod, 2001; Jaszi & Woodmansee, 2003; Seeger, 2005; Boateng, 2011a and b; Anderson, 2013). Originally designed to regulate the cultural production of European nations, IP laws were given international scope through conventions that drew increasing portions of the world into their norms. At the time that those laws were conceived and also when their scope was first extended beyond European national borders in the late nineteenth century, Indigenous peoples, along with much of what is now considered the "Third World," were under European colonial control. In the middle of the twentieth century the global political order changed considerably, giving greater sovereignty to some of those subject peoples. Yet the cultural production of Indigenous and Third World peoples remains subjugated within IP laws and the conceptions of knowledge and culture on which those laws are based.

Although my discussion is mainly of nations in the Third World, I also refer to Indigenous peoples. There are similarities in the issues that arise around the culture of Third World nations and Indigenous peoples. However, it is important to underscore the important differences between the two groups. Most Third World nations share with Indigenous peoples a history of colonization by Europeans through either "indirect" colonization (like Ghana) or settler colonization (like the United States). Where European colonizers did not settle in significant numbers in the territories they controlled, national independence transferred the state and national sovereignty to the original inhabitants of those territories. It must be noted, however, that the state in such nations does not always represent the interests of all its people, some of whom may be marginalized in ways similar to Indigenous peoples in settler territories.

In those territories, independence meant autonomy for settlers from their European nations of origin. In the US, for example, independence meant British settlers wresting control of the state from the British kingdom. For the Indigenous people whose territory had been seized by those settlers, settler-led independence did not translate into independence for them. Rather it meant continued subjugation that Indigenous peoples still experience in many forms in the present – not only in the United States but also in nations like Canada, Australia, and Brazil. Despite their shared history of colonization, and the similarity in the consequences of colonization for their cultures, Indigenous peoples in settler societies do not share Third World countries' status of nation states with full membership in international organizations. That status is contingent on full sovereignty as nation states and enables members to shape international policy and law, including intellectual and cultural property laws. Although Indigenous peoples have long insisted that such organizations pay attention to their interests, the final outcomes are decided by member nations.

It is also important to explain my use of the term "Third World" despite its Cold War connotations of a hierarchy of a democratic/capitalist Western European and North American First World, a socialist/communist Second World, and a Third World of mostly former colonies (many of which also identified as politically "non-aligned" with members of the First and Second Worlds). I do not use the term "Third World" in an endorsement of the relegation of those regions of the world and their people to third place behind Western nations and the former communist bloc. Rather, informed by some postcolonial scholarship, I use it to signal the structural location of the Third World in global arrangements of power established during colonization. I also use the more current term "global South" interchangeably with "Third World."

In this chapter, I argue that the unequal treatment of different kinds of knowledge and culture in IP laws is a result of the cultural specificity of those laws. It is also a result of the processes by which IP laws attained the status of universal norms. Those processes are bound up with the history of empire and colonization that created structures of dominance over today's Indigenous and Third World peoples – or the people of the global South. I further argue that significant elements of those structures and their underlying premises remain and help to account for the current place of Indigenous and Third World knowledge and culture in IP law. As a result of those structures and premises, IP laws locate the knowledge and culture of people of the global South outside art and science – forms of cultural production granted protection under copyright and patent laws. That exclusion leaves Third World and Indigenous knowledge and culture vulnerable to appropriation (Boateng, 2011a and b; Anderson, 2013).

In this chapter I adopt a critical perspective that is materialist in paying attention to structures of power. I am also attentive to the cultural dimensions of power. My approach is informed by the insights of African feminist scholars like Amina Mama (1997) and Desiree Lewis (2004) who have noted the problems with European and North American knowledge production about Africa in the past as well as the ways that external agendas and priorities continue to shape African knowledge production. My analysis also draws on the work of African philosophers and literary scholars like Emmanuel Eze (2008) and Kwaku Korang (2004), who have noted how European conceptions of history and modernity placed African people outside both.

In tracing the history of the location of the global South in structures established during the colonial period I also situate the knowledge and cultural production of the South within the same historical and political context. Further, by drawing attention to the location of the South and its cultural forms in the current global order, I show the continuity in the logics underpinning the past history and present reality of the South, including its location in IP and cultural property regimes. I argue that despite the wave of mid-twentieth century decolonization, there has been little change in the status of most former colonies in the global economy.

I first outline the shift from direct economic, military and political dominance of colonial territories to less direct forms of dominance in the second half of the twentieth century. I then briefly outline the history of IP laws, focusing on their cultural specificity. I place that history in the context of the history of direct and indirect dominance of the global South during and after colonization. I also discuss the increasing importance of IP in the regimes through which dominance occurs as knowledge, information, and culture have become important economic commodities. I also outline the history of cultural property (CP) laws as an additional site for the protection of culture. I undertake a comparative analysis of the discourses of CP and IP laws for what they suggest about different kinds of culture.

I argue that the purported differences between the cultural production of people of the global South, on the one hand, and members of industrialized societies, on the other, are not so much qualitative or intrinsic as a function of their location in different regimes of cultural production. I therefore use the same terminology to refer to all kinds of cultural production rather than following the convention of using adjectives like "Indigenous" and "traditional" to refer to the cultural production of Indigenous and Third World people. Such adjectives have the effect of placing different kinds of knowledge and cultural production in an unequal relationship, reinforcing the structural inequities between the people who produce them.

I further argue that the cultural contingency of IP laws not only makes them unsuited to the protection of Indigenous and Third World knowledge and culture, but also sets a precedent for considering alternative or additional conceptions of culture that reflect more fully the wide range of cultures of property that exist among all the different groups that constitute the global community. I also argue that assuming an easy fit between the culture of the global South and cultural property laws reflects the same conceptions of knowledge and culture that are used to exclude the culture of the South from IP law. Therefore, rather than providing an alternative or supplement to the protection offered by IP laws, cultural property laws simply marginalize the cultural forms they protect.

I locate the case of Ghana in this historical and legal context as I discuss Ghana's efforts to protect the culture of Ghanaian peoples – that is, the people of the different ethnic groups that make up the nation of Ghana. In protecting locally produced culture as national culture, the Ghanaian state does not always represent the interests of all its citizens. Those citizens sometimes contradict the state as they identify individuals, communities, and ethnic groups as the rightful custodians of the culture that they produce (Boateng, 2011a and b). Bearing those contradictions in mind, I critically examine Ghana's protection of its people's culture and consider the implications of its use of the different legal and policy frameworks of IP and CP to protect different kinds of culture. I also consider what are some of the cultures of property that Ghanaian peoples offer for rethinking and expanding the options provided by intellectual and cultural property laws.

Colonial orders in the postcolonial age

In order to understand the place within IP law of the knowledge and culture of the peoples of the global South, it is important to situate the law in the historical processes through which such nations and peoples came to occupy their current location in the global order. Starting in the fifteenth century with the innovations that made transoceanic travel possible, European states began to take control of the lands and people that they encountered through those journeys in a process of colonization that continued into the early twentieth century.

Although that colonization was undertaken by different European powers including Spain, Portugal, Britain, France and the Netherlands, there was little variation in its underlying logics. Those logics included the expansion of European imperial territories, the conversion of "heathens" to Christianity, and views of land use that deemed unexploited land to be "terra nullius" or empty, even when it was occupied and its resources used by its original inhabitants (Whitt, 2009). The concept of terra nullius was important in justifying settler colonization in which Europeans took over the lands of Indigenous peoples across the Americas and also in Australia, New Zealand and Southern Africa.

An important additional justification for settler colonization came from the invention of theories of race that placed Europeans at the top of a hierarchy of the different races they encountered (Omi & Winant, 1994). The invention of race harnessed "science" to ongoing projects of empire and was used to justify centuries of enslavement in which millions of Africans were forcibly transported to the Americas to work on plantations established by European colonizers. Toward the end of the nineteenth century, with the official end of slavery and the need for raw materials to feed industrialization, European powers met in Berlin from 1884 to 1885 and divided the continent of Africa among themselves. As with the colonies established earlier in Asia and the Americas, the economic focus in African colonies was on resource extraction and colonial economies were structured toward these ends. As a result, local African populations shifted from agricultural production for local food needs to "cash crops" for export.

The three decades immediately following WWII saw a wave of decolonization as nations in large parts of Africa and Asia successfully gained independence from European colonial powers. By then most settler-colonies had become independent nations in struggles led by the descendants of settlers who sought and gained autonomy from their respective imperial powers. As noted earlier, independence in those colonies meant continued rule by the descendants of Europeans and made little difference to the sovereignty of Indigenous people. In colonies that experienced indirect rule, however, independence took the form of the transfer of the colonial state to Indigenous populations, and the conversion of those colonies into modern nation states. This was the process by which the British colony of the Gold Coast became the independent nation of Ghana.

In many instances, independence in territories that experienced indirect colonization has turned out to be nominal, as those territories have labored under the weight of adverse global economic arrangements established under colonization. Many have continued as producers of primary goods designated for extraction based on the needs of former colonial powers and of the US, which emerged from World War II as the leading world power. Although a number of independent nations tried to shift the base of their economies from primary products to industries producing finished or semi-finished goods, few have been successful and, for the most part, colonial economic structures remain in place – especially in Africa. In Ghana, primary goods from the agricultural and mining sectors account for a significant portion of the economy, although services have replaced agriculture as the largest sector (World Bank). The high dependence on primary agricultural and mineral goods has made nations like Ghana vulnerable to market fluctuations in the prices of those goods, and several have foundered economically.

These developments have been exacerbated by struggles over the state by competing political actors including the military. In Ghana, Kwame Nkrumah, the country's first head of state, was deposed in 1966 in a military coup that some claimed was backed by the CIA (Grundy, 1968). Apart from his importance as a nationalist leader, Nkrumah was notable for identifying post-independence economic subjugation by colonial and other external powers as "neo-colonialism." He was also a proponent of socialism in a period marked by Cold War tensions between the US and Soviet Union. However, his significant failings as a national leader cannot be discounted as a factor in his downfall.

The military overthrow of Nkrumah was the beginning of almost three decades of military rule briefly punctuated by two civilian governments whose terms were cut short by military coups. Until the first transfer of power from one civilian government to another in 2002, therefore, changes in government in Ghana occurred mostly without the consent of the governed. With the combination of Nkrumah's increasingly autocratic rule by the time of his overthrow, and arbitrary rule by unaccountable military governments, the custodians of the postcolonial Ghanaian state bear some responsibility for the country's adverse fortunes since independence. The external factors outlined earlier are unquestionably important in understanding the position of Ghana and other Third World nations in the current global order. However, as Abebe Zegeye and Maurice Vambe have warned, it is important not to gloss over or romanticize the shortcomings of African states like Ghana (2006).

As a result of this history, and as several postcolonial scholars have observed, the European dominance of colonized peoples did not come to a complete stop with the end of formal colonization. Rather, such scholars argue, that dominance has continued in what some, following Nkrumah, characterize as neo-colonialism or (as Jacqui Alexander calls it) "flag independence" (Alexander, 1994). In the period since the end of World War II, the United States has emerged as the leading global power, and a number of scholars have characterized its post war position in the global order as an imperial one (Loomba, 1998).

The intellectual terra nullius

Operating in tandem with the history of physical dominance and resource extraction during and after the colonial era is the cultural history that elevated European systems of knowledge and cultural production over those of subject peoples around the globe. The colonial period coincided with the rise of systems of knowledge production in Europe that came to be known as the "Enlightenment." The Enlightenment inaugurated "modern science" in which knowledge was based on observation and measurement rather than on religious authority, as had previously been the case. Alongside subjects like physics and botany, scholars of the period sought to account for the inhabitants of the territories that were being colonized by European powers.

Colonial knowledge production served primarily to establish those societies' difference from, and inferiority to, Europeans in scholarship that supported the colonial project. Subject peoples in the Americas, Africa, and parts of Asia were deemed "primitive," "barbaric" and "savage" and their cultural artifacts were desecrated, stolen as curios and relocated to museums in European capitals. In addition, colonizers dismissed as "superstition" the knowledge of local communities in African and other territories (Zegeye & Vambe, 2006).

The new modes of European knowledge production combined with the spread of empire to render those systems of knowledge production hegemonic, and European educational systems were imposed in place of Indigenous ones. Drawing on Michel Foucault's insights into the operation of knowledge as a mechanism of power, Michael Doxtater has described these processes by which Europeans devalued and displaced local modes of knowledge production as "colonial-power-knowledge" (Doxtater, 2004). That colonial-power-knowledge has been the target of critical scholarship in Indigenous studies. Scholars in this area have therefore drawn attention, and sought to restore value, to Indigenous modes of knowledge production (Doxtater, 2004; Smith, 2005; Million, 2009; Zegeye & Vambe, 2006).

The study of the global South has continued to focus on its presumed distance from or proximity to Western Europe and North America, reflecting the interests of the Western academy and the power structures in which it is embedded. With the end of official colonization after the end of WWII, the study of the global South shifted from its overt link with Western dominance. However, the postwar emergence of development studies kept intact colonial epistemologies of Third World inferiority. Growing out of post-WWII theories of "modernization," and informed by the construction of poverty as a site of scientific intervention in the late nineteenth and early twentieth centuries, development was commonly construed as an evolutionary process in which "developing nations" were encouraged to achieve the conditions of industrialized nations in Western Europe and North America (Escobar, 1995).

Both modernization and development have been challenged based on both their demonstrated failures and their flawed premises that fail to take into account the structural causes of development (Rogers, 1978; Cardoso & Faletto, 1979; Escobar, 1995). The second half of the twentieth century also saw the emergence of postcolonial studies, which has posed important challenges to the eurocentric assumptions of colonial cultural anthropology and development studies. However, modernization has remained a dominant theme in the study of the global South, and the nations of the South are measured by the extent to which they modernize. For the most part, those nations have acquiesced with the imperative to modernize in the terms established by the West. Rather than imagining and establishing radically different ways of ordering social and political life based on Indigenous institutions and norms, nations like Ghana have chosen to adopt and adapt the "modern" forms inherited from colonial powers.

The devaluation of Indigenous modes of knowledge and cultural production from the global South is an important factor in the status of such knowledge and culture in IP law. The first IP laws emerged in Europe at the time that Enlightenment thought was leading to changes in ideas of human subjectivity and science. As a result, where cultural production had been collective and built openly on existing work, copyright laws institutionalized new conceptions of cultural production as individual and original, de-emphasizing links to existing work. IP laws therefore conceived of knowledge, culture and their alienability in ways that were new to Europe and also very specific to European nations. They represented ways of conceiving of knowledge and culture that were by no means universal but culturally specific.

European global dominance – a dominance shared by settler nations like the US, Canada and Australia – led to the globalization of the conceptions of knowledge and cultural production embedded in the IP laws of Western European nations in the eighteenth and nineteenth centuries. Although the laws themselves were not globalized until the late twentieth century (Oguamanam, 2004), their basic precepts were embedded in national laws around the world as former colonies became independent and adopted "modern" laws. For example, in Ghana those laws were simply British colonial laws that were gradually modified to reflect national priorities. However, their underlying premises were often left intact, and this was the case with the IP and CP laws that Ghana inherited from Britain.

These conceptions of knowledge and cultural production have proved inimical to the interests of peoples of the global South in the twentieth and twenty-first centuries. As these peoples have sought protection for their knowledge and cultural production, their ways of producing that knowledge and culture have been held to the standards embedded in IP law, and they have been deemed ineligible for protection by those standards ostensibly because they are not produced according to the individualistic subjectivity and creativity privileged by IP law (Anderson, 2005). In fact, the differences between Western norms of creativity and those in the cultural production of the South are not always as extreme or as absolute as claimed (Boateng, 2011a and b, 2013). Yet, rather than being protected, the culture and knowledge of the global South has been treated as a kind of intellectual terra nullius by external groups and individuals who use them as the basis for "artistic" creations and "scientific" discovery. As I show in the next section, developments in both national and international IP regulations in the late twentieth and early twenty-first centuries have only worsened this problem.

Global economic power in the age of information

Where colonization operated primarily through the direct control of territories and peoples using military, political and economic force, dominance in the post-WWII era has occurred through both direct and indirect means such as political and economic pressure exerted by the main world powers bilaterally and multilaterally. While feminist political scientists like Marianne Marchand and Anne Sisson Runyan (2011) have identified military power as a feature of US power and a factor of continuing importance in the contemporary world order, economic and political pressure have become key means of exercising power in the global economy. Economic power is exercised bilaterally between nations and also multilaterally through institutions like the World Bank and International Monetary Fund (IMF).

By the 1980s Ghana and several other nations in Africa and beyond were deeply indebted to the World Bank and IMF and subject to conditions imposed by those agencies. Also known as the Bretton Woods institutions, the World Bank and IMF were created after WWII to finance the rebuilding of Western Europe. Towards the end of the twentieth century those institutions' primary focus shifted, as they became major lenders to former colonies. The 1980s also marked the rise of neoliberal economic policies that identified the market as more efficient and desirable than the state in distributing social goods.

As a condition for securing loans from the World Bank and IMF, several Third World nations were obliged to implement "Structural Adjustment Programs" (SAPs) that mandated such market-centered policies. The combined result of these external and internal factors is that political independence of African and other Third World nations has not been matched by economic independence or advancement. As a result, even though they are full members of international institutions like the UN because of their formal status as sovereign nation states, they have very little influence in the decision making of those institutions. The adverse consequences of that lack of influence are especially evident in the era of the World Trade Organization (WTO).

In the final decade of the twentieth century, the WTO emerged from the Bretton Woods institutions as an important means of coordinating the economic activities of member states and a key site for the exercise of global economic dominance (Aoki, 1998). By the time of its creation, information had become a major component of several national economies in what some identified as a progression from an industrial to an information age. Some of those nations, like the US, grew impatient with the UN-based World IP Organization (WIPO) as a means of safeguarding their economic interests in information. One source of frustration came from the relatively democratic procedures that gave all members an equal say in the organization's decisions (Ryan, 1996). Prior to the WTO era, individual nations exercised a lot of discretion in the nature and extent of IP protections that they accorded each other's cultural production (Oguamanam, 2004).

Consequently, the US and other major industrialized nations turned to the international trade arena where the General Agreement on Tariffs and Trade (GATT) was in the process of being reformed. In 1995 GATT was replaced by the WTO and one of the major agreements within the WTO was the Agreement on Trade Related Aspects of IP (TRIPS). Instead of the one-nation-one-vote procedures of WIPO, TRIPS provided the alternative of "linkage-based bargaining" in which bargaining power determined states' ability to influence decision making (Ryan, 1996). With TRIPS, industrialized nations created IP norms that were legally binding and enforceable in ways that the conventions and agreements of WIPO were not. At the same time, it should be noted that despite its relatively democratic principles, WIPO cannot be viewed as existing apart from and in opposition to the WTO and TRIPS. Rather, as Keith Aoki observed, there has been an interpenetration of the "'public international institutions' of the UN with the 'private' IMF, World Bank and WTO" (1998: 14).

It is important to note that the linking of IP to trade was not in itself unique or unprecedented, since IP laws have had economic significance from their first inception in national laws. In the words of Chidi Oguamanam, "Chiefly, IPRs are capitalist creations, designed to serve the market economy and advance commercial interests as a matter of priority over cultural sensitivities" (2004: 145). Accordingly, the first international IP agreements, the Paris Convention for the Protection of Industrial Property (1883) and the Berne Convention for the Protection of Literary and Artistic Works (1886), were enacted by European nations seeking to regulate access to their culture as it began to circulate beyond national borders. IP laws can therefore be viewed as intrinsically bound up with the commodification and economic circulation of knowledge and culture (Bettig, 1996; Oguamanam, 2004).

The advent of TRIPS reinforced this economic function of IP protection. In doing so, it reflected the priorities of the United States in a number of ways. For example, TRIPS makes provision for the patenting of plant material and other life forms (including human biological material). This follows a precedent established in US patent law in 1980 when such protection was first allowed (Aoki, 1998). That precedent was further reinforced by cases such as that of John Moore who unsuccessfully sued the Regents of the University of California for an interest in the lucrative patents derived from his spleen by doctors who treated him at the university's Los Angeles medical center (Boyle, 1996). In a discussion of such practices in the Third World. Keith Aoki cites an article by Lisa Belkin in the *New York Times Magazine* in January 1998, reporting the harvesting of samples from people in a number of nations including Saudia Arabia, Ghana and Nigeria (Aoki, 1998: 46).

The provision in TRIPS that globalizes the IP protection of such practices beyond the US law is of particular importance for Indigenous people and local communities in Third World nations. As several critical legal scholars have argued along with Indigenous and Third World scholars and activists, much of the plant life that has become amenable to such protection originates in communities that do not benefit from the protections granted under TRIPS and national laws (Posey & Dutfield, 1996; Oguamanam, 2004). However, the protections are granted not to those communities but to those who can successfully claim to have identified and isolated the key ingredients in such plants and other biological (including human) material. The protections in question cover those methods of identification and isolation. In both the global North and South, the persons whose bodily material is exploited and privatized under such provisions also do not benefit from that exploitation.

In sum, as different kinds of information gained in value towards the end of the twentieth century, IP laws became important means of their regulation both nationally and internationally. The US, which in the nineteenth century "was considered to be the 'Barbary Coast' of IP" emerged as international IP enforcer-in-chief (Aoki, 1998: 24–25). It led the move to establish international IP regulation primarily as a trade issue structured by the Bretton Woods institutions and was successful in shaping the new TRIPS regime to its national IP norms, reflecting changes in those norms that were new in IP history and mandating them for the rest of the world. If IP norms have been malleable in the hands of the US, allowing the protection of new creative forms (such as software) and previously exempt forms (such as plant, animal and human material), they have proved unyielding in the face of the demands of Indigenous and Third World people for the protection of their knowledge and culture. As I discuss in the next section, a close examination of the bases on which IP norms have expanded and contracted so far suggests that there is scope for expanding them further in the interests of Indigenous and Third World people.

Cultural property: Alternative or backwater?

Cultural property laws appear to provide an alternative space for the protection of knowledge and culture from Indigenous peoples and Third World nations. It is worth remembering, however that those laws were not originally conceived with Indigenous peoples and the global South in mind. The first international cultural property convention, the Hague Convention for the Protection of Cultural Property in the Event of Armed Conflict (1954), was a direct outcome of the Second World War and a response to the Nazi theft of cultural goods from people – especially Jewish people – in the territories they controlled. The language of the convention also suggests that it was a response to the wartime bombing of immovable cultural property – as much in Cologne, Germany, as in Coventry, England.

As important and necessary as the convention was in signaling the international community's abhorrence at Nazi cultural appropriation, and regret at both Nazi and Allied destruction of major European cultural sites, it is telling that the parties to the convention did not appear to view the appropriation of Indigenous and other subject peoples' culture as equally constituting theft and destruction. At the time the convention was signed, most of Africa was still under the colonial control of some of the parties to the convention. However, subsequent conventions governing cultural property have been more inclusive of the kinds of cultural property stolen by colonial powers. Those conventions include the UNESCO Convention on the Means of Prohibiting and Preventing the Illicit Import, Export and Transfer of Ownership of Cultural Property (1970), and the UNESCO Convention for the Protection of the World Cultural and Natural Heritage (1972).

The description of cultural property in the 1970 convention includes the kinds of culture taken from Indigenous peoples and Third World nations under colonization, such as "products of archaeological excavations (including regular and clandestine) or of archaeological discoveries; elements of artistic or historical monuments or archaeological sites which have been dismembered; antiquities more than one hundred years old, such as inscriptions, coins and engraved seals; objects of ethnological interest" (UNESCO, 1970: 4). However, even as they acknowledge and provide the basis for both the protection and potential restitution of cultural goods, these descriptions conceive of cultural property in terms of European and North American ideas of science (archaeological discoveries), art and history (antiquities) and conceptions of the human (ethnological interest). They map onto the categories of colonial knowledge production where people deemed as the Other are indistinguishable from their artifacts. If cultural property laws seem better suited than IP laws to the protection of the culture of Indigenous peoples and the global South, the ways that they conceive of culture are as troubling as the exclusions of IP law. In addition, major international cultural property conventions assign cultural property primarily to national rather than sub-national groups like Indigenous peoples in nations such as Australia or ethnic groups in nations like Ghana.

Naomi Mezey (2007) has identified a preservationist tendency in cultural property laws that, contrary to the fluidity and dynamism of culture, render it static and frozen. This is, in part, a result of cultural property's focus on identifying culture with specific groups of people, and in emphasizing property at the expense of culture. She states, "The paradox of cultural property is that it deals in culture and yet distorts and mummifies culture in its dealings with it. Cultural property not only misses the point, but perpetuates potentially harmful notions about cultures and groups in the name of trying to protect and preserve them" (2007: 2026). Using as her point of departure the controversy that led to the retiring of the University of Illinois' mascot, Chief Illiniwek, Mezey argues instead for a focus on hybridity and cultural fusion even when, as in the case of Chief Illiniwek, members of a dominant group (white Americans) appropriate the culture of a subjugated group (Native Americans).

Mezey's discussion does not extend to IP laws, but it is productive to consider those laws in relation to her main objection to cultural property. In Mezey's argument, the preservationist tendencies of cultural property are invoked ostensibly in the interests of Native Americans, and Native American culture is rendered static in order to prevent the harm from its appropriation in the figure of Chief Illiniwek. It can be argued that IP law operates similarly to fix certain conceptions of what is and is not art and science in ways that exclude Indigenous culture and knowledge from protection (Anderson, 2005). It can further be argued that if cultural property norms were successfully invoked in the case of Chief Illiniwek, IP laws have not been as accommodating of the cultural interests of the global South. In a way, the two sets of law mirror each other while resting on similar conceptions of Indigenous and Third World people. The way that Ghana has used both kinds of law to protect local culture points to IP laws as the pre-eminent regulatory site for the protection of culture.

Cultures of property in Ghanaian intellectual and cultural property laws and policies

Ghana's IP laws began as British colonial laws when the territory was still the British colony of the Gold Coast. The first copyright law, for example, was the Imperial Copyright Act of 1911 (Amegatcher, 1993). This was revised in 1960, 1985 and, most recently, in 2005 with each revision more closely reflecting both national interests and pressure from Ghanaian groups, especially musicians. The country also has industrial property laws that have reflected differing national priorities in the course of Ghana's history since it gained independence in 1957. For example, for the last quarter of the twentieth century, Ghana's industrial property laws included a *sui generis* textile designs registration decree originally aimed at protecting the local textile industry (Government of Ghana, 1973). IP has therefore been an active site of legislation and legal reform throughout Ghana's history as an independent nation.

By contrast, Ghana has no cultural property laws as such. Rather, it has laws setting up institutions charged with handling issues relating to culture. Those institutions are the Museums and Monuments Board (GMMB) which, according to the Board website was established "in March 1957 – on the eve of Ghana's independence – as a result of the merger of the then interim Council of the National Museum of the Gold Coast and the Monuments and Relics Commission" (GMMB, 2016). The legal instrument behind the merger was the Museum and Monuments Board Ordinance, a statute of the Gold Goast. In 1969 the Ordinance was repealed and replaced by the National Museum Act, which is still in force. In 1990, the government of Ghana passed the National Commission on Culture Law, establishing a second body charged with responsibility for Ghanaian culture. The Commission served as Ghana's Ministry of Culture and was eventually replaced by the Ministry of Chieftaincy and Culture and, most recently, by the Ministry of Tourism, Culture and the Creative Arts.[1] The law setting up the National Commission on Culture is still in force and gives that body (and its successors) oversight over the Museums and Monuments Board and other institutions including the

National Theatre of Ghana, the Ghana Dance Ensemble, and the Bureau of Ghana Languages. Finally, in 2004, the Commission drew up a national cultural policy.

The language of the National Museum Act is evocative of the definitions of cultural property discussed earlier in addressing the sale, export and preservation of "antiquities" and "monuments." In this, it is reflective of the Eurocentric conceptions of the culture of the South. The National Commission on Culture Law suggests a wider understanding of culture, that includes "the arts" as well as "cultural heritage" and "cultural workers," while the National Cultural Policy provides more specificity in its discussion of different areas of Ghanaian culture including "the arts" and "heritage assets." The GMMB website further expands on cultural heritage and identifies key elements of Ghana's cultural heritage as:

- A varied collection of Forts and Castles, built and occupied by the Portuguese, Dutch, Danes, Swedes, Germans, French, British and Brandenburg-Prussians between the 15th and 20th Centuries
- Ten ancient Asante Traditional Buildings dating from the 17th Century to the early 20th Century
- Mosques in Northern Ghana
- Artefacts such as pots, stools, musical instruments, textiles, clothing, leather works, weapons, tools, carvings, masks, jewellery, ritual dolls

(GMMB, 2016)

Additional elements of that heritage include: "Adinkra symbols, Carved wooden stools, Festivals of the various ethnic groups, Gold weights, Kente cloth, Musical genres such as highlife and hiplife, Traditional and contemporary musical instruments, Traditional dances, Traditional ethnic music" (GMMB, 2016). While these elements of Ghanaian cultural heritage are evocative of some of the definitions and categories of cultural property, they are only indirectly constituted as objects of protection through legally established cultural institutions rather than directly under cultural property law.

The cultural property policy of 2004 defines culture as "the totality of the way of life evolved by our people through experience and reflection in our attempt to fashion a harmonious coexistence with our environment" (NCC, 2004: 9). The policy is also significant in emphasizing dynamism as a feature of Ghanaian culture. It states, culture is "a dynamic phenomenon . . . established by our concept of Sankofa, which establishes linkages with the positive aspects of our past and the present." Sankofa symbolizes returning to the past to retrieve what has been forgotten, but the 2004 policy states that it also "affirms the co-existence of the past and the future in the present. It therefore embodies the attitude of our people to the interaction between traditional values and the demands of modern technology within the contemporary international cultural milieu" (NCC, 2004: 9).

Significantly, it is in the area of IP law that Ghana has tried to protect cultural forms originating from within its borders. For example, the textile designs registration decree of 1973 included the designs of Indigenous adinkra and kente cloth in its protection. Beginning in 1985, those designs were also protected under copyright law as elements of folklore, which the law defined to include elements of oral and material culture (Government of Ghana, 1985, 2005). In 2003 when Ghana passed a geographical indications law for the first time in its history, it included cultural items like kente cloth in the goods protected by the law (Government of Ghana, 2003).

While the protection of culture in Ghana is somewhat vague in the context of the legal and policy provisions that most resemble those of cultural property law, it is much clearer in the provisions of IP law. This seems to reflect the status of IP law as the dominant site of cultural protection especially in the WTO/TRIPS era of the late twentieth and early twenty-first century. This legal choice on the part of Ghana is especially interesting given the view that some of the cultural forms it protects under IP laws are ineligible for such protection. Indeed, Ghana's copyright protection of adinkra and kente designs seems to confirm that view because the provisions of the law try to fit adinkra and kente to the law rather than fitting the law to local norms of authorship guiding the production of adinkra and kente cloth.

For example, in keeping with Western conventions of copyright protection, Ghana's law only protects the *expressions* of kente and adinkra designs and not adinkra and kente cloth per se. However, the designs have their greatest value when expressed in the medium of cloth, and the copyright protection of the expressions alone is therefore inadequate (Boateng, 2011a and b). In addition, when Ghanaian activists protested against the state (rather than individuals or communities) claiming the rights to local culture when such culture was first included in copyright law in 1985, the state's response was to recognize individual authorship of such culture in the 2005 revision of the law. However, communities and ethnic groups continue to be excluded from holding the rights to such culture. National cohesion has been invoked as a justification for that exclusion, but in privileging the state and individuals over communities, the copyright law imposes norms of authorship that are at variance with the local norms that guide the production of adinkra and kente and other kinds of local Ghanaian culture (Boateng, 2011a and b).

It is clear from these limitations that Ghana's legal protection of local culture is far from perfect even though at first glance it appears to chart new ground in using IP law to protect cultural forms that are typically held to be ineligible for such protection. By separating designs from the medium of cloth, the law runs the risk of fragmenting what it protects. Similarly, making provision for the authorship rights of individuals but not of ethnic groups and communities also fragments local authorship norms by privileging individual over collective rights even though the authorship of many local cultural forms (including adinkra and kente cloth designs) is both individual and collective (Boateng, 2011a and b).

Ultimately, therefore, Ghana's copyright protection of local culture reinforces the dominant Eurocentric authorship norms of IP law far more than it challenges them. Similarly, Ghana's CP policies, especially regarding the cultural heritage listed at the GMMB website, begin with and simply add onto Western conceptions of such property. The cultural policy of 2004 goes a little further in conceiving of culture as dynamic and also in addressing itself to the conditions of cultural production that make dynamism possible. It does this by identifying the promotion of the arts (including "traditional arts") as one of its goals and, unlike the GMMB, it distinguishes between the arts and "heritage assets". The discussion of those heritage assets returns to the language of some international CP conventions in emphasizing recovery of stolen heritage assets. When it comes to culture conceived as "heritage," therefore, the national cultural policy comes closer to the GMMB and is also suggestive of international CP norms.

Conclusion

Ghana's IP protection of local culture stops well short of a radical interrogation or reimagining of culture that goes beyond the simple preservation of the end products of cultural processes to consideration of the conditions of cultural production that might offer new insights for legal norms of protection. CP, as implied in the GMMB's category of "cultural heritage" and the cultural policy's "heritage assets" also does not appear to go much beyond Western conceptions of such property. In both IP and CP (to the extent that Ghana has CP laws and policies), local and indigenous culture are ultimately fixed in ways that continue to be dominated by Western norms of culture and its protection. That fixing occurs through IP laws that uphold the convention of the individual or corporate/state author and owner of cultural production while CP policy fixes culture by conceiving of it in terms of antiquity and heritage.

When it comes to IP and CP, therefore, there seems to be a reluctance on the part of Ghanaian lawmakers and some policymakers to go far beyond the conceptions of culture and property embedded in Western IP and CP laws. Some of that reluctance may be a function of Ghana's paradoxical situation as a society that seeks simultaneously to assert its modernity through laws that stay close to Western standards, while asserting its distinctiveness through cultural processes and products that have long been deemed non-modern. In resolving that contradiction, Ghana has so far tended to come down on the side of the cultures of property embedded in Western IP and CP frameworks in a kind of ongoing cultural neocolonialism. However, the cultural policy of 2004 disrupts this somewhat in making a distinction between arts and heritage assets. In making that distinction, it provides a potential basis for reimagining the protection of local culture in ways that incorporate Indigenous and local norms.

Note

1 I am grateful to Zagba Oyortey, Director of the Ghana Museums and Monuments Board, for pointing out these changes.

Bibliography

Alexander, M. Jacqui. "Not Just (Any) Body Can Be a Citizen: The Politics of Law, Sexuality and Postcoloniality in Trinidad and Tobago and the Bahamas." *Feminist Review* 48(Autumn), 1994: 5–23.

Amegatcher, Andrew Ofoe. *Ghanaian Law of Copyright*. Accra, Ghana: Ghana Law Publishers, 1993.

Anderson, Jane. "The Making of Indigenous Knowledge in Intellectual Property Law in Australia." *International Journal of Cultural Property* 12, 2005: 347–373.

Anderson, Jane. "Anxieties of Authorship in the Colonial Archive." In Cynthia Chris and David Gerstner (eds.) *Media Authorship*. New York: Routledge, 2013: 229–246.

Aoki, Keith. "Neocolonialism, Anticommons Property, and Biopiracy in the (Not-so-Brave) New World Order of International Intellectual Property Protection." *Indiana Journal of Global Legal Studies* 6(1, Fall), 1998: 11–58.

Bettig, Ron. *Copyrighting Culture: The Political Economy of Intellectual Property*. Boulder, CO: Westview Press, 1996.

Boateng, Boatema. *The Copyright Thing Doesn't Work Here: Adinkra and Kente Cloth and Intellectual Property in Ghana*. Minneapolis: University of Minnesota Press, 2011a.

Boateng, Boatema. "Whose Democracy? Rights-based Discourse and Global Intellectual Property Rights Activism." In Robin Mansell and Marc Raboy (eds.) *The Handbook of Global Media and Communication Policy*. Malden, MA: Blackwell, 2011b.

Boateng, Boatema. "The Hand of the Ancestors: Time, Cultural Production and Intellectual Property Law." *Law and Society Review* 47(4), 2013: 943–973.

Boyle, James. *Shamans, Software, and Spleens: Law and the Construction of the Information Society*. Cambridge, MA and London: Harvard University Press, 1996.

Cardoso, Fernando Henrique and Enzo Faletto. *Dependency and Development in Latin America*. Berkeley: University of California Press, 1979.

Coombe, Rosemary. *The Cultural Life of Properties: Authorship, Appropriation and the Law*. Durham, NC: Duke University Press, 1998.
Doxtater, Michael G. "Indigenous Knowledge in the Decolonial Era." *American Indian Quarterly* 28(3/4, Summer–Autumn), 2004: 618–633.
Drahos, Peter and Susy Frankel. "Indigenous Peoples' Innovation and Intellectual Property: The Issues." In Peter Drahos and Susy Frankel (eds.) *Indigenous Peoples' Innovation: Intellectual Property Pathways to Development*. Canberra: Australian National University E Press, 2012.
Escobar, Arturo. *Encountering Development: The Making and Unmaking of the Third World*. Princeton, NJ: Princeton University Press, 1995.
Eze, Emmanuel Chukuwudi. "Language and Time in Postcolonial Experience." *Research in African Literatures* 39(1), 2008: 24–47.
GMMB (Ghana National Museums and Monuments Board). "The Material Cultural Heritage of Ghana." http://www.ghanamuseums.org/material-cultural-heritage.php (accessed February 22, 2016).
Government of Ghana. National Museum Act, 1969.
Government of Ghana. Textile Designs (Registration) Decree, 1973.
Government of Ghana. National Commission on Culture Law, 1990.
Government of Ghana. Geographical Indications Act, 2003.
Government of Ghana. Copyright Act (Act 690), 2005.
Grundy, Kenneth W. "The Negative Image of Africa's Military." *The Review of Politics* 30(4), 1968: 428–439.
Jaszi, Peter and Martha Woodmansee. "Beyond Authorship: Refiguring Rights in Traditional Culture and Bioknowledge." In Mario Biagioli and Peter Galison (eds.) *Scientific Authorship: Credit and Intellectual Property in Science*. New York: Routledge, 2003: 195–223.
Korang, Kwaku Larbi. "Where is Africa? When is the West's Other? Literary Postcoloniality in a Comparative Anthropology." *diacritics* 34(2), 2004: 38–61.
Lewis, Desiree. "African Gender Research and Postcoloniality: Legacies and Challenges." In S. Arnfred, B. Bakare-Yusuf, E. Waswa Kisiang'ani, D. Lewis, O. Oyewumi, and F. Chioma Steady (eds.), *Codesria Gender Series 1. African Gender Scholarship: Concepts, Methodologies and Paradigms*. Dakar, Senegal: Council for the Development of Social Science Research in Africa, 2004: 27–41.
Loomba, Ania. *Colonialism/Postcolonialism*. New York: Routledge, 1998.
McLeod, Kembrew. *Owning Culture: Authorship, Ownership and Intellectual Property Law*. New York: Peter Lang, 2001.
Mama, Amina. "Shedding the Masks and Tearing the Veils: Cultural Studies for a Post-Colonial Africa." In A. Imam, A. Mama, and F. Sow (eds.), *Engendering African Social Sciences*. Dakar, Senegal: Council for the Development of Social Science Research in Africa, 1997: 61–80.
Mamdani, Mahmood. *Citizen and Subject: Contemporary Africa and the Legacy of Late Colonialism*. Princeton, NJ: Princeton University Press, 1996.
Marchand, Marianne H. and Sisson Runyan (eds.) "Introduction." In *Gender and Global Restructuring: Sightings, Sites and Resistances, 2nd Edition*. New York: Routledge, 2011.
Mezey, Naomi. "The Paradoxes of Cultural Property." *Columbia Law Review* 107, 2007: 2004–2046.
Million, Dian. "Felt Theory: An Indigenous Feminist Approach to Affect and History." *Wicazo Sa Review* 24(2), 2009: 53–76.
NCC (National Commission on Culture). *The Cultural Policy of Ghana*, 2004.
Oguamanam, Chidi. "Localizing Intellectual Property in the Globalization Epoch: The Integration of Indigenous Knowledge." *Indiana Journal of Global Legal Studies* 11(2), 2004: 135–169.
Omi, Michael and Howard Winant. *Racial Formation in the United States: From the 1960s to the 1990s, 2nd Edition*. New York: Routledge, 1994.
Posey, Darrell and Graham Dutfield. *Beyond Intellectual Property: Toward Traditional Resource Rights for Indigenous Peoples and Local Communities*. Ottawa: IDRC, 1996.
Rogers, Everett. "The Rise and Fall of the Dominant Paradigm." *Journal of Communication* 28(1), 1978: 64–69.
Ryan, Michael P. *Knowledge Diplomacy: Global Competition and the Politics of Intellectual Property*. Washington, DC: Brookings Institution Press, 1996.
Seeger, Anthony. "Who Got Left Out of the Property Grab Again: Oral Traditions, Indigenous Rights, and Valuable Old Knowledge." In Rishab Ghosh (ed.) *CODE: Collaborative Ownership and the Digital Economy*. Cambridge, MA: The MIT Press, 2005: 75–84.
Sell, Susan and Christopher May. "Moments in Law: Contestation and Settlement in the History of Intellectual Property Law." *Review of International Political Economy* 8(3), 2001: 467–500.

Smith, Andrea. "Spiritual Appropriation as Sexual Violence." *Wicazo Sa Review* 20(1), 2005: 97–111.
United Nations. *State of the World's Indigenous Peoples*. New York: UN Department of Economic and Social Affairs, 2010.
UNESCO. Final Act of the Intergovernmental Conference on the Protection of Cultural Property in the Event of Armed Conflict. Paris, France: UNESCO, 1954.
UNESCO. Convention on the Means of Prohibiting and Preventing the Illicit Import, Export and Transfer of Ownership of Cultural Property. Paris, France: UNESCO, 1970.
UNESCO. Convention for the Protection of the World Cultural and Natural Heritage. Paris, France: UNESCO, 1972.
Whitt, Laurelyn. *Science, Colonialism, and Indigenous Peoples*. New York: Cambridge University Press, 2009.
World Bank. "World Development Indicators." http://databank.worldbank.org/data/reports.aspx?source=2&country=GHA&series=&period= (accessed February 22, 2016).
World Intellectual Property Organization. http://www.wipo.int/about-wipo/en/history.html (accessed June 9, 2015).
Zegeye, Abebe and Maurice Vambe. "African Indigenous Knowledge Systems." *Review (Fernand Braudel Center)* 29(4), 2006: 329–358.

PART IV

Cultural property beyond the state

Jane Anderson and Haidy Geismar

As the Introduction to this volume makes clear, the category of cultural property has historically drawn together histories of thinking about property and cultural identity in the context of national sovereignty and an international community that is still scaled to the nation-state. As such, cultural property reflects both social and political theory and is also located historically within the very specific trajectories of the nation-state in global contexts of warfare, colonialism, and capitalism particularly as they have been instantiated in the nineteenth and twentieth centuries. However, in the present many of these relationships and communities are being challenged from a number of different directions. The tensions surrounding the remit and sovereignty of the nation-state, the efficacy of international law and policy and the scope of free markets emerge as a major theme for this volume.

The chapters in this section articulate some of the present-day tensions emerging from more than two hundred years of global capitalism. In a recent exhibition at the ZKM in Karlsruhe, Germany, Bruno Latour and his co-curators invited the visitor to "Reset Modernity" through a series of heavily orchestrated encounters with artworks that interrogate the place of human culture and society in the age of the Anthropocene. The exhibition draws on the trope of friction as established by Anna Tsing: the "awkward, unequal, unstable, and creative qualities of interconnection across difference" (2004: 4) and brings this concept of friction into the often smooth conceptual move between the local and the global. The concept of friction allows us to see the places in which global capitalism is halted or jarred in its encounters with communities, with nature, with alternative scales, and understandings of scale. The first display of the exhibition unpacked the seminal film, book and image project produced by the office of Charles and Ray Eames, *Powers of Ten* (1977). *Powers of Ten* starts with an image of a family picnicking in a park in Chicago and moves both in and out of this image in powers of ten, shifting from the local to the planetary and the cosmic and then back to the local, moving through the human body into the microbial and atomic scale. Several of the artworks, and indeed the exhibition as a whole, intended to "interrupt this smooth glide through space" and in doing so make us aware of the work that goes into allowing us to conceptualize the global from the perspective of the local and vice versa (Latour et al. 2016). All of the chapters in this section effect a similar disruption, intervening in some of the understandings of the relation between the local and the global that are built into commonplace understandings of cultural property, and challenging the ways in which the nation-state is normalized as the reference point for the ordering of property relations, entitlement and sovereignty.

In many ways the smoothing out of scale and friction in the movements between the local and the global has created many of the 'problems' that cultural property both instantiates and emerges to resolve. How do we satisfy the claims of nations whilst creating a commitment to international community? How can we utilize culture as a local resource without it becoming valued only as a global commodity? How do we satisfy ideologies that underpin free markets with our ethical and cultural responsibilities towards historical polities that have not necessarily shared or benefited from these ideologies? How do we manage the relationship between state and market governance? At what scale does cultural identity become a form of sovereignty? Finally, and perhaps most chillingly, if the state is being eroded, what is emerging in its place? Each of the four chapters in this section demonstrates how cultural property is, in the present day, being rescaled to fit new kinds of collectivities, together with the intrinsic ways in which cultural property is implicated in identity politics and the constitution of sovereignty, again at different registers. This section, along with the following on new and emergent forms of cultural property, is a fitting end to the volume: to suggest what we perceive as the future of cultural property – a mechanism to undo, decolonize and transform the relations and borders between states and markets, between localities and global flows whilst also reworking the weave of the national and the international community, defining new forms of sovereignty and new conditions of ethically and responsibly circulating and sharing culture.

Stefan Groth and Regina Bendix explore the work that 'culture' plays in consolidating shared platforms of governance across the European Union. This chapter takes on a new salience in the wake of the referendum held in June 2016 in which the United Kingdom voted to leave the European Union, dubbed 'Brexit'. The result of this referendum, which sent shock waves throughout Europe and beyond, and initiated an instant downturn in the UK economy, might be perceived as a failure in the cultural project of the Union. However, writing from the perspective of continental Europe, Groth and Bendix argue that culture has been a flexible concept allowing for both difference and uniformity to facilitate the construction of a sense of 'European Community' whilst maintaining national diversity. Groth and Bendix explore how the 'culture concept' has been put to many uses within the EU, whose governance structure and policy has been driven largely by economic interests. 'Culture' and the attempts at forging a new European identity have been used to leverage cultural identity, cultural difference and culturally framed values. Importantly however, Groth and Bendix are also concerned to show how (an imagined and performed unified European) culture has been used to gloss over conflicts and inequalities in EU policy and implementation. In the context of the significant refugee crisis that has overwhelmed Europe and was one of the catalysts for the UK referendum result, this chapter encourages a reflection upon the economic and political uses and abuses of the culture concept, paying particular attention to how they are used within EU policy and governance.

In his provocative chapter, 'Who Owns the Bible?', Neil Silberman unpacks some of the assumptions built into cultural property from a global perspective, focusing on the ways in which evangelical Christianity rejects both regions and nations in their understanding of their global reach. His starting point is not the constitution of the Bible as cultural property, but rather the impossibility of thinking about the Bible within this register. Rather than critique the global from the perspective of the local, Silberman forces us to evaluate the ways in which we naturalize certain global positions. His piece provokes a rethink of the global categories of both cultural property and traditional knowledge and of how the ownership of culture may privilege certain constituencies. By wondering whether evangelical, reformist Christians should be considered as cultural property owners because of a claim to a unique form of 'traditional knowledge', Silberman challenges the global definitions of culture that are contained in both mainstream cultural property positions and in their critique. Silberman's chapter asks us to look closely at the ways in which such positions as well as their critiques reference definitions of culture, which as Adam Kuper has observed, often reproduce conservative, romantic anthropological definitions of culture as belonging to bounded, territorially defined groups (2003). He points to the dangers that are embedded within the category of traditional knowledge that has been produced predominately within the UN agency of the World Intellectual Property Organization with very little input from the communities that it seeks to reference and mobilize. The chapter is a cautionary tale about the different ways in which cultural property may be deployed by parties with radically different agendas, networks of power and systems of political leverage.

Paul Tapsell's very personal contribution re-theorizes the national, and criticizes the way in which ideas about Indigenous culture have emerged as a foil for the settler-colonial nation-state. As critics such as Elizabeth Povinelli (2002), Jessica Cattelino (2010) and Audra Simpson (2014) have argued, Indigenous identity exists in a complicated bind – both as conceptually outside the settler-colonial state, yet also over-determined and entangled within that very politics of recognition. Tapsell provides an argument for the 'pre-Indigenous': a category of being that connects to lineages and pasts that refute settler-colonial histories of disconnection and dispossession as they are reflected in the very politics of recognition. Tapsell's formulation of the pre-Indigenous marks a different political point of departure. He rejects the emphasis on the Maori Iwi, glossed as a tribe, arguing that it has emerged as a neoliberal, and neocolonial, tool of state domination. Rather, he argues for a return to the *marae* – the political, spiritual and social centre of Maori communities, and by extension for a genuinely grass-roots perspective on cultural property.

Finally, Rosemary Coombe explores the ways in which cultural property has become a focal point in the global South, channelling new forms of neoliberal governance. Neoliberal collectives – corporately structured cultural polities – both work against the colonial legacy of certain nation-states and create new kinds of entanglements in global markets. On the one hand this might be read as an intensification of culture and cultural identity into new forms of capital accumulation. On the other it can be read as a new form of global resistance to market hegemonies, in which traditional knowledge economies are used to 'assert particular forms of culturally based sovereignty which may exceed the calculus of market economies'. The paradoxes continue – neoliberal governance encourages community empowerment by devolving authority to the grass-roots, but also legitimates the withdrawal of state support for cultural heritage. The recognition of new rights holders has facilitated the emergence of transnational cultural and political movements (and Coombe focuses especially on new Indigenous social movements and economic formations), as well as new transnational markets.

Each of these contributions demonstrates the ways in which cultural property is providing ground for new forms of conceptualization of collective identity and the kinds of entitlement and property that it might produce. From ownership of the idiom, and therefore the authority, of global Christianity, through to the co-option of nature by new forms of neoliberal instrumentality, the state remit over cultural property, so painstakingly built up over the modern era is being both disrupted and eroded. It is here that we see cultural property, once a way to define the material culture most prominently associated with the state, becoming a way to articulate global flows, translations, and transformations that resist both the territorial borders of the state, and the abrogations of state sovereignty.

Bibliography

Cattelino, Jessica. 2010. "The Double-Bind of American Needs-Based Sovereignty." *Cultural Anthropology* 25(2): 235–262.

Kuper, Adam. 2003. "The Return of the Native." *Current Anthropology* 44(3): 389–395.

Latour, Bruno, ed. 2016. *Reset Modernity!* Cambridge, MA: The MIT Press.

Povinelli, Elizabeth A. 2002. *The Cunning of Recognition: Indigenous Alterities and the Making of Australian Multiculturalism.* Durham, NC: Duke University Press.

Simpson, Audra. 2014. *Mohawk Interruptus: Political Life Across the Borders of Settler States.* Durham, NC: Duke University Press.

Tsing, Anna Lowenhaupt. 2004. *Friction: An Ethnography of Global Connection.* Princeton, NJ: Princeton University Press.

16

CULTURE AS A FLEXIBLE CONCEPT FOR THE LEGITIMATION OF POLICIES IN THE EUROPEAN UNION

Stefan Groth and and Regina F. Bendix

Introduction

"Culture" plays a pivotal role for the European Union (EU) (Shore 2006) and other transnational European institutions and organizations. In fields as diverse as tourism, rural development, education, and law, culture is framed strategically as a flexible concept mediating between member state interests, integrating diverging perceptions, and creating acceptance for the EU's goals and policies amongst its citizens. Despite the current breadth of initiatives and programs on culture – from "Capitals of Culture" to "Heritage Labels" and "Work Plans for Culture" – the inclusion of culture is a relatively new development in conventions and legal frameworks of the EU itself.[1] Official EU documents do not even reference the term "culture" until 1969 (Cunningham 2001: 121). In 1992, the "culture clause" of the Maastricht "Treaty on the European Union" (TEU, European Economic Community 1992: Art. 167) gave legal basis to EU cultural policies, stressing the cultural diversity of the Union.[2] Despite this late accentuation and inertia of "culture" in official policy and legislation, it is now pervasive in many fields of the EU. Be it by stressing the "common" in European heritage or the "national and regional diversity" in the EU, culture has become a pivotal and cross-cutting concept in the EU, mobilized by a diverse range of actors for identity politics and economic policies, and used for its symbolic power.

The EU is an emergent economic, political, and territorial formation. Seeking not least to counteract the devastations brought about by warring nation states and attendant nationalist ideologies during World War II, a path was sought to create a federation of European states (Monnet 1961; Lecerf 1965; cf. Brinkley 1991). Foregrounding the benefits of economic cooperation, six countries signed the Treaty of Rome which brought forth the European Economic Community (EEC) as well as EURATOM, a body cooperating in the development of nuclear energy in 1958. In 1973, additional states joined the EEC, a common, supranational governance structure was established, and in 1979 the first direct, democratic elections to the European Parliament were held. In the post-1989 years, numerous former Eastern Bloc nations applied for EU membership, leading to vast territorial expansion and an ever more complex federal administration, admitting more young state economies to benefit from EU economic programs, and – as has been evident over the past decade – great burdens for ailing state economies to uphold the terms of membership. Keeping with the predominance of economic motivation for cooperation, the EU established a joint currency in 2002, the Euro. At the time of this writing, 28 states are EU members and of those, 19 are also members of the Eurozone. Economic interests are not free of tensions and monetary currency not devoid of national(ist) significance. Thus campaigners for and against joining the EU in individual countries considering membership often raised political as well as cultural concerns – for instance, the Austrians worried that they might have to let go of regional nomenclatures for food specialties (Löffler 1997). In Norway, along with Iceland the only non-EU member among the Nordic countries, the pro and contra EU sentiment across the political party spectrum led to a narrow rejection in the referendum to join in 1972, although parliament had been strongly in favor; the rejection forced the government to step down (cf. Miles 1996).[3] In Germany, citizens hung on to coins of their national currency, the *Deutsche Mark*, as an icon of national identity as much as from fear that the new Euro might go under quickly. Euro coins, in turn, are imprinted with iconography of European as much as national significance, signaling the effort to shape a joint identity while offering space for cultural diversity.

In the course of roughly five decades of first planning and then slowly establishing this federation of European states, fundamentally economic interests have brought forth not just a governance structure, but also a number of treaties that contribute to socio-cultural changes. Most important among these is the Schengen Treaty of 1985 which lifted border controls between member states and granted free mobility to EU citizens within the Schengen-area.[4] The standardized passport of EU citizens simultaneously serves as the given national passport and an EU flag represents the federation, with all the nation state flags remaining intact as well. EU citizens simultaneously are also national citizens of their given place of birth or registration. They thus are flexible citizens as theorized by Aihwa Ong. Observing actors within emergent free-trade zones in developing contexts, she formulated a "concept of graduated sovereignty to denote a series of zones that are subjected to different kinds of governmentality and that vary in terms of the mix of disciplinary and civilizing regimes" (1999: 7). Thomas Biolsi made use of "Ong's remarkably provocative description of graduated sovereignty" (2005: 240) to explore what he termed "imagined geographies" available to indigenous subjects in negotiating economic, political, and legal opportunities afforded to them as dual citizens of their tribe as well as the United States. EU citizens contribute to and confront the complex maze of policy of both nation state and EU, and fostering cultural identification remains a goal of both entities.

The development of EU culture and cultural policy is also reflected in the rise of anthropological research on these issues (cf. Bendix and Löfgren 2008: 5).[5] The diagnosis of the "Europeanization" in diverse fields (Borneman and Fowler 1997; Kaschuba 2008a) as well as the construction of an overarching European identity (Shore 1993) led to inquiries into the symbolic functions of the EU (Shore 2013; Abélès, Bellier, and McDonald 1993) and the influence of EU developments on the construction of difference between European and non-European countries (Kaschuba 2008b).[6] Such studies shed light on the interplay between notions of homogeneous and heterogeneous culture within Europe, highlighting the tension between the production of cultural difference, the requirements of cooperation and the construction of a unifying "European spirit." One pervasive aspect of such studies – from anthropology as well as political sciences (Hansen and Williams 1999; Pantel 1999; Fuchs and Klingemann 2011) – is a focus on the legitimizing potential of culture for EU policy, integration and particular interests: how are perceptions of a common European culture, shared cultural values and traits or cultural diversity in the EU framed to contribute to the legitimization of policies and development programs? And what are the properties of "culture" to be adaptable to such a broad range of issues and positions – geared not least toward establishing a sense of culture as property?

As a complex (and conflictual) constellation of national and supranational legislation, multi-scalar bureaucratic apparatus and – poignantly so – imaginaries of an interstate political project concerned with security policy as much as with identity politics, the EU regulates expanding thematic areas. This regulation is shaped not only within official EU bodies, but can just as well emerge from and be influenced by the activities of commercial interest groups, civil society, transnational cooperation or as a reaction to global initiatives such as Millennium Development Goals.[7] Likewise, EU policy principles such as "community-led local development" (CLLD)[8] promote bottom-up approaches conceptualized to have an effect on prospective policy instruments. Ratified EU development programs mobilize significant economic potentials, and EU policies resulting from convoluted negotiation processes on different levels have economic, political, as well as social repercussions, not least in the realm of cultural property.[9] Both in their negotiation and establishment, all of these instruments and policies require procedural as well as normative justification: the values or norms established demand legitimation as do the procedures through which they are to be implemented. The flexibility of the "culture concept" in established EU instruments, we argue here, is used in many of these areas to strategically leverage cultural identity, cultural difference, and culturally framed values to bolster arguments for a diverse range of policies in the EU. Especially with regard to cultural property, culture in its various discursive frames functions as a pragmatic token for the legitimation of economic programs, regulatory frameworks or ethno-nationalistic projects. In these fields, the language of "culture" and its respective linguistic registers are characterized by a high degree of ambivalence and semantic openness. Yet, their pragmatic implications can be harnessed for their potential to bridge tensions, mediate conflicts, and compensate for deficits in legitimation. We thus aim to show in this chapter how "culture" as a flexible concept is used to gloss over conflicts and inequalities of EU policy and its implementation, and how it can veil interests detrimental to the very goals argued for.

In the following sections, this chapter will probe EU cultural policies in the context of cultural property, drawing on conventions and declarations from the EU and its bodies, but also decisions from international organizations like the Council of Europe in the field of cultural property. As central dimensions, in which cultural heritage and property surface in the EU, its conventions and guidelines, we have chosen unity and diversity, cooperation, national sovereignty, and economic policies. We analyze the different notions of culture and their relation to cultural property in European conventions, providing an overview of how central definitions, discourses, and practices of cultural property are being configured in the contemporary context of the European Union. The chapter furthermore elaborates on the EU's preference for normative power and looks at how EU cultural policy functions as "soft power" in foreign relations, paying attention to how conventions normatively frame the protection of cultural property contained therein. How are protection measures and other elements of cultural policy justified, and which principles of justification are made salient in conventions? We hope to show that "culture" and "cultural property" can be considered as flexible shifters in EU policy concepts and as a useful tool for the legitimation of policies. We focus here mainly on some central dimensions in which "culture" features in EU policies, and on how "culture" and its propertization are used to foster processes of Europeanization by means of economic incentives, framed by normative references, and institutionalized as policy on national and supranational levels.

Dimensions of legitimation

EU member state policy is partly decided by EU bodies – the elected European Parliament and Council of the European Union acting as the legislative, the European Commission serving as executive, and the European Council (assembling the heads of member states) providing direction. The European Commission sets the agenda, taking up suggestions from parliament or the council, but shaping the contours of the legislative debate. National parliaments do have agency in the process: if a third of them find that a new policy is in violation of EU principles of subsidiarity, the EU bodies have to review the proposed legislation afresh. Despite relatively clear-cut procedural guidelines and formal requirements, the drafting of EU policy and its subsequent implementation on the national level is a messy process, involving a multitude of actors and diverging views, back channels, trade-offs and bargaining chips. Given that inequalities between EU member states shape this sometimes intransparent process, the question thus arises – both on the level of scholarly discourse (primarily in the political sciences) and empirically – whether and to what extent supranational EU decisions that influence national sovereignty and markets have a legitimate basis – with discussions on a "democracy deficit" of EU governance ensuing (cf. Scharpf 1999; Beetham and Lord 1998; Bellamy and Castiglione 2003). This is as much a theoretical discussion on the possibility of pursuing "just" principles in drafting and implementing policy as it is one of public discourse on specific instruments and the European unification process as a whole. Programs, initiatives and legal frameworks of the EU entail normative references and conceptualize values directed at compensating for such deficits or weak spots in their justification. In the realm of cultural property, the various instruments and frameworks regulating the protection, safeguarding and promotion of culture draw from a relatively stable range of justifications, from economic to human and cultural rights, justice and fairness, as well as the inherent value of culture (cf. Groth and May 2015). These are positioned to normatively justify cultural property instruments. However, the culture concept itself can be used strategically to provide legitimation for policies.

An example can be found in the regulation of European markets in the realm of traditional food specialties. European ethnologist Gisela Welz has traced the genesis of "European products" – that is, foods that would not exist without the European guidelines providing for them (Welz 2009, 2006). This concerns, for instance, geographic indications or GIs, which may have a prior existence as foods but achieve their labeled GI-state only through this EU instrument and its associated regulating principles. Among the regulations one finds prescriptive measures for the specific type and place of production as well as for the place of origin of ingredients which intervene not only in local traditions of production but also in transnational food markets (cf. May et al. 2015). As an example one might look at the *Eichsfelder Feldgieker*, a sausage produced in the Eichsfeld Region of Thuringia, Germany. The Origin's Association of Thuringian and Eichsfeld Sausage and Meat made application for a GI for this sausage on the basis of regional provenience, including the climatic conditions, of the meats used. Among many other factors, the application referred to specifics of production such as the "immediate post-butchering warmth" of the meat, and the traditional herbal mixture worked into the meat; the authors substantiated the "centuries of tradition" behind the product with documentary evidence reaching back to 1718 and dialect proof of existence from 1844.[10] The applicants were successful and received their GI status in 2013 and thus caught up with a competing sausage from the neighboring countryside of Göttingen – the *Göttingen Feldgieker* received its GI for much the same reason already in 2011. The goal of the GI policy is to alter market competition through seals of originality and/or quality and thus to protect regional specialties considered representative for European culinary diversity. Such interventions require justification: they contort competition and grant special rights. To do so, arguments are drawn from culture: cultural diversity, traditional knowledge, and heritage are brought in as reasons for granting special rights. The example illustrates how the normative justification of programs appeals to culture, strategically positioning cultural and regional heritage as important elements in economic policy that establishes one type of cultural property regime. However, as the sausage example illustrates, competitors in adjoining regions (we are talking about perhaps 15 kilometers distance here) may apply for the same cultural-geographic distinction and reduce the economic benefit, not to speak of the cost involved in the application procedure. The GI, in this regard, turns into a form of branding.

This example illustrates the complexity of references to culture in competing for funds and recognition: producers of food specialities are keen to take up the possibility to frame their product as culturally valuable, adding market value and partly also legal recognition to production processes and product composition. This – through their acceptance – both strengthens and reinforces respective policy instruments offered by the EU and contributes to subsequent stages of the policy process. However, with regard to European GI applications, producers may weigh carefully whether it is worth their while to propertize the cultural component of their food product. Gisela Welz in her long-term documentation of Cypriot halloumi propertization could show how the GI, once awarded, pushed small producers out of the consortium, as they could not maintain the EU hygiene standards (Welz 2007), and how the halloumi-GI morphed – from the perspective of competitors in other countries – into a brand with which one could compete, if necessary through the European courts (Welz 2015: 93–111).

European food products are not the only example where the clinching argument justifying the establishment of a new policy is drawn from culture. Cultural heritage programs in the context of the EU are subject to this type of argument as well, so as to justify the need for such conventions and attendant guidelines for their implementation (Kockel 2013). There is a strong discursive link here between identity politics and policy. Constructing a common heritage builds on the idea of universal European values and a European identity – all of which, as Máiréad NicCraith (2012: 23) has shown, are at heart a political project and an opportunity to legitimize both cultural heritage and property. Wolfgang Kaschuba continues this train of thought, arguing that a distinctive cultural heritage opens up the "ideological basis for constructions of cultural difference" (Kaschuba 2008b: 36). Needless to say, actors within different nation states and with divergent ideological persuasions will take advantage of these opportunities, desist or change their mind. One of the more spectacular cases in Germany occurred in the city of Dresden. Here, the citizens voted to go ahead with the construction of a new bridge across the Elbe river even though this meant that the city would lose the UNESCO World Heritage status awarded in 2004, due to the loss of the unique landscape written into the award (Peselmann and Socha 2010).[11]

Anthropological and ethnological research has focused on these questions from several vantage points.[12] They contribute to an understanding of the symbolic legitimation of the EU and its programs, including the intricacies and power asymmetries connected with it. Critics demand, for instance, more inclusiveness in the realm of cultural heritage and property, opposing "authorized heritage discourses" that protect hegemonic notions of what is heritage (Smith 2006) and push aside hybrid and marginal cultural forms (Lowenthal 1995). "Culture", it has been shown in the vast body of literature over recent years, functions as a useful tool to reproduce hegemonic perceptions about which practices, artifacts, and knowledges are seen as "valuable"; it plays a crucial role for whose voices and interests are considered in the regulation of property regimes and features in the configuration of financial flows in development, tourism, and heritage programs. As Haidy Geismar has shown, this does not necessarily imply the path of dependency of cultural property instruments following institutionalized and authorized notions of culture and forms of regulation (2013). Rather, such dynamic constellations hint at the potentials of culture as a flexible concept which can be harnessed by different sets of actors and translated into various discourses. The flexibility entails – and this is crucial for grasping the valuation and valorization processes surrounding morsels of culture – divergent associations with regard to what kind of culture is envisioned: these range from a classist denotation of "high" culture to an anthropologically outdated notion of holistic, clearly bounded regional or ethnic culture (Bendix 2015).

Noteworthy in such discussion in the context of the EU is the focus on integration inside Europe, and not on the EU's role in proffering cultural legitimacy beyond the state and regional level. Questions of legitimacy, however, reach beyond the EU: the normative dimensions of legal and political frameworks such as conventions and declarations influence foreign relations of the EU as well. Especially as the EU prefers a "norms over force" approach in foreign policy (Laïdi 2008),[13] the ways in which stances on policy issues are framed in conventions, treaties or position papers of the EU are relevant for multilateral negotiations and global cooperation. The importance (as well as the pervasiveness) of such a stance is illustrated, for example, by the role that culture and perceptions of "unbroken cultural continuity over a very long timescale" and a "benefit from an immense accumulation of cultural heritage" in the EU play in EU–China cooperation (Lisbonne de Vergeron 2015: 4). This facilitates the establishment of cooperation frameworks due to culture as the EU's perceived "comparative advantage in soft power globally" (ibid.: 5).

The culture concept is thus used not only to justify cultural property frameworks, but perceptions about cultural property can also be positioned to legitimize policies in other areas. Within member states of the EU, between them, and in the foreign relations of the EU, there are struggles for interpretation regarding the implications of the use of culture as a flexible concept. As it is a means to absorb criticism, gloss over contradictions and reproduce perceptions about "valuable" culture and the "right" methods to protect or safeguard culture, it has become a powerful tool in EU discourse. There are thus several overlapping areas of tension with regard to notions of culture in EU conventions.

Between unity and diversity

Preserving diversity vis-à-vis a unifying approach to common European heritage is one such area. Giving legal basis to EU cultural policies in 1992, the "culture clause" of the Maastricht "Treaty on the European Union" (TEU, European Economic Community 1992: Art. 167, ex Article 151 TEC) stresses the cultural diversity of the Union while simultaneously highlighting common cultural elements of EU member states:

> The Union shall contribute to the flowering of the cultures of the Member States, while respecting their national and regional diversity and at the same time bringing the common cultural heritage to the fore.

The respect for national and regional diversity on the one hand and the need for unity on the other is a common theme in debates on cultural diversity (Carlier 2010). For the EU, the balance between the two mediates in crucial ways between local, national and regional identity politics. Adopted as the EU's official motto in 2000, "Unity in Diversity" "signifies how Europeans have come together, in the form of the EU, to work for peace and prosperity, while at the same time being enriched by the continent's many different cultures, traditions and languages."[14]

Unity versus diversity also surfaces in the context of cultural property. Cultural anthropologist Reinhard Johler argues that the Europe of the EU has "grown to be the most important agent of the cultural, and even more so an agent encouraging diversity" (Johler 2010: 39). EU programs addressing this realm intend to generate not only economic but also political and cultural surplus by nurturing cultural heritage (ibid.). In other words, despite or because of joint and unifying EU efforts, it is the national preservation of heritage that is fostered through EU funds. As Susan Smith put it, "the presence of Europe has made the sameness and difference of social life our prime political interest," whereby difference is ascertained through distinguishability and plurality of cultural heritage (Smith 1999, cited in Johler 2010: 41). Sameness, in this formulation, comes about not through a new and shared cultural heritage that unites member states or citizens, but rather through the shared processes of producing diverse heritages and cultural products. Laurajane Smith similarly criticizes what she terms authoritative heritage discourse for the institutionalized, hegemonic processes which many states have brought forth to emphasize difference (Smith 2006). For instance, the opportunity to compete for the European Heritage Label is attached to a list of criteria established by the European Commission. The applicants thus need to narrate their potential European heritage according to those criteria which entail facets such as bringing "to life the European narrative and the history behind it. They are about much more than aesthetics."[15]

Heritage making has been termed a metacultural operation (Kirshenblatt-Gimblett 2004) – though its omnipresence has turned the meta into a traditional bureaucratic-cultural practice of its own, taking in time and effort priority over the vernacular practices that it seeks to insert into the "global hierarchy of value" (Herzfeld 2003). Heritage making requires knowledge of the standardized language through which cultural forms and practices can be turned into valuable cultural properties for a worldwide market of appreciation and visitation. Europe gains in plurality, not in unity. The "Faro Convention on the Value of Cultural Heritage for Society" by the Council of Europe from 2005[16] as much as the UNESCO heritage instruments is a policy that produces cultural diversity in the sense of a next-to-one-another; it does not acknowledge internal differentiation or hybridization. The kind of local and regional difference anthropologists have found for instance in the realm of year cycle festivities cannot figure in such supranational cultural valorization schemes. Should there be competing applicants, actors need to negotiate a ranking and preferably jointly support the winner. This programmatic concept of culture fosters cultural diversity as long as it is conceived to be morsels of culture around the globe, relying on an outdated, holistic concept of culture. Ownership claims for hybridized, creole, mixed cultural expressions are legally still more difficult to conceptualize (cf. Noyes 2014).

Nonetheless, a look at the conventions confirms that this is a development that actors within EU institutions have desired, for it is communicated quite openly. Thus, we read in the "European Agenda for Culture in a Globalising World":

> In the debate on intercultural and cultural dialogue and on what is meant by "culture", it is often understood that culture unites people together rather than being a moderator of differences. In this context, Jean Monnet could be quoted: those young people "acquainted with all that is great and good in different cultures, without ceasing to look to their own lands with love and pride, they will become Europeans".[17]

Positioning culture more as a mediator for distinctiveness, and less as a means to generate elements of common culture is as important for the construction of European identity (Shore 2013) in general as it is for fields such as regional development or culinary diversity. However, the processes that produce this distinctiveness with recourse to cultural heritage favor hegemonic forms of "authentic" and authorized culture, limiting the influence of local communities in the shaping of their piece of diversity (cf. Welz 2007; Hafstein 2014; Smith 2006). The use of the culture concept in the realm of cultural diversity thus legitimizes a streamlining of cultural forms following perceptions of culture that work for the benefit of institutionalized frameworks, and less for the strengthening of minority perspectives, subversive practices, or community empowerment.

Cooperation and mutual understanding

There is another complex of EU policies working with cultural legitimation that is directly connected to the nexus of unity and diversity. It concerns cooperation and understanding among EU member states: what are the limits of the EU motto of unity? It is particularly the harmonization of instruments and programs that is at issue. Processes and procedures are to be streamlined and a common language is to be developed for the realm of cultural property and heritage. Thus equipped, one can seek to impress and draw boundaries to the outside. The preamble of the European Cultural Convention of the Council of Europe from 1954 illustrates cooperation and mutual understanding from this perspective:

> For the purpose, among others, of safeguarding and realising the ideals and principles which are their common heritage; understanding of one another among the peoples of Europe; to safeguard and encourage the development of European culture; languages, history and civilisation of the others and of the civilisation which is common to them all.
>
> *(Council of Europe 1954)*

"Culture, history and civilisation" serve as a comprehensive if vague definition of culture with which – after World War II – a rhetorical bridge is built among states formerly at war with one another. It draws boundaries vis-à-vis the outside and works for understanding within, without letting go of national or local differentiations. One finds similar articulations in the Convention for the Protection of the Architectural Heritage of Europe (1985), the European Convention on the Protection of the Archaeological Heritage (1992, revised), and the European Landscape Convention (2000). An example illustrating the workings of this common language and streamlining is the program European Cultural Capitals. The program seeks to relate what is special about a city and country in connection with the European project; touristic interest in the cultural capitals is seen as an additional benefit fostering mutual understanding. The incentive to participate in the European Capital of Culture is strongly orchestrated from the top, but opportunities for competition are interpreted also as mobilizing forces. The EU selects for every year two countries that will be hosting such a capital, one in an old and one in a young EU state.[18] The two countries are nominated six years before it is their turn "to perform". Within the state, cities may apply to be considered for the title and vigorous planning ensues which is reported in the regional and national press. The finalists are visited by a final selection panel. In Germany for instance, public interest and support for the four cities ultimately competing for the title for 2010 was quite intense, with opinions sharply divided between those who favored Chemnitz as a recovering city in the former GDR and those who favored Essen as an unlikely (yet ultimately victorious) representative of the post-industrial wasteland turned heritage area. As European ethnologist Daniel Habit illustrated, the interplay between the program's Europeanization strategy and the cultural logics on the ground in choosing and implementing the capitals at least somewhat redresses a perspective that foregrounds the top-down nature of this program (2011). Simultaneously, the Council of the European Union keeps adjusting the parameters of what kind of culture is to be foregrounded in the application, as shown in Gisela Welz's assessment of Cypriot cities competing for the 2017 title. Nicosia, though praised for its rich and multicultural heritage and lively young art scene, lost to the smaller city of Paphos. The selection committee here saw greater attention paid to the present-day cultural impact of immigration which had been emphasized in the call for nominations (2015: 140–144).

In their effort to foster cultural inroads to Europeanization, the programs we are discussing here invariably model a top-down implementation of ideas, however well intended. There are, naturally, actors who simply refuse participation and cultural initiatives that fail, such as the nearly invisible Europe Day (May 5) and the European Flag Day (May 9). But programs promising economic benefit through measures of circumscribing and elevating facets of culture have an appeal – so much so that there are also actors upset that they are excluded from participation. Thus there is a group of European villages whose leaders were incensed that only cities and not villages could become cultural capitals of Europe. After some initial planning, twelve villages from twelve EU nations joined under the heading of "cultural village of Europe." Villagers travel from one to another village to foreground and "discover the forgotten local level."[19]

Naturally, culture is thus also evident as a project of resistance and negotiation, not only as local projects are framed in the rhetoric of EU cultural policy, but also as a way to counter and contradict official programs by local initiatives as well as by nation states positioning themselves against EU majority decisions or mainstream policies by referencing the special role of culture. Perhaps the most prominent example for this is the French "exception culturelle": emerging – as a concept in multilateral negotiations – from trade negotiations in 1993, it "refers to the exemption of cultural goods" from trade agreements on the grounds that the very nature of cultural goods, as public goods, makes them unsuitable for commodification in a competitive market (Laborde 2001: 723; cf. Collarde 2000). France was, based on its longstanding cultural policies designating a special role to audiovisual goods in trade issues, the driving force behind the "exception culturelle," which was later adopted by the EU as a whole. Currently, the concept has been emphasized again in the context of TTIP (Transatlantic Trade and Investment Partnership) negotiations between the EU and the US – again, France being one of the major proponents (Bartsch 2014). The case of the "exception culturelle" illustrates how a member state's preference for a largely "uncommodified" cultural sector led to a hesitant change in EU cultural policy – and this preference was all the while partly motivated by a protectionist economic rationale. Thus, EU policy making in the realm of culture as well as in other fields does not necessarily emanate from shared positions: it is contingent upon power relations, country-specific trajectories of policy preferences, and constellations of interest in spatio-temporal contexts.

Looking at such convention texts as well as program language, the conceptual flexibility in the formulations becomes clear: it is a flexibility that would seem to ease the tension between the concepts of unity and diversity. By keeping culture relatively undefined, potential conflicts between perceptions of national culture versus regional differentiations and European values can be veiled. Such a degree of cultural relativity, especially with regard to cultural property, provides leeway for separate ownership on the one hand, and for the endurance of cultural practices that might be deemed incompatible with values proclaimed by the EU. In contestation between national frameworks and regional movements such as in Catalonia (Noyes 2003, 2007; Crameri 2008), cultural property provides both discursive registers and regulatory tools to transgress and transform policies. It allows a broad range of actors and organizations to link up to the culture concept and draw from its legitimating potential as well as from cultural property instruments. It can then be used to leverage against both member states and regional networks, to deny funding requests on the basis of cultural integrity and to reject policy proposals citing a misfit of inherent cultural values.

Common heritage as enabler of national cultural sovereignty

From the vantage point of the EU, culture, it would appear, is utilized particularly to strengthen national identity and cultural sovereignty. To this end, initiatives described so far were developed, implemented, and if necessary, adjusted. European ethnologists have long discovered and analyzed the state's role in administering folk culture (Rassem 1979). They have also long examined state-based cultural politics and its contribution to generating "second hand folk culture" (Moser 1962) and conducted a productive discussion concerning "folklorism" (cf. Bendix 1988). Yet despite global or European contexts within which heritage programs blossom, states achieve new prominence in the planning and implementing of cultural heritage (cf. Bendix, Eggert, and Peselmann 2013; Groth, Bendix, and Spiller 2015; Hauser-Schäublin 2011).

With regard to the division of tasks, the European Parliament formulates that it is the member states that are responsible for cultural policy, while the Union may provide support, help with coordinating efforts, or establish complementary measures.[20] Thus regional cooperation and coordination balances with national arrangements. Transnational regulation for the protection of cultural heritage is generally arranged in a fashion that provides nation states with more regulatory power over cultural production (Kurin 2005), a shift evident also from the perspective of international law (Mißling 2010). Gisela Welz suspects that the intention to support traditional economies cannot really succeed precisely because of the way in which measures to protect, for instance, cultural knowledge become subject to state regulation and inspection. Protective measures generate standardized "larger, more elite nationalized forms of cultural enterprise" (Welz 2007) and marginal, heterogeneous forms of traditional knowledge and heritage are pushed to the margins. Valdimar Hafstein similarly emphasizes that the protection of cultural heritage by the state very often dispossesses and incapacitates local actors of their vernacular culture (Hafstein 2014).

The cultural heritage instruments on the European level facilitate this development. The direct protection and safeguarding of cultural heritage are a further central element for the legitimation of European cultural policies. In the "European Parliament resolution of 10 April 2008 on a European agenda for culture in a globalising world," one reads:

> Without denying the fact that it is wholly desirable to take as open an attitude as possible to every other culture, the European Union has a very special duty to safeguard Europe's cultural richness, implying that the European cultural heritage, in all its dimensions, must, by every means, be preserved, disseminated, and shared both within and outside the Union.

In connection with earlier international efforts to safeguard culture against destruction in war or looting (cf. Splettstößer and Tasdelen 2015), current instruments and measures to safeguard, protect or promote cultural heritage and property are a forceful argument in cultural heritage debates (cf. Groth and May 2015). Despite their framing as a European safeguarding project, however, they mostly strengthen national identity and cultural sovereignty by embedding measures in a larger context – the role of the state in such processes remains strong or even grows stronger (cf. Bendix, Eggert, and Peselmann 2013).

As "'culture' became the central strategic resource of European self-perceptions" (Kaschuba 2008b: 36), cultural affiliations as the "ideological basis for the construction of cultural difference" have become "fundamental imaginaries of social order in modern Europe" (ibid.). National elements of heritage, thus, are central in efforts to protect and safeguard culture, legitimized by European notions of unity despite their fostering of authorized diversity. Paradoxically, by arguing for the protection or safeguarding of cultural property, community involvement (Adell et al. 2015) and diversity, the flexibility of the culture concept allows for the strengthening of hegemonic discourses. This may be seen in the growth of populist and right-wing parties in countries such as Greece, Austria, and France where cultural nationalism against the European Union is an important platform. At the time of writing, when the United Kingdom voted with a small majority to leave the Union, the stakes of culture have become even higher.

Culture and economic policies

Culture is increasingly built into the legitimation of economic measures and has grown into a pillar in the conception of economic policy. A report from 2014 concerning cultural heritage in the EU thus states:

> Cultural heritage is a significant force for 21st century Europe. Not only is it at the heart of what it means to be European, it is being discovered by both governments and citizens as a means of improving economic performance, people's lives and living environments. . . . Evidence demonstrates that relatively modest investment in cultural heritage can pay substantial dividends. These can be taken economically but also in terms of improving environmental sustainability and social cohesion.[21]

The economic (and environmental) potential of cultural heritage is highlighted in conjunction with its inherent values for identity politics. Similar to the case of regional development or food specialties, programs investing in cultural heritage are legitimized by a mix of cultural and economic factors. Another emblematic example is the initiative "Creative Europe 2014–2020." This endeavor builds arguments for extensive support measures on Europe's cultural diversity as it warrants hope for creative innovation and prospective revenues:

> The Commission noted that the Union needs to provide more attractive framework conditions for innovation and creativity. In that regard, cultural and creative sectors are a source of innovative ideas that can be turned into products and services that create growth and jobs and help address societal changes.[22]

Culture has accrued legitimating potential for stimulation packages both in the EU and between EU member states, within and beyond the creative sector. Simultaneously, there are groups of actors who hope for economic gain in associating themselves with stimuli such as the heritage conventions. This link between economic and cultural regimes of justification illustrates how legitimation gaps may require multiple points of reference to be stopped.

Crafts associations and guilds, waning as a professional sector all over Europe, have had some success in gaining distinction for their cultural property: traditional knowledge and forms of association. The French guilds have been included in the UNESCO intangible heritage list (Adell 2013). The German bakers have been trying to be nominated for this list as well; with the cultural prestige gained they hope to turn the tide in the struggle of craft breads versus industrialized baking and encourage young people to apprentice again despite the unattractive work hours (Bendix 2014). German brewers, dumpling makers, and other trade sectors line up with dossiers intended to turn their traditional knowledge into properties worthy of national and world heritage.

On the other hand, if arguments are not sufficient to garner political support, the economic potentials of culture and cultural heritage can be used to supplement the justification of a project such as the value of heritage status for tourism (Schnepel, Girke, and Knoll 2013; Salazar 2012; Camp, Eggmann, and Taufer 2015; cf. also Groth 2013). Similarly, with regional development programs the EU seeks to structurally support particular landscapes. These are landscapes which combine both the "special" as a unique trait of a region as well as the "typical" that stands representative for something larger, for the nation state or for Europe. Cultural anthropologist Reinhard Johler has demonstrated how reference to culture assists in this simultaneous differentiation and unification of landscape. "Culture landscapes" and "regional heritage" become the normative justification for funds to protect landscape (Johler 2001: 89; cf. also Johler 2002). What has been successfully used to attract tourists also assists in the acquisition of European funds, both with recourse to culture and cultural heritage. Thus, varying actors draw from the culture concept in the realm of cultural property to legitimize and foster their interests not necessarily aligned with those which are proclaimed on the surface.[23]

Culture as "soft power"

In addition to its functioning on behalf of the relation between European states and the European process of integration, culture plays a significant role for the external relations of the European Union. An early example is the Copenhagen Declaration on European Identity. Drafted amidst the first oil crisis and tensions in the Middle East following the Yom Kippur War of October 1973, the then nine member states of the EC explicitly posited the declaration as a foreign policy tool "to achieve a better definition of their relations with other countries and of their responsibilities and the place which they occupy in world affairs."[24] The development of this convention can partly be explained by the geopolitical situation of that time (cf. Hill and Smith 2000: 92). The oil-producing countries were willing to embargo the EU and the US (ibid.), creating the need for the EU to position itself with its own voice. The convention was an attempt to formulate a (in part) common European identity and to present a shared foreign policy. Accordingly, Anker Jørgensen, then president of the community and Danish prime minister, declared at the end of the summit:

> The nine countries affirm their common will that Europe should speak with one voice in important world affairs. They adopted the declaration on the European identity, which defines, with the dynamic nature of the Community in mind, the principles which are to underlie their action.[25]

Mainly framed in the language of identity, the declaration alludes to the "common heritage" and the "rich variety of their national cultures." This early example shows that the EU also uses non-economic aspects in its external relations in order to argue for its role in the world. An approach to external relations that uses neither military nor economic means is called soft power, i.e. the ability to influence the behavior of other states in a way that is conducive to one's interests without military or economic pressure (Nye 2008). Immaterial values such as human rights, solidarity, peace, fairness, rule of law, good governance, or sustainable development are central to soft power. Its success on the international level would be determined by the ability of the EU to pursue the same goals as one might have sought through military or economic power based on these immaterial values.

The relations of Europe with the rest of the world after the Cold War have been increasingly determined by normative principles such as the immaterial values outlined above (Manners 2002). The EU shows a preference for soft power (Laïdi 2008; Jones 2009–2010) and, in their external relations, uses less military force or economic incentives and more soft power, thus working with references and justifications drawing from universal principles (Tulmets 2007; Michalski 2005). What is important is not necessarily the actual interest in pursuing such norms, but the framing and legitimizing effort as well as the pursuit of strategic goals by means of soft power. Further, distinguishing between "hard" and "soft" power as well as separating military and economic incentives from other, more "cultural" and "soft" factors is to a large extent a theoretical exercise with limits in its implementation. Crucial, however, is that the concept is mirrored in how the EU positions itself in many cultural policy debates. Soft power is in this regard not idealistic; rather, it is a foreign policy tool that can aid in the diffusion of norms, prompting countries that strive for cooperation with the EU to streamline their policies in accordance with EU norms.

Similarly, this European preference for norms can be illustrated with regard to EU cultural policy with the statement of Androulla Vassiliou, EU Commissioner for Education, Culture, Multilingualism and Youth in a 2014 press release:

> Culture is a vital part of our collective European identity and helps to underpin our shared values such as respect for human rights, diversity and equality. Cultural diplomacy is an opportunity for us to share these values and our European culture with other countries. Developing a more active and dynamic role for European culture on the international stage is one of my key priorities. Used intelligently, I believe this "soft power" can benefit the EU and its Member States in their relations with the wider world.[26]

With the treaty of Maastricht and its culture clause, the idea that culture is a means of soft power in the EU's external relations has gained a legal basis. With the European Agenda for Culture from 2007, the EU decided that the "'promotion of culture as a vital element in the Union's international relations' is one of the three strategic objectives of the European Agenda for Culture,"[27] alongside "cultural diversity and inter-cultural dialog, and culture as a catalyst for creativity."[28] Of course, soft power is not "pure": while the theoretical concept outlines a contra-factual distinction, soft power is intermingled with elements of hard power as external relations entail economic incentives via trade agreements or military cooperation as part of security policies. A clear-cut distinction between the two is, in the face of the economic and geopolitical potentials of culture for development and a broad range of industries – from media to pharmaceuticals to education – empirically improbable. However, the role of norms in the context of cultural property goes beyond mere hard power, and soft power aspects feature prominently in multilateral instruments and negotiations.

The self-positioning of the EU as a soft power and norm entrepreneur includes an element of competition that places the EU and its member states into a state of competition both with other states and their norms and their economic and military resources and strategies. In the European Parliament resolution on a "European Agenda for Culture in a Globalising World" from 2008, Europe portrays itself as the cradle of culture and universal values. Not only hard goods, but also "soft goods" like attention, the legitimacy of norms, and prestige (Werron 2012) feature in the competition between states for the ability to determine what the "right" norms are (Manners 2002: 23). States themselves, but also NGOs, civil society or indigenous groups are of relevance for the evaluation of these questions. As "universalized third parties" (Werron 2012: 339), they feature in the processes determining which norms are perceived as legitimate or just. In multilateral negotiations on cultural heritage and property as well as the resulting conventions and instruments, states calibrate their interests in terms of the direct economic effects and policy implications to be expected. However, they also consider how shared norms contribute to the enforcement and justification of their interests. Richard Kurin has argued that efforts to position culture as soft power "must go well beyond the most elite of arts and culture to the grass roots",[29] and thus benefit from cultural heritage beyond "high culture". For an understanding of EU policy with regard to culture this is an important point, as cultural policy needs to be adjusted accordingly to meet these requirements of norm alignment.

One example for the successful implementation of soft power in the realm of cultural heritage is UNESCO's first culture convention on world heritage from 1974. The influence of European norms in this convention is visible in the fact that the greatest concentration of world heritage sites is in Europe. As a result of the nomination process, mostly European monuments and sites have been inscribed on the list (cf. Eggert and Mißling 2015). This is due to how the convention frames the concept of heritage (Brumann 2014). The perception of cultural heritage enshrined in the convention (and other UNESCO policies) follows specifically European and Western norms (Hafstein 2014; cf. also Groth 2009) and adds to the prestige of the EU and its member states as well as to the legitimacy of said norms. Of import is not only the protected or safeguarded cultural heritage itself, in this case the number of heritage sites, but also – in the sense of the soft power concept – the values behind safeguarding instruments such as the 1974 UNESCO convention. In the convention's framing, these values are defined in predominantly European terms. The instrument and its normative justification position the EU as a central and successful norm entrepreneur and as the creator of crucial values in this context, as is expressed also in the Lisbon Treaty:

> Drawing inspiration from the cultural, religious and humanist inheritance of Europe, from which have developed the universal values of the inviolable and inalienable rights of the human person, freedom, democracy, equality and the rule of law.

In addition, the "Faro Convention on the Value of Cultural Heritage for Society" by the Council of Europe from 2005[30] shows how European organizations make use of soft power. In the text, the link between human rights and cultural heritage is made for the first time in an international legally binding agreement (cf. Zagato 2015) with the formulation that "every person has the right to engage with the cultural heritage of their choice". Of course, such normative references for the justification or strengthening of policy are relatively inconsequential if they are not followed by a specific implementation of norms in policy. It is easy to "do good" by arguing with norms or universal values, specifically in the context of cultural heritage (cf. Labadi 2013) and with reference to cultural or human rights.

In multilateral negotiations, external relations or in building cooperation between the EU and other actors, conventions such as the Faro framework and the norms enshrined in them can be leveraged as a strategic or rhetorical device. For an understanding of EU policy and practice in the field of cultural heritage and property, the EU's stance on culture as soft power is an important element. An example is multilateral negotiations on traditional knowledge and intellectual property in the World Intellectual Property Organization (WIPO). In this context, the EU as well as EU member state representatives stress that they are in favor of safeguarding cultural diversity and argue for the recognition of the value of culture for traditional and indigenous cultures.[31]

However, such expressions of a generalized appreciation or favoring of values can function as communicative strategies (cf. Groth 2012: 78ff.) deployed to counter demands from stakeholders. In the WIPO example, the EU foregrounds the importance of culture for economic policies and innovations, arguing that – similar to the EU's agenda on culture – culture and intellectual property rights to culture are important driving forces for creativity and innovation. Accordingly, an argument is made by the EU against the claims of indigenous groups for changes in IP law by making reference to culture and dimensions of cultural diversity, cultural creativity and cultural heritage. In applying soft power in this context, an effort is made to convince other states – mainly those of the Global South – to share the EU's preferences for cultural property rights and not demand far-reaching changes in patent law.[32] Factually, then, in this context the flexibility of the culture concept is used to argue against claims for cultural and human rights by referring to economic and developmental potentials of culture for various social sectors. Soft power, thus, does not necessarily presuppose the enforcement of "just" norms, but rather places policies in competition for the most convincing incentives while drawing from the legitimizing potential of the culture concept. This is the case for soft power when applied by the EU as a political actor in multilateral negotiations: here, EU member states have assigned EU bodies – mainly the EU Commission – to represent the interests of member states and to negotiate on their behalf. Notwithstanding, soft power can also be a means to create internal coherence within the EU, to reinforce power asymmetries or to put up resistance against the streamlining of supranational policy based on EU decisions. Especially as – following the "unity in diversity" motto – culture acts more as a mediator for distinctiveness than as a means to create common cultural elements, the culture concept is both flexible and powerful enough to work on different levels, thus being compatible for use in foreign policy, within the EU as well as in national and local contexts – both for and against EU mainstream policies.

Conclusion: Flexible culture, cultural property, and the EU

This chapter has analyzed how culture and cultural heritage are positioned in EU conventions and policy both within the Union and in the context of external relations, in terms of when and how a concept of culture is used to justify policy measures, bridge tensions between diverging interests, and bolster strategic positions with recourse to normative principles. The aspects of unity and diversity, cooperation, national sovereignty, economic policies, and soft power emerge as central dimensions within which culture and more specifically cultural heritage and property play a role in EU conventions and frameworks. The ways in which culture is positioned in EU policy has significant bearing on national discourses and processes of implementation. Policy issues and programs are framed in the language and discourse of cultural property and provide useful points of reference for their justification in various fields. Policy initiatives relating to culture itself – such as cultural heritage programs or the protection of traditional knowledge – or to related topics – such as geographic indications or the creative industries – are partly legitimized by the EU using arguments based on culture, a common heritage, or shared normative principles. There are a number of diverging justification schemes for the regulation of culture in international instruments, including economic interests, human and cultural rights, fairness, justice, and the inherent value of culture (cf. Groth and May 2015). However, culture itself can be used to legitimize and justify policies in diverse fields, and the principles of justification made pertinent in the course of doing so are accordingly a central aspect for understanding EU cultural policy.

In the context of EU conventions and policy, the "culture concept" is thus used as a justification for diverse measures and compensates for deficits of legitimacy. The legitimizing potential of culture is not limited to economic programs for rural development, the strengthening of a European identity, campaigns for the creative industries, or the safeguarding of cultural diversity. It is further central to the external relations of the EU and European cultural policies in their international dimensions, also in the realms of cultural heritage and cultural property. The culture component in the wielding of soft power has so far not been scrutinized in depth. Several facets are of special interest in this context: the number of cultural heritage sites and the ability to secure grants or funding are relevant criteria for measuring success, but the enforcement or acceptance of norms encapsulated in conventions is relevant as well, as they carry with them the prestige of the EU as a region and the weight of the coalition of cooperating states.

Culture and cultural heritage fulfill multiple legitimizing functions in EU policy: they justify the authorized heritage discourse and mediate the tension between the need for some degree of unity in the EU and member states' insistence on diversity and national distinctiveness. Furthermore, "common heritage" and shared cultural values feature in the promotion of cooperation and mutual understanding between EU member states and citizens, enable or strengthen national sovereignty by means of cultural policy, and legitimate safeguarding measures as well as economic policies. Lastly, they function as crucial tools for external relations with regard to the EU's role as a soft power.

These functions partly contradict each other, or at least are positioned in a very diverging manner: the proclamation of unity is in contrast with the strengthening of national sovereignty and identities where unity is mostly present in streamlined forms and processes, but not in content; cultural arguments are strategically used to achieve political and economic goals; and norms or soft power are foregrounded to pressure other states towards streamlining policies. Both on the conceptual and on the terminological level, these contradictory or diverging functions are enabled by the flexibility of their framing in conventions and policies.

As they are kept only vaguely defined and are outlined in a broad sense with little context, "culture", "cultural heritage", and "cultural property" remain flexible and easy to use strategically, especially as part of soft power. They are useful because they can be connected to a broad range of different issues – e.g. cultural heritage, culture and creativity, or culture and human rights – and are able to bridge tensions between different perceptions – e.g. of unity and diversity and requirements – e.g. regarding the regulation of safeguarding measures for cultural heritage or traditional food specialties.

As concepts, they are flexible because they can denote both shared culture and distinct culture, be used as a means of differentiation between cultural characteristics on various levels (within states, between states, and between the EU and others), relate to different policy realms such as innovation frameworks, human rights principles, cultural diversity, education, intellectual property, and the creative industries. As terms, their vagueness and ambiguity keeps them open to interpretation, depending on the context in which they are used. The semantic indeterminacy and pragmatic definition depending on context and policy dimension characterizes "culture" and "cultural heritage" as shifters – referential indexes whose reference shifts regularly, depending on the variables of the communicative context in which they are used (Silverstein 1976; cf. Groth 2012: 100ff). They are strategically deployable (Urciuoli 2000) as they can be used to refer to varying contexts of use. The indeterminacy and variability of shifters means that "culture" can, depending on context and audience, denote both the concept of a shared European or a distinct national culture, highlight economic aspects of the cultural sphere or foreground safeguarding principles.

Shifters facilitate ambiguity, which in turn brings forth differences in the implementation of cultural policy, as has been shown with UNESCO's culture conventions (cf. Bendix, Eggert, and Peselmann 2013). Shifters also provide the kind of leeway that may be unwanted in policy areas where legal certainty is required, such as intellectual property legislation in the context of traditional knowledge. Flexibility, for instance, is problematic when culture and cultural heritage have a legitimating function and are thus connected to normative principles. Shifting meaning might then decouple normative principles from action which in turn would have a temporarily adverse effect on the strategic and legitimizing functions of culture in policy contexts. Claiming the value of human rights to be inherent in the common heritage of Europe – such as formulated in the Lisbon Treaty – while at the same time pragmatically negating human rights claims in multilateral negotiations on cultural property is an example of this (cf. Groth 2012). Culture as soft power, but also as part of the other dimensions pertinent for EU policies outlined in this chapter, partly hinges on this perceived normative legitimacy of policy (but also, of course, on power relations and economic incentives). If the respective cultural policy or culture convention is perceived as unjust, biased, hegemonic, or exclusive, it loses the strategic potential it is often harnessed for, at least temporarily. A critical engagement with the uses of culture as a flexible concept for the legitimation of policies within the EU as well as in foreign policy contexts thus needs to take into account how such normative legitimacy is constructed, how contradictions between rhetorical uses of the culture concept and pragmatic implementations are glossed over, and how the interplay between local, regional, national, and supranational levels is configured. Especially in cultural property and cultural heritage contexts in as well as outside the EU, references to normative contents of the culture concept as well as its relation to issues of unity, diversity, and national sovereignty feature strongly in legitimizing policies as we have aimed to show here. How culture gains traction and is made useful as a flexible concept in a broad range of policy arenas not necessarily directly related to cultural property issues will, in the face of the pervasiveness of cultural property and heritage discourses, be a topic for anthropology for years to come.

Acknowledgements

Elements of this chapter were presented by Stefan Groth at the Centre for Global Cooperation Research at the University of Duisburg-Essen as well as at the Department of European Ethnology at the University of Bonn; thanks are due to the stimulating and helpful comments of both audiences.

Notes

1 The Treaty of Rome (TEEC), establishing the European Economic Community (EEC) in 1957, as one of the significant first steps towards the EU, did not include any provisions on cultural policy. A fact sheet of the European Parliament on "cultural policy" remarks that the TEEC preamble makes

reference "to culture as a factor capable of uniting people and promoting social and economic development". However, the preambular language of the treaty's unamended original version does not include this passage. (Jean Monnet, one of the "founding fathers" of the European Community, is said to have remarked that "if we were to do it all again we would start with culture" [cf. Shore 1993, 785], although Shore in a later paper points to the lack of evidence for this quote [2006, 8].)

2 Other European organizations more explicitly flagged the importance of culture for the European project from early on. The European Cultural Convention, drafted by the members of the Council of Europe (COE) (then Belgium, Denmark, France, Germany, Greece, Iceland, Ireland, Italy, Luxembourg, the Netherlands, Norway, Sweden, Turkey, and the United Kingdom [cf. http://conventions.coe.int/Treaty/Commun/ChercheSig.asp?NT=018&CM=&DF=&CL=ENG, accessed March 10, 2015]) in 1954, obliges signatories "to safeguard and to encourage the development of its national contribution to the common cultural heritage of Europe" (Council of Europe 1954, Art. 1) in an effort "to safeguard and encourage the development of European culture" (ibid., preamble). The term "common cultural heritage" constitutes a crucial point of reference for the COE's Faro Framework Convention on the Value of Cultural Heritage for Society (Council of Europe 2005), linking cultural heritage to human rights issues and the concept of "community" (cf. Zagato 2015).

3 Like a number of other European countries, Norway is a member of the European Economic Area (EEA) which facilitates a good amount of economic benefits but is also subject to a number of European Union regulations. Other national parliaments, such as Switzerland's, have repeatedly tried to convince their citizens to join the EU and have failed to win the popular vote. Yet Switzerland, too, participates in a number of EU programs which, however, have come under great fire in the last decade, due to the enormous rise of the right-wing populist Swiss People's Party.

4 At the time of this writing, the refugee crisis caused by the Syrian civil war, the aftermath of the Arab Spring and the rise of the Islamic State in the course of 2015 has repeatedly led to border closings and thus contestation of the Schengen agreement.

5 Early anthropological studies mostly focused on small-scale local research and the links of community studies to regional and global patterns (e.g. Cole 1977; cf. Welz 2011). Now, much emphasis is placed on questions of identity formation and Europeanization.

6 There are studies on the impact of EU institutions on local identities and conceptions of place (Siivonen 2002; Frykman 2002), questions of citizenship and migration (Frykman 2008) alongside debates on cultural integration (Shore 2006), xenophophia and cultural chauvinism (Shore 1993; Gingrich and Banks 2006), and discourses of racism (Wodak and Reisigl 1999; Silverstein 2005). A growing body of research scrutinizes migration policies and their influence in the EU (e.g. Green 2013; Transit Migration Forschungsgruppe 2007).

7 Cf. https://ec.europa.eu/europeaid/policies/european-development-policy/eu-millennium-development-goals_en (checked January 23, 2017).

8 Cf. http://ec.europa.eu/regional_policy/sources/docgener/informat/2014/community_en.pdf (checked January 23, 2017).

9 All official languages of EU member states have to be included which adds to the complexity and slowness of the process – and provides many work opportunities for interpreters.

10 Cited from "Antrag auf Eintrag einer geografischen Angabe oder einer Ursprungsbezeichnung Eichsfelder Feldgieker/Eichsfelder Feldkieker". In DE Markenblatt Heft 36 vom 05.09.2008, Teil 7a-aa, pp.46516–46518.

11 As Welz has observed, "the cultural operation of 'unmaking' heritage has hardly been theorized" (2015: 157). Dresden and the Elbe valley are a key example, proving that in contrast to the laborious and long effort required for heritage and thus cultural property making, exiting from it or being thrown out of a propertizing framework can be a speedy matter.

12 In addition to scrutinizing the pervasive power of the heritage regime and its impact on the state's relation to communities and its generation of massive bureaucracies (Bendix, Eggert, and Peselmann 2013), there have been studies looking more broadly at the interface of governmentality and EU integration (Walters and Haahr 2005) in the construction of Europe (Bellier and Wilson 2000). The increase of a European public sphere and its role contribute to understanding this complex (Eriksen 2005) as does a grasp of the influence yielded by "Eurocrats" (Shore 2013) and of the everyday culture of the European Commission and the European Parliament (Abélès 1992). A further important point is how democracy and collective identity interact (Habermas 1999), how national and regional identities interact and how inclusive an EU identity can be (Peckham 2003).

13 Cf. also the "Normative Power Europe" (NPE) concept (Manners 2002).

14 Cf. http://europa.eu/about-eu/basic-information/symbols/motto/index_en.htm (accessed March 10, 2015).
15 See "European Heritage Label, http://ec.europa.eu/programmes/creative-europe/actions/heritage-label/index_en.htm (accessed January 24, 2016).
16 See http://www.coe.int/t/dg4/cultureheritage/heritage/Identities/default_en.asp (checked January 23, 2017).
17 See http://eur-lex.europa.eu/legal-content/EN/TXT/?uri=uriserv:OJ.CE.2009.247.01.0032.01.ENG (checked January 23, 2017).
18 Cf. "European Capitals of Culture", http://ec.europa.eu/programmes/creative-europe/actions/capitals-culture_en.htm (accessed January 23, 2016).
19 "European Villages of Culture", http://www.cultural-village.com/ (accessed January 23, 2016). Martina Häußer wrote her ethnographically based, unpublished masters thesis on the German village that forms part of this group and accompanied the villagers on one such trip to France (Häußer 2013).
20 See http://www.europarl.de/de/europaundsie/politikfelderaz/kulturundbildung.html (checked January 23, 2017).
21 See http://bookshop.europa.eu/en/getting-cultural-heritage-to-work-for-europe-pbKI0115128/ (checked January 23, 2017).
22 See http://eur-lex.europa.eu/legal-content/EN/TXT/?uri=CELEX:32013R1295 (checked January 23, 2017).
23 Cf. May et al. (2017) for case studies in the context of geographic indications for food specialities.
24 See http://www.cvce.eu/content/publication/1999/1/1/02798dc9-9c69-4b7d-b2c9-f03a8db7da32/publishable_en.pdf (checked January 23, 2017).
25 See http://www.cvce.eu/content/publication/1999/1/1/3a5ed1b6-00da-486e-a85d-88b60f05ce1d/publishable_en.pdf (checked January 23, 2017).
26 IP-14–382EN Press Release, Androulla Vassiliou, Commissioner for Education, Culture, Multilingualism and Youth, see http://europa.eu/rapid/press-release_IP-14-382_en.htm (checked January 23, 2017).
27 See http://eur-lex.europa.eu/legal-content/EN/TXT/?uri=uriserv:OJ.C_.2007.287.01.0001.01.ENG (checked January 23, 2017).
28 IP-14–382EN Press Release, Androulla Vassiliou, Commissioner for Education, Culture, Multilingualism and Youth, see http://europa.eu/rapid/press-release_IP-14-382_en.htm (checked 23 January, 2017).
29 See http://www.folklife.si.edu/resources/pdf/TS_Fall07.pdf (checked 23 January, 2017).
30 See http://www.coe.int/t/dg4/cultureheritage/heritage/Identities/default_en.asp (checked 23 January, 2017).
31 "The EU continued to believe that one of the most important achievements of the Committee had been to recognize the importance of TK, TCEs and GR to traditional and indigenous cultures worldwide. . . . It continued to support the Committee's spirit of open and responsible collaboration, and looked forward to further progress in the form of consensus solutions" (WIPO/GRTKF/IC/12/9: 10–11).
32 This also relates to the question of how notions of justice are conceptualized in such multilateral negotiations. To what extent the EU or other soft power actors are able to prevent the framing of cultural issues under negotiations as global justice issues (cf. Groth and Döpking 2015), and not as technical or procedural issues is thus another facet of soft power.

Bibliography

Abélès, Marc. 1992. *La Vie Quotidienne au Parlemenet Européenne*. Hachette.

Abélès, Marc, Irene Bellier, and Maryon McDonald. 1993. *Approche Anthropologique de la Commission Européenne*. Brussels: European Commission.

Adell, Nicolas. 2013. "Un Tour sur Soi. Les Bons Usages de la Nostalgie en Compagnonnage". *Ethnologie Française* 43(1): 85–96.

Adell, Nicolas, Regina F. Bendix, Chiara Bortolotto, and Markus Tauschek, ed. 2015. *Between "Imagined Communities" and "Communities of Practice": Participation, Territory and the Making of Heritage*. Göttingen: Göttingen University Press.

Bartsch, Marlen. 2014. "The Return of the Cultural Exception and its Impact on International Agreements". *Global Media Journal* 4(1): 1–12.

Beetham, David, and Christopher Lord. 1998. *Legitimacy and the European Union*. London: Longman.

Bellamy, Richard, and Dario Castiglione. 2003. "Legitimizing the Euro-'Polity' and Its 'Regime'". *European Journal of Political Theory* 2(1): 7–34.

Bellier, Irene, and Thomas M. Wilson, ed. 2000. *An Anthropology of the European Union. Building, Imagining, and Experiencing the New Europe*. Oxford: Berg.

Bendix, Regina. 1988. "Folklorismus: The Challenge of a Concept". *International Folklore Review* 6: 5–15.

Bendix, Regina F. 2014. "Daily Bread, Global Distinction? The German Bakers' Craft and Cultural Value-Enhancement Regimes". In *Edible Identities: Exploring Food and Foodways as Cultural Heritage*, edited by Ronda L. Brulotte and Michael A. diGiovine. Farnham, UK: Ashgate.

Bendix, Regina F. 2015. "Patronage and Preservation: Heritage Paradigms and Their Impact on Supporting 'Good Culture'". In *Between Imagined Communities and Communities of Practice: Participation, Territory and the Making of Heritage*, edited by Nicholas Adell, Regina F. Bendix, Chiara Bortolotto, and Markus Tauschek, pp. 219–234. Göttingen: Göttingen University Press.

Bendix, Regina F., and Orvar Löfgren. 2008. "Rethinking Europe as a Field for European Ethnology". *Ethnologia Europaea* 38(1): 5–7.

Bendix, Regina, Aditya Eggert, and Arnika Peselmann. 2013. "Introduction: Heritage Regimes and the State". In *Heritage Regimes and the State*, edited by Regina Bendix, Aditya Eggert, and Arnika Peselmann, pp.11–20. Göttingen: Göttingen University Press.

Biolsi, Thomas. 2005. "Imagined Geographies. Sovereignty, Indigenous Space, and American Indian Struggle". *American Ethnologist* 32(2): 239–258.

Bomberg, Elizabeth, John Peterson and Richard Corbett, eds. 2012. *The European Union. How Does it Work?* 3rd ed. Oxford: Oxford University Press.

Borneman, John, and Nick Fowler. 1997. "Europeanization". *Annual Review of Anthropology* 26(1): 487–514.

Brinkley, Douglas. 1991. *Jean Monnet: The Path to European Unity*. Basingstoke, UK: Macmillan.

Brumann, Christoph. 2014. "Shifting Tides of World-Making in the UNESCO World Heritage Convention: Cosmopolitanisms Colliding". *Ethnic and Racial Studies* 37: 2176–2192.

Camp, Marc-Antoine, Sabine Eggmann, and Barbara Taufer, ed. 2015. *Reiseziel: Immaterielles Kulturerbe: Ein interdisziplinärer Dialog*. Zürich: Chronos.

Carlier, Jean-Yves. 2010. "Regional Integration and Cultural Diversity: The Case of European Citizenship". In *Cultural Diversity and the Law: State Responses from Around the World*, edited by Alison Dundes Renteln, Marie-Claire Foblets, and Jean-François Gaudreault-DesBiens, pp. 763–778. Brussels: Bruylant.

Cole, John W. 1977. "Anthropology Comes Part-Way Home: Community Studies in Europe". *Annual Review of Anthropology* 6(1): 349–378.

Collarde, Susan. 2000. "French Cultural Policy: The Special Role of the State". In *Contemporary French Cultural Studies*, edited by William Kidd and Siân Reynolds, pp. 38–51. London: Routledge.

Council of Europe. 1954. "European Culture Convention". Strasbourg.

Council of Europe. 2005. "Framework Convention on the Value of Cultural Heritage for Society (Faro Convention)". Strasbourg.

Crameri, Kathryn. 2008. *Catalonia: National Identity and Cultural Policy 1980–2003*. Cardiff: University of Wales Press.

Cunningham, Collette B. 2001. "In Defense of Member State Culture: The Unrealized Potential of Article 151(4) of the EC Treaty and the Consequences for EC Cultural Policy". *Cornell International Law Journal* 34(1): 119–163.

Eggert, Aditya, and Sven Mißling. 2015. "Das UNESCO-Übereinkommen von 2003 zur Erhaltung des Immateriellen Kulturerbes". In *Kultur als Eigentum: Instrumente, Querschnitte und Fallstudien*, edited by Stefan Groth, Regina F. Bendix, and Achim Spiller, pp. 61–82. Göttingen: Göttingen University Press.

Eggert, Aditya, and Arnika Peselmann. 2015. "Heritage und die Chimäre der Governance". In *Kultur als Eigentum: Instrumente, Querschnitte und Fallstudien*, edited by Stefan Groth, Regina F. Bendix, and Achim Spiller, pp. 141–163. Göttingen: Göttingen University Press.

Eriksen, Erik Oddvar. 2005. "An Emerging European Public Sphere". *European Journal of Social Theory* 8(3): 341–363.

European Economic Community. 1992. "Treaty on the European Union" (Maastricht Treaty).

Frykman, Jonas. 2002. "Place for Something Else: Analysing a Cultural Imaginary". *Ethnologia Europaea* 32(2): 47–68.

Frykman, Maja Povrzanovic. 2008. "Beyond Culture and Identity: Places, Practices, Experiences". *Ethnologia Europaea* 38(1): 13–22.

Fuchs, Dieter, and Hans-Dieter Klingemann. 2011. *Cultural Diversity, European Identity and the Legitimacy of the EU*. Cheltenham, UK: Edward Elgar.
Geismar, Haidy. 2013. *Treasured Possessions: Indigenous Interventions into Cultural and Intellectual Property*. Durham, NC: Duke University Press.
Gingrich, Andre, and Marcus Banks, ed. 2006. *Neo-Nationalism in Europe and Beyond. Perspectives from Social Anthropology*. Oxford: Berghahn Books.
Green, Sarah. 2013. "Borders and the Relocation of Europe". *Annual Review of Anthropology* 42(1): 345–361.
Groth, Stefan. 2009. "Kulturen Im Gespräch: Interview Mit Valdimar Hafstein". *Kulturen* 2: 40–47.
Groth, Stefan. 2012. *Negotiating Tradition: The Pragmatics of International Deliberations on Cultural Property*. Göttingen: Göttingen University Press.
Groth, Stefan. 2013. "Allmendgemeinschaften und Cultural Commons in der Diskussion um kulturelles Eigentum". In *Kultur_Kultur. Denken, Forschen, Darstellen. 38. Kongress der Deutschen Gesellschaft für Volkskunde in Tübingen vom 21. bis 24. September 2011*, edited by Reinhard Johler, Christian Marchetti, Bernhard Tschofen, and Carmen Weith, pp. 59–65. Münster: Waxmann.
Groth, Stefan. 2015. "Between Society and Culture: Recognition in Cultural Heritage Contexts". In *Between Imagined Communities and Communities of Practice: Participation, Territory and the Making of Heritage*, edited by Nicholas Adell, Regina F. Bendix, Chiara Bortolotto, and Markus Tauschek, pp. 55–81. Göttingen: Göttingen University Press.
Groth, Stefan, and Lars Döpking. 2015. "Clustering Justice: Über normative Dimensionen kulturellen Eigentums". In *Kultur als Eigentum*, edited by Stefan Groth, Regina Bendix, and Achim Spiller, pp. 417–448. Göttingen: Göttingen University Press.
Groth, Stefan, and Sarah May. 2015. "Von Schutz bis Verwertung: Zielsetzungen und Begründungsmuster von Rechtsinstrumenten im Bereich kulturellen Eigentums". In *Kultur als Eigentum*, edited by Stefan Groth, Regina Bendix, and Achim Spiller, pp. 102–120. Göttingen: Göttingen University Press.
Groth, Stefan, Regina F. Bendix, and Achim Spiller, ed. 2015. *Kultur als Eigentum: Instrumente, Querschnitte und Fallstudien*. Göttingen: Göttingen University Press.
Groth, Stefan, Peter-Tobias Stoll, and Miriam Sanmukri. 2015. "Das zwischenstaatliche Komitee der WIPO zu geistigem Eigentum an traditionellem Wissen, traditionellen kulturellen Ausdrucksformen und genetischen Ressourcen". In *Kultur als Eigentum: Instrumente, Querschnitte und Fallstudien*, edited by Stefan Groth, Regina F. Bendix, and Achim Spiller, pp. 18–29. Göttingen: Göttingen University Press.
Habermas, Jürgen. 1999. "Braucht Europa eine Verfassung? Eine Bemerkung zu Dieter Grimm". In *Die Einbeziehung des Anderen. Studien zur politischen Theorie*, edited by Jürgen Habermas, pp. 185–191. Frankfurt am Main: Suhrkamp.
Habit, Daniel. 2011. *Die Inszenierung Europas? Kulturhauptstädte zwischen EU-Europäisierung, Cultural Governance und lokalen Eigenlogiken*. Münchner Beiträge zur Volkskunde, Volume 40. Münster: Waxmann.
Hafstein, Valdimar T. 2009. "Intangible Heritage as a List: From Masterpieces to Representation". In *Intangible Heritage*, edited by L. Smith and N. Akagawa, pp. 93–111. London: Routledge.
Hafstein, Valdimar T. 2014. "Protection as Dispossession: Government in the Vernacular". In *Cultural Heritage in Transit: Intangible Rights as Human Rights*, edited by Deborah Kapchan, pp. 25–57. Philadelphia: University of Pennsylvania Press.
Hansen, Lene, and Michael C. Williams. 1999. "The Myths of Europe: Legitimacy, Community and the 'Crisis' of the EU". *JCMS: Journal of Common Market Studies* 37(2): 233–249.
Häußer, Martina. 2013. "Kulturdörfer Europas. Eine Fallstudie zum Schachdorf Ströbeck". Unpublished Masters Thesis in Cultural Anthropology/European Ethnology, Göttingen University.
Hauser-Schäublin, Brigitta, ed. 2011. *World Heritage Angkor and Beyond: Circumstances and Implications of UNESCO Listings in Cambodia*. Göttingen: Göttingen University Press.
Hertz, Ellen. 2015. "Bottoms. Genuine and Spurious". In *Between Imagined Communities and Communities of Practice: Participation, Territory and the Making of Heritage*, edited by N. Adell, R. F. Bendix, C. Bortolotto and M. Tauschek, pp. 25–58. Göttingen: Göttingen University Press.
Herzfeld, Michael. 2003. *The Body Impolitic: Artisans and Artifice in the Global Hierarchy of Value*. Chicago: University of Chicago Press.
Hill, Christopher, and Karen E. Smith, ed. 2000. *European Foreign Policy: Key Documents*. London: Routledge.
Johler, Reinhard. 2001. "Wir müssen Landschaft produzieren. Die Europäische Union und ihre 'Politics of Landscape and Nature'". In *Natur – Kultur. Volkskundliche Perspektiven auf Mensch und Umwelt*, edited by A. Schneider, R. W. Brednich, and U. Werner, pp. 77–90. Münster: Waxmann.
Johler, Reinhard. 2002. "Local Europe. The Production of Cultural Heritage and the Europeanisation of Places". *Ethnologia Europaea* 32(2): 7–18.

Johler, Reinhard. 2010. "Kulturelles Erben: Eine europäische Zustandsbeschreibung". In *Erb.gut? Kulturelles Erbe zwischen Wissenschaft und Gesellschaft*, edited by Karl C. Berger, Margot Schindler, and Ingo Schneider, pp. 35–47. Vienna: Österreichisches Museum für Volkskunde.
Jones, William J. 2009–2010. "European Union Soft Power: Cultural Diplomacy and Higher Education in Southeast Asia". *Silpakorn University International Journal* 9–10: 41–70.
Kaschuba, Wolfgang. 2008a. "Europäisierung als kulturalistisches Projekt? Ethnologische Beobachtungen". In *Kulturwissenschaftliche Europaforschungen*, edited by Hans Joas and Friedrich Jaeger, pp. 204–225. Baden-Baden: Nomos.
Kaschuba, Wolfgang. 2008b. "Cultural Heritage in Europe: Ethnologists' Uses of the Authentic". *Anthropological Yearbook of European Cultures* 17(2): 34–46.
Kirshenblatt-Gimblett, Barbara. 2004. "Intangible Heritage as Metacultural Production". *Museum International* 56(1/2): 52–65.
Kockel, Ulrich. 2013. "Borders, European Integration and UNESCO World Heritage: A Case Study of the Curonian Spit". In *Heritage Regimes and the State*, edited by Regina F. Bendix and Arnika Peselmann, pp. 227–246. Göttingen: Göttingen University Press.
Kurin, Richard. 2005. "Regulating Culture?" *Anthropology News* 45(9): 28.
Labadi, Sophia. 2013. *UNESCO, Cultural Heritage, and Outstanding Universal Value: Value-Based Analyses of the World Heritage and Intangible Cultural Heritage Conventions*. Lanham, MD: AltaMira Press.
Laborde, Cécile. 2001. "The Culture(s) of the Republic: Nationalism and Multiculturalism in French Republican Thought". *Political Theory* 29(5): 716–735.
Laïdi, Zaki. 2008. *Norms over Force: The Enigma of European Power*. Basingstoke: Palgrave Macmillan.
Lecerf, Jean. 1965. *Histoire de l'Unité Européenne*. Paris: Gallimard.
Lisbonne de Vergeron, Karine. 2015. "China–EU Relations and the Future of European Soft Power: A Strategy for a European Cultural Diplomacy". LSE Ideas Strategic Update 15.4. http://www.lse.ac.uk/IDEAS/publications/reports/pdf/European-Soft-Power.pdf (checked 23 January, 2017).
Löffler, Klara. 1997. "Zum Beipsiel Erdäpfelsalat. Variationen zum Thema Nationalisierung". *Österreichische Zeitschrift für Volkskunde* 100: 35–53.
Lowenthal, David. 1995. "Heritages for Europe". *International Journal of Cultural Property* 4(2): 377–381.
Manners, Ian. 2002. "The Normative Power of the European Union in a Globalised World". In *EU Foreign Policy in a Globalised World: Normative Power and Social Preferences*, edited by Zaki Laïdi, pp. 23–37. London: Routledge.
May, Sarah. 2013a. "Cheese, Commons, and Commerce. On the Politics and Practices of Branding Regional Food". *Ethnologia Europaea* 43(2): 62–77.
May, Sarah. 2013b. "Making Traditional Food? Local Interpretations of European Protection Systems". In *Return to Traditional Food*, edited by P. Lysaght, H. Jonsson, and A. Bursted, pp. 278–287. Lund: Lund University.
May, Sarah, Katia Laura Sidali, Achim Spiller, and Bernhard Tschofen, ed. 2017. *Taste, Power, Tradition: Geographical Indications as Cultural Property*. Göttingen: Göttingen University Press.
Michalski, Anna. 2005. "The EU as a Soft Power: The Force of Persuasion". In *The New Public Diplomacy: Soft Power in International Relations*, edited by Jan Melissen, pp. 124–144. Houndmills, UK: Palgrave Macmillan.
Miles, Lee, ed. 1996. *The European Union and the Nordic Countries*. London: Routledge.
Mißling, Sven. 2010. "Die UNESCO-Konvention zum Schutz des immateriellen (Kultur-) Erbes der Menschheit von 2003: Öffnung des Welterbekonzepts oder Stärkung der kulturellen Hoheit des Staates?" In *Die Konstituierung von Cultural Property*, edited by Regina Bendix, Kilian Bizer, and Stefan Groth, pp. 91–114. Göttingen: Göttingen University Press.
Monnet, Jean. 1961. *La Communauté Européenne et l'Unité de l'Occident*. Lausanne: Centre de Recherches Européennes. École des H.E.C., Université de Lausanne.
Moser, Hans. 1962. "Vom Folklorismus in unserer Zeit". *Zeitschrift für Volkskunde* 58: 177–209.
NicCraith, Máiréad. 2012. "Europe's (Un)common Heritage(s)". *Traditiones* 41(2): 11–28.
Noyes, Dorothy. 2003. *Fire in the Plaça: Catalan Festival Politics after Franco*. Philadelphia: University of Pennsylvania Press.
Noyes, Dorothy. 2007. "Voices in the Provinces: Submission, Recognition, and the Making of Heritage". In *Prädikat Heritage. Wertschöpfungen aus kulturellen Ressourcen*, edited by Dorothee Hemme, Markus Tauschek, and Regina Bendix, pp. 32–52. Münster: LIT.
Noyes, Dorothy. 2014. "Heritage, Legacy, Zombie: Burying the Undead Past". In *Cultural Heritage in Transit: Intangible Rights as Human Rights*, edited by Deborah A. Kapchan, pp. 58–86. Philadelphia: University of Pennsylvania Press.

Nye, Jr., Joseph S. 2008. "Public Diplomacy and Soft Power". *The Annals of the American Academy of Political and Social Science* 616(1): 94–109.
Ong, Aihwa. 1999. *Flexible Citizenship. The Cultural Logics of Transnationality*. Durham, NC: Duke University Press.
Pantel, Melissa. 1999. "Unity-in-Diversity: Cultural Policy and EU Legitimacy". In *Legitimacy and the European Union: The Contested Polity*, edited by Thomas Banchoff and Mitchell Smith, pp. 46–65. London: Routledge.
Peckham, Robert Shannan, ed. 2003. *Rethinking Heritage: Cultures and Politics in Europe*. London: I.B. Tauris.
Peselmann, Arnika. 2009. "Creating and Dealing with Cultural Heritage in the Erzgebirge Region – A Field Report". *Journal of Ethnology and Folkloristics* 3(2): 65–74.
Peselmann, Arnika and Philipp Socha. 2010. "Cultural Property und das Heritage Regime der UNESCO. Parallelen in ideellen und wirtschaftlichen Inwertsetzungsprozessen von kulturellen Elementen". In *Die Konstituierung von Cultural Property*, edited by R. Bendix, K. Bizer and S. Groth, pp. 65–87. Göttingen: Göttingen University Press.
Rassem, Mohammed H. 1979. *Die Volkstumswissenschaft und der Etatismus*. Mittenwald: Mäander.
Salazar, Noel B. 2012. *Envisioning Eden: Mobilising Imaginaries in Tourism and Beyond*. Oxford: Berghahn Books.
Scharpf, Fritz W. 1999. *Governing in Europe. Effective and Democratic?* Oxford: Oxford University Press.
Schnepel, Burkhard, Felix Girke, and Eva-Maria Knoll, ed. 2013. Kultur All Inclusive. Identität, Tradition und Kulturerbe im Zeitalter des Massentourismus. Bielefeld: transcript.
Shore, Cris. 1993. "Inventing the 'People's Europe': Critical Approaches to European Community 'Cultural Policy'". *Man* 28(4): 779–800.
Shore, Cris. 2006. "'In Uno Plures' (?) EU Cultural Policy and the Governance of Europe". *Cultural Analysis* 5: 7–26.
Shore, Cris. 2013. *Building Europe: The Cultural Politics of European Integration*. Abingdon: Routledge.
Siivonen, Katriina. 2002. "Does the European Union Leave Room for Local Identities? Locality as a Cultural Semiotic". *Ethnologia Scandinavica* 32: 63–77.
Silverstein, Michael. 1976. "Shifters, Linguistic Categories, and Cultural Description". In *Meaning in Anthropology*, edited by K. H. Basso and H. A. Selby, pp. 11–55. Santa Fe: School of American Research Press.
Silverstein, Paul A. 2005. "Immigrant Racialization and the New Savage Slot: Race, Migration, and Immigration in the New Europe". *Annual Review of Anthropology* 34(1): 363–384.
Smith, Laurajane. 2006. *The Uses of Heritage*. London: Routledge.
Smith, Susan J. 1999. "The Cultural Politics of Difference". In *Human Geography Today*, edited by Doreen Massey, John Allen, and Philip Sarre, pp. 129–150. Cambridge, UK: Polity.
Splettstößer, Anne, and Alper Tasdelen. 2015. "Der Schutz beweglicher materieller Kulturgüter auf internationaler und nationaler Ebene". In *Kultur als Eigentum: Instrumente, Querschnitte und Fallstudien*, edited by Stefan Groth, Regina F. Bendix, and Achim Spiller, pp. 83–96. Göttingen: Göttingen University Press.
Stoll, Peter-Tobias, and Sven Mißling. 2015. "Cultural Property und das Völkerrecht: Prinzipien des Kulturvölkerrechts". In *Kultur als Eigentum: Instrumente, Querschnitte und Fallstudien*, edited by Stefan Groth, Regina F. Bendix, and Achim Spiller, pp. 249–272. Göttingen: Göttingen University Press.
Tasdelen, Alper. 2015. "Das völkerrechtliche Regime der Kulturgüterrückführung". In *Kultur als Eigentum: Instrumente, Querschnitte und Fallstudien*, edited by Stefan Groth, Regina F. Bendix, and Achim Spiller, pp. 229–248. Göttingen: Göttingen University Press.
Transit Migration Forschungsgruppe, ed. 2007. Turbulente Ränder. Neue Perspektiven auf Migration an den Grenzen Europas. Bielefeld: transcript.
Tulmets, Elsa. 2007. "Can the Discourse on 'Soft Power' Help the EU to Bridge Its Capability-Expectations Gap?" *European Political Economy Review* 7: 195–226.
Urciuoli, Bonnie. 2000. "Strategically Deployable Shifters in College Marketing, or, 'Just What Do They Mean by 'Skills' and 'Leadership' and 'Multiculturalism'?" Language and Culture Symposium, Working Paper.
Von Lewinski, Silke, ed. 2004. *Indigenous Heritage and Intellectual Property. Genetic Resources, Traditional Knowledge and Folklore*. The Hague: Kluwer Law International.
Walters, William, and Jens Henrik Haahr. 2005. *Governing Europe. Discourse, Governmentality and European Integration*. London: Routledge.
Welz, Gisela. 2006. "Europäisierung als qualkulatives Regime". In *Turn to Europe: Kulturanthropologische Europaforschungen*, edited by Kerstin Poehls and Asta Vonderau, pp. 11–25. Berliner Blätter 41. Münster: LIT Verlag.

Welz, Gisela. 2007. "Europäische Produkte: Nahrungskulturelles Erbe und EU-Politik. Am Beispiel der Republik Zypern". In *Prädikat Heritage. Wertschöpfungen aus kulturellen Ressourcen*, edited by Dorothee Hemme, Markus Tauschek, and Regina Bendix, pp. 323–336. Münster: LIT.

Welz, Gisela. 2009. "Eine Chronik des Scheiterns europäischer Umweltpolitik: Der Konflikt um die Halbinsel Akamas in der Republik Zypern". In *Projekte der Europäisierung. Kulturanthropologische Fallstudien*, edited by Gisela Welz and Annina Lottermann, pp. 143–162. Frankfurt am Main: Kulturanthropologische Notizen.

Welz, Gisela. 2011. "Epistemische Orte: Gemeinde und Region als Forschungsformate. Zur Einführung". In *Epistemische Orte*, edited by Antonia Davidovic-Walter, Gisela Welz, and Anke S. Weber, pp. 9–19. Frankfurt am Main: Institute für Kulturanthropologie und Europäische Ethnologie.

Welz, Gisela. 2015. *European Products. Making and Unmaking Heritage in Cyprus*. Oxford: Berghahn.

Werron, Tobias. 2012. "Worum konkurrieren Nationalstaaten? Zu Begriff und Geschichte der Konkurrenz um 'weiche' globale Güter". *Zeitschrift für Soziologie* 41(5): 338–355.

Wodak, R., and M. Reisigl. 1999. "Discourse and Racism: European Perspectives". *Annual Review of Anthropology* 28(1): 175–199.

Zagato, Lauso. 2015. "The Notion of 'Heritage Community' in the Faro CoE Convention: Its Impact on the European Legal Framework". In *Between Imagined Communities and Communities of Practice: Participation, Territory and the Making of Heritage*, edited by Nicholas Adell, Regina F. Bendix, Chiara Bortolotto, and Markus Tauschek, pp. 141–168. Göttingen: Göttingen University Press.

17
THE BIBLE AS CULTURAL PROPERTY?
A cautionary tale

Neil Asher Silberman

Introduction

Is the Bible[1] cultural property? The answer to that question seems obvious, for few Christian or Jewish religious leaders, humanities scholars, heritage policymakers, legal experts, or even secularized members of the general public in most world regions would deny that it *is* cultural property, at least in a generalized sense.[2] Indeed, the Bible meets the main criteria that international heritage organizations (chief among them, UNESCO) use to distinguish cultural heritage properties from other cultural forms and creative expressions. The Bible is accorded special reverence as both tangible artifact and intangible religious tradition; it plays a central role in shaping community identity; and many of its core narrative components have been passed down, from generation to generation over almost two millennia in substantially unchanged form (Tov 2011). As a rich compendium of religious lore, genealogies, histories, symbols, metaphors, and turns-of-phrase, the Bible's epic tales of Creation, Deluge, wandering Patriarchs, and Exodus from slavery to freedom contain a vast treasury of cultural symbols, folktales, historical narratives, and moral lessons shared – and variously interpreted – by the world's approximately 2.2 billion Christians and 14 million Jews.[3]

Yet if the Bible fulfills criteria normally used to characterize cultural property, who does it belong to and exactly what kind of cultural property would it be? Those questions have clear legal and political ramifications, for in recent decades, lawyers, archaeologists, ethnographers, and heritage professionals all over the world – deeply concerned with an unprecedented scale of looting, theft, and destruction of tangible cultural heritage (Kila and Zeidler 2013; Brodie et al. 2001; Ehlert 2013) and the alarming loss of indigenous languages, time-honored spiritual traditions, and other forms of intangible heritage (Brown 2005; Kuprecht 2013) – have developed a complex typology of cultural property categories and stakeholders. They have also developed a range of specialized legal instruments and strategies to identify the rightful owners and ensure the protection, conservation, or safeguarding of each type (Carr 2012; Anderson 2009).

There is no question that certain *physical* copies of the Bible, namely ancient biblical manuscripts such as the Dead Sea Scrolls and the Aleppo Codex, illuminated Bibles from medieval Europe, and Gutenberg Bibles qualify as "works of art; manuscripts, books and other objects of artistic, historical or archaeological interest" enshrined as cultural property in the 1954 Hague Convention (UNESCO 1954) and accepted by subsequent international conventions that have codified legitimate ownership rights to specific biblical texts. In some cases, title is disputed between rival nation-state claimants, as in the decades-long dispute between Israel, Jordan, and Palestine over the legal title to the Dead Sea Scrolls (Silberman 1995). In other cases, ethnic communal institutions have been recognized as the rightful owners, as in the case of a rare Bible and other Hebrew books smuggled out of Nazi Germany without proper title and sold at auction by Southeby's in 1984. The New York State Supreme Court later ordered Southeby's to cancel the sale and redistribute the books to Jewish institutions that were identified as legal successors to ownership (Blaustein 1985). In yet other cases, the right to transfer ownership was never questioned; in 1987, a copy of the Gutenberg Bible was sold to a prominent bookseller for $4.9 million at Christie's New York (Goldman and Quigley 1987), a fifteenth century Italian-printed Pentateuch was sold in 2014 to a private collector for $3.8 million at Christie's Paris (Jewish Telegraphic Agency 2014), and the most expensive copy of a biblical text ever sold – the Bay Psalm Book – the first book printed in America, garnered a record-breaking price of $14.2 million for another collector at Sotheby's New York (Van Biema 2013). In all of these cases, specific copies of the Bible were unquestioningly viewed as moveable property, whose ownership was both exclusive and transferable, like other types of private goods.

Yet the Bible is, of course, of much wider cultural significance than the ownership or monetary value of its rarest exemplars. It has a far wider intangible cultural and religious significance as well. One need only think of the millions of mass-produced Gideon Bibles tucked in hotel room nightstands from Singapore to Sao Paulo and the tens of millions of inexpensive paperback Bibles and biblical tracts translated into hundreds of languages by missionary organizations all over the world (Carroll 1998). Even for nonbelievers, the Bible, used as a ritual object in swearing-in ceremonies and other civic procedures, has an intangible value that differentiates it from other books and certainly from other kinds of intellectual property.

Indeed, some communities of believers, such as the members of the currently politically influential "Christian Reconstruction" Movement in the United States, see the Bible as not only a guide to spiritual salvation, but a central component of their collective identity (Brook 2011; Ingersoll 2015). For the Reconstructionists and the larger community of American "evangelicals" who share a fundamental belief in the inerrancy of scripture (Dochuk 2012; Franzen and Griebel 2013), "Bible belief" is an inseparable, indeed, essential core of their social existence – an authoritative source of basic wisdom about cosmology, human history and destiny, economics, family values, gender roles, and sexual taboos. In short, to the American biblical fundamentalists who see the United States as a divinely directed nation[4] the Bible unquestionably embodies "knowledge, know-how, skills, practices and representations" that are "expressed through language, oral traditions, feelings of attachment towards a place, memories, spirituality and worldview."

That is precisely how the 2003 UNESCO Convention for the Safeguarding of the Intangible Cultural Heritage defines the category "knowledge and practices concerning nature and the universe" (UNESCO 2003). That landmark convention recognizes that this and other categories of tradition, belief, ritual, and cultural expression should be eligible for inscription and international recognition on the UNESCO Intangible Cultural Heritage Representative List (and more generally, on matters of technical terminology, see Van Zaten 2004).

By 2015, there were already 46 inscribed examples of "knowledge and practices concerning nature and the universe" on the UNESCO Representative List of the Intangible

Cultural Heritage of Humanity, among which are the "Andean Cosmovision of the Kallawaya" of Bolivia (2008), "Places of memory and living traditions of the Otomí-Chichimecas people of Tolimán" of Mexico (2009), the "Wayuu normative system, applied by the Pütchipü'üi" of Venezuela (2010), the "Kyrgyz epic trilogy: Manas, Semetey, Seytek" of Kyrgyzstan (2013), and "Practices and expressions of joking relationships in Niger" (2014). So why not the tent-meeting, revivalist reading and preaching of the Bible, which is the living tradition of specific communities in what has come to be called America's "Bible Belt" (Dochuk 2012)?

For one thing, UNESCO requires that only intangible heritage that is nominated and promoted by a particular nation-state – or congenial alliance of states that are signatories to the convention – be considered for inscription. But even putting aside this nationalistic hurdle to the inscription of intangible tradition,[5] I would suggest that there is an element that might disqualify the Bible in the minds of many. It is the seeming absence of an existential threat to the survival of biblical traditions and the wider religious and ethnic identities of which they are a part.

The UNESCO convention preamble explicitly notes that cultural endangerment is one of the key rationales for its existence, noting that "the processes of globalization and social transformation, alongside the conditions they create for renewed dialogue among communities, also give rise, as does the phenomenon of intolerance, to grave threats of deterioration, disappearance and destruction of cultural heritage" (UNESCO 2003). Indeed, the choice of the term "safeguarding" over such familiar heritage alternatives as "preservation" or "conservation" is a clear indication that cultural survival rather than cultural taxidermy is seen as the ultimate goal (Schmitt 2008). A growing body of scholarly literature suggests that the safeguarding of intangible heritage in the face of the economic changes and unprecedented cultural homogenization brought about by globalization has helped – or will help – strengthen the autonomy of indigenous peoples and other colonized or marginalized groups (e.g. Onciul 2015; Kapchan 2014; Bakker and Müller 2010).

And here is the paradox: while the Bible is considered by many post-colonialist scholars to have been an instrument of social control and colonial oppression from which indigenous peoples and marginalized communities now must struggle to liberate themselves (Prior 1997; Haynes 2002), the neo-fundamentalist Bible activists mentioned above also proclaim their determination to defend their way of life. Whether it is a "War on the Bible" waged by a materialistic and amoral global order (Maltby 2013), the refusal of public schools to teach the biblical story of creation as a legitimate and factually accurate tradition (Berkman and Plutzer 2010), the perceived blasphemy of court-ordered positions on reproductive choice, gay rights, and same sex marriage (Grenz 1990), or the prohibition of prayer in schools and display of the Ten Commandments in courthouses and other public places (Martin 2005), these controversies are all seen by Christian Reconstructionists and the wider American evangelical community as part of an all-out offensive against America's "authentic" Christian culture by a dangerous and oppressive secular humanism (Green 2015; Hartman 2015).

Indeed, whatever one may think of the merits of these assertions, they are undergirded by a distinctive type of cultural relativism not incompatible with the rhetoric of multiculturalism. For at the heart of the biblical faith of the Christian Reconstructionists is a foundational belief in presuppositionalism, namely the conviction that all systems of human knowledge – secular humanism and science no less than a biblical worldview – are equally based on acts of faith (Ingersoll 2015: 19–22). In that sense, the fundamentalist biblical tradition can be seen by its adherents as a legitimate defense of their cultural identity. Yet while the protection of the endangered intangible heritage of indigenous peoples and marginalized communities (however mythic and "unscientific" they may be from a "western" perspective) is enshrined in a UNESCO convention, the demands of biblical neo-fundamentalist groups are widely dismissed as backward and dangerously authoritarian (e.g. Bivins 2003). Kuper (2003) and Holtorf (2009) have both highlighted the structural parallelism of liberatory and reactionary expressions of indigeneity. Yet what are the intellectual and bureaucratic frameworks that have conditioned such divergent attitudes toward the various expressions of traditionalism?

Many types of "traditional knowledge" or only one?

Are the efforts of indigenous peoples to retain ownership and control of their ancient traditions comparable to the demands of biblical fundamentalists? Or are they, each in their distinct political contexts, asserting rights to entirely different things? In this section I would like to explore the concept of "traditional knowledge," a term that has become central to legal and administrative discussions of cultural property ownership and the rights to control its use (O'Connor 2003). Yet it is also a term – used by a range of advocates, organizations, communities, and claimants with differential access to decision- and policy-making power – that has so far proved exceptionally difficult to define (Matsui 2015).

I have already mentioned the recognized domain of "knowledge and practices concerning nature and the universe" within the 2003 UNESCO Intangible Heritage Convention, but that is an exceedingly wide category that has, in practice been applied both to inherited skills for dealing with nature and the universe, as well as to intangible traditions about them. Potentially more relevant to the topic of this chapter are the efforts of the World Intellectual Property Organization (WIPO) to define a distinct category of "Traditional Knowledge" as intellectual property.[6] In fact, as Anderson (2009, 2010) has described in detail, WIPO has had a long history of active involvement in issues of traditional knowledge, beginning in the 1960s, with the incorporation of what had previously been known as "folklore" into the existing international intellectual property regime. This concept of traditional knowledge as legally protected intellectual property, first raised by nation-states in the developing world, is quite different from UNESCO's celebratory and commemorative approach, for it reduces the protection of cultural tradition to the regulation of economic ownership rights. Yet the two bureaucratic strategies gradually converged in the language of the 2007 UN Declaration of the Rights of Indigenous Peoples (United Nations General Assembly 2007) in which the linkage of indigenous peoples with the need for international protection of "cultural rights" played an important role. The Declaration called all states to ensure indigenous peoples' rights "to revitalize, use, develop and transmit to future generations their histories, languages, oral traditions, philosophies, writing systems and literatures," yet it did so in a way that mapped closely to western legal ideas of clearly delineated governmental authority over economic resources. Indeed, during the 25 years that it took this Declaration to come to fruition, WIPO also began to work on drafts of a global intellectual property framework for the legal protection of traditional knowledge, defined as "knowledge, know-how, skills and practices that are developed, sustained and passed on from generation to generation within a community, often forming part of its cultural or spiritual identity" (World Intellectual Property Organization 2015).

This approach to traditional knowledge through legal and bureaucratic mechanisms is unambiguously situated in a uniform, globalized consciousness. Indeed while "traditional knowledge" is recognized as a single, discrete category of intellectual property within existing international legal frameworks, the multiplicity of understandings of what traditional knowledge actually *is* and what role it *plays* in particular social contexts is all too often elided, ignored, or lost. Traditional knowledge apples, oranges, chalk, and cheese are thus all forced into a single category of exclusive property ownership, leading to almost inevitable conflict over the validity of legal claims to certain bodies of traditional knowledge, disputes over whether certain inherited ideas or knowledge actually *are* "traditional knowledge," and uncertainty about how and why particular claims are being made. The process of developing definitive answers to these questions through court battles and legal precedent serves only to further homogenize and globalize the concept of "traditional knowledge" – rather than to preserve the distinctiveness of specific bodies of traditional knowledge in any way.

The convergence in WIPO and UNESCO approaches to the safeguarding of "traditional knowledge" is, in fact, a clear reaction by global institutions to the relentless commodification of traditional practices and expressions), not necessarily a dedication to the preservation of cultural and literary productions from the past. As Linnekin noted, "the selection of what constitutes tradition is always made in the present; the content of the past is modified and redefined according to a modern significance. . . . Cultural revivalists search for an authentic heritage as the basis for ethnic distinctiveness; as they rediscover a culture they also create it" (1983: 241). In that sense, the identification of a selective constellation of cultural traits as "traditional knowledge" can also be seen as an act of strategic essentialism that wittingly or unconsciously drapes contemporary identity in timeless garments (Spivak, Landry, and MacLean 1996: 214). Traditional knowledge is not necessarily a category originally created by indigenous peoples themselves who are, arguably, somewhat confined within it, and have been thus ironically encouraged to utilize a rigid scheme of essentialized identity (once so useful for "othering" colonial subjects) as a vehicle for revitalizing and creatively reshaping contemporary communal identity to achieve some degree of political recognition and politico-economic autonomy (again, as Kuper 2003 pointed out).

It is, in fact, eerily similar to the mode in which the public defense of fundamentalist, literalist biblical belief is waged. The protectionist attitude toward the Bible is not based on abstract principles of human rights or cultural diversity, but on the fact that it is actually seen as absolute, singular truth – conveyed by God to Moses, the Hebrew prophets, and the early Christian apostles in a timeless and unchanging form. It is the canon; it is the "authorized version" whose continuous evolution, transformation, and reinterpretation over the centuries is stubbornly denied. Like the conservative judicial proponents of constitutional "originalism," biblical literalists earnestly believe that their traditional knowledge is the same as it always has been and is stubbornly, even cosmically, impervious to change (Smith and Tuttle 2010).

For its most militant adherents, the Bible is not only a tradition but a truth. Yet traditional knowledge in the sense in which it is sometimes defended and intended to be protected by international frameworks consists of diverse cultural expressions, not universal truths or missionizing ideologies. This stark contrast between orthodoxy and multiculturalism is actually indistinguishable the present categorical form of "traditional knowledge." While the biblical Reconstructionists see secular humanist science as their mortal enemy, the relationship of indigenous traditional knowledge to secular humanist epistemology is far more complex. Western scholarship has been central in creating and describing the typologies of traditional knowledge and western legal and bureaucratic frameworks have become the most powerful means for its protection. It could even be said that the very category of traditional knowledge is modern secular humanism's own projection of its antithesis.

The danger of an authorized version

If 250 years of the critical study of the Bible has taught us anything, it is that the Bible is not a single, seamless composition dictated by God to prophets and apostles, or even composed as a coherent body of systematic theology. As modern biblical studies, supplemented by archaeology (Finkelstein and Silberman 2002; Horsley and Silberman 2002), have now clearly indicated, the Bible contains a complex stratigraphy of folktales, histories, poems, laws, and incantations accumulated by various editors and authors in various places and times (Pelikan 2006). In a literary sense, the Bible is a pastiche of expressions of resistance and exercises of domination, with new layers of tradition added as historical and social contexts changed. It is impossible here to summarize all the complex contemporary theories about development of biblical literature, but suffice to say that canonization of the Hebrew Bible was a process of the eventual incorporation of an eighth-century BCE anti-establishment prophetic tradition into seventh-century BCE Judean royal ideology. The spiritual ferment of a diasporic revivalist movement in Babylonian exile during the sixth century BCE led to a puritanical theocracy in the Persian vassal province of Yehud in the fifth century (Satlow 2014). The canonization of the New Testament underwent a similarly dynamic process (Mack 2013). In almost every case, the literary expressions that were incorporated and further elaborated in the Bible expressed a movement of resistance to the inequalities of the established order that – in the fullness of time – were subsequently utilized by the established order to divide the faithful from the heretics.

If we fast forward to the European Reformation, the same thing happened again – this time facilitated by a new technology. The movements of protest in northwestern Europe against the ecclesiastical hierarchy of the Roman Church were spearheaded by charismatic preachers like Martin Luther and John Calvin, who urged a return to the simple, traditional knowledge of the Scriptures, translated into the contemporary vernacular. In England, the early English translations of Wycliffe and, later, Tyndale, made available to the public in printed versions seemed to pose a danger to Crown and Church. These translations acted to domesticate the spiritual independence movements with King James's "Authorized Version" of 1611. Naturally the transformations did not stop there, with new interpretations and translations of Scripture produced to engage in the evolving forces of Enlightenment humanism that threatened unquestioning scriptural faith. The current selective constellation of "traditional" biblical lifeways – focused on patriarchy, individualism, and condemnation of "Big Government" as a threat to "religious liberty" – is the product of a particular late twentieth century context (Dochuk 2012).

I would suggest that the process of traditional knowledge-making, as illustrated by the centuries-long evolution of the Bible, can be charted at least in its broad outlines:

1. a self- or externally recognized group claims its right to autonomy by declaring and demonstrating its adherence to selective aspects of a body of traditional knowledge;
2. the observance and defense of that strategically constituted body of cultural tradition/knowledge becomes the normative factor in defining its authenticity;
3. that knowledge is formalized, textualized, and publicly recognized as the orthodox iteration of the community's belief system and the basis of its claims to autonomy.

The contemporary heritagization process conforms quite closely to this pattern. The 2003 UNESCO Intangible Heritage Convention requires a painstaking process of formal documentation (in fact, textualization) of each ritual, skill, and/or knowledge tradition that is to be considered for recognition and inscription on a global heritage list (UNESCO Intergovernmental Committee for the Safeguarding of Intangible Cultural Heritage 2015). The requirements for the legal recognition of traditional knowledge as intellectual property require an even greater level of codification of essential characteristics and ideational boundaries. This closely resembles the well-known (neo-) colonial strategy of registration and bureaucratization as instruments of social control (Mitchell 2002; Scott 1998).

If the primary object of cultural property protection is to conserve the world's cultural diversity and to empower the cultural vitality of long marginalized peoples, perhaps that diversity should be sought not only *between* recognized cultural groups but *within* them as well. The current legal and bureaucratic frameworks cannot handle this kind of intra-community complexity, as the categorical terms of "traditional knowledge" are based on essentialized wholes, not contextualized, often conflicted realities. Madhavi Sunder expressed this point succinctly in the realm of cultural property by contrasting the urgent (if essentialized) quests for "cultural survival" with the desirability of promoting intragroup "cultural dissent" (Sunder 2001). For cultural diversity is not just a matter of cataloguing and displaying multiple exemplars stripped of their social and political context like pinned butterflies or mineral samples in a global cabinet of curiosities – nor is it the unquestioned allegiance to a codified body of traditional knowledge that is presented as timeless and immutable. It is perhaps the encouragement of cultural creativity with inherited traditions and active intercultural communication that may actually create new hybrid identities – not through sanctifying preexisting sovereignties, but through the creative interaction of tradition and contemporary challenges.

How then to achieve recognition of cultural difference, if an indigenous or marginalized group's spokespersons and advocates must speak in the terminology of globalized heritage bureaucracy to achieve their distinctive socio-cultural objectives – or even be heard? To gain international recognition and some measure of political recognition of indigenous rights and legal protection for collective control of cultural resources, an immutable cultural character, it seems, must be created and canonized.[7] And that newly imagined or selectively included bundle of cultural traditions, fixed in time and recognized as "authentic," defies the very nature of shared culture and identity, which is in a constant process of transformation as generations come and go, particular interests gain or lose power, and new external challenges and stimuli are met.

One might question the idea that any intergovernmental mechanism such as UNESCO or WIPO can definitively and impartially identify the "proper" use of a body of traditional knowledge. Indeed, this has haunted all the WIPO Inter-Governmental Committee meetings over the last 15 years (Anderson 2010). This culturally hegemonic tendency directly brings up the question investigated at length by Sunder in her essay about cultural dissent. For no human group is ever completely unanimous in its thinking about any subject, certainly not about the "orthodox" practice of culture. Moreover, with the succession of generations and changing socio-economic-environmental challenges, even those cultural values that are shared inevitably shift (Gracia 2003). Thus the body of what is identified as "traditional knowledge" at any given moment in history is something of a snapshot of cultural process in action – never pure, never completely original, usually contested, and always to a significant degree hybrid. The fundamentalist calls for a return to the "traditional knowledge" of the Bible offer clear evidence of the danger of privileging a certain orthodoxy that is constituted in the present yet represented as an eternal, unchanging element of communal identity.

So what are we to make of the seeming parallelism between the "traditional knowledge" claims of biblical fundamentalists and indigenous peoples? Does the militant defense of biblical Creationism and the uncompromising opposition to same-sex marriage, for example, carry the same moral weight as the defense of indigenous and aboriginal claims that are deeply vested in particular geographically and environmentally specific cultural processes and expressions? Do both really seek to defend the same kind of cultural belief systems that are actually in danger of being lost – not just disobeyed?

More important, can such essentially external legal and policy initiatives actually help safeguard the cultural vitality of any community and help to preserve the world's cultural diversity without directly addressing the economic and political factors that endanger them both? There is something inconsistent and perhaps even oxymoronic about the universal ideal of cultural diversity. As Fraser points out in her criticism of Habermas's vision of a single public sphere: there is either the convenient fiction of a single public domain from which many are silently excluded due to racial, cultural or economic factors or there is the recognition of multiple publics and the salutary effect of what she terms "discursive contestation," which, she suggests, help "partially to offset, although not wholly to eradicate, the unjust participatory privileges enjoyed by members of dominant social groups" (Fraser 1990: 68).

This concept of discursive contestation can perhaps help clarify the issues at stake in demands for the protection of what amounts to essentialized culture. Does it expand the space of discursive contestation or does it constrict it to serve the interests of a particular ruling group? In his analysis of the so-called "War on Christianity," Christopher Duerringer pinpoints a central rhetorical weakness of identity politics (2013), in which the de-historicization of essentialized cultures, each depicted as immutable and eternal, can offer cover for attempts by hegemonic groups "to reframe policies aimed at restorative justice and pluralism as unjust, unprovoked offenses against a natural order" (2013: 323).

In that sense, we face a double act of cultural appropriation in the current efforts to safeguard intangible cultural heritage through legal instruments and policies: on the one hand, marginalized and oppressed communities are compelled to appropriate the language of cultural essentialism through the available international bureaucratic categories. On the other hand, the language of victimization is conveniently appropriated by once powerful and hegemonic orthodoxies. Both are, I would suggest, problematic acts of intellectual commodification that have different motivations and different political implications. And that is perhaps the most important cautionary lesson that framing the Bible as cultural property can provide. The dynamic, nebulous, and unfinished bodies of inherited knowledge that we have come to regard as cultural heritage or intangible cultural property are forms of scripture and sacral articulations that inspire and energize every community to sanctify their distinctiveness and protect their collective welfare and collective futures. Yet even as these heritage scriptures are fleeting, they are forever susceptible to canonization as every generation's Sacred Writ. We must be aware that our own perceptions of tradition are not timeless, but are always subject to change, transition and transformation. Subsequent generations and emerging hybrid cultural-political-sexual identities will almost inevitably attempt to overthrow the static and essentialized bureaucratic categories of "traditional knowledge" that we are now canonizing as "cultural property."

Acknowledgments

I would like to thank the editors, Professors Jane Anderson and Haidy Geismar, for their patience, encouragement, and invaluable editorial suggestions during the long development of this chapter. I also want to express my gratitude to Professor Margie Purser of Sonoma State University for discussions that finally headed me in what I hope is the right direction after what seemed to be endless conceptual dead ends.

Notes

1 The precise definition of the term "Bible" is a matter of denominational perspective. For Jews, it consists of the Pentateuch or Five Books of Moses (also known as the Torah), the Prophets, and the so-called

"Writings," amounting to 24 books in all. The Christian canon adds the New Testament (consisting of the Gospels, the Apostolic Letters, and the Book of Revelation, amounting to another 27 books). But denominational differences within the Christian world create substantial complexity, with the Roman Catholic Church also recognizing the books of Tobit, Judith, 1 and 2 Maccabees, the Wisdom of Solomon, Sirach, and Baruch as part of the "Old Testament," and the Protestant canon usually setting them apart as the Apocrypha. There are yet other discrepancies between the canons of the Armenian, Coptic, Ethiopian, Georgian, Greek Orthodox, Russian Orthodox, and Syriac churches. Suffice it to say that Jaroslav Pelikan's *Whose Bible Is It?* (2006) asks the right question and offers some clues.

2 As the most general and inclusive definition of the term "cultural property" as it potentially relates to the Bible and the codified traditional knowledge of other groups, I use the relevant section of Article 1a of the Hague Convention for the Protection of Cultural Property in the Event of Armed Conflict (UNESCO 1954): "movable or immovable property of great importance to the cultural heritage of every people, such as monuments of architecture, art or history, whether religious or secular … manuscripts, books and other objects of artistic, historical or archaeological interest; as well as … important collections of books or archives or of reproductions of the property defined above." More specific questions regarding legal ownership are covered by subsequent UNESCO Conventions and national legislation, though not without internal contradictions and gaps (Francioni 2012).

3 The source for these population numbers, approximate for 2010, is a demographic report of the Pew Research Center as part of the Pew-Templeton Global Religious Futures Project (Pew Research Center 2015).

4 The same could be said of other contemporary fundamentalists who see their native lands as the focus of biblical prophecy and eschatological destiny such as the British Israelites (Wilson 1968) and Israeli settlers on the West Bank influenced by the teachings of Rabbi Abraham Kook (Inbari 2012)

5 As Anderson (2010) quite rightly observes, the member-nation representatives of various United Nations bodies (such as UNESCO and the World Intellectual Property Organization), being the only recognized decision- and policy-makers, have a decisive voice in determining which cultural expressions are to be officially recognized and protected – and which are to be disowned or ignored: "While the role and responsibility of national governments to work towards the development of meaningful outcomes is now a priority, there are many different elements that affect both willingness and capacity to do so" (Anderson 2010: 4). Obviously, the cultural expressions of communities that are perceived as antagonistic or damaging to cohesive national governance are rarely promoted in international fora (see, for example, Smith 2007).

6 Traditional knowledge is actually one element of a triad of WIPO concerns, which also includes folklore and genetic resources (Anderson 2009: 174).

7 To take but one example, in the United States, the process of federal recognition of Native American tribes includes the requirements that "the petitioning entity have been identified by reliable external sources on a substantially continuous basis as an Indian entity since 1900;" that it has maintained political authority or influence on a substantially continuous basis; that it present a governing document, or if it does not have a formal governing document, a statement describing its membership criteria; and, from a biological/genetic perspective, requires that the current members of the petitioning group, as a whole, descend from a historic tribe or tribes which amalgamated (Bureau of Indian Affairs 1997). Of course, even with the acceptance of nuanced interpretations of these criteria, continuity is paramount.

Bibliography

Anderson, Benedict. 2006. *Imagined Communities: Reflections on the Origin and Spread of Nationalism*. Revised edition. London: Verso.

Anderson, Jane. 2009. *Law, Knowledge, Culture: The Production of Indigenous Knowledge in Intellectual Property Law*. Cheltenham, UK; Northampton, MA: Edward Elgar.

Anderson, Jane. 2010. "Discursive Disorder: Power, Authority and Politics in Indigenous Intellectual Property." Presented at the *Sawyer Seminar on Knowledges, Ways of Knowing and the Postcolonial University*, University of Cape Town, February 23.

Anderson, Jane, and Kimberly Christen. 2013. "'Chuck a Copyright on It': Dilemmas of Digital Return and the Possibilities for Traditional Knowledge Licenses and Labels." *Museum Anthropology Review* 7(1–2): 105–126.

Bakker, Karel Anthonie, and Liana Müller. 2010. "Intangible Heritage and Community Identity in Post-Apartheid South Africa." *Museum International* 62(1–2): 48–54.

Berkman, Michael, and Eric Plutzer. 2010. *Evolution, Creationism, and the Battle to Control America's Classrooms*. Cambridge: Cambridge University Press.
Bivins, Jason C. 2003. *The Fracture of Good Order: Christian Antiliberalism and the Challenge to American Politics*. Chapel Hill: University of North Carolina Press.
Blaustein, Joette Milians. 1985. "Why Is This Sale Different from All Other Sales – Abrams v. Sotheby Parke Bernet, Inc." *Cardozo Arts & Entertainment Law Journal* 4: 139.
Boym, Svetlana. 2007. "Nostalgia and Its Discontents." *Hedgehog Review*. https://pdfs.semanticscholar.org/cfcb/eba8cb80315ffebfcf16fe4d17fa6f31286e.pdf, last accessed March 29, 2017.
Brodie, Neil, Jennifer Doole, Colin Renfrew, and McDonald Institute for Archaeological Research, eds. 2001. *Trade in Illicit Antiquities: The Destruction of the World's Archaeological Heritage*. Cambridge; Oakville, CT: McDonald Institute for Archaeological Research; David Brown.
Brook, Joanna L. 2011. "Reclaiming America for Christian Reconstruction: The Rhetorical Constitution of a 'People'." University of Massachusetts Amherst. http://scholarworks.umass.edu/open_access_dissertations/424/, last accessed March 29, 2017.
Brown, Michael F. 2005. "Heritage Trouble: Recent Work on the Protection of Intangible Cultural Property." *International Journal of Cultural Property* 12(1): 40–61.
Bureau of Indian Affairs. 1997. "The Official Guidelines to the Federal Acknowledgment Regulations 25 CFR 83." Washington, DC: US Department of the Interior.
Carr, David. 2011. *The Formation of the Hebrew Bible: A New Reconstruction*. 1st edition. New York: Oxford University Press.
Carr, Gerald. 2012. "Protecting Intangible Cultural Resources: Alternatives to Intellectual Property Law." *Michigan Journal of Race and Law*. 18: 363–390.
Carroll, Robert P. 1998. "Lower Case Bibles: Commodity Culture and the Bible." In *Biblical Studies/Cultural Studies: The Third Sheffield Colloquium*, edited by J. Cheryl Exum and Steven D. Moore, 266:46–69. Journal for the Study of the Old Testament Supplement Series. Sheffield: Sheffield Academic Press.
Dochuk, Darren. 2012. *From Bible Belt to Sunbelt: Plain-Folk Religion, Grassroots Politics, and the Rise of Evangelical Conservatism*. New York: W. W. Norton & Company.
Duerringer, Christopher. 2013. "The 'War on Christianity': Counterpublicity or Hegemonic Containment?" *Southern Communication Journal* 78(4): 311–325.
Edelman, Diana, and Ehud Ben Zvi, eds. 2014. *The Production of Prophecy: Constructing Prophecy and Prophets in Yehud*. London: Routledge.
Ehlert, Caroline. 2013. *Prosecuting the Destruction of Cultural Property in International Criminal Law, with a Case Study on the Khmer Rouge's Destruction of Cambodia's Heritage*. Leiden: Brill.
Ehrman, Bart. 2011. *The New Testament: A Historical Introduction to the Early Christian Writings*. 5th edition. New York: Oxford University Press.
Fleming, Daniel E. 2012. *The Legacy of Israel in Judah's Bible: History, Politics, and the Reinscribing of Tradition*. Cambridge: Cambridge University Press.
Francioni, Francesco. 2012. "Public and Private in the International Protection of Global Cultural Goods." *European Journal of International Law* 23(3): 719–730.
Franzen, Aaron B., and Jenna Griebel. 2013. "Understanding a Cultural Identity: The Confluence of Education, Politics, and Religion within the American Concept of Biblical Literalism." *Sociology of Religion* 74(4): 521–543.
Fraser, Nancy. 1990. "Rethinking the Public Sphere: A Contribution to the Critique of Actually Existing Democracy." *Social Text* 25/26: 56–80.
Fredriksen, Paula. 2006. "Mandatory Retirement: Ideas in the Study of Christian Origins Whose Time Has Come to Go." *Studies in Religion/Sciences Religieuses* 35(2): 231–246.
Goldman, John J., and Eileen V. Quigley. 1987. "Gutenberg Bible Is Sold for Record $4.9 Million." *Los Angeles Times*, October 23.
Gracia, Jorge J. E. 2003. *Old Wine in New Skins: The Role of Tradition in Communication, Knowledge, and Group Identity*. Milwaukee, WI: Marquette University Press. http://site.ebrary.com/id/10022590, last accessed March 29, 2017.
Green, Steven K. 2015. *Inventing a Christian America: The Myth of the Religious Founding*. Oxford: Oxford University Press.
Grenz, Stanley James. 1990. *Sexual Ethics: An Evangelical Perspective*. Westminster: John Knox Press.
Hartman, Andrew. 2015. *A War for the Soul of America: A History of the Culture Wars*. Chicago: University of Chicago Press.

Haynes, Stephen R. 2002. *Noah's Curse: The Biblical Justification of American Slavery*. Oxford: Oxford University Press.
Holtorf, Cornelius. 2009. "A European Perspective on Indigenous and Immigrant Archaeologies." *World Archaeology* 41(4): 672–681.
Horsley, Richard A., and Neil Asher Silberman. 2002. *The Message and the Kingdom: How Jesus and Paul Ignited a Revolution and Transformed the Ancient World*. Minneapolis, MN: Fortress Press.
Hurtado, Larry W. 2014. "Fashions, Fallacies and Future Prospects in New Testament Studies." *Journal for the Study of the New Testament* 36(4): 299–324.
Inbari, Motti. 2012. *Messianic Religious Zionism Confronts Israeli Territorial Compromises*. Cambridge: Cambridge University Press.
Ingersoll, Julie. 2015. *Building God's Kingdom: Inside the World of Christian Reconstruction*. New York: Oxford University Press.
Jewish Telegraphic Agency. 2014. "1482 Torah Book Fetches Record $3.87 Million at Paris Auction." *Jerusalem Post*, May 2. http://www.jta.org/2014/05/01/news-opinion/world/torah-book-fetches-record-3-87-million-at-paris-auction, last accessed March 29, 2017.
Kapchan, Deborah, ed. 2014. *Cultural Heritage in Transit: Intangible Rights as Human Rights*. Philadelphia: University of Pennsylvania Press.
Kila, Joris, and James A. Zeidler. 2013. *Cultural Heritage in the Crosshairs: Protecting Cultural Property during Conflict*. Leiden: Brill.
Kuper, Adam. 2003. "The Return of the Native." *Current Anthropology* 44(3): 389–402.
Kuprecht, Karolina. 2013. *Indigenous Peoples' Cultural Property Claims: Repatriation and Beyond*. New York: Springer.
Leone, Massimo. 2013. "The Semiotics of Fundamentalist Authoriality." *International Journal for the Semiotics of Law-Revue Internationale de Sémiotique Juridique* 26(1): 227–239.
Linnekin, Jocelyn S. 1983. "Defining Tradition: Variations on the Hawaiian Identity." *American Ethnologist* 10(2): 241–252.
Mack, Burton L. 2013. *Who Wrote the New Testament?: The Making of the Christian Myth*. New York: Harper Collins.
Maltby, Paul. 2013. *Christian Fundamentalism and the Culture of Disenchantment*. Charlottesville: University of Virginia Press.
Martin, William. 2005. *With God on Our Side: The Rise of the Religious Right in America*. New York: Broadway Books.
Matsui, Kenichi. 2015. "Problems of Defining and Validating Traditional Knowledge: A Historical Approach." *International Indigenous Policy Journal* 6(2): Article 2.
Mitchel, Timothy. 2002. *Rule of Experts: Egypt, Techno-Politics, Modernity*. Berkeley: University of California Press.
O'Conor, Bernard. 2003. "Protecting Traditional Knowledge." *Journal of World Intellectual Property* 6(5): 677–698.
Onciul, Briony. 2015. *Museums, Heritage and Indigenous Voice: Decolonizing Engagement*. New York: Routledge.
Pelikan, Jaroslav. 2006. *Whose Bible Is It?: A Short History of the Scriptures*. Reprint edition. Harmondsworth: Penguin Books.
Pew Research Center. 2015. "The Future of World Religions: Population Growth Projections, 2010–2050." Washington, DC: Pew Research Center. Accessed December 29. http://www.pewforum.org/2015/04/02/religious-projections-2010-2050/, last accessed March 29, 2017.
Prior, Michael. 1997. *The Bible and Colonialism: A Moral Critique*. Sheffield: Bloomsbury T&T Clark.
Römer, Thomas. 2015. *The Invention of God*. Cambridge, MA: Harvard University Press.
Satlow, Michael L. 2014. *How the Bible Became Holy*. New Haven, CT: Yale University Press.
Schmitt, Thomas M. 2008. "The UNESCO Concept of Safeguarding Intangible Cultural Heritage: Its Background and Marrakchi Roots." *International Journal of Heritage Studies* 14(2): 95–111.
Scott, James C. 1998. *Seeing Like a State: How Certain Schemes to Improve the Human Condition Have Failed*. New Haven, CT: Yale University Press.
Silberman, Neil A. 1995. *The Hidden Scrolls: Christianity, Judaism, and the War for the Dead Sea Scrolls*. New York: Putnam Penguin.
Smith, Laurajane. 2007. "Empty Gestures? Heritage and the Politics of Recognition." In *Cultural Heritage and Human Rights*, edited by Helaine Silverman and D. Fairchild Ruggles, pp. 159–171. New York: Springer.

Smith, Peter J., and Robert W. Tuttle. 2010. "Biblical Literalism and Constitutional Originalism." GWU Legal Studies Research Paper, no. 502. http://papers.ssrn.com/sol3/papers.cfm?abstract_id=1561933, last accessed March 29, 2017.

Spivak, Gayatri Chakravorty, Donna Landry, and Gerald M. MacLean. 1996. *The Spivak Reader: Selected Works of Gayatri Chakravorty Spivak*. New York: Routledge.

Sunder, Madhavi. 2001. "Cultural Dissent." *Stanford Law Review* 54: 495–567.

Syn, Roger. 2001. "Copyright God: Enforcement of Copyright in the Bible and Religious Works." *Regent University Law Review* 14(1): 1–34.

Tov, Emanuel. 2011. *Textual Criticism of the Hebrew Bible*. 3rd edition. Minneapolis, MN: Fortress Press.

UNESCO. 1954. "Convention for the Protection of Cultural Property in the Event of Armed Conflict."

UNESCO. 1954. 2003. "Convention for the Safeguarding of the Intangible Cultural Heritage." http://www.unesco.org/culture/ich/index.php?lg=en&pg=00006, last accessed March 29, 2017.

UNESCO Intergovernmental Committee for the Safeguarding of Intangible Cultural Heritage. 2015. "Nomination Form." http://www.unesco.org/culture/ich/doc/src/ICH-02-2017-EN.doc, last accessed March 29, 2017.

United Nations General Assembly. 2007. "United Nations Declaration on the Rights of Indigenous Peoples." http://www.converge.org.nz/pma/DRIPGA.pdf, last accessed March 29, 2017.

Van Biena, David. 2013. "Bay Psalm Book Auction Smashes Record For Print Book With $14,200,000 Sale Price From Sotheby's." *Huffington Post*, November 27. http://www.huffingtonpost.com/2013/11/27/bay-psalm_n_4350120.html, last accessed March 29, 2017.

Van Zaten, Wim. 2004. "Constructing New Terminology for Intangible Cultural Heritage." *Museum International* 56(1–2): 36–44.

Wilson, J. 1968. "British Israelism." *The Sociological Review* 16(1): 41–57.

World Intellectual Property Organization. 2015. "Traditional Knowledge." Accessed December 30. http://www.wipo.int/tk/en/tk/, last accessed March 29, 2017.

18

BEING PRE-INDIGENOUS

Kin accountability beyond tradition

Paul Tapsell

E Ranginui, takoto mai. Takoto mai ra e uri o Te Aporotanga. Takoto i te wahangutanga o te tangata i te okiokinga pumau tatau katoa. Ka mohiotia e te katoa, na te maramatanga, te tohungtanga, te aroha hoki i waenganui i a koe i whakataki i te ritenga tika ki ahau e noho ana nei i taku tauiratanga. Na reira e kore koe e wareware. E taku rangatira moe mai, moe mai, moe mai ra i roto i nnga ringaringa a te Ariki.

Kua hoatu taku taonga ki a koe, nga taonga o toku tupuna, te patu pounamu me tw kuru tongarerewa.

Kia kania te pounamu ka kitea he kakano kino ranei, je kahurangi ranei: ki te kin otaku taonga, he ahakoa kia tae ki te Kuini; ki te kino, mana e whakahoki mai. Kahore he mea e takoto ana i roto i ahau. E hara inaianei toku taonga, no Tuhourangi, tuku iho ki a Uenukukopako ki a Whakaue. Wahia ena mere kia kite koe e painga i te kinonga ranei.

Ko tenei e oku hoa, e te Makarini e Te Mete, heoi an otaku taonga kua hoatu na ki a korua. Na ra aka pai rawa, ka kino, kia tae aku korero ki te Kuini.

He taonga nui hoki aku korero.

I have given you my taonga, the treasures of my ancestors, namely the patu pounamu and the kuru tongarerewa.

My taonga are not of today; they are of the time of Tuhourangi, by whom they were left to Uenukukopako and by him to Whakaue. Let these greenstones be split, that you may find out their worthiness. It is necessary to cut the greenstone to ascertain whether its grain be bad, or be kahurangi – the finest quality. If my taonga be regarded as of little value, still let them be sent to the Queen; and if they are rejected by her, she may return them. I have withheld nothing.

Now, my friends, Mr McLean and Mr Smith [representatives of the Crown], I have handed all my taonga over to you. Whether they be good, or whether they be bad, let my words [pledge] reach the Queen.

For my pledge is a great taonga indeed.

(Tapsell 2000:176)

Being Native

This thought piece provides a counter, narrative-framed perspective of being labeled "the *Other*" and the ways in which this has been built into understandings of cultural property in

Figure 18.1 Children of Ohinemutu *c.* 1900.
Source: Photographer unknown. Private collection.

museums and beyond. My aim is to highlight some of the elisions that suffuse the category of "Indigenous" in the context of Aotearoa/New Zealand (NZ) and to counsel caution in the turn towards the Indigenous in providing an alternative to settler-colonial constructions of ownership and sovereignty over culture. In past writings I have highlighted definition-transformations that museums have imposed on *taonga* (treasured Māori ancestral belongings), reflecting the political contexts curators have been grappling with, one decade to the next, since colonization (Tapsell 1995, 1998, 2000). On reflection, I have come to realize I too have been subjected to similar shifting ascriptions: in the 1970s, I was raised as a descendant of *(Ngati) Whakaue*; in the 1980s I was part of an ethnic *Māori* renaissance; in the 1990s I was branded as a *native anthropologist*; in the 2000s I was referenced as a *neo-traditionalist*; and today I am apparently an *Indigenous scholar*. Despite these multiple positions, in this chapter I offer views from a "source (kin-marae) community" or a *pre-Indigenous* perspective to the cultural heritage (anthropology and museums) sector on what constitutes "being a Native of Aotearoa/New Zealand." I open with the solemn speech of Ngamoni Te Rangi Piere given to the Crown in 1860. His words contain reference to *Kuru Tongarerewa*, a famous taonga of great antiquity. I close this chapter with a lament also referencing that same *Kuru Tongarerewa*, which in 1993 was sung to the Crown by my elders, the grandchildren of Ngamoni Te Rangi Piere. However performed, *Kuru Tongarerewa* is a heart-wrenching *taonga*, conveying ideas about the complexity of death as understood by us, Ngāti Whakaue of the Arawa confederation of tribes in Waiariki (the geothermal region of the central North Island, NZ), especially when gifted/performed in marae (Māori kin-community) contexts. In further exploring facets of "being native" in New Zealand (NZ), I next take a historical journey examining what it has meant to be *Māori* (normal/ordinary/Indigenous) in key periods, from pre-1840 Treaty of Waitangi times through to the watershed exhibition, *Te Maori* in the 1980s. From this historical discussion, I then focus on a contemporary context exploring motivations behind the 1990s urban-led shift of self-identification away from local communities "*marae/hapū*" toward a more "globalized-tribal" or "*Iwi*" identity. Generally iwi means "tribe," but I am interested in problematizing this understanding beyond its taken-for-granted usage. I next provide an overview of the intersections between being *Indigenous*, the *Iwification* of Treaty of Waitangi settlements and the active role NZ museums have played in the political (re)imagining of a biculturally framed twenty-first-century nation. What are the implications for curators who seek to "co-produce" cultural belongings – *taonga* – that have been captured within nationalized, if not corporatized, spaces of Indigenous representation of the "Māori" people? I conclude my chapter with thoughts on being *pre-Indigenous*, raising questions regarding today's widespread usage of the terms *Iwi* and *Indigenous* to pre- and/or proscribe ideological boundaries of ethnic/cultural difference in museums in NZ. These implanted identities obscure the centrality of hapū (autonomous Māori kin group) and cross-generational understandings of treasured ancestral belongings/taonga from a source community perspective, in NZ embodied in the marae – central plaza/space of the village/pa-kainga. Not unlike their colonial predecessors, museums wittingly or unwittingly continue to play a central role in imagining or "Imagineering" a nation of two peoples, conveying politically loaded ideology, like biculturalism, to a trusting public.

As a descendant of Whakaue and a grandchild of Enid Tapsell who helped to establish the Rotorua Museum, I was raised amongst taonga. Her 1960s museum stepped outside convention. It provided a secure place for Ngāti Whakaue/Te Arawa's most treasured taonga to be both viewed and protected under loan agreements by which they could be uplifted at a moment's notice to participate on marae. Looking back over my short life, I note taonga, like *Te Kahumamae o Pareraututu* (Tapsell 1997), are now less engaged within, if not disappearing altogether from, Māori communities. This appears to be occurring at the same pace that many marae are also struggling to remain vibrant in communities, and are in some cases collapsing, both metaphorically and literally. This double-edged retreat of kin accountability and genealogically encoded knowledge is inversely proportional to today's all-pervasive Indigenous-framed rhetoric of being "Iwi."

When did this paradigm shift occur? I cannot speak for other tribes, but I believe I am at least qualified to provide a kin-shaped insight from the perspective of being Ngāti Whakaue as once understood by my grandparents' generation. To bring focus to this shift, one particular taonga stands out: *Kuru Tongarerewa*, a revered (tapu) name reaching back to ancient times. It denotes a mythically powerful greenstone (pounamu/nephrite) of the finest grain (kahurangi), associated with the initial Pacific voyages of discovery tens of generations ago. *Kura Tongarerewa* has become a taonga of such power its very existence is transcendental, reflecting more than 3,000 years of oceanic consciousness. It is a cross-generational manifestation of *mana* (ancestral authority/power), *tapu* (revered/restricted) and *kōrero* (narrative/oratory) that exists beyond tangible/physical form. In Ngāti Whakaue, the name *Kura Tongarerewa* is/was carefully used with great respect. When a much-loved young person died suddenly, my tribal elders poetically compared him or her to the *Kuru Tongarerewa* in an attempt to express the deepness of loss, heartfelt by all.

I know of three times when the name *Kuru Tongarerewa* was prestated (ceremonially performed, gifted and/or bestowed) beyond our mourning ceremonies (tangihanga). The first marked an occasion in 1860 when Ngāti Whakaue/Te Arawa leader Ngamoni Te Rangi Piere offered our metaphorical heart to Queen Victoria for her inspection, laying it open so she might judge our worthiness as her Treaty partner and make good her promise to protect our lands, people and resources (see above). The second time was in 1989 when Ngāti

Whakaue answered the call of Te Ati Awa/Ngāti Toa (the local kin groups of Wellington) to bestow the name *Kuru Tongarerewa* on the Crown's newly proposed Museum of New Zealand (Tapsell 1998: 292). And the third, not unrelated to the second, was the 1993 re-presentation of *Kuru Tongarerewa*, but this time directly to the new Museum of New Zealand's board chair while visiting Rotorua (Ibid.: 292–294). His visit was part of the newly enacted (1992) Museum of New Zealand / Te Papa "Tongarewa" consultation tour, seeking tribal mandates nationwide to implement new Māori policies. Ngāti Whakaue expressed their disappointment in the new Māori name of the museum "Te Papa Tongarewa," which appeared to be a nonsensical corruption of our most precious taonga *Kuru Tongarerewa.* The elders eloquently, but firmly, sought explanation around the fate of their original 1989 gifting of *Kuru Tongarerewa* to the Crown. Its Māori consultants argued that while the spelling had changed, the intent of the gift had not been deliberately overlooked or altered. As a compromise, they offered to take it back to Wellington for board consideration: that the name be integrated and thus read *Te Papa Kuru Tongarerewa.* Ngāti Whakaue were not unhappy with this proposal as the essence of their taonga remained intact. The formal speech-making proceedings with the new museum board chair then closed with the elders singing a chant (*moteatea*) that referenced *Kura Tongarerewa*, thus completing Ngāti Whakaue's direct re-gifting while simultaneously reinstating its *tapu* (ancestrally prescribed restrictions, see below).

At a deeper level, this 1993 meeting marks the point when elders at home began realizing that Ngāti Whakaue/Te Arawa's urban-living descendants, especially those working in government ministries in the capital had splintered beyond marae kin connection context. At the 1993 meeting it was revealed that one of our own, who had lived in Wellington most of his adult life had been directly involved in developing the *Te Papa Tongarewa* name, likely without ever knowing his own marae elders had been the 1989 source of *Kuru Tongarerewa* (via local Te Ati Awa/Ngāti Toa kin communities of Wellington). He was present at the 1993 meeting, but neither showed surprise, nor offered any defense nor provided explanation. He even knew our lament. The heart of *Kura Tongarerewa* may well have been splintered by the Crown, but aided and abetted by our very own who did not seek mandate or make themselves accountable to their home marae communities. As one of my dear aunts repeatedly said from that day on: "We are our own worst enemies."

Being Māori

I opened my chapter with the *Kuru Tongarerewa* story to signal the complexities that underscore the recognition and production of identity in the context of nearly two hundred years of settler colonialism. Being Native remained a deep-seated cross-cultural boundary marker until the 1980s. The traveling exhibition *Te Maori* (Mead 1984) marks a watershed moment when New Zealand (NZ) museums re-examined their role as interpreters of things Māori. It was initiated by the AFA (American Federation of Arts) and AGMANZ (Art Galleries and Museums Association of NZ) in the late 1970s, seeking to exhibit primitive Māori art in prestigious US galleries. The touring exhibition comprised 174 Māori carvings curated out of NZ museums. It opened at the Metropolitan Museum of Art in New York in 1984 with an unprecedented Māori traditional dawn ceremony. Thereafter, it visited St Louis Art Gallery, DeYoung in San Francisco and the Field Museum in Chicago before returning in 1986 to tour NZ (Mead 1986). The politically framed bicultural imagining created in this exhibition (Dibley 1996) shifted an economically struggling nation toward a more Pacific-centered identity (Tapsell 2011). In other words, *Te Maori* helped NZ move from being almost exclusively British-focused to a shared cultural identity more located in the Pacific. Māori

Figure 18.2 Children at Opononi Wharf, 2010.
Source: Photographer: Krzysztof Pfeiffer.

cultural property – formerly viewed in most museums as artificial curiosities, primitive curios, specimens, artifact, primitive art, became known internationally as *taonga*, translated as Māori *art* (Mead 1984; Tapsell 1997) – shifted from exclusive representations of "native other" to inclusive symbols of one nation. This ontological shift toward an inclusive indigenous definition, but simultaneously coopting its cultural representation for use in an exclusive global art discourse, raised new tensions regarding who actually carried the right to define taonga in museum contexts (Tapsell 2003, 2011; also see Tapsell 2000 regarding the Pukaki example of cooption, and rights of definition beyond source community horizons).

The origin of the 1980s shift of power over definitions of Māori cultural identity extends back over many generations. At its heart was the breakdown of kin accountability and cross-generational knowledge transmission in the late 1800s, but this only became more widely apparent as families moved away from their home communities in the mass rural–urban migration that occurred after World War Two. The pre-Indigenous values of tribal (hapū) society – as once fiercely maintained by distinctive marae communities and described in Article 2 of the Treaty of Waitangi in the assertion of the chiefly authority (tino rangatiratanga) over and from lands (whenua), people (kainga) and taonga – appeared to be under threat from our own, now being raised in cities. How did we get to this point?

In recent decades, "being *Māori*" has equated to "being Indigenous," coinciding also with the Treaty of Waitangi (post-) claim settlement era (from the late 1980s). In previous times, the customary use of the term "Māori" denoted anything that was "normal" or clear of contamination, the classic example being *wai-Māori* or ordinary water. Not surprisingly, when Europeans first began crossing our Pacific beaches in the late 1700s (Dening 1980), the local kin groups of at least 700 distinct and autonomous tribal marae communities saw themselves as normal or *Māori* in counter-distinction to the arriving strangers. The hapū was the primary term of identification, defining kin-based communities, focused around marae, which represent the core social, economic and political unit of Māori society, denoted by prefixes like *Ngati.* . . . or *Ngai* . . . , *Te Aitanga.* . . . or *Whanau a.* . . . meaning the people descended from. . . . Hapū fiercely maintain customary kin-authority of, over and from surrounding access to estates and resources (mana o te whenua). As translated in Kawharu (1989: 316–321), the 1840 Treaty of Waitangi (with the British Crown) promised to uphold the exclusive authority (tino rangatiratanga) of tribal leaders (rangatira) over all their tribal (hapū) lands (whenua), people/marae (kainga) and treasured belongings (taonga) (Article 2) as well as conferring upon them the rights and duties of British citizenship (Article 3). This last article was especially important to those rangatira exporting produce to the lucrative Australian goldfields market (potatoes were the primary export on tens of rangatira-owned and operated sailboats crossing the Tasman sea between 1830 and the 1850s (Petrie 2006).

By the mid-1850s, if not earlier in some parts of the North, the economic monopoly of rangatira over NZ commerce began to shift into colonial control (Petrie 2006). This decade of increasing Māori economic marginalization was fundamentally aided and abetted by a land-hungry settler government keen to take control of primary production. Rather than honouring the Treaty and its stated promise to protect the exclusive authority of rangatira, the Crown set about undermining the economic and political control Māori were still attempting to exercise within the fledgling colony (Walker 1990). The 1850s' collapse happened at a time when NZ's first settler government was constituted, and when British immigration was increasing exponentially. The 1852 decline coincided with the establishment of NZ's first museum (in Auckland) and also the time when colony-controlled steamships began operating. Auckland bankers colluded with the Crown seeking transfer of fertile lands of Waikato, Bay of Plenty and Taranaki in lieu of unpaid debts as rangatira struggled to keep their over-capitalized mills and sailing ships operating through the 1850s' economic decline (Petrie 2006). In 1861 Governor Grey returned for a second term, neutralizing the two most powerful rangatira of NZ by presenting Te Rauparaha to Te Wherowhero as his captive (Burns 1983). This divide and rule action removed the threat of a combined Māori nation attack and freed Grey to build the Great South Road on which his British and colonial regiments were mobilized to invade the Waikato (Walker 1990). Rangatira from across NZ petitioned their Treaty partner (the Crown) to desist from deliberate economic destabilization of their control over resources. With the introduction of the 1863 New Zealand Settlements Act tensions boiled over and a confiscation-fuelled war shut down the means of subsistence for many tribes, especially those seen as "rebellious." Numerous hui (meetings on marae) were hosted by influential rangatira seeking to regroup and reaffirm boundaries in the face of a common enemy (Ibid). Being Māori was no longer about being normal: it was about survival in the face of a colonial machine hell-bent on land acquisition – legislated confiscation – by force if need be. The resulting 1860s–1880s' conflicts, seizures, alienations and incarcerations rendered rangatira and their marae communities destitute of lands and waterways. Settlers and British soldiers, who referred to the battles as the Māori Wars, were allotted 100+ acre blocks, which they cleared for farms (Ibid.). Only today, descendants of those original settlers are beginning to understand the cross-generational cost of excluding Māori from their own nation, resulting from the violent civil dispossession of lands once owned by marae/hapū under the mantle of their rangatira who were equally British under Article 3 of the Treaty. While the colonizers grew wealthy, dispossessed Māori, like my grandfather, were forced to become laborers on their alienated lands, digging ditches, building fences, felling forests and laying roads in order to put food on the table. Marae impoverishment was deepened by waves of epidemics like dysentery, tuberculosis, dropsy and influenza and high infant morbidity. By 1900 the New Zealand/British colony of over one million people (compared with 2,000 in 1840 and 60,000 in 1860) controlled most of the nation's 66 million acres and all associated ocean, waterways and fisheries (Ibid.; Pool 1991). Meanwhile Māori numbers had dropped to 40,000 (compared with over 70,000 in 1840 and 60,000 in 1860) and life expectancy was less than 30 years of age (Walker: 114). Māori spirituality became a new unifying vehicle of survival. While the Pākehā community still referred to themselves as British, they were now coming to call the New Zealander Natives *Maoris* in a derogatory manner, stigmatizing my grandparents' generation as dumb, lazy, foul-smelling. This generation was raised in a climate of politically prescribed and museologically validated racial inferiority: a dying race in the final throes of extinction.

Through the pre-World War One efforts of Māori politicians such as James Carroll, Apirana Ngata, Peter Buck, Maui Pomare, Hone Heke Ngapua, and other mission-school-educated sons of rangatira, along with women leaders, not least Te Puea Herangi and Guide Makareti Papakura, "being Māori" was reaffirmed as a title of pride. Their new health interventions assisted in arresting the population decline (e.g. Tohunga Suppression Act 1907; Jones 2012). "Māori" symbolism was overtly applied to the Māori All Blacks, Māori art and the Māori Contingent of World War One who fought gallantly in European theaters of war and became nationally recognized. This demonstrable right of British citizenship as promised under Article 3 of the Treaty resulted in a highly successful recruitment of Māori from most tribes (some exceptions being in the Waikato, Taranaki and Bay of Plenty who had suffered the 1860s' wars more brutally than most) with many dying at Gallipoli, the Somme and Passchendaele. But on return not much had changed. The 1918 influenza epidemic, brought home by returning soldiers, hit marae communities seven times harder than the Pākehā population (Rice 2012: 86). While Pākehā comrades were awarded lands and pensions for service to the king, the isolated marae communities' experience of landless associated poverty, despair, depression and death deepened. With a new war on the horizon Apirana Ngata in particular, who later rose to Deputy Prime Minister, successfully established the 28th Māori Battalion in an effort to again prove the worth of Māori through fighting for the Crown in foreign lands (Ngata 1943). Only after the 28th Māori Battalion's spectacular World War Two campaigns in Greece, North Africa and Italy did Ngata's dream of Māori becoming respected by Pākehā as their citizen equals get realized. (This came at great cost: the 28th Māori Battalion recorded the highest World War Two casualty rate of any battalion; Soutar 2008).

Full of pride and a sense of independence, these young Māori soldiers returned to their rural homes as a post-World War Two booming economy took hold across NZ's towns and cities. The allure of urban-living opportunities was irresistible (Walker 1990; Kawharu 2014). In the 1950s young Māori like my father made strategic decisions to migrate away from their impoverished marae locales and find steady employment in towns and cities. Also on offer were government-funded housing, education and health services. Not only was my father's generation able to explore individuality beyond the tribal horizon, but they were also able to escape the cross-generational poverty that had paralyzed their economically isolated communities since the end of NZ's nineteenth century civil wars (Kawharu 1989). But this escape came at a price – a forgoing of marae-based identity in favor of a more generic Māori identity. When the 1970s' economic downturn hit New Zealand, thousands of Māori nuclear families had become well and truly locked into an urban isolated way of life (Tapsell 2014). Not that returning home to make a living was a possibility. The Crown had long since alienated marae communities' most fertile hinterlands into a nationalized infrastructure of settler-owned rural production of agriculture (beef, dairy, sheep), horticulture (fruit and vegetables) and aquaculture (fresh water and ocean fisheries).

The tribal migration into cities was unprecedented, reaching its peak in the late 1960s, but it still continues today. As a matter of survival in a foreign milieu, descendants banded together to form "Māori" or pan-tribal organizations (Gagné 2013; Rosenblatt 2002; Tapsell 2002), aiding access to particular employment opportunities in competition with other ethnic groups, not least Pākehā and Pacific Islanders. Being Māori in cities also opened up access to state-funded education, housing and health benefits otherwise unavailable if one remained on tribal homelands. This new form of Māori identity threatened to overwhelm local marae which had become swamped by urbanization because of where their land was. For example, the Ōrākei community of Auckland was inundated – rendered invisible – by tens of thousands of young incoming Māori and Pacific Islanders seeking a better way of life (Kawharu 1975). Not until the 1991 Orakei Act did the Crown again acknowledge the Ōrākei community as the local/home marae of Central Auckland. Thereafter they have partnered with the Crown in providing essential services, like health, available to all peoples now living in the vicinity of their ancestral lands. Three decades after World War Two, New Zealand's sense of sovereign, Pacific-framed identity began emerging after Britain entered the European Economic Community. Almost overnight New Zealand's taken-for-granted British citizenship was dismantled. British passports were replaced by New Zealand ones, flying the Union Jack disappeared and we were no longer required to sing "God Save the Queen" before school or at the movies. The black jersey and silver fern came to symbolize international difference from Britain. Then in 1972 New Zealand's rowing eight won gold at the Munich Olympics at which our unofficial anthem "God of Nations" was played, triggering its 1977 official adoption (Swarbrick 2014) by an eager nation seeking to stand apart on its own terms, full of pride. Notwithstanding the rise of very public Māori land protests throughout the 1970s, coinciding with a major economic downturn, the 1984 international touring *Te Maori* Art Exhibition swept throughout the nation, daring two peoples – Māori and Pākehā (British colonial descendants) – to dream of a biculturally-constructed nation built on the promises embedded in the 1840 Te Tiriti o Waitangi (Treaty of Waitangi): the ultimate boundary of negotiated partnership in a NZ context. Led by Minister of Internal Affairs, Hon. Peter Tapsell, the Museum of New Zealand Project (then known as Te Marae o Aotearoa) became an imagined vehicle by which the nation could focus its emerging sense of bicultural identity in a South Pacific context (Dibley 1996; Tapsell 2011). At the same time, museums began reinventing themselves around Māori cultural property, openly calling them taonga. Meanwhile hundreds of lineal meters of grievance-laden Waitangi Tribunal Claims' archives were being produced, exposing the depth of dishonorable actions instigated by the Crown against Māori tribes. This acceleration in Treaty-associated evidence was a direct response to the Tribunal being granted the ability to retrospectively investigate grievances dating back to the 1840 signing of the Treaty (Treaty of Waitangi Amendment Act 1985). By the mid-1990s, museum-held taonga – isolated from source communities since the nineteenth century – began reflecting their urban-raised Māori descendants' deep-felt sense of alienation from marae, ancestral estates and not least their cultural property. The late 1980s' search to meaningfully engage with their cultural identity through museums post-*Te Maori* was now overshadowed by urban-led Māori repatriation protests, accusing the Crown and its museums of stealing their ancestors (Tapsell 1998). Meanwhile wider tribes came head to head with their own relations sitting on newly formed urban Māori authorities, disintegrating the 1980s' sense of unity that *Te Maori* had momentarily created. For the first time, the organizing concept "Iwi" came to the public fore as Māori divided themselves accordingly, urban or tribal, brother versus brother in a bitter legal fight for control over the Crown-agreed return of 50 percent of NZ's fishing quota to Māori (Tapsell 2002).

Being Iwi

Where did this word "Iwi" come from? In earlier times, iwi (not using a capital "i") was applied to a group of related kin communities who temporarily realigned their hapū (principal social, political, economic kin group(s) underpinning marae) under a common, but more distant ancestor (Ballara 1998). This kin-driven coalition was inherently unstable and only lasted for as long as required to ameliorate a profound crisis, overcome a shared challenge or mutually benefit from an external opportunity. Thereafter the iwi disbanded to its constituent, but fiercely independent hapū/marae communities. While the term iwi was also used to refer to a general gathering of people, like at a hui, its modern-day reformation, Iwi (capital I) is very different and has direct implications in and beyond NZ's museums.

If we take a closer look at the Treaty of Waitangi, in Article 2 "hapū" is the identified kin group, represented by rangatira who wield exclusive authority (tino rangatiratanga) over their lands (whenua), people/marae communities (kainga) and treasured ancestral belongings (taonga). For all its usage today, the word iwi does not feature in the 1840 Treaty of Waitangi. Yet, the Crown, museums and general public openly refer to Iwi as Treaty partners with whom to engage. So where did this radical shift of iwi meaning occur, successfully overwriting tribal marae sovereignty – tino rangatiratanga – and distracting us from properly understanding the customary tribal values of hapū/marae still represented by museum-held taonga?

Through the late 1980s into the 1990s the Crown, the Waitangi Tribunal, NZ courts and Privy Council ultimately redefined the customary concept of Iwi as a politically potent

Figure 18.3 Ngāti Whakaue / Te Arawa welcome Pukaki home, Ohinemutu 1997.
Source: Photographer: Hamish Macdonald.

boundary marker of pan-tribal/ethnic difference (Belgrave et al. 2003). The 1990 Runanga Iwi Act triggered the modern-day globalizing of tribal trusts (regional amalgamation of kin land holdings established by the nineteenth Native/Māori Land Court (Kawharu 1977)) into legally recognized Iwi (corporate) organizations or RIOs (Tapsell 2014). Literally overnight legally constituted boardrooms representing shareholding land interests gained Iwi status and came to be recognized by the Crown as legally mandated tribal voices. This directly challenged kin marae leadership who had previously maintained exclusive customary authority for tens of generations, but which the Crown had ignored or undermined since 1843 (Ibid.). In 1991 the Runanga Iwi Act was repealed, but the newly elected government did not hesitate in taking advantage of the recently reorganized corporate Iwi organizations. In 1991 it launched a new direct negotiation initiative with recognized Iwi (Ministry for the Treaty of Waitangi Negotiations) that conveniently overstepped the Waitangi Tribunal hearing process and its presentation of overwhelming evidence demonstrating the systematic devastation inflicted on every marae community of NZ.

With the passage of its 1992 Act, the Museum of New Zealand/Te Papa Tongarewa Project (Te Papa) took the lead in promoting "Iwi–Crown" relationships within a Treaty discourse of bicultural partnership. In the mid-1990s, it was at the forefront of coining bicultural labels such as Iwi-Māori/Iwi-Pākehā alongside Taonga-Māori/Taonga Pākehā and Tangata-Whenua versus Tangata-Tiriti, denoting Māori as the first Iwi/peoples in distinction to later Pākehā arrivals who entered NZ under Te Tiriti/Treaty of Waitangi (Tapsell 1998).

In 1998, when Te Papa opened it had firmly embedded an Iwi exhibitionary policy, inviting different Iwi groups to display themselves in the new Mana Whenua gallery on a two-to-three-year rotation cycle. Not surprisingly, the actual mana whenua tribes of Wellington – Ngāti Toa/Te Ati Awa – were treated as but two Iwi among many, mirroring the way the Ōrākei community had also been excluded from hosting *Te Maori* at the Auckland Art Gallery in 1987 (Tapsell 1998). Interestingly, Te Papa's Mana Whenua space is located on the Māori side of the fourth floor between the Treaty of Waitangi talking post display, the "Taonga-Māori" permanent exhibition and the multifunctional, multi-cultural pan-Iwi marae space named Te Marae: Rongomaraeroa (Tapsell 2005). This taonga-Māori assemblage of Iwi-focused displays and functions acted as an ideologized traditional counterpoint to the rest of the fourth floor dedicated to modern NZ exhibitions of "Taonga-Pākehā": fine art and culture (Williams 2005).

By the late 1990s, the "Iwi" descriptor had successfully replaced pre-1990 "Māori" usage. Government departments, schools, hospitals and not least legally reorganized tribal authorities appeared to adopt Iwi as if it had always been the natural order of Treaty-framed Māori society. Being Iwi placed you on the Crown's radar for negotiation. Lost in this political confusion of everything being termed Iwi was the tribal marae community from which both urban-raised descendants and museum-held taonga originated. Associated customary leadership roles based on tried and tested ancestral values of kin accountability, *intellectual belonging* (IB) and service were submerged by a new generation of urban-raised Māori working in museums post-*Te Maori*. They claimed exclusive rights to define boundaries without formal recourse to their employers, let alone local or source communities (Tapsell 2011). Back in the tribal domains male-dominated Iwi boards, comprising elected trustees, began delivering services and benefits to their legally prescribed membership of listed owners, shareholders or beneficiaries. Their frame of reference to act on behalf of communities was western-legally defined as opposed to being marae-defined. Kin accountability was now, therefore, being prescribed very differently – by individualized democracy rather than kin-consensus succession – compared with my elders' pre-1990s era.

The 1990s can be seen as the "Iwification" decade of Māori. Almost without exception, NZ tribes went down the Crown-prescribed Iwification corporate/fiscal boardroom track, leaving behind hapū/marae identities. Regional museums in Taranaki, Whanganui, Rotorua and Tai Rawhiti were not initially swayed as they had already developed reliable lines of tribal marae accountability concerning their museum-held taonga and ancestral human remains (Tapsell 2016). The most notable was the Auckland Museum. In the mid-1990s, it enacted a Taumata-a-Iwi / Māori Advisory Committee (TAI) under its 1996 Auckland War Memorial Museum Amendment legislation. Initially designed to represent all Iwi across the nation, the TAI vision was revised by Ngāti Whātua o Ōrākei with the support of neighboring tribes, Tainui and Ngāti Paoa, so it might more accurately reflect the Māori values inherent in all taonga and ancestral human remains resting in the Auckland Museum (Tapsell 2006a). The TAI was thus recast to more appropriately provide customary accountable advice, reflecting the marae communities from which all taonga originated (Kawharu 2006). Unlike Te Papa where the Māori staff take on the role of Tangata Whenua (host Iwi) on a pan-Iwi marae (located on the fourth level of the building), the Auckland Museum utilizes its Taumata-a-Iwi (representing the host hapū/marae community of Auckland) to ritually create a customary marae space by which visiting source communities might be properly received as part and parcel of accessing their museum-held taonga while resting on another tribe's ancestral domain (Tapsell 2011, 2015).

On the wider Treaty settlement horizon, by the mid-2000s the direct negotiation pathway became a route by which claimants could sit down with the Crown concerning their claim. The Crown successfully coaxed disparate tribes across regions to form large natural groupings (LNGs) and enter into a collectively negotiated global settlement under one legally recognized Iwi entity. The resulting post-settlement Iwi authorities – also called PSGEs (Post-Settlement Governance Entities) or RIOs (Crown Recognized Iwi Organizations) – sought regional museums' recognition as the exclusively mandated local tribal voice, usurping established marae elders' lines of accountability to taonga. One example of which I have direct experience is Te Pumautanga o Te Arawa, formed under an act of parliament in 2007. This post-settlement multi-tribal Iwi entity, representing not inconsiderable capital holdings, has imposed its Crown-legitimized and -funded corporate status to dominate representation on the Rotorua Museum's Te Pukenga Koeke (Māori advisory committee), successfully overriding the once dominant customary voice of the local marae elders of Ngāti Whakaue. These corporate-organized Iwi have generally marginalized their tribal marae, which today provide little more than a convenient annual general meeting venue where PSGE/RIOs might demonstrably deliver economically operational reports to their "Iwi" shareholders/beneficial owners. They are fashioned on a corporate "office" model, requiring legally embedded processes of democracy (protecting individual's beneficial rights and shareholdings) to elect trustees/directors. This has completely obscured, confused, undermined and depowered the customary succession of tens of generations of carefully transferred knowledge-based "kin" belonging modes of leadership as once represented by rangatira. Urban Māori organizations – non-kin membership-based by virtue of residential location – have similarly organized themselves and built up large corporate entities not averse to partnering with PSGEs to deliver benefit to all "Iwi" living in their shared catchments (e.g. Waipereira Whanau Trust, Ōrākei and Tainui work together to deliver Māori health programs in the Auckland City region).

Being Indigenous

It was during the late 1980s/early 1990s' "Iwi" proliferation that most of my third-generation urban-raised Māori students were born. In the wake of *Te Maori*, their parents (my

Figure 18.4 Opening of Ko Tawa Exhibition, Australian Museum, Sydney, 2007.
Source: Photographer: Krzysztof Pfeiffer.

generation) proudly identified themselves as Māori: *Iwification* of all things Māori was still a decade away. My students' parents were the first generation of Māori from elsewhere to grow up in cities: raised beyond our grandparents' marae-centred universe. But some of us of that generation were still near enough to home to maintain meaningful links with our indulging, tribally orientated grandparents. For most of my generation, however, *Te Maori* was the first time, after the 1977–1984 recession, that we came face-to-face again with our marae-based elders and previously obscured museum-held ancestors, like Pukaki (Tapsell 2000). This reunion became three way and it repeated itself four times, in four metropolitan museums/galleries upon another tribe's confiscated ancestral estates.[1] All of NZ was swept up by *Te Maori*. It was the beginnings of a bicultural imagining as Pākehā New Zealanders discovered their own sense of Indigeneity beyond being British (Dibley 1996) and set a new course of economic engagement with neighboring Pacific rim nations using Māori branding to identify national uniqueness. Despite the rise of multiple urban-based Māori voices in the media like Ranginui Walker (1987), Māori had little impact or inclusive say in the new biculturally driven economic direction. Meanwhile the "old world" of marae-associated kin accountability as still being practiced by relatives living on ancestral homeland (hau kainga) became so obscure, it was near invisible to the general public.

A main casualty of this era was cross-generational transmission of unique, marae-based genealogically encoded knowledge (mātauranga/whakapapa), primarily due to geographical separation of marae elders from their urban-raised grandchildren (mokopuna). Tangihanga (mourning ceremony) is arguably the main cultural ceremony that brings relatives from near and far back together. And even then that is but a shadow of what I experienced as a child: a moment up to five days long, when my whole community halted everyday work to mourn the loss. The person who laid in state on our marae represented a life crisis – leaving a void, both emotionally and practically. On her/him would lie particular taonga of our ancestors especially pertinent to specific genealogical lines. Some of these taonga came from our local museum, held in trust until required for such occasions. On the final night we would all pack into the marae and sit at the feet of our elders to listen to the *poroporoaki* – the final farewell to the departing spirit. The last speaker would identify or be identified as the successor to all the knowledge and skills the deceased once contributed to our community. It was beyond argument and the taonga resting on the departed became witness to this occasion, embodying yet another layer of *korero* (narrative) before disappearing from sight like a tui bird darting back into our native bush (Tapsell 1997).

The taonga that toured in *Te Maori*, like Pukaki, Tiki and Uenuku, were once active participants in the life-crisis cycle of everyday marae living of singularly particular kin communities. The colonization process ripped both land and taonga from these communities and converted the latter into objectified examples of Native otherness. In 1984 *Te Maori* started out as a US-touring Māori art exhibition of exactly that, but by its 1987 NZ conclusion it had touched a whole nation and the taonga were no longer depictions of ancestors, they were the ancestors. Even so, all these taonga remained the legal property of museums. In due course the holding museums at least have learned you cannot have it both ways – to call them taonga – ancestral belongings – contradicts ideas of legal ownership, tipping NZ into a challenging new era of negotiated custodianship across three decades of fast-changing Māori/marae leadership and in some cases – for example Pukaki (Tapsell 2000) – resulting in remarkable returns to marae (source) communities (Tapsell 2006b).

From the late 1980s, being Māori had become a positive self-ascription reflected through clothing, skin art, language, scholarships, museums, art galleries, treaty settlements, national anthem, literature, radio, television. It also empowered a new generation of settler descendants to identify themselves as *being Pākehā* (King 1985). As I now explain to my students who generally have never heard of *Te Maori* until my class, this exhibition is recognized for heralding the Māori renaissance (Walker 1990; McCarthy 2007, 2011). *Te Maori* was the catalyst behind development of today's taken-for-granted Iwi-Māori sense of pride. They are aghast when I explain I grew up in an era when barbers refused to provide Māori with haircuts; Māori had to sit downstairs at the movies (upstairs being reserved for Pākehā only) and Māori were not permitted to drink in lounge bars at the pub. But after *Te Maori*, New Zealand's international market profile was quick to cash in on our nation's emerging Brand Māori. Led by Te Papa, other national brands including Air New Zealand, Aotearoa Fisheries, Tourism Board, Venice Biennale artists and the All Blacks also sought to leverage a global market that was willing to pay to experience NZ's unique Māori point of difference. Since the late 1990s Māori have also become internationally recognized by other First Nation ethnicities as the Indigenous people of the South Pacific islands of Aotearoa. Yet back home on the marae – the source of Māori identity – the word Indigenous remained a foreign concept beyond association with plants, animals or Indians. Kin-accountable nomenclature, like *Ngāti* this or *Ngai* that, still prevailed. In the early 1990s the Resource Management Act's reference to Kaitiakitanga challenged Pākehā ideas of custodianship over privately controlled resources (Kawharu 2003) while at the same time raising questions over intellectual property rights of native flora, fauna and cultural intellectual property (WAI 262 1991). From the 2000s the UN Declaration of Rights of Indigenous Peoples (2007) along with influential writings around Indigeneity from within and beyond Māori academia (e.g. Smith 1999) built on the 1990s' legislative challenges and began to shape urban-raised Māori individuals' self-identification as "Indigenous" (with a capital "I"). Being Indigenous is a shared narrative of colonization that provides Māori today with a passport of exclusive identity to very real market opportunities and a sense of belonging, evolving out of a digitally accessible era of interconnection and entrepreneurship without borders.

My annual challenge to students is to wind back the clock to a time prior to the Indigenous era, to a time of genealogical accountability as represented by the kin-philosophy of *whakapapa* (genealogical ordering of all things in the universe) under which their grandparents were raised. Through narrative I gently begin introducing them to another way of knowing: one that is (or was) dynamically perpetuated by learned elders on ancestral/tribal estates. Each year's new raft of students take my Indigenous Development papers – Whakapapa and Marae 302, and Taonga and Museums 402 – seeking to better understand from a Māori perspective the unique trajectory underpinning Indigeneity today. In contrast to two decades ago, the majority of today's Māori students attending University of Otago have limited if any contact with their source marae communities and elders. Like the Otago Museum-held taonga across the road, they too are generally disconnected from the lived realities of their home people (hau kainga) and their dialect, customs and not least kin-community marae (as opposed to urban marae (Tapsell 2002)). Nevertheless, many young Māori have learned to speak a homogenized version of our language via university studies and proudly access Māori and Iwi scholarships to assist their academic aspirations. But are they being encouraged to explore beyond the academy and return across their ancestral horizon to the marae communities from where their "Māori" identity originates? The gap is widening between being Māori in the cities and being Māori back home in depopulated marae communities. Latest statistics (New Zealand Statistics Census 2013) suggest over 90 percent of Māori now dwell in urban areas compared with pre-World War Two when it was less than 20 percent (Pool 1991). The Māorimaps.com fieldwork (2010–2014 survey of 770 tribal marae of NZ) reflected this runaway diaspora, visually documenting the extent of human resource depletion and structural decay, now beginning to enter its fourth generation (Tapsell 2014).

My favourite image I use when teaching is of Pukaki resting on his marae in Rotorua. I muse with my students about what it might have been like the day Pukaki left our marae on October 2, 1877, bidding his people farewell, my great grandparents' generation, to embark on an extraordinary life beyond our tribal horizon. While three generations of Ngāti Whakaue arrived, lived and died back in Rotorua, Pukaki was himself meeting millions of people, including artists like Gauguin, state leaders and British royalty while he reposed alongside his cousin Tiki in Auckland Museum. He then led *Te Maori* across the United States and back through NZ before deciding to reappear on his marae like a blazing comet 120 years later (Tapsell 2000).

Most of my students are Māori. They are surprised to learn every one of NZ's tribal marae communities still continue carrying their own distinctive dynamic knowledge system (whakapapa), representing unbroken chains of Pacific identity that reach back thousands of years. I explain how these are the same tribal marae out of which all museum-held taonga originate. Like these taonga, I reposition my keen audience to also see themselves as sharing the same origin story: products of 175 years of Māori tribal society upheaval. They have been born into the business end of a brutal colonization trajectory that began when the British Crown first transgressed the Treaty of Waitangi in 1843. I pose my classes challenging questions: How did you get here? What is a source community? If they are Māori, I might ask them, do they know their marae? With each year that passes fewer and fewer of my Māori students have any formative engagement with their marae communities, let alone elders. Through publications and first person narrative I guide their academic dissection of tangihanga (mourning rituals), but always with an eye of preparing them for the time they might return home to experience one for themselves. And in due course I hope they will fully realize that every tribal marae in NZ has its very own set of unique customs, idioms and practices, setting each kin group apart as distinct autonomous communities. Taonga like Pukaki represent ritually encoded systems of knowledge. They form the backbone of marae identity, especially during tangihanga where they are ritually performed to ameliorate the crisis of death, heal cross-generational wounds and mark kin succession, all the while representing an outward expression of the marae community's customary authority over their estates (mana *o te* whenua).

While my Māori students may lack direct contact with their ancestral marae, nevertheless they are part of today's generation of urban-raised descendants who maintain a strong sense of *Iwi* affiliation. Access to Iwi scholarships and other RIO/PSGE-controlled benefits assists in this sense of identity, not to mention keeping down student loans. Less obvious, however, is any meaningful (re)connection of these Iwi scholarships to hapū identity via marae, which no longer appear to provide any tangible benefit to our youth, at least in monetary terms. Like lands and other resources, museum-held taonga that have also returned as part of a treaty settlement are thereafter administered by the PSGE, not by the marae community from which they were originally alienated. Yet another tension associated with today's settlements and to which my students remain oblivious until they begin my paper.

When my students discover that museum-held taonga – marae-performed symbols of kin identity – are casualties of Crown-alienated ancestral lands and resources, they begin to reflect on their own trajectories that have led to them being raised away from their marae communities. In the wake of colonial land alienation marae across NZ struggled to survive. Taonga were often the first to depart, ending up in nineteenth-century metropolitan-located collections while three generations later their descendants followed a similar trajectory, into the same urban dislocations. Identification of the pathway by which taonga and descendant have independently arrived in metropolitan areas enables remedies to begin to be applied and to assist reestablishment of a dynamic, genealogically engaged sense of well-being and kin-connectedness.

The ultimate goal of my university seminars, associated readings and searching questions is to shift a new generation of Māori thinkers from their taken-for-granted ideas of Indigeneity and Iwification to a realization that being "Māori" is built on a deeper and profoundly complex set of kin relationships. These are predicated on a prescribed set of responsibilities, obligations, accountabilities and duties uniquely associated with the 770 surviving tribal marae of NZ (Te Potiki National Trust 2008). Once my students have addressed their own ancestral trajectory from marae community to urban descendant they are better equipped to research and explore the potential pathways by which Ancestral Human Remains and taonga have also left source community landscapes and entered museums and/or associated global markets of exchange (i.e. auction houses/private collections). The constant throughout this research-directed exploration is the pivotal importance of ancestral marae, associated rituals of kin-belonging and the central role taonga still play in the last remaining marae ritual, the tangihanga. Sooner or later they come to realize that colonization is ongoing and just as legislatively brutal today as in the nineteenth century. Crown-privileged Iwi entities (Kawanatanga in Article 1) are now completing what the Crown began: the undermining and dismantling of the last surviving expression of tino rangatiratanga: the marae (kainga), which the Crown promised to protect (Article 2). Unless immediately addressed the nineteenth-century colonial end game of rendering the social, political and economic centers of the tribal Māori universe extinct will come to pass, marking the end of a more than 3,000-year-old former Pacific-wide marae civilization. Taonga like Pukaki will thereafter lose their performative power that requires marae-activated contexts. Without descendants' ongoing engagement the mana, tapu and korero of taonga risk becoming diminished, severed and redefined, perhaps forever, from any future genealogically framed horizon of kin-associated identity.

Are museums still the answer or is there another way to reach out to the new generation of disconnected Māori? Will museum-held taonga ever be legally set free to again circulate between marae in customary-governed (lore) contexts of belonging, reciprocity and kin-accountability? I still dream of such a future. When I was growing up I thought all museums were like my grandmother's: a place where our most treasured ancestral belongings (taonga) were kept safe – on loan – until such time they might be urgently required by kin communities (marae) to assist amelioration of a life crisis (tangihanga). Over the coming years I came to realize the tribally engaged uniqueness of the Rotorua Museum where I held my first curatorial appointment. It was a time when an Indigenous label to anything but a natural history specimen was foreign, at least to me. Until I went to university in the 1980s even calling myself Māori was foreign. First and foremost I was Ngāti Whakaue, mai Maketu ki Ohinemutu. Notwithstanding spending my teenage years in Wellington and then South Auckland, I used to think Māori was a label applied to those who grew up in cities disconnected from their marae homes. But by 1990 I became more aware of the colonial agenda and how urbanization was a direct result. Fast-forward to 2016 and it is now my generation's grandchildren growing up in an urban era of competing ethnic identities. Being Māori today is not straightforward. Digital interconnectivity via social networking sites (SNS) has transnationalized ideas of being Indigenous beyond state boundaries.

Meanwhile museums' ongoing fixation on "cultural property" vis-à-vis ownership remains all-pervading despite the report findings of WAI 262. Marketing departments have come to dominate the heritage sector output. Within NZ, museums have geared up to capture a share of the fastest-growing industry, tourism. Taonga-related imagery is used widely to leverage our bicultural nation's unique Indigenous point of difference. The sector can argue it has also done much to enter into new spaces of source community engagement and initiated co-production. The Auckland Museum's *Ko Tawa* Project led the way from 2003 to 2008 before it radically shifted focus to a marketing strategy under new directorship. *Ko Tawa* was a traveling "turn-key" exhibition of famous taonga presented to or acquired by Capt. Gilbert Mair, a famous nineteenth-century New Zealander. Three-way sharing of knowledge between curators (Auckland Museum), local kin community (Orakei marae) and source (marae) communities (of the taonga) was the co-production heart of *Ko Tawa*. It toured through regional museums, hosted by numerous marae and was exhibited in Auckland, Wellington and Sydney. Apart from *Ko Tawa*, the fundamental issue of recognizing and accommodating kinship-based value systems of belonging – inherent in museum-held ancestral representations worldwide – still remains the core challenge to modern-day curatorship. Contact zones, source communities, co-curatorship, co-knowledge creation are modern-day terms, indicating general acceptance of "Other" value systems, which can be neither ignored nor dismissed as ossified realms of past traditions. Many of my curatorial colleagues would agree that an exhibitionary praxis of dynamic reciprocity is essential to any twenty-first-century representation of indigeneity in a museum and seek to integrate first voices, First Nations. Done well, exhibitions of *Other* ways of being can illuminate, enlighten and provide new and equally valid, but different, systems of engaging our shared universe of knowledge. Not to take away from my well-meaning colleagues, but until institutional governance shifts from a generally exclusive ethic of financially framed *western* world values and paid convenience of Indigenous consultants, curators will always be challenged by their principal funders, source communities and not least, home kin communities (Tapsell 2011, 2015). Governance within colonial memory institutions not only needs to recognize the cross-generational obligations carried by local (home) kin communities – on whose lands museums stand throughout the colonized world – but also provide governance space for their home kin leaders to assist in the complex engagement of source communities (from where ancestral items, objects or things resting in colonial museums originated) over and above engaging convenient one-stop Indigenous collaborators who are not necessarily mandated by either home or source communities. As explained in previous writings (Ibid.) inclusion of home kin leaders is key to successful source communities' engagement. The NZ exemplar of *Ko Tawa* has not been lost on our international colleagues. The recent Musqueam curated exhibition named "c̓əsnaʔəm: City before the City" was simultaneously exhibited at three Vancouver venues, the Museum of Anthropology, Musqueam First Nation Centre and the Museum of Vancouver, taking the *Ko Tawa* model of co-production to a whole new level of visitor engagement (2015). The National Museum of Australia recently embedded the idea of co-production by intensively engaging home and source communities in a co-curated space, producing its Australian landmark exhibition, *Encounters* (2015). The very act of home elders opening the museum's front door and inviting source communities across the threshold to reengage with their ancestors not only rebuilds respect for the holding institution, but releases new ways of understanding "cultural property" – a three-way praxis of co-production as first practiced when *Ko Tawa* visited Sydney. If museums, however, disregard the kin authority represented by the underlying ancestral landscape (mana *o te* whenua) on which their institutions stand, they are effectively dictating, setting or promoting a political agenda of what they think it means to be Māori/Indigenous within their four walls. This continuing practice, driven by fiscal policies set by museum boardrooms, effectively suggests museums are generally remaining complicit in the ongoing colonization and systemic dismantling of the wider tribal world.

Being pre-Indigenous

New Zealand's colonial history suggests obfuscation of our taonga, representing our once dynamic marae-based value system was no accident. The current generation of young Māori, including those who come to university are today's continuation of a sophisticated and still evolving colonization process. They have been mostly raised in an urban vacuum, drawing on digital media-fueled ideas of Indigenous identity, often believing taonga are property to be owned; their ancestors were naïve, violent and uneducated; and being Māori is about modern Iwi beyond tribal primitivism. Even the most tapu of terms, rangatira (in customary times rangatira was sparingly applied to a visionary leader of her/his kin communities: they were willing to lead by example in service to wider kin, past and present, even if it meant sacrificing one's own life so future generations might survive and hopefully prosper), has been colonized and like the term taonga, is also applied widely today in and beyond Māori/Iwi/Indigenous contexts.

The redefining of taonga – post-*Te Maori* – to fit the Crown's agenda of biculturalism laid the foundation for urban-raised Māori to find a new place to reaffirm their Māori identity in counter-distinction to Pākehā, validating a nation state of a Treaty partnership imagining (Tapsell 1998). The question now is whether the new and emerging urban-raised generation of *Indigenized/Iwified* youth have become irreversibly disconnected from their ancestral marae, taonga and values? Without intervention, they appear to represent the end game of 175 years of deliberate, systematic colonization. They are our Generation "I." In 1987 nationally respected elder Rev. Māori Marsden accused the Crown of being complicit in the ongoing deliberate undermining of marae communities. He prophesized our children will grow up and become *he tuporo teretere – drifting logs* on the tide of humanity. Three decades later, his

Figure 18.5 Headstone unveiling of a rangatira, Reweti, 2007.
Source: Photographer: Krzysztof Pfeiffer.

words appear to be prophetic, not least describing the disproportionate Māori homelessness dominating 2016 media (Mana Magazine 2016). What part can museums yet play to reconnect our grandchildren to their ancestral past being swept away by an ethnic driven wave of Indigenized present?

My previous writings have been built on me being centered on my marae looking across the horizon to the rest of the world. Today our marae descendants live alongside our museum-held taonga in that rest of the world. For them, the novel is also beyond the horizon, but this now includes their own source marae, which for most would be even more foreign, uncomfortable and perplexing than being dropped into the French countryside. The element of embarrassment, anxiety and in some cases outright fear of being found ignorant, a stranger on your own marae, is a major barrier to descendant reconnection. But as the co-produced *Ko Tawa* Project marae fieldtrips proved, such fear is unfounded as home elders are just overjoyed to receive home and embrace their grandchildren from the cities (Tapsell 2015). The depopulation crisis is very real for rural marae communities. They desperately need youth replenishment or else most tribal marae will die in our lifetime – www.māorimaps.com has visually documented at least 100 marae having already succumbed and been abandoned (Tapsell 2014).

As an engaged kin community descendant I view the current Indigenous-framed *Iwification* of Māori as a sophisticated continuation of colonization in New Zealand: deepening disconnection of people (tangata) from their ancestral soil (whenua). Without continuation of marae-prescribed genealogical connection – the performative role of taonga in appropriate marae contexts, like tangihanga (Tapsell 2011) – the source of kin-individuals' ancestry vis-à-vis spiritual well-being (*wairua*) is disrupted. How can we break the spiral of disconnection? The still developing picture of colonization is not pretty, but it is critical we understand it if future

Māori are to find a pathway to success that does not discard the core kin-values of Māori identity, represented by whenua, marae and taonga. These values are core to not only museum-held taonga, but also today's Māori diaspora, both sharing the same urban migration trajectory across their ancestral marae communities' horizons. The values underpinning both ancestral taonga and living descendants are the same – mana, tapu, korero – but only during marae-like rituals of performance do they become truly apparent. Knowledgeable elders are key to unlocking this shared source identity. They are qualified to genealogically link ancestor to resource/estate to living community through dynamic rituals of performance as expressions of whakapapa (Ibid.). But in many marae districts elders who can truly collapse time and bring taonga to life are becoming few and far between. Done correctly, taonga performed on their home marae become the living representation of ancestors (*tupuna*) whose bones (*ko-iwi*) are embedded in the surrounding estates (whenua), sharing their breath (*ha/hau*) with us, the living (tangata), while evoking a deep sense of kin-belonging (whakapapa) as we stand proud in our ancestry (turangawaewae) on our source marae (kainga).

On balance, the *Iwification* of Māori has become all pervading: a convenient delivery mechanism of tribal identity in absentia that does not require the individual to make themselves accountable to their kin or marae. As a name on a beneficiary roll, the individual Māori can access RIO/PSGE benefits and opportunities, validating a globally Indigenized sense of First Nationhood. Thus the 1990s' introduction of Iwi identity, with Te Papa as the ideological promoter, became the novel manifestation of being Indigenous in a New Zealand context beyond kin marae accountability. As *Iwification* takes a deeper hold, will the pre-Indigenous marae-based value system of kin belonging, responsibility, accountability, obligation, duty and service (rangatiratanga) to those passed, living and still to be born (whakapapa) survive? And what role will museum-held taonga play in such a future – reflections of a past era or active leaders in future, three-way co-produced exhibitions? From my "native anthropologist" perspective I provide a glimpse beyond neo-traditionalism (to borrow from McCarthy 2007) by which disciplines like museums, anthropology and art history might access a deeper appreciation of some of the not insignificant internal tensions and challenges being experienced by a once very tribally orientated people. Today's individualistically driven generation of *Indigenized* youth – the *Gen-I* (recently popularized by US President Obama's 2015 launch of Generation Indigenous aimed at young Native Americans) – is emerging from an urban milieu of competing ethnicities on a digitally global scale.

For this generation in NZ, being Indigenous with a capital "I" encompasses their sense of *Iwi-Māori* distinctiveness in much the same way other First Nation peoples have globalized their own identities, using digital media beyond national borders. In the NZ case, ideas of Indigeneity have emerged from urban centers more focused on ethnic (Iwi-Māori) difference with mainstream colonizer (Iwi-Pākehā) settler populations than with source kin communities (hapū/marae) and their customarily prescribed ancestral values (Tapsell 2002). Not unlike my elders' *Kura Tongarerewa* experience in 1993 the marae values of museum-held taonga – *mana, tapu* and *korero* – are today being split apart, redefined, abstracted and/or overwritten by our own urban-raised relations working in and beyond Crown organizations, TLAs, museums and educational institutions. Pre-Indigenous values of marae-framed kin accountability, belonging and service are part of my generation's fading memory. Our grandchildren are now entering a complex world of emerging Gen-I exhibitionary narratives based on individualized Māori success in an urbane, Iwi-framed, post-colonial global market of Indigenization.

In 2005 the last of my Ngāti Whakaue elders who sang *Kura Tongarerewa* passed on to the next world, taking with her all this taonga once represented in her marae-centered universe.

Meanwhile the name Te Papa has successfully embedded itself in NZ consciousness, a reconstructed metaphor, representing today's colonial tide of Iwification.

Takiri ko te ata, kia whakamau au	At the strike of dawn, I prepare myself
Nga uru whetu riki e i, ka rere kopu	The small stars above, disappear into the abyss
Ko taku tau peange i, tenei ka ora mai	Perhaps my loved one will come alive in my dreams
Hoki mai e tama e i, tenei te moenga	Return my son, to your bed
E taku te ahuru e i, ehara taku tau	Where you can rest in peace, my treasured one
I te tau mai e i, he kuru tongarerewa . . .	Was no ordinary person, he was of great value
Naku i ahua e i, i roto i te whare tapu	I moulded him in the womb
E whakatau ana hoki e i, ki te mau o te tao	To become an expert with the spear so it might
Titaha atu range e i, nga titahatanga	Demonstrate his grace and prowess, which he
I raro te waipuna e i, kia whakarewa ia	Practiced in a special place to the highest level
To kiri kai mata e i, to matarau nui	He is a young man, in the prime of his life
Ka moe i te hau na I	But he has been taken by the wrath of Tu
Ka riro hoki range e i, atutahi ma Rehua	By Rehua to the stars of the highest heaven
Wahio ki muri nei e i, tangi kau ko te mapu	I am left behind, weeping from my soul
E kai ana hoki e i, i te ate whainene	As if my heart is being eaten
E waho ana koe e i, hai kotikoti hono	We had hoped you would remain to unite us
Taku whakaruruhau e i	To be everybody's protector
Mo te rarangi mokai e tama e	And to lead us into battle

(Tapsell 1998: 293)

Acknowledgements

First and foremost, I gratefully acknowledge Dr. Merata Kawharu for her invaluable editorial assistance in preparing this chapter – ka nui te mihi! I am also extremely appreciative of assistance provided by the New Zealand Royal Society's Marsden Fund for the projects: "*Transformations of entrepreneurial Māori tribal leadership*"; and "*Te Ao Hou: Transforming worlds in New Zealand 1900–1950.*"

Note

1 I.e. Orakei in Auckland Art Gallery; Te Ati Awa/Ngāti Toa in National Museum, Wellington; Ngai Tahu ki Otautahi in McDougall Art Gallery, Christchurch; and Kai Tahu ki Otakou in Otago Museum, Dunedin.

Bibliography

Auckland War Memorial Museum Amendment Act, 1996. [http://www.legislation.govt.nz/act/local/1996/0004/10.0/DLM83637.html] accessed 26 June 2016.

Ballara, A., 1998. *Iwi: The Dynamics of Māori Tribal Organisation from c.1769 to c.1945.* Wellington. Victoria University Press.
Belgrave, M., M. Kawharu & D. Williams (Eds.), 2005. *Waitangi Revisited: Perspectives on the Treaty of Waitangi.* Melbourne. Oxford University Press.
Burns, P., 1983. *Te Rauparaha: A New Perspective.* Auckland. Penguin Books.
ċesnaʔem: The City Before the City, 2015. Museum of Anthropology at UBC. [www.moa.ubc/portfolio_page/citybeforecity/] accessed 26 June 2016.
Dening, G., 1980. *Islands and Beaches: Discourse on a Silent Land: Marquesas.* Melbourne. Melbourne University Press.
Dibley, B., 1996. Museum, Native, Nation: Museological Narrative and Postcolonial Nation Identity Formation. Unpublished M.A. Thesis – Department of Sociology, University of Auckland.
Gagné, N., 2013. *Māori in the City.* Toronto. University of Toronto Press.
Generation Indigenous, 2014. [http://whitehouse.gov/blog/2015/02/12/white-house-launches-generation-indigenous-native-youth-challenge] accessed 25 June 2016.
Jones, R., 2012. Rongoā – Medicinal Use of Plants – The Impact of Colonisation. In *Te Ara – The Encyclopedia of New Zealand.* [www.TeAra.govt.nz/en/rongoa-medicinal-use-of-plants/page-5] accessed 26 June 2016.
Kawharu, I. H., 1975. *Orakei: A Ngati Whatua Community.* Wellington. New Zealand Council for Educational Research.
Kawharu, I. H., 1977. *Maori Land Tenure.* Oxford. Clarendon Press.
Kawharu, I. H. (Ed.), 1989. *Waitangi: Maori and Pakeha Perspectives of the Treaty of Waitangi.* Auckland. Oxford University Press.
Kawharu, M. (Ed.), 2003. *Whenua: Managing Our Resources.* Auckland. Reed Publishing.
Kawharu, M. 2006. Ko Tawa and the Taumata-a-Iwi. In *Ko Tawa: Māori Ancestors of New Zealand – Gilbert Mair Collection*, pp. 154–181. Auckland. David Bateman.
Kawharu, M. (Ed.), 2014. *Maranga Mai! Te Reo and Marae in Crisis.* Auckland. Auckland University Press.
King, M., 1985. *Being Pakeha Now: Reflections & Recollections of a White Native.* Auckland. Penguin NZ.
McCarthy, C., 2007. *Exhibiting Maori: A History of Colonial Cultures of Display.* Wellington. Te Papa Press.
McCarthy, C., 2011. *Museums and Maori: Heritage Professionals and Indigenous Collection, Current Practice.* Wellington. Te Papa Press.
Mana Magazine. There's No Place Like Home. 127. [www.co.nz/archive/issue-127/housing.html] accessed 25 June 2016.
Mead, S. M. (Ed.), 1984. *Te Maori: Maori Art from New Zealand Collections.* New York. Abrams.
Mead, S. M., 1986. *Magnificent Te Maori: Te Maori Whakahirahira.* Auckland. Heinmann.
Museum of New Zealand/Te Papa Tongarewa Act, 1992. [www.legislation.govt.nz/act/public/1992/0019/latest/dlm260204.html] accessed 26 June 2016.
National Museum of Australia, 2015. *Encounters: Revealing Stories of Aboriginal and Torres Strait Islander Objects from the British Museum.* Canberra. National Museum of Australia Press.
Ngata, A. T., 1943. *The Price of Citizenship: Ngarimu, VC.* Wellington. Whitcombe & Tombs.
O'Regan, G., 1997. *Bicultural Development in Museums of Aotearoa: What Is the Current Status? Ki te Whakamana i te Kaupapa Tikanga-a-rua ki roto i nga Whare Taonga o te Motu: Kei hea e tu ana?* Wellington. Museum of New Zealand Te Papa Tongarewa National Services in partnership with Museum Association of Aotearoa New Zealand Te Ropu Hanga Kaupapa Taonga.
Petrie, H., 2006. *Chiefs of Industry: Maori Tribal Enterprise in Early Colonial New Zealand.* Auckland: Auckland University Press.
Pool, I., 1991. *Te Iwi Maori: A New Zealand Population, Past, Present, and Projected.* Auckland. Auckland University Press.
Rice, G., 2012. Epidemics – The Influenza Era, 1890s to 1920s. In *Te Ara – The Encyclopedia of New Zealand.* [www.TeAra.govt.nz/en/epidemics/page-4] accessed 26 June 2016.
Rosenblatt, D., 2002. Titirangi Is the Mountain: Representing Maori Community in Auckland. Special Issue of *Pacific Studies.* Moddell, J. (Ed.) 25(1/2):117–140. March/June 2002. Hawaii. Brigham Young University.
Runanga Iwi Act, 1990. [www.nzlii.org/nz/legis/hist_act/ria19901990n125155.pdf] accessed 26 June 2016.
Runanga Iwi Act Repeal Act, 1991. [www.legislation.govt.nz/act/public/1991/0034/latest/whole.html] accessed 26 June 2016.

Smith, L. T., 1999. *Decolonising Methodologies: Research and Indigenous Peoples*. Dunedin. University of Otago Press.
Soutar, M., 2008. *Nga Tama Toa: The Price of Citizenship – C Company 28 (Maori) Battalion 1939–1945*. Auckland. David Bateman.
Statistics New Zealand. 2013. 2013 Census. [www.stats.govt.nz/Census] accessed 26 June 2016.
Swarbrick, N., 2014. National Anthems – History of God Defend New Zealand. In *Te Ara – The Encyclopedia of New Zealand*. [www.TeAra.govt.nz/en/nationalanthems/page-2] accessed 26 June 2016.
Tapsell, P., 1995. Pukaki: Te Taonga o Ngati Whakaue ki Rotorua. Unpublished M.A. Thesis, University of Auckland.
Tapsell, P., 1997. The Flight of Pareraututu. *Journal of the Polynesian Society*. December 1997. Vol. 106. No. 4, pp. 323–374.
Tapsell, P., 1998. Taonga: A Tribal Response to Museums. Unpublished Doctorate of Philosophy thesis – Museum Ethnography, Pitt Rivers Museum. Oxford University.
Tapsell, P., 2000. *Pukaki: A Comet Returns*. Auckland. Reed Publishing (NZ).
Tapsell, P., 2002. Marae Identity in Urban Aotearoa New Zealand. In "Moral Communities". Special Issue of *Pacific Studies*. Moddell, J. (Ed.) 25(1/2): 141–171. March/June 2002. Hawaii. Brigham Young University.
Tapsell, P., 2003. Beyond the Frame: An Afterword. In *Museums and Source Communities: A Routledge Reader*, pp. 242–251. L. Peers & A. Brown (Eds.). London. Routledge.
Tapsell, P., 2005. From the Sideline: Tikanga, Treaty Values and Te Papa. In *Waitangi Revisited: Perspectives on the Treaty of Waitangi*, pp. 266–282. Belgrave, M., Kawharu, M. and Williams, D. (Eds.). Melbourne. Oxford University Press.
Tapsell, P., 2006a. The Genesis of the Taumata-a-Iwi, Tamaki Paenga Hira. In *View to the Future*, pp. 8–17. Auckland. Museum Circle, Auckland Museum.
Tapsell, P., 2006b. *Ko Tawa: Māori Ancestors of New Zealand – Gilbert Mair Collection*. Tapsell, P. (Ed.). Auckland. David Bateman.
Tapsell, P., 2011. Aroha Mai: Whose Museum? In *The Routledge Companion to Museum Ethics: Redifining Ethics for the Twenty-First-Century Museum*. Marstine, J. (Ed.). London & New York. Routledge.
Tapsell, P., 2014. Crisis, What Crisis? In *Maranga Mai! Te Reo and Marae in Crisis*, pp. 35–64. Kawharu, M. (Ed.). Auckland. Auckland University Press.
Tapsell, P., 2015. Ko Tawa: Where Are the Glass Cabinets? In *Museum as Process: Translating Local and Global Knowledge*, pp. 262–278. Silverman, R. (Ed.). London & New York. Routledge.
Tapsell, P., 2016. Museums as Cemeteries: Do the Living Really Matter? In *Challenging the Dichotomy: The Licit and the Illicit in Archaeological and Heritage Discourses*, pp.197–218. Field, L., Watkins, J. and Gnecco, C. (Eds.). Tuscon. The University of Arizona Press.
Treaty of Waitangi Amendment Act, 1985.[www.nzlii.org/nz/legis/hist_act/towaa19851985n148306/] accessed 26 June 2016.
United Nations Declaration of Rights of Indigenous Peoples, 2007. 61/295, General Assembly, 13 September. [www.un.org/esa/socdev/unpfii/documents/DRIPS_en.pdf] accessed 26 June 2016.
WAI 262, 1991. Indigenous Flora and Fauna and Cultural Intellectual Property Claim. In *Ko Aotearoa Tenei: A Report into Claims Concerning New Zealand Law and Policy Affecting Maori Culture and Identity* (2011). Wellington. Department of Justice. [https://forms.justice.govt.nz/search/Documents/WT/wt_DOC_68356054/KoAotearoaTeneiTT1W.pdf] accessed 26 June 2016.
Walker, R. J., 1987. *Nga Tau Tohetohe – The Years of Anger*. Auckland. Penguin Books.
Walker, R. J., 1990. *Ka Whawhai Tonu Matou – Struggle Without End*. Auckland. Penguin Books.
Williams, P., 2005. *A Breach on the Beach: Te Papa and the Fraying of Biculturalism*. [www2.le.ac.uk/departments/museumstudies/museumsociety/documents/volumes/williams.pdf] accessed 26 June 2016.
Te Potiki National Trust, est. 2008. Te Potiki National Trust: A Web Based Charitable Organization, Linking Descendant Communities With Tribal Marae. [www.maorimaps.com] accessed 26 June 2016.

19

FRONTIERS OF CULTURAL PROPERTY IN THE GLOBAL SOUTH

Rosemary J. Coombe

Introduction: Political economies and political ecologies of cultural properties

This chapter delineates the features of a distinctive terrain – emerging political economies and political ecologies in which cultural property's futures in the Global South are likely to unfold and aspirations for alternative futures politically articulated in a culturally possessive fashion. The position is advanced by way of a contribution to the anthropological literature on "actually existing neoliberalism" (Clarke, 2008; Collier, 2006, 2012; Ferguson, 2009; Hilgers, 2010, 2012; Gershon, 2011; Goldstein, 2012) as an uneven or variegated field of market-oriented regulatory restructuring (Brenner, Peck & Theodore, 2010), with special emphasis on informational capitalism and new forms of cultural governmentality. These include extensions of trade-based intellectual property (IP), *in situ* means for protecting genetic resources and traditional knowledge (TK), regimes for safeguarding intangible cultural heritage, and new forms of conservation management.

Although the growth and spread of IP, heritage, and biodiversity regimes might be seen primarily as spreading commodified relationships throughout the Global South (e.g. Cutler, 2011; Farhat, 2008; Fernando, 2003), we suggest that attempts to embed allegedly universal market-based exchange relations are met with assertions of local specificities and desires for autonomy in what Polanyi (1944) recognized as the "double movement" of the commodity – and anthropologists have historically understood as the dialectical relationship between property and personhood. Under new forms of neoliberal governmentality, collective attachments to cultural goods are cultivated and communities identified as subjects by diverse legal instruments, transnational agencies, corporate attentions, and global policy norms that focus on local cultural assets as significant goods and capacities. Cultural assets, however, may also figure as political resources under conditions in which occupying the subject position of an indigenous, local, or traditional community is a means to seek transnational support, development aid, recognition, political alliances, and distinctive forms of citizenship. Cultural properties are thus increasingly integral to the assertion of new governmentalities, autonomies, and sovereignties.

This chapter will delineate some of the changing social and institutional conditions under which cultural properties are configured as economic and political resources in struggles that are likely to become more evident in the political economies of informational capitalism. I also show how hybridized natural and cultural landscapes – socionatures – emerge in contemporary political ecologies; the biocultural turn in conservation discourse and practice has encouraged new forms of environmental governmentality that emphasize customary community norms for managing biodiversity and genetic resources in plants, or both, in "cultural landscapes." This has encouraged communities to assert revitalized forms of customary, traditional, or living law in a nascent "ontological" turn in heritage and cultural property management which suggests that legal pluralism may be the new frontier on which property's cultures multiply.

Neoliberal governmentalities and cultural communities

Many critical scholars of global political economy understand neoliberalism not as an ideology, and not as a withdrawal of the state, but as a reconfiguration of the state through processes of uneven regulatory restructuring in which a wide range of actors and authorities now exercise governmental powers over individuals and groups (Braithwaite, 2008; Drahos, 2014; Grabosky, 2013; Himley, 2012) which tends to intensify the "uneven development of regulatory forms across places, territories and scales" (Brenner, Peck & Theodore, 2010: 184). Such "variegated neoliberalism" emphasizes market-based relationships focused on property and contract, as well as new technologies of certification and audit, through which local goods and local governance are rendered legible and "effective governance is measured with reference to asset management ... and the capacity to foster accumulation" (Comaroff, 2011: 45). Neoliberal governmentalities constitute collectivities as responsible community subjects through intervention, auditing, and monitoring (Brenner, Peck, & Theodore, 2010; Coombe, 2011a, 2011b; Creed, 2006; Rose & Miller, 2010) in development projects in which they must make their cultural or "traditional" assets legible for new forms of investment (Bennett, 1998, 2000; e.g. Coffey, 2003; Coombe & Weiss, 2015; Wilson, 2008).

Recent work on heritage management explores a new distribution of governmental powers in which nations, sovereignties, territories, and rights are reconfigured. Rather than a simple abandonment of heritage management to local authorities, we witness a multiplication of authority in new coalitions of agencies, joint partnerships, public–private alliances, and multiscalar assemblages of NGOs, international authorities, and multilateral institutions (Coombe, 2012: 378). An interpenetration of civil society, state, and market forces is increasingly the norm. Exploring heritage governance in the Caribbean, for example, Philip Scher (2011, 2014) shows how the reconfigured neoliberal state operates through dispersed interventions. These include the transnational and decentralized institutional oversight made necessary by the diversification of cultural markets to encourage tourism, foster foreign direct investment, promote product differentiation, and otherwise capitalize upon cultural resources for sustainable development. This involves the use of IP such as geographical indications to mark local cultural goods and new practices of nation and place-branding, in which collective cultural distinctions are resources to be managed in accordance with "best practices" in fields of expertise that may also implement novel forms of social control.

Anthropologists have long recognized that neoliberal government operates via technologies of subjectification (Hilgers, 2010; Ong, 2007) that cultivate new responsibilities and autonomies. The moulding of new subjectivities is crucial to harnessing cultural goods and practices as heritage resources, optimizing agents to maximize their advantages as autonomized entities in a process that instills social agents with possessive attitudes and proprietary rights to engage in extended market relations. Neoliberal government operates not so much by controlling or limiting activities but by relying upon the "empowerment" of capacitated citizens and self-organized communities "capable of bearing a kind of regulated freedom" (Rose & Miller, 2010: 272). Through the use of archives and cultural inventories, TK registers, mappings and countermappings, for example, cultural resources are rendered legible in ways that promise to maximize local autonomy even as they subject communities to new forms of discipline and surveillance.

Neoliberal government is supported by globalizing processes driven by information technologies in which culture is not only drawn into relations of economic exchange but becomes a force of production in its own right (Long & Labadi, 2010). In a political economy of capital accumulation that privileges informational goods, the use of local cultural specificity as a means of capturing monopoly rents has accelerated (Harvey, 2001). Ironically, this is a strategy proffered in response to global capitalist forces that are understood to be culturally homogenizing (Ray, 2003); investments in local cultural resources for endogenous development are perceived to counter resulting "losses" of cultural diversity. Such investments in locality, culture, and tradition may also, paradoxically, afford unique resources and opportunities for political creativity which Harvey marks as "one of the key spaces of hope" (2001: 109).

We have elsewhere explored the centrality of trade-based IP and digital and genetic technologies to new forms of capital accumulation in so-called knowledge economies (Coombe, 2016; Coombe & Turcotte, 2012; Turcotte, 2016), which have extended commodified exchange relations into new zones of life and livelihood. Simultaneously, the imposition of IP has triggered widespread resistance in new social movements that demand recognition for other forms of human inscription, creativity, and innovation. For example, in opposition to the TRIPS Agreement, indigenous women in the Philippines forged farmers' movements to assert their rights to cultivate and save seed, actively resist patents, and exercise plant breeder's rights while forging seed exchange networks they characterized as a form of intercultural dialogue (Wright, 2008a, 2008b). They also rejected public domain and common heritage arguments, describing their agricultural stewardship as a locally significant tradition on which they based rights, not via possession, but through inalienable responsibilities of nurture. Such food security coalitions have scaled up into new social movements that project the need to protect culturally based food sovereignties that exceed the calculus of market economies (for examples, see Counhihan & Siniscalchi, 2014).

Even within international institutions, the propriety of trade-based IP's commodity logic for cultural goods has been challenged in conversations in which anthropologists have been active interlocutors. Take the "safeguarding" of intangible cultural heritage under UNESCO's 2003 Convention. The concept was developed specifically to avoid the use of the word "protection," which had negative connotations resulting from earlier negotiations about how "folklore" could or should be protected as IP. "Cultural heritage" was considered a more appropriate term because of its acceptance by delegates in deliberations on the content of international indigenous rights (Coombe & Turcotte, 2015). Negotiators sought to recognize the dynamism of "traditions" and find "capacitating" mechanisms to maintain their vitality as vehicles for social reproduction (Blake, 2009, 2014). The implementation of the regime inevitably created new forms of government through regulatory intervention, and lent itself to new forms of cultural marketing and merchandizing (Bendix, 2009).

Means of safeguarding were ideally to be designed to respect the values, practices, and norms of local communities in activities such as community management of cultural landscapes (Albert, Richon, Vinals & Witcomb, 2012; Disko, 2012; Kuutma, 2012a, 2012b; Rössler,

2006, 2012) and the use of TK and local cultural institutions to manage threats posed by climate change (Rodriguez-Navarro, 2015; Tano, 2015). The new regime was intended "to hold safe" the attachment of social collectives to practices, forms, and expressions significant to them and to maintain the social bonds that constitute this significance. Despite the considerable controversy these requirements have provoked, the principle of community participation is now operative in all areas of UNESCO activity (De Cesari, 2012). Given that communities have no natural boundaries and, in many jurisdictions, no juridical stature, we might anticipate that such norms will invite instrumental behaviour, be challenged by states (Meskell, 2013) and entrenched elites (Brumann, 2015) – or captured to buttress their own powers (Hertz, 2015), demand unwarranted social sacrifice (Meskell, 2009), and/or put excessive pressure on under-resourced residents (Lafrenz-Samuels, 2010). They may also enjoin more ethical orientations in new forms of public–private partnership (Di Giovane, 2015), provide points of political leverage for community claims (e.g. Leblon, 2012; Lydon, 2009), and platforms to assert cultural rights (Coombe & Weiss, 2015).

Community relations to heritage governance are not, however, limited to UNESCO auspices; it is more appropriate to think about "assemblages of different patrimonial paradigms . . . creative contact zones between different heritage logics that compete against one another or that are combined in synergistic ways" (Tauschek, 2012: 196). The newly "responsibilized" community that stewards local cultural resources is a global subject position with diverse policy provenance; communities are intervened in through a number of regulatory regimes. Global environmental norms of preserving and maintaining TK, international IP policies for the protection of traditional cultural expressions (TCEs), and NGO promotion of cultural industries to further sustainable development all confront "communities" with diverse, overlapping demands and incentives to register, map, create inventories of, and devise new plans for the valuation of their cultural resources (Forsyth, 2012: 1).

Heritage as a resource is mobilized through the energies of states and corporations, NGOs and regional associations, UN bodies and civil society movements, all of which have particular interests in empowering communities as entrepreneurs, owners, stewards, custodians, or guardians of scarce and endangered forms of knowledge, difference, and distinction. While governmental practices may attempt to identify and attach groups to the kinds of heritage most easily managed as commodifiable resources, they do not necessarily succeed. It is "important to look not just at the forms of collective and individual identity promoted by practices of government, but also at how particular agents negotiate these forms – at how they embrace, adapt, or refuse them" (Inda, 2005: 11) and the "forms of political possibility" that neoliberalism's freedoms and autonomies afford (Ferguson, 2009). Elsewhere (Coombe, 2016; Coombe & Weiss, 2015), we have suggested that the "congenitally failing" quality of neoliberal government also marks the point of entry for imaginative assertions of propriety – proprietary rights framed in terms of community values, well-being, *bien vivr* ("good life"), or *Sumak Kawsay* ("living well"), to name but a few local articulations. The forms of autonomy people assert may not necessarily accord with those that authorities demand, and authorities may sometimes reshape practices to better align with the politics of the governed.

Property and personhood at the intersection of globalization and autonomy

Political economists understand the globalization of international law as privileging the commodity form in governance regimes dominated by a limited form of exclusive property rights serving market interests in a "new constitutionalism" (Cutler, 2011; Cutler & Gill,

2015). The TRIPS Agreement (and bilateral successor regimes) is seen as a central pillar in this architecture, with IP being a form of enclosure that encourages proprietary conceptions of sovereignty, identity, and autonomy (Cutler, 2011: 29). So-called minimum standards for IP "purport to create an equal playing field for all" (49), but operate as hard law sanctions enabling dispossession of intangible goods and protecting private regimes of accumulation. Meanwhile, soft law, which entails more diverse parties articulating different norms and values, proliferates in the margins (Anderson, 2012). From this perspective, IP is one of the most powerful forces disembedding elements of human lifeworlds from social and ecological contexts.

The anthropological study of IP has added considerable nuance to this position, prompting a revitalization of the anthropology of property that has focused on the conditions under which culture becomes proprietary and properties become cultural. IP protects the intangible dimensions of significant forms through material means of enforcement in market economies. Symbolic or signifying media are inscribed in material forms that are publicly accessible, if not freely available, cultural goods around which capital interests, public affect, social identification, group identities, and material needs cathect (Coombe, 1998).

Early anthropological inquiry was preoccupied with liberal distinctions between public and private goods and concomitant distinctions between a commons and its commodification, emphasizing how IP restricted cultural expression, the flow of genetic resources, and access to necessary goods (e.g. Brown, 1998; Brush, 1998; Handler, 1991; Napier, 1994). Later work complicated these simple distinctions, and critically explored their history and political consequence in colonial and postcolonial contexts (Bowrey & Anderson, 2009; Sunder & Chander, 2004). The expansion of IP to new subject matter and new areas of the world along with proliferating forms and norms of heritage have revitalized anthropological interest in the interrelationships between property, personhood, and propriety (e.g. Brown, 2010; Comaroff & Comaroff, 2009; Coombe, 2009; Hirsch, 2010; Humphrey & Verderey, 2004; Meurer & Perry, 2003; Strathern, 2001; Strathern & Hirsch, 2004).

> Attempts to spread capitalist market relationships into new geographical, cultural, and informational fields inevitably encounter resistance because they intervene in existing social relations that shape the way these new commodity relations are interpreted, reconfigured or refused … The result is not uniformity but rather a proliferation of institutional, discursive, cultural and material "frontiers" in the power-laden crucible of making and remaking property relations. And in this remaking, universals are actively reshaped, taking particular hybrid forms . . . as the grip of the universal meets the ways of being, knowing and living in a particular place.
>
> *(Prudham & Coleman, 2011: 12)*

Indeed, property refers to a set of social relationships between people that allocate rights and responsibilities. Capitalist market economies continue to spread, but property is not and has never exclusively entailed absolute rights or monopolies of use. Rather, property is relational, specific, bounded, and limited. Identities are often attached to fields of obligation and entitlement, and the introduction of new forms of commodification often undermines such attachments. People may resist such disruptions by reviving and politicizing old patterns of economic relationship, informal rights and norms, and moral economies (expressed as "traditional" or "customary") in what Polanyi (1944) describes as the commodity's "double movement." This process may be intensified when formal property rights are extended to include TK, traditional cultural expressions (TCEs), or forms of intangible heritage designated as especially important to group identity. These are significant sites for struggle, knowledge mobilization, and identity formation since they are "more than rights to assets: they are constitutive of the production of subjectivities – individual and collective – among rights holders" (Prudham & Coleman, 2011: 14). New forms of property emerge at the nexus of capitalist globalization and struggles for autonomy.

Legal anthropologists have long considered issues of property and personhood to be dialectically related (Meurer & Schwab, 2006; Napier, 2002; Strathern, 1999, 2001); the forms of subjectivity that IP imagines, constructs, and projects into social worlds have been a fruitful area of inquiry. The early anthropological study of IP turned to those whose creative activities were not historically covered by IP, did not conceive of their lifeworlds and livelihood resources within Western proprietary terms, encountered and appropriated forms of cultural governance alien to them, consciously resisted or refused these legal mandates, or learned to interpret IP "otherwise" (e.g. see overview in Coombe, 2018; Geismar, 2013). Anthropological preoccupations with the lack of propriety in using IP rights to "protect" the intangible cultural resources of others (e.g. Brush, 1998; Brush & Stabinsky, 1996; Dove, 1996) soon evolved into a broader inquiry into the ethics of cultural appropriation and cultural research in an era in which community relationships to knowledge were subjects of both IP and human rights deliberation (Coombe, 2009).

The extension of the commodity form to more intangible cultural goods was also resisted; social counter-movements emerged at the turn of the century to insist that IP should not be governed entirely by market-based economic considerations (Halbert, 2005). Developing country governments, other UN bodies, and NGOs put new pressure on the World Intellectual Property Organization (WIPO) to forge IP norms and practices that fulfilled a wider range of human rights and development objectives more relevant to the communities whose collective creative work had been outside its purview. WIPO addressed the need to protect TK and ensure "access and benefit sharing" under the Convention on Biodiversity (CBD), while reaching out to "new beneficiaries" to consider their customary means of managing knowledge-based resources in complementary strategies of cultural governmentality. Most early WIPO efforts seemed dedicated to ensuring that CBD objectives were operationalized in contractual terms that privileged market-based exchanges between corporations, state institutions, and communities, but the organization also became more transnational, sending out regional "fact-finding missions" in 1999 to ascertain the needs and values of collective holders of TK assets. Founded in 2000, the Intergovernmental Committee on Intellectual Property, Genetic Resources, Traditional Knowledge and Traditional Cultural Expressions (IGC) began to actively engage communities as holders of IP in TK, as well as TCEs (formerly the domain of UNESCO under the rubric of folklore). WIPO's new programs served to build "capacity" or "empower" local communities, while creating new non-state markets for WIPO expertise. A new institutional logic of "governing from a distance" becomes apparent.

The IGC was accused of encouraging "tribal entrepreneurialism" amongst "premoderns" forced to assert rights to genetic resources and TK within "the framework of privatized and alienable assets" (Farhat, 2008: 216). Certainly the interpellation of collective entrepreneurial subjects is one aspect of IGC efforts, but it also acknowledges the specificity of sacred forms of knowledge, outlines non-proprietary means through which cultural rights may be protected, stresses the need for free, prior, and informed consent (FPIC) with respect to the use of indigenous TK and genetic resources in contested ancestral territories, advises against the freezing of dynamic traditions, and increasingly recognizes customary laws as potential *sui generis* regimes for protection to be made legible to external actors by way of new databases,

TK Labels, and digital libraries. In so doing, it acknowledges that issues of cultural property are imbricated in regulatory restructurings in which development, conservation, heritage concepts, and community identities are being mutually reconfigured. It also indexes the human rights context in which WIPO, as a UN organization, must legitimate its activities. Indigenous Peoples have long intervened in these deliberations, moreover, in attempts to make commodity considerations subservient to the realization of indigenous rights of self-determination.

Emerging fields of IP involving genetic resources, TK, and TCE have fostered the articulation of new forms of collective identity, conflict, and contestation. Many of the earliest anthropological studies addressed how these new policy objectives were implemented, adopting a simple social constructionism in which "communities" were shown to be the romanticized projections of outside groups, instrumentally forged for gain, impossible fictions, or vested with "invented" traditions by foreign NGOs which thereby created new forms of local inequality based on spurious cultural grounds (e.g. Li, 2000). Cory Hayden's (2003a, 2003b) work on Mexican bioprospecting and Shane Green's allegations about the "incorporation" of "the Aguaruna" people in the Peruvian Amazon by virtue of the recognition of their TK of local plant resources (Green, 2004) were widely cited examples. The latter narrative addressed shifting indigenous identities, the need to organize on ever-higher scales of legibility to negotiate with transnational actors, and the international alliances that resulted in the world's first indigenous "know-how agreement," providing shared benefits in the form of royalties from resulting patents. The process clearly necessitated new forms of community definition, incorporation, and deliberation, resulting in great hopes, dashed expectations, and ultimately, division and disillusionment. Critics read it as a great tragicomedy that, unsurprisingly, illustrated the constructed nature of cultural identity and the artefactuality of both tradition and community.

In later work Green (2009) provides a more empathetic reflection on the painful process of entrepreneurial ethnogenesis in the region that few of bioprospecting's early anthropological critics seem to consider. He investigated how Aguaruna leaders "customized" the indigenous and environmentalist subject positions offered to them through their rights-based political work in the region. Avoiding the simple readings of collective self-essentialism and corporate victimization to which his earlier work lent itself, he explored how new forms of inclusive citizenship and transnational solidarities were forged in these endeavors. Revitalizations of traditional institutions (such as the *ipaamamu*) helped leaders create greater economic and political security for regional groups in neoliberal governmental activities of biodiversity conservation through which they decided which market values to accept, how, and to what ends.

Many anthropologists rejected the new emphasis upon "tradition" and "community" in the areas and subject matter to which rights might extend to "new beneficiaries" (traditional agriculture and handicrafts, traditional environmental knowledge (TEK), traditional medicine, etc.) as constructed and reified, romanticized, and rhetorically exaggerated (Agrawal, 1995; Agrawal & Gibson, 1999; Gupta, 1998; Li, 2002). Others countered that critics' apolitical positioning failed to consider the aspirations of people dependent upon subsistence resources in the Global South and the transnational political economies and political ecologies in which they were inevitably immersed (Affif & Lowe, 2007; Briggs, 1996; Brosius, Tsing & Zerner, 1998, 2005; Tsing, 1999, 2003, 2005). Later work explored the processes and practices of translation by which "traditions" came to be articulated for modern science, commerce, and other fields of knowledge and power (de la Cadena, 2004; Dove, 2007; Fish, 2006; Gatmaytan, 2003; Nadasdy, 2005, 2007; Reddy, 2006; West, 2005) as people made their communities, identities, and assets legible to new authorities, new auditors, new investors, and new political allies.

Indigenous Peoples figure prominently in anthropological debates about the propriety of extending property rights on cultural grounds and anxieties about culturally possessive claims (e.g. Brown, 1998, 2003, 2005). They were historically compelled to assert rights claims on cultural grounds in international fora structured by the hegemony of modern nation state polities and liberal political principles. As non-state parties who did not understand themselves as minorities – and whose very claims were based on refusing the stigmatized status that made their assimilation a modern state priority – they could claim the protection of international human rights laws only through the cultural rights provisions of the Covenant on Civil and Political Rights (Cutler, 2011: 41). Although such protections historically applied only to individuals, indigenous leaders were allowed to submit early cases against state violations of obligations to protect minority cultural rights on behalf of larger collectives. Deprived of the capacity to assert self-determination in "national" terms, claims to autonomy were increasingly framed as rights to protect ways of life rooted in cultural attachments to territory (Gibbs, 2005). These were eventually recognized as the first human rights held by collectives.

New forms of collective cultural property are increasingly based on cultural rights principles, grounded in the larger field of human rights (Shaheed, 2011) which compel peoples to represent their traditions within liberal political frameworks – engendering diverse projects of traditional revitalization (Clifford, 2013; Hirtz, 2003). These projects must inevitably be locally interpreted; they must be rendered "in the vernacular" (Levett & Merry, 2009; Merry, 2009; Preis, 2009). The culture thereby discerned is thus never "traditional" in a primordial sense, but an articulation of how people interpret their histories and desired futures in contexts in which they encounter new values. As Anna Tsing recounts, people in Kalimantan had to engage with the concept of gender equity when they started considering themselves as indigenous or customary communities (2005). Similar patterns of articulation have been explored at the conjuncture of neoliberal government, liberal equality norms, and indigenous identifications in southern Mexico (Altamirano-Jimenez, 2013; Hernandez-Castillo, 2002; Speed, 2007; Speed, Hernandez-Castillo & Stephen, 2006; Speed et al., 2009).

The longstanding need to articulate indigenous rights within the prism of cultural rights may have been designed to depoliticize the former, but it has succeeded in politicizing the latter, particularly as the concept of heritage has been operationalized across UN organizations in a rights-based, rather than an exclusively proprietary framework. Indigenous Peoples and their rights, however, are not recognized exclusively by state legislatures or international Conventions, but in transnational networks that involve multilateral institutions, development banks, environmental and development NGOs, corporate social responsibility platforms, and new social movements (Coombe, Malik & Griebel, forthcoming). The anthropological and aesthetic understandings of culture that oriented international law (Holder, 2008) enabled some Indigenous Peoples to protect rights of access to ancestral lands and resources, but did not adequately accommodate issues of environmental sustainability, communal provisioning, or meaningful forms of governance significant to indigenous aspirations for autonomy (Corntassel, 2008). Indigenous Peoples' movements adopted the culturalized principle of "development with identity" to combine claims for the protection of land-based livelihoods with development projects congruent with local values (Tauli-Corpuz, 2008).

Environmental conservation and the "biocultural turn" in heritage management

Environmental politics increasingly provide the values, rhetorical vehicles, and practices through which cultural goods are identified and embraced. In rights-based conservation and development practice, biological and cultural diversity have been so continuously interwoven over the past 25 years that the hybridized "biocultural diversity" is now a common noun and a new norm (Coombe, 2016). The biocultural turn in environmental and development policy discourses since the 1990s reflects a growth in concern with sustaining livelihood resources, respecting minority identities, and facilitating the participatory rights of local residents in conservation management – often in opposition to national interests in economic modernization or globally uniform models for nature conservation (Buergin, 2015: 2028).

Efforts to value, protect, or safeguard TK have taken place in diverse fora but their early evolution in a culturalized indigenous rights framework continues to be referenced in the rhetoric of UN bodies and new social movements alongside the political principles of free, prior, and informed consent (FPIC), and, increasingly, community protocols that prioritize indigenous self-determination. Even in regions where indigeneity is politically contested as a relevant form of identification, local communities are engaged as potential partners in protecting forests, mitigating climate change, and providing environmental services. Environmental NGOs consider such *in situ* approaches as superior to IP for "protecting" TK while securing sustainable livelihoods in more "resilient" cultural landscapes (Ruiz-Mallen & Corbera, 2013). Community-conserved area management principles, codes of conduct for research, culturally appropriate forms of biodiversity and knowledge documentation, criteria for environmental and cultural impact assessments, *sui generis* regimes drawing upon customary law, and women's capacity-building describe some emerging cultural proprieties.

When taking possession of such projects, many peoples assert not their rights, but their historical obligations to steward biocultural heritage. Natural Justice, for example, is an NGO that now evokes the "right to responsibility" as empowering communities to use TEK to maintain and develop resilient landscapes and sustainable livelihoods (Jonas & Jonas, 2013). The responsibilities that communities assert may be rather different than the responsibilizations that regulatory restructurings impose. Local socioecological actions, events, and identifications are not merely derivative of extra-local economic and political structurations (West, 2005: 233), but activities in which legal discourse, regulatory technologies, and rights norms are taken up in new political articulations that combine normative rhetorical resources from indigenous, environmental, conservation, heritage, and human rights regimes in culturalized management and enterprise (Pretty et al., 2009). Culturalized claims articulated in possessive relationships to traditions have long surpassed the early models provided by trade-related IP and bioprospecting contracts under neoliberal government and informational capital. Those simple proprietary models are often rejected in favor of more flexible assemblages or "regulatory toolkits" to achieve multiple objectives (Forsyth, 2013; Forsyth & Farran, 2015). People encounter concepts of IP, TEK, biodiversity, and heritage through global investments, development projects, new social movements, NGO attentions, environmental lawyers, and engaged anthropologists and thereby find new ways to position themselves in global policy articulations.

Latin America was host to some of the earliest biodiversity projects, particularly in "megabiodiverse" Colombia. In the early 1990s, grassroots preparation for negotiations of global environmental governance under the CBD coincided with constitutional recognition of the country's multiethnic character. Critical ethnographic studies (Asher, 2009; Asher & Ojeda, 2009; Escobar, 1998; 2008; Ulloa, 2005; Wilshusen, 2006) illustrate how early biodiversity government gave rise to place-based movements in Latin America popularizing rights-based rhetorical frames for expressing identities through cultural attachments to territories. These expressly rejected Western IP models that separated knowledge from nature and failed to recognize biodiversity as itself a vernacular technology (e.g. Hurtado, 1999).

Neoliberalization produces new socionatures at the conjuncture of policy landscapes, multiscalar regulatory restructuring, and local political dynamics. Markets and market proxies are used as tools for environmental governance, including biotechnological innovation, patent expansion, and certifications of origin in extended commodity chains (Coombe, 2016; Coombe, Ives & Huizenga, 2014). Anthropologists report possessive attachments to and heightened reflexivity about biocultural knowledge throughout Latin America, where rural peoples are familiar with biodiversity as a global asset, global valorizations of ethnobotanical knowledge, and corporate holdings of IP in bioengineered seeds derived from traditional landraces (Fitting, 2011; Rhoades, 2013). In both Amazonian and Andean regions the bio-diverse properties of ecosystems came to be understood locally as heritage goods in territories toward which new ethics of care and affective connection were expressed (Yates & Bakker, 2013) in movements which stressed alternative ontologies or traditional cosmologies as the grounds for new rights (de la Cadena, 2010; Tsing, 2009). From 2000 to 2005, Robert Rhoades directed an ethnographic research project in which anthropologists and other specialists worked with Quechua-speaking communities in the Cotacachi Canton, Ecuador, to understand their territories, agricultural practices, resources, and TK (Rhoades, 2006). In the process, Indigenous Peoples began to consider these as aspects of cultural heritage they should recover and repatriate. Other nearby biodiversity projects used ethnicity as a marketing tool to promote cultural tourism to ethnic gardens and eco-hostels. For Rhoades (2013), such projects were suspect – not, it seems, because they marketed cultural properties, but because they did not give priority to local needs, values, and interests.

There is a longer history and a transnational context in which these activities should be positioned. Neoliberal investments in indigenous social capital in the region go back to the early 1990s and World Bank financing of Prodepine in Ecuador (which deposited Bank funds directly to an institution run by indigenous organizations). Such attentions involved extensive practices of community-based governmentality – tenure regularization, cultural mappings of significant resources, identifications of traditional goods, and the marking of these as typical products – coupled with capacity building (training in ethnography, participatory planning, and project management). Such early "ethnodevelopment" projects were considered depoliticizing because they focused on cultural assets to be developed by entrepreneurial subjects and failed to address structural racism or acknowledge indigenous agency (Andolina, Radcliffe & Laurie, 2005). Such criticism gave way to a closer exploration of how communities adopted these subject positions to assert more concrete forms of autonomy (Andolina, Radcliffe & Laurie, 2009), which corresponded with the articulation of "development with identity" (Rhoades, 2006) as a substantive form of collective self-determination globally endorsed by the UN Permanent Forum on Indigenous Issues in 2010 (Sena, 2010).

Anthropologists are divided in their assessments of Latin American ethnic marketing and cultural rights assertions. Some consider these primarily as by-products of neoliberal governmentality under the generic term "neoliberal multiculturalism" (e.g. Colloredo-Mansfeld, 1998; De Hart, 2010; Hale, 2002, 2004; Wilson, 2008). Others claim that neoliberalism has been "interrupted" since the turn of the century (Goodale & Postero, 2013) via "post-multicultural" projects committed to decolonizing agendas, resulting in "postdevelopment" or even a nascent "postneoliberalism" (Escobar, 2010; Gustafson & Fabricant, 2011; Natera, 2013; Postero, 2007; Ramirez, 2011). Geographers Yates and Bakker (2013) view Latin American postneoliberalism as encompassing a diverse set of political projects that attempt to reorient the market economy towards social needs in a political ethics of local participation. This involves cultural self-determination at a variety of scales, often revitalizing "traditional" political norms and institutions, such as the *ayllu* in land reform, traditional models of communal labor and provisioning in economics, pluricultural relationships in national constitutions, intercultural communication in citizenship, and new knowledge networks for community governance. Anthropologists working in Peru, Bolivia, Colombia, and Ecuador argue that the pluricultural imaginaries now projected in the region are creative articulations that do not wholly align with neoliberal cultural governmentalities (Erazo, 2010, 2013; Gustafson & Fabricant, 2011; Postero, 2007; Rappaport, 2005).

When, with transnational support and international funding, indigenous leaders in Latin America made the revitalization of cultural identity the centerpiece of development efforts in the 2000s, the loss of traditional crops and TEK become a rationale both for attracting investments and claiming territorial rights. Villagers in Cotacachi, Ecuador worked with anthropologists to document and preserve knowledge of plants, establish community seed farms and cultivate biodiversity gardens "symbolic of the recovery of our traditions" (Fueres, Flores & Ramos, 2013: 111) in weekly *mingas* (communal labor parties). Communities share their cosmovisions and socionatural lives in *Pachamama* ("Mother Earth," recently given national constitutional stature) through the Farm of the Ancestral Future and the new tourism certification "Runa Tupari" ("meet indigenous people" in Quechua). Anthropologist Virginia Nazarea found that there was no local linguistic term for "nature" or "conservation," but community members easily expressed affective attachments to plant genetic resources as cultural traditions. The relationships of equality and anti-paternalism that researchers wanted to forge with the community, the community considered as ethically relevant to their relationships with plants. Nurturing biodiversity assumed literal terms as an "expanding web of emotional attachment to the land, to rural places, mindful lifestyles, and wholesome food" (Nazarea, 2013: x).

In situ conservation techniques are increasingly understood by those seeking to steward them in the Andes as a form of cultural repatriation – from modern institutions such as genetic resource banks where these are treated as inert resources to living local landscapes where they will continue to reciprocally evolve with peoples and their traditional institutions (Graddy, 2013). "Development with identity" includes place-based techniques for agrobiodiversity conservation and Indigenous Peoples have incorporated these into their agendas for self-determination and food sovereignty, leveraging global environmental policy norms to protect, maintain, and encourage indigenous agricultural knowledge systems. Aymara scholar Tirso Gonzales (2013) argues that indigenous socionatures are founded on language, territory, spirituality, and worldview. If for some anthropologists this must be considered an "essentialist" claim based upon "romantic" notions, its proponents view it as based upon scientifically validated evidence of internationally affirmed correlations between language, distinctive worldviews, and biodiversity (a process summarized in Coombe, 2016).

Biodiversity and TEK now assemble universities, international agencies, NGOs, scientists, biotechnology researchers, and corporations in new social movements with indigenous, *campesino*, or other "local" communities. The latter have come to nominate their knowledge of plant properties as cultural heritage, grounds of identity, a rationale for territorial defense, and the justification for new autonomies. Stewardship of local biocultural diversity, therefore, might be considered a "not-quite-neoliberal" subject position (Anthias & Radcliffe, 2013) embraced as a space of opportunity and responsibility. Cultural diversity and community distinctions are expressed through biological diversity and practices for its care. Municipal food fairs feature the "food of our ancestors" and seed exchanges are ritually celebrated as means to increase socio-ecological resilience. In Bolivia, traditional landraces animate festive ritual exchanges between communities and their cultural preservation informs climate change justice movements, food security policy, agricultural education, and crop research priorities (Zimmerer, 2013).

Chris Shepherd's ethnographic study of community sustainability efforts in three regions of the Peruvian Andes (2010) shows how identifying and locating *in situ* biodiversity conservation measures put a new face on Andean culture. These activities made TEK more visible and indigenous communities more legible for investments in their development and their own participatory government. Coincident with the emergence of thousands of Latin American NGOs in the 1980s, a pro-Andean movement focused on the *campesino* and later the indigenous community as an autonomous expression and agent of Andean cultural revival. Coalitions of middle class urban dissenters, indigenous intellectuals, scientists, anthropologists, and local universities mobilized around bilingual education, health, and agriculture to integrate TK, indigenous technologies, and languages into more autonomous development projects. Thousands of Andean technologies were documented as forms of viable TK for conservation purposes.

In the 1990s, the movement became more overtly culturalized, linking agroecology to revitalized Andean cosmologies, to assert that Andean peoples held *in situ* practices and resources not only relevant, but crucial to the conservation of global biodiversity (Brush, 2000; Gonzales, 2000). These movements took advantage of CBD and WIPO policies in globally recognized hotspots of agrobiodiversity (in tubers, maize, and quinoa), and garnered the support of anthropologists, ethnobotanists, local NGOs, and development funding agencies. Alongside regional social movements, scientists and activists cultivated opportunities with and for resident *campesino* communities to revive and capitalize upon their own TK. Such *in situ* conservation programs revitalized pride in an Andean identity – long denigrated under modern agricultural paradigms as the economic, intellectual, and moral basis for rural poverty.

> However, this local knowledge-practice was not "just there." Actors framed it according to what many anthropologists would now recognize as "cultural essentialism" – that is to specify and restrict the qualities, knowledges, and practices that are claimed to belong to a particular "culture." This essentialism was not wrong. Rather it was selective. The particular modus of "cultural selection" was, however, consistent with the conditions for the success of agrobiodiversity as it was still cultivated by many campesinos in the fields. The principal marker of cultural authenticity was, for these actors, ritualized agrocentric life, the existence of particular forms of community organization (based on traditional authorities), and innumerable farming practices that were construed as revolving around and nurturing the chacra and its all-animate contents. . . .
>
> *(Shepherd, 2010: 634–635).*

Many *campesinos* were ambivalent and had to be convinced to revive long neglected social relations based on the *ayllu*, the collective spirit of communal work, ritualized seed exchange and systems of traditional authority. Few abandoned modern forms of agriculture entirely. Andean social movement actors worked to instill solidarity with an Andean regional cultural identity, while situating these practices within cosmologies that expressed ideal human and nonhuman relations and ultimately, they learned to argue, made a larger contribution to a global humanity that needed Andean agrobiodiversity to redress the problems facing modern forms of agriculture.

In areas where the Green Revolution had made few inroads, villages long characterized as sites of abject poverty were now privileged sites for investment. This was precisely because crop diversity and TK was more recently integral to community survival. Some elderly residents, working precariously in seasonal wage employment, still remembered the hundreds of native varieties of potato, corn, and other crops that grew in the *chacras* where they received their primary education. Many of them were willing to fuse these old memories with new project goals when *in situ* projects were operationalized after 2000. In some areas, over seven years, "agrobiodiversity had increased tenfold in potato, sixfold in maize, and substantially in the other seven crops that the project targeted" (Shepherd, 2010: 638). Such biodiversity cultivation efforts were also harnessed in community park management, tourist services, and product development, providing new sources of employment for Andean peoples (Coombe & Griebel, 2014; Coombe & Weiss, 2015).

Proponents of these activities describe them as an "agroecological revolution" actively blending advances in agroecological science with indigenous knowledge systems to enhance food security, conserve natural resources, empower peasant organizations, and bring new benefits to small farmers (e.g. Altieri & Toledo, 2011). They do so through energy-efficient, biodiverse, resilient, and sustainable agricultural systems in a transition away from fossil fuel and monocultural, chemically based, export-oriented production. Agroecology is now incorporated into the vision of *La Via Campesina*, a transnational agrarian movement that works in synergy with organized Indigenous Peoples.

It is beyond the scope of this chapter to survey the numerous scientific arguments offered in favor of such approaches to global conservation, food sovereignty, and rural security in the face of climate change and acknowledgments of the anthropocene. Nor do I have the capacity to evaluate claims that "traditional agroecosystems have the potential to bring solutions to many uncertainties facing humanity in a peak oil era of global climate change and financial crisis" (Altieri & Toledo, 2011: 591). I would, however, caution against seeing such efforts in purely local terms. Such agroecological movements forge relationships of reciprocity and communication between farming communities across transnationally linked social movements, in which TK and TK innovations scale up for widespread distribution and adaptation to new contexts – even when they are grounded in traditional cosmovisions. It is probably stretching the concept too far to regard these as cultural properties. Nonetheless, other autonomies and ontologies articulated in culturally possessive terms are clearly emergent in such practices and ideals.

Like proponents of Andean culture, Amazonian indigenous movements have more successfully projected conceptions of territory, TK, and biodiversity within a broader cultural rights framework (Vadjunec, Schmink & Greiner, 2011). Ancestral histories are woven into forests which are sources for traditional medicines and their integration into health care systems, protection of TK attracts support for bilingual education, and management of archaeological sites may provide sustainable employment positions from which to steward cultural landscapes (Caruso, 2014; Cepek, 2011a, 2011b, 2012; Hutchins & Wilson, 2010). Here too, community-based cultural enterprises that might have originated in neoliberal governmentalities have been adopted, adapted, or appropriated for other ends.

Since the early 1990s, community-based cultural development projects initiated by international and Quito-based NGOs in Napo Province, Ecuador, have enabled indigenous leaders to shape people into a new and distinctive citizenry (Erazo 2010: 1032). Although international NGOs sought to provide new forms of income generation less environmentally destructive than cattle ranching or the cultivation of local cash crops, Kichwa leaders have encouraged these local cultural industries (e.g. agricultural cooperatives, ecocultural tourism, and traditional ceramics) as collective projects to assert traditional indigenous cosmologies and emergent political identities.

People in this region historically lived in extended networks of biological and ritual kin-groups rather than in bounded communities, but their leaders reinterpreted their histories to make new futures possible. Communities, anthropologist Julia Erazo argues, were forms of social organization strategically structured in the latter half of the twentieth century to defend lands, resources and ways of life from colonial aggression; they have become the social basis for indigenous national participation. Communal market-based enterprises do not have a history of sustained viability, but indigenous optimism about them may not be primarily focused on profit. Ethnographically observing such projects in the Ecuadorian Amazon over fifteen years, Erazo became convinced that such cultural industries served political rather than economic objectives. Even in the absence of NGO support, leaders continued to promote these collective activities because they shaped indigenous citizens, "actively engaged with the larger community rather than simply their patrilineal kinship groups" (Erazo, 2010: 1020), providing the social empowerment necessary for long-term land use planning and livelihood strategies.

Greater autonomy for ethnic minorities in Latin America is a political project of government in which peoples actively constitute themselves as culturally distinct groups that express "not an unchanging cultural essence, but a utopian project rooted in their reflections on indigenous culture" (Erazo, 2010: 1022) which are transmitted to other Indigenous People recognized as having their own cultural properties in new forms of pluricultural citizenship (for example, Erazo, 2013; Escobar, 2008; Gow, 2008; Osco, 2010; Natera, 2013; Rappaport, 2005; Shepherd, 2015; Walsh, 2010; Yates, 2014). Indigenous rights organizations have become indigenous governing organizations that inculcate greater public engagement. From obtaining bilingual secondary schools to campaigns against oil drilling, co-operatives, peasants' unions, and collectives of various kinds have used community cultural enterprise to achieve political objectives. Cultural governmentality, in short, takes place on diverse scales, by diverse agents, for diverse ends.

Protecting possessive attachments: Legal pluralism and new ontologies of property

Meaningful challenges to neoliberalism are emerging in a fashion that rhetorically combines resources from cultural, environmental, and collective rights traditions to "agitate for fundamental ruptures with the symbolic organization of colonial modernity" (Goodale & Postero, 2013; Natera, 2013: 254). For those who consider the modern predominantly to be a colonial power matrix, the category of the "cultural" as it is evolving in rights-based discourses (Appadurai, 2013; Rajagopal, 2003) offers affordances other than those provided by neoliberal governmentalities under conditions of informational capitalism. Cosmologies increasingly ground and shape rights claims (for example, Osco, 2010; Tsing, 2009). Certainly, the "modern constitution" (Latour, 1993, 2004) – in which culture was conceived either as national state patrimony or a limited basis for state recognition of minorities – has been fundamentally disrupted by others seeking to stake alternative claims and responsibilities, overcome colonial forms of dispossession, and aspire to "amodern" futures.

Divisions between natural and cultural properties are breaking down in numerous policy domains. Postcolonial or postdevelopment perspectives emphasize the way that this nature/culture dualism is received and opposed by marginalized groups who reject the dominance of this dualism in Western ontologies in the service of decolonization. As an "epistemological device" it dates back only to the last third of the nineteenth century in Europe (Descola, 2013). Although it may have no exact counterparts in other social traditions, there are now specialized fields of archaeology, heritage practice, biology, and ecology with bodies or experts dedicated to conservation in one domain or the other, holding global influence:

> We can see that culture–nature dualism need not have been "natural" to the Global South in order for it to have powerfully framed modern environmental policy and programs there, any more than the classic "authorized" heritage discourse needed to have roots in the cultures of the South in order to embed itself in modern heritage systems and to take on an aura of naturalness there.
>
> *(Byrne & Ween, 2015: 96).*

Scholars and activists increasingly reject this basis for dividing conservation and safeguarding activities, with Indigenous Peoples particularly insisting that their own ontologies are better suited for local governance of meaningful places and landscapes. Science and technology scholars assert that "[t]raditional societies do not live in harmony with nature; they are unacquainted with it" (Latour, 2004: 232). Agrarian groups may inhabit terrain in which ancient agricultural infrastructure, for example, is so intrinsic to the landscape that the "nature" they recognize is inextricably cultural. Anthropologists have long recognized indigenous socionatures, in which the kinship between human and other species creates social worlds of mutual responsibility. As Byrne and Ween remind us, heritage practice is evolving, particularly in Australia and Southeast Asia (e.g. Brockwell, O'Connor & Byrne, 2013), to incorporate such ontologies in heritage management practice; often "precolonial archaeological sites and artifacts can become 'catalysts' for the reproduction in contemporary indigenous society of the knowledge systems they represent" (Byrne & Ween, 2015: 97).

Recognition of the Western bias in the World Heritage Convention has prompted a revisiting of the ways in which the culture/nature divide tended to replicate a division between the West and the rest, or Europe and its others, with respect to the selection of cultural and natural sites. Since the early 1990s, a greater acknowledgment of how humans have shaped so-called natural environments and Indigenous Peoples' dynamic living relationships with World Heritage landscapes has impelled new hybrid categories, such as cultural landscapes, for nominations (Lennon, 2012; Rössler, 2012, 2006), resulting in a slow movement towards establishing indigenous co-management of protected areas in regions of the world where Indigenous Peoples and their rights are recognized.

Critics suggest that the ways in which "management" has been historically understood in such contexts tends to depoliticize relationships of inequality (Nadasdy, 2005) and continues to disadvantage Indigenous Peoples who are constrained by systems incompatible with their knowledge practices and custodial obligations (Baird, 2012). Even where TK is supposed to guide management decisions, local engagement may be largely encouraged only with respect to activities such as providing tourist goods and visitor education, rather than made integral to natural resource management (Ween & Columbi, 2013). If this is the case in countries where indigenous rights *are* recognized, most states have little interest in recognizing Indigenous Peoples as such – let alone their custodial rights with respect to heritage sites – and international rights norms are still largely unrecognized in most levels of state civil service and bureaucratic practice.

International recognition of the role of local communities, however, is evident in new practices such as collaborative management of protected areas (CMCPs), and new territories called indigenous community conserved areas (ICCAs). Thousands of globally protected areas are home to peoples dispossessed of livelihood resources under modern conservation paradigms which are now understood to violate human rights (Kothari, 2008). These areas may well evolve into relatively autonomous zones in which indigenous cultural norms have stature (Kothari, Camille & Brown, 2013). Indeed, they are key frontiers for articulating customary or "living law" (Stevens, 2014; Tobin, 2014), claiming indigenous identities, valuing TK, and asserting heritage rights. The International Union for the Conservation of Nature (IUCN), which has responsibilities for UNESCO World Heritage sites, recently adopted biocultural diversity as a policy principle with concomitant commitments to indigenous rights, FPIC, and community governance (Hill et al., 2011; Oviedo & Puschkarsky, 2012). This will inevitably raise issues of how to respect customary law (IUCN & CEESP, 2010) and the prospect of new fields of legal pluralism in cultural landscape governance. The IUCN, like other UN bodies, functions in a global policy arena where "cultural heritage" includes biocultural resources as well as *in situ* protections for TK (Shaheed, 2011: 9), and human rights norms oblige social actors to obtain community FPIC before engaging in development activities that put community cultural resources at risk.

Even if we are skeptical about the capacities of rights-oriented organizations to impose their ideals on states and corporations, we must acknowledge that there are significant incentives for peoples to represent and recognize themselves as culturally constituted collectives when their lands and livelihoods are at stake. We should indeed be ambivalent, if not outraged, when the cultural rights claims of communities provide the primary political leverage for ethnically distinct marginalized peoples facing displacement, dispossession, food insecurity, and loss of subsistence resources. Hundreds of thousands of peasants in Southeast Asia practicing what has historically been called "swidden" or more pejoratively, "slash and burn" agriculture experience their traditional way of life disappearing in the face of state-supported investments in rubber and palm oil plantations that promise to turn them into a landless precariat without social security (Coombe & Malik, 2017; Li, 2014). Declarations that shifting agriculture is the cultural heritage of Southeast Asia's Indigenous Peoples, essential to the preservation of global biodiversity, and the source of valuable local knowledge and innovation for engaging climate change seem obvious, trite, and despairing; they express grossly limited but still absolutely necessary points of leverage in struggles we seem to have lost other vocabularies to wager.

Still, critical heritage scholars are cautiously optimistic that the hegemonic global extension of Western ontological dualisms in heritage and nature conservation is waning:

> in the early twenty-first century we witness a counter-trend, manifest in a plurality of heritage practices and a plurality of "heritages" (i.e. alternative conceptions of heritage), which accompanies the growing assertiveness of countries in Asia, Latin America, and Africa, and of indigenous peoples globally . . . working within and against the global machinery of World Heritage to create new models of environmental management framed in terms of a pluriverse, acknowledging the co-existence of multiple lifeworlds and different, co-existing, attributions of subjectivity and agency.
>
> *(Byrne & Ween, 2015: 106)*

Such pluralities emerge partly from a decline in the power of Western global models and ontologies, but also by virtue of "the reworking of conservation ideas and practices that indigenous and Southern societies have taken from the North," interpreting and adapting these for new ends. Revisiting Nadasdy's thesis of indigenous dispossession in a recent study of Ashaninka community co-management of ancestral territories as protected areas in Amazonian Peru, Emily Caruso concluded that such projects were neither inherently "empowering nor disempowering, but the fruit of constant negotiations" (2011: 610), in which new autonomies might emerge in assertions of agency based on indigenous ontologies.

The management of cultural properties in authorized zones of autonomy guarantees neither emancipation nor sustainability. By this point it should be apparent that the concept of autonomy is itself paradoxical under conditions of neoliberal governmentality; it does not function normatively in any self-evident way in programs for the management of cultural property. The "right" to autonomously manage goods significant to a community's cultural identity is one that is simultaneously advanced as a strategy of neoliberal government and as a rubric for political self-determination. Determining when this is a matter of political subjugation and when it is a tactic of collective subject formation requires ethnographic study attentive to regimes of power, negotiation, and interlocution at multiple scales where issues of recognition and redistribution demand scrutiny. Assertions of cultural properties lend themselves to diverse projects of "empowerment".

If norms of community autonomy are sometimes linked to new agencies of self-determination, being recognized as responsible for safeguarding cultural resources may also invest communities in "economies of abandonment" (Povinelli, 2011). The mapping of community cultural resources in twenty-first-century Japan, for example, enrolls residents in participatory projects of cataloguing significant local attributes (Love, 2013). This governmental project "activates" rural residents in "treasure hunts" in which they come to see the areas in which they live as places rich in unique goods. Designed to spur local sustainability in the face of economic decline, these projects of community mapping emphasize "self-propelled" stewardship as residents are collectively motivated to preserve territories holding resources of cultural value. "Treasure hunts" are responses to processes of neoliberal decentralization in recessionary Japan and the withdrawal of tax subsidies from a depopulating countryside. This devolution of responsibility "organizes rural inhabitants to participate in acts of self-recognition – to generate a distinctive and reaffirming notion of their collective identity" (Love, 2013: 114) based in the localities they steward. Experts tutor them in locating and inscribing things "important to an area's way of life" (116), encouraging residents to take up enterprises such as renewed marketing of rural heritage foods and revival of ancestral industries through which community competition will "diminish needs for central government supports" (120).

In neoliberal governmental conditions – in which powers are decentralized and devolved and entrepreneurial and independent cultural communities are promoted by state and international agencies – territorial autonomy may no longer serve as the horizon for transformative politics (Hale, 2011: 204). If some indigenous communities have been targeted for ethno-developmental investment, others find that territorial recognition and autonomy is a state mapping of and for enclosure and economic neglect. Securing territory may provide a resource base, limited rights, but extensive responsibilities, new procedures, endless meetings and modest employment prospects, but few means "to challenge either the market-based disciplines of the global economy or persisting state authority as the ultimate arbiter of communities' political affairs" (205). Hale's work with communities engaged in participatory mapping suggested the need to shift emphasis from devolutions of authority to self-sustaining forms of production. Such forms of autonomy, moreover, appear to be most successful under conditions where communities are transnationally linked to others and to transnational social movements, as our considerations of Andean and Amazonian community cultural heritage projects made apparent.

Eric Hirsch (2016) offers a recent instance of heritage project work in the Colca Valley in Peru, where communities are allegedly subject to competitive projects of "development with identity" implemented by international agencies invested in a revalorization of indigeneity vested in intangible cultural goods. Sierra Sur is a project co-financed by the International Fund for Agricultural Development (IFAD). According to Hirsch, its mission statement insists "that development is no longer about imposing improvements and offering handouts, but now entails 'facilitating' growth for Andean 'citizens, agents of their own development through competitively awarded investments'" (103) in indigenous human capital. As one coordinator of the project explained, development is not an imposition, but merely incentivizes "the freedom to seek these traditions." To receive assistance (one of the few forms of welfare locally available) it is "imperative to identify with and display a recognizable Colcan indigeneity" (104). As Hirsch describes them, such competitions designate the most worthy indigenous entrepreneurs in pedagogical practices through which local communities are encouraged to valorize "what they have" (104) by marketing products to augment rural incomes. Such projects "place the burdens of development on its participants" through territorial investments in "sustainable land use and recuperated indigenous practice" (105). Hirsch sees such activities as externally initiated forms of neoliberal cultural governmentality that actively construct indigenous subjects who internalize these valorizations to their detriment.

In the absence of any understanding of the global policy contexts framing these projects or the rights norms which inform international organizations like IFAD, without consideration of the historical agencies, social movements, and aspirations of Andean Indigenous Peoples, any acknowledgment of how regional agroecology movements have attracted investments into the region, or the political projects of decolonization through which "development with identity" is locally configured, it is all too easy to dismiss such enterprises and presume that neoliberal cultural governmentality instills autonomy only as a recipe for social abandonment. Such limited inquiries rule out of order the exploration of if and how international development projects are customized for local exigencies and/or respond to community objectives as expressed in local participatory deliberations. The political economies and political ecologies in which cultural properties become legible for investment, intervention, and insurgency however, are too complex to justify such simplistic local analyses. Neoliberal cultural governmentalities figure at the nexus of social change in topographies of emergent political articulation and agency that must be explored as complex, multiscalar assemblages.

Conclusion

Globalization, informational capitalism, and neoliberal governmentalities position anthropologists within increasingly distributed and dispersed legal and policy frameworks and institutional circuits of power, knowledge, and normative discourse, in which the sites and stakes of cultural claims have proliferated and expanded. In international rights norms, cultural heritage rights are now tied to membership in specific communities rather than to national citizenship (Shaheed, 2011). International NGOs assert heritage protections once limited to globally recognized Indigenous Peoples to forest-dwelling, pastoralist, and other "communities" whose livelihood resources are at risk (Coombe, Malik & Griebel, forthcoming, 2018). Domestic courts extend principles of aboriginal rights based on cultural attachments to communal properties to rural minorities more generally (Huizenga, n.d.). Regional development banks and transnational environmental organizations are increasingly proactive in naming, blaming, and shaming states and corporate actors whose activities and development projects affect livelihood resources of rural peoples represented as communities holding rights premised upon collectively held cultural heritage.

Culturalized identities, indigenous resurgence, and new attachments to cultural properties are not merely derivative by-products of neoliberal governmentality and informational capital, but tenuous accomplishments of political articulation under new conditions of globalizing power, diverse market measures, and new forms of governmentality in which disciplines are imposed and responsibilities asserted and distinctive fields for political articulation are afforded. If the vocabularies of political indigeneity now extend to embrace a greater range of the world's most marginalized peoples (Coombe, Malik & Griebel, 2017), this may be because they enable traditions to serve as dynamic resources for imagining alternative futures. As James Clifford puts it, if neoliberalism opens possibilities for culturally based movements, channeling diversity in particular ways, the politics of the possible is not thereby exhausted: "spaces opened from above are also being [re]created from below" (2013: 39). The regulatory fields of power, knowledge, and recognition in which contingent assemblages of identity are forged are charged with contradictions, shaped by diverse rhetorical frames, and governed through technologies which offer their own affordances. Numerous transnational regimes animate and provide incentives for cultural collectivities to assemble, multiplying their needs, resources, and capacities to assert themselves as political subjects of various kinds. Mapping this shifting terrain and the ethical and epistemological questions it poses will be a major challenge facing scholars exploring cultural properties in (not quite) neoliberal futures.

Acknowledgments

I thank Laura Fox, Masters student in the Communication and Culture Program at York University who provided excellent research and editorial assistance on this chapter. This study continues and is closely related to research work I have done collaboratively over several years with a group of postdoctoral fellows and graduate students (Nicole Aylwin, Melissa Baird, Marc Griebel, Daniel Huizenga, Sara Ives, Ali Malik, Joe Turcotte, Lindsey Weiss) in coauthored publications herein referenced. When making reference to this work I use the authorial "we."

Bibliography

Affif, S. & Lowe, C. (2007). Claiming indigenous community: Political discourse and natural resource rights in Indonesia. *Alternatives: Global, Local, Political* 32 (1), 73–97.

Agrawal, A. (1995). Dismantling the divide between indigenous and scientific knowledge. *Development and Change* 26 (3), 413–439.

Agrawal, A. & Gibson, C. (1999). Enchantment and disenchantment: The role of community in natural resource conservation. *Word Development* 27 (4), 629–649.

Albert, M. T., Richon, M., Vinals, N. & Witcomb, A. (Eds.). (2012). *Community Development through World Heritage*. Valencia: UNESCO.

Altamirano-Jimenez, I. (2013). *Indigenous Encounters with Neoliberalism: Place, Women and the Environment in Canada and Mexico*. Vancouver: UBC Press.

Altieri, M. A. & Toledo, M. (2011). The agroecological revolution in Latin America: Rescuing nature, ensuring food sovereignty and empowering peasants. *Journal of Peasant Studies* 38 (3), 587–612.

Anderson, G. (2012). Beyond "constitutionalism beyond the state," *Journal of Law and Society* 39 (3), 359–383.

Andolina, R., Laurie, N. & Radcliffe, S. (2005). Ethnodevelopment: Social movements, creating experts and professionalising indigenous knowledge in Ecuador. *Antipode* 37 (3), 470–496.

Andolina, R., Laurie, N. & Radcliffe, S. (2009). *Indigenous Development in the Andes: Culture, Power, and Transnationalism*. Durham, NC: Duke University Press.

Anthias, P. & Radcliffe, S. (2013). The ethno-environmental fix and its limits: Indigenous land titling and the production of not-quite-neoliberal natures in Bolivia. *Geoforum* 64, doi:10.1016/j.geoforum.2013.06.007.

Appadurai, A. (2013). *The Future as Cultural Fact: Essays on the Global Condition*. London: Verso.

Asher, K. (2009). *Black and Green: Afro-Colombians, Development, and Nature in the Pacific Lowlands*. Durham, NC: Duke University Press.

Asher, K., & Ojeda, D. (2009). Producing nature and making the state: Ordenamiento territorial in the Pacific lowlands of Colombia. *Geoforum* 40, 292–302.

Baird, M. (2012). The breath of the mountain is my heart: Indigenous cultural landscapes and the politics of heritage. *International Journal of Heritage Studies* 19 (4), 327–340.
Bakker, K. (2010). The limits of "neoliberal natures": Debating green neoliberalism. *Progress in Human Geography* 34 (6), 715–735.
Bendix, R. (2009). Heritage between economy and politics: An assessment from the perspective of cultural anthropology. In L. Smith & N. Akagawa (Eds.), *Intangible Heritage* (253–269). London: Routledge.
Bennett, T. (1998). *Culture: A Reformer's Science*. London: Sage.
Bennett, T. (2000). Acting on the social: Art, culture and government. *American Behavioral Scientist* 43 (9), 1412–1428.
Blake, J. (2009). UNESCO's 2003 Convention on Intangible Cultural Heritage: The implications of community involvement in "safeguarding." In L. Smith & N. Akagawa (Eds.), *Intangible Heritage* (45–73). New York: Routledge.
Blake, J. (2014). Seven years of implementing UNESCO's intangible heritage convention: Honeymoon period or the "seven-year itch?" *International Journal of Cultural Property* 21, 291–304.
Bowrey, K. & Anderson, J. (2009). The politics of global information sharing: Whose agendas are being advanced? *Social and Legal Studies* 18 (4), 479–504.
Braithwaite, J. (2008). *Regulatory Capitalism: How it Works, Ideas for Making it Work Better*. Cheltenham, UK: Edward Elgar.
Brenner, N., Peck, J. & Theodore, N. (2010). Variegated neoliberalization: Geographies, modalities, pathways. *Global Networks* 10 (2), 182–222.
Briggs, C. L. (1996). The politics of discursive authority in research on the "invention of tradition." *Cultural Anthropology* 11 (4), 435–446.
Brockwell, S., O'Connor, S. & Byrne, D. (Eds.). (2013). *Transcending the Culture–Nature Divide in Cultural Heritage: Views from the Asia-Pacific Region*. Terra Australia 36. Canberra: ANU E-Press.
Brosius, P., Tsing, A. & Zerner, C. (1998). Representing communities: History and politics of community-based natural resource management. *Society and Natural Resources* 11 (2), 157–168.
Brosius, P., Tsing, A. & Zerner, C. (Eds.). (2005). *Communities and Conservation: Histories and Politics of Community-Based Natural Resource Management*. Walnut Creek, CA: AltaMira Press.
Brown, M. (1998). Can culture be copyrighted? *Current Anthropology* 39 (2), 193–222. [The article is followed by comments from several other anthropologists.]
Brown, M. (2003). Cultures and copyrights. In M. Brown (Ed.), *Who Owns Native Culture?* (43–68). Cambridge, MA: Harvard University Press.
Brown, M. (2005). Heritage trouble: Recent work on the protection of intangible cultural property. *International Journal of Cultural Property* 12 (1), 40–61.
Brown, Michael F. (2010). Culture, property, and peoplehood: A comment on Carpenter, Katyal, and Riley's "In Defense of Property." *International Journal of Cultural Property* 17, 569–579.
Brumann, C. (2015). Community as Myth and Reality in the UNESCO World Heritage Convention. In N. Adell, R. F. Bendix, C. Bortolotto & M. Tauschek (Eds.), *Between Imagined Communities and Communities of Practice: Participation, Territory and the Making of Heritage* (273–290). Göttingen: Göttingen University Press.
Brush, S. (1999). Bioprospecting the public domain. *Cultural Anthropology* 14 (4), 535–555.
Brush, S. (2000). The issues of in situ conservation of crop genetic resources. In S. B. Brush (Ed.), *Genes in the Field: On-farm Conservation of Crop Diversity* (3–26). Rome: International Plant Genetic Resources Institute.
Brush, S. B. & Stabinsky, D. (Eds.). (1996). *Valuing Local Knowledge: Indigenous People and Intellectual Property Rights*. Washington, DC: Island Press.
Buergin, R. (2015). Contested rights of local communities and indigenous peoples in the context of the biocultural turn in environmental and development discourses. *Modern Asian Studies* 49, 2022–2062.
Byrne, D. & Ween, G. B. (2015). Bridging cultural and natural heritage. In Lynn Meskell (Ed.), *Global Heritage: A Reader* (94–111). New York: Wiley-Blackwell.
Caruso, E. (2011). Co-management redux: Anti-politics and transformation in the Ashaninka Communal Reserve, Peru. *International Journal of Heritage Studies* 17 (6), 608–628.
Caruso, E. (2014). State governmentality or indigenous sovereignty? Protected area comanagement in the Ashaninka Communal Reserve in Peru. In S. Stevens (Ed.), *Indigenous Peoples, National Parks, and Protected Areas: A New Paradigm Linking Conservation, Culture and Rights* (150–171). Tucson: University of Arizona Press.

Cepek, M. (2011a). Expression, instrument and obstacle: The social life of Indigenous rights discourse in Cofan political practice. Montreal: Paper presented at the annual meeting for the American Anthropological Association.

Cepek, M. (2011b). Foucault in the forest: Questioning environmentality in Amazonia. *American Ethnologist* 38 (3), 501–515.

Cepek, M. (2012). *A Future for Amazonia: Randy Borman and Cofán Environmental Politics*. Austin: University of Texas Press.

Clarke, John. (2008). Living with/in and without neoliberalism. *Focaal—European Journal of Anthropology* 51, 135–147.

Clifford, J. (2013). *Returns: Becoming Indigenous in the Twenty-First Century*. Cambridge, MA: Harvard University Press.

Coffey, M. K. (2003). From nation to community: Museums and the reconfiguration of Mexican society under neoliberalism. In J. Bratich, J. Packer, & C. Macarthy (Eds.), *Foucault, Cultural Studies and Governmentality* (207–242). Albany: SUNY Press.

Collier, S. J. (2006) Global assemblages. *Theory, Culture and Society* 23 (2–3), 399–401.

Collier, S. J. (2012). Neoliberalism as big leviathan, or ... ? A response to Wacquant and Hilgiers. *Social Anthropology* 20 (2), 186–195.

Colloredo-Mansfeld, R. (1998). Dirty Indians, radical Indigenas, and the political economy of social difference in modern Ecuador. *Bulletin of Latin American Research* 17 (2), 185–205.

Comaroff, J. (2011). The end of neoliberalism? What is left of the Left. *The Annals of the American Academy of Political and Social Science* 637 (1), 141–147.

Comaroff, J. L. & Comaroff, J. (2009). *Ethnicity, Inc.* Chicago: University of Chicago Press.

Coombe, R. J. (1998). *The Cultural Life of Intellectual Properties: Authorship, Alterity and the Law*. Durham, NC: Duke University Press.

Coombe, R. J. (2005). Protecting traditional environmental knowledge and new social movements in the Americas: Intellectual property, human right or claims to an alternative form of sustainable development? *Florida Journal of International Law* 17 (1), 115–136.

Coombe, R. J. (2009). The expanding purview of cultural properties and their politics. *Annual Review of Law and Social Sciences* 5, 393–412.

Coombe, R. J. (2011a). Possessing culture: Political economies of community subjects and their properties. In M. Busse & V. Strang (Eds.), *Ownership and Appropriation* (105–127). London: Berg Publishers.

Coombe, R. J. (2011b). Cultural agencies: "Constructing" community subjects and their rights. In M. Biagioli, P. Jaszi & M. Woodmansee (Eds.), *Making and Unmaking Intellectual Property* (79–98). Chicago: University of Chicago Press.

Coombe, R. J. (2012). Managing cultural heritage as neoliberal governmentality. In R. Bendix, A. Eggert, A. Peselmann & S. Mißling (Eds.), *Heritage Regimes and the State* (375–389). Göttingen: Göttingen University Press.

Coombe, R. J. (2016). The knowledge economy and its cultures: Neoliberalism and Latin American reterritorializations. *HAU: Journal of Ethnographic Theory* 6 (3), 247–275.

Coombe, R. J. (forthcoming, 2018). Intellectual property. In C. Greenhouse (Ed.), *The Anthropology of Politics, Law and Power*. A volume in H. Callon (Ed.), *International Encyclopedia of Anthropology*, 12 volumes. London: Wiley Blackwell.

Coombe, R. J. & Griebel, M. (2014). An amodern territory: Working potatoes and properties in an era of informational capital. Paper presented at the Alternative Property Practices Symposium, International Institute for the Sociology of Law, Onati, Spain, April 4. Available at: http://rcoombe.blog.yorku.ca/presentation/an-amodern-territory-working-potatoes-and-properties-in-an-era-of-informational-capital/.

Coombe, R. J., Ives, S. & Huizenga, D. (2014). Geographical indications: the promise, perils and politics of protecting place-based products. In M. David & D. Halbert (Eds.), *Sage Handbook on Intellectual Property* (207–223). Thousand Oaks, CA: Sage Publications.

Coombe, R. J. & Malik, S. A. (2017). Rethinking the work of geographical indications in Asia: Addressing hidden geographies of race and gendered labour. In I. Calboli & N. L. W. Loon (Eds.), *Geographic Indications at the Crossroads of Trade and Development in Asia* (87–121). Cambridge: Cambridge University Press.

Coombe, R. J., Malik, S. A. & Griebel, M. (forthcoming, 2018). Culturalised properties in neoliberal futures: Frontiers of dispossession and indigenous assertion. In C. Antons & W. Logan (Eds.), *Intellectual Property, Cultural Property and Intangible Cultural Heritage*. London: Routledge.

Coombe, R. J. & Turcotte, J. F. (2012). Cultural, political, and social implications of intellectual property laws in an informational economy. In UNESCO-EOLSS Joint Committee (Eds.), Culture, Civilization and Human Society, in *Encyclopedia of Life Support Systems (EOLSS)*, Oxford, UK.

Coombe, R. J. & Turcotte, J. F. (2015). Indigenous cultural heritage in development and trade: Perspectives from the dynamics of cultural heritage law and policy. In A. Connolly (Ed.), *Cultural Heritage Rights: A Reader* (275–310). Dartmouth, UK: Ashgate Publishing.

Coombe, R. J. & Weiss, L. (2015). Neoliberalism, heritage regimes and cultural rights: Politics in assemblage. In Lynn Meskell (Ed.), *Global Heritage: A Reader* (42–68). New York: Wiley-Blackwell.

Corntassel, J. (2008). Toward sustainable self-determination: Rethinking the contemporary indigenous-rights discourse. *Alternatives: Global, Local, Political* 33 (1), 105–132.

Creed, G. W. (2006). The seductions of community: Reconsidering community. In G. W. Creed (Ed.), *The Seductions of Community: Emancipations, Oppressions, Quandaries* (1–20). Santa Fe, NM: SAR Press.

Cutler, A. C. (2011). The globalization of international law, indigenous identity, and the new constitutionalism. In W. Coleman (Ed.), *Property, Territory, Globalization* (29–45). Vancouver: UBC Press.

Cutler, A. C. & Gill, S. (Eds.). (2015). *New Constitutionalism and World Order.* Cambridge: Cambridge University Press.

De Cesari, C. (2012). Thinking through heritage regimes. In R. Bendix, A. Eggert & A. Peselman (Eds.), *Heritage Regimes and the State* (399–413). Göttingen: Göttingen University Press.

De Hart, M. C. (2010). *Ethnic Entrepreneurs: Identity and Development Politics in Latin America.* Stanford, CA: Stanford University Press.

De la Cadena, M. (2004). Commentary on "Agricultural hybridity and the 'pathology' of traditional ways …": the challenges of translation analysis for the ethnography of "development." *Journal of Latin American Anthropology* 9 (2), 278–283.

De la Cadena, M. (2010). Indigenous cosmopolitics in the Andes: Conceptual reflections beyond "politics." *Cultural Anthropology* 25 (2), 334–370.

Descola, P. (2013). *Beyond Nature and Culture.* Chicago: University of Chicago Press.

Di Giovane, M. (2015). The ethics of participation, community formation and governmentality in Unesco's World Heritage Program. In N. Adell, R. Bendix, C. Bortolotto & M. Tauschek (Eds.), *Between Imagined Communities and Communities of Practice: Participation, Territory and the Making of Heritage* (83–110). Göttingen: Göttingen University Press.

Disko, S. (2012). World heritage sites and indigenous communities: The importance of adopting a human rights-based approach. In M. T. Albert, M. Richon, N. Vinals & A. Witcomb (Eds.), *Community Development through World Heritage* (16–27). Valencia: UNESCO.

Dove, M. (1996). Center, periphery and bio-diversity: A paradox of governance and a developmental challenge. In S. Brush and D. Stabinsky (Eds.), *Valuing Local Knowledge: Indigenous People and Intellectual Property Rights* (41–67). Washington, DC: Island Press.

Dove, M. (2007). Perceptions of local knowledge and adaptation on Mount Merapi, central Java. In R. Ellen (Ed.), *Modern Crises and Traditional Strategies: Local Ecological Knowledge in Island Southeast Asia* (238–262). New York and London: Berghahn Books.

Drahos, P. (2014). Regulatory capitalism, globalization and the end of history. *Intellectual Property Law and Policy Journal* 1, 1–23.

Erazo, J. (2010). Constructing Indigenous subjectivities: Economic collectivism and identity in the upper Amazon. *Development and Change* 41 (6), 1017–1039.

Erazo, J. (2013). *Governing Indigenous Territories: Enacting Sovereignty in the Ecuadorian Amazon.* Durham, NC: Duke University Press.

Escobar, A. (1998). Whose knowledge, whose nature? Biodiversity, conservation, and the political ecology of social movements. *Journal of Political Ecology* 5, 53–82.

Escobar, A. (2008). *Territories of Difference: Place, Movements, Life, Redes.* Durham, NC: Duke University Press.

Escobar, A. (2010). Latin America at a crossroads: Alternative modernizations, post-liberalism, or post-development? *Cultural Studies* 24 (1), 1–65.

Farhat, R. (2008). Neotribal entrepreneurialism and the commodification of biodiversity: WIPO's displacement of development for private property rights. *Review of International Political Economy* 15 (2), 206–233.

Ferguson, B. G. & Morales, H. (2010). Latin American agroecologists build a powerful scientific and social movement. *Journal of Sustainable Agriculture* 34 (4), 339–341.

Ferguson, J. (2009). The uses of neoliberalism. *Antipode* 41, 166–184.

Fernando, J. (2003). NGOs and production of Indigenous knowledge under the condition of postmodernity. *The Annals of the American Academy of Political and Social Science* 590 (1), 54–72.

Fish, A. (2006). The commodification and exchange of knowledge in the case of transnational commercial yoga. *International Journal of Cultural Property* 13 (2), 189–206.
Fitting, E. (2011). *The Struggle for Maize: Campesinos, Workers, and Transgenic Corn in the Mexican Countryside*. Durham, NC: Duke University Press.
Forsyth, M. (2012). Lifting the lid on the community: Who has the right to control access to traditional knowledge and expressions of culture? *International Journal of Cultural Property* 19 (1), 1–31.
Forsyth, M. (2013). How can traditional knowledge best be regulated? Comparing a proprietary rights approach with a regulatory toolbox approach. *Contemporary Pacific* 25 (1), 1–31.
Forsyth, M. & Farran, S. (2015). *Weaving Intellectual Property Policy in Small Island Developing States*. Cambridge: Intersentia.
Fueres, M., Flores, R. & Ramos, R. (2013). Saving our seeds: An indigenous perspective from Cotachachi, Ecuador. In V. Nazarea, R. Rhoades & J. E. Andrews-Swann (Eds.), *Seeds of Resistance, Seeds of Hope* (107–114). Tucson: University of Arizona Press.
Gatmaytan, A. B. (2003). Advocacy as translation: Notes on the Philippine experience. In P. Brosius, A. L. Tsing, & C. Zerner (Eds.), *Communities and Conservation: Histories and Politics of Community-Based Natural Resource Management* (459–476). Walnut Creek, CA: AltaMira Press.
Geismar, H. (2013). *Treasured Possessions: Indigenous Interventions into Cultural and Intellectual Property*. Durham, NC: Duke University Press.
Gershon, I. (2011). Neoliberal agency. *Current Anthropology* 52 (4), 537–555.
Gibbs, M. (2005). The right to development and indigenous peoples: Lessons from New Zealand. *World Development* 33 (8), 1365–1378.
Goodale, M. & N. Postero (Eds.) (2013). *Neoliberalism interrupted: Social change and contested governance in contemporary Latin America*. Palo Alto, CA: Stanford University Press.
Goldstein, D. (2012). Decolonizing "actually existing neoliberalism." *Social Anthropology* 20 (3), 304–309.
Gonzales, T. (2013). Sense of place and Indigenous People's biodiversity conservation in the Americas. In V. D. Nazarea, R. Rhoades & J. E. Andrews-Swann (Eds.), *Seeds of Resistance, Seeds of Hope: Place and Agency in the Conservation of Biodiversity* (85–106). Tucson: University of Arizona Press.
Gonzales, T. A. (2000). The cultures of seed in the Peruvian Andes. In S. B. Brush (Ed.), *Genes in the Field: On-farm Conservation of Crop Diversity* (193–216). London: Lewis.
Grabosky, P. (2013). Beyond responsive regulation: The expanding role of non-state actors in the regulatory process. *Regulation and Governance* 7 (1), 114–123.
Graddy, T. G. (2013). Regarding biocultural heritage: In situ political ecology in the Peruvian Andes. *Agriculture and Human Values* 30 (4), 587–604.
Green, S. (2004). Indigenous people incorporated? Culture as politics, culture as property in contemporary bioprospection deals. *Current Anthropology* 45 (2), 211–237.
Green, S. (2009). *Customising Indigeneity: Paths to a Visionary Politics in Peru*. Stanford, CA: Stanford University Press.
Gupta, Akhil. (1998). *Postcolonial Developments: Agriculture in the Making of Modern India*. Durham, NC: Duke University Press.
Gustafson, B. & Fabricant, N. (2011). Introduction: New cartographies of knowledge and struggle. In N. Fabricant & B. Gustafson (Eds.), *Remapping Bolivia: Resources, Territory, and Indigeneity in the Plurinational State* (1–29). Santa Fe, NM: School for American Research.
Halbert, D. J. (2005). *Resisting Intellectual Property*. London: Routledge.
Hale, C. (2002). Does multiculturalism menace? Governance, cultural rights and the politics of identity in Guatemala. *Journal of Latin American Studies* 34 (1), 485–524.
Hale, C. (2004). Rethinking Indigenous politics in the era of the "Indio Permitido". *Nacla Report on the Americas. Report on Race* (Part 1), 16–21.
Hale, C. (2005). Neoliberal multiculturalism: The remaking of cultural rights and racial dominance in Central America. *Political and Legal Anthropology Review* 28 (1), 10–19.
Hale, C. (2006). *Mas que un Indio (More than an Indian): Racial Ambivalence and Neoliberal Multiculturalism in Guatemala*. Santa Fe: School of American Research Press.
Hale, C. (2011). Resistance, pur qui? Territory, autonomy and neoliberal entanglements in the empty spaces of Central America. *Economy and Society* 40 (2), 184–210.
Handler, R. (1991). Who owns the past? History, cultural property and the logic of possessive individualism. In B. Williams (Ed.), *The Politics of Culture* (63–74). Washington, DC: Smithsonian Institution Press.
Harvey, D. (2001). The art of rent: Globalization, monopoly and the commodification of culture. In L. Panitch & C. Leys (Eds.), *Socialist Register 2002: A World of Contradictions* (93–110). London: Merlin Press.

Hayden, C. (2003a). *When Nature Goes Public: The Making and Un-making of Bioprospecting in Mexico*. Princeton, NJ: Princeton University Press.
Hayden, C. (2003b). From market to market: Bioprospecting's idioms of inclusion. *American Ethnologist* 30, 359–371.
Hernandez-Castillo, R. A. (2002). National law and indigenous customary law: The struggle for justice of Indigenous women in Chiapas, Mexico. In M. Molyneux & S. Razavi (Eds.), *Gender Justice, Development, and Rights* (384–412). Oxford: Oxford University Press.
Hertz, E. (2015). Bottoms, real and spurious. In N. Adell, R. Bendix, C. Bortolotto & M. Tauschek (Eds.), *Between Imagined Communities and Communities of Practice: Participation, Territory and Communities of Practice* (25–57). Göttingen: Göttingen University Press.
Hilgers, M. (2010). The three anthropological approaches to neoliberalism. *International Social Science Journal* 61 (202), 351–364.
Hilgers, M. (2012). The historicity of the neoliberal state. *Social Anthropology* 20 (1), 80–94.
Hill, R. et al. (2011). Empowering indigenous peoples' biocultural diversity through World Heritage cultural landscapes. *International Journal of Heritage Studies* 17 (6), 571–591.
Himley, M. (2012). Regularizing social extraction in Andean Peru: Mining and social mobilization in an era of corporate social responsibility. *Antipode* 42 (2), 394–416.
Hirsch, E. (2010). Property and persons: New forms and contests in the era of neoliberalism. *Annual Review of Anthropology* 39, 347–360.
Hirsch, E. (2016). Mediating indigeneity: Public space and the making of political identity in Andean Peru. *Political and Legal Anthropology Review* 39 (1), 95–109.
Hirtz, F. (2003). It takes modern means to be traditional: On recognizing indigenous cultural minorities in the Philippines. *Development Change* 34 (5), 887–917.
Holder, Cindy. (2008). Culture as an activity and human right: An important advance for indigenous peoples and international law. *Alternatives: Global, Local, Political* 33, 7–28.
Huizenga, D. (n.d.) Articulations of aboriginal title, Indigenous rights and living customary law in South Africa. Winner of the 2016 Canadian Law and Society Association Roderick A. MacDonald Graduate Student Essay Prize.
Humphrey, C. & Verdery, K. (Eds.) (2004). *Property in Question: Value Transformation in the Global Economy*. Oxford: Berghahn.
Hurtado, L. M. (1999). Access to the resources of biodiversity and indigenous peoples. *Beyond Law*. Special Issue. Biological and Cultural Diversity Challenges and Proposals from Latin America 6 (18–19), 143–155.
Hutchins, F. & Wilson, P. C. (Eds). (2010). *Editing Eden: A Reconsideration of Identity, Politics, and Place in Amazonia*. Lincoln: University of Nebraska Press.
Inda, J. X. (2005). Analytics of modern: An introduction. In J. X. Inda (Ed.), *Anthropologies of Modernity: Foucault, Governmentality, and Life Politics* (1–20). Oxford: Wiley-Blackwell.
International Union for the Conservation of Nature (IUCN) & Commission on Environmental, Economic and Social Policy (CEESP). (2010). Bio-cultural diversity conserved by Indigenous peoples and local communities – examples and analysis: Companion document to IUCN/CEESP Briefing Note No. 10. Tehran; London: IUCN, CEESP.
IUCN. (2011). Report submitted by IUCN to the Tenth Session of the United Nations Permanent Forum on Indigenous Issues. Document E/C.19/2011/CRP.8. 2. Retrieved from http://undesadspd.org/IndigenousPeoples/UNPFIISessions/Tenth.aspx.
Jonas, H. & Jonas, H. (2013). Reforming rights to support responsibilities. In H. Jonas, H. Jonas & S. M. Subramanian (Eds.), *The Right to Responsibility: Resisting and Engaging Development, Conservation and the Law in Asia* (206–229). Institute for Advanced Studies, Malaysia: Natural Justice and United Nations University.
Kingfisher, C. & Maskovsky, J. (2008). Introduction: The limits of neoliberalism. *Critique of Anthropology* 28 (2), 115–126.
Kothari, A. (2008). Protected areas and people: The future of the past. *Parks* 17, 23–34.
Kothari, A., Camille, P. & Brown, J. (2013). Conservation as if people also mattered: Policy and practice of community-based conservation. *Conservation & Society* 11 (1), 1–15.
Kuutma, K. (2012a). Communities and the contested representational politics of ownership. Final Report: The First ICH Researchers Forum: The Implementation of UNESCO's 2003 Convention (pp. 42–51). Retrieved from www.irci.jp/assets/files/2012_ICH_Forum.pdf.
Kuutma, K. (2012b). Between arbitration and engineering: Concepts and contingencies in the shaping of heritage regimes. In R. Bendix, A. Eggert & A. Peselman (Eds.), *Heritage Regimes and the State* (21–36). Göttingen: Göttingen University Press.

Lafrenz-Samuels, K. (2010). Material heritage and poverty reduction. In S. Labadi & C. Long (Eds.), *Heritage and Globalization* (202–217). London: Routledge.
Latour, B. (1993). *We Have Never Been Modern*. Cambridge, MA: Harvard University Press.
Latour, B. (2004). *Politics of Nature*. Cambridge, MA: Harvard University Press.
Leblon, A. (2012). A policy of intangible cultural heritage between local constraints and international standards. In R. Bendix, A. Eggert & A. Peselman (Eds.), *Heritage Regimes and the State* (97–120). Göttingen: Göttingen University Press.
Lennon, J. (2012). Cultural landscape management: International influences. In K. Taylor & J. Lennon (Eds.), *Managing Cultural Landscapes* (45–69). London and New York: Routledge.
Levett, P. & Merry, S. E. (2009). Vernacularization on the ground: Local uses of global women's rights in Peru, China, India and the United States. *Global Networks* 9 (4), 441–461.
Li, T. M. (1999). Marginality, power and production: Analysing upland transformations. In T. M. Li (Ed.), *Transforming the Indonesian Uplands: Marginality, Power and Production* (1–46). Amsterdam: Harwood Academic Publishers.
Li, T. M. (2000). Articulating Indigenous identity in Indonesia: Resource politics and the tribal slot. *Comparative Studies in Society and History* 42 (1), 149–186.
Li, T. M. (2002). Engaging simplifications: Community-based resource management, market processes, and state agendas in upland Southeast Asia. *World Development* 30 (2), 265–283.
Li, T. M. (2014). *Social Impacts of Oil Palm in Indonesia: A Gendered Perspective from West Kalimantan*. Occasional Paper 124. Bogor, Indonesia: Center for International Forestry Research.
Long, C. & Labadi, S. (2010). Introduction. In S. Labadi & C. Long (Eds.), *Heritage and Globalization* (1–16). London: Routledge.
Love, B. (2013). Treasure hunts in rural Japan: Place making at the limits of sustainability. *American Anthropologist* 115 (1), 112–124.
Lydon, J. (2009). Young and free: The Australian past in a global future. In L. M. Meskell (Ed.), *Cosmopolitan Archaeologies* (28–47). Durham, NC: Duke University Press.
Merry, S. E. (2009). Legal transplants and cultural translation: Making human rights in the vernacular. In M. Goodale (Ed.), *Human Rights: An Anthropological Reader* (265–302). Malden, MA: Wiley-Blackwell.
Meskell, L. (2009). The nature of culture in Kruger National Park. In L. M. Meskell (Ed.), *Cosmopolitan Archaeologies* (89–112). Durham, NC: Duke University Press.
Meskell, L. (2013). UNESCO and the fate of the World Heritage Indigenous Peoples Council of Experts (WHIPCOE). *International Journal of Cultural Property* 20 (2), 155–174.
Meurer, B. & Perry, R.W. (Eds.). (2003). *Globalization Under Construction: Governmentality, Law and Identity*. Minneapolis: University of Minnesota Press
Meurer, B. & Schwab (Eds.). (2006). *Accelerating Possession: Global Futures of Property and Personhood*. New York: Columbia University Press.
Nadasdy, P. (2005). The anti-politics of TEK: The institutionalisation of co-management discourse and practice. *Anthropologica* 47 (2), 215–232.
Napier, A. D. (1994). Saving or enslaving: The paradox of intellectual property. *Journal of the Anthropological Society of Oxford* 25 (1), 49–58.
Napier, A. D. (2002). Our own way: On anthropology and intellectual property. In J. MacClancy (Ed.), *Exotic No More: Anthropology on the Front Lines* (287–318). Chicago: University of Chicago Press.
Natera, M. A. C. (2013). Postscript: Insurgent imaginaries and post-neoliberalism in Latin America. In M. Goodale & N. Postero (Eds.), *Neoliberalism Interrupted: Social Change and Contested Governance in Contemporary Latin America* (249–268). Stanford, CA: Stanford University Press.
Nazarea, V. D. (2006). Local knowledge and memory in biodiversity conservation. *Annual Review of Anthropology* 35, 317–335
Nazarea, V. D. (2013). Temptation to hope: From the "idea" to the milieu of biodiversity. In V. Nazarea, R. Rhoades & J. E. Andrews-Swan (Eds.), *Seeds of Resistance, Seeds of Hope* (19–41). Tucson: University of Arizona Press.
Novellino, D. (2007). Talking about kultura and signing contracts: The bureaucratization of the environment on Palawan Island (the Philippines). In C. Maida (Ed.), *Sustainability and Communities of Place* (82–105). New York; Oxford: Berghahn.
Ong, A. (2007). Neoliberalism as a mobile technology. *Transactions of the Institute of British Geographers* 32 (1), 3–8.

Osco, M. F. (2010). Ayllu: Critical thinking and (an)other autonomy. In M. Blaser, R. De Costa, D. Mc Gregor, & W. Coleman (Eds.), *Indigenous Peoples and Autonomy* (27–48). Vancouver: University of British Columbia Press.

Oviedo, G. & Puschkarsky, T. (2012). World heritage and rights-based approaches to nature conservation. *International Journal of Heritage Studies*. Special Issue. World Heritage and Human Rights: Preserving our Common Dignity through Rights-based Approaches 18 (1), 285–296.

Peck, J. & Theodore, N. (2012). Reanimating neoliberalism: Process geographies of neoliberalisation. *Social Anthropology* 20 (2), 177–185.

Polanyi, K. (2001 [1944]). *The Great Transformation: The Political and Economic Origins of Our Time*. Boston: Beacon Press.

Postero, N. (2007). *Now We Are Citizens: Indigenous Politics in Postmulticultural Bolivia*. Stanford, CA: Stanford University Press.

Povinelli, E. A. (2011). *Economies of Abandonment: Social Belonging and Endurance in Late Liberalism*. Durham, NC: Duke University Press.

Preis, A. (2009) Human rights as cultural practice: An anthropological critique. In M. Goodale (Ed.), *Human Rights: An Anthropological Reader* (332–355). Oxford: Wiley Blackwell.

Pretty, J., Adams, B., Berkes, F., Ferreira de Athayde, S., Dudley, N., Hunn, E., Maffi, L., Milton, K., Rapport, D., Robbins, P., Sterling, E., Stolton, S., Tsing, A., Vintinnerk, E. & Pilgrim, S. (2009). The intersections of biological diversity and cultural diversity: Towards integration. *Conservation and Society* 7 (2), 100–112.

Prudham, S. & Coleman, W. D. (2011). Introduction: Property, territory and globalization. In W. D. Coleman (Ed.), *Property, Territory, Globalization: Struggles over Autonomy* (1–28). Vancouver: UBC Press.

Radcliffe, S. (2012). Development for a post-neoliberal era? Sumak Kawsay, living well and the limits of decolonization in Ecuador. *Geoforum* 43 (2), 240–249.

Rajagopal, B. (2003). *International Law from Below. Development, Social Movements and Third World Resistance*. Cambridge: Cambridge University Press.

Ramirez, P. M. (2011). Cartographies of Indigenous Power. In N. Fabricant & B. Gustafson (Eds.), *Remapping Bolivia: Resources, Territory, and Indigeneity in the Plurinational State* (30–45). Santa Fe, NM: School for American Research.

Rappaport, J. (2005). *Intercultural Utopias: Public Intellectuals, Cultural Experimentation and Ethnic Pluralism in Colombia*. Durham, NC: Duke University Press.

Ray, C. (2003). *Culture Economies: A Perspective on Local Rural Development in Europe*. Centre for Rural Economy: University of Newcastle upon Tyne.

Reddy, S. (2006). Making heritage legible: Who owns traditional medical knowledge? *International Journal of Cultural Property* 13 (2), 161–188.

Rhoades, R. (Ed.) (2006). *Development with Identity: Community, Culture and Sustainability*. Boston: CABI Press.

Rhoades, R. E. (2013). When seeds are scarce: Globalization and the response of three cultures. In V. Nazarea, R. E. Rhoades & J. E. Andrews-Swann (Eds.), *Seeds of Resistance, Seeds of Hope: Place and Agency in the Conservation of Biodiversity* (262–286). Tucson: University of Arizona Press.

Rodriguez-Navarro, G. E. (2015). Traditional knowledge: An innovative contribution to landscape management. In K. Taylor, A. St. Clair & N. J. Mitchell (Eds.), *Conserving Cultural Landscapes: Challenges and New Dimensions* (277–294). New York and London: Routledge.

Rose, N. (1999). *Powers of Freedom: Reframing Political Thought*. Cambridge: Cambridge University Press.

Rose, N. & Miller, P. (2010). Political power beyond the state: Problematics of government. *British Journal of Sociology* 61 (1), 271–303.

Rössler, M. (2006). World Heritage cultural landscapes: A UNESCO flagship programme. *Landscape Research* 31 (4), 333–353.

Rössler, M. (2012). Partners in site management, A shift in focus: Heritage and community involvement. In M. T. Albert, N. Richon, M. J. Vinals & A. Whitcomb (Eds.), *Community Development Through World Heritage* (World Heritage Papers No. 31) (27–31). Paris: UNESCO World Heritage Centre.

Ruiz-Mallen, I. & Corbera, E. (2013). Community-based conservation and traditional ecological knowledge: Implications for social-ecological resilience. *Ecology and Society* 18 (4). Retrieved from http://dx.doi.org/10.5751/ES-05867-180412. Accessed March 29, 2017.

Sena, K. (2010). Indigenous peoples: Development with culture and identity articles 3 and 32 of the United Nations Declaration on the Rights of Indigenous Peoples (PFII/2010/EGM). Department of Economic and Social Affairs. Division for Social Policy and Development Secretariat of the Permanent Forum on Indigenous Issues. New York: United Nations. Retrieved from http://www.un.org/esa/socdev/unpfii/documents/Paper%20submitted%20by%20Kanyinke%20Sena.doc. Accessed March 29, 2017.

Scher, P. (2011). Heritage tourism in the Caribbean: The politics of culture after neoliberalism. *Bulletin of Latin American Research* 30 (1), 7–20.

Scher, P. (2014). The right to remain cultural: Is culture a right in the neoliberal Caribbean? In D. Kapchan (Ed.), *Cultural Heritage in Transit: Intangible Rights as Human Rights* (87–112). Philadelphia: University of Pennsylvania Press.

Shaheed, F. (2011). Report of the independent expert in the field of Cultural Rights. United Nations General Assembly, Human Rights Council, Seventeenth Session. Doc A/HRC/17/38, 2011. Retrieved from http://www.unesco.org/new/fileadmin/MULTIMEDIA/HQ/CLT/images/Report%20of%20Farida%20Shaheed.pdf. Accessed March 29, 2017.

Shepherd, C. J. (2010). Mobilizing local knowledge and asserting culture. *Current Anthropology* 51 (5), 629–654.

Speed, S. (2007). *Rights in Rebellion: Indigenous Struggle and Human Rights in Chiapas*. Stanford, CA: Stanford University Press.

Speed, S., Hernandez-Castillo, R. A. & Stephen, L. eds. (2006). *Dissident Women: Gender and Cultural Politics in Chiapas*. Austin: University of Texas Press.

Speed, S., Blackwell, M., Hernandez-Castillo, R. A., Sieder, R., Sierra, M. T., Ramirez, R., Macleod, M. & Herrera, J. (2009). Remapping gender, justice, and rights in the Indigenous Americas: Toward a comparative analysis and collaborative methodology. *Journal of Latin American and Caribbean Anthropology* 14 (2), 300–331.

Stevens, S. (2014). Advancing the new paradigm: Implementation, challenges and potential. In S. Stevens (Ed.), *Indigenous Peoples, National Parks, and Protected Areas: A New Paradigm Linking Conservation, Culture and Rights* (283–312). Tucson: University of Arizona Press.

Strathern, M. (1999). Potential property: Intellectual rights and property in persons. In M. Strathern (Ed.), *Property, Substance and Effect: Anthropological Essays on Persons and Things* (161–178). London: Athlone Press.

Strathern, M. (2000). Multiple perspectives on intellectual property. In K. Whimp & M. Busse (Eds.), *Protection of Intellectual, Biological and Culture Property in Papua New Guinea* (47–61). Canberra: Asia Pacific Press; Port Moresby: Conservation Melanesia.

Strathern, M. & Hirsch, E. (Eds.). (2004). *Transactions and Creations: Property Debates and the Stimulus of Melanesia*. Oxford: Berghahn Books.

Sunder, M. & Chander, A. (2004). The romance of the public domain. *California Law Review* 92 (5), 1331–1374.

Tano, M. (2015). Climate and the transformation of landscapes: Building and strengthening Indigenous knowledge systems and institutions to manage threats to cultural landscapes. In K. Taylor, A. St. Clair & N. Mitchell (Eds.), *Conserving Cultural Landscapes: Challenges and New Directions* (325–340). New York: Routledge.

Tauli-Corpuz, V. (2008). The concept of indigenous people's self-determined identity or development with identity and culture: Challenges and trajectories. Tebtebba Foundation on behalf of UNESCO. CLT/CPD/CPO/2008/IPS/02. Retrieved from http://portal.unesco.org/culture/en/files/37745/12197591975Concept_paper_Indigenous_Peoples__Development_with_Identity.pdf/Concept%2Bpaper%2BIndigenous%2BPeoples%2B%2BDevelopment%2Bwith%2BIdentity.pdf. Accessed March 29, 2017.

Tauschek, M. (2012). The bureaucratic texture of national patrimonial politics. In R. Bendix, A. Eggert & A. Peselmann (Eds.), *Heritage Regimes and the State* (195–212). Göttingen: Göttingen University Press.

Tobin, B. (2014). *Indigenous Peoples, Customary Law and Human Rights: Why Living Law Matters*. New York: Routledge.

Tsing, A. L. (1999). Becoming a tribal elder and other green development fantasies. In T. M. Li (Ed.), *Transforming the Indonesian Uplands: Marginality, Power and Production* (159–202). Amsterdam: Harwood Academic.

Tsing, A. L. (2003). Agrarian allegory and global futures. In P. Greenough & A. Tsing (Eds.), *Nature in the Global South* (124–166). Durham, NC: Duke University Press.

Tsing, A. L. (2005). *Friction: An Ethnography of Global Connection*. Princeton, NJ: Princeton University Press.

Tsing, A. L. (2009). Adat/Indigenous: Indigeneity in motion. In C. Gluck & A. L. Tsing (Eds.), *Words in Motion: Toward a Global Lexicon* (40–64). Durham, NC: Duke University Press.

Turcotte, J. F. (2016). Creative transformation and the knowledge-based economy: Intellectual property and access to knowledge under informational capitalism. PhD dissertation, York University, August 9, 2016.

Ulloa, A. (2005). *The Ecological Native: Indigenous Peoples' Movements and Eco-Governmentality in Colombia.* New York: Routledge.

UNESCO. (2003). Convention for the Safeguarding of the Intangible Cultural Heritage. Retrieved from http://www.unesco.org/culture/ich/en/convention

Vadjunec, J., Schmink, M. & Greiner, A. L. (2011). New Amazonian geographies: Emerging identities and landscapes. *Journal of Cultural Geography* 28 (1), 1–20.

Walsh, C. (2010). Development as buen vivir: Institutional arrangements and decolonial entanglements. *Development* 53 (1): 15–21.

Ween, G. B. & Colombi, B. (2013). Two rivers: The politics of wild salmon, indigenous rights and natural resource management. *Sustainability* 5 (1), 478–495.

West, P. (2005). Translation, value, and space: Theorizing an ethnographic and engaged environmental anthropology. *American Anthropologist* 107 (4), 632–642.

Wilshusen, P. (2006). Territory, nature, and culture: Negotiating the boundaries of biodiversity conservation in the Colombian Pacific Coast region. In S. Brechin, P. Wilshusen, C.L. Fortwangler, & P. West (Eds.), *Contested Nature: Promoting International Biodiversity with Social Justice in the Twenty-First Century* (73–88). Albany, NY: SUNY Press.

Wilson, P. (2008). Indigeneity, neoliberalism and social engineering in Ecuador's Amazon. *Critique of Anthropology* 28 (2), 127–144.

Wright, S. (2008a). Locating a politics of knowledge: Struggles over intellectual property in the Philippines. *Australian Geographer* 39 (4), 409–426.

Wright, S. (2008b). Globalizing governance: The case of intellectual property rights in the Philippines. *Political Geography* 27 (7), 721–737.

Yates, J. (2014). Historicizing ethno-development: Kamoyaq and political economic development across governance regimes in the Peruvian Andes. *Journal of Historical Geography* 46 (1): 53–65.

Yates, J. & Bakker, K. (2013). Debating the "post-neoliberal turn" in Latin America. *Progress in Human Geography* 38 (1), 62–90.

Zimmerer, K. S. (2013). Environmental governance through "speaking like an environmental state" and respatialising resources: Ethical livelihood concepts in Bolivia as versatility or verisimilitude? *Geoforum* 64, 314–324.

PART V

New and experimental forms of cultural property

Jane Anderson and Haidy Geismar

As debates about cultural property evolve in tandem with broader social and political issues and events, Merryman's model of two ways of thinking about cultural property has splintered into many more (Merryman 1986; Bauer 2008). The constituents or claimants of cultural property have expanded from an initial dialogue between the national and the international to include many more grass-roots constituencies (from Indigenous communities through to the descendants of Jewish families systematically dispossessed during World War Two). In turn, following cultural theory and property theory more broadly, cultural property is no longer understood to be simply material culture, things we have collective rights in, but rather is perceived as the rights in relation to an assemblage of subjects, objects, processes and practices (Strathern 1999). The form of cultural property has also expanded away from antiquities, monuments and museum pieces, to include digital technologies, immaterial practices, medicinal knowledge, dance, music, sport and so on.

The emergence of new stakeholders, new territories, new sovereignties and new legal regimes is both produced by and produces new forms of cultural property. It also produces provocations and ambivalences: provocations in the sense that there are real challenges to liberal conceptualizations of the individual and property, and ambivalences in the sense that the state is no longer perceived as the primary site for cultural regulation. Thinking through these provocations and ambivalences, George Marcus observes that the claims of Indigenous peoples, for instance, are provocative because they 'define a form of cultural property that does not respect the nation-state but instead stands for the exclusive Other that operates within and across the boundaries of nation-states' (Marcus 1998: 233). This might also be understood as a politics of refusal (Simpson 2014) or as a form of counter-heritage (Byrne 2014). As a result of active disruptions to the traditional status quo of cultural property many of its new forms are experimental – cultural property regimes and discourses are being extended to intellectual property, to traditional knowledge, to pharmaceutical knowledge and even to the human body. Other forms of cultural property emerge from long-standing intersections and tensions between processes of marketization and commodification, and understandings of the public, the commons, national and universal heritage. In this section our contributors explore the intersections between cultural property discourses, the material world and the multiple relationships that shape and are shaped by these engagements.

Sita Reddy unpacks debates around the claiming of yoga as cultural property by India as a nation-state. Reddy highlights the ways in which yoga is in fact an 'invented tradition' that comes into being as a recognizable form of cultural property in the moments it becomes global. In this moment of recognition a very particular form of twentieth-century neoliberal nationalism is simultaneously mobilized and Reddy details this response as well as its consequences. The twentieth-century history of yoga as a form of fitness and lifestyle philosophy, both outside and within India, underscores the imaginary of yoga as an ethnically, spiritually and nationally delineated practice. By complicating the usual binary between culturally invested community engagement and corporate engagement, Reddy invites us to appreciate the ways in which new forms of cultural property also serve older ambitions, for instance in support of neoliberal nationalism. Here Reddy points to the paradox of both making and undoing cultural property at the same time. Yoga, because of its global distribution, can no longer function as cultural property of the state; it merely serves as a prop to reinforce a national imaginary that is cloaked in a variety of deliberate exclusions and omissions.

In a twist that layers past national politics and history with emergent ideas of property and collective memory, Lee Douglas explores the ways in which post-Franco Spain is coming to terms with its troubled history through emerging forms of restitution and historical memory that result in the recognition of new kinds of evidence of the past, from skeletal remains through to oral history and family documents. The efforts of citizen-scientists to presence the disappeared of Franco's regime is a political movement that exposes the complicity of the archive in state projects of oppression. Forensic anthropologists, alongside artists, historians and family members, labour to make this past, focusing attention on bodily remains of ancestors and oral histories in order to establish new articulations of cultural property from *within* the state but not *of* the state. In this emergent form an active critique of the state as the responsible authority is legitimately leveraged, since it is through the violence of the state towards its people that this new kind of cultural property has emerged.

Jane Anderson and Maria Montenegro's piece explores the ways in which the digitization of cultural property has created a new mode of social interaction and new protocols and collaborative frameworks for governing the circulation of digital media. Focusing on two instances of negotiation and collaboration – the Zuni reworking of the 1923 Shalako film held at the American Museum of Natural History and the *Local Contexts* project (an initiative to build new licences and labels for traditional knowledge within digital archiving platforms) – Anderson and Montenegro highlight how the digital circulation of cultural property encodes new forms of entitlement and sovereignty over cultural property, but in ways that are very different from the usual interventions into intellectual and cultural property rights. *Local Contexts* is in fact a hack of Creative Commons, itself a hack of intellectual property. *Local Contexts* insists that cultural property become an idiom within intellectual property – that attention be paid to the perpetual and enduring collective rights that are inscribed within digitized and digital culture. Both intellectual property law and Creative Commons focus on the rights of individual authors to maintain copyright or to give it up. *Local Contexts* recalibrates this domain to the "third space" of cultural property (see the Introduction to this volume). In the emergent domain of negotiated rights and permissions, cultural exchange is encapsulated by the notion of protocols and the development of meaningful practices of collaboration must also attend to the legal legacies of ownership that are being perpetuated in the transition to the digital.

In a similar vein, Shannon Faulkhead, John Bradley and Brent McKee explore the ways in which animations have come to mediate and make tangible Aboriginal language, allowing for a re-articulation through wide circulation of digital media of Aboriginal rights and sovereignties over cultural tradition, and therefore land. The dynamic objectification of storytelling through animation permits a greater visibility and circulation for Aboriginal language, and the discourse of cultural property leverages this visibility into a project of cultural revitalization with very specific activations of community agency. These animations also upend some of the binaries inherent within cultural property discourses. Put together collaboratively they reflect both Aboriginal knowledge and Euro-American visual culture. They reference the property protocols of both Aboriginal law and Western intellectual property, presenting us with an intercultural property artefact.

Marama Muru Lanning examines the tensions between corporate interest and cultural property surrounding the national allocation of different rights and entitlements to water in Aotearoa New Zealand. Maori investments in economic hydroelectric ventures signal the ways in which culture and economy are linked in contemporary cultural property claims. Fundamentally, Muru Lanning's work joins that of other Maori theorists who ask what a Maori national economy, or a Maori business world would look like (Spiller et al. 2010). These questions have been framed by Jean and John Comaroff as 'Ethnicity, Inc' (2009). The Comaroffs are interested in the ways in which ethnicity has become a new form of neoliberal instrumentalism, structuring new kinds of corporate engagement. However, they focus on the ways in which ethnicity is coopted into commodity flows and neoliberal frameworks. Muru Lanning focuses on the ways in which *taonga* (Maori cultural treasures) flow into these new structures and demand new forms of engagement. What does an economy look like when the river itself is a stakeholder? Muru Lanning's work joins a wave of new property theorists who critique the market from the vantage point of nature itself – assigning sovereignty to rivers, forests and the animal world (Kohn 2013). This is now a global movement, most famously supported by Ecuador including the Rights of Nature in its new constitution (Republic of Ecuador 2008).

In thinking about new and experimental forms of cultural property Douglas, Anderson and Montenegro, and Faulkhead, Bradley and McKee's contributions focus on the ways in which unexpected or novel forms of cultural property provide lucid articulations of historical memory and injustice as well as materializing cultural claims within new national frameworks. By contrast, Lanning's and Reddy's contributions focus on the ways in which ancient forms – Maori relations to waterways, and the system and practice of yoga – are being reforged as resources, highlighting in both cases the impossibility of purifying processes of cultural production and commodification. The emergence of new and experimental forms of cultural property demonstrate that the future for cultural property is intimately entangled in global markets, the boundaries of the state, but also a vital point of critique that privileges not just the collective over the individual or corporation but also the material and immaterial forms of property, demanding an engagement with the non-human as well as human world. We hope that this will gain traction in the age of the anthropocene, which is making clear the stakes of our relationship to the environment.

Bibliography

Bauer, Alex. 2008. "New Ways of Thinking about Cultural Property: A Critical Appraisal of the Antiquities Trade Debate." *Fordham International Law Journal* 31(3): 690–724.

Byrne, Denis. 2014. *Counterheritage: Critical Perspectives on Heritage Conservation in Asia.* New York: Routledge.

Comaroff, John L., and Jean Comaroff. 2009. *Ethnicity, Inc.* Chicago: University of Chicago Press. http://www.loc.gov/catdir/toc/ecip0828/2008040972.html.

Kohn, Eduardo. 2013. *How Forests Think: Toward an Anthropology Beyond the Human*. Berkeley: University of California Press.
Marcus, George. 1998. "Censorship in the Heart of Difference: Cultural Property, Indigenous Peoples' Movements and Challenges to Western Liberal Thought." In Robert Post (ed.), *Censorship and Silencing: Practices of Cultural Recognition*. Los Angeles: Getty Research Institute.
Merryman, John. 1986. "Two Ways of Thinking about Cultural Property." *American Journal of International Law* 80(4): 831–853.
Republic of Ecuador. 2008. *The Constitution of Ecuador*. https://www.constituteproject.org/constitution/Ecuador_2008.pdf
Simpson, Audra. 2014. *Mohawk Interruptus: Political Life Across the Borders of Settler States*. Durham, NC: Duke University Press.
Spiller, Chellie, Ljiljana Erakovic, Manuka Henare, and Edwina Pio. 2010. "Relational Well-Being and Wealth: Māori Businesses and an Ethic of Care." *Journal of Business Ethics* 98(1): 153–169.
Strathern, Marilyn. 1999. *Property, Substance, and Effect: Anthropological Essays on Persons and Things*. London; New Brunswick, NJ: Athlone Press.

20

WHO OWNS YOGA?

Transforming traditions as cultural property

Sita Reddy

The year 2015 was a year of extraordinary ferment in yoga's changing practice, and increasing propertization, around the world. On June 21, International Yoga Day, the Indian Prime Minister Narendra Modi and his newly appointed Minister of Yoga declared their intention to get Geographical Indication trademark status for yoga to establish its Indian origins. This followed continuing efforts by the Indian government to compile a digital archive of yoga postures or *asanas* as part of the Traditional Knowledge Digital Library, whose original intent was to prevent its cultural theft and appropriation by the West. May 2015 saw the latest court ruling in the Bikram Choudhury copyright case that has roiled the yoga community for more than ten years since Bikram Yoga first laid copyright claim to yoga as intellectual property. Nor was cyber-yoga quiet in these heritage claims. Earlier in the year, there was a high-profile attempt by YogaGlo, the largest online yoga company in the US, to secure a patent for its yoga videos. Meanwhile, yoga has been at the center of a series of disputes over its religious origins – ranging from two legal cases, one in the US, the other in India, attempting to ban yoga in public schools (on the claim that "it's too Hindu"), to an effort by the Hindu American Foundation to "Take Back Yoga" from celebrity culture (on the claim that "it's not Hindu enough"). And all of these legal disputes over yoga's cultural authenticity or historical origins say nothing about the rash of distinctly *non*-Hindu yoga styles to have mushroomed in secular (Stiles Yoga) as well as Christian contexts in the US (Praise Moves). If 2015's diversity was any guide, contemporary yoga practice may not even have to *be* Indian any more to be culturally meaningful to its global practitioners. Perhaps yoga in the twenty-first century need no longer be defined by its geographical origins or its physical connection to place.

Who owns contemporary yoga? Is yoga a religion? An exercise brand? A commodity? A cultural resource to be propertized? Is cultural *property*, in fact, at the heart of yoga's transformation in the modern age? Are the anxieties about yoga's origins – geographical, religious, national – driving its diverse expressions and heritage claims of ownership in an era of increasing commercialization? It certainly seems so. The irony is that most of these disparate ownership claims over yoga as cultural property are premised on two disputable 'facts': a) that yoga *asanas*, or modern postural yoga – seen as the bedrock of contemporary yoga – have existed since time immemorial (they have not); and b) that yoga is essentially part of, or has always been part of, Hindu Vedic orthodoxy (it is not).

This chapter will focus on a small handful of these legal cases and narratives to map the changing landscape of cultural ownership debates around yoga. It will end by drawing on interdisciplinary research behind a major art exhibition on the visual genealogy of yoga – *Yoga: The Art of Transformation* – to show two things through the visual historical record. First, that modern postural yoga or *asanas*, especially the standing *asanas*, as we know them, are not as old as we think they are. For example, the *Surya Namaskar* (the 'sun salutation' *asana* sequence at the heart of the California public school case mentioned above) is, as anthropologists and historians have shown, an early twentieth-century 'invented tradition' in Hobsbawm and Ranger's definition of the term (Hobsbawm and Ranger, 1983). And second, the exhibition shows that yoga has roots not in Hindu orthodoxy but in heterodox Saiva and Tantric traditions. In fact, the earliest visual evidence we have of a sequence of standing *asanas* is from a sixteenth-century medieval Sufi text written in Persian and translated from the Sanskrit: namely, the extraordinary *Bahr-Al-Hayat.* Yogic *practice*, it seems, especially those practices that we can trace historically through the visual record, has always been global, heterodox, and plural.

Yoga, in the contemporary

Even with tangible or built heritage, cultural property and heritage protection discussions can go around in circles, feeding off each other like a Jungian ourobouros chasing its own tail. Nowhere is this circularity, this rehashing of old arguments, more visible than in ownership claims over *intangible*, emergent, and evolving cultural practices like yoga. As we now know from contemporary yoga the world over, this centuries-old form of mind-body discipline is nothing if not adaptive to current contexts. An entire literature has emerged to describe what Mark Singleton (2010) calls the changing forms of 'transnational Anglophone yoga,' or what Joseph Alter (2004) terms contemporary yogic heteropraxy. But yoga's own etymology may be instructive in pointing to a peculiar irony within these transformations. The Sanskrit word yoga means union or link (between mind and body) and it is etymologically related to the English 'yoke,' which in this case refers to the union between mind and body in the quest for spiritual enlightenment. Yoke could, however, also be interpreted to mean yoked to history, chained to a pre-determining past. And indeed, twenty-first-century yoga practice, in all its diversity, seems mired in its preoccupations with distant pasts, yoked to its own heritage claims of singular authenticity and classical origins – all of which puts yoga at the very epicenter of cultural property debates in this anxious age.

Even compared with other years, 2015 was uncommonly busy for these propertizing claims over yoga's past. So perhaps it is as good a place as any to start discussions of yoga *as* cultural property. I should begin with the caveat that like most history, this chapter is fiction. It is not a lie or alternative fact; it is an honest, even accurate, account of these heritage stories and narrative claims. But in the process of telling and re-telling and recovery of heritage, in particular intangible heritage, as property, there are gaps that become visible, contradictions that reveal themselves as fault-lines, and unintended consequences of making this heritage legible, or visible, or even commercially viable. So it is with contemporary yoga's heritage claims. Heritage, after all, is just one form of social remembrance and reflection upon the past, not always the most effective. Indeed, as Jacques Derrida reminds us in *Archive Fever* (1998), archival remembering is often as much about forgetting as it is about remembering. In the act of seeing, each seer creates an image and forgets the rest; in the act of remembering, each account selects memories and erases others; in the act of telling, each teller creates a set of stories that persist as original, authentic and true.

As stories go, this one may in fact be somewhat static and repetitive, and replete with predictable plot-lines about ancient pasts. At one level, this is because of the things I study (invented traditions that hark back to classical golden ages and medieval decline), the cultural biographies I trace, and the international regime of heritage policy that makes it difficult, sometimes even impossible, for intangible cultural heritage to move easily, cross borders, and transcend boundaries – despite all assurances to the contrary – whether these boundaries are social, museological or legal. My heritage story may lack good plot-lines but it has a supporting cast that includes the entire family of cultural and intellectual property cousins (trademark, patents, copyright) rubbing up against each other to protect the protagonist, modern yoga, in its various identity claims as Indian, or as Hindu, or even just as exercise regimen.

2015 was rife with these propertizing claims over yoga's origins in its changing practice around the world. Yoga is now the ultimate global commodity, and everyone seems to want in on its ownership, from the Indian government to gurus in swank California studios, as yoga gets caught in a web of claims and counterclaims, and problems of visibility and legibility even as it spins into orbit in the heritage pantheon.

To begin with, as mentioned earlier, in one of the more public claims at the national level, the Indian Prime Minister, Narendra Modi announced that he wants to claim Geographical Indication status for yoga to establish its Indian origins and thus prevent its appropriation by or in the West. This follows continuing efforts by the Indian government to compile a digital archive of yoga *asanas*, the Traditional Knowledge Digital Library, in an effort not only to avoid its cultural theft by non-Indian nationals but also to establish its 'correct' practice amongst the same audiences. At the other end of the global spectrum, there are efforts by international multilateral organizations, such as UNESCO, to push for yoga to be considered an Olympic sport, replete with all the competitive nationalism that they may inspire. 2015 also saw the latest court ruling in the Bikram Choudhury copyright case that has shaken the yoga community since 2002 when he began to make copyright claims for his sequence of Bikram Yoga. Earlier in the year, there was a high-profile attempt by YogaGlo, the largest online yoga company in the US, to secure a patent for its method of filming yoga classes, which may have been unsuccessful in proving innovation but remains notable in that the patent was requested in the first place. Meanwhile, yoga has been at the center of a series of disputes over its religious origins – including two legal cases, one in the US (*US v. Sedlock*), the other in India (All India Muslim Personal Law Board campaign), attempting to ban yoga in public schools on the claim that 'it's too Hindu,' and an effort by the Hindu American Foundation to Take Back Yoga from celebrity culture, on the claim that 'it's not Hindu enough.'

In turn, everyone seems to be not only defending their version of authentic yoga, but offending, getting offended, and drawing lines of ownership and communities of belonging and 'right practice' – Hindus, Indians, sadhus and Nath yogis, the wealthy, the poor, Christians, women who pray, women who don't. And all of these legal disputes over authenticity say little about the rash of distinctly non-Hindu yoga styles to have mushroomed in secular as well as Christian contexts in the US. If this diversity is any guide, contemporary transnational yoga practice no longer has to *be* Indian or look Indian to be culturally meaningful to its practitioners. Could it be that yoga's cultural identity in the twentieth century is both deeply defined by geography but no longer determined by its origins? Is it possible that contemporary yoga has, in fact, been *un*yoked from place?

How did this come about? This zeal for moral certainty about what cultural property belongs to whom, and where it is literally, physically, from. Was it always thus? After all, medieval yoga in the twelfth century was marked by a remarkably fluid transcendence beyond regional boundaries and sectarian lines. Given this continuing diversity of contemporary practitioners, who owns twenty-first-century yoga? And, as I posed earlier, what is yoga exactly? Is yoga a religion? An exercise brand? A commodity? A cultural resource to be propertized? Is cultural property, in fact, at the heart of yoga's transformation in the modern age? Are the anxieties about yoga's origins – geographical, religious, national – driving its diverse expressions in an era of increasing commercialization and propertization? It certainly seems so.

What follows is a very short attempt to tease out some of these longer (and more historically entrenched) arguments and newer heritage claims. This chapter will attempt to map some of the more recent cases, tracing ways in which yoga, the gentle art of transformation, was itself transformed in the twenty-first century. Drawing on interdisciplinary research behind a major 2013 art exhibition on the visual genealogy of yoga – *Yoga: The Art of Transformation* – it will focus on a small handful of these cases to map the changing landscape of cultural ownership debates around changing yoga, as it transformed itself in reaching out to transnational audiences everywhere. Perhaps yogic *practice*, contrary to current more nationalistic claims, was always already global.

Yoga as India's cultural property

One place to begin unraveling these various threads is with recent governmental claims that yoga is – or should be – India's distinct cultural property, a *national* resource to be controlled by the state. On June 21, 2015, International Yoga Day, Prime Minister Narendra Modi, and his newly appointed Minister of Yoga, Shripad Yesso Naik, announced their intention to seek Geographical Indication status for yoga. Just the creation of the new Minister's position in itself is an indication of Modi's continuing efforts, since he took office, to have yoga recognized as an *Indian* practice grounded in the Hindu tradition. There has been an ongoing effort to incorporate yoga into India's schools; to introduce it as a palliative therapy in hospitals and as a remedial program in prisons; and to include it in police academies as a training tool. Meanwhile, the Traditional Knowledge Digital Library, which has already worked at compiling Ayurvedic knowledge to prevent patent theft, continues with a government archive documenting at least 1,500 yoga *asanas* – a library of videos demonstrating practitioners doing yoga the proper way, which represents a centralized response to unofficial guides with more grassroots or idiosyncratic bases. These efforts are part of the current government's larger Made in India campaign, which includes plans to improve the country's public infrastructure and manufacturing sector. From a cynical standpoint, all of these efforts to establish yoga's Indianness, including Naik's appointment, might be akin to a strategic business move – to claim a segment of what has become a lucrative multi-billion-dollar yoga industry in the US. And here lies the irony: to cash in on yoga's transnational success story, it appears that India, from the cultural property point of view, must first show yoga to *be* Indian. The *cultural* work with a GI status or a digital database of yoga like TKDL is to produce and manufacture this yoke to Indianness, the yoke being both historical anchor as well as lifeline to aspired futures.

Seeking Geographical Indication status for yoga, however, may be neither that simple nor straightforward. Within cultural property categories, a Geographical Indication is essentially a trademark – a formal acknowledgement of the importance of geography, or location, to a specific product. Described another way, it's a measure of the centrality of place to cultural identity, typically used in food products such as Champagne grapes or Camembert cheese. But while Geographical Indications are given by a country's government trade office, they were essentially established by TRIPS (that is, Trade-Related aspects of Intellectual Property Rights, administered by the World Trade Organization) and thus there is no larger regulatory international body like the United Nations that can resolve international disputes. The US

Patent and Trade Office acknowledges this vagueness and, as a result, countries with an ownership claim on this or that culturally specific product (for example, Champagne wine or Mysore silks) have no way of challenging them. This seems to be a nature of the market, with the US continuing to sell products without always verifying their cultural origins.

With yoga, on the other hand, it would be difficult to establish a concrete geographical connection or a definitive link with any one place. Unlike, for example, Champagne – which is made from grapes grown in a particular region with distinct soil content and chemistry – yoga has no *terroir*, i.e. it cannot be linked with either land or region.[1] There are of course genealogical schools and traditions of yoga – each of which does come from specific places, and indeed, some yoga forms can be linked to a region or state (e.g. Bihar School). But practically speaking, securing a Geographical Indication for yoga would be nearly impossible, even though legal scholars point out that it is more a rhetorical claim to establish a foundational mythology that uses an idea of the law to secure the strategic fiction. Indeed, although yoga originated in South Asia, its *transnational* practice – including the many diverse forms that have emerged, such as elder yoga, Stiles yoga, hot yoga, doga, nude yoga – makes it difficult to argue that its Indian origins are always essential to its essence or contemporary meaning.

Moreover, even if all the conditions for Geographical Indication status were met, international enforcement would be a logistical nightmare. While protection within the country might still be within the realms of possibility, keeping tabs on every yoga studio in the world would be practically impossible. Furthermore, even though the government is providing significant resources toward the effort, it would need an effective bureaucracy to regulate yoga, which in all probability would not be easy to implement. Ultimately, it looks like little will change anytime soon for the US yoga industry and its current population of 20 million practitioners. But it is easy to understand why the Indian government would explore the possibility: yoga classes and the accompanying products are a $10 billion a year industry. Global yoga sells, and propertizing it through geography or national identity is one way of attempting to claim one's share.

Whose yoga? "Not Hindu enough"

With all these economic and cultural resources at stake, it is not surprising that there is a debate about yoga's true origins, and who, if anyone, it ultimately belongs to – in other words, who owns it. It is also not surprising that the global yoga market – and what Mark Singleton calls "transnational Anglophone yoga" – is replete with versions and variants of yoga that have no recognizable similarity to those in India. The Western fascination with yoga can be traced back to the 1960s, when a generation was hungry for a spirituality and practice different from their parents' religious beliefs. Religious studies scholar Catherine Albanese (2006), for instance, suggests that metaphysical religion is at least as important as evangelicalism in shaping American religious history and practice, and in identifying what makes them distinctive.[2] And in this context, at least in the US, diasporic yoga was a means by which traditional Christian thought could be blended with Eastern philosophy. Even earlier, the nineteenth-century philosopher and religious teacher Swami Vivekananda presented yoga as a system of philosophical practice that balanced Eastern spiritualism and Western materialism, a form of practice that could be seen as Eastern corrective to the excesses of Western capitalism and commodification.[3]

These days, however, many Americans view yoga as little more than an exercise regimen, which means that the practice has more or less been broken off from its millennia-old Hindu philosophical roots, or even from Vivekananda's synthesis of the nineteenth century. A few years ago, yoga's near-complete transition from spiritual practice to trendy fitness and exercise regimen was marked by a spirited debate, which flared up again in 2015. Incensed by American yoga's lack of religious connotation or acknowledgement, Sheetal Shah, a senior director at the Hindu American Foundation (HAF), an organization devoted to celebrating this hyphenated religious identity among Indian diasporics, contacted the publication *Yoga Journal* to ask why it had never linked yoga to Hinduism. *Yoga Journal*'s unsatisfactory responses, in Shah's view, prompted her to launch an initiative called Take Back Yoga to highlight yoga's Hindu roots. In response to Shah's campaign, groups across the religious spectrum questioned whether there was a place in the ancient practice for practitioners of other faiths, and whether it was possible for any religion to 'own' yoga in the first place (taking the example of Yahweh yoga). Others wondered if religious twists on yoga were contrary to the vision of Vivekananda, who first introduced yoga to the West in 1893 at the World Parliament of Religions at the Chicago World's Fair. Indeed, Vivekananda's message of East meets West, body meets mind, through yoga seemed to privilege the practice for secular practitioners or those of any religious bent, rather than orthodox believers of a particular faith.

Prior to Shah's Take Back Yoga campaign, the *Washington Post* published a series of dialogues between another HAF member, Dr. Aseem Shukla, and the physician-author Deepak Chopra, arguing over yoga's provenance. While the HAF maintained that the West ignores the connection between Hinduism and yoga, Chopra and many yoga instructors have pointed to the Sanskrit invocations peppered throughout a typical yoga practice as evidence that proper dues were being paid. Moreover, Chopra argued that yoga's connection to Hinduism might be weaker than often presumed, given that the archaeological record suggests that yoga predates early Hindu scriptures.

Today, the HAF says that Take Back Yoga is a misnomer. They say they were simply interested in highlighting yoga's Hindu roots without insisting that it must be practiced by people of a specific religion. Even so, as described in new statements and position papers, they still seem to care deeply about the distinction between *true* yoga's respect for the past and American yoga's relatively superficial concerns. For Shah, the ultimate goal of yoga remains that of *moksha,* or spiritual liberation. But for many others, apparently, there's a very different angle from which to approach the issues of cultural ownership and religious origins of yoga: its underlying Hinduism. Or not. Indeed, these differences in goals point to the multiple searches for *religious* authenticity that yoga gets caught up in.

If there's a coda here, it is to suggest that while yoga does not belong to Hinduism or Hindus, the fact remains that it has been presented as such – symbolically, ritually, in yoga classes the world over – even as its philosophical base, which is of course *derived* from Hinduism, often gets reduced or understood strictly as exercise regimen in the local gymnasium.

Whose yoga? "Too Hindu for school"

The opposite claim – that yogic exercise qua exercise was far too 'Hindu' to be taught in public schools – also found its way through the courts in 2015, both in the US and in India. In April 2015, a California appeals court ruled that a school district in Encinitas could incorporate yoga into physical education classes, rejecting a challenge by parents who said the millennia-old discipline violates religious freedom provisions in California's constitution, which are broader than those in the US Constitution.

The constitutional gatekeeping around public schools has managed to keep out a variety of religious activity in recent history – student prayers at football games, Bible readings in class, pictures of Jesus. Yoga was just one in a long line of practices to be accused of overly religious content (by plaintiffs) and, given the separation of church and state in the Constitution, a practice that ought to be off-limits in secular public schools. The yoga *asanas* taught by instructors in Encinitas's nine schools were adapted from Ashtanga yoga, which was popularized by Sri K. Pattabhi Jois, an eminent Indian yoga teacher who died in 2009. Literally meaning eight limbs, *ashta anga* includes among these limbs the union with the divine.

The plaintiffs, Stephen and Jennifer Sedlock, who sued on behalf of their two children, portrayed yoga in their court briefs as "a Hindu religious exercise or practice that is simultaneously physical and religious." Court briefs argued that the Jois Foundation funded the yoga program and trained the instructors, with a 'mission' to disseminate his religious notions. At the heart of the California case is the *surya namaskar*, the sun salutation series of exercises shared by Ashtanga as well as other forms of yoga, which was taught as part of a rigorous exercise regimen to students of all ages. Somewhat ironically, the Sedlocks were (and are) represented by the National Center for Law & Policy, a group that defends the religious rights of Christians.

The Encinitas public school case itself actually began a few years earlier. After parents complained in 2012 of yoga's religious overtones, the school district stripped the program of Sanskrit and any references to the spiritual or divine, including a description of the curriculum that said yoga brings out 'the inner spirit of the child.' The *asanas*, or as the school district calls them, 'poses', have child-friendly and neutral names, such as 'the boat' (for *utkanasana*) while the lotus pose (*padmasana*) was renamed 'crisscross applesauce.' A lower court found the program was 'devoid of any religious, mystical or spiritual trappings' although this process of renaming *asanas* in order to expunge yoga of all religious content is interesting in itself. The California Fourth District Court of Appeal agreed. The court's ruling stated "It is clear that while yoga may be practiced for religious reasons, it cannot be said to be inherently religious or overtly sectarian. In the absence of evidence that the District's program advances religion, no religious coercion is present."

According to the chief counsel of the National Center for Law & Policy, the family is considering its legal options, on the premise that "No other court in the past fifty years has allowed public school officials to lead children in formal religious rituals." If the school cases point to anything, it is the ironic ways in which twenty-first-century yoga's propertization rests on identity claims that are not just nationalistic but religious or secular, as the case may be.

Who owns yoga's copyright?

And finally, last but certainly not least, there is the controversy surrounding Bikram Chaudhury's 'Hot Yoga' sequence of *asanas* and his decade-long attempt to copyright his version of yoga. On October 14, 2015, the US District of Appeals for the Ninth Circuit ruled that a sequence of poses performed in a heated room – Bikram Chaudhury's 'Hot Yoga' Sequence (as it is called) – was not entitled to copyright protection under the law. To the jubilation of more than six hundred yoga studio franchises of the Bikram sequence across the country, the legal case in a federal appeals court, *Bikram Yoga College v. Evolation Yoga*, effectively ended a decade-long battle in the courts in which Choudhury had attempted to claim monopoly over his sequence of 28 poses, repeatedly and aggressively suing for copyright infringement.

All those copyright claims took a blow when the court ruled that Chaudhury does *not* hold the exclusive right to teach the series of poses and breathing exercises he developed. The legal fight had in some ways epitomized the struggle between traditional yoga practice, with its focus on spiritual healing and poses that are ostensibly thousands of years old, and the modern multibillion-dollar industry that has sprung up to sell that practice to the public. Chaudhury and the Bikram College/Hot Yoga enterprise had long threatened other instructors with legal action, warning them that without his authorization, they could not use the sequence of 28 poses made famous at his Los Angeles-based studio and its franchises. Anyone who wanted to teach the sequence had to pay a licensing fee and adhere to a number of other specifications, such as the correct temperature (103°F) and length of class (90 minutes), quality of lighting, specific training for instructors, and so on.

But in the court's opinion, Judge Kim McLane Wardlaw wrote, "Consumers would have little reason to buy Choudhury's book if Choudhury held a monopoly on the practice of the very activity he sought to popularize." "The Sequence," as the series is known, is an "idea, process or system designed to improve health. Choudhury can copyright *expressions* of that idea – books, diagrams, movies – but he can't copyright its execution any more than a surgeon can stop other doctors from mimicking his techniques."

From all media accounts, yoga studios around the country and their practitioners were relieved at the ruling, which, they said, would allow them to continue to focus on teaching yoga, rather than worry about copyright violation of a yoga empire that was motivated by greed. Needless to say, the Bikram Yoga College made the opposite claims over the decade – that it was the *unaffiliated* studios and teachers of the practice who were stealing and modifying the Bikram sequence without regard to the safety or health of the hapless clients. Remarkably, each side made similar arguments and hurled it at the other – namely, that it was the innocent 'clients' who got hurt in this trend toward unfettered yoga capitalism and commodification.[4]

Over the last decade, a number of studio owners had settled out of court with Choudhury to avoid a prolonged legal battle. The California-based Open Source Yoga Unity was among the first to challenge Choudhury's copyrights, although the cases were eventually settled out of court. In 2011, Choudhury took on Yoga to the People, a pay-what-you-can chain of studios in New York opened by one of his former students. Ultimately, that case was also settled. Yoga to the People's owners agreed to stop teaching Bikram-style Hot Yoga to bring an end to the suit. But it prompted the US Copyright Office to issue a new policy clarifying that individual yoga poses are not subject to copyright laws, the same way a choreographer cannot lay claim to an individual ballet step.

It's interesting to note that the legal case in question behind the recent 2015 ruling originated when Mark Drost, a former Bikram acolyte, left to found Evolation Yoga in 2008. Drost was committed to continuing to use the Bikram sequence in his own way, and when Choudhury sued for copyright infringement, he refused to settle. The opening statement on Drost's website declared, "We wanted to establish that you can't *own* [emphasis mine] yoga sequences. Traditionally, you take a teacher's training and move forward with it."

In the end, if the decade-long struggle over copyrighting yoga established anything, it was that cultural ownership of something as complicated as twenty-first-century yoga is no simple matter. Since copyright seems to be the chosen form of intellectual property struggle for intangible or digital heritage, as opposed to, for example, patents (which need to show innovation) or trademarks (usually pursued by corporate entities), the Bikram case also shows that copyright ownership itself can as easily be contested in principle and in practice; that intangible heritage can be propertized for infringement as easily as it can be reclaimed for the public domain. While the Bikram Yoga copyright case was neither a nationalist claim (as was the Indian government's Geographical Indication application) nor a religious claim (as in the public school cases), it remained an individual claim outside India for a very specific transformation of yoga's practice. As such, one can argue that these transformations of yoga as commodity – national, religious, or health care – are key to the transformative idea of yoga *as* cultural property. Thus at a material level, unyoking yoga from traditional forms of production seems to exist alongside its re-yoking to new forms of commodity fetishism and new relations of cultural production.

Yoga and the art of modern transformations

Through all these swirling arguments of ownership and belonging over yoga, both in India and abroad, there are two presumptions that seem to lie at the very core of yoga's heritage claims: one, that modern postural yoga – the core of exercise regimens today – is more than a millennium old, dating back intact to at least the time of Patanjali's *Yoga Sutras* in the fifth century CE. And two, that this ancient yoga had orthodox Hindu roots and origins, not heterodox ones. The *visual* record of yoga, however, tells a quite different story, or set of stories, belying both presumptions.

In 2013, the Smithsonian's Arthur M. Sackler Gallery of Asian Art presented an interdisciplinary art exhibition *Yoga: The Art of Transformation* that relied on this visual genealogy to trace the story of yoga's transformations, many of which were able to show definitively that yoga's heritage claims are neither that old nor that orthodox.[5] Visual genealogies of yoga are rarely seamless, often revealing themselves most clearly at times of change. Through what Christopher Pinney calls 'visual eruptions' of earlier images, they suggest that what we take for granted today in modern yoga and therefore in modern yoga's cultural property cases – the emphases on *asana* (posture), *vinyasa* (sequential movement), and specific *asana* sequences (such as *surya namaskar* or sun salutation, the *asana* sequence at the center of the school ban cases) – are neither millennia-old nor rooted in ancient texts, but of relatively recent vintage. While their roots certainly run deep, modern postural yoga, and *surya namaskars* in particular, are in fact twentieth-century invented traditions.

This history can be fairly specific if we start looking for illustrated treatises that actually depict postural yoga or standing *asanas* in pictorial form as opposed to mere verbal descriptions of them in earlier texts. Interestingly, these visual depictions can rarely be traced before the twentieth century. In what follows, I offer a smattering of the key illustrated texts and media that trace this story in the visual record. One of the earliest illustrated compilations of yoga *asanas*, for example, is a 1907 history of fakirs in German by Richard Schmidt titled *Fakire und Fakirtum im Alten und Modernen India. Fakire und Fakirtum* was unusual because it included not only negative perceptions of yogis as 'petty thieves and swindlers,' as was common in Western popular media and travelogues of the time, but also a reclamation of classical, text-based yoga. Its comprehensive account of hatha yoga included eighty-seven watercolors of *asanas* drawing on artistic styles of early nineteenth-century illustrated manuscripts, such as the *Jogapradipika* painted in the Kangra style or the Mysore Palace's Tanjore-style *Sritatvanidhi*.

Each of the illustrated *asanas* in *Fakire und Fakirtum* is isolated and labeled and identified in Devanagari script, and the watercolor medium and unpainted ground is typical of nineteenth-century Company School (*kampani kalam*) paintings, which native artists produced for foreign patrons. Seen individually, the paintings are elegant but unremarkable, executed in what Partha Mitter calls the "conceptual mode of art followed by Indian artists since antiquity": shallow, flat, two-dimensional outlines of figures that lack Western perspective. But, taken together, *Fakire und Fakirtum*'s watercolors offer a complete visual archive of all the classical *asanas* outlined in medieval hatha yoga texts, such as *Hathayogapradipika* and *Gheranda Samhita*. It was thus possibly the earliest inspiration for Indian yoga pioneers like Swami Kuvalayananda and T. Krishnamacharya, who in the early twentieth century developed what would become modern postural yoga practice.

Schmidt's *Fakire und Fakirtum* was a precursor of the instructional manuals of *asanas* published in the 1920s, when figurative, two-dimensional, conceptual models gave way to the naturalistic, objective representations of photographic realism as yoga was assimilated into the modern. A key transitional text in this visual history is *Yogasopana Purvacatushka*, compiled by Yogi Ghamande in 1905 – described by Mark Singleton as "perhaps the first and only self-help yoga manual to use a half-tone block print reproduction technique." *Yogasopana* (literally, 'stair-way to heaven') includes thirty-seven detailed black-and-white line drawings of *asanas*, all modeled by Ghamande himself. This exquisite volume broke new ground in depicting naturalistic, muscled, yogic bodies, prefiguring photographic *asana* manuals by two decades, and is particularly important to a visual genealogy of yoga because it was conceived as a practical postural yoga manual in the twentieth century. Interestingly, *Yogasopana* was likely printed using the same half-tone block printing process used by one of the best-known early contemporary artists in India, Raja Ravi Varma – from the hypothesis that the artists may have shared space in Mysore Palace with T. Krishnamacharya's famous yogasala (yoga hall).

As with art, so with reinventions of yoga *asanas*. If there is a single text (and eponymous *asana* series) in the early twentieth century that embodies the transformation of yoga through its intersections with bodybuilding and physical culture through an *asana* sequence, it is Pratinidhi Pant's *Surya Namaskars*, first published in 1929 and revised and republished five times before 1940. The book's title refers to the sun salutation exercise that may well be the single best-recognized *asana* sequence or yoga meme in postural yoga today – and of course is at the very center of the bans on yoga in schools, both complainants claiming (from opposite ends) that sun worship is too Hindu for public schools (California) or too Hindu for the Indian nation (India).

Surya namaskar is routinely invoked by contemporary practitioners as an ancient feature of Indian civilization, although it is thoroughly modern. While it is often difficult to trace the exact genealogy of specific sequences, historians agree that the creation of the modern *surya namaskar* system can be attributed to Pratinidhi Pant, who was the then raja of Aundh. Pant chose to illustrate the first edition of *Surya Namaskars* with monochromatic prints of schematic, two-dimensional figures performing ten *asanas* in the original series. Later editions include photographs of all ten *asanas*, evidence of the new photographic realism that was changing perceptions of yogic bodies in the early twentieth century. Either way, *Surya Namaskars* (the book) sits at an important historical nexus of yoga, bodybuilding and physical education in India during the early twentieth century. Pant's project of health reform clearly fit with ongoing political, medical and cultural trends, but was also unique in its emphasis on the relationship between body discipline and nationalism in modern India. He was a devoted bodybuilder and practitioner of the Eugene Sandow method who popularized the *surya namaskar asana* sequence as an indigenous bodybuilding technique. In gymnasia, this sequence became a practical expression of the unique blend of yoga-physical fitness through an internal regimen of body conditioning on the one hand and indigenous bodybuilding on the other. It was only later, in the 1930s, that it was absorbed into yoga routines, in some part due to the popularity of Pant's book.

Other illustrated yoga manuals made similar connections with Western models of physical culture, such as the Scandinavian Ling exercise system. A classic case in point is M. R. Jambunathan's 1941 *The Yoga Body Illustrated*, which promised the reader 'a strong and beautiful body' through the practice of yoga. Among the best-known early printed *asana* manuals, these publications presented yoga *asanas* as body-conditioning techniques that could lead to bodily perfection and, therefore, happiness. Both books exemplify the absorption of postural yoga by physical culturalists in the early twentieth century, the promotion of hatha yoga exercise as part of a larger, highly aestheticized physical culture regime based on Western models. During this period, books like *The Yoga Body Illustrated* reflected an identifiable shift in yogic body practice – from hatha yoga's perfection of the body (the conquest over the 'material') to modern fitness models based on Western ideals of physique and strength. Swami Kuvalayananda's *Yoga Mimansa*, which first made the link between yoga, health and science in the 1920s was another classic case in point. And as such, these manuals anticipated by several decades all the other photographic manuals of *asanas* that followed: Theos Bernard's *Hatha Yoga* in 1941 and, later in the 1960s, works by Indra Devi, B. K. S. Iyengar and Vishnudevananda.

Similar attempts to link hatha yoga with physical culture and muscle control occurred in the transnational context. During the first decades of the twentieth century, early proponents of yoga in the United States included Yogendra, Ramacharaka, Yogi Gherwal and Yogi Wassan, but they also extended to alternative healthcare practitioners who drew on New Thought philosophies. An early example of this therapeutic synthesis is Albrecht Jensen's 1920 *Massage and Exercise Combined*. The book, endorsed by American alternative health luminary W. A. Kellogg, identified psychophysiological methods of muscle control as Indian yoga techniques. It thus recast yoga as a muscle-based physical culture for a new generation of American alternative health enthusiasts who would not have easily encountered hatha yoga through other routes.

For all their transformative potential in producing new forms of *asana*, static print and photographic technologies of visual reproduction were thoroughly eclipsed by the extraordinary reach of moving images and film in the early twentieth century, especially when these new media were used by a legendary twentieth-century practitioner to disseminate yoga's dynamic potential as sequential movement and transformative practice available to everyone. Such was the case in 1938 when the Mysore maharaja, Krishnaraja Wodiyar, sponsored an early film of T. Krishnamacharya – the father of modern yoga – demonstrating a series of flowing *asana* sequences. For the first time in history, these yoga sequences could be showcased around the country to non-students: 'imagined communities' in pre-independence India, united through shared pasts and invented future.

In other words, even this first *archival* film on standing yoga's origins is old but not that old. Partly filmed in black-and-white and partly in color, the archival 57-minute silent film is a composite of rare footage showing a 50-year-old Krishnamacharya demonstrating advanced postures in linked sequences that are both hypnotic and inspiring. He is accompanied by several other practitioners, young and old, male and female, including his then-student B. K. S. Iyengar. In the grainy, eight-minute opening sequence, the camera focuses on a young Iyengar, who performs a series of difficult seated *asana* positions, what seems to be a modified version of Ashtanga Advanced A Series, in an unidentified outdoor location. The next segment (ten minutes long) features close-ups of Krishnamacharya doing a series of seated *nauli* and *pranayama* exercises, the grace and elegance of the linking *vinyasas* matched only by the control required to sustain each position. In the short sections that follow, the camera moves indoors to feature two women and two children (performing *asanas* synchronously), ending in a sequence where Krishnamacharya demonstrates a set of balancing exercises with the children, more reminiscent of an acrobatic circus act. The film ends with a black-and-white sequence outdoors, against a backdrop of unidentified mountains, in which Krishnamacharya dazzles the viewer with a tightly choreographed series of difficult inversions and headstands.

At the time the film was made, Krishnamacharya was the resident teacher in the Mysore Palace, where he created his own yoga synthesis, combining hatha yoga practice, British and

Swedish calisthenics, and the gymnastic and wrestling traditions of Karnataka. Moving images or silent film offered the perfect dynamic and public medium through which these *vinyasas* could be presented for the first time in pre-independence India. This impulse to spread the gospel of new yoga through regular demonstrations was both democratizing – it introduced yoga to unprecedented new audiences – and competitive, attracting students who might otherwise have gone the way of Western gymnastics. The maharaja sent Krishnamacharya all over South India on this 'propaganda work,' and the teacher's debut on celluloid was conceived as part performance piece, part spectacular enticement to introduce yoga to mass audiences.

Throughout the film, the slow, almost languorous, aesthetic of unfolding *asanas* complements the camera's rigorous focus on the practitioner; the dynamic linking *vinyasas* provide both sequential narrative and connective tissue for the story of modern postural yoga in India. The film achieves many things at once: it is cultural archive as well as museum artifact; live theater as well as historical documentation of a tradition in the making. In the late 1930s, it was a cinematic innovation in visualizing modern yogic practice, but also part of a larger project of public dissemination that relied heavily on a nationalist physical culture.

Located somewhere between documentary and ethnography, the film's narrative-free sequences of *asanas* encode their own hidden visual histories, much like a palimpsest. It can be seen as a performative spectacle that recalls earlier performances of fakirs and yogis but was reinvented for nationalist audiences eager to see yoga as indigenous exercise. If this film footage suggests one thing, it is that new ways of representing *asana* led directly to new ways of perceiving yoga, and therefore, of practicing yoga, performing yogic identities and inhabiting yogic bodies.

This archival film footage was the very last exhibit in the Sackler Gallery's exhibition *Yoga: The Art of Transformation* (as displayed in Washington, DC) and as such, provides an excellent endpoint for a chapter on yoga's transformations in the twenty-first century. Indeed, one of the striking elements in the exhibition was the visual connection between at one end the static, three-dimensional *portrayals* of movement and hatha yogic transformation, to the other end with two-dimensional medium of archival film, which demonstrated how dynamic – how *transformative* – yoga could be in actual performative practice. Through this extraordinary film, the exhibition was able to suggest that twenty-first-century yoga, modern postural yoga, might have begun at that very moment – when static, individual *asanas* were visually and publicly transformed by a contemporary master into a sequence of *asanas* seamlessly woven together through a combination of breath, rhythm and yogic alchemy.

From there it's a very short hop to new ways of propertizing yoga *asanas* in the twenty-first century, or at least to new ways of making these claims over modern postural yoga *as* property. In a world marked by increasing media cacophony and image saturation, we are reminded that these first visual representations and technologies of modern postural yoga not only transformed practice and the medium, they actually created the message. As we have seen through the various claims over yoga's heritage as property, life does imitate art – yogic lives can and often do closely imitate yogic art. Yokes to the past can sometimes be counterproductive if they end up yoking or determining yoga's future trajectories, even the range of its possible transformations.

Ultimately, yoga as we know it today, or rather the modern postural *asana* sequences that are under cultural dispute *as* property, do not go back to hoary antiquity – for the most part, they are no more than a century old. By using the past to solve the question of ownership, yoga has tied itself into proverbial knots, in the process stretching and transforming both history and itself. In the end, when answering the question of who owns yoga – whether the proposed owner is the nation, or religion, or an individual teacher intending to copyright the past – one can only say that it is a complicated million-dollar answer that will morph with the times, or with the particular genealogy one is able to unearth. But change that question to who owns yoga *asana*? And therein lies a tale, or three.

Notes

1 *Terroir* as a concept has been discussed in relation to cultural heritage, by this author and others, and has been applied to heritage management by Alexander Bauer (2009).
2 See for instance Catherine Albanese (2006).
3 For a more detailed version of Vivekananda's synthesis of yoga, see Sita Reddy (2013).
4 The fact that the term used in the arguments was 'clients' rather than practitioners is additionally interesting, thus indicating the bias toward yoga seen not so much as neutral practice but as a commodity, which yoga's clients had to buy into and consume rather than believe in or practice.
5 I was co-curator of the Modern Transformations section of this exhibition, and thus some of this section is drawn from my catalogue essay on Modern Postural Yoga in the beautifully produced exhibition catalogue, *Yoga: The Art of Transformation*, edited by Debra Diamond, Smithsonian Books, 2013. Readers are encouraged to visit the catalogue preview site and consult the catalogue for a taste of the extraordinary artworks and interdisciplinary research that were part of this exhibition at the Sackler Gallery: http://www.asia.si.edu/support/yoga/catalogue-preview.asp.

References

Albanese, Catherine. 2006. *America: Religion or Religions*, Belmont, CA: Wadsworth Press.

Alter, Joseph. 2004. *Yoga in Modern India: The Body Between Science and Philosophy*. Princeton, NJ: Princeton University Press.

Anderson, Jane and Kim Christen. 2013. '"Chuck a Copyright on It": Dilemmas of Digital Return and the Possibilities for Traditional Knowledge Licenses and Labels'. *Museum Anthropology Review* 7, no. 1–4: 105–126.

Anderson, Benedict. 1983. *Imagined Communities: Reflections on the Origins and Spread of Nationalism*, London: Verso Editions.

Bauer, Alexander. 2009. *Heritage Management*, Vol. 2, No. 1 (Spring), pp. 81–104.

Bikram's Yoga College v. Evolation Yoga, No. 13–55763. United States Court of Appeals for the Ninth Circuit, 2015.

Bell, Joshua, Kimberley Christen and Mark Turin, eds. 2013. 'After the Return'. *Museum Anthropology Review* 7, no. 1–2: 1–263.

Derrida, Jacques. 1995. 'Archive Fever: A Freudian Impression', *Diacritics*, Vol. 25, No. 2 (Summer), pp. 9–63.

Hobsbawm, Eric and Terrence Ranger. 1992. *The Invention of Tradition*, Cambridge University Press.

Jambunathan, M. R. 1941. *The Yoga Body Illustrated*, Madras: Jambunathan Book Depot.

Mitter, Partha. 1992. *Much Maligned Monsters: History of European Reactions to Indian Art*, Chicago: University of Chicago Press.

Pant, Pratinidhi, Raja of Audh. 1929. *Surya Namaskars*, Bombay: Orient Longmans.

Reddy, Sita, 2006. 'Making Heritage Legible: Who Owns Traditional Medical Knowledge?' *International Journal of Cultural Property*, Vol. 13, No. 2 (May), pp. 161–188.

Reddy, Sita, 2013. 'Vivekananda and Rational Spirituality' in D. Diamond, ed. *Yoga: The Art of Transformation*, Washington, DC: Smithsonian Books.

Singleton, Mark. 2010. *Yoga Body: The Origins of Modern Posture Practice*. New York: Oxford University Press.

Schmidt, Richard. 1907. *Fakir und Fakirtum in Alten und Modernen India*, Germany.

United States v. Michael Sedlock, United States Court of Appeals for the Fourth District, 2015.

Yogi Narayana Ghamande. 1931. *Yogasopana Purvacatushka*, Bombay: Tukarama Book Depot.

21

BONES, DOCUMENTS AND DNA

Cultural property at the margins of the law

Lee Douglas

Analyzing objects through a cultural property framework draws our attention to the constitutive role of culture – to how "identity is asserted and difference claimed through expressive activities that deploy meaningful forms" (Coombe 1998: 23). It also elucidates the very complex processes through which objects are mobilized to make meaning – how they are used to constitute and produce new forms of knowledge. Theories regarding the intangibility of culture (Brown 2003; Appiah 2006) and anthropological analyses of the "new kinds of entitlement and processes of claim making" (Geismar 2013: 3) that emerge in relation to local formulations of ownership have become increasingly useful in attempts to track how objects – and, indeed intangible objects, such as oral histories and folklore – are invested with particular kinds of value. They also aid in untangling the diverse ways in which a language of rights can be deployed to make claims to and over particular forms of shared cultural knowledge. By considering the relationships between particular cultural objects, regimes of value, and definitions of ownership, many anthropological discussions of cultural property examine how the law is activated, subverted, and creatively deployed in order to make or prohibit rights claims over objects and the forms of knowledge embedded within them. In many cases where cultural property becomes the subject of heated debate, the law becomes an important arena in which power and hegemony can be both exerted and resisted. As Rosemary Coombe describes, the "law provides [the] means and forms for legitimating and contesting dominant meanings and the social hierarchies that they support" (1998: 29). In these contexts, the law is a domain in which claims are asserted, validated, or denied, thereby becoming an important "mediator for identifying and interpreting" (Aragon & Leach 2006: 623) particular forms of indigenous or local knowledge (see also Anderson 2005; Merry 1998).

How, then, might we approach objects and forms of knowledge that are not controlled, regulated, or overlooked by the law? In the absence of legal frameworks capable of mediating, identifying, or interpreting particular forms of knowledge, how can we make sense of claims that are made through objects – both tangible and intangible – and that seek to constitute particular forms of cultural value? Can a cultural property framework prove useful when analyzing objects and testimonies that do not reside in museums and national collections or that do not neatly fit into the category of cultural heritage? This chapter – and the photographs that accompany it – will examine an unruly corpus of objects, data, and testimonies that are central to the assertion of claims to new, alternative forms of historical, cultural knowledge in contemporary Spain. These objects and testimonies are unearthed – both literally and metaphorically – in mass grave exhumation projects that seek not only to recuperate the remains of those who fell victim to twentieth-century fascism, but also to change dominant historical narratives about the Spanish Civil War (1936–1939) and the ensuing Franco dictatorship (1939–1975). The human remains, personal objects, and archival documents exhumed and the testimonies collected in these endeavors are mobilized to create new forms of knowledge about the recent past. However, this evidence exists at the margins of Spanish law. Unlike other crime investigations, exhumations are not overseen by legal procedure. Only in some limited cases are the objects and human remains collected in these events treated as archaeological patrimony.[1] The testimonies gathered in these endeavors, in contrast, are never treated as bearing a patrimonial value. However, they are invested with multiple forms of social and historical value, and they are mobilized to produce and constitute new forms of shared cultural knowledge. It is, in fact, their position outside the law that makes them potent objects through which different collectivities make claims to the recent past. By considering how these claims are made, this chapter will outline provocative new ways to think about cultural property and its relationship to the law.

***

Initiated in 2000, the Spanish Historical Memory Movement is a grassroots, civil society-led initiative that advocates for the rescue and recovery of individual and collective narratives regarding political violence exerted during the Spanish Civil War and the fascist dictatorship that followed it. Since its inception, this Movement, although heterogeneous in form,[2] has consistently turned to forensic science as a tool for unearthing and making public the material traces of Spain's violent past.[3] Combating the lasting effects of a post-dictatorship Amnesty Law – which prohibits defining Franco's victims as victims of crime – and the persistence of public discourses that hail collective forgetting as a mode of social and political modernization (Aguilar 2002; Labanyi 2002; Resina 2000), the Movement emphasizes recuperation – the retrieval of genetic, documentary, and narrative evidence – as a strategy for recasting individual loss and social marginalization as part of a larger phenomenon of state-sponsored, systematic violence (Espinosa et al. 2004). In this context, mass grave exhumation projects, specifically, initiatives that focus on the location, exhumation, and identification of individuals who fell victim to Spanish fascism, form part of a complex constellation of emerging social practices, whereby individuals and collectivities produce and mobilize new forms of knowledge about the recent past. In seeking to widen, amplify, and call into question dominant historical narratives that exclude the voices of victims and their surviving kin, the Movement produces new forms of historical knowledge that are grounded in shared, culturally produced ideas about the "facticity" and "objective" truth-telling capacities of scientific practice (Daston 1994; Daston & Galison 2007; Fleck 1979; Latour & Woolgar 1979).

Following the death of dictator Francisco Franco in 1975, Spain entered a democratic transition that focused on the promotion of political and social consensus. In this process, forms of collective remembrance were replaced by cultural forgetting. With the ratification of Spain's Amnesty Law in 1977, amnesia was judicially institutionalized (Aguilar 2002). For the kin of those who fell victim to Francoist violence, this legal framework, paired with dominant discourses regarding the need to move forward by never looking back, reinforced the idea that kin-based narratives regarding intimate experiences with political repression were not apt for public circulation. For many, this meant that complex histories of forced disappearance, social and economic marginalization, and everyday forms of violence not only would be unrecognized by the Spanish state, but also would fail to be woven into dominant historical accounts of the war and its aftermath. The turn to forensic science battles cultural amnesia and legal amnesty through its ability to resurface evidence that helps undo the traditions of historical silence and erasure imposed by the dictatorship and the Spanish Transition. In the absence of courts of law equipped to deal with the genetic, osteological, and documentary evidence unearthed and made public in mass grave exhumation projects, forensic practice invests human remains, DNA samples, archival documents, and family photographs – objects that simultaneously resurface in these events – with scientific value. In their interactions with this new corpus of "hard" evidence and scientifically validated material, forensic experts, victims' kin, memory activists, and local researchers make new claims regarding the events of the past. These claims, however, do not fit neatly into a discourse of rights that is legible to national law. These scientifically grounded acts of recuperation and retrieval occur at the unruly boundaries of legal procedure – a space in which the "objects of evidence" (Engelke 2009) regarding a particular collective history can be collected, but not submitted to or managed by courts of law.

The processes of recuperation and retrieval implicit in exhumation projects require the coming together of multiple forms of knowledge. Techno-scientific expertise is deployed in order to make sense of the human remains contained within mass graves. Forensic methods, carefully deployed by team members, make it possible to individualize skeletons, to estimate the age, sex, and stature of each victim, and to collect other forms of evidence – personal objects, bullet casings, and body placement – that can illuminate how and by what means victims were killed. However, this techno-scientific expertise can only be activated when paired with other forms of local knowledge.[4] Testimonies given by victims' kin are crucial in attempts to locate mass graves. Individual memories and community hearsay provide important data regarding how political repression was exerted and experienced in these local contexts. Kin-based knowledge – despite its fragmented form – helps reconstruct the events leading up to particular acts of violence. It also sheds light on the everyday, political lives of victims. When woven together, these bits and pieces of local, kin-based knowledge allow forensic experts to make connections between the osteological, genetic evidence that they exhume and a more complex historical narrative that describes not only the crime being investigated, but also the events surrounding these acts of disappearance. Similarly, archival documents extracted from state and municipal archives, as well as photographs and personal letters culled from the homes of victims' kin, help further elucidate violent events and the social and political contexts in which they were embedded.

Mass grave exhumations in Spain are "para"-forensic events (see Holmes & Marcus 2005). Evidence is collected "as if" it was to be submitted to courts of law. It is, however, this "as if" status that is mobilized to make claims to historical knowledge that is embedded in the objects and narratives that are recuperated and produced in these endeavors. Standing outside the purview of the law, forensic and narrative evidence is transformed into forensic reports, doctoral dissertations, history texts, and documentary films. Photographs of unearthed mass graves – mounds of skeletons framed and put on view – are sequenced in public exhibitions, newspaper articles, and art books. They are plastered onto posters held high during memory marches. Memorials are erected. Dossiers lined with documentation and forensic analyses are compiled. Some of them are submitted to NGOs and international human rights organizations. Others are carefully guarded in the homes of victims' kin and the archives at research centers. Through these forms of production and mobilization, historical "truth" is questioned, re-fashioned, and re-constituted. New narratives rooted in the "objectivity" of scientific practice are invested with forms of historical, political, and social value. Although this knowledge remains illegible to the law – unrecognized by the state and not incorporated into educational curricula – it is from this outsider position that members of the Historical

Memory Movement make powerful claims to amplify and deepen the official record, to recognize and validate all that has been silenced and made to disappear.

***

The objects, narratives, and knowledge recuperated and produced in Spanish mass grave exhumation projects are not legally defined as "cultural property." In fact, their very existence and circulation – their constitution and amplification – are products of attempts to recover and value events and experiences that have been silenced, left out, and unrecognized by dominant historical narratives, the very narratives that are produced in national museum collections and circulated in school textbooks and educational curricula. It is from this position outside the law – in the limbo between national patrimony, scientific object, and judicial evidence – that these cultural forms are deployed to make claims to a more nuanced historical record. Deploying a language of human rights that resonates transnationally but falls flat locally, forensic experts, memory activists, and victims' kin – among others – seek to present new forms of knowledge to the Spanish public in an attempt to undo a culture of amnesty and amnesia that threatens to make these objects and the knowledge embedded in them irrelevant. If we take seriously Coombe's suggestion that "The imaginative making of meaning is the quintessential human act, and culture is both its practice and its products" (1998: 44), Spanish mass grave exhumations and the creation and circulation of knowledge that are part and parcel of these endeavors are most certainly cultural forms. In fact, it is their exclusion from legal procedure and official state forms of recognition and their entanglement with scientific practice that make them powerful tools for expressing new forms of entitlement and creating novel, effective forms of historical claim making. If law is able "to generate signs and forms – signifying forms – through which difference is constituted and given meaning" (Ibid.: 29), exclusion from legal procedure creates new subject positions from which difference can also be wielded to make powerful claims over objects and the knowledge they represent.

In one of several essays on local knowledge, Clifford Geertz describes at length the relationship between fact and law. In his analysis, he identifies the "skeletonization of the fact" as a social process that defines the "[narrowing of] moral issues to a point where determinant rules can be employed to decide them" (1983: 170). For Geertz, legal process is the site where this reduction occurs. In Spain and in the context of the Historical Memory Movement, it is science that helps skeletonize facts. It is through the discovery and presentation of evidence – objects that are themselves skeletonized in very literal forms – that new moral categories and imperatives are developed. How these categories and imperatives are made to mean in cultural terms coincides with similar processes of social action through which recovered objects and testimonies are animated in order to constitute new, valid forms of historical knowledge. They also coincide with the assertion of a language of rites that claims these cultural objects as a collective form of patrimony that must be re-inserted into mainstream historical narratives and re-claimed, indeed recognized, by the Spanish state. Although Geertz is concerned with how the legal representation of facts is deployed to create particular shared social norms, his discussion of law as "a distinctive manner of imagining the real" (Ibid.: 173) is a thought-provoking way to approach areas of social life that exist at the margins of legal procedure. In the process of asserting claims to new forms of historical knowledge, the Historical Memory Movement imagines new possibilities regarding what can and *should* be recognized. In this way, the objects, testimonies, and forms of knowledge exhumed in these endeavors are heavy with cultural meaning. Perhaps more importantly, they also provide new modes of cultural-making that challenge long-term structures of silence and forgetting.

Images of recuperation: photographs of the Spanish historical memory movement

Figure 21.1 A local newspaper in the Province of Burgos publishes an article about an exhumation conducted near the town of Monte de Estépar in the summer of 2014.
Source: Lee Douglas

Figure 21.2 Memory activists await the arrival of representatives from the United Nations Working Group on Enforced or Involuntary Disappearances in Madrid, September 2013.
Source: Lee Douglas

Figure 21.3 At the same event, a memory activist holds a large *pancarta*, or banner, with a photo-collage of images extracted from newspapers.
Source: Lee Douglas

Figure 21.4 The kin of the disappeared carry portraits of their missing loved ones as they await the arrival of UN representatives.
Source: Lee Douglas

Figure 21.5 A memory activist displays a poster-collage that includes images of his disappeared kin and copies of documents extracted from a military archive.
Source: Lee Douglas

Figure 21.6 The forensic investigation carried out in Monte de Estépar resulted in the location of four mass graves and 96 cadavers, which were exhumed in July of 2014 and March of 2016.
Source: Lee Douglas

Figure 21.7 Once skeletons are individualized and documented *in situ*, forensic team members remove them and place them in large boxes in preparation for their transport to the laboratory.
Source: Lee Douglas

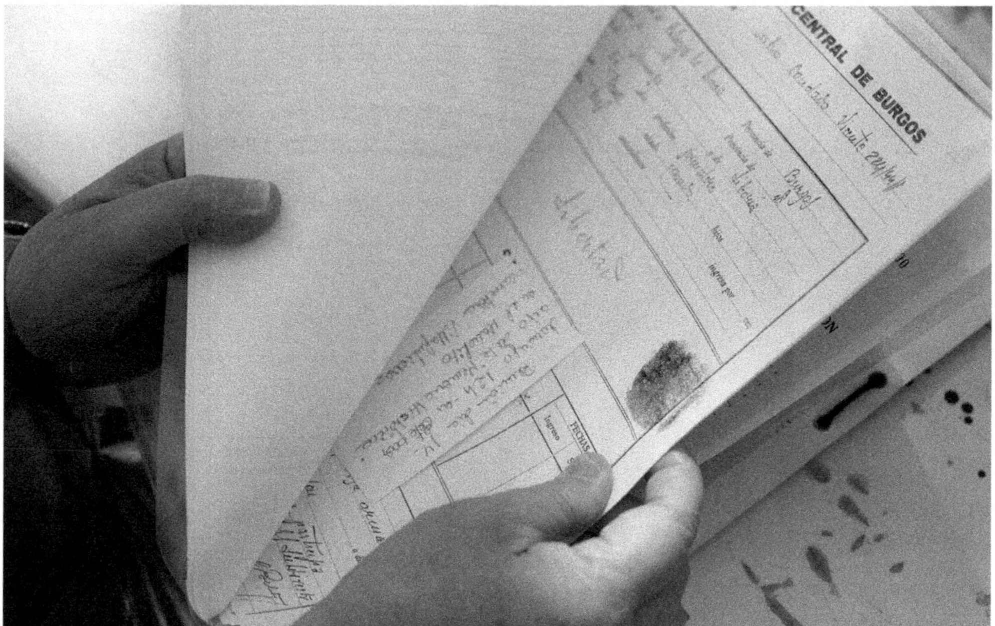

Figure 21.8 Victims' kin and community members routinely attended the exhumation carried out in Monte de Estépar.
Source: Lee Douglas

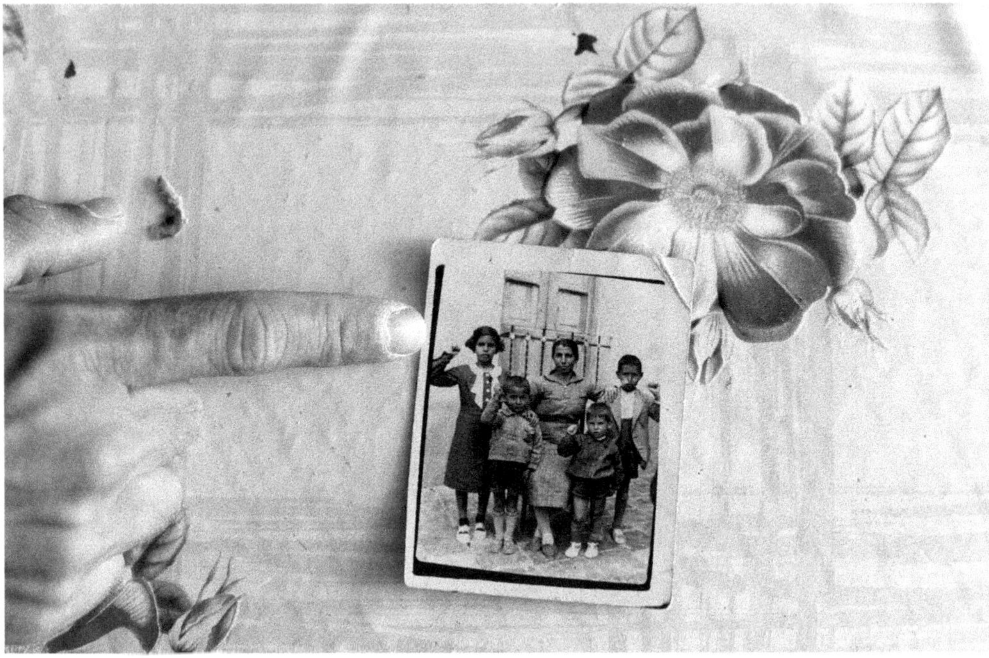

Figure 21.9 A young historian and archaeologist from the town of Oropesa de Toledo collects testimonies from community members who were small children during the Spanish Civil War and the ensuing dictatorship.
Source: Lee Douglas

Figure 21.10 Felisa Herrero, the granddaughter and niece of two women who were extra-judicially killed after Francoist troops entered the town of Oropesa de Toledo in August of 1936, holds a family portrait that she keeps in her sewing room.
Source: Lee Douglas

Figure 21.11 A magazine clipping from the makeshift archive kept in the home of a villager from Oropesa de Toledo.
Source: Lee Douglas

Figure 21.12 A memorial located on the hill in Monte de Estépar where four mass graves were located.
Source: Lee Douglas

Figure 21.13 Victims' kin and members of a local memory association in the town of Calera y Chozas participate in the memorial event, in which remains recovered during an exhumation were returned to families and community members.
Source: Lee Douglas

Acknowledgements

I would like to thank Juan Montero Gutiérrez for his insightful comments regarding exhumations and patrimony in contemporary Spain. The visual essay that accompanies this text includes photographs taken in a variety of contexts and places. With that in mind, I am indebted to Ricardo Moreno and Felisa Herrero from Oropesa de Toledo, who shared their experiences and photographs with me. My fieldwork in Oropesa would not have been possible without Ricardo's incredible expertise and guidance. I would also like to extend my gratitude to members of the technical-scientific team that conducted the Monte de Estépar exhumation in July of 2014, the second site where many of these images were taken. In particular, I would like to thank the project directors Francisco Etxeberria Gabilondo (Aranzadi Sciences Society), Juan Montero Gutiérrez (Provincial Coordinating Committee for the Recovery of Historical Memory – Burgos), Ignacio Fernández de Mata (University of Burgos), as well as the incredibly talented student volunteers who made this work possible. Both Lourdes Herrasti and Jimi Jiménez from the Aranzadi Sciences Society provided guidance regarding the publication of the images taken during this exhumation. Finally, I would like to extend my sincerest thanks to Haidy Geismar and Jane Anderson for the invitation to contribute this chapter and its accompanying images to this volume.

Notes

1 On September 23, 2011, the Official State Gazette, also known as the BOE, made public the "Protocol for Carrying out Exhumations of Victims of the Spanish Civil War and the Dictatorship," which

outlined a detailed methodology to be followed in all mass grave exhumation projects (see Etxeberria 2011). The Protocol was elaborated in compliance with the Spanish Historical Memory Law passed in 2007. It suggests that all archaeological interventions completed as part of mass grave exhumation projects should follow the precautions outlined in Law 16/1985 that oversees the treatment of archaeological patrimony. A select group of Autonomous Communities, including Aragón and later Asturias and Castille-La Mancha, have developed local historical memory protocols that take into account the archaeological treatment of objects that may have patrimonial significance. The case of Aragón is unique in that this Autonomous Community has passed legislation that situates mass grave exhumations under the administrative tutelage of the General Office of Cultural Patrimony (Montero 2010: 73). However, as noted by archaeologist Juan Montero Gutiérrez (2010), there is a vast difference between national and regional protocols and the creation of laws that define these initiatives as part of a larger national project to recuperate national patrimony (see also González Ruibal 2007, 2009). Mass grave exhumation projects, like many historical memory practices in Spain, face a legal void that makes it difficult to define how the objects recuperated in these endeavors should be treated.

2 It is important to note that the Spanish Historical Memory Movement, also known as the Movement to Recover Historical Memory is complex and heterogeneous. Local, regional, and national iterations of historical memory struggles – and the political claims and tensions between different groups of memory activists working at these different levels – mean that the Movement cannot be described in simple, homogeneous, or national terms (Ferrándiz 2014). However, as noted, the Movement has been consistent in its uptake of forensic science as a tool in the struggle to make new claims to alternative historical narratives. In this chapter, I will refer to this phenomenon in general terms in order to address how the objects and narratives recuperated in these investigations might be framed as a kind of cultural property and what implications this might have in terms of widening discussions about how different forms of knowledge and culture are re-claimed in post-violence contexts where the crimes of the past are not legally or judicially recognized.

3 In September 2000, Emilio Silva, a journalist and the grandson of a *desaparecido* (or disappeared person) advocated for the exhumation of a mass grave located on the outskirts of Priaranza del Bierzo in León. Local hearsay and family narratives inherited by Silva confirmed that in October 1936 several men had been rounded up, extra-judicially killed, and dumped into a ditch at the edge of town. Members and volunteers of the Association for the Recovery of Historical Memory worked side-by-side with members of the Aranzadi Forensic Team, uncovering and recuperating the bodies of 12 men. The remains included those belonging to Silva's paternal grandfather. Although community exhumations of mass graves had been common in the late 1970s and early 1980s in Spain, this was the first time that the remains of victims of fascist repression were exhumed and identified through the application of scientific methods and the use of genetic DNA testing (Silva & Macías 2003).

4 For an ethnographic description of the relationship between techno-scientific expertise and kin-based knowledge, see "Mass Graves Gone Missing: Producing Knowledge in a World of Absence" (Douglas 2014).

Bibliography

Aguilar, Paloma. 2002. *Memory and Amnesia: The Role of the Spanish Civil War in the Transition to Democracy*. New York: Bergen Books.

Anderson, Jane. 2005. "The Making of Indigenous Knowledge in Intellectual Property Law in Australia." *International Journal of Cultural Property*, 12(3): 345–371.

Appiah, Anthony Kwame. 2006. *Cosmopolitanism: Ethics in a World of Strangers*. New York: W. W. Norton.

Aragon, Lorraine V. and James Leach. 2008. "Arts and Owners: Intellectual Property Law and the Politics of Scale in Indonesian Arts." *American Ethnologist*, 35(4): 607–631.

Brown, Michael F. 2003. *Who Owns Native Culture?* Cambridge, MA: Harvard University Press.

Coombe, Rosemary. 1998. *The Cultural Life of Intellectual Properties: Authorship, Appropriate, and the Law*. Durham, NC: Duke University Press.

Daston, Lorraine. 1994. "Marvelous Facts & Miraculous Evidence in Early Modern Europe." In *Questions of Evidence: Proof, Practice, & Persuasion Across the Disciplines*. H. J. Harootunian, J. Chandler, and A. Davidson, eds. Chicago: University of Chicago Press.

Daston, Lorraine and Peter Galison. 2007. *Objectivity*. Cambridge, MA: MIT Press.

Douglas, Lee. 2014. "Mass Graves Gone Missing: The Production of Knowledge in a World of Absence." *Culture & History*, 3(2): e022.

Engelke, Matthew. 2009. "The Objects of Evidence." In *The Objects of Evidence: Anthropological Approaches to the Production of Knowledge*. M. Engelke, ed. Oxford: Blackwell Publishing.

Espinosa Maestre, Francisco, Julián Casanova, Conxita Mir and Francisco Moreno Gómez. 2004. *Morir, Matar, Sobrevivir: La Violencia en la Dictadura de Franco*. Madrid: Editorial Critica.

Etxeberria Gabilondo, Francisco. 2011. "Exhumaciones Contemporáneas en España. Las Fosas Communes de la Guerra Civil." *Boletín Galego de Medicina Legal y Forense*, 18(1): 13–28.

Ferrándiz, Francisco. 2014. *El Pasado Bajo Tierra. Exhumaciones Contemporáneas de la Guerra Civil*. Madrid: Anthropos.

Fleck, Ludwik. 1979. *Genesis and Development of a Scientific Fact*. Chicago: University of Chicago Press.

Geertz, Clifford. 1983. "Local Knowledge: Fact & Law in Comparative Perspective." In *Local Knowledge: Further Essays in Interpretative Anthropology*. New York: Basic Books.

Geismar, Haidy. 2013. *Treasured Possessions: Indigenous Interventions into Cultural and Intellectual Property*. Durham, NC: Duke University Press.

González Ruibal, Alfonso. 2007. "Making Things Public: Archaeologies of the Spanish Civil War." *Public Archaeology* 6(4): 203–226.

González Ruibal, Alfonso. 2009. "Arqueología y Memoria Histórica." *Patrimonio Cultural de España* 1: 103–122.

Holmes, Douglas & George Marcus. 2005. "Cultures of Expertise and the Management of Globalization: Toward the Refunctioning of Ethnography." In *Global Assemblages: Technology, Politics, & Ethics as Anthropological Problems*. Ong Aiwha & Stephen Collier, eds. Oxford: Blackwell

Labanyi, Jo. 2002. "Engaging with Ghosts; or, Theorizing Culture in Modern Spain." In *Constructing Identity in 20th-Century Spain*. Jo Labanyi, ed. Oxford: Oxford University Press.

Latour, B. & S. Woolgar. 1979. *Laboratory Life. The Construction of Scientific Facts*. Beverly Hills: Sage Publications.

Merry, Sally. 1998. "Legal Pluralism." *Law & Society Review* 22(5): 869–901.

Montero Gutiérrez, Juan. 2011. "Exhumando el Legado Material de la Represión Franquista. De la Percepción Social a la Encrucijada Jurídica y Patrimonial." In *Recorriendo la Memoria/Touring Memory*. Jaime Almanza Sánchez, ed. Oxford: Archeopress.

Resina, José Ramón. 2000. "Introduction." In *Disremembering the Dictatorship: The Politics of Memory in the Spanish Transition to Democracy*. José Ramón Resina, ed. Amsterdam: Rodopi.

Silva, Emilio and Santiago Macías. 2003. *Las Fosas de Franco*. Madrid: Temas de Hoy.

22

COLLABORATIVE ENCOUNTERS IN DIGITAL CULTURAL PROPERTY

Tracing temporal relationships of context and locality

Jane Anderson and Maria Montenegro

Introduction

In April 2015 the British Museum opened the exhibition *Indigenous Australia: Enduring Civilization* with a parallel collaborative exhibition titled *Encounters*, opening at the National Museum of Australia in Canberra in November 2015. Developed and advertised as the first major exhibition that the British Museum has offered on Aboriginal and Torres Strait Islander peoples as part of thriving and living cultures, it makes visible previously unknown and unseen Aboriginal and Torres Strait Islander material culture from the museum's extensive collection of about 6,000 items.

There are many 'firsts' with this exhibition from the British Museum standpoint. These include the collaboration with an overseas institution within the country from which these objects derived; the planned parallel exhibition that will see around 170 objects from the British Museum collection travel, temporarily, to Australia; that the exhibition was curated by the first Indigenous Australian curator to hold a staff position at the British Museum, Gaye Sculthorpe; the consultation and engagement of 25 different Indigenous communities within Australia; and that new and previously unknown knowledge about items within the collection emerged through these consultations adding value and meaning to the collection itself. All these 'firsts' speak to some significant changes that are occurring within the international museum community with regard to, and perhaps more importantly, with respect for the historical conditions that led to the existence of these collections in the first place and the contemporary custodians, owners and stewards who remain vitally connected to this material.

The institutional recognition of existing peoples and communities who have an interest in these collections that exceed the traditional 'public' that such exhibitions have usually been constructed for is well overdue. Much recent work has been produced that focuses on the changes in museological practice that are a result of emerging new relationships with 'source communities' within what Ruth Phillips refers to as 'museums' second age' (Phillips 2003; Peers and Brown 2003; Kreps 2009; Boast 2011; Lonetree 2012; Harrison 2013; Krmpotich 2014). For non-tribal institutions these emerging relationships offer new possibilities for knowing and making sense of collections as well as the opportunity to develop reflective and more sensitive policies that can address the multiple forms of structural exclusion that have largely positioned source communities outside the institutional machine.

The time it has taken to arrive at this new place increasingly characterized by what might be termed 'collaborative encounters' reveals what is actually at stake here and for whom. For institutions, foundational understandings about the role and function of the museum itself, the conditions under which collections were produced, and a breaking apart of presumed stable categories like 'the public' have had to occur. Yet reassembling the museum with attention to the epistemological, ideological and physical violences that underpin these sites and their collections still presents various difficulties. For instance, certain legal and social entitlements that are embedded within the institution and importantly entwined through and within the collections themselves, remain as colonial traces and tethers that practically prevent certain possibilities and relationships from emerging. The legal ownership of collections, secured through either real property or intellectual property law remains as a pressing problem that is very difficult to unravel for even the most seasoned legal counsel. In almost all jurisdictions there is no option for retro-actively reasserting the 'correct' authorship or ownership, even if this could be agreed upon by all parties (Anderson 2013).

For the source communities from where these collections derive, ongoing challenges are in making their diverse connections to these collections legible within institutions where the driving Western discourses continue to privilege ideas and notions of property and ownership. For instance, the very indexes, classificatory frames and metadata models describing collections function to stabilize these discourses primarily through a privileging of certain fragments of information – the name of the collector, how it was acquired by the museum, the date of the acquisition, the place and date of the collection and a general statement of the collection. This archival systematization, promoted by George Dorsey in 1899, is as simple as it is fragmentary and it now means that there are few classificatory options and alternatives available for considering the items within these collections as not objects at all, but as ancestors, beings, belongings that continue to need, hold and convey ongoing responsibility, care and relationality (Hays-Gilpin and Lometewama 2013; Krmpotich and Peers 2013). Despite the multiple ways in which this has been pointed to, written about and experienced within institutions themselves through direct instances of engagement and repatriation, an epistemic break in understanding and speaking about the institutional 'object' as a source community 'belonging' or 'being' has been incredibly difficult to address in practice.

In 2015 it was impossible for the British Museum exhibition to avoid the uncomfortable histories of its Aboriginal and Torres Strait Islander collection. Ameliorating this politics was, in part, why there was a parallel exhibition planned in Australia to begin with, why there were extensive 'consultations' with Indigenous communities, and why the National Museum of Australia's Indigenous Reference Group was engaged in the project. In a nice parallel movement, these combined elements attentive to the current political climate for displaying items of a colonial encounter go on to affect the credibility of the British Museum exhibition. As the National Museum of Australia's acting director stated in early press reporting about the exhibition in 2013: 'I think, honestly, that this is the most important work we're [the NMA] doing this decade' (Neill 2013). The consultations themselves led to a realization that is occurring within many similar contexts: that information currently held about collections or identification about items themselves is largely fragmentary or incorrect. We will return to what the larger implications of this are for institutions, for communities and for the larger knowledge production about Indigenous peoples and cultures within the chapter. For now, however, it illustrates an important political shift that institutions now know that they need to 'consult' in some way, in order to correct mistakes in the historical record, in the catalogue and in the display of this material. But this consultation still opens the door to the problem that the British Museum, as well as other institutions, is keen to avoid: the claims of ownership to the collections themselves. As Henrietta Fourmile Marrie, who has been at the forefront of asking questions about who owns these collections since the early 1980s (Fourmile Marrie 1988) asks, 'Why do the British Museum want them [the collections]? It has no relevance to them as a people. It has no relevance to their culture; it has more importance to us here' (Neill 2013). This question continues to reverberate and to produce a variety of positions within museology contexts. Nicholas Thomas, for instance, identifies such (anthropology) collections as 'always also historical collections: they are the products of, the evidence for, and maybe even the memorials to entangled histories.' (Thomas 2010: 8–9). Clementine Deliss, previously the Director of the Weltkulturen Museum in Frankfurt takes a different stand, making an argument that the ethnographic museum today is 'chronically deficient' and a place of 'sickness', in part because of what it holds and how it came to hold it (Deliss 2015).

Amidst such concerns, the British Museum offered its own (compromised) model of 'return' through the parallel exhibition. This model of return might more accurately be described as 'visitation'. In this model, return is temporally limited: only experienced for a short period, as the objects come for a visit and then are 'returned' to where it is implied that they really 'belong' – in the UK at the British Museum.

There should be no doubt that even with the collaborative turn that underpins this exhibition, the British Museum has been very careful about what national (Australian) legislative frameworks are now in place to make sure that any material that travels to Australia will be 'returned' to the UK. There is a paradigmatic shift here in the possibilities that a framework of 'return', as articulated by James Clifford for instance, can have (Clifford 2013). For both institutions involved in this exhibition, the British Museum and the National Museum of Australia, there was no desire to see a repeat of the 2004 Dja Dja Warung case wherein several 1850s bark etchings on loan in Australia from the British Museum and Kew Gardens were initially prevented from returning to the UK by a unique piece of Australian cultural heritage legislation, the Protection of Moveable Cultural Heritage Act 1986 (Willis 2008). In the fallout from the case, including the temporary injunction keeping the material in Australia, the subsequent lifting of the injunction by the Federal Court and its return to the UK, a new piece of legislation, the Protection of Cultural Objects on Loan Act 2013 was introduced. This new legislation creates legal surety for the international institution in the sense that nothing that is loaned from an international institution for an exhibition in Australia can have any ownership or repatriation claim made to it. It illustrates exactly where the power relations around the idea of return, and its articulation in practice, remain. This pushes any repatriation/return claims back into the non-legislative, non-structured, non-binding spaces of good will and institution to community forms of temporal negotiation.

We use this story of the British Museum exhibition to begin our chapter for several key reasons. Firstly, it reveals what kinds of inter-institutional and community collaboration, activity and engagement have become necessary for institutions wanting to create exhibitions that draw upon Aboriginal, Torres Strait, Native American or First Nation collections. This kind of work is what institutions have to do now if they want to maintain some public-relation credibility for the exhibition itself. In doing so they have to open, just slightly, a conversation over the thornier question about the role and function of the ethnographic museum today.

However, how that actually gets dealt with differs from institution to institution and much more could be read into the British Museum example. Secondly, we are interested to further explore the multi-faceted dimensions of collaborative encounters within and between institutions and local communities, and to ask to what extent these can result in a decentring of the property and ownership paradigm that continues to tether these collections to the institution itself, rather than to the context from which they derive and in which they continue to have meaning. Finally we are largely focusing on what all this looks like for digital collections. In this regard, we follow a trajectory of inquiry set by Faye Ginsburg, Kim Christen and Haidy Geismar about the hidden assumptions, unaddressed power differentials and the way in which the digital folds traditional paradigms of classification, ordering and property back into itself (Ginsburg 2008; Christen 2012; Geismar 2013). In thinking through ongoing questions of what collaboration is and means for the various parties involved, we are also asking how do museums engage (or fail to engage) with Indigenous communities, philosophies and cultural production and what are the implications of these questions for future museum practices and articulations of Indigenous agency?

Collaborative encounters

Collaboration has become one of the major themes of critical museology and museum anthropology in the current moment. In a US context, abundant literature has been written about this subject since the passage of the Native American Graves Protection and Repatriation Act (NAGPRA) in 1990 and the opening of the National Museum of the American Indian in Washington, DC in 2004 (Simpson 1996; Mithlo 2004; Srinivasan *et al.* 2010; Colwell-Chanthaphonh 2010; Kreps 2009, 2011a, 2011b; Lonetree 2012; Atalay 2012; Krmpotich and Peers 2013; Shannon 2014). Concepts such as 'contact zone' (Clifford 1997); 'source communities' (Peers and Brown 2003); 'second museum age' (Phillips 2005); 'neocolonial collaboration' (Boast 2011); 'digital return' (Boast & Enote 2013); and 'curatorial responsibilities' (Harrison 2013) have been coined and used to illustrate the complexity of the power relations involved in museum collaborative encounters, as well as to set the guidelines for more authentic forms of collaboration and reciprocal curation of Native American collections. However, despite this extensive critique on collaboration theory, it is surprising how little has changed regarding the ways non-tribal museums relate, interact and 'collaborate' with tribal communities. Specifically, museums still feel the need to exercise control, still fear sharing their authority with the Native communities they themselves invite to participate, and they seem even more afraid of change. Moreover, some question if it is even possible for Western, mainstream museums to ever truly become decolonized, given their colonial legacies and their location in the power structure of dominant societies (Kreps 2011b). This section focuses on certain practical perspectives of where Native communities, museums and museum professionals are at today in relation to collaboration. It will also critically assess the possibilities, temporalities and limitations of collaboration, and the principles that should guide collaborative relationships and their outcomes.

Over the last two decades, Native communities and tribal museums in the United States have been striving to reposition themselves in new and dynamic ways to better understand the culture of Western museums and their channels of influence, and fostering a movement that promotes real participation in and authentic collaboration with these institutions. As Indigenous peoples gain more control and assert more agency within museum collections – urging the rethinking of conventional ways of interpreting and circulating their cultural heritage – the power dynamics and asymmetries between museums and Native communities are being slowly transformed. Today, it makes sense to almost every museum with these kinds of collections that the representation of Native cultures cannot be adequately accomplished without some kind of base-line engagement or, better still, collaboration with the originating communities. Notwithstanding the mistakes and missing information within institutional documentation records and metadata, non-tribal museums are acknowledging first, that they must be held accountable to the communities affected by colonial collecting practices of dispossession and second, that consultation is not enough to get at that problem. Institutions have a greater responsibility to pursue deeper and more engaged reciprocity with the peoples through whose very collections, the status and existence of the museum has been built.

Collaboration is the word of the moment. In the programme for the 2015 annual meeting of the Association of Tribal Archives, Libraries and Museums (ATALM), for instance, the preponderance for using the term in a panel's title description evidenced both concern for this new paradigm as well as advocacy for projects that have some collaborative component. The conference entitled 'New Encounters: Communities + Collections + Museums' at the National Museum of Australia held in March 2016 also foregrounded the need for collaboration as a means for connecting museums with source communities (NMA 2016). This leads to some important questions about what collaboration is and means, what it is being deployed to signify and what kinds of similarities in practice it can meaningfully align. It also means interrogating the nature of the partnerships that are being established between the communities and institutions involved, questioning their conditions of equity and responsibility (Colwell-Chanthaphonh 2010). Is collaboration defined by the outcome of the encounter between Native communities and non-tribal collecting institutions? By the kind of relationship itself that both parties build during those encounters? Or by the process involved in the achievement of both groups' goals throughout the collaboration?

Jim Enote, the Executive Director of the A:shiwi A:wan Museum and Heritage Center in Zuni, New Mexico and one of the leaders of what might be termed a 'museum collaboration movement' (Montenegro 2015) stresses that collaboration is more than a sharing of information. Moreover, authentic collaboration goes beyond a shared vision; it requires all participants to work around the same purpose to build – to 'co-elaborate' – a common product that must make sense to every person involved in the process in the same way. Collaboration, he insists, is the elaboration of a 'story' between two or more entities that must agree to the terms of how the story should be told, and as such, requires an active participation of the different cultures involved and between their unique ways of knowing (Enote 2014a). This does not mean that both systems of knowledge need to be merged into one, but that some effort to bridge them appropriately is required. The process of collaboration then is not only in detailing the *how* of collaboration but also *what* can be produced from it; namely, how by putting different ways of knowing in tension, collaboration potentially produces a new space for negotiation, cooperation and dialogue, a virtual knowledge space in which Indigenous knowledge traditions and Western science can be critically evaluated but not annulled or absorbed into one authorized voice – a third space in which new knowledges can be produced and re-interpreted (Mithlo 2004; Smith 2012; Nakata and David 2010; Turnbull 2012; Enote 2014a).

There will be multiple ways of getting to this third space, but certainly this kind of idea about collaboration necessarily requires a resolve to address historical and contemporary power imbalances between the communities and institutions participating in the collaborative process. This includes developing short- and long-term agreements designed together by both groups; ensuring that all parties equally and reciprocally benefit from the collaboration and its outcomes; and integrating diverse ways of knowing and thinking throughout the collaboration. As Anishinabe archaeologist and scholar Sonya Atalay (2012) points out, the most critical tool for successful collaboration is will – the willingness to share power, authority and control and the willingness to work together to develop benefits that will affect both parties in the long term (Colwell-Chanthaphonh 2011; Atalay 2012; AIATSIS 2013). Reciprocity is central to every collaborative endeavour; the challenge, however, is to appropriately define what the benefits will be and to determine to whom they shall go. Informed by her work on community-based participatory research, Atalay (2012) stresses that authentic collaboration demands that community members should be directly and actively involved in every stage of the collaborative encounter, and that each participant should bring some kind of resource to the collaboration – such as knowledge, labor, economic resources and capacity building – in order to develop a shared sense of ownership of the outcome. Teasing out these necessary components in more explicit ways allows for subtle and not so subtle shifts in power to communities involved, and along with the tribal representatives' participatory involvement, has the potential to enable museum curators, anthropologists and archaeologists to overcome the museum field's colonial inheritance, allowing space for Native individuals and communities to make epistemic shifts in how knowledge is produced by also calling into question the authoritative voice of the 'museum expert'.

Collaboration then, according to Enote, Atalay and Colwell-Chanthaphonh actually requires quite specific intentions and practices. This means that not every museum practice involving Indigenous peoples should be considered 'collaborative' despite a political desire to name them as such. There are different degrees and levels of collaboration and it is imperative that we use the term carefully and draw the differences between collaboration and what are merely consultation practices. This is the case with repatriation efforts conducted in the United States under the 1990 Native American Graves Protection and Repatriation Act (NAGPRA), for instance, which originated as a response to a legal obligation that does not necessarily imply an ongoing relationship or an agreement of different understandings between the communities and institutions involved (see for instance, Gould and Benton in this volume). Similarly, the review by Native representatives of Indigenous collections held in mainstream repositories should not be automatically identified as a form of collaboration either, since typically tribal delegations bring information into the museum, enhance the catalogue descriptions and associated data, but do not take anything back to their home communities. Moreover, it is usually the museum that dictates what should be reviewed and under what terms, not allowing a space for the communities to negotiate and get what would really benefit them from these encounters. Apache scholar Nancy M. Mithlo (2004) poses that real inclusion of Indigenous peoples and knowledge into the museum implies relying on Indigenous research methodologies. Robust collaboration between museums and Indigenous peoples should enable Native communities to choose what objects to review, what topics to study, which methodology to use and which theoretical and practical purposes to pursue. One example of this kind of collaboration is the Reciprocal Research Network (RRN), an online tool aimed at the reciprocal and collaborative research about cultural heritage from the Northwest Coast of British Columbia, co-developed by the Musqueam Indian Band, the Stó:lō Nation/Tribal Council, the U'mista Cultural Society and the Museum of Anthropology at the University of British Columbia. The RRN is grounded in the belief that originating communities should have a major voice in shaping research questions and should benefit from the new knowledge that is produced. On the RRN, First Nations communities are not just collaborators but co-developers of the project – they have voice in both the direction and the decision-making processes at all levels (Rowley 2013). The RRN recognizes and privileges Indigenous concepts, epistemologies and realities by adapting a culturally responsive information system to culturally diverse traditions of knowledge management and by accommodating Indigenous rights to traditional knowledge.

Finally, while many multivocal exhibitions taking place at non-tribal museums include Native 'voice' in their narrative, they often end up dismissing larger concerns about authorship, integrity and authority. The most compelling recent example of this is the 2015 show at the Metropolitan Museum of Art in New York *The Plains Indians: Artists of the Earth and the Sky*, wherein the ongoing colonial practice of taking Native belongings and their relationality, power and meaning to each other, to their families, custodians and caretakers across time and transforming these into decontextualized 'objects' of aesthetic wonder, was perpetuated. As curator Joe Horse-Capture explained, 'A few years ago, I was approached to contribute to the [Plains Indian] exhibition catalog, and my first question was, "Who are the Native partners?" No partners, but plenty of Native consultants. This formula, where Native people are consultants to the project and the non-Native organizers reserve the option to reject their input, is problematic' (Horse-Capture 2015).

What happened in *The Plains Indians* exhibition – a mainstream museum favouring (Western) aesthetics over context – resonates with the curatorial strategies that have been underpinning new 'ethnographic' museums such as the Musée du Quai Branly in Paris, which holds vast collections from Indigenous peoples from Africa, Asia, Oceania and the Americas. The Quai Branly has been openly criticized for marginalizing the histories and social context of the cultures and objects represented in its collections, by concealing or eliminating almost any form of interpretative text and privileging the experiences of 'illusion' and 'wonder' provoked by the 'work of art' (Clifford 2007). Collaborative exhibitions that centre ideas of collaboration as articulated above should prioritize Native peoples as curators (or co-curators) and organizers, not just as consultants. This is the case of the exhibition that opened in March 2016 at the National Museum of the American Indian in New York *Unbound: Narrative Art of the Plains*, in which historical and contemporary ledger art, along with objects, artworks and digital displays were arranged side by side. Curated by Emil Her Many Horses, a member of the Oglala Lakota Nation in South Dakota, *Unbound* emphasized the aesthetic as much as the historical aspect of the objects on display, connecting past and present and therefore embedding the exhibition's narrative with context and locality, bringing to life the stories and identities of those who were represented in the show.

The potential for conflicting or alternative views in the interpretation and representation of museum collections by tribal members inspired James Clifford's application of Mary Louise Pratt's concept of the 'contact zone' to the museum. The term has been largely criticized by several scholars and museum professionals (Mithlo 2004; Lynch 2011; Smith 2012; Srinivasan *et al.* 2010; Boast 2011; Boast & Enote 2013) who argue that, even though Clifford makes evident the power imbalance in the contact zone, in some way he underestimates the museum's need to exercise control and manipulate consensus even in an apparent collaborative setting. Mithlo takes this critique even further, by pointing out that what might be seen as an advocacy of inclusion of tribal members into the museum practice can also be read as another burden imposed on Native peoples, who are expected to fill and bridge conceptual gaps within the museum narrative (Mithlo 2004). As in all collaborative and partnering situations between museums and source communities, we must consider what the terms of collaboration are and who is setting, defining and managing them.

Collaboration that is attentive to history, politics and power should actively work to integrate different systems of knowledge, avoiding the validation of one way of knowing over the other. It is not enough to incorporate Native points of view by just consulting with the communities about how objects should be interpreted or represented; by doing so the museum perpetuates the asymmetries of power of colonial knowledge production. On the contrary, the integration of local knowledge into the collaborative process should be ongoing with museum professionals incorporating Indigenous protocols, frameworks and traditional knowledge into how collections are circulated, preserved, accessed, curated, researched and 'owned' (Smith 2012). This also, increasingly, means addressing the very hard question of the *legal* rights in materials. For some communities, the legal rights are a critical first issue that must be addressed before any future relationships can be developed. This speaks powerfully to the historical role of law, and of copyright in particular, as a serious and deliberate tool of colonial dispossession. Thus understood, re-asserting tribal ownership (often defined in multiple ways) becomes one of the only ways that tribes can be taken seriously as equal partners at the institutional table making decisions about the futures of circulating, accessing and sharing these belongings.

The issues around circulation and use of Indigenous cultural heritage take on a new dimension due to the increasing movement of these collections into digital formats. Digital objects create new negotiations around access, care and ownership between non-tribal collecting institutions and Native communities, as well as new expectations and social engagements between these communities and the digital. Digital technologies enable various forms of collaboration by allowing the coexistence of multiple voices, diverse systems of knowledge and layers of meaning within museum narratives, interpretative materials and collections management systems, thus recognizing cultural narratives from the source as valid and legitimate (Geismar 2013; Christen 2015). However, as a dynamic platform for circulating materials, tribal communities also have anxieties about this and the capacity to maintain locally based protocols around the circulation of particular domains of cultural property and traditional knowledge. Here the anxiety is that with the introduction of digital technologies into the museum/archive, culturally sensitive objects that are now digitized – along with the information and *misinformation* they have attached – will circulate without restrictions on the Web. This radically opens up a range of inadequate contexts of viewing by inappropriate audiences (see Myers 2012, 2014 for further elaboration). Therefore, and now that cultural heritage is more accessible than ever before, it becomes crucial that museum experts, when collaborating with Native communities, take into account Indigenous protocols and epistemologies regarding how these cultural materials should be interpreted, retrieved, ascribed and shared. We must not only think critically about collaboration, but also about the media that is facilitating collaborative efforts, and how very particular forms of collaboration and very particular knowledge hierarchies are upheld.

In view of the risks that the digital age implies regarding access to and circulation of traditional knowledge, some Native communities are adopting critical and reflexive approaches towards using new technologies to control the dissemination and sharing of sensitive and/or wrong information about their cultural heritage. The inaccuracies and misinformation within archival material, plus the incomplete information within photographs' captions and films' inter-titles, for instance, have motivated tribal members to develop a counter-discursive Indigenous imaginary that is key to their contemporary self-production, self-determination, cultural rights and political sovereignty (Ginsburg 2008). By using digital technologies, some tribal communities like Zuni, for instance, are working collaboratively with museums and archives in order to re-narrate and re-inscribe archival material, thus re-signifying colonial narratives and regaining control over their cultural heritage. Within a US context, *The Shalako Film Revisited* and the increasing number of communities testing the Traditional Knowledge (TK) Labels are examples of these efforts at imagining new Indigenous orders of interpretation and meaning making. Here the project is to privilege and place as central local community rules, expertise and authority.

Temporality and spirituality in collaboration: *The Shalako Film Revisited*

In 2011, a delegation of Zuni religious leaders and staff from the A:shiwi A:wan Museum and Heritage Center at Zuni, New Mexico (AAMHC) were reviewing the Zuni collection at the American Museum of Natural History (AMNH) in New York City as part of a multi-year National Park Service Native American Graves Protection and Repatriation Act Documentation grant. The collection reviews led to an enduring partnership between the AAMHC and the AMNH to work collaboratively towards the development of *Amidolanne*, a Zuni-based digital repository of Zuni collections enabling Zuni to add commentary to standardized museum descriptions of their cultural materials. While the majority of the work at AMNH involved reviewing Zuni ethnographic, anthropologic and archaeological objects, Barbara Mathé, then Head of the Library and Special Collections at AMNH, invited the Zuni group to visit the museum's Special Collections of photographs and films. The collections unexpectedly included a film titled *The Shalako Ceremonial at Zuni, New Mexico*, a silent ethnographic film shot in 1923 by filmmaker Owen Cattell, by the request of Clark Wissler, then chair of the AMNH. Mathé was not aware at the time of the relevance the material would have for the Zuni delegation, nor could she possibly have anticipated the outcomes the film's viewing would entail.

As the name implies, *The Shalako Ceremonial at Zuni, New Mexico* is a film about the Sha'lak'o ceremony – an important part of the collective Zuni ceremonial life. Sha'lak'o, a year-round assemblage of ceremonial activity, is a major occasion near the conclusion of the Zuni ceremonial year and when all of Zuni prepares to welcome their ancestors back home – both physically and spiritually. The large two-day public ceremony is held in late November or early December with the purpose of sending out the old year and setting the appropriate conditions for a fertile new year to come (Bunzel in Isaac 2007). Sha'lak'o relates to the story of creation and emergence of the Zuni people and the migration of their ancestors to find the centre of the world – Halona:wa Idiwana'a – which is where the Pueblo of Zuni is currently located. Sha'lak'o is an essential part of the Zuni world and an educational rite for the younger generations of Zuni – during the ceremony, the Sha'lak'o bless the community and their homes along with bringing with them the knowledge and history of the ancestors to bestow on the Zuni families (Isaac 2007). There have been years when it has been discussed among the community whether Sha'lak'o should be open to non-Zunis and non-Natives or not. In Zuni, knowledge is restricted and controlled by a complex hierarchical system in order to ensure its appropriate use. One of the fundamental aspects of Zuni ways of knowing is that knowledge is partitioned into public and private spheres: Zuni is divided into religious groups, societies and clans, and the membership within each group is determined by gender, age and family position within the religious leadership. There are prerequisites that determine how knowledge should be acquired, who receives knowledge and when the right moment is to receive it (Isaac 2007). These circumstances are reflected in Sha'lak'o, where many ceremonies take place in the kivas or within other private locations. Many more Sha'lak'o rituals take place outside the Zuni village and are restricted as well; some are not supposed to be seen by outsiders or even by Zuni who do not belong to certain religious hierarchies; others cannot be witnessed by anyone other than the Sha'lak'o participants themselves.

However, Sha'lak'o has attracted a large number of non-Zunis, anthropologists and ethnographers to the Pueblo over the past century. *The Shalako Ceremonial at Zuni, New Mexico* stands as one of the consequences of that fascination for Zuni esoteric knowledge. During the summer of 1923, in order to supplement the written documentation of the Hendricks-Hodge

Expedition in the Southwest (1917–1923), filmmaker Owen Cattell shot eleven ethnographic films depicting Zuni lifeways and cultural practices at the request of the Museum of the American Indian. Cattell received an invitation from some Zuni leaders to come back to the Pueblo that same year in order to make a moving picture record of Sha'lak'o (Wegner 2009). Cattell went back to Zuni in late November as agreed, but this time funded by the American Museum of Natural History with the additional support of the Southwest Society. However, when Cattell arrived at Zuni, he encountered several problems and difficulties regarding the shooting of the ceremony. The community was divided: while some of the officials and priests in power apparently allowed the recording of the ceremony, an important group of Zuni were actively opposed to that permission – they did not wish to have the pictures taken (Wenger 2009: 185). The controversy around the recording of the ceremony can be seen in the film in three different instances: first, in a scene where the six Sha'lak'o are to enter the village at the same time, the film only depicts five of them likely because one objected to being photographed; second, the disagreement of some members of the community is represented by the image of a Zuni man standing in front of the camera; and finally, Cattell closes the film with inter-titles explaining he was restricted from recording the entire ceremony, although he does not explain why.

The contemporary issues over whether non-Zunis and non-Natives should be allowed to attend Sha'lak'o are directly related to the shooting of *The Shalako Ceremonial at Zuni, New Mexico*, and the questions around access to and circulation of imagery of Zuni ceremonialism. From that time, the Zuni community has developed a collective understanding of how important it is to control the circulation of their cultural heritage with the outside world, and this shared consensus is communicated via posted signs around the middle village (Belarde-Lewis 2011). Today, even though the two-day public portion of the Sha'lak'o ceremony is open to outsiders, all Zuni oppose visitors photographing or recording it; they all share the concern of outsiders shifting Sha'lak'o meaning from a religious to a spectacle kind of event; they worry about tourists and other non-Native people duplicating or mimicking the ceremony as has happened at the Smoki museum and Koshare museum; and they all share the desire to prevent non-Zuni depictions of Zuni ceremonialism outside Zuni. Zunis see any kind of images taken by outsiders as a clear sign that sacredness and esoteric knowledge has leaked from Zuni's partitioned system of ceremonial knowledge control; photographs and films are seen as circulation of this knowledge outside their original contexts. The making of the film *The Shalako Ceremonial at Zuni, New Mexico* refers to a historical turning point for Zuni over the use of documentary media by outsiders. According to Jim Enote, the confrontation of the ancestors with Cattell in 1923 is when Zunis first decided that no filming or recording of Zuni ceremonies would ever be allowed at the Pueblo again, and many other Indigenous communities followed the same decrees (Enote 2013).

Collaborative formations of control and ownership of digital cultural property

While watching the film at the AMNH, the Zuni delegation felt conflicted, shocked and distressed; they knew about the existence of a shorter version of the film and have seen it, but they had never seen the entire 23-minute film. Besides the fact that a film like this should have never been made, it reveals some restricted parts of the ceremony – esoteric ceremonial scenes that are not supposed to be seen by non-Sha'lak'o-initiated men. They also noticed that the inter-titles of the film were mostly incorrect and that some of the sequences of the ceremony were misidentified as well; the film was full of shortcomings due to the lack of contextual information.

Once the Zuni representatives finished viewing the film, they could not but show their concern regarding the misidentification of the ceremony and the potential circulation of the film itself. AMNH staff do not know who else – besides the National Museum of the American Indian – has a copy of the analogue film and therefore, it is impossible to know how many other digital copies could be circulating online and/or in various collections. The Zuni delegation, aware of their inability to stop the film's circulation, decided to mitigate the dissemination of the misrepresented film by controlling its message. In 2013, the AAMHC came to an agreement with the AMNH in order to produce a new community-edited remake of the film using a digital copy. The collaborative project consisted of three main interventions in the footage.

First, the Zuni participants added their own inter-titles to the film, graphically different from the originals. This allowed them to correct the misinformation and inaccuracies within the film's interpretative text yet not delete the original interpretations, evidencing that the original inter-titles were wrong and that knowledge from the source is needed for interpreting culturally sensitive visual culture. Additionally, a piece of the film depicting a part of the ceremony that should not be seen by anyone who is not a Sha'lak'o initiate was cut out of the newly edited digital version; new inter-titles were added to explain the edit, which is shown by a black screen that lasts the length of the sensitive section (Mathé 2014). Finally, voiceover in Zuni language was added to the film; this voiceover is much more detailed than the inter-titles and its main purpose is to supplement the images with contextual information, making the film an educational tool for the Zuni community. The Zuni voice and new inter-titles add important commentary about how the shooting of Sha'lak'o affected the community's unity and shaped the subsequent prohibition against recordings at Zuni – effects that are not mentioned in the original film.

The AMNH, in conjunction with the AAMHC, sought funding for this project from the National Film Preservation Foundation. The technical work was done by AMNH staff while the intellectual work was done in its entirety by Zuni religious leaders Ronnie Cachini, George Yawakie and Octavius Seowtewa, along with AAMHC's Director, Jim Enote, and AAMHC's Museum Technician Curtis Quam. The new digital version of the film allowed the community to re-signify, accommodate and even transform digital contents from the original film. The original film footage, in which Indigenous subjectivity was not taken into account, becomes evocative in the new digital version holding collective, accurate and authentic narrative from the source.

Aside from redressing the imbalance of the past, *The Shalako Film Revisited* also stands as an educational tool for cultural revitalization within a Zuni context. According to Jim Enote, the new film allows Zunis to understand why they are who they are, and it gives an opportunity to Zunis who do not belong to the private spheres of knowledge to learn about an important part of their culture. Archives are sites from which information can be retrieved and in some situations can be spaces of knowledge production. The showing of the new film at the AAMHC sparks emotions, memories and stories among the viewers, reviving a sense of belonging to a collective identity (Montenegro 2015). *The Shalako Film Revisited* affirms that religious traditions in Zuni have been performed in the exact same way for decades, and provides Zuni youth with visuals they can use to supplement the oral descriptions they constantly hear of the past – the film generates the environment for Zuni members to re-interpret the original film, according to their own experience, every time they view it.

Once the successful collaborative work conducted by both museums on repurposing *The Shalako Ceremonial at Zuni, New Mexico* was done, the Zuni representatives realized there were several issues around the access, circulation and ownership of the new version of the film that were not clear. They raised the question of copyright in the new version as well as other questions concerning the circumstances under which the new film could be shown and seen, as well as how the old unedited film could be shown and seen. The original *The Shalako Ceremonial at Zuni, New Mexico* is in the public domain, which means that the film can be seen and used by everyone without authorization. While limits can be placed, for instance maintaining a non-digital copy that requires a physical visit to the institution that holds it, without a special policy in relation to sensitive materials that governs the actions of the institution, it can still be viewed. (On this point see the recent Protocols for the Treatment of Sensitive Materials recently produced by the American Philosophical Society 2015). On the other hand, the physical property in the original film canisters is owned by the AMNH – the institution that hired Cattell to make the film. The AMNH Film Collection Record continues to credit Cattell as the film's author. This original authorship and credit remains problematic as it suggests continued ownership, or at least infers a misleading proprietary connection, even if the work is in the public domain. This incorrect 'authorship' from a Zuni perspective perpetuates mistakes about authority and who can and should speak for this film. As the 'subjects' of the film, and not their legal copyright owners, Zunis not only have no control over the life of the material – where it is being housed and the conditions regarding its circulation and access – but they must also secure permission from the 'author' or 'owner' – in this case the AMNH – in order to reuse this film that documents their own lives, customs and cultural practices (Anderson 2013). Of course, 'copyright', 'ownership' and 'authorship' are subjective qualities or characteristics derived from a non-Zuni world. Zuni would maintain the images are Zuni no matter what and no matter the time period (Enote, personal communication, 2016).

However, staff at AMNH – including the museum's legal counsel upon consultation – agreed that the Zunis should own the copyright over the new digital film, since they are the ones who created the new intellectual content, and in fact a new copyright (derivative) work. As the copyright holders of the renewed version of the film, Zunis do have the right to control the access to and the circulation of at least that copy. When the Zuni delegation proposed to the AMNH to collaborate on remaking the film in order to 'at least control its message', they did not just mean correcting the inaccuracies and shortcomings of the original footage, but also controlling when, how and where to share it. Thus, the AMNH agreed with the AAMHC that the new film should only be shown where there is a Zuni person present to narrate the story both of Sha'lak'o and of the collaborative work both groups undertook to rearticulate the film. This specific negotiation over the terms of access and circulation demonstrates that ownership and control become two different trajectories for action when it comes to the protection of Indigenous archives. This is because conventional intellectual property law does not allow for nuanced Zuni forms of ownership over the film and its routes of circulation, thus the community negotiated a different approach that importantly requires Zuni presence when watching the new film. The innovation that the community has made in enacting control over this and all of their cultural materials offers an example of an alternative regime of power, authority and political sovereignty. What the community is trying to correct are the messages of two different but interrelated stories: on one hand the story that is misidentified in the original film – the misinformation, the incorrect succession of events and the lack of contextual information – while on the other hand, the story of *who* controls access to *what*; how this has been historically determined and enforced; and how it is being unsettled with this new film.

The partnership between the AMNH and the AAMHC can be linked to a wider project of decolonization wherein the record is set straight and where collaboration becomes a tool of power sharing, community-driven authorship, identity revitalization and social change. The collaborative work around *The Shalako Film Revisited* involved examining the ways in which the Zuni community experiences ownership and property, and incorporating their understandings of what is needed for resignifying the film as well as controlling its circulation, access and future use. However, while the labour around rearticulating the film did not strike difficulties regarding the collaborative process itself, it did raise several questions concerning the way in which collaboration works when there is collective knowledge production involved. For example, to whom in Zuni should the copyright be ascribed: to the team that edited the film, to the AAMHC, to the tribal government? Will the real property ownership of the original film ever be transferred to the Zuni community? These questions illustrate two kinds of limitations that can arise from dealing with Indigenous cultural property: first, that there are responsibilities both of the museums and the source communities when collaborating in projects where a reduced group speaks on behalf of a larger group, and second that the collaboration paradigm is often contradictory to intellectual property laws and the Western decision-making model – both have proven to be inadequate to protect multivocal cultural knowledge productions (Anderson & Christen 2013). This is one of the main reasons why collaboration in these kinds of cases becomes crucial: solutions to situations involving the sensitive management of Indigenous digital cultural property often lie outside the legal domain, and thus depend on the will, ethics, labour and creativity of the people and institutions involved. The challenge is for museum professionals, archivists and researchers to fashion their idea of collaboration alongside the communities with whom they work, in order to develop guidelines that will benefit both parties in the long term.

Reciprocal and informed sharing of cultural property

The problem of who legally owns and is the 'author' of the Shalako film, and any derivative works made from it, raises questions of how intellectual property law in general and copyright in particular, intersects archives and affects forms of collaboration. In the United States, for at least the last 25 years, a primary focus has been directed towards institutional responsibility for the unethical, insensitive and violent treatment of Native American ancestors and belongings. It is only recently that more focused attention has turned to intellectual property as an area of law equally complicit in the taking and exclusion of Indigenous peoples from their cultural heritage. As the above example illustrates, Zuni concerns about the ownership of the film reflect greater anxieties about access and circulation and the inability of Western legal frameworks to accommodate cultural rules regarding these. (For a similar expression of anxiety from a Hopi perspective see Anderson, McElgunn and Richland 2016).

The opening of archives, museums and libraries to Indigenous individuals and communities has made visible the intricate networks of colonial law that are wrapped around and embedded within these collections. The domain of copyright is particularly insidious because it embeds relations of power and entitlement into the very structure of the archive itself, for instance in the indexes and catalogues that are organized around the author/owner. This structural dimension renders largely invisible the colonial process of appropriation and resource extraction that copyright is integrally involved in. Moreover, copyright normalizes a whole range of ideals of circulation, ranging from normative perceptions of the public domain to open access. This normalization has consequences in practice, especially when

Indigenous communities coming to the archive seeking new relationships point to the cultural particularity of these concepts.

Navigating and negotiating around copyright is hard for communities and institutions alike. However, institutions have a different range of resources available and all have some kind of legal counsel that they receive support from, with the most iconic institutions having legal counsel in house. Indigenous communities have a range of attorneys and legal services available, but few have meta-legal copyright expertise. This is largely because among the various areas of law requiring community-based expertise, from Federal Indian Law, to contracts, to employment and commercial law interests, intellectual property and copyright are a late addition. The difference in access to this area of law greatly affects what kinds of negotiations are possible, especially in asserting alternative perspectives about circulation and access, as negotiations around the Shalako film aptly demonstrate.

Local Contexts is an online platform (www.localcontexts.org) developed in 2012 to offer legal and educational support for Indigenous management and negotiation over cultural heritage collections held in cultural institutions nationally and internationally. It was specifically designed to address two inter-related problems. The first is the abovementioned access to legal information about intellectual property and copyright in order to advance options for communities engaged in negotiations around the 'ownership' and 'authorship' of their cultural heritage collections. The second is a developed strategy to deal with a more specific problem emanating from the copyright/archive/author nexus – that Indigenous communities are rarely the legal owners or authors of their cultural heritage. This is because copyright is either held by third parties (the researcher, film-maker, photographer or institution, etc.) or has expired in the 'work' and it now falls into the public domain where no one can be an owner/author. This means that regardless of ongoing cultural associations, obligations, responsibilities and rules, this material cannot be repositioned through an Indigenously ordered framework of control and access.

In its fourth year of development, and with recent support from the National Endowment for the Humanities (Division of Preservation and Access), *Local Contexts* is continuing to build up its infrastructure for supporting information about intellectual property and the various implications for decision making at a tribal level. This is being done in conversation with the project's advisory council, its four tribal partners testing the TK Labels (Stó:lō First Nation, Musqueam First Nation, Karuk Tribe and the Penobscot Nation) and other tribal users of the site including tribal museums like Ziibiwing Center for Anishinabe Culture and Lifeways. This work has led, for instance, to the inclusion of template documents like Memorandums of Understanding and examples of other public tribal documents. For instance, the Karuk Tribe in northern California has contributed a range of their own community documents that have been developed and approved by the Karuk Tribal Council in the last year. This knowledge sharing through the very documents themselves allows access to tribally negotiated frameworks increasingly required to establish equitable and community oriented practices for research collaboration and the future sharing of cultural heritage.

Alongside this legal support, *Local Contexts* has developed a new digital labelling system for cultural heritage materials, the Traditional Knowledge (TK) Labels. As a largely educative initiative, an underlying premise for the labels was that they could be utilized by communities that are unable to assert legal control over their collections. In this sense, while they cannot 'correct' the legal ownership from a community/tribal perspective, they can assert the ongoing tribal, community and even family relationships, obligations and responsibilities that are embedded in this material. Moreover, these relationships of responsibility can finally be included as part of the digital, metadata and catalogue records associated with this material. In this very act of labelling and pointing back to the contemporary local contexts from which these materials derive their meaning and continue their networks of responsibility, there is a disruption in the presumed stability of the asserted legal ownership. With the labels, particularly the Attribution Label, the collector as author/owner is partially denaturalized, and another kind of understanding about these belongings is made possible. Other labels point to different concerns about access and use, much like those expressed by Zuni in relation to the Shalako film, for instance, conveying restrictions based on gender and/or initiate rights, or conveying significance of material because of its totemic, esoteric or spiritual power.

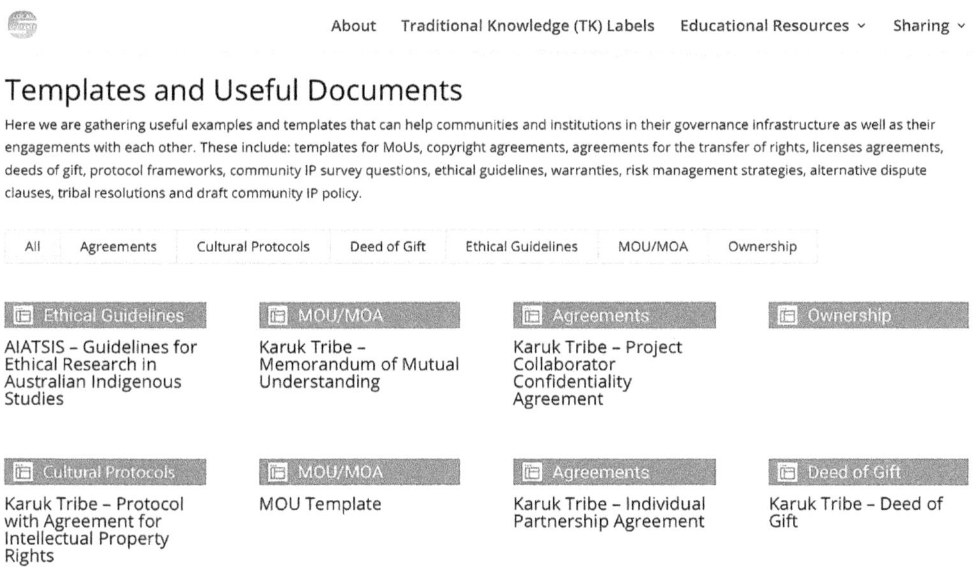

Figure 22.1 Screenshot from *Local Contexts*.
Source: www.localcontexts.org

On one level the TK Labels offer themselves as a specific device for the development of collaborations between Native/First Nation and Indigenous communities and institutions over the futures of access and sharing, particularly in a digital environment. They prioritize direct dialogue and negotiation because the label text cannot be written by institutions; they require detail, nuance and importantly approval that resides at a tribal level. Through this there is an important turn towards privileging the multiple forms of owning and stewarding and the relationships of responsibility to heritage materials that span generations and contexts from an Indigenous standpoint. Reorienting these belongings and knowledges through local community epistemological framing not only changes how meaning about them can be made, but also the centrality of the relationships required to facilitate that meaning.

The labels are also being utilized within community contexts for projects that do not necessarily involve negotiations with institutions, but that still engage with digital publics, variously constituted, being invited to engage with specific community history and experiences of colonialism in the present. As one example, the Sq'éwlets Band of the Stó:lō Nation in Canada have been working through Virtual Museums Canada and Simon Fraser University to develop an educational website that explains Sq'éwlets history, cultural heritage and engagement with the discipline of archaeology to Sq'éwlets and non-Sq'éwlets audiences. (See http://www.digitalsqewlets.ca/index-eng.php.) One problem identified early in the project was how to convey Sq'éwlets expectations regarding access, ownership and use of materials on the website itself. While the site is being designed for a global public, but especially a Canadian public that has patchy and largely minimal information about Canada's First Nations peoples, and has been developed and vetted through community protocols, workshops and regular discussions, there remained the problem of conveying specific cultural expectations of seeing and using this material. Representatives working with the Sq'éwlets Band, Dave Schaepe, Natasha Lyons and Kate Hennessey offered the idea of *Local Contexts* and the TK Labels at community meetings as a means to develop answers to these questions. Initial interest in hearing more about these options developed into a full-scale workshop where Sq'éwlets representatives from the whole community adapted five of the TK Labels for purposeful Sq'éwlets use. The labelling function was able to convey Sq'éwlets expectations and protocols of access to the range of publics that will engage with this website. In doing so it serves an important role in adding an extra level of information about the digital content, educating users about culturally specific expectations for using significant cultural heritage materials in a non-legal frame. Significantly this also includes providing appropriate means of attribution and acknowledgement for any future use of this material. The Sq'éwlets adaptation and implementation of the TK Labels provides an additional set of local and culturally specific guidelines for reading and engaging with content provided on the site, and it also points to the network of relationships that work to give the material shared on this site its meaning. To this end, the educational goals of the site are amplified and the digital expression of this material has expanded and embedded metadata for re-use in other community or third party contexts.

The Traditional Knowledge Labels developed by the Sq'éwlets community directly reflect community negotiated and agreed-upon concerns and needs about access and use of cultural heritage derived from the Sq'éwlets community itself. In the below screenshot from the website digitalsqewlets.ca, the TK Label icons are found in the top right hand corner under the Virtual Museums Canada logo. Clicking on the image opens a box that explains the label and its intentions from a Sq'éwlets perspective. In this example, making a label about name and attribution simultaneously points to a historical paradigm of misnaming and misattributing Sq'éwlets cultural heritage, whilst at the same time correcting the historical record and creating possibilities for future engagement.

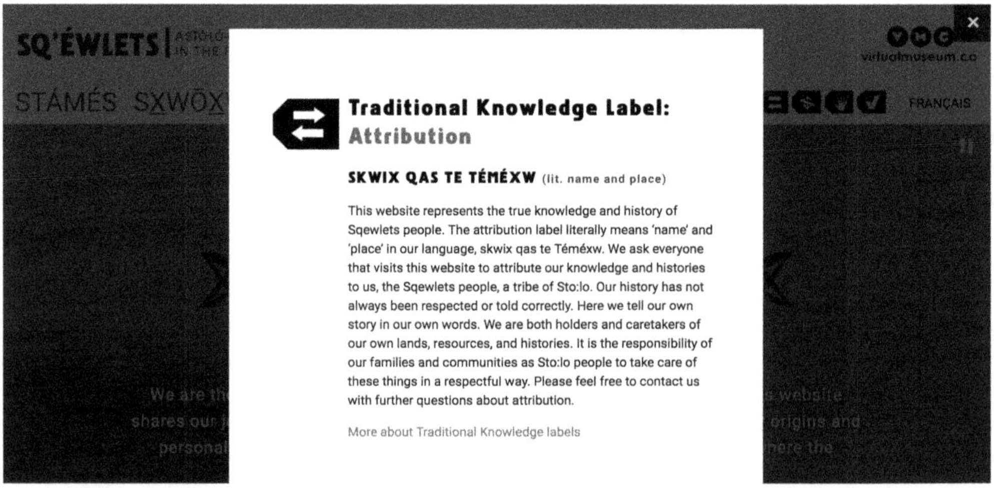

Figure 22.2 Attribution Label on Sq'éwlets website.
Source: http://digitalsqewlets.ca/index-eng.php

The application of the TK Labels to this Sq'éwlets cultural heritage website functions to localize meaning. It gives any user who encounters the site more information about the Sq'éwlets community's intentions and expectations in sharing their culture and cultural heritage in a digital environment. Importantly, the intent for sharing is being explained through Sq'éwlets terms and language, with recognition of and respect for the special cultural rules that govern knowledge and its connection to history, to people and families, and importantly to tribal territory. The idea of labelling gets at one part of the problem of access, circulation and management of cultural property that figure as urgent needs to be addressed in the future management and stewardship of Native/First Nations digital cultural heritage.

Conclusion: The collaborative transit of cultural property

The three case studies we have looked at throughout this chapter – the British Museum's *Indigenous Australia: Enduring Civilization* exhibition with its parallel collaborative exhibition at the National Museum of Australia, *The Shalako Film Revisited*, and digital initiative *Local Contexts* and the TK Labels – illustrate how institutions are re-orienting their practices. Indigenous and non-Indigenous groups are increasingly collaborating to de-centre the power of collecting institutions, defy the hierarchies of conventional documenting and interpretative practices, and build more culturally responsive information systems guided by Indigenous concepts, epistemologies and realities. In this chapter, we wanted to explore the multifaceted dimensions of the collaborative turn in institutional engagement with their collections and the communities to which they belong. The collaboration between the British Museum and the National Museum of Australia is an unprecedented example of inter-institutional collaboration involving the active participation of 25 Indigenous Australian communities. It is propelled forward by political climates that demand this kind of work, public relations concerns and recognition that it can lead to enhanced knowledge about collections. *The Shalako Film Revisited* is the outcome of the collaborative work and a long-term relationship between a non-tribal museum and a Native community reworking the terrain of an early ethnographic encounter that was unbalanced and insensitive to Zuni community protocols for sharing. *Local Contexts* is a further example of the possible forms of collaboration between scholars and tribal members, and between tribal members and non-tribal collecting institutions holding Indigenous cultural property and its increased routes of circulation in digital forms.

As museums are collaborating more and more with Native peoples at different levels and Indigenous peoples are instigating and leading a movement in the spirit of 'pure collaboration' (Enote 2015), more questions than answers are being raised. Now that collaboration is a reality it is necessary to think critically on what Colwell-Chanthaphonh calls the 'problem of collaboration' as well as on what the future of genuine collaboration from multiple party perspectives looks like. Can we really talk about collaboration when issues of ownership, authorship and control of Native collections remain unaddressed, unclear and unresolved?

This takes us back to the British Museum example, where the institution fashioned a temporary model of 'return' through what was really a visitation or short-term sharing of part of the museum's collection on Aboriginal and Torres Strait Islander material culture to Australia. The proprietary logics here are deeply entrenched, and this is regardless of how 'much' of the material has appropriate provenance documentation. The hard work remains addressing both the ethical and the legal rights and the subsequent claims of multiple communities over their cultural heritage. For the British Museum there remain questions about the outcomes of this collaboration in real and meaningful ways, especially about what will be the long-term benefits for the 25 communities who enriched and enhanced the content within the British Museum's catalogue. There are a number of different positions here, but there clearly remains a problem that the basic and foundational proprietary interests in this collection largely went overlooked (by some) and therefore remained practically unaddressed. This speaks powerfully to how these proprietary regimes continue to condition institutional and community relationships of collaboration and engagement. As Henrietta Fourmile Marrie said in response to the imminent return of her grandfather's material:

> It is with a heavy heart that I stand here today . . . and look at the many items which have been brought here . . . It came this far, his spirit . . . [is] within those items, that spirit had returned home . . . and in two weeks time that spirit will be gone again . . . we will miss him, again.
>
> *(Daley 2016)*

While there certainly have been many 'new encounters' through this 'collaborative' exhibition, some of the structural and legal violence of the first encounter(s), those that led to these collections leaving their communities and the country in the first place, remains.

The future of collaboration is now foregrounded by issues of ownership and authorship of Native collections. Unless institutions deal with these issues they are still holding power and perpetuating colonial dynamics of dispossession. Learning to let things go still falls under an institution's good will and ethics. As pointed out throughout this chapter, as well as in the abundant literature on the subject, Western legal frameworks have largely proved insufficient to meet Indigenous peoples' claims to their objects, belongings and knowledge. Repatriation laws, such as NAGPRA in the United States, are only valid at a national level and only require the repatriation of human remains along with sacred and funerary associated objects and objects of cultural patrimony. NAGPRA certainly has its contests in application and delivery, but it is also so specific that it leaves out other vital community material such as language documents and audiovisual materials like photographs and films. These are precisely the materials that communities, in a post-NAGPRA environment, are especially concerned with accessing and negotiating ownership over. With no national policies, frameworks or even adequate advice, collaboration still has very real limits.

Acknowledgements

We would like to acknowledge and thank Jim Enote for allowing us to write about the *Shalako Film Revisited* project and share his ideas around what a museum collaboration movement should look like. We also want to thank people involved in the project who generously shared their experiences and time. At the American Museum of Natural History, we thank Nell Murphy and Barbara Mathé. Special thanks to Cynthia Chavez-Lamar for allowing Maria Montenegro to participate in the negotiations between the A:shiwi A:wan Museum and the NMAI Archive Center. We would also like to thank Kim Christen, Robin Boast, Sonya Atalay, Fred Myers, Faye Ginsburg, Haidy Geismar, Sabra Thorner, Kate Hennessey, Natasha Lyons, Dave Schaepe, Andrea Geyer and Ashley Hunt for multiple conversations, engagements and collaborations that fed into and have been woven through this chapter.

Bibliography

American Philosophical Society. 2015. *Protocols for the Treatment of Indigenous Materials.* https://amphilsoc.org/library/protocols-for-indigenous-materials Last Accessed: March 3, 2016.

Anderson, Jane. 2013. "Anxieties of Authorship in the Colonial Archive." In *Media Authorship*, edited by C. Chris and D. Gerstner, 1–17. London: Routledge.

Anderson, Jane and Kim Christen. 2013. "'Chuck a Copyright on It': Dilemmas of Digital Return and the Possibilities for Traditional Knowledge Licenses and Labels." *Museum Anthropology Review* 7, no. 1–2: 105–126.

Anderson, Jane, Hannah McElgunn, and Justin Richland. 2016. "Labeling Knowledge: The Semiotics of Immaterial Cultural Property and the Production of New Indigenous Publics." In *Engaging Native American Publics*, edited by B. Meeks, P. Krotisky and E. Nevins. London: Routledge.

Atalay, Sonya. 2012. *Community-Based Archaeology: Research with, by, and for Indigenous and Local Communities.* Berkeley: University of California Press.

Australian Institute of Aboriginal and Torres Strait Islander Studies (AIATSIS). 2011. *Guidelines for Ethical Research in Australian Indigenous Studies.* http://aiatsis.gov.au/research/ethical-research/guidelines-ethical-research-australian-indigenous-studies Last Accessed: March 31, 2016.

Belarde-Lewis, Miranda. 2011. "Sharing the Private in Public: Indigenous Cultural Property and Online Media." iConference, Seattle, WA, February 8–11.

Boast, Robin. 2011. "Neocolonial Collaboration: Museum as Contact Zone Revisited." *Museum Anthropology* 34, no. 1: 56–70.

Boast, Robin, and Jim Enote. 2013. "Virtual Repatriation: It is Neither Virtual nor Repatriation." In *Heritage in the Context of Globalization: Europe and the Americas*, edited by P.F. Biehl and C. Prescott. New York: Springer Briefs in Archaeology.

Christen, Kim. 2009. "Access and Accountability: The Ecology of Information Sharing in the Digital Age." *Anthropology News* 50, no. 4: 4–5. Seattle: Washington State University.

Christen, Kim. 2012. "Does Information Really Want to Be Free?: Indigenous Knowledge and the Politics of Open Access." *International Journal of Communication* 6: 2870–2893.

Christen, Kim. 2015. "Tribal Archives, Traditional Knowledge, and Local Contexts: Why the "s" Matters." *Journal of Western Archives* 6, no. 1: 1–19.

Clifford, James. 1991. "Four Northwest Coast Museums: Travel Reflections." In *Exhibiting Cultures: The Poetics and Politics of Museum Display*, edited by Ivan Karp and Steven D. Lavine. Washington, DC: Smithsonian Institution Press.

Clifford, James. 1997. "Museums as Contact Zones." In *Routes: Travel and Translation in the Late Twentieth Century*, edited by James Clifford, 188–219. Cambridge, MA: Harvard University Press.

Clifford, James. 2007. "Quai Branly in Process." *October* no. 120: 3–23.

Clifford, James. 2013. *Returns: Becoming Indigenous in the Twenty-First Century.* Cambridge, MA: Harvard University Press.

Colwell-Chanthaphonh, Chip. 2010. "The Problem of Collaboration? Reflections and Engagements of Inclusivity, Reciprocity, and Democracy in Museum Anthropology." *Western Humanities Review* 64, no. 3: 49–63.

Daley, Paul. 2016. "Indigenous Treasures, Briefly on Loan to Australia, Are about to be Taken Away – Again." *The Guardian*, March 22, 2016. http://www.theguardian.com/australia-news/postcolonial-blog/2016/mar/22/indigenous-treasures-briefly-on-loan-to-australia-are-about-to-be-taken-away-again Last accessed: March 31, 2016.

Deliss, Clementine. 2015. "The Sick Museum." Radio Web Macba (RWM). http://rwm.macba.cat/en/sonia/clementine-deliss/capsula Last accessed: March 27, 2016.

Enote, Jim. 2013. *The Shalako Film Revisited* [film]. 23 mins. Zuni Pueblo, New Mexico: A:shiwi A:wan Museum and Heritage Center.

Enote, Jim. 2014a. Negotiations at the Smithsonian National Museum of the American Indian, Washington, DC, September 24.

Enote, Jim. 2014b. "Museum and Source Community Responsibilities in Collection Reviews." Lecture, Minpaku – National Museum of Ethnology, Osaka, Japan, October 6.

Enote, Jim. 2015. Museum Manifesto. Museum Summit, Association of Tribal Archives, Libraries and Museums (ATALM) Annual Conference. Washington, DC, October.

Enote, Jim. 2016. Personal communication.

Fourmile Marrie, Henrietta. 1988. "Who Owns the Past? – Aborigines as Captives of the Archives." Aborigines Making History Conference, Canberra, May 1988.

Geismar, Haidy. 2013. "Defining the Digital." *Museum Anthropology Review* 7, no. 1–2: 254–263.

Ginsburg, Faye. 2008. "Rethinking the Digital Age." In *The Media and Social Theory*, edited by David Hesmondhalgh and Jason Toynbee, 127–144. New York: Routledge.

Harrison, Rodney. 2013. "Reassembling Ethnographic Museum Collections." In *Reassembling the Collection: Ethnographic Museums and Indigenous Agency*, edited by Rodney Harrison, Sarah Byrne and Anne Clarke, 3–35. Santa Fe, NM: School for Advanced Research Press.

Hays-Gilpin, Kelley, and Ramson Lomatewama. 2013. "Curating Communities at the Museum of Northern Arizona." In *Reassembling the Collection: Ethnographic Museums and Indigenous Agency*, edited by Rodney Harrison, Sarah Byrne and Anne Clarke, 259–283. Santa Fe, NM: School for Advanced Research Press.

Horse-Capture, Joe. 2015. "Native People Have a Story to Tell – Their Own," Indian Country Today Media Network. http://indiancountrytodaymedianetwork.com/2015/04/25/horse-capture-native-people-have-story-tell-their-own-160144 Last accessed: March 27, 2016.

Isaac, Gwyneira. 2007. *Mediating Knowledges. Origins of a Zuni Tribal Museum*. Tucson: University of Arizona Press.

Isaac, Gwyneira. 2015. "'Get to Know Your World': An Interview with Jim Enote, Director of the A:shiwi A:wan Museum and Heritage Center in Zuni, New Mexico." In *Museum Transformations. International Handbook of Museums*, edited by Annie E. Coombes and Ruth B. Phillips. Oxford: Blackwell.

Kreps, Christina. 2009. "Indigenous Curation, Museums, and Intangible Cultural Heritage." In *Intangible Heritage*, edited by Laurajane Smith and Natsuko Akagawa. New York: Routledge.

Kreps, Christina. 2011a. "Non-Western Models of Museums and Curation in Cross-cultural Perspective." In *A Companion to Museum Studies*, edited by Sharon Macdonald. Malden, MA: Blackwell.

Kreps, Christina. 2011b. "Changing the Rules of the Road: Post-colonialism and the New Ethics of Museum Anthropology." In *The Routledge Companion to Museum Ethics: Redefining Ethics for the Twenty-First-Century Museum*, edited by Janet Marstine. New York: Routledge.

Krmpotich, Cara. 2014. *The Force of Family: Repatriation, Kinship and Memory on Haida Gwaii*. Toronto: University of Toronto Press.

Krmpotich, Cara and Laura Peers. 2013. *This is Our Life: Haida Material Heritage and Changing Museum Practice*. Vancouver: University of British Columbia Press.

Lonetree, Amy. 2012. *Decolonizing Museums. Representing Native America in National and Tribal Museums*. Chapel Hill: University of North Carolina Press.

Lynch, Bernadette T. 2011. "Collaboration, Contestation, and Creative Conflict: On the Efficacy of Museum/Community Partnership." In *The Routledge Companion to Museum Ethics: Redefining Ethics for the Twenty-First-Century Museum*, edited by Janet Marstine. New York: Routledge.

Mathé, Barbara. 2014. "Whose Pictures are These? Indigenous Community Access and Control of Digital Archives." Lecture, Girona, 2014: Arxius/Industries Culturals.

Mithlo, Nancy M. 2004. "Red Man's Burden. The Politics of Inclusion in Museum Settings." *American Indian Quarterly* 28, no. 3–4: 743–763.

Montenegro, Maria. 2015. "Setting the Record Straight: Indigenous Agency and Digital Technologies within a Critical Social Movement of Museum Collaboration." Master's thesis, program in Museum Studies, New York University (unpublished).

Myers, Fred. 2012. "Censorship from Below: Aboriginal Art in Australian Museums." In *No Deal: Indigenous Arts and the Politics of Possession*, edited by T. Berman. Santa Fe, NM: School for Advanced Research.

Myers, Fred. 2014. "Showing Too Much or Too Little: Predicaments of Painting Indigenous Presence in Central Australia." In *Performing Indigeneity*, edited by Glenn Penny and Laura Graham. Lincoln: University of Nebraska Press.

Nakata, M. and B. David. 2010. "Archaeological Practice at the Cultural Interface." In *Handbook of Postcolonial Archaeology*, edited by J. Lydon and U. Rizvi, 429–444. Walnut Creek, CA: Left Coast Press.

National Museum of Australia (NMA). 2015. http://www.nma.gov.au/whats-on/events/new_encounters_conference. Last Accessed: March 31, 2016.

Neill, Rosemary. 2013. "British Museum and National Museum of Australia Host Dual Indigenous Exhibition." *The Australian*, October 5, 2013. http://www.theaustralian.com.au/arts/review/the-collectors/story-fn9n8gph-1226731746376 Last accessed: March 31, 2013.

Peers, Laura, and Alison K. Brown. 2003. "Introduction." In *Museums and Source Communities*, edited by Laura Peers and Alison Brown, 3–16. New York: Routledge.

Phillips, Ruth. 2003. "Community Collaboration in Exhibitions: Toward a Dialogic Paradigm. Introduction." In *Museums and Source Communities*, edited by Laura Peers and Alison Brown, 155–171. New York: Routledge.

Phillips, Ruth. 2005. "Re-placing Objects: Historical Practices for the Second Museum Age." *Canadian Historical Review* 86, no. 1: 83–110.

Rowley, Susan. 2013. "The Reciprocal Research Network: The Development Process." *Museum Anthropology Review* 7, no. 1–2: 22–43.

Shannon, Jennifer. 2014. *Our Lives: Collaboration, Native Voice, and the Making of the National Museum of the American Indian*. Santa Fe, NM: School for Advanced Research.

Simpson, Moira. 1996. *Making Representations: Museums in the Post-Colonial Era*. New York: Routledge.

Smith, Linda Tuhiwai. 2012. *Decolonizing Methodologies. Research and Indigenous Peoples*. London: Zed Books.

Srinivasan, Ramesh, Jim Enote, Katherine M. Becvar and Robin Boast. 2010. "Diverse Knowledges and Contact Zones within the Digital Museum." *Science, Technology, & Human Values* 35, no. 5: 735–768.

Thomas, Nicholas. 2010. "The Museum as Method." *Museum Anthropology* 33, no. 1: 6–10.

Turnbull, David. 2012. "Performativity and Complex Adaptive Systems: Working with Multiple Narratives across Knowledge Traditions." *Studia UBB. Philosophia* 57, no. 1: 9–32.

Wenger, Tisa. 2009. *We Have a Religion: The 1920s Pueblo Indian Dance Controversy and American Religious Freedom*. Chapel Hill: University of North Carolina Press.

Willis, Elizabeth. 2008. "The Law, Politics, and 'Historical Wounds': The Dja Dja Warrung Bark Etchings Case in Australia." *International Journal of Cultural Property* 15, no. 1: 49–63.

23

ANIMATING LANGUAGE

Continuing intergenerational Indigenous language knowledge

Shannon Faulkhead, John Bradley and Brent McKee

Introduction

2011 saw the birth of the Monash Country Lines Archive (MCLA) programme that reassessed existing academic processes in Indigenous Australian language preservation and community engagement. Working on the premise that Indigenous Australian communities already have the infrastructure to continue and preserve their language through intergenerational learning, MCLA decided to support this system of learning instead of changing it or introducing something new. Through the use of 3D (three-dimensional) animation as tools to re-engage and revitalize interest in language continuation, Indigenous communities are working in partnership with MCLA in the protection of their cultural and intellectual property contained within their languages.

Li-Yanyuwa li-Wirdiwalangu

The Yanyuwa animation project was the impetus for the MCLA programme. This project captured seven Yanyuwa Country Line narratives in 3D animation, through a partnership between *li-Yanyuwa li-Wirdiwalangu* (Yanyuwa elders group) (Borroloola, NT), and Monash University (2008–2010).[1] At 20 years of age John Bradley began working with the Yanyuwa people of Borroloola over 30 years ago, first as a school teacher, then as an academic to address fears of loss of their cultural and intellectual property through the disengagement of the young ones and the Yanyuwa language.[2] Through this kinship and friendship relationship the old people began to record their language in the hope that it could be used to re-engage the younger generations in their language. Together they discovered ways to record knowledge and information whose existence was untranslatable into the static forms of the written word. The Yanyuwa traditional artistic expression is poetry, song, and performance. Although they have visual artists today, they do not have a pre-colonial tradition of visual art. They were interested in Bradley's drawings of their stories and songs, but it was when he illustrated the dreaming stories as an atlas that the Yanyuwa declared they needed 'images that moved' for their stories to be told properly – this was where animation as a tool for language continuation originated, as a way of preserving what in the West we might call cultural heritage, but what the Yanyuwa called Law. Whilst the use of animations was grounded in research that supported animation as a tool for cross-cultural communication and cross-generational knowledge sharing,[3] the choice of 3D animation format was chosen after the li-Yanyuwa li-Wirdiwalangu viewed every form of animation available and they did not like any of them for various reasons. Then one day Dr Tom Chandler[4] approached John Bradley and asked if he had anything he would like animated using 3D animation. Chandler had been using 3D animation for archaeological recreations of Angkor Wat.[5] These were shown to the Yanyuwa and they said yes. This was the style of animation they wanted based on the 3D animation's ability to translate their stories and characters, and rebuild country in a way that was relevant to them; they wanted their stories to 'look real.' The Yanyuwa decided the way to test the 3D animation format, and the academic team that was to animate the story.

The Yanyuwa's choice of 3D animation continued into the MCLA programme, with communities having the choice of using the realism of this form of animation, or using their community/country's art in a 3D format.

The Monash Country Lines Archive

The MCLA programme was developed in 2011 with funding from Alan and Elizabeth Foundation[6] for an Australia-wide five-year programme. There was already interest from other communities to use 3D animation to assist in language continuation through the telling of their stories. The MCLA needed to be a decolonizing space through a collaborative, co-creative journey between the partners – Indigenous, non-Indigenous, community, and academics. Based on previous collaborative partnerships two strategies were identified for the MCLA[7] programme: copyright of the animations was to be retained by the story owners/holders, and the partnerships and timelines were to be community based, not academic. MCLA considered these essential to affirm Indigenous communities' rights in the protection of their cultural and intellectual property.

Animating languages

The authors of this chapter are the main members of the MCLA team. This chapter has been divided into three sections based on each of the author's expertise and written from self-reflexive positioning:

1. Bradley explores the *Importance of Learning Indigenous Languages* through his friendship and kinship relationships with the li-Yanyuwa li-Wirdiwalangu (Yanyuwa elders group) (Borroloola, NT). Throughout this 30-plus year relationship, the li-Yanyuwa li-Wirdiwalangu and Bradley have been grieved that the young people could not speak Yanyuwa, and were therefore growing up not knowing or understanding the Laws and responsibilities of their lands.
2. *MCLA Strategies* looks at how the MCLA programme was built. Whilst MLCA is an academic programme, Faulkhead writes on how this does not need to be in opposition to the rights of Indigenous peoples in the protection of their cultural and intellectual property.
3. The final section is *Animating Language and Country* by McKee. McKee reflects on how as an animator, his animation processes changed when he began visiting Indigenous peoples' countries and being able to create and re-create their stories the way they see them, instead of through photos.

Importance of learning Indigenous languages

'How do we give the kids ears?'

Yanyuwa elder 2011[8]

In June of 2010 a senior Yanyuwa[9] elder died. He was 75 years old. In all of those 75 years he never left his country; he spoke and sang Yanyuwa language 'like the old people long dead'; he knew the Law of the country; and yet he could also speak with authority in English to the many research scientists, government officials and others who travelled across his country. Because of his great wealth of knowledge and formidable intellect, this man was respected widely. With his death the Yanyuwa lost 'the book and volume of his brain.'[10] A library had gone from the country of the Yanyuwa people. Over the last 35 years far too many 'volumes of encyclopaedic minds' have died in the Yanyuwa community. This old man was just one of so many older Indigenous people both in Australia and worldwide whose deaths create a vast lacuna that is terribly hard to fill.

Facilitated by the words of Yanyuwa elders conveyed to John Bradley, this chapter's introductory discussion has been shaped both in terms of an academic engagement, and the cultural place and value of the animations. This two-way conversation about the Yanyuwa animation project[11] began when the first animation was shown to Yanyuwa families eight years ago; this was the point where for first time their language and country were seen animated. The first animation was a short section of a song line: a senior Yanyuwa woman felt that if we could animate a song, then anything could be animated; it was also a song associated with her mother's clan, and already the last senior men associated with it had died. We start here with Yanyuwa words, Yanyuwa voices, and family sentiment in regards to the animations themselves and the sharing of these cultural expressions of Law and family to a wider audience.

Graham Friday, a senior Yanyuwa elder, has reflected on the animations as they now stand as a body of work, and said:

> Those animations are our Law, Yanyuwa Law; it is not Law for any other group of people in Australia, no one else. Our old people are dying, they have died too quick, so we had to think of ways to teach our kids so they can know something about their country. We are really happy for these animations, young people, old people we really like them. Let me tell you, people on the outside looking at them, people on the outside, 'whitefellas or blackfellas' they have nothing to say, nothing at all, those animations, well, that's the choice we make, we have to do what we can, we do not want our kids to sit around with nothing in their heads.[12]

These sentiments were echoed by Dinah Norman, the 85-year-old matriarch of the Yanyuwa community and one of the last fluent speakers of Yanyuwa:

> I sit here and I look at these young people, all of them, my grandchildren and all these other children, they do not speak Yanyuwa, they do not hear Yanyuwa, they have not seen the ceremonies of the old people, they do not know, they are in ignorance of all these things, some of them know the country because their parents and grandparents take them, but still they do not know the Law, the Law from the old people. I sit with my grandchildren and I look at the stories (animations) on TV, I am so happy that they are there, I teach my children the Law from the country

> when they are watching, we are talking about the country and family, maybe, maybe they will learn some of the stories, a little bit of the Law.[13]

Dinah Norman's son Leonard Norman was present when his mother spoke these words, and he followed up by saying:

> You know those animations are really important to us Yanyuwa people, they are helping to keep our country strong, as *kardirdi* [mother's brother] Graham said we are making our own choices about how to teach kids. . . . I am telling you, no one, not one European or Aboriginal has anything to say about this, we make choices, if they are right or wrong we make them.[14]

The distress caused by the old man's death, and that of other elders, and the great burden carried by elders faced with a reality of language loss and a breakdown in understandings of Law amongst young people, echoes through the statements made by Graham, Dinah, and Leonard. Their comments reveal the great burden of responsibility that they face in the safeguarding of their Law and culture. It is in this context that people make decisions and activate choices as to the best ways to maintain Law and culture for their children, grandchildren, and great grandchildren. The fact that Yanyuwa families make choices that involve collaborations and creative projects involving non-Yanyuwa and non-Indigenous people is historically embedded in a tradition they hold of developing carefully considered cross-cultural relationships that they see are built upon principles of mutual respect.

Yanyuwa country was settled by Europeans as late as 1886, and its culture recorded in minor detail in 1901 by ethnographers Spencer and Gillen.[15] Detailed research on the culture as an autochthonous people with a unique language, epistemology, and spirituality only started in the 1980s, at which point, Yanyuwa people, long inured to non-Indigenous disruption of their culture and lifestyles, were intent on and able to control how they were represented. This was both empowering and threatening as the mediation they engaged in – creating films, television programmes, dictionaries, books – was necessarily conducted in English and by a dwindling team of culturally knowledgeable elders. These ventures into Western media and forms of expression were designed for their own children and those outsiders respectful of the power of Law and culture, in the fervent hope that they could document powerful knowledge before it was too late, and archive it for future unimaginable uses by their own people.

Australians have slowly learnt how to read the publicly available spiritual content of these works, mainly in the first instance through print text and large gallery exhibitions and more recently the National Indigenous Television programming on SBS, and to respect what is silently withheld from outsider scrutiny. This was in part due to the Western concept of scholarly endeavour with the belief that everything could and should be studied. With Indigenous voice penetrating studies and representations of Indigenous cultures, this is slowly changing with Indigenous protocols infiltrating all mediums. The affect inhering in such works is palpable and it speaks in many voices and almost effortlessly across the cultural divide. Such works are a splendid starting point for understanding Aboriginal culture in the classroom. Yanyuwa treasures, though, are linguistic – song poetry, oratory and ritual songlines and performance – rather than visual. It is indeed a more challenging exercise to foster understanding of affect using such resources which do not readily translate into Western media, and that is precisely the challenge that is faced when Yanyuwa permit public screenings of the animations to a wider audience of viewers.

The West has a long and inglorious history of dismissing Indigenous social formations and the moral orders that go with them, relinquishing to the category of 'traditionalism' or 'nativism' leftover from an undesirable past. Indigenous social formations have proven to be incredibly resilient across time despite attempts at cultural annihilation through multiple forms of colonialism. Across the country Indigenous peoples have managed to maintain some form of extended kinship network that forms the basis of their identity. The onus remains on the settler state to learn to appreciate, work with, and accommodate these social formations rather than trying to wish them out of existence. This is imperative because of the richness and complexity that characterizes Indigenous social formations, and because the Yanyuwa worldview has much to offer the West in terms of deep ecological knowledge, spirituality, and ways of relating to the world around us.

What is very rarely fully appreciated in everyday Australian contexts is how Indigenous networks of kinship and the affective ties they bring are often made invisible by the academic and governmental processes which draw out of this complexity an essentialized understanding of Aboriginality and 'Indigenous affairs'. This leads to a myth of 'pan-Aboriginality' where the specificity of Indigenous cultural expressions, group politics, discreet languages, and political histories is overlooked and undervalued. Beyond this, Yanyuwa ways of knowing are not museum pieces; they are not relics of a former cultural order. Yanyuwa culture has changed and is changing in response to contact with the encroaching mainstream society. What has historically been compromised and remains threatened are levels of control over the processes of representation. Early colonial writing and ethnographic curiosity made many Indigenous Australians captives of the archives, powerless to control the means by which their cultures were represented or recorded. This remains a threat for Indigenous people in Australia, where the countries of Indigenous populations are invoked in myths and mythical narratives for the purposes of tourism, political campaigning, policy development, and international showcases. The Yanyuwa (like many other Indigenous groups worldwide) are uncompromising in their desire to move from being prisoners of the archives to self-determine and voice their aspirations for themselves, rather than to be spoken for by the state or academia.

Sadly, many senior members of the Yanyuwa community have passed away in the last decade. As a result, the community faces a crisis in the maintenance of Yanyuwa language and cultural expressions, and therefore the long-held means by which social formations and moral orders were constructed and presented across generations. In 1979 there were approximately 260 speakers of the Yanyuwa language.[16] Today there are only five semi- to full-time speakers, and they have for some time sought the means to record and share their language and Law in ways that are engaging and captivating for their children and young adolescents. The five remaining speakers of the language face the daunting task of maintaining the language and developing educational programmes within the restraints of limited funding and training in language maintenance strategies and a mainstream schooling system that prioritizes English in the classroom. Today the Yanyuwa population is made up almost entirely of middle and younger generations of people, striving to find a place in the world both as individuals and more importantly as Yanyuwa families with a shared and collective identity that is deeply embedded in social memory.

The Yanyuwa animation project is best seen as part of a cumulative strategy that has been building since the 1980s when Yanyuwa first started to engage in various forms of research and recording with linguists, anthropologists, archaeologists, ethnomusicologists, filmmakers, scientists, and lawyers. Drawing together Yanyuwa knowledge of the country and new technologies of visual-digital representation represents a further evocation of Yanyuwa ancestral narratives as present memory. The animation project involved the production of digital animations of ancestral narratives and songlines in both Yanyuwa and English language versions. To date a series of digital presentations of Yanyuwa ancestral narratives and songlines have been produced for Yanyuwa families, under their guidance and direction. Digital renderings of Yanyuwa Law allow a compression of time (ancestral knowledge/ contemporary encounter) and space (bringing visuals and a sense of country to the television screen or computer) that results in a proximity and immediacy for young and old viewers in the moment of sitting down and watching the animations. In the watching of these animations it is not loss that is comprehended but rather the sharing of knowledge that relates to the intimate spaces of kinship and country, and perhaps the possibilities that other engagements with technology will occur in the future.

Yanyuwa cultural treasure, made up of a body of stories, some of which have associated songlines, was first systematically made available in print form in 1988.[17] This was achieved with an inter-subjective methodology that saw Yanyuwa tell their ancestral stories to John Bradley, who then drew what he was hearing, with guidance and reflection from the narrator and other family members who happened to be around. This subsequently became the basis for an increasingly sophisticated series, and methods, for recording Dreaming[18] material. The Yanyuwa, along with many other Indigenous groups around Australia, have become keenly aware that other forms of inscription are important, not just for themselves but also for those who stand outside their communities. For many communities there is a fierce willingness to share and a need to be heard. For the Yanyuwa people specifically, Bradley's bilingual illustrated anthology was attentive to the site-specificity of Yanyuwa narratives and to the special significance of multiple sacred sites, some with particularly high affective charge. But like so many Western representations of mythological material, it was limited by its presentation in a particular form of media, namely a book, which restricts its potential readership to children with a proficiency in reading English, and literary and anthropological scholars with a particular interest in Indigenous knowledges. It has also been restricted in its capacity to tell the narratives of Yanyuwa country in that this text has been delimited, defined, and classified according to a restrictive Western definition of oral mythological narratives, including creation myths, legends of sun, moon and stars, and animals, and moral tales.

Print representations of Yanyuwa narratives (and Indigenous narratives generally) have several inherent limitations: they fail to distinguish between different kinds of oral storytelling practice, and to mark whether the context is a storytelling session for children or adepts, or whether the version is a fully fledged performance complete with archaic poetic language, music, dance, and perhaps intended for an audience restricted on gender lines. Most significantly, these narratives are often told *in situ*, with the part of the narrative relevant to a particular moment, locale, or action. Context is a given, and superfluous to the narrative, as the objects and places referred to are evident to a Yanyuwa auditor, and the narrative may begin *in media res* as narrative elements relevant to place are foregrounded, and the continuities of those parts of the story that belong in other places (because Yanyuwa stories move across country) are left for another oration.

The sense of the centrality of place to narrative is easily occluded in print texts, and very few anthologies of Indigenous Dreaming narratives pay any attention at all to this central element. Another element not deeply appreciated in Western representations of Indigenous Dreaming narratives is that orations and songs are owned by those with a claim to the particular parcels of land spoken about or sung in the narrative, a notion that is anathema in the West where knowledge is considered freely available to those who seek it. Furthermore, European tales for children frequently get reduced to 'just-so' and moralizing tales. By contrast, Yanyuwa Dreaming narratives typically have cross-age auditors, many of whom are adepts who are not 'spoken down to', and the narratives perform a great variety of functions from articulating the sacredness of the web of life and the kin relationships between the human and more-than-human worlds, to more mundane purposes like demonstrating how one might recognize a hidden water source, or know how to detoxify poisonous plants and render them nutritious. In other words, real learning through narrative and song is an expression of deep kinship ties and can be location specific. 127 years after white contact, these narratives inevitably carry a political freight palpable to their owners, and speaking to a history of deep colonizing, dispossession, and despoliation of sacred places by post-contact land use practices such as grazing and mining interests.

The Yanyuwa animation project was from the outset committed to moving away from crystallizing manifestations of cultural expression, and aims to reproduce, with integrity, the vitality and affect of Yanyuwa narrative. The animations stand before generations of young people as aspirational motivators for finding and anchoring identity. They are dynamic constructions based on knowledge that is held by elders of the community, who have a responsibility to make them present for a younger generation that carries the burden of stepping up as a generation of future elders and leaders equipped with the knowledge to manage, care for, and carry country, Law, and some semblance of a Yanyuwa way. The burden for both elders and younger members of the community is profound. Through decision-making processes the Yanyuwa, in conjunction with anthropologists and digital animators and information technology specialists, have found a suite of mechanisms to illustrate ancestral beginnings in a manner that honours their ongoing presence in country.

Whilst elders are in a position of remembering and can call into being a social memory of Yanyuwa culture, middle and younger generations of Yanyuwa are not always equipped with an established knowledge of language and ancestral narrative. It is imperative that this knowledge, in some form or another, be present when younger people are in a position to seek it. The Yanyuwa animation project is one way of ensuring the knowledge is present and available in generationally relative formats for young people to grasp it when ready. The transmission of an understanding of Yanyuwa Law and culture is considered a vital step in the development of self-esteem and wellbeing among younger generations who, according to elders, lack a sense of what it means to be a proper 'Yanyuwa person' in the world today. For Yanyuwa elders, sharing of and looking after cultural information must take place in settings where the integrity of the knowledge is acknowledged, where there exist the social, cultural, political, and emotional supports to fully understand what is encountered. Conscious decisions are made as to whether these supports exist.

Similarly, for young Yanyuwa, knowledge must be present in a manner that speaks to them, that resonates with the world that they know. It is in response to such a reality that Yanyuwa families have undertaken projects, aimed at bridging gaps in knowledge and encouraging the cross-generational transmission of Yanyuwa culture. These are considered pivotal in the construction of mainstream and culture-based educational programmes to teach younger generations of Yanyuwa just what it means to be *li-Anthawirriyarra* (how they refer to themselves). In a world where Yanyuwa elders often feel 'things move too fast' and cannot contain the power of Yanyuwa narrative, Yanyuwa youth want access to their culture on terms that appeal to their generation. The terms of engagement and knowledge acquisition are heavily dependent upon and influenced by the desire to know, and having the conditions to support forms of knowledge in a shifting world of meaning, or at least to find connectivity between new knowledge and existing knowledge. For young and old, all exchange of cultural information is prefaced by the question, 'What is the place for this knowledge?'

The completed animations comprise a set of nine 3D animations. These animations capture Yanyuwa representation of self and culture without the external gaze that represents Indigenous peoples as 'other'. They offer what print-based recordings of Yanyuwa Law and culture cannot. They capitalize on the highly visually literate X and Y generations and on the new capabilities of 3D animation, offering faithful recreations of actual Yanyuwa landscapes, peopled with realistic creatures. The landscapes have been built from a combination of satellite, photographic images and site-specific sketches, and lay out the many landscape forms that exist in Yanyuwa country, and the surprising variety of them. For the non-Yanyuwa viewer who knows this country simply as 'dry sclerophyll savannah', the depiction of mangrove, ant-hill plains, rocky escarpments, islands, lagoons and lightly forested plains, all with their own distinctive moving Dreamings and geo-political and geo-physical land unit designations, indicates a different way of being in place, a greater intimacy in the encounter with the world around. What captures Yanyuwa affective responses is the memory of the ceremony and strong feelings evoked by the song and dance. For non-Yanyuwa viewers, the sheer aesthetic beauty of the images has its own pay-off, but increasingly as settler-descendant Australians learn more about Indigenous Australian matters they begin too to sense some of the affective power that is central to a Yanyuwa rendering of their stories.

Traditional oral cultures and new technologies of digital media are underwritten by different imperatives, and there is an ever-present colonial dilemma of the risks of commodifying, exoticizing, and othering cultural groups and their knowledges. The non-Yanyuwa learner inevitably relies on his/her cultural paradigms and needs reassurance that the journey is productive and mutually illuminating. The journey outlined, which saw the creation of the Yanyuwa animation project, has led to Yanyuwa families finding new and more effective ways of communicating their Dreaming narratives and their affective ties to kin, country, and Law. This has been and remains an energizing multi-disciplinary and bicultural framework in which Indigenous and non-Indigenous people came together to achieve something that they each thought was important and meaningful. This is a project with huge educational potential not only for understanding the Dreaming narratives themselves, but also for cross-cultural exchange of a truly post-colonial kind. What the stories potentially teach a non-Yanyuwa listener/viewer is the difference between Western 'hearings' of stories and Yanyuwa ontology. The beginning of this understanding is country, not imagined but actual, with its embedded affect, which is then overlain with kinship, and even more intense affect, which connects people and all aspects of their world – other people, places, ancestors, spirits, country, animals, elements, and so on.

Monash Country Lines Archive strategies for decolonization

Of the original 274 languages and 600 dialects of Indigenous Australia, approximately only 20 remain strong today; that is approximately 20 languages that are still being spoken by all generations in a community and are still being passed on. However only about 12 percent of Indigenous people still speak these languages at home. This is even more devastating when you take into account that many of the dialects are inherently equal in terms of linguistic structure and complexity to the actual languages.

These figures combined with the connection between language, cultural knowledge and history (as illustrated in the section *Importance of learning Indigenous languages*) provide the urgency of the MCLA programme[19] for Indigenous communities, whilst providing the purpose: to assist communities in the continuation of Indigenous Australian languages through the use of 3D animations. Each partner group is vastly different in terms of language knowledge: some have fluent language speakers while in others language revitalization and recovery is one of the purposes of the community engaging with MCLA.

> Displacing systematic discrimination against Indigenous peoples created and legitimized by the cognitive frameworks of imperialism and colonialism remains the single most crucial cultural challenge facing humanity. Meeting this responsibility is not just a problem for the colonized and the oppressed, but rather the defining challenge for all peoples. It is the path to a shared and sustainable future for all peoples.[20]

Since colonization of Australia in 1788, Indigenous Australians' ability to pass their knowledge onto the next generations through intergenerational learning, to address intergenerational trauma,[21] and to share their cultural knowledge beyond their community on their own terms has been severely restricted.[22] We have adopted the decolonizing method of reconciling research:

> Reconciling research is envisaged as a collaborative, co-creative journey, in this case between members of the academy, Indigenous communities and the archival community. It validates multiple sources of knowledge and promotes the use of multiple methods of discovery, implementation and dissemination of knowledge.[23]

Faulkhead joined the MCLA programme as the Senior Research Fellow and project manager after a proposal had been developed and funded. Whilst the programme had been developed based on Bradley's work with the Yanyuwa, we were now going Australia wide, and we needed to create MCLA as a decolonizing[24] space. Decolonization requires casting out many Western concepts of research and ownership and starting anew, to end the effects of colonization upon a country's original peoples by both the colonized and colonizers.[25] This was our starting point.

Growing the MCLA programme was both very clear and vague. Nine years working for a Victorian Indigenous cultural centre meant Faulkhead had heard almost every horror story of academic hierarchal research methods;[26] similar stories led to the development of Australian research protocols for working with Indigenous Australian peoples to prevent future harm from research.[27] Two primary strategies were proposed that the Monash academic team supported unconditionally. The first was the ownership of the animations, and the other that each community group be an individual partnership with its own timelines. It would be wrong to suggest that this was an easy development process. It took months of self- and group reflection and discussion.

The continuum of Indigenous knowledge (i.e. written – oral – animations – oral – etc.) is one that most Indigenous peoples are no longer willing to share without retaining their intellectual property. Any programme that did not recognize this position could jeopardize relationships by being viewed as 'another group that want to control Indigenous intellectual and cultural property for themselves.' This fixed the first strategy for MCLA as recognizing that intellectual property laws and rights (including copyright) do not adequately represent Indigenous concepts of ownership, and has been used to their detriment over the years.[28] Australian copyright law assigns copyright to Monash University as the creators of the animations. Whilst this is one of many issues with current (and historical) copyright laws, the law does allow for copyright to be signed over to another party; Monash could legally sign copyright back to the story owners/community groups. If Monash University did not do this, then the MCLA programme would be viewed as 'stealing' or even 'owning' Indigenous intellectual property and knowledge, a continuation of colonizing processes.[29] This is often reinforced by the first question asked by community groups being: 'Who owns the animations?' As soon as we say that they do, we get 'Good. Now we can talk.'

Whilst the first strategy was a given for the Monash team, strategy two needed more thought. The proposed structure was based around an advisory committee that oversaw the MCLA programme. Apart from the Monash representatives, the committee's membership would include representatives from the community groups participating in the MCLA programme, and their membership was for as long as their knowledge was being modelled and translated into 3D animations. Whilst this adhered to Indigenous research protocols in Australia, this was not going to work for the MCLA programme. It meant that other community groups would have a say in the direction of animations other than their own, and was based on the assumption that each community would be sequential in that the first community that was partnered with would produce the first animation. This in effect contradicted the first strategy in terms of intellectual property, whilst not allowing community groups time to develop their animations in their own timeframe; the academic team would be dictating the timelines instead of them being developed as part of the partnership. After pondering and dismissing this structure we needed to replace it with something that reflected the proposed partnership model. We then realized we already had a model based on Bradley's work with the Yanyuwa – each community group should be an individual partnership under the MCLA programme. The research team would be developed as part of the partnership process and would provide the direction for that animation project. As for timelines, each animation project, to date, reflects the complexity and diversity of opinions within communities, as well as the conflicting demands on the individual members' time. We have partnered with community groups where four years has resulted in two animations, another is only now ready to animate, whilst another took a year to create the animation, but another two years to go through community approval – 'We do not deny that community research partnerships are messy, complex and time consuming, but this experience can also make the research fun and beneficial on so many levels.'[30]

We had two strategies to implement in a way that could also address Monash University research requirements such as ethics. The obvious solution was a Memorandum of Understanding (MOU). With feedback provided by the first community groups to engage with the MCLA programme, we developed a draft MOU. As this included agreements regarding copyright, the legal advice was that this document should be a Memorandum of Agreement (MOA). The MOA is edited by each partnership to address the purpose and requirements of their animation project. Once developed, the MOA becomes the agreement and research description for each community for Monash University Human Research Ethics approval.

The MCLA programme also addresses the long-term preservation of Indigenous language, culture, and narratives in digital and multimedia forms as an act of decolonization of the archive. It recognizes the importance of preserving Indigenous stories, narratives, and culture as part of a living, interactive community archive that is used as tools for intergenerational learning. This supports the MCLA archival concept that both the individual animations and the animation series are storing Indigenous knowledge records as an archive. However, the archival concept of the MCLA programme is more than this.

An archive is often mistaken as a physical institution/building that stores physical records of the past. However, the broader (and truer) definition of archive encompasses 'oral and written records, literature, landscape, dance, art, the built environment, and artefacts.'[31] This definition is being applied and researched – especially in colonized countries and where Indigenous and minority communities' records are still being stored orally within the community or on country. Faulkhead's research[32] explores this definition with Indigenous Australian communities as archival repositories. Whilst the 3D animations and models are an archive collection,[33] they are also tools to access Indigenous oral records. Through intergenerational viewing of the animations, people begin to share stories that are associated with the story being viewed – the knowledge being shared moves from the animation archive and into community and personal archives. As we say, the animations are not the end product, but the beginning to learning language and the knowledge it contains. It is this conceptual understanding of Indigenous knowledge as an archive that supports the existing infrastructure of intergenerational learning. If a community is an archive, then it needs to be able to share that knowledge/records with the next generation for continued life – as Bradley previously stated, the death of an Indigenous elder is a loss of a library. This is the situation when intergenerational sharing has not occurred.

The MCLA programme is situated at the nexus of leading edge virtual heritage modelling and 3D animation technologies, archival science, Indigenous studies, and anthropology, and the needs of both Indigenous communities and the wider Australian community relating to Indigenous cultural heritage. It is highly innovative in bringing together a unique combination of multidisciplinary expertise and the expert domain knowledge of Indigenous communities, and enabling knowledge and skills transfer and mutual learning. The MCLA programme is also an exemplar of reconciling research, partnership research between Indigenous and non-Indigenous researchers, and Indigenous communities. It provides a best-practice model for ethical, community-centred, participatory research. Partnership research allows projects to constantly evolve[34] as the research develops, and to address issues as they arise. Regardless of guidelines, principles, and ethics, there will always be actions or processes undertaken that will need to be addressed. That is why MCLA advocated for partnership research that allows for self-reflexivity by the team and to discuss and work through processes or problems that occur within the research.

Animation language and country

Animation allows complexity to be interpreted visually. Many of the animation projects have a primary aim of teaching and learning for their own community, with a secondary aim of sharing to other communities – they are made for themselves first and foremost. How the animations are interpreted depends on the knowledge they already have. An Indigenous elder will be able to read the Law, for others the country, or for others to be exposed to Indigenous voice.

3D animation provides solutions that other forms of animation cannot offer, where real world objects and life forms can be digitally modelled. While animation dates back almost a century, it is important to distinguish the medium of 3D animation from traditional hand-drawn animation or other forms of 2D (two-dimensional) animation created on computers. The fundamental difference is that 3D animation derives from a digital space not of images but from a modelled space that is very similar to those used in architectural and engineering simulations, medical vizualisation and 'virtual reality' applications. Essentially, it is the sculpting of this complex world made up of many thousands, and sometimes millions, of different 3D models that constitutes the research behind the animations. The objects, data and records produced and gathered by this project have the potential to become a national asset as a living and growing archive of Indigenous Australia, as well as being an exciting tool for e-learning.[35] This area is currently being researched as a PhD study.[36]

As discussed above, the Yanyuwa chose 3D animation over every other animation form due to its realism. This has been reinforced through comments from community groups wanting to work with the MCLA programme, such as 'We don't want Walt Disney.' This comment and others are due to Indigenous narratives, stories, and history being often been reduced to children's stories or myths. This has offended some elders and communities. Whilst these animations are to teach and engage the younger generations, they are not to be 'children's stories.'

The younger generation's engagement with the animations is evident through the constant change in the technology used to share the animations. The Yanyuwa project animations were burnt onto DVDs and posted to the families for distribution. Some of the young ones worked out how to copy the animations and started sharing them with family via Bluetooth on their phones. Now they are shared through Dropbox links, memory sticks, and via the web. As well as on the MCLA website, the Yanyuwa animations are available on ABC Splash and the Endangered Languages Project.[37]

The process adopted in creating the 3D animations is one where the community group and MCLA team work together. The MCLA programme also uses digital technologies to create opportunities for Indigenous Australian communities to record, store and transmit narratives of history, language, and culture through 3D animation, with the first decision usually being the look of the animation. Whilst some groups want the realism that re-creates their country prior to colonization, others prefer the look and feel of artwork from their community.

Following is the journey taken by Brent McKee, the lead animator on the MCLA programme, from animating blind to describing how visiting country and meeting people whose language he was animating brought a new dimension, depth, and understandings to his work that he now recognizes was absent from his early work. McKee is a non-Indigenous animator who started working with the MCLA programme as a Master's student.

Connecting country and animation

In the early days of animating the Yanyuwa animation project, the digital recreation of culturally specific and often sacred landscapes was done solely by photo reference and satellite images. At that time, the animators had little to no first-hand experience of landscapes outside Melbourne, situated in south-eastern Victoria, Australia, a temperate-to-cool climate area comprised mostly of farmland and forest, a far cry from the blistering heat of the tropical savannah of the Gulf of Carpentaria.

From these photo references and the use of Google Maps satellite images, the animators were able to create something that was stylistically representative of the landscape that the narratives or songlines were connected to. The colour of grasses and water bodies were matched to that of the photos. The location of the country also impacted on the colour and images. For example, the same species of trees would be completely different if from the far north of Australia, much closer to the equator, where intense light results in a hot, bright, sun-cooked landscape, compared with the cool country of south-eastern Australia. These differences were difficult to appreciate from the photos, and it was sometimes challenging for communities to identify what the difference was between their country and the digital images.

When completed the animations were sent to the community for input and approval. It was important for the communities to be able to see that these digital landscapes captured the essence of their landscape. However, there is only so much that can be captured of a particular landscape from photo references alone. This problem was discovered after we produced

Figure 23.1 Yanyuwa Country.
Source: © Brent McKee

a very different animation after visiting the country that we were animating. It was obvious to the whole team that first-hand experience of the country and people was imperative to the successful creation of truly representative landscapes.

This visit was in 2010 when the animators were given the opportunity to visit Yanyuwa country for research into the next series of animations. This also gave the animators a chance to evaluate landscapes that had previously been animated.

While up until this point, the Yanyuwa community had been happy with the representations of their landscapes, it became apparent to the animators that they had missed so much of the essence of the landscapes, an essence that can only be comprehended with familiarity. Being present on the landscape with the Yanyuwa people opened up a whole new world of imaging and representing specific landscapes. It was no longer felt that we were outsiders working on a project that we had no personal connection with.

On this journey, the animators experienced the three main aspects of Yanyuwa traditional narratives – Country, Kin, and Law. The Country was where the narrative belonged – the stage in which it is set – the Kin, the performers, and the performance is the Law. Each aspect is as important as the others and completely interconnected a continuum linking people and country. Understanding this interdependency was crucial in understanding the essence beneath the Dreaming narratives of the Yanyuwa people.

With this newfound understanding came a much more ‘eyes open’ approach to visualizing landscapes. The animators began to notice certain nuances that had not been apparent before, nuances that make each landscape unique, such as the way light passed through leaves at a certain time of day or the way the colour and transparency of water varies depending on its depth and clarity, or how the density, height, and thickness of trees and grasses change as the amount of light varies or the way the colour of light changes depending on the time of day.

When creating digital representations of culturally specific landscapes, being aware of these unique aspects is critical in capturing a landscape's essence, an essence that the animators now feel can only be grasped through first-hand experience. It is this sense of experience that becomes an important part of decolonizing the images of an Indigenous people's country. There are important issues associated with this whereby it has become critical for the animator to visit the country to be animated, to sense it and understand it in a way that even the most detailed image cannot. This is also due to having to listen to Indigenous people talk about their country and to the animator watching people moving through the country to be animated.

Currently the MCLA is working with a number of Aboriginal communities across Australia, each one in a completely unique country – the Taungurung of central Victoria, a temperate climate area of winding rivers and mountainous forest; the Yanyuwa of coastal north-western Australia, with its large expansive beaches and flat plains of light woodland and termite hills; or the Garrwa of inland Northern Territory, with its hot red rocky earth of sprawling hills and valleys, just to name a few. Each community offers a unique challenge for the animators to capture the essential qualities of each landscape, the qualities that make that

Figure 23.2 Yanyuwa Country. Monash Country Lines animation still from *Ngurdungurdu (The Tiger Shark)* 2009.
Source: © Yanyuwa Families, Borroloola, NT. http://artsonline.monash.edu.au/countrylines-archive/tiger-shark-and-the-rock-wallaby-ngurdungurdu-kulu-a-buluwardi/ [accessed 25 November 2016].

Figure 23.3 Garrwa Country. Monash Country Lines animation still from *Purdiwan (Pretty One)* 2014.
Source: Photo © Brent McKee. Monash Country Lines animation still © Garrwa People, Borroloola, NT. http://artsonline.monash.edu.au/countrylines-archive/purdiwan-pretty-one-2014/

Figure 23.4 Yagun Gulinj Wiinj (How Man Found Fire). Monash Country Lines animation still.
Source: © Dolodanin-dat Animation Project Group, Taungurung People, Vic. http://artsonline.monash.edu.au/countrylines-archive/yagun-gulinj-wiinj-how-man-found-fire-2016/

Figure 23.5 Marlukarra Ngarrkadabawurr: Karnanganjanyi (Emu Hunters of Excellence). Monash Country Lines animation still.
Source: © Garrwa People, Borroloola, NT. http://artsonline.monash.edu.au/countrylines-archive/marlukarra-ngarrkadabawurr-karnanganjanyi-emu-hunters-of-excellence-2015/

landscape unique and sacred to that community, qualities that can only truly be comprehended with first-hand experience.

Conclusion

Each of the Yanyuwa cultural recording projects that has been undertaken over the last few decades, including the books,[38] films,[39] and the animations[40] are testament to cultural survival in very real terms. Furthermore, they enact crucial post-colonial and trans-cultural conversations that involve nothing less than understanding that all ways of knowing are necessarily provisional and dynamic, and mutually enriching. From a discussion of these various media and their uses for Yanyuwa and outsider education, there emerges a dynamic decolonizing tension that warrants active acknowledgement. This springs forth from the different teaching and learning constituencies that create and then encounter Yanyuwa cultural recordings and presentations. In fact, the Yanyuwa animation project is an excellent starting point to teach decolonizing methods and theory to a wide audience of non-Indigenous people. The specifics of who this audience will be remains to be seen, as presently the animations have been created only for Yanyuwa families, who at present are nurturing this body of knowledge in the quest for cross-generational knowledge transfer. Amongst the elders and their extended family groups, there is a constant flow of discussion taking place as to where the animation project goes from this point. The conversations continue an ongoing effort of safeguarding powerful Yanyuwa knowledge for generations of young people who will stand up strong in their country and remember the lives, stories, affection, and love of their old people. These are the choices that the Yanyuwa have made, along with the many Indigenous groups across Australia that are now working with us. Animation is a bridge between the past and present, but it also a technology of expanded horizons that opens up areas that were previously closed because of the form of media (books, images, print) and their relatively static take on time, place, movement, and meaning. There are important considerations about the decolonial possibilities for not only sharing knowledge but also how technology is opening up further important discussions about these issues too. This is of course a conversation filled with the anxiety that elders reasonably express about the 'speeding-up' of all things in their lives. In the animations time can be compressed, but there are important factors here about how the animations find a place where things are not faster or slower, but perhaps more entangled and engaged. There are important issues here, beyond this chapter, to explore and it is something the MCLA needs to research more deeply, because there is an entanglement of both colonial and decolonial matters that exist not always in opposition to each other.

Based on 30 years of struggle by one community to re-engage their young ones in language and complementary understanding of the continuum between country and people in the care, health, and wellbeing of both, the MCLA programme acknowledges and honours the diversity of needs and history of each community we work with. We are currently working with nine Indigenous Australian languages and the people who aim to continue them.

Our chapter explores issues that suggest that translating texts, working with oral traditions that through processes of coloniality have become 'frozen' on paper, and practising animation not only complement each other, but are essential to restore and revivify local place-based histories that belong to various Indigenous groups that we have worked with. We have been able to base these conclusions on research across Australia. We have recorded many forms of oral traditions from the various Indigenous families we work with. In doing so we have used a phenomenological approach to suggest a model of research and use of technology that highlights the intersubjective experience in the formation of stories, graphics, sounds, and completed animations. In this instance then intersubjective experience refers to a view that considers human experience to be included in and constituted by our engagement with the world in all its various manifestations. By applying an expanded sense of what we do as an 'intersubjective practice' to studies of languages, literature, and history we move to a place whereby we can recognize the importance of our own participation in the relational dynamics between the people we work with and what it is we are seeking to understand. Such a view of research and technology, therefore, takes into account our personal experience with the narratives and the people who own them. These narratives are drawn from rich oral traditions and are tied to places; therefore, the process of animating must also develop a relationship with the places that need to be animated. It is both the spoken and sung traditions that highlight a relationship to the importance of place and this becomes a site of valuable material for critical thought in regards to the process associated with animation.

As many of us in academia are aware, there can be a tendency to theorize away from reality as it is lived and known. This can be particularly problematic when we analyse and interpret narratives that are associated with a worldview far from our own. Such materials appear reified and disassociated from life, even when attempts are made to contextualize their use, production, and distribution. As a result, practices of intellectualization applied to such texts may solidify the living human experiences they represent into theories and conceptual models that alienate us from the vital experiences we want to understand.

Thus our work, our research, is dependent on relationships and travel and knowing country, and attempting to see and feel this as far as is possible. Ultimately this can only be achieved when the academic guise is dropped so that we learn to listen to what Indigenous people want from us. This is not always an easy task, but it is one that we learn from and ultimately affects every animation that we work on.

With technology continually changing, we are often asked how can the animations succeed long term? The uniqueness of this programme is that we are not trying to recreate or produce a new method of knowledge storage and exchange, but to support that which has always existed – intergenerational knowledge sharing. Therefore, the continued use of the animations is not our primary outcome; instead it is that languages continue, live, are revived. Through the continuation of languages we believe that health and wellbeing of the community will improve as knowledge is gained and shared. Whilst we will endeavour to preserve these animations as archive, we also recognize that the intellectual property and copyright owners of the animations will have final say as to what happens in the future.

The MCLA programme is a collaborative and co-creative journey that is producing a form of cultural property. It is a programme that is attempting to decolonize our corner of the university as much as possible. This process produces shared outcomes where all parties contribute and are acknowledged, but with the shared objective that these animations are Indigenous intellectual and cultural property. Their primary purpose is as tools for community intergenerational learning, in the communities' endeavour to protect the cultural and intellectual property contained within their languages. This formal academic recognition of Indigenous ownership of their cultural and intellectual property is a reconciling research method that not only acknowledges the complexity and traumas that many Indigenous communities are experiencing, but also that the university does not need to 'own' research for it to benefit both the community partners and the academy. Whilst there are easier ways to undertake this form of research, they would not be nearly as satisfying . . . or fun.

Notes

1 The Yanyuwa animation project was developed through the kin relationship and friendship between the Yanyuwa elders and John Bradley as a progression of their preservation endeavours of the knowledge contained in their language. Funding to build these animations was from small philanthropic grants, and later a government grant as part of an Australian Research Council project.

2 At 20 John Bradley was sent to teach Aboriginal children in a school at remote Borroloola, on the Gulf of Carpentaria in far north Australia. But it is the teacher who is educated by the Yanyuwa elders and their families. Over three decades he learns their language and their country, becoming intimately

drawn into other ways of being, both practical and spiritual. With passion and pride they teach him their songlines, relating what they know and value – ancestors, kin, allegiances; places, plants, animals; seasons, ceremonies, stories – and the spirit that sustains all. This is the Yanyuwa families' and Bradley's journey.

Bradley, J. and Yanyuwa Families. 2010. *Singing Saltwater Country*. Sydney: Allen and Unwin.

3 This chapter presents some of the complexities of language and knowledge transmission in relation to choices by Yanyuwa elders to animate their Law: Bradley, J., G. Friday, A. Kearney, and L. Norman. 2010. '"These Are The Choices We Make": Animating Saltwater Country', *Screening the Past*, 31.

4 Dr Tom Chandler – MCLA team member based in the SensiLab, Faculty of Information Technology, Monash University. Chandler provides coordination, technical support and advice for the animation team on the MCLA animations.

5 Angkor Wat http://ngm.nationalgeographic.com/2009/07/angkor/angkor-animation [Accessed March 31, 2016].

6 After seeing the Yanyuwa animations in 2010, Dr Alan Finkel AM and Dr Elizabeth Finkel recognized their importance in the continuation and preservation of language and were inspired to establish the MCLA programme through five-year funding from the Finkel Foundation. This gift along with the financial and in-kind support from Monash University has enabled MCLA to partner with Indigenous communities from across Australia.

7 The MCLA team is a cross-disciplinary programme of Monash University, between the Monash Indigenous Centre (MIC), Faculty of Arts and the SensiLab, Faculty of Information Technology. The team is: MIC – Associate Professor John Bradley and Dr Shannon Faulkhead; SensiLab – Mr Brent McKee and Dr Tom Chandler.

8 Pers. comm. Graham Friday with John Bradley, 2009.

9 Yanyuwa country is 1,000 kilometres south-east of Darwin, the south-west Gulf of Carpentaria. The nearest town is Borroloola, which has a population of about 1,000 people, of which 60 percent are Indigenous Australians derived from the four language groups of Yanyuwa, Marra, Garrwa and Gudanji. Sixty kilometres south of Borroloola, on the McArthur River, is one of the biggest deposits of lead silver and zinc, which is currently being mined. The country of Yanyuwa people is the tidal limits of the McArthur River, Wearyan River, and also the mouth of the Robinson River. Their country also includes the Sir Edward Pellew Group of Islands. The largest of these islands is Vanderlin island at approximately 25 kilometres in length. The Yanyuwa people are saltwater people; they call themselves *li-Anthawirriyarra* – the people whose spiritual and cultural heritage is from the sea. Indigenous land ownership has never been relinquished. However, whilst some of Yanyuwa country has been 'won' back through the arduous land rights process, other parts of Yanyuwa country are now part of pastoral leases and mining developments. Yanyuwa clan boundaries still overlie all Yanyuwa country, regardless of today's ownership, showing each individual's relationship to the land and sea and all that it contains through their father's fathers, mother's father, mother's mother and father's mother. Thus while we might usually see boundaries as marking exclusion, each boundary in this instance is a way of acknowledging special and specific relationships that people have to the land and sea.

10 Evans, N. 2010. *Dying Words. Endangered Languages and What They Have To Tell Us*. Chichester and Malden, MA: Wiley-Blackwell, p. 9.

11 Yanyuwa Animation Project consists of nine animations created with the li-Yanyuwa li-Wirdiwalangu at Borroloola. Seven of these animations were created from 2008 to 2010 as a separate project, and two animations as part of the MCLA programme.

12 Verbal correspondence between Graham Friday and John Bradley, 2010.

13 Verbal correspondence between Dinah Norman and John Bradley, 2010 Translated from Yanyuwa, into English, by John Bradley.

14 Verbal correspondence between Leonard Norman and John Bradley, 2010.

15 Spencer, B., and F. J. Gillen. 1969. *The Northern Tribes of Central Australia*. Oosterhout: Anthropological Publications, and Spencer, B., and F. J. Gillen. 1912. *Across Australia*. Volumes 1 and 2. London: Macmillan.

16 Bradley, J., and Yanyuwa Families. 2016. *Wuka nya-nganunga li-Yanyuwa li-Anthawirriyarra: Language for Us, the Yanyuwa Saltwater People: A Yanyuwa Encyclopaedic Dictionary*, Volumes 1 and 2. North Melbourne, Australia: Australian Scholarly Publishing.

Bradley, J., and A, Kearney. 2008. *Report on Remote Learning Partnership Project: Borroloola Community*. Consultancy Report to the Northern Territory Department of Employment, Education and Training, pp. 12–16

17 Bradley, J. 1988. *Yanyuwa Country: The Yanyuwa People of Borroloola Tell the History of their Land.* Richmond, Victoria: Greenhouse.

18 *Dreaming* is a distinctly Indigenous Australian construction and is central to Indigenous Australian peoples' social life and has a central place in constituting their lived world. Its central pillar is being able to see immutable relationships in regard to time, space, and personhood. Because the Dreaming touches so many dimensions of life it possesses no single or finite significance. Its interpretation and understanding is context driven and dependent. It is a projection into a symbolic space of various social processes and its social meaning can only ever be understood when we are able to relate it to the particular circumstances of those who are using it.

19 The Monash Country Lines Archive (MCLA) is a collaborative Monash University project between the Monash Indigenous Centre (MIC), Faculty of Arts and the Faculty of Information Technology with a team of Monash researchers, digital animators, and postgraduate students from the Monash Indigenous Centre, Faculty of Arts and the Faculty of Information Technology. The Monash Country Line Archive demands intellectual engagement in regards to issues associated with how best to construct a living archive that is a decolonized space in which communities are happy to see their material stored. It also provides an exciting place for scholars to work and share knowledge. More information is available at: http://artsonline.monash.edu.au/countrylines-archive/.

20 Daes, Erica Irene. 1999. United Nations Working Group on Indigenous Peoples at the UNESCO Conference on Education, July. As cited in: Battiste, Bell, and Findlay, 'Decolonizing Education in Canadian Universities: An Interdisciplinary, International, Indigenous Research Project', p. 82.

21 Atkinson, Judy. 2002. *Trauma Trails, Recreating Song Lines: The Transgenerational Effects of Trauma in Indigenous Australia.* North Melbourne: Spinifex Press.

22 Faulkhead, Shannon. 2009a. 'Narratives of Koorie Victoria'. PhD thesis. Clayton: Monash University.

23 McKemmish, S., S. Faulkhead, and L. Russell. 2011. 'Dis-Trust in the Archive: Reconciling Records'. *Archival Science*, 11(3–4): 211–239, p. 220.

24 Smith, Linda Tuhiwai. 1999. *Decolonizing Methodologies: Research and Indigenous Peoples.* London: Zed Books.

25 Nehrez, Samia as quoted in: hooks, bell. 1992. *Black Looks: Race and Representation.* Boston, MA: South End Press, p. 1.

26 Adams, Karen and Shannon Faulkhead. 2012. 'This Is Not a Guide to Indigenous Research Partnerships'. *Information, Communication & Society*, 15(7). doi:10.1080/1369118X.2012.709260.

27 Examples of research protocols include:

a) Australian Institute of Aboriginal and Torres Strait Islander Studies. 2000. *Guidelines for Ethical Research in Indigenous Studies.* Canberra: Australian Institute of Aboriginal and Torres Strait Islander Studies. Available at: http://www.aiatsis.gov.au/research/ethical-research/guidelines-ethical-research-australian-indigenous-studies [Accessed March 28, 2016].

b) National Health and Medical Research Council (NHMRC). 2006. *Keeping Research on Track: A Guide for Aboriginal and Torres Strait Islander Peoples About Health Research Ethics*, National Health and Medical Research Council (NHMRC). Available at: http://www.nhmrc.gov.au/publications/synopses/e65syn.htm [Accessed March 28, 2016].

28 Anderson, J. 2013. 'Anxieties of Authorship in the Colonial Archive'. In *Media Authorship.* Edited by C. Chris and D. Gerstner. New York: Routledge Press.

29 Janke, T. 2009. *Writing up Indigenous Research: Authorship, Copyright and Indigenous Knowledge Systems.* Sydney: Terri Janke and Company. Available at: http://www.terrijanke.com.au/#!writing-up-indigenous-research/o7pdb [Accessed March 28, 2016].

30 Adams, Karen and Shannon Faulkhead. 2012. 'This Is Not a Guide to Indigenous Research Partnerships'. *Information, Communication & Society*, 15(7). doi:10.1080/1369118X.2012.709260.

31 McKemmish, Sue. 2005. 'Traces: Document, Record, Archive, Archives'. In *Archives: Recordkeeping in Society*, edited by Sue McKemmish, Michael Piggott, Barbara Reed and Frank Upward, 1–20. Wagga Wagga, New South Wales: Centre for Information Studies, Charles Sturt University, p. 3.

32 Examples:

a) Faulkhead, S. 2009b. 'Connecting Through Records: Narratives of Koorie Victoria'. *Archives and Manuscripts*, 37(2): 60–88.

b) Faulkhead, S. 2009a. 'Narratives of Koorie Victoria'. PhD thesis, Clayton: Monash University.

33 As being explored by Narissa Timbery's PhD research, Visualising Country: Archiving 3D Models.

34 Faulkhead, Shannon, Lynette Russell, Diane Singh, and Sue McKemmish. 2007. 'Is Community Research Possible within the Western Academic Tradition?' In *Researching with Communities: Grounded Perspectives on Engaging Communities in Research.* Andy Williamson and Ruth DeSouza, eds. Auckland: Muddy Creek Press, pp. 39–56.

35 The term e-learning refers to computer-enhanced training. E-learning is usually delivered via a personal computer. It includes learning delivered by other communications technologies. Methods include online lectures, tutorials, simulations, job aids, games, and more. It is an approach to facilitate and enhance learning through both computer and communications technology. Such devices can include personal computers, CDROMs, television, MP3 Players, and Mobile Phones. Communications technology enables the use of the Internet, email, discussion forums, collaborative software, classroom management software, and team learning systems. E-learning may also be used for distance learning and is also considered a form of flexible learning.

36 Narissa Timbery's PhD research, Visualising Country: Archiving 3D Models, is to develop a conceptual model for an archival system to house 3D models created in the MCLA project. This will be informed by specifications and guiding principles that have been developed with community based on their specific needs.

37 Websites: Monash Country Lines Archive http://artsonline.monash.edu.au/countrylines-archive/.
ABC Splash http://splash.abc.net.au/.
Endangered Languages Project http://www.endangeredlanguages.com/lang/4317/guide.

38 a) Bradley, J. 1988. *Yanyuwa Country: The Yanyuwa People of Borroloola Tell the History of their Land.* Melbourne: Greenhouse Publication.
b) Bradley, J., M. Holmes, D. Norman, A. Isaac, J. Miller and I. Ninganga. 2006. *Yumbulyumbulmantha ki-awarawu (All Kinds of Things from Country) Yanyuwa Ethnobiological Classification.* Ngulaig Monograph, St Lucia: Aboriginal and Torres Strait Islander Unit, University of Queensland.
c) Bradley, J., with Yanyuwa Families, and N. Cameron. 2003. *Forget About Flinders. An Indigenous Atlas of the Southwest Gulf of Carpentaria.* Brisbane, Australia: J.M. McGregor (Limited Edition).
d) Bradley, J., and Yanyuwa Families. 2010. *Singing Saltwater Country.* Sydney: Allen and Unwin.
e) Bradley, J., and Yanyuwa Families. 2016. *Wuka nya-nganunga li-Yanyuwa li-Anthawirriyarra: Language for Us, the Yanyuwa Saltwater People: A Yanyuwa Encyclopaedic Dictionary*, Volumes 1 and 2. North Melbourne: Australian Scholarly Publishing Ptd Ltd.

39 a) *Ka-wayawayama* (Aeroplane Dance). Film Australia, 1992.
b) *Buwarrala Akarriya* (Journey East). Marndaa Productions, 1988.
c) *Kanymarda Yuwa* (Two Laws) Red Dirt Films, 1981.

40 *Yanyuwa families of Borroloola.* Monash Country Lines Archive. http://artsonline.monash.edu.au/countrylines-archive/the-yanyuwa-families-of-borroloola/ [Accessed February 4, 2016].

Bibliography

Adams, Karen and Faulkhead, Shannon. 2012. 'This Is Not a Guide to Indigenous Research Partnerships'. *Information, Communication & Society*, 15(7). doi:10.1080/1369118X.2012.709260.

Anderson, J. 2013. 'Anxieties of Authorship in the Colonial Archive'. In *Media Authorship*, edited by C. Chris and D. Gerstner. Abingdon: Routledge.

Atkinson, Judy. 2002. *Trauma Trails, Recreating Song Lines: The Transgenerational Effects of Trauma in Indigenous Australia.* North Melbourne: Spinifex Press.

Australian Human Rights Commission. 2010. *The Community Guide to the UN Declaration on the Rights of Indigenous Peoples.* Canberra.

Australian Institute of Aboriginal and Torres Strait Islander Studies. 2000. *Guidelines for Ethical Research in Indigenous Studies.* Canberra: Australian Institute of Aboriginal and Torres Strait Islander Studies. Available at: http://www.aiatsis.gov.au/research/ethical-research/guidelines-ethical-research-australian-indigenous-studies [Accessed March 28, 2016].

Bradley, J. 1988. *Yanyuwa Country: The Yanyuwa People of Borroloola Tell the History of Their Land.* Richmond, Victoria, Australia: Greenhouse.

Bradley, J., and A. Kearney. 2008. *Report on Remote Learning Partnership Project: Borroloola Community.* Consultancy Report to the Northern Territory Department of Employment, Education and Training, pp. 12–16.

Bradley, J., and Yanyuwa Families. 2010. *Singing Saltwater Country.* Sydney: Allen and Unwin.

Bradley, J., and Yanyuwa Families. 2016. *Wuka nya-nganunga li-Yanyuwa li-Anthawirriyarra- Language for Us, the Yanyuwa Saltwater People: A Yanyuwa Encyclopaedic Dictionary*, Volumes 1 and 2. North Melbourne, Australia: Australian Scholarly Publishing.

Bradley, J., with Yanyuwa Families, and N. Cameron. 2003. *Forget About Flinders. An Indigenous Atlas of the Southwest Gulf of Carpentaria*. Brisbane, Australia: J.M. McGregor (Limited Edition).

Bradley, J., G. Friday, A. Kearney, and L. Norman. 2010 '"These Are The Choices We Make": Animating Saltwater Country'. *Screening the Past*, 31.

Bradley, J., M. Holmes, D. Norman, A. Isaac, J. Miller, and I. Ninganga. 2006. *Yumbulyumbulmantha ki-awarawu (All Kinds of Things from Country) Yanyuwa Ethnobiological Classification*. Ngulaig Monograph. St Lucia: Aboriginal and Torres Strait Islander Unit, University of Queensland.

Daes, Erica Irene. 1999. United Nations Working Group on Indigenous Peoples at the UNESCO Conference on Education, July. As cited in: Battiste, Bell, and Findlay, 'Decolonizing Education in Canadian Universities: An Interdisciplinary, International, Indigenous Research Project', p. 82.

Evans, N. 2010. *Dying Words. Endangered Languages and What They Have To Tell Us*. Chichester and Malden, MA: Wiley-Blackwell.

Faulkhead, Shannon. 2009a. 'Narratives of Koorie Victoria'. PhD thesis. Clayton, Australia: Monash University.

Faulkhead, Shannon. 2009b. 'Connecting Through Records: Narratives of Koorie Victoria'. *Archives and Manuscripts*, 37(2): 60–88.

Faulkhead, Shannon, Lynette Russell, Diane Singh, and Sue McKemmish. 2007. 'Is Community Research Possible within the Western Academic Tradition?' In *Researching with Communities: Grounded Perspectives on Engaging Communities in Research*, edited by Andy Williamson and Ruth DeSouza. Auckland: Muddy Creek Press, pp. 39–56.

hooks, bell. 1992. *Black Looks: Race and Representation*. Boston, MA: South End Press.

Janke, T. 2009. *Writing up Indigenous Research: Authorship, Copyright and Indigenous Knowledge Systems*. Sydney: Terri Janke and Company. Available at: http://www.terrijanke.com.au/#!writing-up-indigenous-research/o7pdb [Accessed March 28, 2016].

McKemmish, Sue. 2005. 'Traces: Document, Record, Archive, Archives'. In *Archives: Recordkeeping in Society*, edited by Sue McKemmish, Michael Piggott, Barbara Reed and Frank Upward. Wagga Wagga, New South Wales: Centre for Information Studies, Charles Sturt University, pp. 1–20.

McKemmish, S., S. Faulkhead, and L. Russell. 2011. 'Dis-Trust in the Archive: Reconciling Records'. *Archival Science*, 11(3–4): 211–239.

National Health and Medical Research Council (NHMRC). 2006. *Keeping Research on Track: A Guide for Aboriginal and Torres Strait Islander Peoples About Health Research Ethics*. National Health and Medical Research Council (NHMRC). Available at: http://www.nhmrc.gov.au/publications/synopses/e65syn.htm [Accessed March 28, 2016].

Smith, Linda Tuhiwai. 1999. *Decolonizing Methodologies: Research and Indigenous Peoples*. London: Zed Books.

Spencer, B., and F. J. Gillen. 1912. *Across Australia*, Volumes 1 and 2. London: Macmillan.

Spencer, B., and F. J. Gillen. 1969. *The Northern Tribes of Central Australia*. Oosterhout: Anthropological Publications.

24

ANCESTORS FOR SALE IN AOTEAROA-NEW ZEALAND

Marama Muru-Lanning

Māori are passionately concerned about the appropriation of natural resources in their ancestral territories through processes of colonisation and more recently privatisation. *Kaitiakitanga* (guardianship) is a fundamental Māori concept that over the past three decades has been intimately linked with the protection and wellbeing of natural resources. This chapter explores the complex and diverse nature of Māori responses to the recent wave of electricity-generating asset privatisations in Aotearoa-New Zealand. I ask: how does the privatisation of natural resources, those used in hydro, geothermal and wind electricity generation and that are referred to by Māori as *taonga* (treasures), *tūpuna* (ancestors), *whānau* (family) and *atua* (supernatural beings) alter Māori understandings of their ancestral territories and their relationships with the Crown? Furthermore, the chapter also examines what kaitiakitanga of natural resources means in contemporary times, and how Māori understand their role as *kaitiaki* (guardians) in the context of privatising freshwater and geothermal resources. My aim is to show how Māori negotiate and understand their kaitiaki commitments even though their experiences and responses to privatisation may be different. These questions highlight the challenges when competing discourses come together and when cultural property moves away from the more straightforwardly negotiated domain of museums and collections, which have a long history of power sharing and collaboration, into the private sector.

Privatising the electricity companies

This work sits within the broader context of debates and discussion among Māori about the national government's privatisation of electricity-generating assets in 2013 and 2014. On 29 January 2011, the Prime Minister, John Key, announced New Zealand was dangerously in debt and to alleviate the problem his government intended to partially privatise the country's electricity-generating assets. The assets to be sold included Mighty River Power, Genesis Energy Limited and Meridian Energy. When the Government first proposed the sales, some Māori leaders indicated a desire to buy shares in the companies (Tahana 2011). At the outset, Waikato leader Tukoroirangi Morgan announced that his *iwi* (tribe), Waikato-Tainui, in their capacity as kaitiaki of the Waikato River, were excited by the prospect of buying shares in Mighty River Power and Genesis Energy which produce much of New Zealand's electricity and are located on the Waikato River within his tribe's ancestral territory. In an effort to reassure New Zealanders that the assets would be in safe hands if bought by Māori, Morgan explained "iwi won't sell [their shares], the investments are intergenerational" (Gifford 2011). However, Morgan's position on Waikato-Tainui becoming shareholders in the electricity companies changed after the New Zealand Māori Council challenged the Government's privatisation strategy and water-ownership policy. The Māori Council, a statutory body, who view themselves as kaitiaki of natural resources that Māori have interests in, urged all Māori to reject the privatisations until Māori property rights in freshwater were determined (Misa 2012; Water Claimants 2013). To stop the privatisations the Māori Council submitted a claim to the Waitangi Tribunal requesting an urgent hearing of the sales of the electricity assets. This was followed by a second part to their strategy in February 2012, where the Māori Council and 10 co-claimant iwi and *hapū* (subtribes) filed a claim for freshwater and geothermal resources in the High Court. This was not the first claim for legal recognition of Māori proprietary rights in water. There are others, many of which date back to the nineteenth century. The Māori Council's argument was that the asset sales, in particular the sale of Mighty River Power which was scheduled to be sold first, were detrimental to Māori interests in freshwater. They disputed that if the electricity-generation companies were partially privatised, the new private owners were not bound by the Crown's Treaty responsibilities and would not be obliged to engage in remedies for the loss of Māori property rights in water. The Māori Council argued that Māori continued to have:

> unsatisfied or unrecognized proprietary rights in water, which have a commercial aspect, and that they are prejudiced by Crown policies that refuse to recognize those rights or to compensate for the usurpation of those rights for commercial purposes.
> *(Waitangi Tribunal 2012:1)*

On 13 March 2012, the Waitangi Tribunal granted an urgent hearing of the claim on the grounds that the claimants were likely to suffer significant irreversible prejudice and that the claim addressed Crown actions and policies of national importance.

Treaty of Waitangi claims have been a significant feature of New Zealand race relations and politics since 1975. Over the last 40 years, New Zealand governments have provided opportunities for Māori iwi and hapū to seek redress for Crown breaches that were outlined in the Treaty of Waitangi of 1840. Because the Treaty of Waitangi has limited legal standing, the primary means of registering and researching Treaty claims is through the Waitangi Tribunal. Waitangi claims are settled through negotiations between Māori tribal and government representatives. On 24 August 2012, the Tribunal released its interim full report which recommended that the Government postpone the electricity asset sales until the issue of freshwater rights had been resolved between the Crown and Māori iwi around the country. The Tribunal's finding was based on its conviction that proceeding with the partial privatisations would reduce the Government's ability to properly address outstanding claims to water and geothermal resources. The Tribunal's interim report also indicated that Māori interests in waters used by the electricity companies were in the nature of ownership, stating:

> Our generic finding is that Māori had rights and interests in their water bodies for which the closest English equivalent in 1840 was ownership rights, and that such rights were confirmed, guaranteed, and protected by the Treaty of Waitangi, save to the extent that there was an expectation in the Treaty that the waters would be shared with the incoming settlers.
> *(Waitangi Tribunal 2012)*

Māori gather to debate the issues

On 13 September 2012, at the invitation of the Māori King, Tuheitia Paki, almost one thousand Māori gathered at Tūrangawaewae Marae to discuss Māori water rights. The group included hereditary chiefs, elected iwi leaders, Māori academics, activists, politicians, and representatives from the Iwi Leaders Forum, the Māori Council and the Māori Women's Welfare League. After speeches from key leaders, Sir Tumu Te Heuheu, Sir Edward Taihakurei Durie and Emeritus Professor Ranginui Walker, King Tuheitia declared: "We [Māori] have always owned the water. . . . [in the Waikato region] we have never ceded our mana [ancestral prestige] over the river to anyone" (Young 2012a). While the Prime Minister was not invited to attend the gathering, he responded to King Tuhetia's comments in the media with "King Tuheitia's claim that Māori have always owned New Zealand's water is just plain wrong". He went on to say that "all the advice the government had received was that the common-law position that no-one owned the water stands" (Young 2012b). Subsequently, the water rights issue became a topic of national significance with opposition political parties accusing John Key and his government of trying to undermine Māori. Green Party co-leader Metiria Turei who attended the Māori pan-tribal meeting stated "Mr Key is trying to divide and rule Māori" (Radio New Zealand 2012). Turei further expressed "there is an entrenched resistance by some powerful New Zealand institutions against recognising Māori as indigenous people with an international indigenous identity that is independent from the Crown."

However, against the wishes of many Māori, and non-Māori New Zealanders, Mighty River Power and Meridian Energy were partially privatised in 2013 and Genesis Energy followed in 2014.

Māori understandings of natural resources

Before the arrival of Europeans, Māori society had its own concept of land, water and resource ownership (Firth 1929:338–339). Often land, water and other natural resources belonged to more than one tribal group. Each tribe's rights and uses could be quite different. For instance, one tribe may have had the rights to harvest birds in an area at a particular time of the year, while another tribe may have had the fishing rights for the area and a third tribe may have had the rights to grow crops (Firth 1929:43; Ballara 1998:194–195, 197). According to Mead, this system of tribal co-operation in cultivation and the sharing and redistribution of resources inhibited any trend towards individualism and the individual ownership of land and freshwater (2003:282). Contests over land, freshwater and natural resources were also a regular occurrence between tribal groups (Jones and Biggs 1995:138). While exclusive rights to lands and resources were extremely rare, tribes constantly disputed and negotiated their rights with one another (Ballara 1998:200). Disputes between tribes had just as much to do with "acting out of a responsibility and an obligation to care" as they did with protecting their economic and political interests (Gulliver 1979:193). Indeed, recurrent disputing and negotiating meant that tribal boundaries and rights to natural resources were flexible. Claims were typically linked to inherited *mana* (authority and prestige) over land and resources as well as a tribe's occupation and use of it. Ballara describes how ancestral claiming was practised:

> the land and resources which a Māori has best claim to is that which [he] has had handed down to him from his ancestors to himself. Yet descent from an owning ancestor alone was insufficient; it had to be from an ancestor whose descendants had continued to occupy it. Descendants who lived elsewhere eventually lost their

> rights – their claims grew cold. Inheritance of land was from that limited group of ancestors known to have first cleared and cultivated or otherwise used the resources of the land, and who had handed down their rights from generation to generation of people also occupied the land.
>
> *(1998:200)*

Acknowledging that a range of opinions exist goes a long way in helping to understand some of the problems associated with Māori conceptions of resource ownership. The key point is that Māori claim "rights" (which may also be interpreted as responsibilities and obligations) to exercise authority over particular resources, and in the twenty-first century they are forced to make sense of English common law and their own customary understandings of ownership. Whatever the different conceptions of ownership are, be it possessive individualism, collective ownership, shared rights in property or variable ownership, another way of interpreting this debate is that it is more to do with claims to status and power. Claims to ownership are important not least because they also provide a vehicle for legitimising status within and between competing tribal groups.

Lands and natural resources which are regarded by Māori as "taonga" are at the heart of many Treaty claims (Waitangi Tribunal 1998:84). This is because Article 2 of the Treaty of Waitangi guarantees Māori "possession" of their taonga (Kawharu 2000:365). The Waitangi Tribunal's definition of taonga is a "valued possession, or anything highly prized," and "may include any material or non-material thing having cultural or spiritual significance for a given tribal group" (Wheen and Ruru 2004:100). Not surprisingly, there is a large body of literature on the concept of taonga, some of which claims that taonga act as symbols of important relationships (see Tapsell 1997, 2000, 2006; Henare 2005). When Weiner wrote about taonga, she compared the concept to the *kula* system of exchange in Melanesia and exchanges of fine mats in Samoa (1992:46). Weiner proposed that taonga are important things that cannot be alienated from earlier possessors. She described taonga not only as valuable Māori heirlooms which carry the identity of people and their pasts but also as things that are imbued with the power and prestige of the people who possessed them. Therefore to gain another person's taonga is to acquire their rank, name and history (1992:64). She made the point that:

> Some things, like most commodities, are easy to give. But there are other possessions that are imbued with the intrinsic and ineffable identities of their owners which are not easy to give away. Ideally, these inalienable possessions are kept by their owners from one generation to the next within the closed context of family, descent group, or dynasty. The loss of such an inalienable possession diminishes the self and by extension, the group to which the person belongs.
>
> *(Weiner 1992:6)*

For Durie, the way taonga are valued varies according to particular customary methods practised by different tribal groups (1998:23). In view of this idea it is possible to see why Māori argue that bodies of water and geothermal resources, which are perceived as taonga cannot be parted from them (Gibbs, Dawson and Bennett 2007:15). Yet, not all Māori use the Treaty of Waitangi's representation of taonga to secure their rights in local lands and resources. Merata Kawharu makes the point that:

> According to some oral traditions, lands, forests, fisheries, *marae* or sacred sites (*waahi* tapu) were not necessarily termed *taonga* (cf. Waitangi Tribunal 1996:54). To do so

> would have made common place their status and said nothing about the particular qualities of each. Environmental resources were considered on their own merits and potential within a holistic scheme that is the universe. Thus land was referred to as *whenua* rather than *taonga*, sacred waters as *wai tapu* rather than *taonga* and so on. *(2000:365)*

In previous works I have demonstrated how Waikato iwi perceive the Waikato River to be their *Tūpuna Awa* (River Ancestor). Kamira Binga Haggie, from Turangawaewae Marae of Waikato iwi, described this phenomenon in an interview for Te Papa Museum, where he said "the [Waikato] river is like a tūpuna, an ancestor" (Haggie 1997). However, in stating that the Waikato River is a tūpuna it does not mean that Waikato Māori do not also think that the river is a taonga. Waikato iwi represent their interest in the Waikato River by claiming that the river is their Tūpuna Awa. The concept of Tūpuna Awa shares many of the same understandings as the concept of taonga, that Waikato people cannot be alienated from their ancestor, and the ancestor cannot be alienated from them. Furthermore, some Māori look upon important natural resources as whānau. This is an understanding that Matiu and Mutu demonstrated in their text *Te Whanau Moana: Nga Kaupapa me nga Tikanga: Customs and Protocols*. For over five decades Joan Metge has contributed to the literature of whānau. Early on in her research she made the point that while membership to iwi and hapū is determined by a person's descent from an eponymous ancestor, a person's membership within a whānau is established on different grounds. Metge contended that whānau are a nucleus of people descended through a male and female ancestor, usually a husband and wife. As the ancestors recede, family members group themselves into branches stemming from the dominant personalities among their elders. Over time these branches act with increased independence until eventually all who remember the ancestors have died. Once the elders of the group separate, their descendants become large families in their own right. A consequence of the fission is that whānau membership usually stays at between 30 and 50 people who are distributed among several households (Metge 1976 [1967]:136). While Hirini Mead (2003:212) claimed that a key characteristic of whānau is that its "members are born into it and all are relatives," Metge asserted that whānau groups are inclusive of "people who are attached to its real members by marriage and adoption" (Metge 1995:62–64). In some circumstances, as Matiu and Mutu (2003) illustrate, important natural resources like fish, mountains and rivers are understood to be whanau members as tribal groups and specific natural resources share intertwined histories with one another. Expanding this discussion to Māori understandings of geothermal resources used in electricity generation, some Māori see a direct relationship between geothermal activity and the atua (supernatural being) Ruaumoko, who is the god of earthquakes, volcanoes and seasons. Similarly, wind resources used in electricity generation may also be associated with the atua Tawhirimatea, the god of thunder and lightning, wind, clouds and storms. Different Māori groups comprehend their ancestral territories in iwi-specific ways and therefore fundamental Māori concepts such as kaitiaki, taonga, tūpuna, whānau and atua may have different interpretations.

While human–environmental relationships have become a major field of research inquiry in anthropology in the last three decades, research that is specific to Māori conceptions of environment do not feature strongly in the international literature. I refer to the works of Bender (1993), Hirsch and O'Hanlon (1995), Orlove (2002), Povinelli (1999), Strang (1997, 2004) and Rose (1996) in this sense. Indeed, the absence of Māori case-studies is surprising given that Māori are recognised internationally for progressing Treaty of Waitangi and indigenous rights claims (Ruru 2012; Te Aho 2011; Williams 2001). In anthropology much of the cultural property and human–environment literature is the result of scholars working with Australian aborigines, the peoples of Papua New Guinea and Melanesia and indigenous groups in Central and South America. According to Metge and Webster, Māori resistance to being studied by anthropologists after the 1980s is a key reason for the absence of Māori case-studies in the literature (Webster 1998:170–187).

Mighty River Power in New Zealand

To better understand the relationship between the electricity companies and Māori some background information about the company Mighty River Power is helpful. New Zealand's electricity industry has undergone major reforms since the mid-1980s. In 1986, in the context of radical restructuring of the state, the Government announced its intention to reform the generation and transmission sectors of the electricity industry. The first of these reforms occurred in 1987 when the Electricity Corporation of New Zealand (ECNZ) became a state-owned enterprise (SOE) operating in much the same way as a private company. Subsequently, ECNZ created a subsidiary, Transpower, to run its transmission assets. The reforms continued in 1993 under the Electricity Act (1992), which removed distributors' statutory monopolies and the obligation to supply electricity. As well, the Electricity Market Company Ltd, M-co, was established to assist the electricity market framework for wholesale trading. One year later Transpower was separated from ECNZ and set up as a stand-alone SOE. The changes continued in 1995 when ECNZ split into two competing SOEs, namely ECNZ and Contact Energy. In 1998 a range of reforms were announced by the Government which included selling Contact Energy and the separation of transmission lines from the energy generation business (Muru-Lanning 2010:50–51). These decisions led to splitting ECNZ into three smaller SOEs: 1) Genesis Energy, a thermal, natural gas and LPG electricity generator and retailing company; 2) Meridian Energy, a hydro and wind generator and electricity retailer located primarily in the South Island; and 3) Mighty River Power, a hydro, geothermal and natural gas generator and electricity retailer located in the North Island. Mighty River Power has grown considerably in size and economic productivity since it was established. Depending on demand, Mighty River Power produces between 16 per cent and 22 per cent of New Zealand's electricity supply of which 80 per cent is derived from hydro generation. The company's hydro generating system comprises eight dams and nine power stations on the Waikato River. The rest of the company's electricity generation results from a gas-fired power station in South Auckland and five geothermal power stations that it co-owns with individual Māori tribes in the Taupo and Rotorua regions.

Energy-driven relationships with Māori

The Waikato River is the largest natural resource that Mighty River Power uses in its electricity generation processes. Flowing through the heart of the Waikato region in the Central North Island, the river is the life source of many Māori tribes living along it. These tribes include Ngāti Tūwharetoa, Ngāti Tahu-Ngāti Whaoa, Ngāti Raukawa, Ngāti Koroki, Ngāti Haua and Waikato-Tainui. In 2002, Ngāti Tahu-Ngāti Whaoa's tribal authority signed a Memorandum of Partnership with Mighty River Power. Tribal authority representatives from Waikato-Tainui's tribal executive and the Waikato Raupatu Trust Company also signed one in 2003, as did Ngāti Raukawa.[1] In 2004, Ngāti Tūwharetoa's tribal authority agreed to a five-year strategic business plan with Mighty River Power. These agreements, which express a convergence of intent between the parties and indicate a common line of action, are mostly used in cases where the parties do not propose to create a legal commitment. In general, these Memorandums organise the power relations of, and between, tribal authorities and Mighty River Power. What is intriguing about these types of agreements is that, while they are widely publicised when they are signed, their actual details remain private.[2] In the case of Waikato-Tainui and Mighty River Power, the official reason given for the agreement was to outline the ways in which the two parties would work together to preserve and enhance the Waikato River. Waikato-Tainui and Mighty River Power issued a press release explaining:

> Waikato-Tainui and Mighty River Power, two of the largest stakeholders in the welfare of the Waikato River, have signed a partnership agreement outlining how they will work together to contribute to the future wellbeing of the river. Waikato-Tainui regard the Waikato as their ancestral river while most of Mighty River Power's current electricity generation comes from the eight dams and nine stations along the Waikato. Last night the two organisations signed an agreement outlining the way they would work together to ensure the preservation and enhancement of the river and its surrounds for future generations.
>
> (Scoop Independent News *2003)*

While the nature of the agreement may be largely symbolic some Māori have benefited from their relationship with Mighty River Power in a variety of ways. For example, Waikato-Tainui has gained greater business prominence in the region; they are now recognised nationally for their management of the heritage of the Waikato River, and acknowledged as power-brokers by central government. According to Mighty River Power their relationships with iwi and Māori landowners are instrumental to their business approach which centres on the sustainability of natural resources. This ethos is sometimes compared with Māori understandings of kaitiakitanga.

Kaitiakitanga in the twenty-first century

For Māori, to be kaitiaki exemplifies a duty of care passed down from ancestors to descendants, to nurture and protect places, natural resources and taonga in their territories (Benton et al. 2013:105–114; Kawharu 2000). Using kaitiakitanga as a lens, this work emphasises people, human–environment relationships and the unique socio-cultural aspects of living in New Zealand. As Merata Kawharu points out "kaitiakitanga is more than managing relationships between environmental resources and humans; it also involves managing relationships between people in the past, present and future" (2000:352). Kaitiaki is a fluid concept and can mean different things amongst different groups and can be applied differently amongst members of the same kin group. Importantly, this work provides a broad definition of kaitiakitanga which draws on understandings of kaitiakitanga as relationships between people and the environment that include *taniwha*[3] (Benton et al. 2013:376–378) and encompass responsibilities of guardianship (Marsden 1992:15), Māori environmental ethics (Roberts et al. 1995:15), sustainable resource management (Marsden 1992; Kawharu 2000), collaborative management (Memon and Kirk 2012), governance and so on. Kaitiaki act as both benefactors and beneficiaries in the sense that they protect resources while still acquiring benefits from them (Hayes 1999).

The concept of kaitiaki between Waikato-Tainui and the Waikato River was defined in Waikato Regional Council Policy (1999) as follows:

> 2 MATTERS OF SIGNIFICANCE TO MAORI
> 2.2 Iwi in the Waikato Region
> 2.2.3 Waikato-Tainui
> Waikato-Tainui are currently represented by the Tainui Maori Trust Board. They have never objected to sharing the waterways or its fisheries and its use for recreation. However, it offends Waikato-Tainui to see the waters of the Waikato River and other waterways being depleted and polluted by users. Waikato-Tainui therefore object to the abuse of the River and other waters. The principal concern of Waikato-Tainui as Kaitiaki, is management, restoration and protection of the environment for future generations.

More recently, however, the Waikato River Settlement (2009) has established a new era of kaitiakitanga between Waikato-Tainui iwi and the Waikato River. The Settlement which creates a modern co-management partnership between Waikato-Tainui and the Crown has created among other things fisheries bylaws for the Waikato River. The bylaws allow Waikato-Tainui to carry out traditional management practices to prohibit, restrict and enable fishing for cultural and sustainable reasons (Waikato Raupatu River Trust 2016). The new bylaws include kaitiaki protections such as:

> BYLAW 4: Minimum weight for commercially harvested eels
> No commercial fisher may take or possess any shortfin eel taken within the Waikato-Tainui Fisheries Area weighing less than 300g.
> No commercial fisher may take or possess any longfin eel taken within the Waikato-Tainui Fisheries Area weighing less than 400g.
> BYLAW 5: Maximum weight for commercially harvested eels
> No commercial fisher may take or possess any eel taken within the Waikato-Tainui Fisheries Area weighing more than 2kg.
> BYLAW 6: Prohibition on taking of female migrant longfin eels
> No commercial fisher may take or possess any female longfin eel taken within the Waikato-Tainui Fisheries Area that is in the migratory morphological phase.
> *(Waikato Raupatu River Trust 2016)*

In contrast, Mighty River Power draws its authority and identity from conservation and environmental discourses. This leads the company to refer to itself as steward of natural resources in its corporate domain.

In 2011 Mighty River Power's CEO, Doug Heffernan, and the Chair of Mighty River Power's board, Joan Withers, announced in an article that their company "needed to embed ethical governance in their corporate DNA for its decision to partner with Māori land trust interests to use geothermal resources to power its energy generation strategy" (Institute of Management New Zealand 2011). Heffernan declared:

> Nobody owns our geothermal resources – to get access you must reach an agreement with land owners. Typically, Māori land trusts own the land that sits atop our geothermal reservoirs. When Mighty River saw New Zealand's Maui oil field declining while the need for more energy grew, it saw the geothermal potential. Coincidentally, Māori interests were looking for greater involvement in the development and ownership of their resources.[4]
> *(Institute of Management 2011)*

He went on to say "Māori were effectively disenfranchised by traditional royalty-based resource exploration models as they had no cash to develop their resources" and explained that:

> This motivated Mighty River Power to find ways to allow Māori property owners to participate in a geothermal strategy and simultaneously build equity in the energy business. Electricity generation is a long-term business with projects sometimes taking up to 30 to 50 plus years to complete. There is, therefore, a large risk with investing with electricity generation projects. Mighty River Power's $430 million Nga Awa Purua project on the Rotokawa geothermal field, 14 kilometres northeast of Taupo, is 25 percent owned by the Tauhara North No 2 Māori Land Trust. This project became fully operationally in 2010.

According to Mighty River Power the Tauhara North No 2 Māori Land Trust was earning royalties that were being distributed to its 2,000-plus owners, and in Heffernan's view this particular Māori trust would not have partnered with Mighty River Power unless the company could demonstrate its capacity to manage local geothermal resources sustainably. He asserted:

> They want it for their grandchildren and their grandchildren's children. Sustainability was fundamental to the business proposition.

Both kaitiakitanga and stewardship enable Māori and Mighty River Power to present themselves and their partnership in a positive light with regard to environmental sustainability and the ethical management of natural resources.

Given the significance of freshwater in New Zealand, the Crown has acknowledged the need to set a national direction with regards to both the management of and claims to freshwater. This is addressed in the National Policy Statement on Freshwater Management 2011 (NPS-FM). The NPS-FM sets out objectives and policies to guide local government management of water in an integrated and sustainable way, while still providing for economic growth within set limits relating to water quantity and quality limits. The Statement (amended in 2014) recognises the national significance of freshwater for all New Zealanders. The main focus of the NPS-FM is:

- setting freshwater objectives (goals that describe the desired state of freshwater now or in the future);
- setting limits (the maximum amount of the resource available for use); and
- implementing methods to achieve the freshwater objectives and limits.

In particular, Objective D1 requires regional councils:

> To provide for the involvement of iwi and hapū, and to ensure that tangata whenua values and interests are identified and reflected in the management of fresh water including associated ecosystems, and decision-making regarding freshwater planning, including on how all other objectives of this national policy statement are given effect to.

It also requires local Councils to "take reasonable steps to":

a involve iwi and hapū in the management of fresh water and freshwater ecosystems in the region;

b work with iwi and hapū to identify tāngata whenua values and interests in fresh water and freshwater ecosystems in the region; and

c reflect tāngata whenua (local Māori) values and interests in the management of, and decision-making regarding, fresh water and freshwater ecosystems in the region.

(Ministry for the Environment 2014, Obective D1)

In addition to the NPS-FM objectives, the Waitangi Tribunal recommended that the WAI 2358 Water and Geothermal Claim must remain one of priority, and decided that the Stage 2 inquiry should occur in early 2016. The inquiry was to be after the Crown's consultation on water reform, which finished in February 2016, and before "final" Crown decisions on water reform have been made. Tribunal hearings at that stage will enable the Crown's decisions to be informed by a Tribunal report on the Treaty compliance of the Crown's water reform options. Reflecting the priority status of the Claim, the Tribunal has also directed claimants to begin preparing whatever evidence "will be essential for the evaluation of whichever policy options are distributed for consultation in 2016" (Māori Council 2015).

To date the freshwater and geothermal ownership issue remains unresolved; however, at 2015's Waitangi celebrations John Key advised the Government had conceded in the Supreme Court in 2013 that Māori did have some genuine rights and interests in these natural resources which needed to be worked through. He stated that while "we think there might be quite a gap between what some groups think those rights and interests are . . . there are by catchment, in certain places, rights and interests" (Radio New Zealand 2015).

Conclusion

This chapter introduced the idea that contemporary privatisation processes redefine Māori relationships with their lands, natural resources and ancestral territories. The discussion raised questions of what the Māori term kaitiakitanga means today and explores the moral dilemmas and contradictions that emerge for Māori from the combination of commercial interests that now seem to underpin kaitiakitanga. Indeed, freshwater and other natural resources are vitally important to Māori identities. This chapter explored how Māori reconcile the sale of electricity companies that draw on freshwater and other natural resources understood as taonga (prized treasures), tūpuna (ancestors), whānau (family) and atua (supernatural beings), and how this mediates their duties as kaitiaki. My current research investigates the impact of privatising freshwater and other electricity generating resources in New Zealand. Prior to the privatisations of the electricity generating assets, when the Crown was the sole owner of the companies, Māori capacity to carry out their kaitiaki duties was mediated by their relationship with the Crown. With the partial privatisation of the electricity assets the Government has disposed of its rights to control the electricity company's power stations, dams, resource-use and water intakes to generate electricity. It has introduced a number of new parties – a "bunch of faceless others"– to that longstanding relationship, others who are now entitled to use river and lake waters, geothermal resources and wind in their Generation processes. This discussion introduces a view that subtle shifts in Māori–environment discourse reflect wider social and symbolic struggles, since privatisation serves "first to undo the relations between things and people, and then to remake them in a different form" (Alexander 2009:48).

Importantly, this work further develops ideas that serve to "root" Māori groups (iwi, hapū, and whānau) in particular lands and resources. In addition, it contributes to a type of scholarship that denies the primacy of the Western point of view. Scholars such as Kawharu (2000),

Matiu and Mutu (2003) and Stokes (1997) have used a variety of methods to identify specific iwi–Māori environmental discourses which include: mapping and photographing lands and resources in Māori territories; identifying genealogies, ancestors and tribal sayings that link iwi, hapū and marae to lands and resources; and also defining fundamental Māori concepts such as kaitiakitanga, taonga, tūpuna, whānau and atua to demonstrate the unique relationships that Māori groups have with local lands and resources. These works show how specific Māori groups use their agency to imaginatively create distinct cultural landscapes.

Notes

1 The two signing representatives were Kingi Porima (Chairperson of Waikato-Tainui's tribal executive) and Hemi Rau (CEO of the Waikato Raupatu Lands Trust).
2 See for example, NZPA 'Tainui and Mighty River Power agree on river care' *New Zealand Herald* (8 July 2003); NZPA 'Generator and tribe sign deal' *New Zealand Herald* (9 July 2003); 'Key parties create Waikato River partnership' *Mighty River Power News* (8 July 2003).
3 Taniwha are supernatural creatures in Māori tradition, similar to serpents and dragons in other cultures. They live in oceans, rivers, lakes and caves and are kaitiaki or guardians of the water bodies they reside in.
4 See, for example, The Waikato River Authority, retrieved 11 December 2015 http://www.waikatoriver.org.nz/about-the-waikatoriver/history/.

Bibliography

Alexander, Catherine. 2009. Privatisation: Jokes, Scandal, and Absurdity in a Time of Rapid Change. In Karen Sykes (ed), *Ethnographies of Moral Reasoning: Living Paradoxes of a Global Economy*. New York: Palgrave Macmillan, pp. 43–65.

Ballara, Angela. 1998. *Iwi: The Dynamics of Maori Tribal Organisation from c. 1769 to c. 1945*. Wellington: Victoria University Press.

Bender, Barbara. 1993. *Landscapes, Politics and Perspectives*. Oxford: Berg.

Benton, Richard, Alex Frame and Paul Meredith. 2013. *Te Mātāpunenga: Compendium of References to the Concepts and Institutions of Māori Customary Law*. Wellington: Victoria University Press.

Durie, M. H. 1998. *Te Mana Te Kawanatanga: The Politics of Maori Self Determination*. London: Oxford University Press.

Firth, Raymond. 1929. *The Economics of the New Zealand Maori*. London: Government Printer.

Gibbs, Meredith, Blake Dawson and April Bennett. 2007. Māori Claim to Ownership of Freshwater, *Resource Management Journal* (August): 13–18.

Gifford, Adam. 2011. Iwi Staking their Claim, *New Zealand Herald*, 9 August.

Gulliver, Phillip H. 1979. *Disputes and Negotiations*. New York: Academic Press.

Haggie, Kamira Binga. 1997. Turangawaewae Marae. Video recorded interview with Kamira Binga Haggie Shown at Te Papa National Museum, Wellington.

Hayes, Selwyn. 1999. Defining Kaitiakitanga and the Resource Management Act 1991, *Auckland University Law Review*, 8(3): 893–898.

Henare, A. 2005. *Museums, Anthropology and Imperial Exchange*. Cambridge: Cambridge University Press.

Hirsch, E. and O'Hanlon, M. (eds) 1995. *The Anthropology of Landscape: Perspectives on Place and Space*. Oxford: Clarendon Press.

Institute of Management New Zealand. 2011. Responsible Governance: Maori and Might River Power, *New Zealand Management*, September, p. 38. http://www.management.co.nz/articles/responsible-governance-maori-and-mighty-river-power. Last accessed March 16, 2017.

Jones, P. and B. Biggs. 1995. *Nga Iwi o Tainui: The Traditional History of the Tainui People*. Auckland: Auckland University Press.

Kawharu, Merata. 2000. Kaitiakitanga: A Māori Anthropological Perspective of the Māori Socio-environmental Ethic of Resource Management, *Journal of the Polynesian Society*, 110(4): 349–370.

Māori Council. 2015. Stage 2 Water Claim. http://www.Māoricouncil.com/2015/06/07/heading-stage-2-water-claim-inquiry-scheduled-for-early-2016/. Last accessed March 16, 2017.

Marsden, Māori. 1992. Kaitiakitanga: A Definitive Introduction to the Holistic World View of the Māori. Paper written with Te Aroha Henare for Maruwhenua, Ministry for the Environment.

Matiu, McCully and Margaret Mutu. 2003. *Te Whanau Moana: Nga Kaupapa me nga Tikanga: Customs and Protocols*. Auckland: Reed.

Mead, S. 2003. *Tikanga Maori: Living by Maori Values*. Wellington: Huia Publishers.

Memon, P.A. and N. Kirk, 2012. Role of Indigenous Māori People in Collaborative Water Governance in Aotearoa/New Zealand, *Journal of Environmental Planning and Management*, 55(7): 941–959.

Metge, J. 1976 [1967]. *The Maoris of New Zealand*. London: Routledge and Kegan.

Metge, J. 1995. *The Whaanau in Modern Society*. Wellington: Victoria University Press.

Minhinnick, Nganeko Kaihau. 1989. Kaitiaki. Paper written for the Resource Management Law Reform. Auckland: The Print Centre.

Ministry for the Environment. 2014. Guidance for Implementing the National Policy Statement for Freshwater Management. http://www.mfe.govt.nz/fresh-water/tools-and-guidelines/implementing-national-policy-statement-freshwater-management. Last accessed March 16, 2017.

Misa, Tapu. 2012. Water Claim Really about Māori's Role as Caretakers, *New Zealand Herald*, 16 July.

Muru-Lanning, Marama. 2010. Tupuna Awa and Te Awa Tupuna: An Anthropological Study of Competing Discourses and Claims of Ownership to the Waikato River. Unpublished PhD thesis, The University of Auckland.

New Zealand Government. 1992. Electricity Act 1992 (1992 No 122):55,67(a), 73. http://www.legislation.govt.nz/act/public/1992/0122/latest/DLM281858.html. Last accessed March 16, 2017.

Orlove, Ben. 2002. *Lines in the Water: Nature and Culture at Lake Titicaca*. Berkeley: University of California Press.

Povinelli, Elizabeth A. 1999. Settler Modernity and the Quest for an Indigenous Tradition, *Public Culture*, 11(1): 19–48.

Radio New Zealand. 2012. PM Accused of Divide and Rule over Water Rights, Political News, 8 August, 10.30am. http://www.radionz.co.nz/news/political/112593/pm-accused-of-divide-and-rule-over-water-rights. Last accessed March 16, 2017.

Radio New Zealand. 2015. Deadline Set for Freshwater Deal, Te Manu Korihi News, 5 February, 9.01pm. http://www.radionz.co.nz/news/te-manu-korihi/265413/deadline-set-for-freshwater-deal. Last accessed March 16, 2017.

Roberts, Mere, Waerete, Nganeko Minhinnick, Del Wihongi, and Carmen Kirkwood. 1995. Kaitiakitanga: Māori Perspectives on Conservation, *Pacific Conservation Biology*, 2: 7–20.

Rose, D. 1996. *Nourishing Terrains: Australian Aboriginal Views of Landscape and Wilderness*. Canberra: Australian Heritage Commission.

Ruru, J. 2012. The Right to Water as the Right to Identity: Legal Struggles of Indigenous Peoples of Aotearoa, New Zealand. In F. Sultana and A. Loftus (eds), *The Right to Water: Politics, Governance and Social Struggles*. Abingdon: Earthscan, pp. 110–122

Scoop Independent News, 2003. Key Parties Create Waikato River Partnership Press Release, 8 July. http://www.scoop.co.nz/stories/BU0307/S00083/key-parties-create-waikato-river-partnership.htm. Last accessed March 16, 2017.

Stokes, Evelyn. 1997. Ko Waikato Te Awa: The Waikato River. In E. Stokes and M. Begg (eds), *Te Hononga ki te Whenua: Belonging to the Land People and Places in the Waikato Region*. Hamilton: Waikato Branch NZGS Society, pp. 36–51.

Strang, Veronica. 1997. *Uncommon Ground: Cultural Landscapes and Environmental Values*. Oxford, New York: Berg.

Strang, Veronica. 2004. *The Meaning of Water*. Oxford, New York: Berg.

Tahana, Yvonne. 2011. Iwi Leaders Talk Asset Sales with PM, *New Zealand Herald*, 17 February.

Tapsell, Paul. 1997. The Flight of Pareraututu: An Investigation of Taonga from a Tribal Perspective, *Journal of Polynesian Society*, 106(4): 323–374.

Tapsell, Paul. 2000. *Pukaki: A Comet Returns*. Auckland: Reed Books.

Tapsell, Paul. 2006. *Ko Tawa Maori Treasures of New Zealand*. Auckland: David Bateman.

Te Aho, Linda. 2011. Indigenous Aspirations and Ecological Integrity in Aotearoa, New Zealand. In L. Westra, K. Bosselmann and C. Soskolne (eds), *Globalisation and Ecological Integrity in Science and International Law*. London: Cambridge Scholars Press.

Waikato Raupatu River Trust. 2016. Retrieved 12 April 2016, http://www.wrrt.co.nz/waikato-river-fisheries-bylaws/.

Waikato Regional Council Policy. 1999. Retrieved 12 April 2016, http://www.waikatoregion.govt.nz/PageFiles/20874/2012/Chapter_2.pdf. Last accessed March 16, 2017.

Waitangi Tribunal. 1998. Te Ika Whenua Rivers Report (Wai 212). Wellington: Government Printers.

Waitangi Tribunal. 1999. The Whanganui River Report (Wai 167). Wellington: Government Printers.

Waitangi Tribunal. 2012. The Stage 1 Report on the National Freshwater and Geothermal Resources Claim. Wellington: Waitangi Tribunal.

Water Claimants. 2013. Retrieved 6 June 2014, www.Māoricouncil.com/category/water-claim-2/. Last accessed March 16, 2017.

Webster, Steven. 1998. *Patrons of Māori Culture: Power, Theory, and Ideology in the Māori Renaissance*. Dunedin: University of Otago Press.

Weiner, A. 1992. *Inalienable Possessions: The Paradox of Keeping-While-Giving*. Berkeley, Los Angeles: University of California Press.

Wheen, N. and J. Ruru. 2004. The Environmental Reports. In J. Hayward and N. Wheen (eds), *The Waitangi Tribunal*. Wellington: Bridget Williams Books, pp. 97–112.

Williams, David V. 2001. *Crown Policy Affecting Māori Knowledge Systems and Cultural Practices*. Wellington: Waitangi Tribunal.

Young, Audrey. 2012a. We Own the Water – Māori King, *New Zealand Herald*, 14 September.

Young, Audrey. 2012b. Key Hits Back: Māori King 'Just Plain Wrong' on Water, *New Zealand Herald*, 15 September.

INDEX

For Product Safety Concerns and Information please contact our EU representative GPSR@taylorandfrancis.com
Taylor & Francis Verlag GmbH, Kaufingerstraße 24, 80331 München, Germany

www.ingramcontent.com/pod-product-compliance
Ingram Content Group UK Ltd.
Pitfield, Milton Keynes, MK11 3LW, UK
UKHW050052200926
475702UK00019B/2795
9780367783983